FUNDAMENTALS OF MARKETING:
ADDITIONAL DIMENSIONS
SELECTIONS FROM
THE LITERATURE

Edited by **JACK L. TAYLOR, JR. and JAMES F. ROBB**
Portland State University

MCGRAW-HILL BOOK COMPANY

New York
St. Louis
San Francisco
Düsseldorf
Johannesburg
Kuala Lumpur
London
Mexico
Montreal
New Delhi
Panama
Rio de Janeiro
Singapore
Sydney
Toronto

To
Michael
Susan
Eileen
Kathleen
Pat
and
Sandra

Fundamentals of Marketing:
Additional Dimensions
Selections from
the Literature

Library of Congress
Catalog Card Number 72-153096

07-062990-0

4 5 6 7 8 9 0 B P B P 7 9 8 7 6 5 4

This book was set in Optima
by Black Dot, Inc., and
printed on permanent paper and
bound by The Book Press, Inc.
The designer was Wladislaw Finne;
the drawings were done by
John Cordes, J. & R. Technical Services, Inc.
The editors were Jack R. Crutchfield,
Hiag Akmakjian,
and Cynthia Newby.
Annette Wentz
supervised production.

CONTENTS

PART 3: THE PRODUCT

PART 4: DISTRIBUTION STRUCTURE

PART 5: THE PRICE SYSTEM

PART 6: PROMOTIONAL ACTIVITIES

PART 7: MARKETING IN SPECIAL FIELDS

PART 8: PLANNING AND EVALUATING THE MARKETING EFFORT

PREFACE

The selections in this book represent dimensions and facets of marketing knowledge which fall beyond textbook parameters. The articles are intended for undergraduate and graduate students taking their first course in marketing. Our purpose is to provide additional insights, views, and concepts of basic marketing subjects—to offer an additional level of understanding.

The book is divided into eight general subject areas for convenience, although different aspects of specific marketing problems are at times developed in several selections. Part One establishes the relationship between marketing and its environment; the selections illustrate that the diversity and dimensions of modern marketing require many types of knowledge and information. Part Two samples the generous literature on the subject of the market and discusses how information is assembled and used in making marketing decisions. Part Three adds a decisive continuum to any discussion on product planning and development; topics include the symbolic dimensions of a product, fashion, and visual design. Part Four, on distribution structure, captures the dynamics, excitement, challenges, problems, and opportunities of a changing distribution system. Part Five examines some perplexing problems surrounding price and pricing policy; these selections establish the relationship between price, cost, and value as perceived by the buyer. Part Six focuses on promotional functions and provides an overview of the firm's communication activities as they relate to advertising, personal selling, and sales promotion. Part Seven, covering marketing in special fields, examines views on the marketing of services and different phases of international marketing. Part Eight contains a sample of the literature on planning and evaluating the marketing effort; corporate models, consumerism, marketing's commitment to economic development, its growing social responsibility, and the communication revolution are among the subjects probed.

We are indebted to the authors and publications represented in this collection. Special acknowledgment and thanks are due to Maureen Taylor for her assistance in developing the manuscript. We are grateful to Hiag Akmakjian and Cynthia Newby for their skill and help in charting the final production of the manuscript. We are especially appreciative and indebted to William Stanton of the University of Colorado and Robert Carter of McGraw-Hill Book Company for their encouragement, support, and confidence. We hope that the book will challenge students to read further into the many interesting dimensions of marketing.

Jack L. Taylor, Jr.
James F. Robb

AUTHOR-
TITLE-
SOURCE INDEX

CORRELATION OF TAYLOR AND ROBB READINGS WITH CHAPTERS OF SELECTED PRINCIPLES OF MARKETING TEXT BOOKS

CHAPTER NUMBER

TEXT	1	2	3	4	5	6	7	8	9	10	11	12	13
Stanton **Fundamentals of Marketing, 3/e**	1-4	5-7	8-11	12,13	14,15	16,17	18,19	20	←——— 21-23 ———→				←
McCarthy **Basic Marketing: A Managerial Approach**	←——— 1-7 ———→		54	8-11	←—— 12-20 ——→ 48,51	45,50	46				←——— 21-23 ———		
Beckman & Davidson **Marketing, 8/e**	5,6	1,2,4 51,52	54,36	←——————— 12-20 ———————→			45⟩		←——————— 24-28 ———————				
Staudt & Taylor **A Managerial Introduction to Marketing, 2/e**	1-3	←—5-6—→ 52		47	4,7,45 11	8,48	←—— 12-20 ——→		46	9 53	←——— 21-23 ———		
Buskirk **Principles of Marketing: The Management View, 3/e**	5,6	2,4 7,47	8-11	12,20, 48	49	←—— 13-19 ——→		45	3 ←— 21-23 —→			←	
Holloway & Hancock **Marketing in a Changing Environment**	1-2	4-6		←—— 12-19 ——→		50	7,48	45		54	52	←8-11→	
Phillips & Duncan **Marketing Principles & Methods, 6/e**	1-4 49,51, 52		←— 12-19 —→	45	50	←							
Converse, Huegy & Mitchell **Elements of Marketing, 7/e**	4,51	1-3 5-6 52	7	12-19 45,50	38-44					30-34	54		←
Sturdivant & Others **Managerial Analysis in Marketing**	7,53	51	54	←12-20→ 45,50		1-4 52 46	21-23	38-44	←30-37→		←—— 24-29 ——→		
Wentz & Eyrich **Marketing Theory & Application**	1-4	←—5-6—→			47,49 53	51,52			←——12-20—— 45,50		←—— 30-37 ——→		
Kotler **Marketing Management Analysis, Planning, & Control**	1-4	13,45 50,51	12,19	15,16 18	7,48	52	47		8-11 17	5-6,14 49	53		←21-23

1. Top row of numbers represents chapters in each of the texts

2. Numbers in all other squares represent readings in Taylor & Robb

14	15	16	17	18	19	20	21	22	23	24	25	26	27	28	29	30	31	32	33
——— 24-29 ———→				← —— 30-37 —— →				← —— 38-44 —→		9	45	46	47,48	49	50-52	53,54			
→		← —— 24-29 ——→					53	←38-44→		← —— 30-37 —— →					47,49		52		
→			21-23 46,47	←30-37→			53	←38-44→	29	29			7,48	8-11		49	3,50		
→	← —— 24-29 ——→							← —— 38-44 ——→			54	← 30-37 →			49	10,49	50	51	
24-29 ——→			←30-37→		←38-44→ 53					50,52	36,54	46	1,51						
20,47 49	21-23	30-37	24-29	←38-44→		←1-2→ 51	46	3,53											
——— 24-27 ———→			20					8-11 47,48	21-23, 46	← 28-29 →			38-44 53	←30-37→				54,56	
——— 24-27 ——→						20		8-11 48	47 49	53	←21-23→ 46	46	28-29	35-37	38-44				
←5-6→ ←8-11→ 49 47,48																			
← 21-23 → 46		←24-29→		←38-44→		← —— 8-11 —— →								54					
→ 46	30-37	←24-29→		←38-44→		54													

PART
ONE

MODERN MARKETING

Marketing in the "trillion-dollar economy" will, and is, taking on dimensions that have somewhat altered the concept of marketing. Professor Drucker's article outlines the nature and scope of marketing as it relates to economic development. W. W. Rostow develops the concept of a national market and its economic implications to marketing. Theodore Levitt's classic article, "Marketing Myopia," has ever-increasing dimensions when it comes to coping with opportunities in the megamarkets of the trillion-dollar economy. Professor Lazer views marketing as an institution of social control which is instrumental in guiding a culture from a producer's to a consumer's orientation.

Marketing does not operate in a vacuum. It is a necessary part of a synergy that makes America grow. "Systems Theory and Management" by Johnson, Kast, and Rosenzweig develops the necessary elements of the systems concept. Professor Adler points out how the systems approach applies to marketing and represents, in his judgment, *the leading edge in both marketing theory and practice.* The impact of technology on marketing will be significant, says John J. Kennedy. However, it offers a challenge—an opportunity to serve mankind.

More than ever before, the marketer will need to assemble information for decision making. Timothy Joyce devotes thought to this in terms of market research. He illustrates how experts from statistics, economics, psychology, sociology, anthropology, and mathematics have all made contributions in methods, concepts, and findings. Beal and Rogers present an example of a research problem. Their research findings suggest that consumers go "through some process" in acquiring information on goods and services. Cox and Good tell how to build a market information system which can supply the marketer with the needed information on which to base decisions. Robert Ferber concludes this section with a warning about misuse of technical methods in the behavioral sciences; he suggests that market research is a rich field for the creative researcher.

READING 1

MARKETING AND ECONOMIC DEVELOPMENT*

Peter F. Drucker

MARKETING AS A BUSINESS DISCIPLINE

The distinguished pioneer of marketing, whose memory we honor today, was largely instrumental in developing marketing as a systematic business discipline:

*Reprinted from *The Journal of Marketing*, published by the American Marketing Association, vol. 22, no. 3, January 1958, pp. 252–259.

In teaching us how to go about, in an orderly, purposeful and planned way
to find and create customers;
To identify and define markets; to create new ones and promote them;
To integrate customers' needs, wants, and preferences, and the intellectual
and creative capacity and skills of an industrial society, toward the design
of new and better products and of new distributive concepts and processes.

On this contribution and similar ones of other Founding Fathers of marketing during the last half century rests the rapid emergence of marketing as
perhaps the most advanced, certainly the most "scientific" of all functional
business disciplines.

But Charles Coolidge Parlin also contributed as a Founding Father toward
the development of marketing as a *social discipline*. He helped give us the
awareness, the concepts, and the tools that make us understand marketing
as a dynamic process of society through which business enterprise is integrated productively with society's purposes and human values. It is in marketing, as we now understand it, that we satisfy individual and social values,
needs, and wants—be it through producing goods, supplying services, foster-
ing innovation, or creating satisfaction. Marketing, as we have come to understand it, has its focus on the customer, that is, on the individual making
decisions within a social structure and within a personal and social value
system. Marketing is thus the process through which economy is integrated
into society to serve human needs.

I am not competent to speak about marketing in the first sense, marketing
as a functional discipline of business. I am indeed greatly concerned with
marketing in this meaning. One could not be concerned, as I am, with the
basic institutions of industrial society in general and with the management
of business enterprise in particular, without a deep and direct concern with
marketing. But in this field I am a consumer of marketing alone—albeit a
heavy one. I am not capable of making a contribution. I would indeed be
able to talk about the wants and needs I have which I, as a consumer of marketing, hope that you, the men of marketing, will soon supply:—a theory of
pricing, for instance, that can serve, as true theories should, as the foundation
for actual pricing decisions and for an understanding of price behavior; or a
consumer-focused concept and theory of competition. But I could not produce any of these "new products" of marketing which we want. I cannot
contribute myself. To use marketing language, I am not even "effective demand," in these fields as yet.

THE ROLE OF MARKETING

I shall today in my remarks confine myself to the second meaning in which
marketing has become a discipline: The role of marketing in economy and
society. And I shall single out as my focus the role of marketing in the economic development, especially of under-developed "growth" countries.

My thesis is very briefly as follows. Marketing occupies a critical role in
respect to the development of such "growth" areas. Indeed marketing is the
most important "multiplier" of such development. It is in itself in every one

of these areas the least developed, the most backward part of the economic system. Its development, above all others, makes possible economic integration and the fullest utilization of whatever assets and productive capacity an economy already possesses. It mobilizes latent economic energy. It contributes to the greatest needs: that for the rapid development of entrepreneurs and managers, and at the same time it may be the easiest area of managerial work to get going. The reason is that, thanks to men like Charles Coolidge Parlin, it is the most systematized, and, therefore, the most learnable and the most teachable of all areas of business management and entrepreneurship.

INTERNATIONAL AND INTERRACIAL INEQUALITY

Looking at this world of ours, we see some essentially new facts.

For the first time in man's history the whole world is united and unified. This may seem a strange statement in view of the conflicts and threats of suicidal wars that scream at us from every headline. But conflict has always been with us. What is new is that today all of mankind shares the same vision, the same objective, the same goal, the same hope, and believes in the same tools. This vision might, in gross over-simplification, be called "industrialization."

It is the belief that it is possible for man to improve his economic lot through systematic, purposeful, and directed effort—individually as well as for an entire society. It is the belief that we have the tools at our disposal —the technological, the conceptual, and the social tools—to enable man to raise himself, through his own efforts, at least to a level that we in this country would consider poverty, but which for most of our world would be almost unbelievable luxury.

And this is an irreversible new fact. It has been made so by these true agents of revolution in our times: the new tools of communication—the dirt road, the truck, and the radio, which have penetrated even the furthest, most isolated and most primitive community.

This is new, and cannot be emphasized too much and too often. It is both a tremendous vision and a tremendous danger in that catastrophe must result if it cannot be satisfied, at least to a modest degree.

But at the same time we have a new, unprecedented danger, that of international and interracial inequality. We on the North American continent are a mere tenth of the world population, including our Canadian friends and neighbors. But we have at least 75 per cent of the world income. And the 75 per cent of the world population whose income is below $100 per capita a year receive together perhaps no more than 10 per cent of the world's income. This is inequality of income, as great as anything the world has ever seen. It is accompanied by very high equality of income in the developed countries, especially in ours where we are in the process of proving that an industrial society does not have to live in extreme tension between the few very rich and the many very poor as lived all earlier societies of man. But what used to be national inequality and economic tension is now rapidly becoming international (and unfortunately also interracial) inequality and tension.

This is also brand new. In the past there were tremendous differences between societies and cultures: in their beliefs, their concepts, their ways of life, and their knowledge. The Frankish knight who went on Crusade was an ignorant and illiterate boor, according to the standards of the polished courtiers of Constantinople or of his Moslem enemies. But economically his society and theirs were exactly alike. They had the same sources of income, the same productivity of labor, the same forms and channels of investment, the same economic institutions, and the same distribution of income and wealth. Economically the Frankish knight, however much a barbarian he appeared, was at home in the societies of the East; and so was his serf. Both fitted in immediately and without any difficulty.

And this has been the case of all societies that were above the level of purely primitive tribe.

The inequality in our world today, however, between nations and races, is therefore a new—and a tremendously dangerous—phenomenon.

What we are engaged in today is essentially a race between the promise of economic development and the threat of international world-wide class war. The economic development is the opportunity of this age. The class war is the danger. Both are new. Both are indeed so new that most of us do not even see them as yet. But they are the essential economic realities of this industrial age of ours. And whether we shall realize the opportunity or succumb to danger will largely decide not only the economic future of this world —it may largely decide its spiritual, its intellectual, its political, and its social future.

SIGNIFICANCE OF MARKETING

Marketing is central in this new situation. For marketing is one of our most potent levers to convert the danger into the opportunity.

To understand this we must ask: What do we mean by "under-developed"?

The first answer is, of course, that we mean areas of very low income. But income is, after all, a result. It is a result first of extreme agricultural overpopulation in which the great bulk of the people have to find a living on the land which, as a result, cannot even produce enough food to feed them, let alone produce a surplus. It is certainly a result of low productivity. And both, in a vicious circle, mean that there is not enough capital for investment, and very low productivity of what is being invested—owing largely to misdirection of investment into unessential and unproductive channels.

All this we know today and understand. Indeed we have learned during the last few years a very great deal both about the structure of an under-developed economy and about the theory and dynamics of economic development.

What we tend to forget, however, is that the essential aspect of an "under-developed" economy and the factor the absence of which keeps it "under-developed," is the inability to organize economic efforts and energies, to bring together resources, wants, and capacities, and so to convert a self-limiting static system into creative, self-generating organic growth.

And this is where marketing comes in.

Lack of development in "under-developed" countries

1. First, in every "under-developed" country I know of, marketing is the most under-developed—or the least developed—part of the economy, if only because of the strong, pervasive prejudice against the "middleman."

As a result, these countries are stunted by inability to make effective use of the little they have. Marketing might by itself go far toward changing the entire economic tone of the existing system—without any change in methods of production, distribution of population, or of income.

It would make the producers capable of producing marketable products by providing them with standards, with quality demands, and with specifications for their product. It would make the product capable of being brought to markets instead of perishing on the way. And it would make the consumer capable of discrimination, that is, of obtaining the greatest value for his very limited purchasing power.

In every one of these countries, marketing profits are characteristically low. Indeed the people engaged in marketing barely eke out a subsistence living. And "mark-ups" are minute by our standards. But marketing costs are outrageously high. The waste in distribution and marketing, if only from spoilage or from the accumulation of unsalable inventories that clog the shelves for years, has to be seen to be believed. And marketing service is by and large all but non-existent.

What is needed in any "growth" country to make economic development realistic, and at the same time produce a vivid demonstration of what economic development can produce, is a marketing system:

A system of physical distribution;
A financial system to make possible the distribution of goods; and
Finally actual marketing, that is, an actual system of integrating wants, needs, and purchasing power of the consumer with capacity and resources of production.

This need is largely masked today because marketing is so often confused with the traditional "trader and merchant" of which every one of these countries has more than enough. It would be one of our most important contributions to the development of "under-developed" countries to get across the fact that marketing is something quite different.

It would be basic to get across the triple function of marketing:

The function of crystallizing and directing demand for maximum productive effectiveness and efficiency;
The function of guiding production purposefully toward maximum consumer satisfaction and consumer value;
The function of creating discrimination that then gives rewards to those who really contribute excellence, and that then also penalizes the monopolist,

the slothful, or those who only want to take but do not want to contribute or to risk.

Utilization by the entrepreneur

2. Marketing is also the most easily accessible "multiplier" of managers and entrepreneurs in an "under-developed" growth area. And managers and entrepreneurs are the foremost need of these countries. In the first place, "economic development" is not a force of nature. It is the result of the action, the purposeful, responsible, risk-taking action, of men as entrepreneurs and managers.

Certainly it is the entrepreneur and manager who alone can convey to the people of these countries an understanding of what economic development means and how it can be achieved.

Marketing can convert latent demand into effective demand. It cannot, by itself, create purchasing power. But it can uncover and channel all purchasing power that exists. It can, therefore, create rapidly the conditions for a much higher level of economic activity than existed before, can create the opportunities for the entrepreneur.

It then can create the stimulus for the development of modern, responsible, professional management by creating opportunity for the producer who knows how to plan, how to organize, how to lead people, how to innovate.

In most of these countries markets are of necessity very small. They are too small to make it possible to organize distribution for a single-product line in any effective manner. As a result, without a marketing organization, many products for which there is an adequate demand at a reasonable price cannot be distributed; or worse, they can be produced and distributed only under monopoly conditions. A marketing system is needed which serves as the joint and common channel for many producers if any of them is to be able to come into existence and to stay in existence.

This means in effect that a marketing system in the "under-developed" countries is the *creator of small business*, is the only way in which a man of vision and daring can become a businessman and an entrepreneur himself. This is thereby also the only way in which a true middle class can develop in the countries in which the habit of investment in productive enterprise has still to be created.

Developer of standards

3. Marketing in an "under-developed" country is the developer of standards —of standards for product and service as well as of standards of conduct, of integrity, of reliability, of foresight, and of concern for the basic long-range impact of decisions on the customer, the supplier, the economy, and the society.

Rather than go on making theoretical statements let me point to one illustration: The impact Sears Roebuck has had on several countries of Latin America. To be sure, the countries of Latin America in which Sears operates—Mexico,

Brazil, Cuba, Venezuela, Colombia, and Peru—are not "under-developed" in the same sense in which Indonesia or the Congo are "under-developed." Their average income, although very low by our standards, is at least two times, perhaps as much as four or five times, that of the truly "under-developed" countries in which the bulk of mankind still live. Still in every respect except income level these Latin American countries are at best "developing." And they have all the problems of economic development—perhaps even in more acute form than the countries of Asia and Africa, precisely because their development has been so fast during the last ten years.

It is also true that Sears in these countries is not a "low-price" merchandiser. It caters to the middle class in the richer of these countries, and to the upper middle class in the poorest of these countries. Incidentally, the income level of these groups is still lower than that of the worker in the industrial sector of our economy.

Still Sears is a mass-marketer even in Colombia or Peru. What is perhaps even more important, it is applying in these "under-developed" countries exactly the same policies and principles it applies in this country, carries substantially the same merchandise (although most of it produced in the countries themselves), and applies the same concepts of marketing it uses in Indianapolis or Philadelphia. Its impact and experience are, therefore, a fair test of what marketing principles, marketing knowledge, and marketing techniques can achieve.

The impact of this one American business which does not have more than a mere handful of stores in these countries and handles no more than a small fraction of the total retail business of these countries is truly amazing. In the first place, Sears' latent purchasing power has fast become actual purchasing power. Or, to put it less theoretically, people have begun to organize their buying and to go out for value in what they do buy.

Secondly, by the very fact that it builds one store in one city, Sears forces a revolution in retailing throughout the whole surrounding area. It forces store modernization. It forces consumer credit. It forces a different attitude toward the customer, toward the store clerk, toward the supplier, and toward the merchandise itself. It forces other retailers to adopt modern methods of pricing, of inventory control, of training, of window display, and what have you.

The greatest impact Sears has had, however, is in the multiplication of new industrial business for which Sears creates a marketing channel. Because it has had to sell goods manufactured in these countries rather than import them (if only because of foreign exchange restrictions), Sears has been instrumental in getting established literally hundreds of new manufacturers making goods which, a few years ago, could not be made in the country, let alone be sold in adequate quantity. Simply to satisfy its own marketing needs, Sears has had to insist on standards of workmanship, quality, and delivery—that is, on standards of production management, of technical management, and above all of the management of people—which, in a few short years, have advanced the art and science of management in these countries by at least a generation.

I hardly need to add that Sears is not in Latin America for reasons of philanthropy, but because it is good and profitable business with extraordinary growth potential. In other words, Sears is in Latin America because marketing is the major opportunity in a "growth economy"—precisely because its absence is a major economic gap and the greatest need.

The discipline of marketing

4. Finally, marketing is critical in economic development because marketing has become so largely systematized, so largely both learnable and teachable. It is the discipline among all our business disciplines that has advanced the furthest.

I do not forget for a moment how much we still have to learn in marketing. But we should also not forget that most of what we have learned so far we have learned in a form in which we can express it in general concepts, in valid principles and, to a substantial degree, in quantifiable measurements. This, above all others, was the achievement of that generation to whom Charles Coolidge Parlin was leader and inspiration.

A critical factor in this world of ours is the learnability and teachability of what it means to be an entrepreneur and manager. For it is the entrepreneur and the manager who alone can cause economic development to happen. The world needs them, therefore, in very large numbers; and it needs them fast.

Obviously this need cannot be supplied by our supplying entrepreneurs and managers, quite apart from the fact that we hardly have the surplus. Money we can supply. Technical assistance we can supply, and should supply more. But the supply of men we can offer to the people in the "under-developed" countries is of necessity a very small one.

The demand is also much too urgent for it to be supplied by slow evolution through experience, or through dependence on the emergence of "naturals." The danger that lies in the inequality today between the few countries that have and the great many countries that have not is much too great to permit a wait of centuries. Yet it takes centuries if we depend on experience and slow evolution for the supply of entrepreneurs and managers adequate to the needs of a modern society.

There is only one way in which man has ever been able to short-cut experience, to telescope development, in other words, to *learn something*. That way is to have available the distillate of experience and skill in the form of knowledge, of concepts, of generalization, of measurement—in the form of *discipline*, in other words.

THE DISCIPLINE OF ENTREPRENEURSHIP

Many of us today are working on the fashioning of such a discipline of entrepreneurship and management. Maybe we are further along than most of us realize.

Certainly in what has come to be called "Operation Research and Synthesis" we have the first beginnings of a systematic approach to the entrepreneurial task of purposeful risk-taking and innovation—so far only an approach, but a most promising one, unless indeed we become so enamored with the gadgets and techniques as to forget purpose and aim.

We are at the beginning perhaps also of an understanding of the basic problems of organizing people of diversified and highly advanced skill and judgment together in one effective organization, although again no one so far would, I am convinced, claim more for us than that we have begun at last to ask intelligent questions.

But marketing, although it only covers one functional area in the field, has something that can be called a discipline. It has developed general concepts, that is, theories that explain a multitude of phenomena in simple statements. It even has measurements that record "facts" rather than opinions. In marketing, therefore, we already possess a learnable and teachable approach to this basic and central problem not only of the "under-developed" countries but of all countries. All of us have today the same survival stake in economic development. The risk and danger of international and interracial inequality are simply too great.

Marketing is obviously not a cure-all, not a paradox. It is only one thing we need. But it answers a critical need. At the same time marketing is most highly developed.

Indeed without marketing as the hinge on which to turn, economic development will almost have to take the totalitarian form. A totalitarian system can be defined economically as one in which economic development is being attempted without marketing, indeed as one in which marketing is suppressed. Precisely because it first looks at the values and wants of the individual, and because it then develops people to act purposefully and responsibly—that is, because of its effectiveness in developing a free economy—marketing is suppressed in a totalitarian system. If we want economic development in freedom and responsibility, we have to build it on the development of marketing.

In the new and unprecedented world we live in, a world which knows both a new unity of vision and growth and a new and most dangerous cleavage, marketing has a special and central role to play. This role goes:

Beyond "getting the stuff out the back door";
Beyond "getting the most sales with the least cost";
Beyond "the optimal integration of our values and wants as customers, citizens, and persons, with our productive resources and intellectual achievements"—the role marketing plays in a developed society.

In a developing economy, marketing is, of course, all of this. But in addition, in an economy that is striving to break the age-old bondage of man to misery, want, and destitution, marketing is also the catalyst for the transmutation of latent resources into actual resources, of desires into accomplishments, and the development of responsible economic leaders and informed economic citizens.

READING 2

THE CONCEPT OF A NATIONAL MARKET AND ITS ECONOMICS GROWTH IMPLICATIONS*

Walt W. Rostow

I

I can tell you—without flattery—that I believe the skills this organization commands and represents are going to prove critical in the generation ahead to the development of countries and regions which contain a clear majority of the world's population. I have in mind the developing countries of Asia, the Middle East, Africa, and Latin America. I also have in mind the Soviet Union and the countries of Eastern Europe. I would add, parenthetically, that should Communist China come, in time, to formulate a rational and effective development strategy—which it now lacks—marketing in all its dimensions must play there, too, a new and significant role.

II

To understand why this proposition is valid, one must look at the development theories and policies which have been applied to these regions over the past generation, examine where they now stand and where they must go as they move forward in their stages of development.

With a few exceptions, the developing nations of Asia, the Middle East, Africa, and Latin America began their first purposeful stage of modernization by concentrating their efforts in two areas: the production of manufactured goods in substitution for consumer goods imports and the creation of basic infrastructure; that is, roads, electric power, ports, education, etc. Agriculture and the modernization of rural life were systematically neglected, yielding now a dangerous decline in per capita food production in some major regions.

There was a certain legitimacy in these initial priorities. The development of an economy, at its core, consists in the progressive diffusion of the fruits of modern science and technology. Industry is the most dramatic form which modern science and technology assumes; and basic infrastructure is directly required for industrialization.

But there was also an element of irrationality. Agriculture was associated with the period of colonialism and/or with excessive dependence on export markets in industrial countries. It appeared to be second order—and, even, faintly humiliating business, as compared to industrialization.

The combination of these two factors—rational and irrational—has led to a phase of development concentrated largely in a few cities, centered around a few industries, and, as I say, to a systematic neglect of what agriculture could

*Reprinted with permission from *Marketing and Economic Development*, Peter D. Bennet, ed. (Chicago: American Marketing Association, 1965), pp. 11–20.

and must contribute by way of food, industrial raw materials, foreign exchange, and enlarged domestic markets.

The start of industrialization varied in time as among the developing countries of the contemporary world. The Latin American countries generally began just before or during the Second World War, while many others began seriously only in the years after 1945. Some, indeed, have not yet launched their first phase of sustained industrialization. Nevertheless, it is broadly true that we have come to the end or are coming to the end of the phase when the initial, narrow postwar strategy for development can be regarded as viable.

In one developing country after another the perception is spreading that the next phase of development must be based on a systematic diffusion of the modern skills, now largely concentrated in urban areas, out into the countryside; on the making of efficient national markets; and, from this widened basis, on the generation of new lines of diversified exports which alone promise to earn the foreign exchange which the developing countries will need in the years ahead. Only this pattern of widened domestic markets and diversified exports promises to provide the foundation for that deepening of the industrial structure (from consumers goods down to capital goods and the heavy industry sectors) which a modern industrial society requires.

If I may be permitted to use a somewhat private vocabulary,[1] it can be said that during the past generation we have had in many parts of the world a take-off in which the leading sectors have been import-substitution industries in consumer goods fields; and for these nations to move on into the drive to industrial maturity requires that they convert their somewhat isolated urban industrial concentrations into active, dynamic centers which purposefully diffuse the process of modernization out across the nation, while they generate the capacity, on this wider market foundation, to pay their way as they move to full industrialization of their societies.

This is a shorthand approximation of the task for the next generation that lies before the nations within the Free World, which contain most of the population of Asia, the Middle East, Africa, and Latin America; and it is also the problem which must be solved if a modern industrialized China is really going to emerge.

III

The problem in the Soviet Union and much of Eastern Europe is, of course, somewhat different. There the origins of industrialization generally reach back to the last quarter of the nineteenth century—in some regions even earlier. These nations (with certain exceptions) have moved forward in the postwar generation to complete the drive to industrial maturity. They did so under doctrines which made the expansion of heavy industry virtually an object in itself; that is, heavy industry was built either to supply military forces or to build more heavy industry. But they have now come to a stage in their devel-

---

[1]Dr. Rostow refers here to his book, *The Stages of Economic Growth: A Non-Communist Manifesto,* Cambridge University Press, 1960.

opment where Khrushchev was quite right in attacking what he called the "steel eaters." He asked, you may remember, 'What do you want us to do with more steel, eat it?' It is the inevitable—and predicted—slowing down in the heavy industry sectors which mainly accounts for the over-all sluggishness of these economies. They have exhausted the capacity of the heavy industry sectors to lead in the growth process.

Along this way, like the developing countries, the Soviet Union and the countries of Eastern Europe have neglected agriculture. In addition, they have kept it under forms of collective organization which were grossly inefficient in their use of capital and manpower, although collective arrangements are being diluted in parts of Eastern Europe in an effort to provide effective incentives to the farmer.

The next stage of development in the Soviet Union and Eastern Europe must, evidently, be based not merely on a correction of agricultural inefficiency but upon the turning of their relatively mature industrial complexes to supply the things which people want when average income levels reach the point at which they now stand in these countries.

If high rates of growth are to be resumed in the Soviet Union and in Eastern Europe, they will come about by some version of the economic and social revolution which we in the United States began in the 1920's and which began to grip Western Europe and Japan in the 1950's; that is, the revolution centered about the rapid diffusion of the automobile, durable consumers goods, suburban housing, and all the rest of the now familiar package.

I may say in passing that this revolution is not to be understood simply in terms of industrial gadgetry. Behind the desire for a private automobile, a television set, a suburban house with a little grass and a fence, are two profound human desires which, from all we can thus far observe, are universal; namely, a desire for mobility—for getting over the horizon—and a desire for privacy. The gadgets we command represent, simply, the ways modern industry has found to satisfy these deep, legitimate, and decent human desires.

Again, reverting to my own terms, I would say that, just as most of the developing world is in a process of adjustment from take-off to the drive to technological maturity, the Soviet Union and Eastern Europe are in a process of adjustment from their own version of the drive to technological maturity to the age of high mass consumption.

IV

And here, of course, is where marketing comes in.

The modernization of the countryside in the developing countries evidently has many dimensions. We now know enough from practical experience to be able to say that, assuming roads and minimum basic education and assuming, also a certain backlog of relevant agricultural science, there are four necessary and sufficient conditions for an agricultural revolution.

First, the farmer must receive a reliable and fair price for his product.

Second, credit must be available at reasonable rates for him to make the change in the character of his output or the shift in productivity desired.

Third, there must be available on the spot technical assistance that is relevant to his soil, his weather conditions, and his change in either output or in productivity.

Finally, there must be available at reasonable rates two types of industrial products: inputs such as chemical fertilizers, insecticides, and farm tools; and incentive goods—that is, the consumer goods of good quality he and his family would purchase in greater quantity or work harder to get if they were cheaper or if his income were higher.

These four conditions can be satisfied in a good many ways. As I have wandered about the developing areas and studied the evidence available, I have been struck by the variety of institutional forms in which agricultural success stories appear—producers' cooperatives, food processing firms, large commercial farms, etc.; but they all have the characteristic of organizing around the farmer these four necessary and sufficient conditions.

You will note that marketing enters directly into these conditions both ways; that is, marketing from the farm to the city and from the city to the farm.

If the farmer is to receive a fair price for his product without a rise of food prices in the cities, there must be a modernization of marketing arrangements which permits this to happen. No aspect of the developing world troubles me more than the widespread situation where the farmer gets 15 or 20 percent of the selling price of his product—with the selling price in the city high and great wastage occurring along the way.

It is sometimes argued that the fragmented and expensive marketing arrangements which exist for many commodities in developing countries are, simply, an aspect of underdevelopment which will pass away with time and the progress of modernization as a whole. Specifically, it is sometimes pointed out that the modernization of marketing might remove from employment people who are now engaged, even at a low level of productivity.

Three considerations argue against this more complacent line of thought.

First, in many cases the marketing arrangements which confront a farmer in a developing country are what economists call monopsonistic; that is, the individual farmer is confronted with a situation where there is only one intermediary to whom he can sell his product. At the critical point of the harvest season the farmer is at the mercy of such intermediaries. That inequitable bargaining circumstance is often made worse because the purchaser of the farmer's products is often also the only available source of credit to the farmer. In short, traditional marketing arrangements are not only inefficient, they often do not have the competitive characteristics economists implicitly assume.

Second, the gap between prices on the farm and prices to the urban consumer constitutes a quite special barrier between the cities and the countryside, the effects of which must be measured not merely in terms of the alternative employment of labor but in terms of the whole urban-rural relationship. Specifically, archaic marketing arrangements make it unprofitable for the farmer to engage in higher productivity agricultural production; and they thereby reduce not only agricultural output but also the size of the market for manufactured goods. In modernizing marketing relations, we must take into account not merely the possible displacement of labor in the present marketing chains but the total effects on output and markets of what one Latin American president has called the Chinese wall they constitute between the city and the countryside.

Third, quite pragmatically, where modern marketing arrangements have been introduced (through producers' cooperatives, food processing firms, commercial farming, or other arrangements), the process of adjustment in employment in the marketing sector has not, in practice, proved difficult.

In short, I am confident that the modernization of marketing arrangements from the farm to the city is a crusade we can enter with a conviction that the benefits will far outweigh the costs in readjustment.

Looked at from the other side, that is, from the city to the countryside, the modernization of rural life demands new and effective ways of getting to the farmer both the things he needs to increase productivity and incentive goods.

With respect to chemical fertilizers, insecticides, seeds, and farm machinery, there is a role, beyond conventional marketing, to be undertaken by the salesman. It may be regarded as sacrilege by some, but it has generally proved true that the most powerful agent in the diffusion of new agricultural technology has been the commercial firm rather than public institutions set up for technical assistance purposes. I would not for a moment denigrate the role in the United States of the county agent nor of those who have followed in his tradition in the developing areas; but it is simply a fact that there are not enough county agents out working in the villages to do the job in contemporary developing areas. Among other reasons, too many trained agricultural technologists are to be found working in government offices in the capital city rather than in grass roots jobs. A good, pragmatic performance in the diffusion of technical knowledge can be and is being done in many parts of the world by those who have a straight commercial interest in selling their products. The salesman knows he must spend his time with potential customers.

With respect to incentive goods, we must begin by accepting the fact that people in the rural areas of the developing world are poor. Until their income rises, they may not be able to buy a great deal more than they are buying. On the other hand, it is also true that what they can buy in their villages by way of manufactured goods is often shoddy and expensive. We know from the history of rural areas in the United States—even the quite recent experience of the Tennessee Valley area—that the availability of attractive and inexpensive consumer goods can be an important stimulus to production and productivity. Lower prices can yield more purchases in the short run; lower prices and the availability of incentive goods of good quality can yield more output, income, and purchases in the longer run. The same lesson can be observed in Mexico and other developing areas where efforts to increase productivity on the supply side are combined with such incentives.

The technical marketing problem from the city to the countryside consists in finding ways to lower the unit cost of distribution under circumstances where rural markets are scattered and the volume of any one commodity to be sold at any one point is low. The most successful solution in developing countries is, of course, the marketing of beer and soft drinks. The volume of sales, however, is sufficient in this case to support regular truck deliveries even at low levels of rural income. What appears to be required is the development of unified marketing arrangements for a wide range of consumer goods so that the overhead distribution costs for each commodity are reduced.

As I have seen soft drink trucks roll into distant villages, I have often wished they had a trailer attached containing textiles, shoes, household equipment, flashlights, transistor radios, books and the other things the villagers would buy if prices were lower.

Producers' cooperatives, food processing plants, and other substantial institutions in rural areas can often serve as centers for the efficient assembly and distribution of such incentive goods, as well as the fertilizers, insecticides, etc., needed to increase productivity.

v

I have tried to indicate concretely the kind of marketing operations required if those engaged in distribution are to play their part in breaking down the Chinese wall between urban and rural life in developing countries and in assisting in the creation of national markets. The modernization of rural life, which lies at the heart of this structural problem, evidently involves elements which go beyond distribution itself. In our recent letter to the Presidents of the Latin American Republics and to the President of the United States, the Members of CIAP—the Inter-American Committee on the Alliance for Progress —listed seven major elements required to accelerate the modernization of rural life. Aside from more efficient distribution, these were: changes in land tenure in regions of many Latin American countries; changes in certain cases in government agricultural price policies; the expansion of production as well as distribution of chemical fertilizers; expansion and improvement of agricultural credit; the buildup of institutions such as producers' cooperatives and food processing firms; programs of popular cooperation and community development. Within this whole complex of actions designed to break the stagnation and apathy of life and production in rural areas, modern marketing arrangements have, however, a critical role.

The range of specific actions required in the Soviet Union and Eastern Europe is similar to that required in the developing areas; but the nations with Communist regimes confront their inherited commitment to collective institutions for production and distribution. Over the years these have proved generally inefficient and resistant to reform; although reform efforts have been made or are being made in several countries in the area. I know of very few government distribution operations anywhere in the world which have proved effective; and I know of a good many which have required massive subsidy to work at all. The reason is the lack of direct interest on the part of the bureaucrat in pressing for that extra margin of cost cutting and that extra margin of sales which make the difference.

Nevertheless, it is clear that there is a ferment in the Soviet Union and in Eastern Europe centered on the lack of incentives to productivity in agriculture and on methods for making the distribution system more responsive to the interests and tastes of the consumer. There is a growing awareness of the inner contradiction between the modes of organization which have been created in the past out of their ideological commitments and the imperatives of progress. No one can predict the outcome of these debates and the changes in policy that will ensue; but they constitute an interesting and important element for change on the world scene, which is essentially hopeful.

VI

The making of national markets through the more effective linking of urban and rural areas bears directly on the other great task of the developing countries in the years ahead; namely, their need to generate diversified exports. A whole range of special skills and special efforts is needed to market new products abroad. Potential markets must be studied with careful attention to local tastes; distribution channels must be established; regular and reliable flows of supplies must be moved and financed; quality controls must be built up; and efficient production must be generated if the exports are to be competitive. For countries whose first phase of industrialization has taken place internally, behind high tariff barriers which protected the local market, a quite revolutionary shift in mentality is required before business can generate the efficiency to face the winds of international competition. That shift is only beginning to take place in a few Latin American countries at the present time; although, in Asia, Taiwan has made the transition to diversified manufactured exports in good style, and South Korea is well on its way. In highly competitive international markets it does not take many cases of supplies that fail to arrive on time or of uncertain quality for the export effort to be set back.

That branch of the art of distribution concerned with the export trade will evidently be increasingly important in the developing areas in the years ahead.

But there is a further connection worth noting. Historically the export of manufactured goods has usually followed or paralleled the development of a national market. The classic case was that of cotton textiles. Starting with Great Britain, one country after another entered the textile export trade as a kind of reflex to learning how to produce and distribute efficiently within its own national market; for cotton textiles are the first modern manufactured product likely to develop a mass market in a relatively poor country. Other manufactured goods, in turn, have flowed into international channels as they took hold in domestic markets—right down to Japan's booming export of transistor radios. In concentrating in the years ahead on the development of national markets, therefore, the developing countries will also be laying the foundations for the export of those diversified manufactures on which their future foreign exchange earning capacity will substantially rest.

VII

The argument I have tried to lay before you today has a particular significance for the development of economic thought as well as for public policy. Whether we are conscious of it or not, our ways of thinking about the economy are still colored by ideas that go back to the classical economists of the nineteenth century and, indeed, back to the eighteenth century world of the physiocrats. They began to organize their thoughts by focusing on the physical factors of production, notably land and labor. The concept of the widening of the market was introduced and effectively dramatized, of course, by Adam Smith. But what it took to widen the market, beyond physical means of transport, was not generally taken seriously by the founding fathers of modern economic thought. In fact, distribution (and services generally) tended to be ignored or regarded, somehow, as an inferior kind of economic activity. Down to the present day it is difficult to get development economists and policy makers to accord to problems of efficiency in distribution the same attention they give automatically to problems of production, investment, and finance.

For Communists the problem is compounded by the nature of Marxist economics. Karl Marx was, as an economist, rooted in the classical tradition. His propositions perpetuated in a particularly strong form the tendency to denigrate distribution—so much so that it is formally excluded from Communist concepts of national income.

Thus in facing now the tasks of widening the market, both in the developing areas and in the Soviet Union and in Eastern Europe, governments must overcome that most insidious of pressures; that is, the pressures created by the sometimes unconscious acceptance of ideas from the past that obscure the character and priority of current problems.

If I am correct that men must, in the generation ahead, diffuse the process of modernization out over long neglected rural regions, creating new efficient networks of distribution, we shall see not merely new and challenging tasks for those who command the skills of distribution but a new theoretical respect and appreciation for the art of that widening of the market which, for so long, was taken for granted.

READING 3

MARKETING MYOPIA*

Theodore Levitt

Every major industry was once a growth industry. But some that are now riding a wave of growth enthusiasm are very much in the shadow of decline. Others which are thought of as seasoned growth industries have actually stopped growing. In every case the reason growth is threatened, slowed, or stopped is *not* because the market is saturated. It is because there has been a failure of management.

*Reprinted by permission of the publishers from Edward C. Bursk & John F. Chapman, eds., *Modern Marketing Strategy*, Cambridge, Mass.: Harvard University Press, Copyright, 1964, by the President and Fellows of Harvard College, pp. 24–48.

FATEFUL PURPOSES

The failure is at the top. The executives responsible for it, in the last analysis, are those who deal with broad aims and policies. Thus:

● The railroads did not stop growing because the need for passenger and freight transportation declined. That grew. The railroads are in trouble today not because the need was filled by others (cars, trucks, airplanes, even telephones), but because it was *not* filled by the railroads themselves. They let others take customers away from them because they assumed themselves to be in the railroad business rather than in the transportation business. The reason they defined their industry wrong was because they were railroad-oriented instead of transportation-oriented; they were product-oriented instead of customer-oriented.

● Hollywood barely escaped being totally ravished by television. Actually, all the established film companies went through drastic reorganizations. Some simply disappeared. All of them got into trouble not because of TV's inroads but because of their own myopia. As with the railroads, Hollywood defined its business incorrectly. It thought it was in the movie business when it was actually in the entertainment business. "Movies" implied a specific, limited product. This produced a fatuous contentment which from the beginning led producers to view TV as a threat. Hollywood scorned and rejected TV when it should have welcomed it as an opportunity—an opportunity to expand the entertainment business.

Today TV is a bigger business than the old narrowly defined movie business ever was. Had Hollywood been customer-oriented (providing entertainment), rather than product-oriented (making movies), would it have gone through the fiscal purgatory that it did? I doubt it. What ultimately saved Hollywood and accounted for its recent resurgence was the wave of new young writers, producers, and directors whose previous successes in television had decimated the old movie companies and toppled the big movie moguls.

There are other less obvious examples of industries that have been and are now endangering their futures by improperly defining their purposes. I shall discuss some in detail later and analyze the kind of policies that lead to trouble. Right now it may help to show what a thoroughly customer-oriented management *can* do to keep a growth industry growing, even after the obvious opportunities have been exhausted; and here there are two examples that have been around for a long time. They are nylon and glass—specifically, E. I. duPont de Nemours & Company and Corning Glass Works:

Both companies have great technical competence. Their product orientation is unquestioned. But this alone does not explain their success. After all, who was more pridefully product-oriented and product-conscious than the erstwhile New England textile companies that have been so thoroughly massacred? The DuPonts and the Cornings have succeeded not primarily because of their product or research orientation but because they have been thoroughly customer-oriented also. It is constant watchfulness for opportunities to apply their technical know-how to the creation of customer-satisfying uses which accounts for their prodigious output of successful new products. Without a very sophisticated eye on the customer, most of their new products might have been wrong, their sales methods useless.

Aluminum has also continued to be a growth industry, thanks to the efforts of two wartime-created companies which deliberately set about creating new customer-satisfying uses. Without Kaiser Aluminum & Chemical Corporation and Reynolds Metals Company, the total demand for aluminum today would be vastly less than it is.

Error of analysis

Some may argue that it is foolish to set the railroads off against aluminum or the movies off against glass. Are not aluminum and glass naturally so versatile that the industries are bound to have more growth opportunities than the railroads and movies? This view commits precisely the error I have been talking about. It defines an industry, or a product, or a cluster of know-how so narrowly as to guarantee its premature senescence. When we mention "railroads," we should make sure we mean "transportation." As transporters, the railroads still have a good chance for very considerable growth. They are not limited to the railroad business as such (though in my opinion rail transportation is potentially a much stronger transportation medium than is generally believed).

What the railroads lack is not opportunity, but some of the same managerial imaginativeness and audacity that made them great. Even an amateur like Jacques Barzun can see what is lacking when he says:

I grieve to see the most advanced physical and social organization of the last century go down in shabby disgrace for lack of the same comprehensive imagination that built it up. [What is lacking is] the will of the companies to survive and to satisfy the public by inventiveness and skill.[1]

SHADOW OF OBSOLESCENCE

It is impossible to mention a single major industry that did not at one time qualify for the magic appellation of "growth industry." In each case its assumed strength lay in the apparently unchallenged superiority of its product. There appeared to be no effective substitute for it. It was itself a runaway substitute for the product it so triumphantly replaced. Yet one after another of these celebrated industries has come under a shadow. Let us look briefly at a few more of them, this time taking examples that have so far received a little less attention:

● *Dry cleaning*—This was once a growth industry with lavish prospects. In

[1]Jacques Barzun, "Trains and the Mind of Man," *Holiday*, February 1960, p. 21.

an age of wool garments, imagine being finally able to get them safely and easily clean. The boom was on.

Yet here we are 30 years after the boom started and the industry is in trouble. Where has the competition come from? From a better way of cleaning? No. It has come from synthetic fibers and chemical additives that have cut the need for dry cleaning. But this is only the beginning. Lurking in the wings and ready to make chemical dry cleaning totally obsolescent is that powerful magician, ultrasonics.

● *Electric utilities*—This is another one of those supposedly "no-substitute" products that has been enthroned on a pedestal of invincible growth. When the incandescent lamp came along, kerosene lights were finished. Later the water wheel and the steam engine were cut to ribbons by the flexibility, reliability, simplicity, and just plain easy availability of electric motors. The prosperity of electric utilities continues to wax extravagant as the home is converted into a museum of electric gadgetry. How can anybody miss by investing in utilities, with no competition, nothing but growth ahead?

But a second look is not quite so comforting. A score of nonutility companies are well advanced toward developing a powerful chemical fuel cell which could sit in some hidden closet of every home silently ticking off electric power. The electric lines that vulgarize so many neighborhoods will be eliminated. So will the endless demolition of streets and service interruptions during storms. Also on the horizon is solar energy, again pioneered by nonutility companies.

Who says that the utilities have no competition? They may be natural monopolies now, but tomorrow they may be natural deaths. To avoid this prospect, they too will have to develop fuel cells, solar energy, and other power sources. To survive, they themselves will have to plot the obsolescence of what now produces their livelihood.

● *Grocery stores*—Many people find it hard to realize that there ever was a thriving establishment known as the "corner grocery store." The supermarket has taken over with a powerful effectiveness. Yet the big food chains of the 1930's narrowly escaped being completely wiped out by the aggressive expansion of independent supermarkets. The first genuine supermarket was opened in 1930, in Jamaica, Long Island. By 1933 supermarkets were thriving in California, Ohio, Pennsylvania, and elsewhere. Yet the established chains pompously ignored them. When they chose to notice them, it was with such derisive descriptions as "cheapy," "horse-and-buggy," "cracker-barrel storekeeping," and "unethical opportunists."

The executive of one big chain announced at the time that he found it "hard to believe that people will drive for miles to shop for foods and sacrifice the personal service chains have perfected and to which Mrs. Consumer is accustomed."[2] As late as 1936, the National Wholesale Grocers convention and the New Jersey Retail Grocers Association said there was nothing to fear. They said that the supers' narrow appeal to the price buyer limited the size of their

[2]For more details see M. M. Zimmerman, *The Super Market: A Revolution in Distribution* (New York, McGraw-Hill Book Company, Inc., 1955), p. 48.

market. They had to draw from miles around. When imitators came, there would be wholesale liquidations as volume fell. The current high sales of the supers was said to be partly due to their novelty. Basically people wanted convenient neighborhood grocers. If the neighborhood stores "cooperate with their suppliers, pay attention to their costs, and improve their service," they would be able to weather the competition until it blew over.[3]

It never blew over. The chains discovered that survival required going into the supermarket business. This meant the wholesale destruction of their huge investments in corner store sites and in established distribution and merchandising methods. The companies with "the courage of their convictions" resolutely stuck to the corner store philosophy. They kept their pride but lost their shirts.

Self-deceiving cycle

But memories are short. For example, it is hard for people who today confidently hail the twin messiahs of electronics and chemicals to see how things could possibly go wrong with these galloping industries. They probably also cannot see how a reasonably sensible businessman could have been as myopic as the famous Boston millionaire who 50 years ago unintentionally sentenced his heirs to poverty by stipulating that his entire estate be forever invested exclusively in electric streetcar securities. His posthumous declaration, "There will always be a big demand for efficient urban transportation," is no consolation to his heirs who sustain life by pumping gasoline at automobile filling stations.

Yet, in a casual survey I recently took among a group of intelligent business executives, nearly half agreed that it would be hard to hurt their heirs by tying their estates forever to the electronics industry. When I then confronted them with the Boston streetcar example, they chorused unanimously, "That's different!" But is it? Is not the basic situation identical?

In truth, *there is no such thing* as a growth industry, I believe. There are only companies organized and operated to create and capitalize on growth opportunities. Industries that assume themselves to be riding some automatic growth escalator invariably descend into stagnation. The history of every dead and dying "growth" industry shows a self-deceiving cycle of bountiful expansion and undetected decay. There are four conditions which usually guarantee this cycle:

1. The belief that growth is assured by an expanding and more affluent population.

2. The belief that there is no competitive substitute for the industry's major product.

3. Too much faith in mass production and in the advantages of rapidly declining unit costs as output rises.

[3]Ibid., pp. 45–47.

4. Preoccupation with a product that lends itself to carefully controlled scientific experimentation, improvement, and manufacturing cost reduction.

I should like now to begin examining each of these conditions in some detail. To build my case as boldly as possible, I shall illustrate the points with reference to three industries—petroleum, automobiles, and electronics—particularly petroleum, because it spans more years and more vicissitudes. Not only do these three have excellent reputations with the general public and also enjoy the confidence of sophisticated investors, but their managements have become known for progressive thinking in areas like financial control, product research, and management training. If obsolescence can cripple even these industries, it can happen anywhere.

POPULATION MYTH

The belief that profits are assured by an expanding and more affluent population is dear to the heart of every industry. It takes the edge off the apprehensions everybody understandably feels about the future. If consumers are multiplying and also buying more of your product or service, you can face the future with considerably more comfort than if the market is shrinking. An expanding market keeps the manufacturer from having to think very hard or imaginatively. If thinking is an intellectual response to a problem, then the absence of a problem leads to the absence of thinking. If your product has an automatically expanding market, then you will not give much thought to how to expand it.

One of the most interesting examples of this is provided by the petroleum industry. Probably our oldest growth industry, it has an enviable record. While there are some current apprehensions about its growth rate, the industry itself tends to be optimistic. But I believe it can be demonstrated that it is undergoing a fundamental yet typical change. It is not only ceasing to be a growth industry, but may actually be a declining one, relative to other business. Although there is widespread unawareness of it, I believe that within 25 years the oil industry may find itself in much the same position of retrospective glory that the railroads are now in. Despite its pioneering work in developing and applying the present-value method of investment evaluation, in employee relations, and in working with backward countries, the petroleum business is a distressing example of how complacency and wrongheadedness can stubbornly convert opportunity into near disaster.

One of the characteristics of this and other industries that have believed very strongly in the beneficial consequences of an expanding population, while at the same time being industries with a generic product for which there has appeared to be no competitive substitute, is that the individual companies have sought to outdo their competitors by improving on what they are already doing. This makes sense, of course, if one assumes that sales are tied to the country's population strings, because the customer can compare products only on a feature-by-feature basis. I believe it is significant, for example, that not since John D. Rockefeller sent free kerosene lamps to China has the oil industry done anything really outstanding to create a demand for its product. Not even in product improvement has it showered itself with eminence. The greatest single improvement, namely, the development of tetraethyl lead, came from outside the industry, specifically from General Motors and DuPont. The big contributions made by the industry itself are confined to the technology of oil exploration, production, and refining.

Asking for trouble

In other words, the industry's efforts have focused on improving the *efficiency* of getting and making its product, not really on improving the generic product or its marketing. Moreover, its chief product has continuously been defined in the narrowest possible terms, namely, gasoline, not energy, fuel, or transportation. This attitude has helped assure that:

• Major improvements in gasoline quality tend not to originate in the oil industry. Also, the development of superior alternative fuels comes from outside the oil industry, as will be shown later.

• Major innovations in automobile fuel marketing are originated by small new oil companies that are not primarily preoccupied with production or refining. These are the companies that have been responsible for the rapidly expanding multipump gasoline stations, with their successful emphasis on large and clean layouts, rapid and efficient driveway service, and quality gasoline at low prices.

Thus, the oil industry is asking for trouble from outsiders. Sooner or later, in this land of hungry inventors and entrepreneurs, a threat is sure to come. The possibilities of this will become more apparent when we turn to the next dangerous belief of many managements. For the sake of continuity, because this second belief is tied closely to the first, I shall continue with the same example.

Idea of indispensability

The petroleum industry is pretty much persuaded that there is no competitive substitute for its major product, gasoline—or if there is, that it will continue to be a derivative of crude oil, such as diesel fuel or kerosene jet fuel.

There is a lot of automatic wishful thinking in this assumption. The trouble is that most refining companies own huge amounts of crude oil reserves. These have value only if there is a market for products into which oil can be converted—hence the tenacious belief in the continuing competitive superiority of automobile fuels made from crude oil.

This idea persists despite all historic evidence against it. The evidence not only shows that oil has never been a superior product for any purpose for very long, but it also shows that the oil industry has never really been a growth industry. It has been a succession of different businesses that have gone through the usual historic cycles of growth, maturity, and decay. Its over-all survival is owed to a series of miraculous escapes from total obsolescence, of last-minute and unexpected reprieves from total disaster reminiscent of the Perils of Pauline.

Perils of petroleum

I shall sketch in only the main episodes:

● First, crude oil was largely a patent medicine. But even before that fad ran out, demand was greatly expanded by the use of oil in kerosene lamps. The prospect of lighting the world's lamps gave rise to an extravagant promise of growth. The prospects were similar to those the industry now holds for gasoline in other parts of the world. It can hardly wait for the underdeveloped nations to get a car in every garage.

In the days of the kerosene lamp, the oil companies competed with each other and against gaslight by trying to improve the illuminating characteristics of kerosene. Then suddenly the impossible happened. Edison invented a light which was totally nondependent on crude oil. Had it not been for the growing use of kerosene in space heaters, the incandescent lamp would have completely finished oil as a growth industry at that time. Oil would have been good for little else than axle grease.

● Then disaster and reprieve struck again. Two great innovations occurred, neither originating in the oil industry. The successful development of coal-burning domestic central-heating systems made the space heater obsolescent. While the industry reeled, along came its most magnificent boost yet—the internal combustion engine, also invented by outsiders. Then when the prodigious expansion for gasoline finally began to level off in the 1920's, along came the miraculous escape of a central oil heater. Once again the escape was provided by an outsider's invention and development. And when that market weakened, wartime demand for aviation fuel came to the rescue. After the war the expansion of civilian aviation, the dieselization of railroads, and the explosive demand for cars and trucks kept the industry's growth in high gear.

● Meanwhile centralized oil heating—whose boom potential had only recently been proclaimed—ran into severe competition from natural gas. While the oil companies themselves owned the gas that now competed with their oil, the industry did not originate the natural gas revolution, nor has it to this day greatly profited from its gas ownership. The gas revolution was made by newly formed transmission companies that marketed the product with an aggressive ardor. They started a magnificent new industry, first against the advice and then against the resistance of the oil companies.

By all the logic of the situation, the oil companies themselves should have made the gas revolution. They not only owned the gas; they also were the only people experienced in handling, scrubbing, and using it, the only people experienced in pipeline technology and transmission, and they understood heating problems. But, partly because they knew that natural gas would compete with their own sale of heating oil, the oil companies pooh-poohed the potentials of gas.

The revolution was finally started by oil pipeline executives who, unable to persuade their own companies to go into gas, quit and organized the spectacularly successful gas transmission companies. Even after their success became painfully evident to the oil companies, the latter did not go into gas transmission. The multibillion dollar business which should have been theirs went to others. As in the past, the industry was blinded by its narrow preoccupation with a specific product and the value of its reserves. It paid little or no attention to its customers' basic needs and preferences.

● The postwar years have not witnessed any change. Immediately after World War II the oil industry was greatly encouraged about its future by the rapid expansion of demand for its traditional line of products. In 1950 most companies projected annual rates of domestic expansion of around 6% through at least 1975. Though the ratio of crude oil reserves to demand in the Free World was about 20 to 1, with 10 to 1 being usually considered a reasonable working ratio in the United States, booming demand sent oil men searching for more without sufficient regard to what the future really promised. In 1952 they "hit" in the Middle East; the ratio skyrocketed to 42 to 1. If gross additions to reserves continue at the average rate of the past five years (37 billion barrels annually), then by 1970 the reserve ratio will be up to 45 to 1. This abundance of oil has weakened crude and product prices all over the world.

Uncertain future

Management cannot find much consolation today in the rapidly expanding petrochemical industry, another oil-using idea that did not originate in the leading firms. The total United States production of petrochemicals is equivalent to about 2% (by volume) of the demand for all petroleum products. Although the petrochemical industry is now expected to grow by about 10% per year, this will not offset other drains on the growth of crude oil consumption. Furthermore, while petrochemical products are many and growing, it is well to remember that there are nonpetroleum sources of the basic raw material, such as coal. Besides, a lot of plastics can be produced with relatively little oil. A 50,000-barrel-per-day oil refinery is now considered the absolute minimum size for efficiency. But a 5,000-barrel-per-day chemical plant is a giant operation.

Oil has never been a continuously strong growth industry. It has grown by fits and starts, always miraculously saved by innovations and developments not of its own making. The reason it has not grown in a smooth progression is that each time it thought it had a superior product safe from the possibility of competitive substitutes, the product turned out to be inferior and notoriously subject to obsolescence. Until now, gasoline (for motor fuel, anyhow) has escaped this fate. But, as we shall see later, it too may be on its last legs.

The point of all this is that there is no guarantee against product obsolescence. If a company's own research does not make it obsolete, another's will. Unless an industry is especially lucky, as oil has been until now, it can easily go down in a sea of red figures—just as the railroads have, as the buggy whip manufacturers have, as the corner grocery chains have, as most of the big movie companies have, and indeed as many other industries have.

The best way for a firm to be lucky is to make its own luck. That requires knowing what makes a business successful. One of the greatest enemies of this knowledge is mass production.

PRODUCTION PRESSURES

Mass-production industries are impelled by a great drive to produce all they can. The prospect of steeply declining unit costs as output rises is more than most companies can usually resist. The profit possibilities look spectacular. All effort focuses on production. The result is that marketing gets neglected.

John Kenneth Galbraith contends that just the opposite occurs.[4] Output is so prodigious that all effort concentrates on trying to get rid of it. He says this accounts for singing commercials, desecration of the countryside with advertising signs, and other wasteful and vulgar practices. Galbraith has a finger on something real, but he misses the strategic point. Mass production does indeed generate great pressure to "move" the product. But what usually gets emphasized is selling, not marketing. Marketing, being a more sophisticated and complex process, gets ignored.

The difference between marketing and selling is more than semantic. Selling focuses on the needs of the seller, marketing on the needs of the buyer. Selling is preoccupied with the seller's need to convert his product into cash; marketing with the idea of satisfying the needs of the customer by means of the product and the whole cluster of things associated with creating, delivering, and finally consuming it.

In some industries the enticements of full mass production have been so powerful that for many years top management in effect has told the sales departments, "You get rid of it; we'll worry about profits." By contrast, a truly marketing-minded firm tries to create value-satisfying goods and services that consumers will want to buy. What it offers for sale includes not only the generic product or service, but also how it is made available to the customer, in what form, when, under what conditions, and at what terms of trade. Most important, what it offers for sale is determined not by the seller but by the buyer. The seller takes his cues from the buyer in such a way that the product becomes a consequence of the marketing effort, not vice versa.

Lag in Detroit

This may sound like an elementary rule of business, but that does not keep it from being violated wholesale. It is certainly more violated than honored. Take the automobile industry:

Here mass production is most famous, most honored, and has the greatest

---

[4]*The Affluent Society* (Boston, Houghton Mifflin Company, 1958), pp. 152–160.

impact on the entire society. The industry has hitched its fortune to the relentless requirements of the annual model change, a policy that makes customer orientation an especially urgent necessity. Consequently the auto companies annually spend millions of dollars on consumer research. But the fact that the new compact cars are selling so well in their first year indicates that Detroit's vast researches have for a long time failed to reveal what the customer really wanted. Detroit was not persuaded that he wanted anything different from what he had been getting until it lost millions of customers to other small car manufacturers.

How could this unbelievable lag behind consumer wants have been perpetuated so long? Why did not research reveal consumer preferences before consumers' buying decisions themselves revealed the facts? Is that not what consumer research is for—to find out before the fact what is going to happen? The answer is that Detroit never really researched the customer's wants. It only researched his preferences between the kinds of things which it had already decided to offer him. For Detroit is mainly product-oriented, not customer-oriented. To the extent that the customer is recognized as having needs that the manufacturer should try to satisfy, Detroit usually acts as if the job can be done entirely by product changes. Occasionally attention gets paid to financing, too, but that is done more in order to sell than to enable the customer to buy.

As for taking care of other customer needs, there is not enough being done to write about. The areas of the greatest unsatisfied needs are ignored, or at best get stepchild attention. These are at the point of sale and on the matter of automotive repair and maintenance. Detroit views these problem areas as being of secondary importance. That is underscored by the fact that the retailing and servicing ends of this industry are neither owned and operated nor controlled by the manufacturers. Once the car is produced, things are pretty much in the dealer's inadequate hands. Illustrative of Detroit's arm's-length attitude is the fact that, while servicing holds enormous sales-stimulating, profit-building opportunities, only 57 of Chevrolet's 7,000 dealers provide night maintenance service.

Motorists repeatedly express their dissatisfaction with servicing and their apprehensions about buying cars under the present selling setup. The anxieties and problems they encounter during the auto buying and maintenance processes are probably more intense and widespread today than 30 years ago. Yet the automobile companies do not *seem* to listen to or take their cues from the anguished consumer. If they do listen, it must be through the filter of their own preoccupation with production. The marketing effort is still viewed as a necessary consequence of the product, not vice versa, as it should be. That is the legacy of mass production, with its parochial view that profit resides essentially in low-cost full production.

What Ford put first

The profit lure of mass production obviously has a place in the plans and strategy of business management, but it must always *follow* hard thinking about the customer. This is one of the most important lessons that we can learn from the contradictory behavior of Henry Ford. In a sense Ford was both the most brilliant and the most senseless marketer in American history. He was senseless because he refused to give the customer anything but a black car. He was brilliant because he fashioned a production system designed to fit market needs. We habitually celebrate him for the wrong reason, his production genius. His real genius was marketing. We think he was able to cut his selling price and therefore sell millions of $500 cars because his invention of the assembly line had reduced the costs. Actually he invented the assembly line because he had concluded that at $500 he could sell millions of cars. Mass production was the *result* not the cause of his low prices.

Ford repeatedly emphasized this point, but a nation of production-oriented business managers refuses to hear the great lesson he taught. Here is his operating philosophy as he expressed it succinctly:

Our policy is to reduce the price, extend the operations, and improve the article. You will notice that the reduction of price comes first. We have never considered any costs as fixed. Therefore we first reduce the price to the point where we believe more sales will result. Then we go ahead and try to make the prices. We do not bother about the costs. The new price forces the costs down. The more usual way is to take the costs and then determine the price, and although that method may be scientific in the narrow sense; it is not scientific in the broad sense, because what earthly use is it to know the cost if it tells you that you cannot manufacture at a price at which the article can be sold? But more to the point is the fact that, although one may calculate what a cost is, and of course all of our costs are carefully calculated, no one knows what a cost ought to be. One of the ways of discovering . . . is to name a price so low as to force everybody in the place to the highest point of efficiency. The low price makes everybody dig for profits. We make more discoveries concerning manufacturing and selling under this forced method than by any method of leisurely investigation.[5]

Product provincialism

The tantalizing profit possibilities of low unit production costs may be the most seriously self-deceiving attitude that can afflict a company, particularly a "growth" company where an apparently assured expansion of demand already tends to undermine a proper concern for the importance of marketing and the customer.

The usual result of this narrow preoccupation with so-called concrete matters is that instead of growing, the industry declines. It usually means that the product fails to adapt to the constantly changing patterns of consumer needs and tastes, to new and modified marketing institutions and practices, or to product developments in competing or complementary industries. The industry has its eyes so firmly on its own specific product that it does not see how it is being made obsolete.

[4]Henry Ford, *My Life and Work* (New York, Doubleday, Page & Company, 1923), pp. 146–147.

The classical example of this is the buggy whip industry. No amount of product improvement could stave off its death sentence. But had the industry defined itself as being in the transportation business rather than the buggy whip business, it might have survived. It would have done what survival always entails, that is, changing. Even if it had only defined its business as providing a stimulant or catalyst to an energy source, it might have survived by becoming a manufacturer of, say, fanbelts or air cleaners.

What may some day be a still more classical example is, again, the oil industry. Having let others steal marvelous opportunities from it (e.g., natural gas, as already mentioned, missile fuels, and jet engine lubricants), one would expect it to have taken steps never to let that happen again. But this is not the case. We are now getting extraordinary new developments in fuel systems specifically designed to power automobiles. Not only are these developments concentrated in firms outside the petroleum industry, but petroleum is almost systematically ignoring them, securely content in its wedded bliss to oil. It is the story of the kerosene lamp versus the incandescent lamp all over again. Oil is trying to improve hydrocarbon fuels rather than to develop *any* fuels best suited to the needs of their users, whether or not made in different ways and with different raw materials from oil.

Here are some of the things which nonpetroleum companies are working on:

● Over a dozen such firms now have advanced working models of energy systems which, when perfected, will replace the internal combustion engine and eliminate the demand for gasoline. The superior merit of each of these systems is their elimination of frequent, time-consuming, and irritating refueling stops. Most of these systems are fuel cells designed to create electrical energy directly from chemicals without combustion. Most of them use chemicals that are not derived from oil, generally hydrogen and oxygen.

● Several other companies have advanced models of electric storage batteries designed to power automobiles. One of these is an aircraft producer that is working jointly with several electric utility companies. The latter hope to use off-peak generating capacity to supply overnight plug-in battery regeneration. Another company, also using the battery approach, is a medium-size electronics firm with extensive small-battery experience that it developed in connection with its work on hearing aids. It is collaborating with an automobile manufacturer. Recent improvements arising from the need for high-powered miniature power storage plants in rockets have put us within reach of a relatively small battery capable of withstanding great overloads or surges of power. Germanium diode applications and batteries using sintered-plate and nickel-cadmium techniques promise to make a revolution in our energy sources.

● Solar energy conversion systems are also getting increasing attention. One usually cautious Detroit auto executive recently ventured that solar-powered cars might be common by 1980.

As for the oil companies, they are more or less "watching developments," as one research director put it to me. A few are doing a bit of research on fuel cells, but almost always confined to developing cells powered by hydro-carbon chemicals. None of them are enthusiastically researching fuel cells, batteries, or solar power plants. None of them are spending a fraction as much on research in these profoundly important areas as they are on the usual run-of-the-mill things like reducing combustion chamber deposit in gasoline engines. One major integrated petroleum company recently took a tentative look at the fuel cell and concluded that although "the companies actively working on it indicate a belief in ultimate success . . . the timing and magni-tude of its impact are too remote to warrant recognition in our forecasts."

One might, of course, ask: Why should the oil companies do anything different? Would not chemical fuel cells, batteries, or solar energy kill the present product lines? The answer is that they would indeed, and that is pre-cisely the reason for the oil firms having to develop these power units before their competitors, so they will not be companies without an industry.

Management might be more likely to do what is needed for its own pre-servation if it thought of itself as being in the energy business. But even that would not be enough if it persists in imprisoning itself in the narrow grip of its tight product orientation. It has to think of itself as taking care of customer needs, not finding, refining, or even selling oil. Once it genuinely thinks of its business as taking care of people's transportation needs, nothing can stop it from creating its own extravagantly profitable growth.

"Creative destruction"

Since words are cheap and deeds are dear, it may be appropriate to indicate what this kind of thinking involves and leads to. Let us start at the beginning —the customer. It can be shown that motorists strongly dislike the bother, delay, and experience of buying gasoline. People actually do not buy gaso-line. They cannot see it, taste it, feel it, appreciate it, or really test it. What they buy is the right to continue driving their cars. The gas station is like a tax collector to whom people are compelled to pay a periodic toll as the price of using their cars. This makes the gas station a basically unpopular institution. It can never be made popular or pleasant, only less unpopular, less un-pleasant.

To reduce its unpopularity completely means eliminating it. Nobody likes a tax collector, not even a pleasantly cheerful one. Nobody likes to interrupt a trip to buy a phantom product, not even from a handsome Adonis or a seductive Venus. Hence, companies that are working on exotic fuel substitutes which will eliminate the need for frequent refueling are heading directly into the outstretched arms of the irritated motorist. They are riding a wave of in-evitability, not because they are creating something which is technologically superior or more sophisticated, but because they are satisfying a powerful customer need. They are also eliminating noxious odors and air pollution.

Once the petroleum companies recognize the customer-satisfying logic of what another power system can do, they will see that they have no more choice about working on an efficient, long-lasting fuel (or some way of de-livering present fuels without bothering the motorist) than the big food chains had a choice about going into the supermarket business, or the vacuum tube companies had a choice about making semiconductors. For their own good the oil firms will have to destroy their own highly profitable assets. No amount of wishful thinking can save them from the necessity of engaging in this form of "creative destruction."

I phrase the need as strongly as this because I think management must make quite an effort to break itself loose from conventional ways. It is all too easy in this day and age for a company or industry to let its sense of purpose become dominated by the economies of full production and to develop a dangerously lopsided product orientation. In short, if management lets itself drift, it invariably drifts in the direction of thinking of itself as producing goods and services, not customer satisfactions. While it probably will not descend to the depths of telling its salesmen, "You get rid of it; we'll worry about profits," it can, without knowing it, be practicing precisely that formula for withering decay. The historic fate of one growth industry after another has been its suicidal product provincialism.

DANGERS OF R&D

Another big danger to a firm's continued growth arises when top management is wholly transfixed by the profit possibilities of technical research and development. To illustrate I shall turn first to a new industry—electronics—and then return once more to the oil companies. By comparing a fresh example with a familiar one, I hope to emphasize the prevalence and insidiousness of a hazardous way of thinking.

Marketing shortchanged

In the case of electronics, the greatest danger which faces the glamorous new companies in this field is not that they do not pay enough attention to research and development, but that they pay *too much* attention to it. And the fact that the fastest growing electronics firms owe their eminence to their heavy emphasis on technical research is completely beside the point. They have vaulted to affluence on a sudden crest of unusually strong general receptiveness to new technical ideas. Also, their success has been shaped in the virtually guaranteed market of military subsidies and by military orders that in many cases actually preceded the existence of facilities to make the products. Their expansion has, in other words, been almost totally devoid of marketing effort.

Thus, they are growing up under conditions that come dangerously close to creating the illusion that a superior product will sell itself. Having created a successful company by making a superior product, it is not surprising that management continues to be oriented toward the product rather than the people who consume it. It develops the philosophy that continued growth is a matter of continued product innovation and improvement.

A number of other factors tend to strengthen and sustain this belief:

1. Because electronic products are highly complex and sophisticated, managements become top-heavy with engineers and scientists. This creates a selective bias in favor of research and production at the expense of marketing. The organization tends to view itself as making things rather than satisfying customer needs. Marketing gets treated as a residual activity, "something else" that must be done once the vital job of product creation and production is completed.

2. To this bias in favor of product research, development, and production is added the bias in favor of dealing with controllable variables. Engineers and scientists are at home in the world of concrete things like machines, test tubes, production lines, and even balance sheets. The abstractions to which they feel kindly are those which are testable or manipulatable in the laboratory, or, if not testable, then functional, such as Euclid's axioms. In short, the managements of the new glamour-growth companies tend to favor those business activities which lend themselves to careful study, experimentation, and control—the hard, practical, realities of the lab, the shop, the books.

What gets shortchanged are the realities of the *market*. Consumers are unpredictable, varied, fickle, stupid, shortsighted, stubborn, and generally bothersome. This is not what the engineer-managers say, but deep down in their consciousness it is what they believe. And this accounts for their concentrating on what they know and what they can control, namely, product research, engineering, and production. The emphasis on production becomes particularly attractive when the product can be made at declining unit costs. There is no more inviting way of making money than by running the plant full blast.

Today the top-heavy science-engineering-production orientation of so many electronics companies works reasonably well because they are pushing into new frontiers in which the armed services have pioneered virtually assured markets. The companies are in the felicitous position of having to fill, not find markets; of not having to discover what the customer needs and wants, but of having the customer voluntarily come forward with specific new product demands. If a team of consultants had been assigned specifically to design a business situation calculated to prevent the emergence and development of a customer-oriented marketing viewpoint, it could not have produced anything better than the conditions just described.

Stepchild treatment

The oil industry is a stunning example of how science, technology, and mass production can divert an entire group of companies from their main task. To the extent the consumer is studied at all (which is not much), the focus is forever on getting information which is designed to help the oil companies improve what they are now doing. They try to discover more convincing advertising themes, more effective sales promotional drives, what the market shares of the various companies are, what people like or dislike about service station dealers and oil companies, and so forth. Nobody seems as interested in probing deeply into the basic human needs that the industry might be trying to satisfy as in probing into the basic properties of the raw material that the companies work with in trying to deliver customer satisfactions.

Basic questions about customers and markets seldom get asked. The latter occupy a stepchild status. They are recognized as existing, as having to be taken care of, but not worth very much real thought or dedicated attention. Nobody gets as excited about the customers in his own backyard as about the oil in the Sahara Desert. Nothing illustrates better the neglect of marketing than its treatment in the industry press:

The centennial issue of the *American Petroleum Institute Quarterly*, published in 1959 to celebrate the discovery of oil in Titusville, Pennsylvania, contained 21 feature articles proclaiming the industry's greatness. Only one of these talked about its achievements in marketing, and that was only a pictorial record of how service station architecture has changed. The issue also contained a special section on "New Horizons," which was devoted to showing the magnificent role oil would play in America's future. Every reference was ebulliently optimistic, never implying once that oil might have some hard competition. Even the reference to atomic energy was a cheerful catalogue of how oil would help make atomic energy a success. There was not a single apprehension that the oil industry's affluence might be threatened or a suggestion that one "new horizon" might include new and better ways of serving oil's present customers.

But the most revealing example of the stepchild treatment that marketing gets was still another special series of short articles on "The Revolutionary Potential of Electronics." Under that heading this list of articles appeared in the table of contents:

- "In the Search for Oil"

- "In Production Operations"

- "In Refinery Processes"

- "In Pipeline Operations"

Significantly, every one of the industry's major functional areas is listed, *except* marketing. Why? Either it is believed that electronics holds no revolutionary potential for petroleum marketing (which is palpably wrong), or the editors forgot to discuss marketing (which is more likely, and illustrates its stepchild status).

The order in which the four functional areas are listed also betrays the alienation of the oil industry from the consumer. The industry is implicitly defined as beginning with the search for oil and ending with its distribution from the refinery. But the truth is, it seems to me, that the industry begins with the needs of the customer for its products. From that primal position its definition moves steadily backstream to areas of progressively lesser importance, until it finally comes to rest at the "search for oil."

Beginning & end

The view that an industry is a customer-satisfying process, not a goods-producing process, is vital for all businessmen to understand. An industry begins with the customer and his needs, not with a patent, a raw material, or a selling skill. Given the customer's needs, the industry develops backwards, first concerning itself with the physical *delivery* of customer satisfactions. Then it moves back further to *creating* the things by which these satisfactions are in part achieved. How these materials are created is a matter of indifference to the customer, hence the particular form of manufacturing, processing, or what-have-you cannot be considered as a vital aspect of the industry. Finally, the industry moves back still further to *finding* the raw materials necessary for making its products.

The irony of some industries oriented toward technical research and development is that the scientists who occupy the high executive positions are totally unscientific when it comes to defining their companies' over-all needs and purposes. They violate the first two rules of the scientific method—being aware of and defining their companies' problems, and then developing testable hypotheses about solving them. They are scientific only about the convenient things, such as laboratory and product experiments. The reason that the customer (and the satisfaction of his deepest needs) is not considered as being "the problem" is not because there is any certain belief that no such problem exists, but because an organizational lifetime has conditioned management to look in the opposite direction. Marketing is a stepchild.

I do not mean that selling is ignored. Far from it. But selling, again, is not marketing. As already pointed out, selling concerns itself with the tricks and techniques of getting people to exchange their cash for your product. It is not concerned with the values that the exchange is all about. And it does not, as marketing invariably does, view the entire business process as consisting of a tightly integrated effort to discover, create, arouse, and satisfy customer needs. The customer is somebody "out there" who, with proper cunning, can be separated from his loose change.

Actually, not even selling gets much attention in some technologically minded firms. Because there is a virtually guaranteed market for the abundant flow of their new products, they do not actually know what a real market is. It is as if they lived in a planned economy, moving their products routinely from factory to retail outlet. Their successful concentration on products tends to convince them of the soundness of what they have been doing, and they fail to see the gathering clouds over the market.

CONCLUSION

Less than 75 years ago American railroads enjoyed a fierce loyalty among astute Wall Streeters. European monarchs invested in them heavily. Eternal wealth was thought to be the benediction for anybody who could scrape a few thousand dollars together to put into rail stocks. No other form of transportation could compete with the railroads in speed, flexibility, durability, economy, and growth potentials. As Jacques Barzun put it, "By the turn of the century it was an institution, an image of man, a tradition, a code of honor, a source of poetry, a nursery of boyhood desires, a sublimest of toys, and the most solemn machine—next to the funeral hearse—that marks the epochs in man's life."[6]

Even after the advent of automobiles, trucks, and airplanes, the railroad tycoons remained imperturbably self-confident. If you had told them 60 years ago that in 30 years they would be flat on their backs, broke, and pleading for government subsidies, they would have thought you totally demented. Such a future was simply not considered possible. It was not even a discussable subject, or an askable question, or a matter which any sane person would consider worth speculating about. The very thought was insane. Yet a lot of insane notions now have matter-of-fact acceptance—for example, the idea of 100-ton tubes of metal moving smoothly through the air 20,000 feet above the earth, loaded with 100 sane and solid citizens casually drinking martinis —and they have dealt cruel blows to the railroads.

What specifically must other companies do to avoid this fate? What does customer orientation involve? These questions have in part been answered by the preceding examples and analysis. It would take another article to show in detail what is required for specific industries. In any case, it should be obvious that building an effective customer-oriented company involves far more than good intentions or promotional tricks; it involves profound matters of human organization and leadership. For the present, let me merely suggest what appear to be some general requirements.

Visceral feel of greatness

Obviously the company has to do what survival demands. It has to adapt to the requirements of the market, and it has to do it sooner rather than later. But mere survival is a so-so aspiration. Anybody can survive in some way or other, even the skid-row bum. The trick is to survive gallantly, to feel the surging impulse of commercial mastery; not just to experience the sweet smell of success, but to have the visceral feel of entrepreneurial greatness.

No organization can achieve greatness without a vigorous leader who is driven onward by his own pulsating *will to succeed*. He has to have a vision of grandeur, a vision that can produce eager followers in vast numbers. In business, the followers are the customers. To produce these customers, the entire corporation must be viewed as a customer-creating and customer-satisfying organism. Management must think of itself not as producing products but as providing customer-creating value satisfactions. It must push this idea (and everything it means and requires) into every nook and cranny of the organization. It has to do this continuously and with the kind of flair that excites and stimulates the people in it. Otherwise, the company will be merely a series of pigeonholed parts, with no consolidating sense of purpose or direction.

In short, the organization must learn to think of itself not as producing goods or services but as *buying customers*, as doing the things that will make people

[6]Op. cit., p. 20.

want to do business with it. And the chief executive himself has the inescapable responsibility for creating this environment, this viewpoint, this attitude, this aspiration. He himself must set the company's style, its direction, and its goals. This means he has to know precisely where he himself wants to go, and to make sure the whole organization is enthusiastically aware of where that is. This is a first requisite of leadership, for *unless he knows where he is going, any road will take him there.*

If any road is okay, the chief executive might as well pack his attaché case and go fishing. If an organization does not know or care where it is going, it does not need to advertise that fact with a ceremonial figurehead. Everybody will notice it soon enough.

READING   4

MARKETING'S CHANGING SOCIAL RELATIONSHIPS*

William Lazer

Marketing is not an end in itself. It is not the exclusive province of business management. Marketing must serve not only business but also the goals of society. It must act in concert with broad public interest. For marketing does not end with the buy-sell transaction—its responsibilities extend well beyond making profits. Marketing shares in the problems and goals of society and its contributions extend well beyond the formal boundaries of the firm.

The purpose of this article is to present some viewpoints and ideas on topics concerning marketing's changing social relationships. The author hopes to stimulate discussion and encourage work by others concerned with the marketing discipline, rather than to present a definitive set of statements. He first presents a brief discussion of marketing and our life style, and marketing's role beyond the realm of profit. This is followed by the development of some ideas and viewpoints on marketing and consumption under conditions of abundance, with a particular focus on changing consumption norms. The last section is concerned with changing marketing boundaries and emerging social perspectives.

MARKETING AND LIFE STYLE

Recent developments in such areas as consumer safety and protection, product warranties, government investigations, and a host of urban issues, including air and water pollution, and poverty, are stimulating thoughtful executives and academicians to pay increasing attention to marketing's fundamental interfaces with society. They highlight the fact that marketers are inevitably concerned with societal norms and life styles of both our total

*Reprinted from The Journal of Marketing, published by the American Marketing Association, vol. 33, no. 1, January 1969, pp. 3–9.

society and societal segments. Since the American economy is a materialistic, acquisitive, thing-minded, abundant market economy, marketing becomes one of the cores for understanding and influencing life styles; and marketers assume the role of taste counselors. Since American tastes are being emulated in other parts of the world such as Europe, Japan, and Latin America, the impact of our values and norms reverberates throughout a broad international community.

Yet a basic difference exists between the orientation of the American life style, which is interwoven with marketing, and the life style of many other countries, particularly of the emerging and lesser-developed countries, although the differences are blurring. American norms include a general belief in equality of opportunity to strive for a better standard of living; the achievement of status and success through individual initiative, sacrifice, and personal skills; the provision and maintenance of a relatively open society with upward economic and social movement; the availability of education which is a route for social achievement, occupational advancement, and higher income. Yet, there are contradictory and conflicting concepts operating within this value system. One contradiction is seen in the conflict between concepts of equality for all on the one hand and the visible rank and status orderings in society. Another conflict much discussed today concerns the conflicts between the coexisting values of our affluent society and the pockets of poverty in the United States.

In their scheme of norms the majority of Americans, even younger Americans, exude optimism in the materialistic productivity of our society. They feel confident that the economic future will be much better than the present, that our standard of living and consumption will expand and increase, that pleasures will be multiplied, and that there is little need to curb desires. They are certain that increasing purchasing power will be made available to them.

This is not to deny the existence of discontent in our economy of plenty, or the challenging and questioning of values. There is evidence that some younger members are critical of our hedonistic culture, of our economic institutions and achievements. Questions have been raised about priorities of expenditures, and authority has been challenged. Various marketing processes and institutions have been attacked. But, by and large, there exists a general expectation of increasing growth, the availability of more and more, and a brighter and better future. As a result of this perspective, economic opportunities and growth are perceived not so much in terms of curbing consumer desires as is the case in many other societies, particularly in underdeveloped economies, but in increasing desires; in attempting to stimulate people to try to realize themselves to the fullest extent of their resources and capabilities by acquiring complementary goods and symbols. Whereas other societies have often hoped that tomorrow will be no worse than today, we would certainly be dismayed if present expectations did not indicate that tomorrow will be much better than today. Similarly, the emerging nations now have rising economic expectations and aspiration levels, and their life style perspectives are changing. They expect to share in the economic abundance achieved by highly industrialized economies.

The growth orientation which reverberates throughout the American society has its impact on our norms and on marketing practices. It is reflected in such marketing concepts and techniques as product planning, new product development, installment credit, pricing practices, advertising campaigns, sales promotion, personal selling campaigns, and a host of merchandising activities.

BEYOND THE REALM OF PROFIT

One of the next marketing frontiers may well be related to markets that extend beyond mere profit considerations to intrinsic values—to markets based on social concern, markets of the mind, and markets concerned with the development of people to the fullest extent of their capabilities. This may be considered a macro frontier of marketing, one geared to interpersonal and social development, to social concern.

From this perspective one of marketing's roles may be to encourage increasing expenditures by consumers of dollars and time to develop themselves socially, intellectually, and morally. Another may be the direction of marketing to help solve some of the fundamental problems that nations face today. Included are such problems as the search for peace, since peace and economic progress are closely intertwined; the renewal of our urban areas which is closely related to marketing development and practices, particularly in the area of retailing; the reduction and elimination of poverty, for marketing should have a major role here; the preservation of our natural resources; the reshaping of governmental interfaces with business; and the stimulation of economic growth. To help solve such problems, in addition to its current sense of purpose in the firm, marketing must develop its sense of community, its societal commitments and obligations, and accept the challenges inherent in any institution of social control.

But one may ask whether social welfare is consonant with the bilateral transfer characteristics of an exchange or market economy, or can it be realized only through the unilateral transfer of a grants economy? This is a pregnant social question now confronting marketing.

Business executives operating in a market economy can achieve the degree of adaptation necessary to accept their social responsibilities and still meet the demands of both markets and the business enterprise. At the very least, the exchange economy will support the necessary supplementary grants economy. Currently we are witnessing several examples of this.[1] The National Alliance for Businessmen composed of 50 top business executives is seeking jobs in 50 of our largest cities for 500,000 hard-core unemployed; the Urban Coalition, composed of religious, labor, government, and business leaders, as well as several individual companies, is actively seeking ways of attacking

[1]For a discussion of this point see Robert J. Holloway, "Total Involvement in Our Society," in *Changing Marketing Systems*, Reed Moyer (ed.) (Washington, D.C.: American Marketing Association 1967 Winter Conference Proceedings, December, 1967), pp. 6–8; Robert Lekachman, "Business Must Lead the Way," *Dun's Review*, Vol. 91 (April, 1968), p. 11; and Charles B. McCoy, "Business and the Community," *Dun's Review*, Vol. 91 (May, 1968), pp. 110–11.

the problem of unemployment among the disadvantaged; and the insurance companies are investing and spending millions for new housing developments in slum areas. It even seems likely that business executives, operating in a market environment, stimulated by the profit motive, may well succeed in meeting certain challenges of social responsibility where social planners and governmental agencies have not.

Governmental agencies alone cannot meet the social tasks. A spirit of mutual endeavor must be developed encompassing a marketing thrust. For marketing cannot insulate itself from societal responsibilities and problems that do not bear immediately on profit. Marketing practice must be reconciled with the concept of community involvement, and marketing leaders must respond to pressures to accept a new social role.[2]

The development of the societal dimensions of marketing by industry and/or other institutions is necessary to mold a society in which every person has the opportunity to grow to the fullest extent of his capabilities, in which older people can play out their roles in a dignified manner, in which human potentials are recognized and nurtured, and in which the dignity of the individual is accepted. While prone to point out the undesirable impact of marketing in our life style (as they should), social critics have neglected to indicate the progress and the contributions that have been made.

In achieving its sense of broad community interest and participation, marketing performs its social role in two ways. First, marketing faces social challenges in the same sense as the government and other institutions. But unlike the government, marketing finds its major social justification through offering product-service mixes and commercially unified applications of the results of technology to the marketplace for a profit. Second, it participates in welfare and cultural efforts extending beyond mere profit considerations, and these include various community services and charitable and welfare activities. For example, marketing has had a hand in the renewed support for the arts in general, the increasing demand for good books, the attendance at operas and symphony concerts, the sale of classical records, the purchase of fine paintings through mail-order catalogues, and the attention being given to meeting educational needs. These worthy activities, while sometimes used as a social measure, do not determine the degree of social concern or the acceptance of social responsibility.

A fundamental value question to be answered is not one of the absolute morality or lack of problems in our economic system and marketing activities, as many critics suggest. Rather, it is one concerning the *relative* desirability of our life style with its norms, its emphasis on materialism, its hedonistic thrust, its imperfections, injustices, and poverty, as contrasted with other life styles that have different emphases. Great materialistic stress and accomplishment is not inherently sinful and bad. Moral values are not vitiated (as many critics might lead one to believe) by substantial material acquisitions. In-

---

[2]Among the recent articles discussing management's new social role are "Business Must Pursue Social Goals: Gardner," *Advertising Age*, Vol. 39 (February, 1968), p. 2; B. K. Wickstrum, "Managers Must Master Social Problems," *Administrative Management*, Vol. 28 (August, 1967), p. 34; and G. H. Wyman, "Role of Industry in Social Change," *Advanced Management Journal*, Vol. 33 (April, 1968), pp. 70–4.

creasing leisure time does not automatically lead to the decay and decline of a civilization. In reality, the improvement of material situations is a stimulus for recognition of intrinsic values, the general lifting of taste, the enhancement of a moral climate, the direction of more attention to the appreciation of arts and esthetics. History seems to confirm this; for great artistic and cultural advancements were at least accompanied by, if not directly stimulated by, periods of flourishing trade and commerce.

MARKETING AND CONSUMPTION UNDER ABUNDANCE

American consumers are confronted with a dilemma. On the one hand, they live in a very abundant, automated economy that provides a surplus of products, an increasing amount of leisure, and an opportunity for a relative life of ease. On the other hand, they have a rich tradition of hard physical work, sweat, perseverance in the face of adversity, earning a living through hard labor, being thrifty, and "saving for a rainy day." There is more than token acceptance of a philosophy that a life of ease is sinful, immoral, and wrong. Some consumers appear to fear the abundance we have and the potential life style that it can bring, and are basically uncomfortable with such a way of life.

Yet, for continued economic growth and expansion, this feeling of guilt must be overcome. American consumers still adhere to many puritanical concepts of consumption, which are relevant in an economy of scarcity but not in our economy of abundance. Our society faces a task of making consumers accept comfortably the fact that a life style of relative leisure and luxury that eliminates much hard physical labor and drudgery, and permits us to alter unpleasant environments, is actually one of the major accomplishments of our age, rather than the indication of a sick, failing, or decaying society. Those activities resulting in the acquisition of more material benefits and greater enjoyment of life are not to be feared or automatically belittled, nor is the reduction of drudgery and hard physical tasks to be regretted.

Some of the very fundamental precepts underlying consumption have changed. For example, consumption is no longer an exclusive home-centered activity as it once was; consumption of large quantities of many goods and services outside the home on a regular basis is very common. Similarly, the hard work and drudgery of the home is being replaced by machines and services. The inherent values of thrift and saving are now being challenged by the benefits of spending and the security of new financial and employment arrangements.[3] In fact, the intriguing problems of consumption must now receive the attention previously accorded to those of physical production.

In essence, our consumption philosophy must change. It must be brought into line with our age of plenty, with an age of automation and mass production, with a highly industrialized mass-consumption society. To do so, the abundant life style must be accepted as a moral one, as an ethical one, as a

---

[3]Some aspects of the economic ambivalence of economic values are discussed by David P. Eastburn, "Economic Discipline and the Middle Generation," *Business Review*, Federal Reserve Bank of Philadelphia (July, 1968), pp. 3–8.

life which can be inherently good. The criteria for judging our economic system and our marketing activities should include opportunity for consumers to develop themselves to the fullest extent, personally and professionally; to realize and express themselves in a creative manner; to accept their societal responsibilities; and to achieve large measures of happiness. Abundance should not lead to a sense of guilt stemming from the automatic declaration of the immorality of a comfortable way of life spurred on by marketing practices.

In our society, is it not desirable to urge consumers to acquire additional material objects? Cannot the extension of consumer wants and needs be a great force for improvement and for increasing societal awareness and social contributions? Is it not part of marketing's social responsibility to help stimulate the desire to improve the quality of life—particularly the economic quality—and so serve the public interest?

In assessing consumption norms, we should recognize that consumer expenditures and investments are not merely the functions of increased income. They stem from and reflect our life style. Thus, new consumption standards should be established, including the acceptance of self-indulgence, of luxurious surroundings, and of non-utilitarian products. Obviously, products that permit consumers to indulge themselves are not "strict necessities." Their purchase does not, and should not, appeal to a "utilitarian rationale." For if our economic system produced only "utilitarian products," products that were absolute necessities, it would incur severe economic and social problems, including unemployment.

Yet some very significant questions may be posed. Can or should American consumers feel comfortable, physically and psychologically, with a life of relative luxury while they are fully cognizant of the existence of poverty in the midst of plenty, of practice of discrimination in a democratic society, the feeling of hopelessness and despair among many in our expanding and increasingly productive economy, and the prevalence of ignorance in a relatively enlightened age? Or, on a broader base, can or should Americans feel comfortable with their luxuries, regular model and style changes, gadgetry, packaging variations, and waste while people in other nations of the world confront starvation? These are among the questions related to priorities in the allocation of our resources, particularly between the public and private sectors and between the national and international boundaries that have been discussed by social and economic commentators such as Galbraith[4] and Toynbee.

These are not easy questions to answer. The answers depend on the perspective adopted (whether macro or micro), on the personal philosophy adhered to (religious and otherwise), and on the social concern of individuals, groups, and nations. No perfect economic system has or will ever exist, and the market system is no exception. Economic and social problems and conflicts will remain, but we should strive to eliminate the undesirable features of our market system. And it is clear that when abundance prevails individuals and nations can afford to, and do, exercise increasing social concern.

Toynbee, in assessing our norms and value systems (particularly advertis-

[4]John K. Galbraith, "The Theory of Social Balance," in *Social Issues in Marketing*, Lee E. Preston (ed.), (Glenview, Illinois: Scott, Foresman and Company 1968), pp. 247–252.

ing), wrote that if it is true that personal consumption stimulated by advertising is essential for growth and full employment in our economy (which we in marketing believe), then it demonstrates automatically to his mind that an economy of abundance is a spiritually unhealthy way of life and that the sooner it is reformed, the better.[5] Thus, he concluded that our way of life, based on personal consumption stimulated by advertising, needs immediate reform. But let us ponder for a moment these rather strong indictments of our norms and the impact of marketing on our value systems and life style.

When economic abundance prevails, the limitations and constraints on both our economic system and various parts of our life style shift. The most critical point in the functioning of society shifts from physical production to consumption. Accordingly, the culture must be reoriented: a producers' culture must be converted into a consumers' culture. Society must adjust to a new set of drives and values in which consumption, and hence marketing activities, becomes paramount. Buckminster Fuller has referred to the necessity of creating regenerative consumers in our affluent society.[6] The need for consumers willing and able to expand their purchases both quantitatively and qualitatively is now apparent in the United States. It is becoming increasingly so in Russia, and it will be so in the future among the underdeveloped and emerging nations. Herein lies a challenge for marketing—the challenge of changing norms and values to bring them into line with the requirements of an abundant economy.

Although some social critics and observers might lead us to believe that we should be ashamed of our life style, and although our affluent society is widely criticized, it is circumspect to observe that other nations of the world are struggling to achieve the stage of affluence that has been delivered by our economic system. When they achieve it, they will be forced to wrestle with similar problems of abundance, materialism, consumption, and marketing that we now face.

CONSUMPTION ACTIVITIES AND NORMS

The relative significance of consumers and consumption as economic determinants has been underemphasized in our system.[7] Consumption should not be considered an automatic or a happenstance activity. We must understand and establish the necessary conditions for consumption to proceed on a continuing and orderly basis. This has rich meaning for marketing. New marketing concepts and tools that encourage continuing production rather than disruptive production or the placement of consumer orders far in advance, or new contractual obligations, must be developed.[8] To achieve our stated

[5]"Toynbee vs. Bernbach: Is Advertising Morally Defensible?" *Yale Daily News* (Special Issue, 1963), p. 2.
[6]Buckminster Fuller, *Education Automation: Freeing the Scholar to Return to his Studies* (Carbondale, Ill.: Southern Illinois University Press, 1961).
[7]George Katona, "Consumer Investment and Business Investment," *Michigan Business Review* (June, 1961), pp. 17–22.
[8]Ferdinand F. Mauser, "A Universe-in-Motion Approach to Marketing," in *Managerial Marketing —Perspectives and Viewpoints*, Eugene J. Kelley and William Lazer (eds.) (Homewood, Illinois: Richard D. Irwin, Inc., 1967), pp. 46–56.

economic goals of stability, growth, and full employment, marketing must be viewed as a force that will shape economic destiny by expanding and stabilizing consumption.

To date the major determinant of consumption has been income. But as economic abundance increases, the consumption constraints change. By the year 2000 it has been noted that the customer will experience as his first constraint not money, but time.[9] As time takes on greater utility, affluence will permit the purchase of more time-saving products and services. Interestingly enough, although time is an important by-product of our industrial productivity, many consumers are not presently prepared to consume time in any great quantities, which in turn presents another opportunity for marketing. The manner in which leisure time is consumed will affect the quality of our life style.

In other ages, the wealthy achieved more free time through the purchase of personal services and the use of servants. In our society, a multitude of products with built-in services extend free time to consumers on a broad base. Included are such products as automobiles, jet planes, mechanized products in the home, prepared foods, "throw-aways," and leased facilities. Related to this is the concept that many consumers now desire the use of products rather than mere ownership. The symbolism of ownership appears to take on lesser importance with increasing wealth.[10]

We live in a sensate culture, one which stresses materialism and sensory enjoyment. Consumers desire and can obtain the use of products and symbols associated with status, achievement, and accomplishments. Material values which are visible have become more important to a broader segment of society, and marketing responds to and reinforces such norms. But our basic underlying value system is not merely the result of the whims of marketers —it has its roots in human nature and our cultural and economic environments.

The concept of consumption usually conjures a false image. Consumption generally seems to be related to chronic scarcity. It is associated with hunger, with the bare necessities of life, and with the struggle to obtain adequate food, shelter, and clothing.[11] It is associated with the perception of economics as the "dismal science," with the study of the allocation of scarce resources.

But, it has been noted that in the future consumption and consuming activities will occur in a society suffering from obesity and not hunger; in a society emerged from a state of chronic scarcity, one confronting problems of satiation—full stomachs, garages, closets and houses.[12] Such an environment requires a contemporary perspective and concept of consumption and consumers. It requires a recognition and appreciation of the importance of stimulating the consumption of goods. For consumers will find that their financial capabilities for acquiring new products are outstripping their natural inclinations to do so.

[9]Nelson N. Foote, "The Image of the Consumer in the Year 2000," Proceedings, Thirty-Fifth Annual Boston Conference on Distribution, 1963, pp. 13–18.
[10]Same reference as footnote 8.
[11]Same reference as footnote 9.
[12]Same reference as footnote 9.

But what happens to norms and values when people have suitably gratified their "needs"? What happens after the acquisition of the third automobile, the second color television set, and three or four larger and more luxurious houses? Maslow has noted that consumers then become motivated in a manner different from that explained by his hierarchy of motives. They become devoted to tasks outside themselves. The differences between work and play are transcended; one blends into the other, and work is defined in a different manner. Consumers become concerned with different norms and values reflected in metamotives or metaneeds, motives or needs beyond physical love, safety, esteem, and self-actualization.[13]

The tasks to which people become dedicated, given the gratification of their "needs," are those concerned with intrinsic values. The tasks are enjoyed because they embody these values. The self then becomes enlarged to include other aspects of the world. Under those conditions, Maslow maintains that the highest values, the spiritual life, and the highest aspirations of mankind become proper subjects for scientific study and research. The hierarchy of basic needs such as physical, safety, and social is prepotent to metaneeds. The latter, metaneeds, are equally potent among themselves.

Maslow also makes a distinction between the realm of being, the "B-realm," and the realm of deficiencies, the "D-realm,"—between the external and the practical. For example, in the practical realm of marketing with its daily pressures, executives tend to be responders. They react to stimuli, rewards, punishments, emergencies, and the demands of others. However, given an economy of abundance with a "saturation of materialism," they can turn attentions to the intrinsic values and implied norms—seeking to expose themselves to great cultural activities, to natural beauty, to the developments of those "B" values.

Our society has reached the stage of affluence without having developed an acceptable justification for our economic system, and for the eventual life of abundance and relative leisure that it will supply. Herein lies a challenge for marketing: to justify and stimulate our age of consumption. We must learn to realize ourselves in an affluent life and to enjoy it without pangs of guilt. What is required is a set of norms and a concept of morality and ethics that corresponds to our age. This means that basic concepts must be changed, which is difficult to achieve because people have been trained for centuries to expect little more than subsistence, and to gird for a fight with the elements. They have been governed by a puritanical philosophy, and often view luxurious, new, convenient products and services with suspicion.

When we think of abundance, we usually consider only the physical resources, capabilities, and potentialities of our society. But abundance depends on more than this. Abundance is also dependent on the society and culture itself. It requires psychological and sociological environments that encourage and stimulate achievement. *In large measure, our economic abundance results from certain institutions in our society which affect our pattern of living, and not the least of these institutions is marketing.*

Advertising is the institution uniquely identified with abundance, particu-

---

[13]Abraham Maslow, "Metamotivation," *The Humanist* (May–June, 1967), pp. 82–84.

larly in America. But the institution that is actually brought into being by abundance without previous emphasis or existence in the same form is marketing.[14] It is marketing expressed not only through advertising. It is also expressed in the emphasis on consumption in our society, new approaches to product development, the role of credit, the use of marketing research and marketing planning, the implementation of the marketing concept, the management of innovation, the utilization of effective merchandising techniques, and the cultivation of mass markets. Such institutions and techniques as self-service, supermarkets, discount houses, advertising, credit plans, and marketing research are spreading marketing and the American life style through other parts of the world.

Marketing is truly an institution of social control in a relatively abundant economy, in the same sense as the school and the home. It is one of the fundamental influences of our life style. It is a necessary condition of our high standard of living. It is a social process for satisfying the wants and needs of our society. It is a very formative force in our culture. In fact, it is impossible to understand fully the American culture without a comprehension of marketing. But, unlike some other social institutions, marketing is confronted with great conflicts that cloud its social role.

CHANGING MARKETING BOUNDARIES

We may well ask, what are the boundaries of marketing in modern society? This is an important question that cannot be answered simply. But surely these boundaries have changed and now extend beyond the profit motive. Marketing ethics, values, responsibilities, and marketing-government relationships are involved. These marketing dimensions will unquestionably receive increasing scrutiny by practitioners and academicians in a variety of areas, and the result will be some very challenging and basic questions that must be answered.

We might ask, for example, can or should marketing, as a function of business, possess a social role distinct from the personal social roles of individuals who are charged with marketing responsibilities?[15] Does the business as a legal entity possess a conscience and a personality whose sum is greater than the respective attributes of its individual managers and owners? Should each member of management be held personally accountable for social acts committed or omitted in the name of the business? Answers to such questions change with times and situations, but the trend is surely to a broadening recognition of greater social responsibilities—the development of marketing's social role.

Few marketing practitioners or academicians disagree totally with the concept that marketing has important social dimensions and can be viewed as a social instrument in a highly industrialized society. Disagreement exists, how-

---

[14]David M. Potter, "People of Plenty" (Chicago, Ill.: The University of Chicago Press, 1954), p. 167.
[15]For a discussion of the social responsibilities of executives see James M. Patterson, "What are the Social and Ethical Responsibilities of Marketing Executives?" *Journal of Marketing*, Vol. 30 (July, 1966), pp. 12–15, and K. Davis, "Understanding the Social Responsibility Puzzle," *Business Horizons*, Vol. 10 (Winter, 1967), pp. 45–50.

ever, about the relative importance of marketing's social dimensions as compared to its managerial or technical dimensions.

The more traditional view has been that marketing management fulfills the greater part of its responsibility by providing products and services to satisfy consumer needs profitably and efficiently. Those adopting this view believe that as a natural consequence of its efficiency, customers are satisfied, firms prosper, and the well-being of society follows automatically. They fear that the acceptance of any other responsibilities by marketing managers, particularly social responsibilities, tends to threaten the very foundation of our economic system. Moot questions about who will establish the guidelines, who will determine what these social responsibilities should be, and who will enforce departures from any standards established, are raised.

However, an emerging view is one that does not take issue with the ends of customer satisfaction, the profit focus, the market economy, and economic growth. Rather, its premise seems to be that the tasks of marketing and its concomitant responsibilities are much wider than purely economic concerns. It views the market process as one of the controlling elements of the world's social and economic growth. Because marketing is a social instrument through which a standard of living is transmitted to society, as a discipline it is a social one with commensurate social responsibilities that cannot merely be the exclusive concern of companies and consumers.

Perhaps nowhere is the inner self of the populace more openly demonstrated than in the marketplace; for the marketplace is an arena where actions are the proof of words and transactions represent values, both physical and moral. One theologian has written, "the saintly cannot be separated from the marketplace, for it is in the marketplace that man's future is being decided and the saintly must be schooled in the arts of the marketplace as in the discipline of saintliness itself."[16]

In this context, marketing's responsibility is only partially fulfilled through economic processes. There is a greater responsibility to consumers and to the human dignity that is vital to the marketplace—the concern for marketing beyond the profit motive.

Academicians and executives will be forced to rethink and reevaluate such situations in the immediate future just by the sheer weight of government concern and decisions if by nothing else.[17] In the last year, there have been governmental decisions about safety standards, devices for controlling air pollution, implied product warranties, packaging rules and regulations, the

---

[16]Louis Finkelstein in Conference On The American Character, Bulletin Center for the Study of Democratic Institutions (October, 1961), p. 6.

[17]The reader can gain some insight into government concern from such articles as "Consumer Advisory Council: First Report," in *Social Issues in Marketing*, Lee E. Preston, editor (Glenview, Ill.: Scott, Foresman and Company, 1968), pp. 282–294; Betty Furness, "Responsibility in Marketing," in *Changing Marketing Systems . . . ,*" Reed Moyer, editor (Washington, D.C.: American Marketing Association 1967 Winter Conference Proceedings, December, 1967), pp. 25–27; Galbraith, same reference as footnote 4; Richard H. Holton, "The Consumer and the Business Community," in *Social Issues in Marketing*, Lee E. Preston, editor (Glenview, Ill.: Scott, Foresman and Company, 1968), pp. 295–303; George H. Koch, "Government-Consumer Interest: From the Business Point of View," in *Changing Marketing Systems . . . ,*" Reed Moyer, editor (Washington, D.C.: American Marketing Association 1967 Winter Conference Proceedings, December, 1967), pp. 156–60.

relationship of national brands to private labels, pricing practices, credit practices, and mergers. There have been discussions about limiting the amount that can be spent on advertising for a product, about controlling trading stamps, about investigating various promotional devices and marketing activities. Such actions pose serious questions about marketing's social role. If we do not answer them, others will; and perhaps in a manner not too pleasing, or even realistic.

There need be no wide chasm between the profit motive and social responsibility, between corporate marketing objectives and social goals, between marketing actions and public welfare. What is required is a broader perception and definition of marketing than has hitherto been the case—one that recognizes marketing's societal dimensions and perceives of marketing as more than just a technology of the firm. For the multiple contributions of marketing that are so necessary to meet business challenges, here and abroad, are also necessary to meet the nation's social and cultural problems.

READING 5

SYSTEMS THEORY AND MANAGEMENT*

Richard A. Johnson, Fremont E. Kast, and James E. Rosenzweig

The systems concept is primarily a way of thinking about the job of managing. It provides a framework for visualizing internal and external environmental factors as an integrated whole. It allows recognition of the proper place and function of subsystems. The systems within which businessmen must operate are necessarily complex. However, management via systems concepts fosters a way of thinking which, on the one hand, helps to dissolve some of the complexity and, on the other hand, helps the manager recognize the nature of the complex problems and thereby operate within the perceived environment. It is important to recognize the integrated nature of specific systems, including the fact that each system has both inputs and outputs and can be viewed as a self-contained unit. But it is also important to recognize that business systems are a part of larger systems—possibly industry-wide, or including several, maybe many, companies and/or industries, or even society as a whole.

What does the concept of systems offer to students of management and/or to practicing executives? Is it a panacea for business problems which will replace scientific management, human relations, management by objective, operations research, and many other approaches to, or techniques of, management? Perhaps a word of caution is applicable initially. Anyone looking for "cookbook" techniques will be disappointed. In this book we do not evolve "ten easy steps" to success in management. Such approaches, while seemingly applicable and easy to grasp, usually are shortsighted and superficial. More fundamental ideas, such as the systems concept, are more difficult

*Reproduced by permission from *The Theory and Management of Systems*, New York, McGraw-Hill Book Company, 1963, pp. 3–15.

to comprehend, and yet they present an opportunity for a large-scale payoff.

In this book we shall develop the foundation for management by system. Before turning to aspects concerned primarily with business, it will be necessary to set the stage with certain introductory materials relative to systems in general and concerning an evolving body of knowledge called general systems theory. This background material will provide a basis for relating systems theory to business and for the integration of systems concepts and management. Those readers who are not particularly interested in general systems theory might find it desirable to skip directly to the Prologue, the last few pages of this chapter.

The discussion in this chapter is centered around the following topics:

Systems Defined
General Systems Theory
Systems Theory for Business
Systems Concepts and Management
Prologue
    Pervasiveness of Systems Concepts
    Plan of the Book

SYSTEMS DEFINED

A system is "an organized or complex whole; an assemblage or combination of things or parts forming a complex or unitary whole." The term system covers an extremely broad spectrum of concepts. For example, we have mountain systems, river systems, and the solar system as part of our physical surroundings. The body itself is a complex organism including the skeletal system, the circulatory system, and the nervous system. We come into daily contact with such phenomena as transportation systems, communication systems (telephone, telegraph, etc.), and economic systems.

A science often is described as a systematic body of knowledge; a complete array of essential principles or facts, arranged in a rational dependence or connection; a complex of ideas, principles, laws, forming a coherent whole. Scientists endeavor to develop, organize, and classify material into an interconnected discipline. Sir Isaac Newton set forth what he called the "system of the world." Other examples are "system of politics" and "system of theology." Two relatively well known works which represent attempts to integrate a large amount of material are Darwin's *Origin of the Species* and Keynes's *General Theory of Employment, Interest, and Money.* Darwin, in his theory of evolution, integrated all life into a "system of nature" and indicated how the myriad of living subsystems were interrelated. Keynes, in his general theory of employment, interest, and money, connected many complicated natural and man-made forces which make up an entire economy. Both men had a major impact on man's thinking because they were able to conceptualize interrelationships among complex phenomena and integrate them into a systematic whole. The word system connotes plan, method, order, and arrangement. Hence it is no wonder that scientists and researchers have made the term so pervasive.

The antonym of systematic is chaotic. A chaotic situation might be described as one where "everything depends on everything else." Since two major goals of science and research in any subject area are explanation and prediction, such a condition cannot be tolerated. Therefore there is considerable incentive to develop bodies of knowledge that can be organized into a complex whole, within which subparts or subsystems can be interrelated.

There is an obvious hierarchy of systems that can be created; that is, systems, systems of systems, and systems of systems of systems. For example, the universe is a system of heavenly bodies which includes many subsystems of stars called galaxies. Within one such galaxy, the Milky Way, there is the solar system, one of many planetary systems. Similarly, an organism is a system of mutually dependent parts each of which might include many subsystems. Human life is comprised of microorganisms which form larger systems that are subsystems of the organism as a whole.

While much research has been focused on the analysis of minute segments of knowledge, there has been increasing interest in developing larger frames of reference for synthesizing the results of such research. Thus attention has been focused more and more on over-all systems as frames of reference for analytical work in various areas. It is our contention that a similar process can be useful for managers. Whereas managers often have been focusing attention on particular functions in specialized areas, they may lose sight of the over-all objectives of the business and the role of their particular business in even larger systems. These individuals can do a better job of carrying out their own responsibilities if they are aware of the "big picture." It is the familiar problem of not being able to see the forest for the trees.

This disregard of the total system may be deliberate in the sense that functional or departmental managers are inclined to enhance their own performance at the expense of the total operation. However, it is more likely that such disregard is unintentional, resulting from the inability of decision makers in isolated segments to comprehend the interaction of their decisions with other segments of the business. The focus of systems management is on providing a better picture of the network of subsystems and interrelated parts which go together to form a complex whole.

Before proceeding to a discussion of systems theory for business, it will be beneficial to explore recent attempts to establish a general systems theory covering all disciplines or scientific areas.

GENERAL SYSTEMS THEORY[1]

General systems theory is concerned with developing a systematic, theoretical framework for describing general relationships of the empirical world. A broad spectrum of potential achievements for such a framework is evident. Existing

---

[1]Two articles provide the basis for this section. The name first appeared in an article by Ludwig von Bertalanffy, "General System Theory: A New Approach to Unity of Science," *Human Biology*, December, 1951, pp. 303–361. A more recent discussion, and one more pertinent to the specific task at hand, was that of Kenneth Boulding, "General Systems Theory: The Skeleton of Science," *Management Science*, April, 1956, pp. 197–208.

similarities in the theoretical construction of various disciplines can be pointed out. Models can be developed which have applicability to many fields of study. An ultimate but distant goal will be a framework (or system of systems of systems) which could tie all disciplines together in a meaningful relationship.

One of the most important reasons pointing to the need for a general systems theory is the problem of communication between the various disciplines. Although there is similarity between general methods of approach—the scientific method—the results of research efforts are not often communicated across discipline boundaries. Hence conceptualizing and hypothesizing that is done in one area seldom carries over into other areas where it conceivably could point the way toward a significant breakthrough. Specialists do not seem to communicate with one another. For example:

Hence physicists only talk to physicists, economists to economists—worse still, nuclear physicists talk only to nuclear physicists and econometricians to econometricians. One wonders sometimes if science will not grind to a stop in an assemblage of walled-in hermits, each mumbling to himself words in a private language that only he can understand.[2]

Of course, the conflict of ideas and difficulties of communication are even greater between the various cultures—the scientific, the social sciences, and the humanistic. This conflict has been intensified during the twentieth century.[3]

On the brighter side there has been some development of interdisciplinary studies. Areas such as social psychology, biochemistry, astrophysics, social anthropology, economic psychology, and economic sociology have been developed in order to emphasize the interrelationships of previously isolated disciplines. More recently, areas of study and research have been developed which call on numerous subfields. For example, cybernetics, the science of communication and control, calls on electrical engineering, neurophysiology, physics, biology, and other fields. Operations research is often pointed to as a multidisciplinary approach to problem solving. Information theory is another discipline which calls on numerous subfields. Organization theory embraces economics, sociology, engineering, psychology, physiology, and anthropology. Problem solving and decision making are becoming focal points for study and research, drawing on numerous disciplines.

With all these examples of interdisciplinary approaches, it is easy to recognize a surge of interest in larger-scale, systematic bodies of knowledge. However, this trend calls for the development of an over-all framework within which the various subparts can be integrated. In order that the *interdisciplinary* movement may not degenerate into *undisciplined* approaches, it is important that some structure be developed to integrate the various separate disciplines while retaining the type of discipline which distinguishes them. One approach to providing an over-all framework (general systems theory)

---

[2]Boulding, *op. cit.*, p. 198.
[3]C. P. Snow, *The Two Cultures and the Scientific Revolution*, Cambridge University Press, London, 1959.

would be to pick out phenomena common to many different disciplines and to develop general models which would include such phenomena. A second approach would include the structuring of a hierarchy of levels of complexity for the basic units of behavior in the various empirical fields. It would also involve development of a level of abstraction to represent each stage.

We shall explore the second approach, a hierarchy of levels, in more detail since it can lead toward a system of systems which has application in most businesses and other organizations. The reader can undoubtedly call to mind examples of familiar systems at each level of the following model.

1. The first level is that of static structure. It might be called the level of frameworks. *This is the geography and anatomy of the universe. . . . The accurate description of these frameworks is the beginning of organized theoretical knowledge in almost any field, for without accuracy in this description of static relationships no accurate functional or dynamic theory is possible.*
2. The next level of systematic analysis is that of the simple dynamic system with predetermined, necessary motions. This might be called the level of clockworks. *The solar system itself is of course the great clock of the universe from man's point of view, and the deliciously exact predictions of the astronomers are a testimony to the excellence of the clock which they study. . . . The greater part of the theoretical structure of physics, chemistry, and even of economics falls into this category.*
3. The next level is that of the control mechanism or cybernetic system, which might be nicknamed the level of the thermostat. *This differs from the simple stable equilibrium system mainly in the fact that the transmission and interpretation of information is an essential part of the system. . . . The homeostasis model, which is of such importance in physiology, is an example of a cybernetic mechanism, and such mechanisms exist through the whole empirical world of the biologist and the social scientist.*
4. The fourth level is that of the "open system," or self-maintaining structure. This is the level at which life begins to differentiate itself from not-life: it might be called the level of the cell.
5. The fifth level might be called the genetic-societal level; it is typified by the plant, *and it dominates the empirical world of the botanist.*
6. As we move upward from the plant world towards the animal kingdom we gradually pass over into a new level, the "animal" level, characterized by increased mobility, teleological behavior, and self-awareness. Here we have the development of specialized information-receptors (eyes, ears, etc.) leading to an enormous increase in intake of information; we also have a great development of nervous systems, leading ultimately to the brain, as an organizer of the information intake into a knowledge structure or "image." Increasingly as we ascend the scale of animal life, behavior is response not to a specific stimulus but to an "image" or knowledge structure or view of the environment as a whole. . . . The difficulties in the prediction of the behavior of these systems arises largely because of this intervention of the image between the stimulus and the response.

7. The next level is the "human" level, that is, of the individual human being considered as a system. In addition to all, or nearly all, of the characteristics of animal systems man possesses self-consciousness, which is something different from mere awareness. His image, besides being much more complex than that even of the higher animals, has a self-reflective quality—he not only knows, but knows that he knows. This property is probably bound up with the phenomenon of language and symbolism. It is the capacity for speech—the ability to produce, absorb, and interpret symbols, as opposed to mere signs like the warning cry of an animal —which most clearly marks man off from his humbler brethren.

8. Because of the vital importance for the individual man of symbolic images in behavior based on them it is not easy to separate clearly the level of the individual human organism from the next level, that of social organizations. . . . Nevertheless it is convenient for some purposes to distinguish the individual human as a system from the social systems which surround him, and in this sense social organizations may be said to constitute another level of organization. . . . At this level we must concern ourselves with the content and meaning of messages, the nature and dimensions of value systems, the transcription of images into historical record, the subtle symbolizations of art, music, and poetry, and the complex gamut of human emotion.

9. To complete the structure of systems we should add a final turret for transcendental systems, even if we may be accused at this point of having built Babel to the clouds. There are however the ultimates and absolutes and the inescapables and unknowables, and they also exhibit systematic structure and relationship. It will be a sad day for man when nobody is allowed to ask questions that do not have any answers.[4]

Obviously, the first level is most pervasive. Descriptions of static structures are widespread. However, this descriptive cataloguing is helpful in providing a framework for additional analysis and synthesis. Dynamic "clockwork" systems, where prediction is a strong element, are evident in the classical natural sciences such as physics and astronomy; yet even here there are important gaps. Adequate theoretical models are not apparent at higher levels. However, in recent years closed-loop cybernetic, or "thermostat," systems have received increasing attention. At the same time, work is progressing on open-loop systems with self-maintaining structures and reproduction facilities. Beyond the fourth level we hardly have a beginning of theory, and yet even here system description via computer models may foster progress at these levels in the complex of general systems theory.

Regardless of the degree of progress at any particular level in the above scheme, the important point is the concept of a general systems theory. Clearly, the spectrum, or hierarchy, of systems varies over a considerable range. However, since the systems concept is primarily a point of view and a desirable goal, rather than a particular method or content area, progress can be made as research proceeds in various specialized areas but within a total

[4]Boulding, *op. cit.*, pp. 202–205.

system context. The important aspect of such a hierarchy of system concepts revolves around the critical element of communication. McGrath, Nordlie, and Vaughn express it as follows:

Consequently, while scientists from many fields contribute to the area, and bring with them a wide range of scientific tools, the steps necessary to provide all applicable methods have not as yet been accomplished. This lack leads to less than optimal application of scientific tools, and to relatively ineffective communication among scientists from different fields working on similar problems, which in turn retards the rate of development of the system research field.

The impetus for the present research program comes from recognition of the need for a more systematic catalogue of methods applicable to system research problems, in order to provide a basis for a common language of method by means of which system research scientists can intercommunicate more adequately.[5]

Clearly, general systems theory provides for scientists at large a useful framework within which to carry out specialized activity. It allows researchers to relate findings and compare concepts with similar findings and concepts in other disciplines. With the general theory and its objectives as background, we direct our attention to a more specific theory for business, a systems theory which can serve as a guide for management scientists and ultimately provide the framework for integrated decision making on the part of practicing managers.

SYSTEMS THEORY FOR BUSINESS

The biologist Ludwig von Bertalanffy has set forth a new concept of general systems theory which he calls open systems.[6] The basis of his concept is that a living organism is not a conglomeration of separate elements but a definite system, possessing organization and wholeness. An organism is an open system which maintains a constant state while matter and energy which enter it keep changing (so-called dynamic equilibrium). The organism is influenced by, and influences, its environment and reaches a state of dynamic equilibrium in this environment. Such a description of a system adequately fits the typical business organization. The business organization is a man-made system which has a dynamic interplay with its environment—customers, competitors, labor organizations, suppliers, government, and many other agencies. Furthermore, the business organization is a system of interrelated parts working in conjunction with each other in order to accomplish a number of goals, both those of the organization and those of individual participants.

At times scholars in the field of management have depicted organizations as smoothly running machines. This would coincide with Boulding's second level in the general systems theory, that of "clockwork" systems. Organiza-

[5]Joseph D. McGrath, Peter G. Nordlie, W. S. Vaughn, Jr., *A Systematic Framework for Comparison of System Research Methods,* Human Sciences Research, Inc., Arlington, Va., November, 1959, p. 2.
[6]Bertalanffy, *op. cit.*

tions were described as highly mechanistic and predictable, and the various resources available—men, material, and machines—were manipulated in just that way.

Another common analogy was the comparison of the organization to the human body, with the skeletal and muscle systems representing the operating line elements and the circulatory system as a necessary staff function. The nervous system stood for the communication system. The brain symbolized top-level management, or the executive committee. In this sense an organization was represented as a self-maintaining structure, one which could reproduce. Such an analysis hints at the type of framework which would be useful as a systems theory for business—one which is developed as a system of systems and that can focus attention at the proper points in the organization for rational decision making, both from the standpoint of the individual and the organization.

The scientific-management movement utilized the concept of a man-machine system but concentrated primarily at the shop level. The so-called "efficiency experts" attempted to establish procedures covering the work situation and providing an opportunity for all those involved to benefit—employees, managers, and owners. The human relationists, the movement stemming from the Hawthorne–Western Electric studies, shifted some of the focus away from the man-machine system per se to interrelationships among individuals in the organization. Recognition of the effect of interpersonal relationships, human behavior, and small groups resulted in a relatively widespread reevaluation of managerial approaches and techniques.

The concept of the business enterprise as a social system also has received considerable attention in recent years. The social-system school looks upon management as a system of cultural interrelationships. The concept of a social system draws heavily on sociology and involves recognition of such elements as formal and informal organization within a total integrated system. Moreover, the organization or enterprise is recognized as subject to external pressure from the cultural environment. In effect, the enterprise system is recognized as a part of a larger environmental system.

Over the years, mathematics has been applied to a variety of business problems, primarily internal. Since World War II, operations-research techniques have been applied to large, complex systems of variables. They have been helpful in shop scheduling, in freight-yard operations, cargo handling, airline scheduling, and other similar problems. Queuing models have been developed for a wide variety of traffic- and service-type situations where it is necessary to program the optimum number of "servers" for the expected "customer" flow. Management-science techniques have undertaken the solution of many complex problems involving a large number of variables. However, by their very nature, these techniques must structure the system for analysis by quantifying system elements. This process of abstraction often simplifies the problem and takes it out of the real world. Hence the solution of the problem may not be applicable in the actual situation.

Simple models of maximizing behavior no longer suffice in analyzing business organizations. The relatively mechanical models apparent in the "scientific management" era gave way to theories represented by the "human relations" movement. Current emphasis is developing around "decision making" as a primary focus of attention, relating communication systems, organization structure, questions of growth (entropy and/or homeostasis), and questions of uncertainty. This approach recognizes the more complex models of administrative behavior and should lead to more encompassing systems that provide the framework within which to fit the results of specialized investigations of management scientists.

The aim of systems theory for business is to develop an objective, understandable environment for decision making; that is, if the system within which managers make the decisions can be provided as an explicit framework, then such decision making should be easier to handle. But what are the elements of this systems theory which can be used as a framework for integrated decision making? Will it require wholesale change on the part of organization structure and administrative behavior? Or can it be fitted into existing situations? In general, the new concepts can be applied to existing situations. Organizations will remain recognizable. Simon makes this point when he says:

1. Organizations will still be constructed in three layers; an underlying system of physical production and distribution processes, a layer of programmed (and probably largely automated) decision processes for governing the routine day-to-day operation of the physical system, and a layer of nonprogrammed decision processes (carried out in a man-machine system) for monitoring the first-level processes, redesigning them, and changing parameter values.
2. Organizations will still be hierarchical in form. The organization will be divided into major subparts, each of these into parts, and so on, in familiar forms of departmentalization. The exact basis for drawing departmental lines may change somewhat. Product divisions may become even more important than they are today, while the sharp lines of demarcation among purchasing, manufacturing, engineering, and sales are likely to fade.[7]

We agree essentially with this picture of the future. However, we want to emphasize the notion of systems as set forth in several layers. This connotes basic horizontal organization cutting across typical departmental lines. Thus the systems that are likely to be emphasized in the future will develop from projects or programs, and authority will be vested in managers whose influence will cut across traditional departmental lines. This concept will be developed more fully throughout this book.

Just as a general framework for integrating research activity and conceptualizing in various scientific disciplines would be helpful, a systems theory for business would be helpful as a framework for integrating managerial decisions. Organizations of the future will be developed with distinct layers of activity and with physical processes of production and distribution providing the base. Semiautomated and automated decision making will take place at a second level, which is geared to the basic activity of the organization. Decisions of a nonprogrammed nature will be carried on at higher levels in the organization.

[7]Herbert A. Simon, *The New Science of Management Decision*, Harper & Brothers, New York, 1960, pp. 49–50. (Emphasis by authors.)

However, the focus of attention in the future is likely to turn more and more to patterns of flow throughout the organizations. For example, material flow could be the focal point for decision making, rather than particular activities which take place with regard to the material; that is, the flow of material through the organization would be the primary concern, with secondary concern given to the functionally specialized departmental activities which are established to adjust or transform that material during the flow process. Similarly, flows of other resources such as men and capital could be so considered, thus changing the emphasis from vertical-hierarchical to the material-flow process. Similarly, if organizations could be defined in terms of information-decision systems, a new look in organization structure might be fostered.

SYSTEMS CONCEPTS AND MANAGEMENT

Management is the primary force within organizations which coordinates the activities of the subsystems and relates them to the environment. Management as an institution is relatively new in our society, stemming primarily from the growth in size and complexity of businesses since the industrial revolution. As Drucker says:

The emergence of management as an essential, a distinct and a leading institution is a pivotal event in social history. Rarely, if ever, has a new basic institution, a new leading group, emerged as fast as has management since the turn of this century. Rarely in human history has a new institution proven indispensable so quickly; and even less often has a new institution arrived with so little opposition, so little disturbance, so little controversy. . . . Management, which is the organ of society specifically charged with making resources productive, that is, with the responsibility for organized economic advance, therefore reflects the basic spirit of the modern age. It is in fact indispensable—and this explains why, once begotten, it grew so fast and with so little opposition.[8]

Managers are needed to convert the disorganized resources of men, machines, and money into a useful and effective enterprise. Essentially, management is the process whereby these unrelated resources are integrated into a total *system for objective accomplishment*. A manager gets things done by working with people and physical resources in order to accomplish the objectives of the system. He coordinates and integrates the activities and work of others rather than perform operations himself.

A general theory of management which has evolved in recent years focuses attention on the fundamental administrative processes which are essential if an organization is to meet its primary goals and objectives.[9] These basic managerial processes are required for any type of organization—business, government, educational, social, and other activities where human and physical resources are combined to meet certain objectives. Furthermore, these processes are necessary regardless of the specialized area of management

[8]Peter F. Drucker, *The Practice of Management*, Harper & Brothers, New York, 1954, pp. 3–4.
[9]See, for example, Harold F. Smiddy and Lionel Naum, "Evolution of a 'Science of Managing' in America," *Management Science*, October, 1954, pp. 1–31.

—production, distribution, finance, and facilitating activities. Although the management process has been described in numerous ways, four basic functions have received general acceptance—planning, organizing, controlling, and communicating. They can be defined in terms of systems concepts as follows:

Planning. The managerial function of planning is one of selecting the organizational objectives and the policies, programs, procedures, and methods for achieving them. The planning function is essentially one of providing a framework for integrated decision making and is vital to every man-machine system.

Organizing. The organizing function helps to coordinate people and resources into a system so that the activities they perform lead to the accomplishment of system goals. This managerial function involves the determination of the activities required to achieve the objectives of the enterprise, the departmentation of these activities, and the assignment of authority and responsibility for their performance. Thus the organizing function provides the interconnection, or intertie, between the various subsystems and the total organizational system.

Control. The managerial function of control is essentially that of assuring that the various organizational subsystems are performing in conformance to the plans. Control is essentially the measurement and correction of activity of the subsystems to assure the accomplishment of the over-all plan.

Communication. The communication function is primarily one of the transfer of information among decision centers in the various subsystems throughout the organization. The communication function also includes the interchange of information with the environmental forces.

Although these four managerial functions are listed and described separately, they should not be considered as independent activities, nor is any exact time sequence implied. Adequate performance of these functions is dependent upon the performance of the other three. For example, effective communication and control depends to a major extent upon the adequacy of the organizational structure and the planning process. Thus the total management process involves coordinating all four of these activities in order to meet the over-all objectives of the system.

READING 6

SYSTEMS APPROACH TO MARKETING*

Lee Adler

More and more businessmen today recognize that corporate success is, in most cases, synonymous with marketing success and with the coming of age of a new breed of professional managers. They find it increasingly important not only to pay lip service to the marketing concept but to do something about it in terms of (a) customer orientation, rather than navel-gazing in the factory, (b) organizational revisions to implement the marketing concept, and (c) a more orderly approach to problem solving.

In an increasing number of companies we see more conscious and formal efforts to apply rational, fact-based methods for solving marketing problems, and greater recognition of the benefits these methods offer. While these benefits may be newly realized, there is nothing new about the underlying philosophy; in the parlance of military men and engineers, it is the systems approach. For, whether we like it or not, marketing is, by definition, a system, if we accept Webster's definition of system as "an assemblage of objects united by some form of regular interaction or interdependence." Certainly, the interaction of such "objects" as product, pricing, promotion, sales calls, distribution, and so on fits the definition.

There is an expanding list of sophisticated applications of systems theory —and not in one but in many sectors of the marketing front. The construction of mathematical and/or logical models to describe, quantify, and evaluate alternate marketing strategies and mixes is an obvious case in point. So, too, is the formulation of management information systems[1] and of marketing plans with built-in performance measurements of predetermined goals. But no less vital is the role of the systems approach in the design and sale of products and services. When J. P. Stevens Company color-harmonizes linens and bedspreads, and towels and bath mats, it is creating a product system. And when Avco Corporation sells systems management to the space exploration field, involving the marriage of many scientific disciplines as well as adherence to budgetary constraints, on-time performance, and quality control, it is creating a *service* system.

In this article I shall discuss the utilization of the systems concept in marketing in both quantitative and qualitative ways with case histories drawn from various industries. In doing so, my focus will be more managerial and philosophical than technical, and I will seek to dissipate some of the hocus-pocus, glamor, mystery, and fear which pervade the field. The systems concept is not esoteric or "science fiction" in nature (although it sometimes *sounds* that way in promotional descriptions). Its advantages are not subtle or indirect; as we shall see, they are as real and immediate as decision making itself. The limitations are also real, and these, too, will be discussed.

(Readers interested in a brief summary of the background and the conceptual development of the systems approach may wish to turn to pages 64–65.)

PROMISING APPLICATIONS

Now let us look at some examples of corporate application of the systems approach. Here we will deal with specific parts or "subsystems" of the total marketing system. Exhibit 1 is a schematic portrayal of these relationships.

---

[1]See, for example, Donald F. Cox and Robert E. Good, "How to Build a Marketing Information System," on page 102.

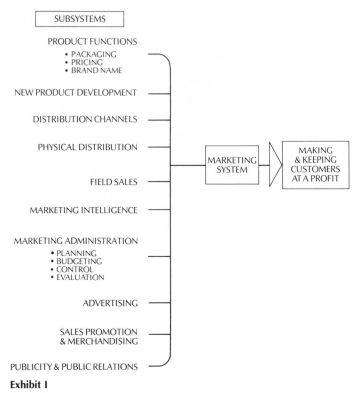

Exhibit I

Marketing subsystems and the total system

Products & services

The objective of the systems approach in product management is to provide a complete "offering" to the market rather than merely a product. If the purpose of business is to create a customer at a profit, then the needs of the customer must be carefully attended to; we must, in short, study what the customer is buying or wants to buy, rather than what we are trying to sell.

In the consumer products field we have forged ahead in understanding that the customer buys nutrition (not bread), beauty (not cosmetics), warmth (not fuel oil). But in industrial products this concept has been slower in gaining a foothold. Where it has gained a foothold, it expresses itself in two ways: the creation of a complete product system sold (1) as a unit, or (2) as a component or components which are part of a larger consumption system.

Perhaps the most eloquent testimony to the workability and value of the systems approach comes from companies that have actually used it. For a good example let us turn to the case of The Carborundum Company. This experience is especially noteworthy because it comes from industrial marketing, where, as just indicated, progress with the systems concept has generally been slow.

Birth of the concept. Founded in 1894, the company was content for many years to sell abrasives. It offered an extremely broad line of grinding wheels, coated abrasives, and abrasive grain, with a reputed capacity for 200,000 different products of varying type, grade, and formulation. But the focus was on the product.

In the mid-1950's, Carborundum perceived that the market for abrasives could be broadened considerably if—looking at abrasives through customers' eyes—it would see the product as fitting into *metal polishing, cleaning,* or *removal systems.* Now Carborundum is concerned with all aspects of abrading—the machine, the contact wheel, the workpiece, the labor cost, the overhead rate, the abrasive, and, above all, the customer's objective. In the words of Carborundum's president, W. H. Wendel:

That objective is never the abrasive per se, but rather the creation of a certain dimension, a type of finish, or a required shape, always related to a minimum cost. Since there are many variables to consider, just one can be misleading. To render maximum service, Carborundum (must offer) a complete system.[2]

Organizational overhaul. To offer such a system, management had to overhaul important parts of the organization:

1. The company needed to enhance its knowledge of the total system. As Wendel explains:

We felt we had excellent knowledge of coated abrasive products, but that we didn't have the application and machine know-how in depth. To be really successful in the business, we had to know as much about the machine tools as we did the abrasives.[3]

To fill this need, Carborundum made three acquisitions—The Tysaman Machine Company, which builds heavy-duty snagging, billet grinding, and abrasive cut-off machines; Curtis Machine Company, a maker of belt sanders; and Pangborn Corporation, which supplied systems capability in abrasive blast cleaning and finishing.

2. The company's abrasive divisions were reorganized, and the management of them was realigned to accommodate the new philosophy and its application. The company found that *centering responsibility for the full system in one profit center* proved to be the most effective method of coordinating approaches in application engineering, choice of distribution channels, brand identification, field sales operations, and so forth. This method was particularly valuable for integrating the acquisitions into the new program.

3. An Abrasives Systems Center was established to handle development work and to solve customer problems.

4. Technical conferences and seminars were held to educate customers on the new developments.

5. Salesmen were trained in machine and application knowledge.

---

[2] "Abrasive Maker's Systems Approach Opens New Markets," *Steel,* December 27, 1965, p. 38.
[3] Ibid.

Planning. A key tool in the systems approach is planning—in particular, the use of what I like to call "total business plans." (This term emphasizes the contrast with company plans that cover only limited functions.) At Carborundum, total business plans are developed with extreme care by the operating companies and divisions. Very specific objectives are established, and then detailed action programs are outlined to achieve these objectives. The action programs extend throughout the organization, including the manufacturing and development branches of the operating unit. Management sets specific dates for the completion of action steps and defines who is responsible for them. Also, it carefully measures results against established objectives. This is done both in the financial reporting system and in various marketing committees.

Quantitative methods. Carborundum has utilized various operations research techniques, like decision tree analysis and PERT, to aid in molding plans and strategies. For example, one analysis, which concerned itself with determining the necessity for plant expansion, was based on different possible levels of success for the marketing plan. In addition, the computer has been used for inventory management, evaluation of alternate pricing strategies for systems selling, and the measurement of marketing achievements against goals.

It should be noted, though, that these quantitative techniques are management tools only and that much of the application of systems thinking to the redeployment of Carborundum's business is qualitative in nature.

Gains achieved. As a consequence of these developments, the company has opened up vast new markets. To quote Carborundum's president again:

Customers don't want a grinding wheel, they want metal removed. . . . The U.S. and Canadian market for abrasives amounts to $700 million a year. But what companies spend on stock removal—to bore, grind, cut, shape, and finish metal—amounts to $30 billion a year.[4]

Illustrating this market expansion in the steel industry is Carborundum's commercial success with three new developments—hot grinding, an arborless wheel to speed metal removal and cut grinding costs, and high-speed conditioning of carbon steel billets. All represent conversions from nonabrasive methods. Carborundum now also finds that the close relationship with customers gives it a competitive edge, opens top customer management doors, gains entree for salesmen with prospects they had never been able to "crack" before. Perhaps the ultimate accolade is the company's report that customers even come to the organization itself, regarding it as a consultant as well as a supplier.

Profitable innovation

The intense pressure to originate successful new products cannot be met without methodologies calculated to enhance the probabilities of profitable

[4]"Carborundum Grinds at Faster Clip," *Business Week*, July 23, 1966, pp. 58, 60.

innovation. The systems approach has a bearing here, too. Exhibit II shows a model for "tracking" products through the many stages of ideation, development, and testing to ultimate full-scale commercialization. This diagram is in effect a larger version of the "New Product Development" box in Exhibit I.

Observe that this is a logical (specifically, sequential), rather than numerical, model. While some elements of the total system (e.g., alternate distribution channels and various media mixes) can be analyzed by means of operations research techniques, the model has not been cast in mathematical terms. Rather, the flow diagram as a whole is used as a checklist to make sure "all bases are covered" and to help organize the chronological sequence of steps in new product development. It also serves as a conceptual foundation for formal PERT application, should management desire such a step, and for the gradual development of a series of equations linking together elements in the diagrams, should it seem useful to experiment with mathematical models.

Marketing intelligence

The traditional notion of marketing research is fast becoming antiquated. For it leads to dreary chronicles of the past rather than focusing on the present and shedding light on the future. It is particularistic, tending to concentrate on the study of tiny fractions of a marketing problem rather than on the problem as a whole. It lends itself to assuaging the curiosity of the moment, to fire-fighting, to resolving internecine disputes. It is a slave to technique. I shall not, therefore, relate the term *marketing research* to the systems approach —although I recognize, of course, that some leading businessmen and writers are breathing new life and scope into the ideas referred to by that term.

The role of the systems approach is to help evolve a *marketing intelligence* system tailored to the needs of each marketer. Such a system would serve as the ever-alert nerve center of the marketing operation. It would have these major characteristics:

- Continuous surveillance of the market.

- A team of research techniques used in tandem.

- A network of data sources.

- Integrated analysis of data from the various sources.

- Effective utilization of automatic data-processing equipment to distill mountains of raw information speedily.

- Strong concentration not just on reporting findings but also on practical, action-oriented recommendations.

Concept in use. A practical instance of the use of such an intelligence system is supplied by Mead Johnson Nutritionals (division of Mead Johnson & Company), manufacturers of Metrecal, Pablum, Bib, Nutrament, and other nutritional specialties. As Exhibit III shows, the company's Marketing Intelligence Department has provided information from these sources:

● A continuing large-scale consumer market study covering attitudinal and behavioral data dealing with weight control.

● Nielsen store audit data, on a bimonthly basis.

● A monthly sales audit conducted among a panel of 100 high-volume food stores in 20 markets to provide advance indications of brand share shifts.

● Supermarket warehouse withdrawal figures from Time, Inc.'s new service, Selling Areas-Marketing, Inc.

Exhibit II

Work flow and systems chart for management of new products.

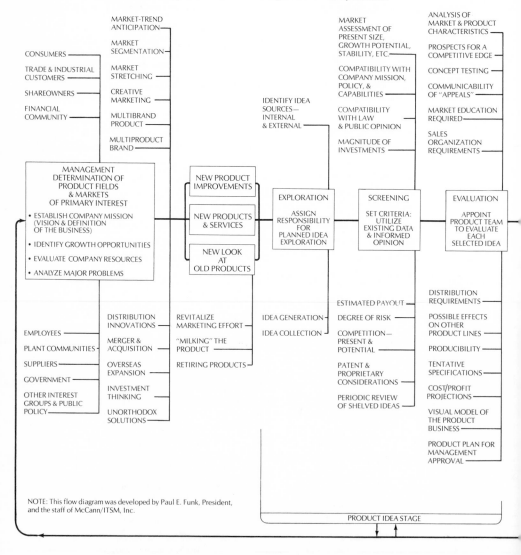

NOTE: This flow diagram was developed by Paul E. Funk, President, and the staff of McCann/ITSM, Inc.

● Salesmen's weekly reports (which, in addition to serving the purposes of sales management control, call for reconnaissance on competitive promotions, new product launches, price changes, and so forth).

● Advertising expenditure data, by media class, from the company's accounting department.

● Figures on sales and related topics from company factories.

● Competitive advertising expenditure and exposure data, supplied by the division's advertising agencies at periodic intervals.

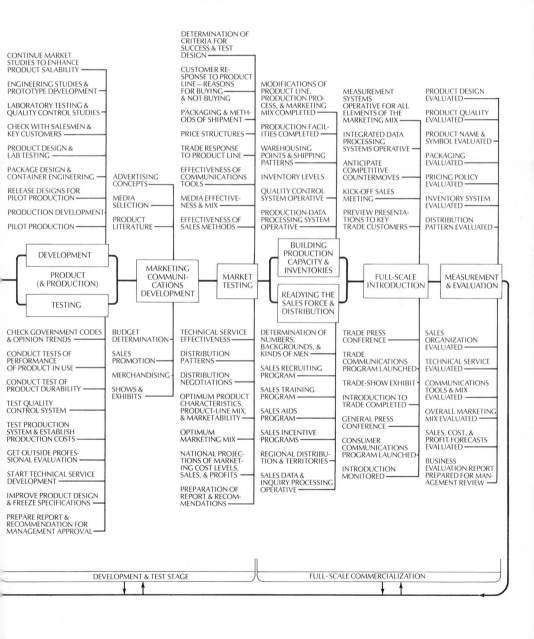

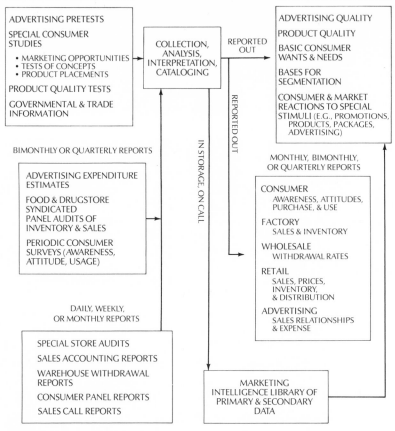

Exhibit III

Mead Johnson's marketing intelligence system.

● A panel of weight-conscious women.

To exemplify the type of outputs possible from this system, Mead Johnson will be able, with the help of analyses of factory sales data, warehouse withdrawal information, and consumer purchases from Nielsen, to monitor transactions at each stage of the flow of goods through the distribution channel and to detect accumulations or developing shortages. Management will also be able to spot sources of potential problems in time to deal with them effectively. For example, if factory sales exceed consumer purchases, more promotional pressure is required. By contrast, if factory sales lag behind consumer purchases, sales effort must be further stimulated.

Similarly, the company has been able to devise a practical measurement of advertising's effectiveness in stimulating sales—a measurement that is particularly appropriate to fast-moving packaged goods. By relating advertising outlays and exposure data to the number of prospects trying out a product during a campaign (the number is obtained from the continuing consumer survey), it is possible to calculate the advertising cost of recruiting such a prospect. By persisting in such analyses during several campaigns, the relative value of alternative advertising approaches can be weighed. Since measurement of the sales, as opposed to the communications, effects of promotion is a horrendously difficult, costly, and chancy process, the full significance of this achievement is difficult to exaggerate.

Benefits realized. Mead Johnson's marketing intelligence system has been helpful to management in a number of ways. In addition to giving executives early warning of new trends and problems, and valuable insights into future conditions, it is leading to a systematic *body* of knowledge about company markets rather than to isolated scraps of information. This knowledge in turn should lead ultimately to a theory of marketing in each field that will explain the mysteries that baffle marketers today. What is more, the company expects that the system will help to free its marketing intelligence people from firefighting projects so that they can concentrate on long-term factors and eventually be more consistently creative.

Despite these gains, it is important to note that Mead Johnson feels it has a long road still to travel. More work is needed in linking individual data banks. Conceptual schemes must be proved out in practice; ways must still be found to reduce an awesome volume of data, swelled periodically by new information from improved sources, so as to make intelligence more immediately accessible to decision makers. And perhaps the biggest problem of the moment, one underlying some of the others, is the difficulty in finding qualified marketing-oriented programmers.

Physical distribution

A veritable revolution is now taking place in physical distribution. Total systems are being evolved out of the former hodgepodge of separate responsibilities, which were typically scattered among different departments of the same company. These systems include traffic and transportation, warehousing, materials handling, protective packaging, order processing, production planning, inventory control, customer service, market forecasting, and plant and warehouse site selection. Motivating this revolution are the computer, company drives to reduce distribution costs, and innovations in transportation, such as jet air freight, container ships, the interstate highway network, and larger and more versatile freight cars.

Distribution is one area of marketing where the "bread-and-butter" uses of the computer are relatively easily deployed for such functions as order processing, real-time inventory level reports, and tracking the movements of goods. Further into the future lie mathematical models which will include every factor bearing on distribution. Not only will packaging, materials handling, transportation and warehouse, order processing, and related costs be considered in such models; also included will be sales forecasts by product, production rates by factory, warehouse locations and capacities, speeds of different carriers, etc. In short, a complete picture will be developed for management.

Program in action. The experiences of the Norge Division of Borg-Warner Corporation point up the values of the systems approach in physical distribution. The firm was confronted externally with complaints from its dealers and distributors, who were trying to cope with swollen inventories and the pressures of "loading deals." Internally, because coordination of effort between the six departments involved in distribution was at a minimum, distribution costs and accounts receivable were mounting persistently.

To grapple with this situation, Norge undertook a comprehensive analysis of its distribution system. Out of this grew a new philosophy. A company executive has described the philosophy to me as follows:

An effective system of physical distribution cannot begin at the end of the production line. It must also apply at the very beginning of the production process—at the planning, scheduling, and forecasting stages. Logistics, in short, is part of a larger marketing system, not just an evaluation of freight rates. We must worry not only about finished refrigerators, but also about the motors coming from another manufacturer, and even about where the copper that goes into those motors will come from. We must be concerned with total flow.

To implement this philosophy, the appliance manufacturer took the following steps:

1. It reorganized the forecasting, production scheduling, warehousing, order processing, and shipping functions into *one* department headed by a director of physical distribution.

2. The management information system was improved with the help of EDP equipment tied into the communications network. This step made it possible to process and report data more speedily on orders received, inventory levels, and the actual movement of goods.

3. Management used a combination of computer and manual techniques to weigh trade-offs among increased costs of multiple warehousing, reduced long-haul freight and local drayage costs, reduced inventory pipeline, and the sales value of an improved "total" product offering. Also assessed were trade-offs between shorter production runs and higher inventory levels, thereby challenging the traditional "wisdom" of production-oriented managers that the longer the run, the better.

4. The company is setting up new regional warehouses.

As a result of these moves, Norge has been able to lower inventories throughout its sales channels and to reduce accounts receivable. These gains have led, in turn, to a reduction of the company's overall investment and a concomitant increase in profitability.

It is essential to note than even though Norge has used operations research as part of its systems approach, many aspects of the program are qualitative. Thus far, the company has found that the development of an all-encompassing model is not warranted because of (a) the time and cost involved, (b) the probability that the situation will change before the model is completed, (c) a concern that such a model would be so complex as to be unworkable, and (d) the difficulty of testing many of the assumptions used. In addition, management has not tried to quantify the impact of its actions on distributor and retailer attitudes and behavior, possible competitive countermoves, and numerous other factors contributing to results.

Toward total integration

The integration of systems developed for product management, product innovation, marketing intelligence, physical distribution, and the other functions or "subsystems" embraced by the term *marketing* creates a total marketing system. Thus, marketing plans composed according to a step-by-step outline, ranging from enunciation of objectives and implementational steps to audit and adjustment to environmental changes, constitute a complete application of systems theory. Further, as the various subsystems of the overall system are linked quantitatively, so that the effect of modifications in one element can be detected in other elements, and as the influences of competitive moves on each element are analyzed numerically, then the total scheme becomes truly sophisticated.

PLUSES & MINUSES

Two elements underlie the use and benefits of systems theory—order and knowledge. The first is a homely virtue, the second a lofty goal. Marketing is obviously not alone among all human pursuits in needing them; but, compared with its business neighbors, production and finance, marketing's need is acute indeed. The application of the systems concept can bring considerable advantages. It offers:

● A methodical problem-solving orientation—with a broader frame of reference so that all aspects of a problem are examined.

● Coordinated deployment of all appropriate tools of marketing.

● Greater efficiency and economy of marketing operations.

● Quicker recognition of impending problems, made possible by better understanding of the complex interplay of many trends and forces.

● A stimulus to innovation.

● A means of quantitatively verifying results.

These functional benefits in turn yield rich rewards in the marketplace. The most important gains are:

A deeper penetration of existing markets—As an illustration, the Advanced Data Division of Litton Industries has become a leader in the automatic revenue control business by designing systems meshing together "hardware" and "software."

A broadening of markets—For example, the tourist industry has attracted millions of additional travelers by creating packaged tours that are really product-service systems. These systems are far more convenient and economical than anything the consumer could assemble himself.

An extension of product lines—Systems management makes it more feasible to seek out compatibilities among independently developed systems. Evidence of this idea is the work of automatic control system specialists since the early 1950's.[5] Now similar signs are apparent in marketing. For example, Acme Visible Records is currently dovetailing the design and sale of its record-keeping systems with data-processing machines and forms.

A lessening of competition or a strengthened capacity to cope with competition—The systems approach tends to make a company's product line more unique and attractive. Carborundum's innovation in metal-removal systems is a perfect illustration of this.

Problems in practice

Having just enumerated in glowing terms the benefits of the systems approach, realism demands that I give "equal time" to the awesome difficulties its utilization presents. There is no better evidence of this than the gulf between the elegant and sophisticated models with which recent marketing literature abounds and the actual number of situations in which those models really work. For the truth of the matter is that we are still in the foothills of this development, despite the advances of a few leaders. Let us consider some of the obstacles.

Time & manpower costs. First of all, the systems approach requires considerable time to implement; it took one company over a year to portray its physical distribution system in a mathematical model before it could even begin to solve its problems. RCA's Electronic Data Processing Division reports models taking three to five years to build, after which holes in the data network have to be filled and the model tested against history. Add to this the need for manpower of exceptional intellectual ability, conceptual skills, and specialized education—manpower that is in exceedingly short supply. Because the problems are complex and involve all elements of the business, one man alone cannot solve them. He lacks the knowledge, tools, and controls. And so many people must be involved. It follows that the activation of systems theory can be very costly.

Absence of "canned" solutions. Unlike other business functions where standardized approaches to problem solving are available, systems must be tailored to the individual situation of each firm. Even the same problem in different companies in the same industry will frequently lead to different solutions because of the impact of other inputs, unique perceptions of the environ-

---

[5] See *Automatic and Manual Control: Papers Contributed to the Conference at Cranford, 1951,* edited by A. Tustin (London, Butterworth's Scientific Publications, 1952).

ment, and varying corporate missions. These factors, too, compound time and expense demands.

"Net uncertainties." Even after exhaustive analysis, full optimization of a total problem cannot be obtained. Some uncertainty will always remain and must be dealt with on the basis of judgment and experience.

Lack of hard data. In the world of engineering, the systems evolved to date have consisted all or mostly of machines. Systems engineers have been wise enough to avoid the irrationalities of man until they master control of machines. Marketing model-builders, however, have not been able to choose, for the distributor, salesman, customer, and competitor are central to marketing. We must, therefore, incorporate not only quantitative measures of the dimensions of things and processes (e.g., market potential, media outlays, and shipping rates), but also psychological measures of comprehension, attitudes, motivations, intentions, needs—yes, even psychological measures of physical behavior. What is needed is a marriage of the physical and behavioral sciences—and we are about as advanced in this blending of disciplines as astronomy was in the Middle Ages.

Consider the advertising media fields as an instance of the problem:

A number of advertising agencies have evolved linear programming or simulation techniques to assess alternate media schedules. One of the key sets of data used covers the probabilities of exposure to all or part of the audience of a TV program, magazine, or radio station. But what is exposure, and how do you measure it? What is optimum frequency of exposure, and how do you measure it? How does advertising prevail on the predispositions and perceptions of a potential customer? Is it better to judge advertising effects on the basis of exposure opportunity, "impact" (whatever that is), messages retained, message comprehension, or attitude shifts or uptrends in purchase intentions? We do not have these answers yet.

Even assuming precise knowledge of market dimensions, product performance, competitive standing, weights of marketing pressure exerted by direct selling, advertising and promotion, and so on, most marketers do not yet know, except in isolated cases, how one force will affect another. For instance, how does a company "image" affect the setting in which its salesmen work? How does a company's reputation for service affect customer buying behavior?

Nature of marketing men. Man is an actor on this stage in another role. A good many marketing executives, in the deepest recesses of their psyches, are artists, not analysts. For them, marketing is an art form, and, in my opinion, they really do not want it to be any other way. Their temperament is antipathetic to system, order, knowledge. They enjoy flying by the seat of their pants—though you will never get them to admit it. They revel in chaos, abhor facts, and fear research. They hate to be trammeled by written plans. And they love to spend, but are loathe to assess the results of their spending.

Obviously, such men cannot be sold readily on the value and practicality of the systems approach! It takes time, experience, and many facts to influence their thinking.

Surmounting the barriers

All is not gloom, however. The barriers described are being overcome in various ways. While operations research techniques have not yet made much headway in evolving total marketing systems and in areas where man is emotionally engaged, their accomplishments in solving inventory control problems, in sales analysis, in site selection, and in other areas have made many businessmen more sympathetic and open-minded to them.

Also, mathematical models—even the ones that do not work well yet —serve to bolster comprehension of the need for system as well as to clarify the intricacies among subsystems. Many models are in this sense learning models; they teach us how to ask more insightful questions. Moreover, they pinpoint data gaps and invite a more systematized method for reaching judgments where complete information does not exist. Because the computer -abhors vague generalities, it forces managers to analyze their roles, objectives, and criteria more concretely. Paradoxically, it demands more, not less, of its human masters.

Of course, resistance to mathematical models by no means makes resistance to the systems approach necessary. There are many cases where no need may ever arise to use mathematics or computers. For the essence of the systems approach is not its techniques, but the enumeration of options and their implications. A simple checklist may be the only tool needed. I would even argue that some hard thinking in a quiet room may be enough. This being the case, the whole trend to more analysis and logic in management thinking, as reflected in business periodicals, business schools, and the practices of many companies, will work in favor of the development of the systems approach.

It is important to note at this juncture that not all marketers need the systems approach in its formal, elaborate sense. The success of some companies is rooted in other than marketing talents; their expertise may lie in finance, technology, administration, or even in personnel—as in the case of holding companies having an almost uncanny ability to hire brilliant operating managers and the self-control to leave them alone. In addition, a very simple marketing operation—for example, a company marketing one product through one distribution channel—may have no use for the systems concept.

APPLYING THE APPROACH

Not illogically, there is a system for applying the systems approach. It may be outlined as a sequence of steps:

1. *Define the problem and clarify objectives.* Care must be exercised not to accept the view of the propounder of the problem lest the analyst be defeated at the outset.

2. *Test the definition of the problem.* Expand its parameters to the limit. For example, to solve physical distribution problems it is necessary to study the marketplace (customer preferences, usage rates, market size, and so forth), as well as the production process (which plants produce which items most efficiently, what the interplant movements of raw materials are, and so forth). Delineate the extremes of these factors, their changeability, and the limitations on management's ability to work with them.

3. *Build a model.* Portray all factors graphically, indicating logical and chronological sequences—the dynamic flow of information, decisions, and events. "Closed circuits" should be used where there is information feedback or go, no-go and recycle signals (see Exhibit II).

4. *Set concrete objectives.* For example, if a firm wants to make daily deliveries to every customer, prohibitive as the cost may be, manipulation of the model will yield one set of answers. But if the desire is to optimize service at lowest cost, then another set of answers will be needed. The more crisply and precisely targets are stated, the more specific the results will be.

5. *Develop alternative solutions.* It is crucial to be as open-minded as possible at this stage. The analyst must seek to expand the list of options rather than merely assess those given to him, then reduce the list to a smaller number of practical or relevant ones.

6. *Set up criteria or tests of relative value.*

7. *Quantify some or all of the factors or "variables."* The extent to which this is done depends, of course, on management's inclinations and the "state of the art."

8. *Manipulate the model.* That is, weigh the costs, effectiveness, profitability, and risks of each alternative.

9. *Interpret the results, and choose one or more courses of action.*

10. *Verify the results.* Do they make sense when viewed against the world as executives know it? Can their validity be tested by experiments and investigations?

Forethought & perspective

Successful systems do not blossom overnight. From primitive beginnings, they evolve over a period of time as managers and systems specialists learn to understand each other better, and learn how to structure problems and how to push out the frontiers of the "universe" with which they are dealing. Companies must be prepared to invest time, money, and energy in making systems management feasible. This entails a solid foundation of historical data even before the conceptual framework for the system can be constructed. Accordingly, considerable time should be invested at the outset in *thinking* about the problem, its appropriate scope, options, and criteria of choice before plunging into analysis.

Not only technicians, but most of us have a way of falling in love with techniques. We hail each one that comes along—*deus ex machina*. Historically, commercial research has wallowed in several such passions (e.g., probability sampling, motivation research, and semantic scaling), and now operations research appears to be doing the same thing. Significantly, each technique has come, in the fullness of time, to take its place as one, but only one, instrument in the research tool chest. We must therefore have a broad and dispassionate perspective on the systems approach at this juncture. We must recognize that the computer does not possess greater magical properties than the abacus. It, too, is a tool, albeit a brilliant one.

Put another way, executives must continue to exercise their judgment and experience. Systems analysis is no substitute for common sense. The computer must adapt itself to their styles, personalities, and modes of problem solving. It is an aid to management, not a surrogate. Businessmen may be slow, but the good ones are bright; the electronic monster, by contrast, is a speedy idiot. It demands great acuity of wit from its human managers lest they be deluged in an avalanche of useless paper. (The story is told of a sales manager who had just found out about the impressive capabilities of his company's computer and called for a detailed sales analysis of all products. The report was duly prepared and wheeled into his office on a dolly.)

Systems users must be prepared to revise continually. There are two reasons for this. First, the boundaries of systems keep changing; constraints are modified; competition makes fresh incursions; variables, being what they are, vary, and new ones crop up. Second, the analytical process is iterative. Usually, one "pass" at problem formulation and searches for solutions will not suffice, and it will be necessary to "recycle" as early hypotheses are challenged and new, more fruitful insights are stimulated by the inquiry. Moreover, it is impossible to select objectives without knowledge of their effects and costs. That knowledge can come only from analysis, and it frequently requires review and revision.

Despite all the efforts at quantification, systems analysis is still largely an art. It relies frequently on inputs based on human judgment; even when the inputs are numerical, they are determined, at least in part, by judgment. Similarly, the outputs must pass through the sieve of human interpretation. Hence, there is a positive correlation between the pay-off from a system and the managerial level involved in its design. The higher the level, the more rewarding the results.

Finally, let me observe that marketing people merit their own access to computers as well as programmers who understand marketing. Left in the hands of accountants, the timing, content, and format of output are often out of phase with marketing needs.

CONCLUSION

Nearly 800 years ago a monk wrote the following about St. Godric, a merchant later turned hermit:

He laboured not only as a merchant but also as a shipman . . . to Den-

mark, Flanders, and Scotland; in which lands he found certain rare, and therefore more precious, wares, which he carried to other parts wherein he knew them to be least familiar, and coveted by the inhabitants beyond the price of gold itself, wherefore he exchanged these wares for others coveted by men of other lands. . . .[6]

How St. Godric "knew" about his markets we are not told, marketing having been in a primitive state in 1170. How some of us marketers today "know" is, in my opinion, sometimes no less mysterious than it was eight centuries ago. But we are trying to change that, and I will hazard the not very venturesome forecast that the era of "by guess and by gosh" marketing is drawing to a close. One evidence of this trend is marketers' intensified search for knowledge that will improve their command over their destinies. This search is being spurred on by a number of powerful developments. To describe them briefly:

● The growing complexity of technology and the accelerating pace of technological innovation.

● The advent of the computer, inspiring and making possible analysis of the relationships between systems components.

● The intensification of competition, lent impetus by the extraordinary velocity of new product development and the tendency of diversification to thrust everybody into everybody else's business.

● The preference of buyers for purchasing from as few sources as possible, thereby avoiding the problems of assembling bits and pieces themselves and achieving greater reliability, economy, and administrative convenience. (Mrs. Jones would rather buy a complete vacuum cleaner from one source than the housing from one manufacturer, the hose from another, and the attachments from still another. And industrial buyers are not much different from Mrs. Jones. They would rather buy an automated machine tool from one manufacturer than design and assemble the components themselves. Not to be overlooked, in this connection, is the tremendous influence of the U.S. government in buying systems for its military and aerospace programs.)

The further development and application of the systems approach to marketing represents, in my judgment, the leading edge in both marketing theory and practice. At the moment, we are still much closer to St. Godric than to the millenium, and the road will be rocky and tortuous. But if we are ever to convert marketing into a more scientific pursuit, this is the road we must travel. The systems concept can teach us how our businesses really behave in the marketing arena, thereby extending managerial leverage and control. It can help us to confront more intelligently the awesome complexity of marketing, to deal with the hazards and opportunities of technological change, and to cope with the intensification of competition. And in the process, the concept will help us to feed the hungry maws of our expensive computers with more satisfying fare.

[6]*Life of St. Godric*, by Reginald, a monk of Durham, c. 1170.

WHAT IS THE SYSTEMS APPROACH?

There seems to be agreement that the systems approach sprang to life as a semantically identifiable term sometime during World War II. It was associated with the problem of how to bomb targets deep in Germany more effectively from British bases, with the Manhattan Project, and with studies of optimum search patterns for destroyers to use in locating U-boats during the Battle of the North Atlantic.* Subsequently, it was utilized in the defeat of the Berlin blockade. It has reached its present culmination in the success of great military systems such as Polaris and Minuteman.

Not surprisingly, the parallels between military and marketing strategies being what they are, the definition of the systems approach propounded by The RAND Corporation for the U.S. Air Force is perfectly apt for marketers:

An inquiry to aid a decision-maker choose a course of action by systematically investigating his proper objectives, comparing quantitatively where possible the costs, effectiveness, and risks associated with the alternative policies or strategies for achieving them, and formulating additional alternatives if those examined are found wanting.†

The systems approach is thus an orderly, "architectural" discipline for dealing with complex problems of choice under uncertainty.

Typically, in such problems, multiple and possibly conflicting objectives exist. The task of the systems analyst is to specify a closed operating network in which the components will work together so as to yield the optimum balance of economy, efficiency, and risk minimization. Put more broadly, the systems approach attempts to apply the "scientific method" to complex marketing problems studied *as a whole*; it seeks to discipline marketing.

But disciplining marketing is no easy matter. Marketing must be perceived as a *process* rather than as a series of isolated, discrete actions; competitors must be viewed as components of each marketer's own system. The process must also be comprehended as involving a flow and counterflow of information and behavior between marketers and customers. Some years ago, Marion Harper, Jr., now chairman of The Interpublic Group of Companies, Inc., referred to the flow of information in marketing communications as the cycle of "listen (i.e., marketing research), publish (messages, media), listen (more marketing research), revise, publish, listen. . . ." More recently, Raymond A. Bauer referred to the "transactional" nature of communications as a factor in the motivations, frames of reference, needs, and so forth of recipients of messages. The desires of the communicator alone are but part of the picture.‡

Pushing this new awareness of the intricacies of marketing communications still further, Theodore Levitt identified the interactions between five different forces—source effect (i.e., the reputation or credibility of the sponsor of the message), sleeper effect (the declining influence of source credibility with the

---

* See Glen McDaniel, "The Meaning of The Systems Movement to the Acceleration and Direction of the American Economy," in *Proceedings of the 1964 Systems Engineering Conference* (New York, Clapp & Poliak, Inc., 1964), p. 1; see also E. S. Quade, editor, *Analysis for Military Decisions* (Santa Monica, California, The RAND Corporation, 1964), p. 6.
† Quade, op. cit., p. 4.
‡ "Communications as a Transaction," *Public Opinion Quarterly*, Spring 1963, p. 83.

passage of time), message effect (the character and quality of the message), communicator effect (the impact of the transmitter—e.g., a salesman), and audience effect (the competence and responsibility of the audience).§ Casting a still broader net are efforts to model the entire purchasing process, and perhaps the ultimate application of the systems concept is attempts to make mathematical models of the entire marketing process.

Mounting recognition of the almost countless elements involved in marketing and of the mind-boggling complexity of their interactions is a wholesome (though painful) experience. Nevertheless, I believe we must not ignore other ramifications of the systems approach which are qualitative in nature. For the world of marketing offers a vast panorama of non- or part-mathematical systems and opportunities to apply systems thinking. We must not become so bedazzled by the brouhaha of the operations research experts as to lose sight of the larger picture.

READING 7

THE IMPACT OF TECHNOLOGY ON MARKETING —A CHALLENGE*

John J. Kennedy

THE NATURE OF TECHNOLOGY AND SCIENCE AND THEIR RELATIONSHIP TO THE SOCIAL AND ECONOMIC ENVIRONMENT

A study of the history of technology reveals differences of opinion as to the nature of technique and science. For example, philosophers of science distinguish between technique and science and, in fact, place great emphasis on points in history when the two merge. Generally, technology refers to methods; the emphasis is application—the pragmatic methodologies developed by one generation and handed on to the next. In contrast, science provides a coherent explanation of why and how. Its mode is ideas. It is a systematic body of knowledge used to theorize on reality. Although technology often implies technique, it is difficult in 1967 to differentiate where technique begins and science ends. It is clear however, that to apply the idea of technique solely to the economic (or marketing) process excludes the impact that technique plays at the human and organizational level. What fosters new techniques? Are there limitations? Should we encourage or discourage innovation? To help view these in perspective, a brief examination of technique is presented.

Technique is lost in antiquity; primitive man had techniques for hunting, fishing, protection, food gathering and so forth and one generation passed

§ See Theodore Levitt, *Industrial Purchasing Behavior* (Boston, Division of Research, Harvard Business School, 1965), p. 25ff.
*Reproduced with permission from *Changing Marketing Systems*, Reed Moyer, ed. (Chicago, American Marketing Association, 1967), pp. 109–112.

those on to the next. And invention created new ones. Advanced techniques such as the refining of silver and gold, glass making, the tempering of weapons, pottery and ship building can be traced to the Near East. In this respect, since the earliest advanced civilizations were in the Middle and Near East, technique is sometimes said to be derived from the East.[1]

Until the Greek civilization, technique is generally not linked with the concept of science. Technique through trial and error, by guesses and sweat raised problems—but it remained for science to theorize and postulate answers. The Greek civilization in the 5th century B.C. in politics and in medicines applied a systematic method for the formulation, development and teaching of hypothesis—and in so doing introduced science. Although technique apparently preceded science—technique began to develop and expand itself only after science appeared. In the present era even a casual analysis reveals that the borderline between science and technique is at best uncertain.

In the centuries following the phenomena of Greece and then Rome, technique expanded; somewhat uncertainly in the span from the 4th to the 14th century—a spurt in the 15th century, a lull until about 1850 and then an explosion that continues to this day.[2] The limited development of technique prevented the Greeks from adequately testing their hypothesis, and although this problem varied in significance in the economic, organizational and human domain, it is generally conceded that the deficiency gap prevented Greek science from advancing even faster than it had.[3] For example, Greek philosophers hypothesized on the atomic structure of matter but lacked the techniques to test the hypothesis.

Science collapsed with the fall of Greece and fell into disrepute and near oblivion from 450 A.D. to about the 12th century when manuscripts of Aristotle brought back from the East during the Crusades renewed interest. This new wave of enthusiasm continued until 1400 and produced theoretical work for example in optics and biology. However, the 1400–1600 period was host to the seeds of the Renaissance and Reformation and interest in science waned. Finally modern science, partly through the personages of Galileo, Bacon, Harvey and Descartes began around 1600.[4] After 1600 it was a matter of accelerated growth, culminating in the explosion of knowledge in the 19th century.[5]

What causes and affects the growth of science and technology? Jacques Ellul in his book, *The Technological Society*, identifies five important factors:

1. A long technical experience.

---

[1]Jacques Ellul, *The Technological Society*, (New York: Alfred Knopf and Co., 1964), p. 27.

[2]An interesting question is whether the current rate of growth will continue, increase or decrease —why, how and when.

[3]Some historians also suggest that Greek philosophy precluded application of technology since wisdom and ideas were goals in themselves.

[4]There is disagreement as to just what modern science is and when it began, but this time period is often used.

[5]See *Science & Social Change*, "Science and Modern Civilization," (Washington: Thornton, Bradhmas Institute, 1939), p. 23.

2. Population expansion.

3. The suitability of the economic environment.

4. The plasticity of the social milieu.

5. The appearance of a clear technical intention.

Each of these is discussed briefly below.

Every modern technical advance had ancestors; every invention has its roots in the residue of past efforts.[6] Every period bears in itself the valuable survivals of past technologies. What appears significant is the formation of a "technical complex" which according to Mumford consists of a series of partial inventions that combine into an ensemble.[7] This unit begins to function when the required number of parts have been assembled, and it trends toward self-improvement.

From about 1000 to about 1750 there was a slow fermentation that permitted the technical miracle of 1850 to occur.[8]

There is a correlation between population growth and technical development; the increase in population generates a need for improved technique. Also the economic environment must be such as to support the time and effort required for technological advance; and the economic milieu must be capable of accepting change.

Perhaps the most important fact is the social aspect; there must be a breakdown of social taboos. For example, in the eighteenth century this involved breaking constraints resulting from religious and moral ideas, judgments concerning actions and the role of man and the ends proposed for life. For techniques to flourish society must be open to new ideas and change.

Another facet of the social aspect is the structure of the social order. Small independent population units that are geographically close do not provide for exchange of ideas and methodologies. Improved communications, transportation and a higher educational level knit the small units into vast, mobile masses of people.

Finally, a clear technical intention is the prime mover. From 1750 to 1850 everybody invented; it was a normal part of life. Such intention had existed in prior cultures. By technical intent is meant to have: (1) a precise view of technical possibilities; (2) the will to attain certain ends; (3) the application in all areas; and (4) the adherence of the whole of society to a conspicuous technical objective. Many causes conspired to produce this phenomenon —certainly the philosophy of Hegel and Marx—but a special factor was the dominance of special self-interest. Drawn by self-interest, the masses went over to the side of technique.

Before 1800, technique was applied in limited, narrow areas, and the activity of sustaining social relations and human contacts predominated over the technical scheme of things. Technique was local, and every technical phe-

---

[6]See Arthur Veerendeel, *Esqusse d'une Histoire de la Technique,* (Brussels: Uromat, 1921) and Lewis Mumford, *Technology Civilization,* (New York: Harcourt, Brace and Company, 1934).
[7]Lewis Mumford, *Techniques and Civilization,* (New York: Harcourt, Brace and Company, 1934).
[8]Charles Moraze, *Essai sur la Civilisation d'Occident,* (Paris: Colin, 1949).

nomenon was isolated. And until the 18th century, techniques evolved slowly and were often directed toward irrational, non-practical diversification. But today technique is characterized by rationality, concentration, immediate application and self-augmentation.

Even this sketchy history of technologies reveals certain questions for the marketing man concerned with the impact of technology on his discipline:

BY THE YEAR 2000

The nature of society in the year 2000 is the subject of a Commission of the American Academy of Arts and Sciences of Harvard University.[9] A similar study has been conducted by Kahn and Wiener of the Hudson Institute.[10] The preliminary findings of the Academy Commission is published in the 1967 Summer issue of *Daedalus*. To attempt to summarize these findings in the limited space allotted does an injustice to these studies and of course introduces the vagueness of qualification necessary with generalizations. But even generalities are adequate for the implications are staggering.

What is immediately apparent is that marketing in the year 2000 will be a function not only of technology but also of the interaction of the social, economic and cultural forces. For example, Daniel Bell, in his introduction article in *Daedalus* identifies four important sources of change:

1. Technology.

2. The diffusion of existing goods and services.

3. The transformation of society into a post-industrial structure with more emphasis of service than production.

4. The relationship of the United States and the rest of the world.

And he concludes that what matters most about the year 2000 are not the products and services that technology might produce, but rather the kind of social arrangements that can deal adequately with the problems we shall confront. These problems will include the problem of social choice and individual values—the question of how to reconcile conflicting individual desires through the political mechanism rather than the market. New social and political forms will be required to permit individual participation in public decisions. Old bureaucratic institutions will be forced to reorganize when faced with the growth of a large educated, professional and technical class that has a desire for breadth, autonomy and a sense of contribution. The new population, communication, and mobility densities could increase stress in society. Finally, "Society becomes more hedonistic, permissive, expressive, distrustful of authority and of the purposive, delayed gratification of a bourgeois, achievement oriented technological world."[11]

[9]Toward the year 2000, "Work in Progress," *Daedalus*, Journal of the American Academy of Arts and Sciences, (Summer, 1967), Cambridge, Mass. This entire issue is devoted to preliminary findings of the commission.

[10]Herman Kahn, Anthony Wiener, *Toward the Year 2000: A framework for Speculation*, (New York: Macmillan, 1967).

[11]Daniel Bell, "The Year 2000—The Projection of an Idea," *Daedalus*, Summer, 1967, p. 645.

Table 1
Basic Trends of Western Society[12]

---

1. Increasingly sensate (empirical, this-worldly, secular, humanistic, pragmatic, utilitarian, contractual, epicurean, or hedonistic) cultures.
2. Bourgeois, bureaucratic, "meritocratic," democratic (and nationalistic?) elites.
3. Accumulation of scientific and technological knowledge.
4. Institutionalization of change, especially research, development, innovation, and diffusion.
5. World-wide industrialization and modernization.
6. Increasing affluence and (recently) leisure.
7. Population growth.
8. Decreasing importance of primary occupations.
9. Urbanization and (soon) the growth of megalopolises.
10. Literacy and education.
11. Increased capability for mass destruction.
12. Increasing tempo of change.
13. Increasing universality of these trends.

On this same subject Kahn and Wiener list thirteen social trends and one hundred technical innovations that we can expect by the year 2000. The thirteen trends are listed in Table 1, and as the reader will note, they support the same general thesis suggested by Bell's quote above. The specific 100 technical innovations, although of interest are less germane and not included here. Our interest is in the overall, broad, technical innovative trends. Mr. Sarnoff, in an article in *Fortune* does just that.[13] The following is taken principally from that source.[14]

Science and technology will advance more in the next thirty-three years than in all the centuries since the cradle of creation. The Western nations alone will be able to produce twice their consumption. The new techniques will include: the protein enrichment of foods, genetic alteration of plant and animals, accelerated germination and growth by electronic means. The desalinization of ocean waters and tapping of vast underground lakes will turn deserts green with lush vegetation. Ultimately laboratories will synthesize highly nutritive foods, and dependence on the soil will end forever.

Extractors and processing techniques will feed the raw materials necessary for industry from ocean waters, the surrounding air and surface rocks. Chemistry will develop additional substitutes for all basic materials and find hitherto unsuspected uses for the 2000 recognized materials in the earth's surface.

The energy at man's disposal is essentially unlimited—the supply of nuclear resources is larger than all the reserves of coal, oil and gas. And conceivably this form of energy could be made obsolete by matter; anti-matter and thermonuclear fusion.

---

[12]Herman Kahn, Anthony Wiener, "The Next Thirty-Three Years: A Framework of Speculation," *Daedalus*, (Summer, 1967), Harvard University, Cambridge, Mass., p. 706, 707.
[13]David Sarnoff, "By the End of Twentieth Century," *Fortune*, (May 1964).
[14]See also "Tomorrow is Here," *Changing Times*, (July 1964); "How Will Marketing Look in 1975," *Printer's Ink*, 1963, "On the Drawing Board—A New America," *Nation's Business*, Sept. 1966).

Science will create means to prolong life. One-hundred years is not an unreasonable expectation, and it will be healthier and more vigorous. Ultra-miniature electronic devices will replace damaged organs and by 2000, complete exchangeability and replacement of vital organs will be a reality. Electronics will replace defective nerve circuits and substitute for sight, speech and touch. Chemistry will rebuild muscles and tissues and science will take an inanimate grouping of simple chemicals and breathe into it the spark of life; man will at last have the capacity to design and maintain his own species.

It will be possible by the end of the century to communicate with anyone, anywhere, at any time by voice, sight or written message. Participants will be in full sight of one another. Individuals equipped with miniature TV trans-mitter-receivers will communicate with one another via radio, switchboard and satellite using personal channels similar to today's telephone. In the year 2000 one to three billion people could be watching the same television pro-gram. And new forms of terrestrial transport will emerge; it is foreseeable that freight will be transported across continents in tens of minutes. No points on the globe will be farther than an hour or two apart and within and among cities, freight will move through underground tubes and will be automatically routed to its destination by computer.

The conditions for rapid technological growth were identified as technical experience, population expansion, a suitable economic environment, a plastic social milieu and a clear technical intent. As the world moves toward the year 2000, various segments of the globe will become ripe for the technological revolution. As more segments become evolved, the process will tend to feed on itself. What contributions can marketing make?

THE ROLE OF MARKETING IN THE TECHNOLOGICAL SOCIETY

What will marketing be in the year 2000? Instant, total communication, speedy, almost immediate distribution, almost push-button computerized design of products to be presented simultaneously to one to three billion people. Almost certainly marketing will be dramatically altered. Today to the large group of consumers, educators and citizens, marketing still connotes advertising—and brain-washing. And the idea that too many people buy too many goods—and that happiness is two cars and a color TV set is a problem that marketing men must face. For example, recently a leading educator stated: "What this University needs is an anti-marketing department—not a marketing department."[15] Is it possible for example, that legislation at the Federal level, will by the year 2000 eliminate persuasive messages? Perhaps only comparative verified facts could be made available for communication to the consuming public through a computerized federal data bank? Since society is concerned with the needs and wants of its members and since mar-keting is partly responsible for the goods and services available for the satis-faction of these needs and wants, is it not inconceivable that this function will not receive an ever increasing attention of government?

[15] A philosopher of science at the University of Notre Dame.

Tomorrow is almost here. Technology and science are but an eyelash away from making yesterday's dreams today's reality. Instant communication, instant movement of goods, instant access to economic and technical data will change the organizational, human and economic techniques of marketing.

Marketing occupies a vital link between an almost limitless production capacity for an almost endless variety of goods and services and the individual with his needs and wants. Could history some day conclude that marketing "dropped the ball?" Marketing scholars may be so concerned with the trees that the forest eludes their vision. The knowledge of consumer behavior, of physical flows, of the transmission and interpretations of symbols and ideas —to name but a few concepts are pregnant with opportunity for application for the acceleration of economic growth of underdeveloped nations, for assisting in the alleviation of slums, or in harnessing the initiative of the have-nots. Has an over-simplified emphasis on profit prevented marketing men (and businessmen generally) from sensing the implication of dealing with the basic and psychological motivations that in effect define patterns of living? Marketing, by stimulating needs and wants and providing for their production and accessibility, is structuring and affecting—however slightly—the way people view life.

What is needed is a philosophy of marketing—a structure of ideas to be applied within recognized constraints of the social, economic and cultural milieu. We need a format to evaluate the use of technology as it relates to marketing in all its awesome dimensions. Our efforts must be twofold: Certainly use—but also against abuse. The history of technology reveals that its nature, growth and use is a function of cultural, social and economic variables. The crystal ball for the year 2000 revealed a wonderland of domination over economic want and the process of life itself. The exciting aspect of marketing is that it can make a contribution to the well-being of man. It is sad but true that an overly simplified view of corporate profit as corporate objectives has provided industry with an easy out from the less pragmatic query as to man's needs and wants.

READING 8

THE ROLE OF THE EXPERT IN MARKET RESEARCH*

Timothy Joyce

Market research is not a practice or a study isolated from other practices or studies. It has drawn freely from certain expert academic fields and will no doubt continue to do so. Further, market research organisations make use of people with expert, specialist training—especially from those fields known broadly as "the social sciences"—both as staff members and consultants.

*Reprinted by permission from *The Journal of the Market Research Society* (formerly) *Commentary*, Winter, 1963, Copyright by the Market Research Society, 39 Hertford Street, London, pp. 19–24.

In this paper I would like to consider: Why has this connection with expert fields existed for market research? What form does it take? And how will it develop?

To tackle these questions, I propose first to examine relevant academic fields and to discuss the contribution made by each to market research to date, and also the contribution which each may potentially make; and second, to draw certain conclusions about how market research *can* or *should* work with these fields, ending with one or two warnings.

The fields which have in the past made a contribution to the development of market research which I want to consider are these, partly in historical and partly in logical order:

Statistics: Economics: Psychology: Social Sciences (including Social Psychology, Sociology and Anthropology): Natural Sciences: Mathematics.

STATISTICS

Historically, the earliest contributions to market research from an expert field were from statistics—in the use of sampling, or the demonstration that a sample could provide information accurate within calculable limits, by comparison with a census, by Bowley and Rowntree especially.

The contributions since made by statistics can be grouped under three headings:

1. The theory of sampling

Here, the contribution made has been to the foundations of the market research business. Users of market research and even a high proportion of the lay public understand that a relatively small sample may be adequate for research purposes if it is selected so as to be representative (though there are aberrations, as when the *Economist* in a leader recently implied that random sampling was less accurate than other sampling methods, assuming evidently that random meant haphazard). It is now very widely realised even outside our business that bias in the selection of the sample must be avoided and that mere size is no guarantee of lack of bias. We shall probably never again see a fiasco of the proportions of the *Literary Digest* poll in the 30's in which a survey based upon a sample of several million voters predicted incorrectly a heavy defeat for Roosevelt.

While statistical theory has given much to sampling practices in field surveys, we may also see the process in reverse—the practitioners themselves adding to statistical theory in tackling the problems peculiar to sample surveys. This is most obviously true of the theory of multi-stage sampling, the need to "cluster" being dictated by practical considerations in most sampling operations. This field is particularly identified with workers at the US Bureau of the Census.

2. Analysis of data

Statistical theory enters at the stage that survey results are being reviewed perhaps most obviously in the computation of levels of significance of confidence limits, and in pronouncing hypotheses confirmed or disconfirmed. It has also contributed to the interpretation of relationships. Measures of association such as correlation coefficients, and multivariate analyses of one sort or another are all now widely used. Attempts to account for the variation in individual responses or the associations between these responses—such as the analysis of variance and factor analysis—are now part of the market researcher's repertoire.

Statistical considerations should also, of course, be taken into account at the design stages of research. The size of the sample and whether or not different sampling fractions should be employed are instances of questions needing to be resolved on statistical grounds when it is known what use is to be made of the data to be collected.

3. Experimental design

Finally, it is necessary to mention the application to a number of market research problems (e.g. product and advertisement research) of the theory of the design of experiments, developed largely by Fisher. As with sampling, one of the main assets which properly conceived experimental designs possess is economy—making it possible for the researcher to get much useful information at relatively low cost.

ECONOMICS

A number of those who did market research in its early days between the wars were economists, and large numbers who have specialised in economics still come to work in market research. It is natural therefore that we should see what market research has learned from economics. Unfortunately, the picture is less clear than in the case of statistics.

There is obvious value for the researcher in "descriptive" economics, describing the structure of the economy and of industry, just as it is useful to anyone in business whose work brings him up against a variety of marketing problems. Wider economic "know-how"—industrial economics, public finance—is also relevant to certain aspects of sales forecasting. In long-term sales forecasting in particular, the forecaster has to take account of economic trends and developments with some knowledge which can take him beyond the simple extrapolation of trends.

However, it is "theoretical" economics which most merit attention in this paper: and here one has to record disappointment. If we take the study of the simplest, most basic economic relationships and occurrences—the theory of consumer choice—we find that the traditional theory is of little use or relevance to us. The main reason for this is the assumption that is made that man is a rational or economic being, acting always in his own interests (or, perhaps more relevant but less tractable, according to what he conceives his own interests to be)—so that he maximises his utility or his expected utility, or lands himself on the highest possible indifference curve, or what you will.

It requires little knowledge of human behaviour (or even just introspection) to realise how inadequate an assumption this is or how far a theory based upon it is divorced from reality. This criticism must still be levelled even at recent attempts to rewrite the theory. It has been pointed out by successive economists over the last fifty years that the early "cardinal utility" formulation of the theory made more assumptions than were strictly necessary to account for rational human behaviour, and all that most economists would now perhaps admit to is the belief in rather weak requirements of consistency in choice. Even these, however, clearly do not stand up as hypotheses accounting for human behaviour—we all at times act contrary to them.

Why has the development of economics at this fundamental point, attempting to account for choices made by individuals, been so unscientific—with so little apparent regard paid to the collection of evidence? The answer appears to be the entangling of the "descriptive" and "prescriptive" functions of theoretical assumptions.[1] Even with new developments such as the theory of games[2] which employs a mathematical model for conflict situations like games, warfare, duopoly and wage bargaining, we find economists talking sometimes as if the theory could explain and predict actual behaviour and sometimes as if it laid down recommended behaviour. This urge to guide decisions seems to have been central to economics, yet in a descriptive theory it is surely out of place, as in other fields—perhaps it is a reaction to the kind of irritation felt by Mark Twain when he said "Everybody talks about the weather, but nobody does anything about it."

One or two recent developments, however, give us grounds for hope. The first is the emphasis laid on a predominantly experimental approach by workers such as Suppes[3] at Stanford, California, where a programme of laboratory experimentation has been embarked upon to test theories of consumer choice in risk-taking situations. They have found that a maximising-utility model of behaviour provides a fair approximation to actual behaviour if the subjective utilities of individuals are a function of, but not equal to, the cash value of the alternatives offered in an experiment—and, a greater departure from traditional theory, if subjective probabilities also are not necessarily equal to actual probabilities.

Second, other workers such as Simon[4] have proposed important modifications to the rationality assumptions. Simon suggests a "principle of bounded rationality" which requires individuals to "satisfice", i.e. to raise themselves above a certain threshold, rather than "maximising"; and suggests that behaviour is rational with respect not to the world as it actually is but to the individual's perception or image of reality.

Finally, under the heading of economic theory we must consider the contribution made by macroeconomics to market research. This has not been very considerable, the main area of interest being demand analysis and the multiple regression analysis of time series explored by Stone and others. Practical application to marketing problems is once again inhibited by the relative

[1] S. Schoeffler, *The Failures of Economics*, Harvard, 1955.
[2] R. D. Luce and H. Raiffa, *Games and Decisions*, New York, 1957.
[3] D. Davidson, P. Suppes and S. Siegel, *Decision Making: An Experimental Approach*, Stanford, 1957.
[4] H. A. Simon, *Models of Man*, New York, 1957.

crudity of the models, which usually take no account of e.g. advertising or other promotional expenditure.

PSYCHOLOGY

The history of the relationship between psychology and market research is so recent and in some ways so clear cut that one is tempted to regard it as a "case history" illustrating how expert fields can help research, leading perhaps to generalising too far from it. The honeymoon of the late 50's is now over and one can view the relationship more objectively now than one would have been able to do just a few years ago.

If one does attempt to get an objective view, one must I think acknowledge that psychology has influenced market research on a large scale at least twice. The first period of influence was in the 40's or perhaps earlier, with the importation of common sense psychology into the business. Perhaps because early researchers read widely, or perhaps because they had a better understanding than most of human behaviour, they for the most part accepted the non-rationality of much consumer behaviour and also the need to word questions in a way which would ensure valid answers—avoiding loaded or leading questions, being suspicious of the question "why", and using indirect methods of establishing the truth in areas where the direct approach may fail, e.g. where there are important inhibitions, fears or feelings of guilt, or a desire to be esteemed, and so on.

The second period which one spontaneously thinks of is the middle and late 50's when there was a wholesale introduction of methods from a number of psychological fields, and the growth of attitude and motivation research. The last (perhaps along with subliminal advertising) achieved lay notoriety, and has probably led quite large numbers of people who have read Vance Packard on the subject to assume that hidden motivational persuasion is what market research is all about.

I would like to consider the nature of this importation under three headings. First, research into human motivations has been aided by such tools as the "depth" interview, i.e. lengthy, informal discussions with respondents on the subject undergoing research, with the object of establishing the saliency of the attitudes and beliefs held by the respondent and of his or her physiological and psychological needs, by projective tests of one sort or another, aiming basically to encourage respondents to reveal their own feelings by describing those of other real or hypothetical people, or by structuring an unstructured situation.

There has been a healthy reaction against overclaims in this area and, in particular, it is now generally recognised that the term "depth interview" is a loose description of something which cannot really be compared with the clinical interview (quite apart from its being unlikely to benefit the respondent directly). The quest for "depth" may be illusory and may also be useless beyond a certain point. It may be amusing to know that behaviour is being influenced by a complex brought about by childhood experiences, but from the marketing point of view there is nothing in retrospect that can be done about these; further, respondents may really be quite ignorant of what the researcher wants to know and no amount of depth interviewing will get it out of them. Politz[5] has argued this persuasively: and the example he quoted which I recall was an amusing one. He established that respondents' views about the pickup of cars they had had experience of bore little relation to the facts about their acceleration. However, analysis showed that there was a strong association between believing that a car had poor pick-up and believing that the accelerator pedal was stiff. Further investigation confirmed that the stiffness or looseness of the pedal was a major factor in influencing opinions about pick-up, obviously with important marketing implications. But this fact emerged from intelligent analysis, not from depth interviewing.

The second area I would like to mention is that of attitude scaling and measurement. Like multi-stage sampling theory, this is again a case where practical research men have made large contributions to theory themselves.

The third area is that of personality measurement. Here again, market research has made its contribution to theory by permitting the administration of personality tests, usually based originally on experiments with small samples of untypical populations such as students, to large samples of the adult population. So far, however, I believe one has to record disappointment. Attempts to validate personality tests by seeing whether different personality groups will react in a predictable manner to different advertising appeals have, to my knowledge, been unpromising. And the factors basic to personality testing are often difficult to grasp or to use—they do not seem to bear much relation to the plain man's vocabulary or choice of terms to describe individual differences, and until communication is established the results of personality tests will remain unused.

Other areas deserve brief mention, such as the use of psychophysical methods in packaging research, or hypotheses derived from learning theory in advertising research. A good text-book of experimental psychology[6] is a useful occasional source of inspiration to the research man.

Market research seems now to have begun a more stable and sensible relationship with psychology. A naive reaction, on the lines of Sam Goldwyn's aphorism "if a man goes to a psychiatrist, he needs his head examined", has been avoided. There are still some dangers. While psychology has avoided the troubles of theoretical economics which I have said I believe to exist, it has troubles of its own. Schools and cults are still far too prevalent in the field.

Looking ahead, one can see several areas in which psychology may further assist market research in the future. We need more basic information about human needs and drives, replacing the instinct lists from a well-meaning but cruder era in psychology. We need more thinking about models of human behaviour, preferably in mathematical and quantitative form; recent developments in decision theory and, from another angle, Lewin's vector psychology[7] are encouraging. We need especially to absorb the work which

[5] A. Politz, *Science and Truth in Marketing Research*, Harvard Business Review, January/February, 1957.
[6] R. S. Woodworth, *Experimental Psychology*, London, 1950.
[7] See D. Snygg and A. W. Combs, *Individual Behaviour*, New York, 1949.

is being done on thinking and concept formation, notably by Bruner and others.[8] I believe this is of great potential importance to brand image and other research areas. We also need to know more about learning and to relate this to response to advertising.

SOCIAL SCIENCE

It is hard to draw dividing lines in the social sciences—all of which are developing rapidly and being popularised on a large scale especially through such journals as "New Society".

1. Social psychology   (the study of interactional processes of human beings)

It has been especially concerned with persuasion, of great interest to us in understanding how advertising works, and with public opinion, prejudice, and stereotypes.

2. Sociology   (the study of society)

A number of concepts developed and used by sociologists are of interest to us—the group; fashion; leadership (particularly of interest to us in opinion leadership, where especially influential people may act as intermediaries between means of mass communication and the public at large); status, peck-order, and social class—studied extensively by such sociologists as Merton and Lloyd Warner.

The methods of sociology are of interest to the market researcher and so in some cases are the findings, for example where the ability to predict social change may affect market forecasts.

3. Social anthropology   (the study of societies)

Traditionally it has been largely concerned with primitive and tribal societies. Studies of modern civilised societies have included surveys of "Middletown" conducted by the Lynds, and those of prewar Mass-Observation. (The most interesting feature of this phenomenon was perhaps the public interest that it attracted—though one critic unkindly suggested that the observers once spent a whole day in Twickenham asking what was the most important thing in life only to find that a majority replied "minding one's own business." The archetypal M-O finding is possibly that of Tom Harrison in "Britain Revisited," where he observed that groups in pubs "drank level", i.e. finished their glasses at precisely the same moment in time for the next round to be bought, and also that *blind* men were able to drink level.) Recent social anthropological studies, such as Michael Young's studies in Bethnal Green and Woodford, have relied to a great extent upon field survey techniques.

Social anthropology is useful to us in so far as it illuminates customs, con-

---

[8]J. S. Bruner, J. J. Goodnow, and G. A. Austin, *A Study of Thinking*, New York, 1956.

ventions and so on—it helps us to know more about the market we are concerned with.

4. Linguistics

Language is an important aspect of social life and it is perhaps logical to consider it here. I would certainly wish to see it included in any discussion of the sources of market research theory and practice. If I had to make a prediction I would guess that its impact over the next 10 or 20 years will be great.

It is obviously relevant to the wording of questions and also the wording and critique of advertising copy that we should know about language actually used and about regional and class differences—so far as the latter is concerned, in terms of both extent of vocabulary and choice of words. Statistical analysis of actual speech may be of use. A recent study, for example, demonstrated that a speaker's use of *um's* and *er's* may reveal the extent to which he is finding it difficult to understand something or to express a point.

One extraordinary feature of present day linguistics is that there is in existence no English dictionary or grammar, apart from the prescriptive ones which lay down usages without necessarily recording actual usages. This deficiency should be met: it is a part of the reason for the difficulties experienced with efficient and idiomatic translation by machine, which is dependent upon having an accurate statement of how language is used.

NATURAL SCIENCES

The natural sciences have made slight contributions to market research in their own right—e.g. the application of food chemistry to product testing. More important, however, has been the use of the scientific method developed principally within the natural sciences.

The key aspects of this are objectivity; the approach which relies upon setting up and testing hypotheses in controlled experiments; and the establishment of hypothetico-deductive systems aiming to account in the simplest manner possible (applying, or some would say hacking about with, Occam's Razor) for observed phenomena.

It is perhaps necessary to deal with the suggestion that the logic of the social sciences is in some way different from that of the natural sciences—possibly e.g. because of the existence of free will as a factor in the former. It is certainly true that the social sciences have developed far more slowly than the natural sciences and that in certain respects more might have been expected in the way of fertile concepts and theories in all social science fields, but I do not myself believe that we have to postulate a difference in principle. The social sciences differ from others in that, in general, they are more complex—a complex physical science such as meteorology illustrates the difficulty this brings; there is more difficulty involved in conducting satisfactory experiments (certain things are ruled out, e.g. one can't kill people and observe the social consequences); and the observer is to some extent at least his own subject, with obvious scope for selective perception and for the rejection of unpalatable theories.

MATHEMATICS

Quite large claims have been made for the last field I want to consider. It has for example been said that while previous stages in market research have owed much to the statistician and psychologist, the next stage will owe much to the mathematician.

The mathematician is interesting because so often he has worked out as a piece of pure mathematics a great deal that can later be taken "off the peg" and applied to real problems. The use made by relativity of tensor analysis is a classic example.

The employment of mathematics in fields such as economics, sociology and biology has grown enormously. It used to be possible to get along as a "literary" economist eschewing any mathematical training, but it is scarcely possible now: and this is increasingly true of the social sciences and of biology.

Will it be true of market research?

The potential value of mathematics for market research is the ability which it provides to construct complex quantitative models, in this case of consumer behaviour, response to advertising and so on. This is a part of the operational research approach, which customarily involves setting up a mathematical model of the system undergoing examination, testing the model for closeness to reality, solving the given problem in the model, and then applying the solution to the real world. OR has been applied now to a wide range of business problems, such as problems involving transportation, inventory control, queueing, blending petroleum oils, and so on. It almost certainly has important potential application to many problems of marketing, notably I believe in the short run to media selection. To judge from the books which have already appeared or which are in the press on mathematical models in marketing, a good deal will be said about these and other applications over the next year or so.

I should perhaps mention that the ability of new generations of computers to digest larger and larger quantities of data sometimes leads the layman to have almost science-fiction faith in their usefulness, and the discussion of computer applications by advertising bodies in the U.S. has given this sort of speculation a second lease of life in our business; we should not ignore the fact that computers are basically simple things, unable to do more than they are told to do.

CONCLUSION

What, then, have these expert fields brought to market research? I would like to sum it as follows:

Methods	Concepts	Findings
(i.e. ways of	(i.e. ways of	(i.e. work we don't
doing things)	looking at things)	have to repeat)

How can market research make the best use of expert knowledge and absorb new developments in these fields? I would like to suggest three main ways.

1. All market researchers should strive at least to know who to go to or where to look to get illumination. Dabbling is not a bad thing, provided that the researcher recognises that he himself needs expert support at certain points, and can be a beneficial thing when it means that resources of expertise are properly used.

2. The "team" working on a market research project, especially but not solely at the planning stage, can ensure that people with different backgrounds can contribute different ideas and viewpoints. Diversity in this sense is, I believe, important to market research outside the fields of statistics, economics and social science just as much as within them. Recruiting market researchers solely among people with these backgrounds seems an unnecessary and perhaps harmful limitation.

3. Highly specialised or peculiar research projects, or other projects where these are handled by a research organisation lacking a wide range of research executive resources, will of course continue to call for consultants who will normally be academic researchers. The use of consultants in some fields, such as psychology, has perhaps declined over the past few years—possibly as more have become full-time staff members; but the demand for outside statistical consultants as at least probity figures will doubtless continue.

I would like to end with three warnings. First, we must avoid the view that an academic field can be swallowed whole. This fallacy was not entirely recognised in the early days of motivation research. Market research is an applied field rather like engineering—which involves knowledge of metallurgy, electronics, mathematics etc., but which has a technique and methodology of its own.

Secondly, the researcher in so far as he acts as a middleman, an intermediary between expert on the one hand and client with problems on the other, must understand what he is being advised to do—he should, for example, avoid using statistical tests in a "recipe book" manner. He should also recognise that terms may differ importantly in different fields.

Thirdly, I believe the researcher has a positive duty to avoid blinding with science. Many problems are really simple, and simple solutions are appropriate. Sometimes he has to resist the use of techniques which are overcomplex but which may have "client appeal". Sometimes there is a temptation to get involved e.g. in attitude scaling where a single question would do the job, in factor analysis where all that is required is that one should look at the correlation matrix, in questions in semantic differential form where a simple yes/no question would in fact be a more sensitive measure of an image given our particular objectives, and so on. I think we have a duty to avoid techniques that are more complicated than they need be.

Having issued these warnings, we can accept with gratitude the gifts of many fields of study to our business and to the guidance we can supply to the manager in aiding his correct solution of his problems.

READING 9

INFORMATIONAL SOURCES IN THE ADOPTION PROCESS OF NEW FABRICS*

George M. Beal and Everett M. Rogers

The rapid advances of science and technology and their implications for homemaking are evident to most of those in the field of home economics. These advances are evident in many areas of research such as human nutrition, food preservation and preparation, textiles and clothing, household equipment, home management, and family relations. Out of the basic research in these areas has come a multitude of technological innovations with the potential of making homemaking easier, more efficient, and more satisfying.

The gap between research-and-development and actual use by the homemaker is of great concern to many groups. The research worker is concerned that his findings be used. The commercial organizations want to sell their new products and services. This gap between development and use is of special concern also to the professional "change agents," those charged with the responsibility of communicating new ideas to the ultimate users and securing their acceptance. The problem of how to diffuse these ideas and practices, especially to adult publics, has long been the special concern of such "change agents" as the home economics teachers, the extension home economists, and those in consumer education. Some research workers have already concerned themselves with the study of how new homemaking ideas are adopted.[1]

Rural sociologists have become increasingly interested in studying the diffusion and adoption of new agricultural practices. Research has been conducted on the adoption of such agricultural innovations as new varieties of seeds, fertilizers, herbicides, and machinery. An intriguing question is whether use of the same concepts, frameworks, and analytical tools in the study of the adoption of homemaking practices would give additional infor-

*Reproduced from *The Journal of Home Economics*, vol. 49, no. 8, October, 1957, pp. 630–634.
[1] For example, see: M. S. Lyle, Educational Needs of Less Privileged Homemakers in a Rural County in Iowa, Research Bull. 392, Agr. Expt. Sta., Iowa State Coll. (Oct. 1952); J. N. Raudabaugh, The Cass County Study, Mimeo. ST-105, Agr. Exten. Serv., Iowa State Coll. (1949); H. C. Abell, The use of scale analysis in a study of differential adoption of homemaking practices, *Rural Sociol.* 17 (1952), pp. 161–165; and E. A. Wilkening, Adoption of Improved Farm Practices, Research Bull. 183, Agr. Expt. Sta., Univ. of Wisc. (Feb. 1953).

mation that would help in understanding how new homemaking practices are adopted.

PURPOSES

Research studies have shown that individuals pass through a process consisting of a series of stages as they adopt a new practice.[2] The purpose of this article is to apply this framework of the adoption process and its stages to the adoption of a relatively new homemaking practice—use of fabrics made from certain man-made fibers. Special emphasis is placed on the sources of information at the various adoption stages. It is hoped that this paper will: (1) acquaint research workers in home economics with some of the concepts and analytical tools currently being used by rural sociologists in adoption studies and (2) give "change agents" some insights into the complexity of the adoption process and the roles that different communication stimuli seem to play in that process.

PROCEDURE

As part of a larger study dealing with the diffusion of farm practices, interviews were obtained in 1955 from 148 farm homemakers residing in the trade area community surrounding a central Iowa village of 420 population. Although the sample is small and there is little basis for generalizing the findings to a larger population, the study does provide data for the two purposes mentioned previously. The community is located in a prosperous corn-hog farming area. The 1950 level of living index for its county was 186, while the state average was 178. For statistical purposes the community may be considered a sample of other similar communities.

Selection of the practice to be studied was based on the criteria that it should have been introduced during the last 15 to 20 years, have applicability in that most homemakers might have use for it and that it require relatively low cost and effort to obtain. Fabrics of nylon, Orlon, and Dacron fulfilled these requirements to an acceptable degree.

Nylon, Orlon, and Dacron were introduced to the public in 1940, 1950, and 1951, respectively.[3] The main advantage of these fabrics was that less time was required for washing, drying, and ironing, and in some cases ironing was not required. These fabrics seemed to wear at least as well as most other fabrics.

The manufacturers, commercial outlets, and "change agencies" presented the merits of these new fabrics to the general public. In spite of some of the obvious advantages of these new fabrics, fewer than half of the homemakers had adopted their use for outer garments such as coats, dresses, blouses, or shirts by 1951, seven years after the first homemaker in our study reported

[2]See: G. M. Beal, E. M. Rogers, and J. M. Bohlen, Validity of the concept of stages in the adoption process, *Rural Sociol.* 22 (1957), in press; and G. M. Beal and E. M. Rogers, forthcoming Research Bulletin, Agr. Expt. Sta., Iowa State Coll. (1957).
[3]N. Hollen and J. Saddler, *Textiles.* New York: Macmillan and Company, 1955, pp. 60–67.

adoption in 1944. At the time of the study, in 1955, about 10 per cent of the homemakers interviewed reported they were not using these fabrics for the garments listed.

THE ADOPTION PROCESS

The adoption of homemaking ideas or practices is the result of the adopter's receiving communication stimuli about the new practice. These stimuli may come from many different sources. Such informational sources might include magazines, radio, television, neighbors, friends, salespeople, home economics teachers, county home economists, and commercial demonstrators. Many of these different communication devices may present information about a single new practice.

One of the propositions that has become evident in the study is that the process of adoption is not a unit act. Rather, it is a complex process of unit acts occurring over a period of time and composed of a stimulus, interpretation, and response. The interpretation of the stimuli is made in terms of past experiences, future expectations, and judgment in relation to these experiences and expectations. It is becoming apparent that in the adoption of complex new ideas, the individual goes through a series of unit acts over a period of time. It is doubtful that this series of unit acts can be broken into discrete, clear-cut, mutually exclusive stages. However, for operational purposes it seems that this complex process may be divided into five stages[4] designated as *awareness, information, application, trial,* and *adoption*. Criteria assigned to each are:

Awareness Stage. The individual is exposed to the idea—he only knows about it, is aware of its existence, but lacks details concerning its use.

Information Stage. The individual is motivated by his curiosity and interest in the new idea. He is attempting to get general and specific information about the idea and is probably trying to get the kind of information that will help him relate it to his other past experiences.

Application Stage. The individual is concerned with making specific application of the practice to his present or predicted situation. This mental trial involves reflection upon past interpretations of similar stimuli and projection into the future in regard to relevant goals and objectives. Relative advantages of the new idea over other alternatives are considered. If the individual decides it may have application to him and his situation, he will make a decision to try out the practice.

---

[4]One of the first more detailed discussions of the concept of stages in adoption was reported in E. A. Wilkening, *op. cit.,* pp. 9–10. Wilkening used four adoption stages in his discussion. G. M. Beal and J. M. Bohlen used the conceptualization of five stages in: The Diffusion Process, Exten. Mimeo. 606, Agr. Exten. Serv., Iowa State Coll. (1954). For the first widely distributed discussion of the five stages, see: *Sub-Committee for the Study of Diffusion of Farm Practices, North Central Rural Sociology Committee,* "How Farm People Accept New Ideas," Spec. Rept. 15, Agr. Exten. Serv., Iowa State Coll. (1955).

Trial Stage. The individual is interested in actually trying out the idea or practice in his own situation. The mental activity involves the specifics of how, what, when, and where. Information regarding techniques and methods is desired rather than evaluative information.

Adoption Stage. Adoption is the decision to make continued use of the idea or practice. The thought process at the adoption stage includes evaluation of, and satisfaction with, the trial and a decision regarding continued use.

OPERATIONALIZING THE ADOPTION PROCESS

An attempt was made to determine the sources of information used by the farm homemakers at the several stages in the adoption process of nylon, Orlon, and Dacron fabrics.[5] The stages were operationalized into actual interview schedule questions as follows: (1) *Awareness.* Where or from whom did you first see or hear about the use of the man-made fabrics, nylon, Orlon, and Dacron for outer garments, such as coats, dresses, and blouses? (2) *Information.* After you first heard about these fabrics, where or from whom did you get additional, more detailed information about them? (3) *Application.* After you had enough information to know quite a lot about these fabrics, where or from whom did you get information that helped you decide whether or not to really try them for yourself? (4) *Trial.* After you decided to try out these fabrics for yourself, where or from whom did you get information or help on where to get them, what kind of care they require, and how to use them? (5) *Adoption.* Once you had tried these fabrics for yourself, how did you decide whether or not to continue using them and actually adopt them?[6]

CATEGORIZING INFORMATIONAL SOURCES

For purposes of analysis, the responses were classified into five main categories:

1. *Mass media*—Radio, television, magazines, and newspapers

2. *Agencies*—High school home economics and Extension Service

3. *Informal*—Relatives, neighbors, and friends

---

[5] The three man-made fibers were grouped together because the pretest showed that the women had difficulty distinguishing between these three fibers, and the general perception of fabrics from new man-made fibers was most important for the purpose of this study. In the subsequent interviewing, the homemakers seemed to group the three fabrics together and answer in relation to them as a group. In the interview questions we used the term "man-made fabrics" as being a simple and easily understood phrase.

[6] A more consistent wording of this question would have been "After you once tried these fabrics for yourself, where or from whom did you get help or information in helping decide whether or not to continue using them and actually adopt them?" Responses to the question as actually worded in the schedule were almost completely in terms of personal satisfaction and decision. It is quite possible that if the question had been worded as suggested above, other communication sources might have been indicated.

4. *Commercial*—Door-to-door saleswomen, store salespeople, direct-mail sales, store displays, and written material with the garments

5. *Self*—Own information, experimentation, and interpretation

There was a highly significant difference in the use of the several sources of information at the various stages. Chi square is 113.2 where significance at the one per cent level with nine degrees of freedom is 21.7.[7]

Awareness Stage. Data in table 1 indicate the relative rank of various sources of information which first made homemakers aware of the new fabrics. Mass media were mentioned most frequently, by 59 per cent; informal contacts, by 16 per cent; commercial sources, by 15 per cent; agencies, by 4 per cent.

Within the major category of mass media, magazines were named most frequently, a combination of magazines and newspapers next most frequently, followed by newspapers, television, and radio, grouped closely together in that order.

Neighbors and friends were named most frequently in the informal contact category. Relatives were named next most frequently, and a combination of relatives, neighbors, and friends was also named.

Store displays and salespeople accounted for almost all of the sources named in the commercial category. Two per cent connected a commercial pamphlet directly to a commercial concern.

The Extension Service and high school home economics department were named in that order of frequency in the agency category.

Information Stage. Informal sources and mass media, both 34 per cent, were the sources named most frequently at the information stage (see table 1). Commercial sources were named by 16 per cent and agencies by 6 per cent. Tags and information attached to garments were named by 2 per cent at this stage. Six per cent stated they were not aware of going through this information stage; they thought they went directly from the awareness to application stage.

Application Stage. As each homemaker concerned herself more specifically with the data needed to make the decision whether or not to actually try the new fabrics for herself, informal sources were utilized most often, by 39 per cent (see table 1). Commercial contacts, named by 31 per cent, were in second place. Six per cent stated they did not get additional evaluative information but utilized information already obtained and their own experiences at this stage. This was categorized as "self." Four per cent stated they went directly from the information to the trial stage.

---

[7]The self category and the adoption stage were omitted from the analysis since their inclusion would have resulted in several cells with an insufficient number of cases for Chi square analysis.

Table 1

Percentage of homemakers who named specific informational sources at stages in the adoption process

Informational Source	Stage in the Adoption Process			
	Awareness	Information	Application	Trial
	per cent	per cent	per cent	per cent
Mass media:	59	34	12	9
Magazines	27	17	5	4
Magazines and papers	17	8	4	2
Papers	6	1	—	—
Television	5	6	1	2
Radio	4	2	2	1
Informal:	16	34	39	18
Neighbors and friends	8	22	21	9
Relatives	6	8	14	8
Relatives, neighbors, and friends	2	4	4	1
Commercial:	15	16	31	40
Store displays and salespeople	13	12	27	13
Clothing tags and information with garment	—	2	2	26
Commercial demonstrations	—	—	—	1
Commercial circulars	2	2	2	—
Agency:	4	6	3	4
Extension Service	2	4	2	2
High school home economics	2	2	1	2
Self:	—	—	6	16
Decided by self with existing information	—	—	6	—
With existing information and own experimentation	—	—	—	16
Other:	6	10	9	13
Don't know and no information	6	4	5	12
Not aware of going through this stage	—	6	4	1
Total	100	100	100	100

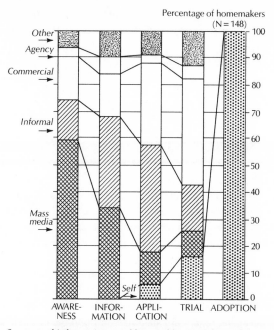

Sources of information used by rural homemakers in the adoption of fabrics made from certain man-made fibers.

Trial Stage. At the trial stage, the individual is seeking specific information on what to buy, where to buy, and how to use and handle the fabrics. Commercial contacts were mentioned most frequently, by 40 per cent (see table 1). The relative importance of information attached to garments may again be noted. Informal contacts were named by 18 per cent, mass media by 9 per cent, and agencies by 4 per cent. Sixteen per cent stated they did not obtain additional information at the trial stage but used only information already gathered at the application stage, or did their own experimentation.

Adoption Stage. All of the respondents stated that their own personal satisfaction with the trial led them to adopt the fabrics, to keep the garments they had purchased, and plan to purchase additional garments made from the fabrics in the future. As pointed out previously, the question was not worded to elicit answers in terms of sources of information utilized at the adoption stage.

RELATIVE IMPORTANCE OF THE SOURCES

Data in the chart give indication of the relative importance that the several sources of information play at the stages in the adoption process. Mass media sources play their most important role at the awareness stage and then decrease in importance throughout the other stages. Informal contacts play their greatest role at the application stage, are also important at the information stage, but less important at the awareness and trial stages. Commercial sources of information play an increasingly important role from the aware-ness through the trial stage. Agencies were mentioned by relatively few home-makers at any stage but played their most important role at the information stage. Self, using only information from a previous stage or information al-ready available or own experimentation, was named increasingly from the application stage, through the trial stage, to the adoption stage, where all of the respondents stated that "self" was the major source of information.

PERSONAL AND IMPERSONAL SOURCES

Another method of categorizing sources of information is in terms of whether the contact is personal or impersonal.

Personal contact is defined as those informational sources where social interaction takes place between two or more people. Included in this category of personal sources of information are: relatives, friends and neighbors, sales-people, agency personnel, and meetings. The category of impersonal sources of information included: farm magazines and papers, newspapers, advertise-ments, radio and television, bulletins, and printed directions attached to the product. In addition to the major categories of personal and impersonal, it was possible to subdivide the four categories of mass media, commercial, informal, and agency into subcategories on the basis of their personal or im-personal nature. The resulting subcategories are: mass media impersonal, commercial impersonal, agency impersonal, informal personal, commercial personal, and agency personal.

Table 2 indicates relative importance of the personal and impersonal sources of information at the five stages in the adoption process.

From table 2 it can be seen that the trend is for impersonal sources to be of decreasing importance through the first three stages and for personal sources to be of increasing importance. At the trial stage, where the individual wants "how to" information, impersonal sources become more important again.

IMPLICATIONS

The data presented in this article have many implications for the "change agent." For example, mass media methods seem to be very effective in inform-ing homemakers that a new practice exists but are less effective in convincing homemakers to try out the new practice. On the contrary, homemakers seem to discuss the product with their friends and relatives before actually trying out new practices and products. Commercial sources of information seem to play their major role at the trial stage when the homemaker has already de-cided to try out the new practice but wants to know where to obtain it and how to use it. The finding of this study was that homemakers are not *influenced* by outside sources into adoption, rather that they primarily decide to adopt a practice on the basis of the results of their own trial.

SUMMARY

In summary, the basic purpose of this paper was to apply the concepts and tools of analysis now being used by rural sociologists in the study of farm

Table 2

Percentage of informational sources categorized as personal and impersonal at the stages in the adoption process

Informational Source	Stage in the Adoption Process				
	Awareness	Information	Application	Trial	Adoption
	per cent	per cent	per cent	per cent	per cent
Impersonal:					
Mass media	59	34	12	9	—
Commercial	2	4	4	27	—
Agency	—	1	—	—	—
Total:					
Impersonal	61	39	16	36	—
Personal:					
Informal	16	34	39	18	—
Commercial	13	12	27	13	—
Agency	4	5	3	4	—
Total:					
Personal	33	51	69	35	—
Self:	—	—	6	16	100
Other:	6	10	9	13	—
Total	100	100	100	100	100

practices to the homemaker adoption of fabrics made of new man-made fibers. It was hoped that this would acquaint those doing home economics research in this area with some of the tools and concepts and also give the "change agents" insights into the complexity of the adoption process. The heuristic conceptualization of the five stages in the adoption process—awareness, information, application, trial, and adoption—was presented. These stages were operationalized and utilized in an empirical field study dealing with the acceptance of fabrics of nylon, Orlon, and Dacron.

The main data presented from the empirical study were related to the sources of information in each of the five stages utilized by farm women. Sources of information were categorized as mass media, informal, agency, commercial, and self. It was found that the various information sources were utilized to a different degree at the several stages.

This adoption process is, of course, only part of the diffusion process. It is an obvious fact that some people adopt new ideas more rapidly than do others. It has been found that people can be categorized by their time of adoption and significant differences in personal, social, and economic characteristics found between these categories. It has also been found that the adoption pattern for many practices approaches a normal curve—there is a slow gradual rate of adoption, a more rapid rate, and then a final decline in the rate of adoption. Further study of the time period over which individuals adopt a homemaking innovation are planned by the authors.

READING 10

HOW TO BUILD A MARKETING INFORMATION SYSTEM*

Donald F. Cox and Robert E. Good

Recently the marketing vice president of a company whose sales volume is $350 million asked, "How should we go about developing a marketing information system? I don't mean one that will keep track of orders and shipments, but a system giving our marketing managers information that will help them make better decisions about pricing, advertising, promotion, product policy, sales force effort, and so forth."

He asked the question of us because, since early 1966, we have been studying the attempts of 15 major U.S. corporations to develop a sophisticated marketing information system, or MIS. We have talked with executives at companies such as Chemstrand, Coca-Cola, General Electric, General Foods, IBM, Lever Brothers, Pillsbury, Schenley, and Westinghouse.

Although this field is relatively new, most of the technical aspects of developing an MIS are no longer an obstacle. Nevertheless, few companies are very far along in taking advantage of an approach which, its users agree, has great potential.

In this article we will attempt to provide some guidelines which might help answer the inquiring marketing vice president—and others with similar questions. First we will present a brief review of some of the characteristics and advantages of a sophisticated MIS, and of the current "state of the art." Then we will identify some of the key decisions which must be made by top management in the MIS development process. In each case we will present a distillation of the experience of the companies studied as an aid in making these critical management decisions.

WHAT IT IS & CAN DO

An MIS may be defined as a set of procedures and methods for the regular, planned collection, analysis, and presentation of information for use in making marketing decisions. This of course is a step beyond logistics systems, which handle inventory control, orders, and so forth.

It is desirable first to differentiate between the two major components of such systems—*support systems* and *operating systems*. Support systems include those activities required to generate and manipulate data—i.e., market research and other data gathering, programming, and data processing. Operating systems are those that use the data as an aid to planning and controlling marketing activities.

This article is concerned mainly with the development of three types of marketing operating systems—those designed for control, for planning, and for basic research. In Exhibit I we summarize some of the applications and

*Reprinted by permission from *Harvard Business Review* vol. 45, no. 3, May–June, 1967, Copyright, 1967 by the President and Fellows of Harvard College; all rights reserved, pp. 145–154.
Authors' note: This is a partial report of a study of the development of marketing information systems which is being supported by the Division of Research of the Harvard Business School.

probable benefits of each type of system (assuming increasing degrees of sophistication) and present examples of systems now operating. The following are examples of marketing systems we have observed, with some of the advantages the companies claim for them.

1. Control systems

These provide continuous monitoring (sometimes through exception reporting) and rapid spotting of trends, problems, and marketing opportunities. They allow better anticipation of problems, more detailed and comprehensive review of performance against plans, and greater speed of response. For instance:

● IBM's Data Processing Division has developed an MIS which district sales managers can interrogate through a time-sharing computer terminal located in an executive's office. A manager punches a typewriter-like keyboard and receives an immediate print-out of information such as:

Sales (or rentals) to date—broken down by product code, type of customer, and branch making the sale.
Sales in relation to goals.
Combinations of information which relate to sales, customer classifications, product codes, and so forth.

The data are current to within three or four days, allowing the manager to keep up to date on marketing problems and opportunities and on progress in relation to goals.

● Schenley has installed the so-called SIMR (Schenley Instant Market Reports) system which allows key executives to retrieve (via video display desk consoles and printers) current and past sales and inventory figures for any brand and package size (or combination) for each of 400 distributors. SIMR furnishes information in less than one second after a query, compared with many minutes or even hours under its former computer and manual system. Furthermore, since the computer does the calculations, managers have great flexibility and near-instant speed of response in making many types of comparisons of sales and inventory positions, such as:

How a brand is doing in any size or in all sizes in any market or in all markets.
How a distributor is doing with a particular brand.
How a bottle size is doing by distributor, state, or region.
How a market is doing by month or has done since the end of the previous fiscal year.

"We can get answers literally while we are still formulating the questions," states Bernard Goldberg, president of Schenley's marketing subsidiary. "Needed information is available so quickly that it helps us think." [1]

---

[1] *Industrial Data Processing Applications Report* (S3), Business Publications International, Division of OA Business Publications, Inc., 1965.

Exhibit I

Benefits possible with a sophisticated MIS

Typical Applications	Benefits	Examples
CONTROL SYSTEMS		
1. Control of marketing costs.	1. More timely computerized reports.	1. Undesirable cost trends are spotted more quickly so that corrective action may be taken sooner.
2. Diagnosis of poor sales performance.	2. Flexible on-line retrieval of data.	2. Executives can ask supplementary questions of the computer to help pinpoint reasons for a sales decline and reach an action decision more quickly.
3. Management of 'ashion goods.	3. Automatic spotting of problems and opportunities.	3. Fast-moving fashion items are reported daily for quick reorder, and slow-moving items are also reported for fast price reductions.
4. Flexible promotion strategy.	4. Cheaper, more detailed, and more frequent reports.	4. On-going evaluation of a promotional campaign permits reallocation of funds to areas behind target.
PLANNING SYSTEMS		
1. Forecasting.	1. Automatic translation of terms and classifications between departments.	1. Survey-based forecasts of demand for complex industrial goods can be automatically translated into parts requirements and production schedules.
2. Promotional planning and corporate long-range planning.	2. Systematic testing of alternative promotional plans and compatibility testing of various divisional plans.	2. Complex simulation models both developed and operated with the help of data bank information can be used for promotional planning by product managers and for strategic planning by top management.
3. Credit management.	3. Programmed executive decision rules can operate on data bank information.	3. Credit decisions are automatically made as each order is processed.
4. Purchasing.	4. Detailed sales reporting permits automation of management decisions.	4. Computer automatically repurchases standard items on the basis of correlation of sales data with programmed decision rules.
RESEARCH SYSTEMS		
1. Advertising strategy.	1. Additional manipulation of data is possible when stored for computers in an unaggregated file.	1. Sales analysis is possible by new market segment breakdowns.

Exhibit I (continued)

2. Pricing strategy.	2. Improved storage and retrieval capability allows new types of data to be collected and used.	2. Systematic recording of information about past R&D contract bidding situations allows improved bidding strategies.
3. Evaluation of advertising expenditures.	3. Well-designed data banks permit integration and comparison of different sets of data.	3. Advertising expenditures are compared to shipments by county to provide information about advertising effectiveness.
4. Continuous experiments.	4. Comprehensive monitoring of input and performance variables yields information when changes are made.	4. Changes in promotional strategy by type of customer are matched against sales results on a continuous basis.

2. Planning systems

These furnish, in convenient form, information the marketing executive requires for planning marketing and sales programs. At least three major consumer goods producers, for example, are developing "data books" for product managers. The books bring together the basic information a product manager needs to formulate annual marketing plans and to "replan" during the course of the year. Putting the information into one book, rather than in a welter of reports, not only saves time, but it also enables all product managers in a group or division to base their plans on the same data. Consequently, their superiors are able to review comparable information quickly when considering the plans for approval.

At a more sophisticated level, planning systems allow simulation of the effects of alternate plans so that the manager can make a better decision. For instance:

● Pillsbury's system enables marketing managers to obtain sales forecasts for each of 39 sales branches, supported by varying levels of trade promotion. The marketing manager asks the question, "What will sales be in each branch if we spend x dollars on trade promotions in comparison with .75x dollars and with 1.2x dollars?" Pillsbury does not claim that the system is perfect—it is obviously no better than the assumptions on which the simulation is based —but it has had a surprisingly good "batting average" in accuracy. It has great value to marketing managers because it allows them to look at alternate plans in each of the 39 sales branches; this was never feasible before.

● A large pharmaceutical company has developed an even more complex model. The company has programmed an artificial panel representing the nation's population of doctors. Every week the company simulates each doctor's prescription decision for every patient he "sees." (Commercial research services are available which provide information on the incidence of symptoms of illness and the "patient mix" of the various medical specialists.) The doctor considers the symptoms "presented" by each patient and decides whether to prescribe a drug and, if so, which type and brand. His decision is based on factors such as his experience with the drug, current attitudes, exposure to the advertising of various brands, exposure to detail men, and word-of-mouth information from other doctors. The simulation even includes a "forgetting routine" which causes a doctor to forget from time to time some of the information he has acquired.

While the company does not disclose how the simulation model is being used, it certainly is capable of generating extremely sophisticated marketing planning. For example, marketing managers can test the effects on share of market and sales of variations in amount, type, and timing of advertising and simultaneously test the effects of variations in frequency of detail men's calls. On a broader basis, the system can be used to screen a number of alternative marketing programs to select the most promising ones to be actually test marketed.

Perhaps the ultimate in sophistication is a marketing planning system which reviews alternatives, then actually makes decisions and takes action. Thus, several large retailing organizations have developed systems that review sales trends and inventories and then place orders for merchandise.

The most advanced unit of this type we have seen is not a marketing system; rather, it buys and sells securities in a stock brokerage house. Still in the future are marketing systems that decide the amount and timing of advertising and price promotions in each of several dozen sales districts.

3. Basic research systems

These systems are used to develop and test sophisticated decision rules and cause-and-effect hypotheses which should improve ability to assess effects of actions and permit greater learning from experience. For instance:

● A large consumer goods company is developing an MIS which, among other things, stores in computer memory the characteristics of each advertisement run (color versus black and white, nature of illustration, amount of copy, and so forth) and readership and attitude change scores for each ad. The purpose is to be able to relate ad characteristics to effectiveness measurements under different conditions and with different types of consumers by systematically studying "experience."

● Most companies find it difficult to relate advertising to sales because there are so many important "uncontrollable" variables which are nearly impossible to take into account in an unsophisticated MIS. One large consumer goods producer has developed an MIS which for the first time allows the company to collect, store, and retrieve advertising, sales, and other marketing data at a level of detail which makes possible much better controlled studies of the relationship of advertising to sales.

CURRENT PROGRESS

The examples which we have presented probably represent the most sophisticated types of MIS now in existence. While we have not surveyed the 500 largest corporations in the country, we have screened more than 50 companies and have reviewed more than 100 current articles on information systems. As far as we have been able to determine, the current state of the art is something like this:

• Very few companies have developed advanced systems, and not all of these are in operation. Some might even best be classified as subsystems, since they relate to only a portion of the marketing decisions made.

• Some companies, perhaps 15, are actively upgrading their systems to a high level. Of these, about half seem to be progressing well; the others have been much less successful.

• Many other companies are contemplating plans to develop sophisticated systems.

The reasons why marketing systems have not developed to the same extent as, say, production, logistics, or financial systems are not "technical." Marketing research technology (data gathering), computer technology (data handling), and analytical procedures (e.g., mathematical model building) are all sufficiently advanced to permit companies to build effective marketing systems.

Although insufficient time has elapsed since the installation of most advanced marketing information systems to allow a precise assessment of benefits, the users of sophisticated systems with whom we have talked are virtually all very enthusiastic about their systems, even though many see room for improvement.

DEVELOPING THE SYSTEM

Because many of the technical problems of developing sophisticated support systems have been solved and many users are gratified over the results, why are there so few advanced marketing information systems in operation? And why have some companies succeeded more than others in realizing the potentials of the MIS?

One characteristic of the more successful companies is striking. In every case, at least some members of top management have seen the promise of the technique and have viewed its development as a top management responsibility. They have devoted a great deal of time, thought, and effort to guiding (and sometimes actually protecting) the development process. Unfortunately, it is widely believed that the job of building an MIS can be turned over to a technical staff group. This has not proved to be the case. Information systems are not merely technical appendages (developed by technical people) that are easily meshed with most existing marketing planning and control systems.

The best way to show why participation of top management is necessary is to pose five key questions which must be answered in the process of instituting a sophisticated MIS. In our opinion, each is a management question:

1. How should we organize to develop a better MIS?

2. How sophisticated should our marketing systems be?

3. What development strategy should we follow—do we attempt to build a "total" system in one move, or in stages?

4. What should be the major characteristics ("macro specifications") of our system?

5. How much should we spend on developing and operating an MIS?

While the field is too new to permit comprehensive and conclusive statements about all its aspects, we can present some guidelines and working hypotheses that are worthy of management's consideration.

Readying the organization

The starting point in organizing for MIS development is not the establishment of a marketing systems group. The starting point is a review and appraisal of the entire marketing organization and of the policies that direct it. As James Peterson, vice president–grocery products marketing at The Pillsbury Company, pointed out to us:

We realized we couldn't develop a marketing control system until we had clearly and sharply defined the responsibilities of our marketing managers. If the system was to measure their performance against plans, we had to specify precisely what each man was accountable for.

Some companies, for instance, have failed to decide whether a product manager is accountable for unit sales and market share, for sales revenue, for marketing profit, or for net profit. Until responsibilities and spheres of activity are clearly defined, it is virtually impossible to build a marketing control system. In fact, specification of who is accountable for what automatically determines many of the control system's characteristics.

Management must next decide how to organize MIS development activities. Our observations show that this is a much more complex problem than might be assumed. Sophisticated systems require the coordinated efforts of many departments and individuals, including:

● Top management.

● Marketing management, brand management.

● Sales management.

● New products groups.

● Market research personnel.

- Control and finance departments.

- Systems analysts and designers.

- Operations researchers, statisticians, and model builders.

- Programmers.

- Computer equipment experts and suppliers.

The contribution of each group of course depends on its specialized talents and interests in the system. Programmers cannot define managers' information needs, and managers usually cannot program. No one person knows enough to accomplish all phases of MIS development.

Furthermore, sophisticated systems do not fall into a company's traditional data handling domains, such as the market research department or the accounting and control department, because an essential feature of a good MIS is that it integrates and correlates marketing and financial data.

Many companies we have observed have not really come to grips with the difficult problem of providing the organizational arrangements and leadership necessary for successful MIS development. They have not answered the question of who is responsible for MIS design, planning, and development. Why is there a leadership vacuum? Partly because top management does not fully appreciate the requirements and implications of the MIS, and partly because it has an understandable reluctance to disturb entrenched and powerful departments.

The approaches which have been tried in an attempt to solve the problems of organization and leadership can be characterized as:

- "Clean piece of paper" approach.

- Committee approach.

- Low-level approach.

- Information "coordinator" approach.

"Clean piece of paper" approach. This involves drawing a new organization chart. The argument goes that the financial and accounting departments and market research departments have developed as much from growing data gathering and processing capability as in response to management information needs. In the pre-computer era, it was rarely possible to correlate marketing and accounting data in a sophisticated manner and on a regular basis for presentation to management. Now it is possible, but the marketing data are supplied by one set of departments and the accounting data by another. In the absence of coordination and compatibility, line management must often do its own correlating. Therefore the "ideal" procedure is to abolish the traditional information gathering and processing departments and establish a management information department.

While this may represent an "ideal" solution, it is not feasible in most companies. Traditions and positions are too well entrenched. Furthermore, it would not solve all the problems. For one thing, it would not ensure the development of an MIS geared to management needs. For another, no management information department could supply all of the data the system needed, such as reports from the field sales organization.

Committee approach. Some companies have established MIS committees. They are excellent vehicles for communicating points of view and for joint learning and sharing in the experience of developing an MIS. They can create shared awareness of compatibility and coordination problems and of the need to resolve them.

The committee approach alone, however, is not the answer. Because meetings and committee assignments consume time, it is difficult to involve busy line managers. Furthermore, it is not easy to get anyone to carry out assignments in addition to his regular job. Finally, a committee of peers, chaired by a peer, is not always able to exert the leadership which may be required. Committees of this kind simply lack "clout." And at times clout may be the only thing that will accomplish necessary changes.

Low-level approach. Some companies have assigned the task of MIS development to a junior member of the market research department—often as a part-time assignment. This reflects a total lack of understanding of the difficulty of the task, and the outcome is predictable. The man, no matter how clever he is, lacks the time and the clout to overcome the organizational and psychological barriers he encounters. Such an assignment has led to the resignation of more than one bright young research man.

Information 'coordinator' approach. Some companies, while retaining traditional departmental boundaries, have appointed a top-level executive to the post of information czar or "coordinator," sometimes called "director of marketing systems." We have observed that men who are capable of understanding both management information needs and systems problems can make substantial progress in MIS development in this position—*when* they enjoy top management support. But it is a delicate position; one coordinator we know preferred not to have any formal title until, after a year, he had established good working relationships with the various departments. Furthermore, even a sensible and sensitive information manager must establish organizational lines that encourage the coordinated efforts of the affected departments and divisions of the company in the design and the accomplishment of the MIS plan.

For many companies this approach has the best chance of success. We suggest that management designate the director of marketing systems as a "prime contractor" who develops MIS plans and specifications, and coordinates and reviews the work of the various "subcontractors" or suppliers contributing to the program. Such a prime contractor-subcontractor approach has proved in military and civilian applications to be effective in handling projects or tasks that require the utilization of many talents and capabilities, not all of which exist in the department or organization directly involved.

For the prime contractor to be effective he must have cost control. It is therefore advisable to use an interdepartmental billing system. The prime contractor is responsible for the overall budget, and negotiates with users (marketing managers) to determine their information needs and to obtain from them the funds required to develop and operate an MIS that would meet these needs. He also arranges to compensate the various supplying departments, such as the systems group for programming, for their services.

Management must also determine the prime contractor's organizational location. It is essential that he represent the department or division which will use (and pay for) the MIS. For a variety of reasons, not one of the companies studied having a central or corporate systems department (responsible for support systems) has designated that group as the "prime contractor" for operating its MIS. They view the corporate systems group as an important supplier of technical advice and of programming and data processing services for the marketing departments. But in the large companies, at least, final authority and responsibility for MIS development, where such authority has been designated, generally rests with the marketing department.

Of the several arguments for this practice, the most important is that the expertise of corporate systems groups is usually in support systems (programming and data processing). Effective development of marketing planning and control systems requires a management, rather than a technical support systems, orientation. Furthermore, effective MIS can be developed only by people who understand users' problems and who can be responsive to users' needs.

How sophisticated?

Someone must decide on the level of sophistication of the MIS to be developed. This decision should, of course, be based on a review of the company's needs and the costs of meeting them.

Equally important, the abilities of managers must be considered. To develop and use effectively some of the more sophisticated systems that have been described, managers must be able to:

● Define specific information needs.

● Develop analytical approaches and models.

● Make explicit their planning, decision-making, and control processes and procedures.

● Interpret and use sophisticated information.

One of the characteristics of the more advanced MIS is automation of certain aspects of the marketing management process. But it is first necessary to make the process explicit. For instance, to develop exception-reporting systems, managers' exception or "control" criteria must be articulated. Simulation models cannot be built into the system until managers have spelled out the characteristics of the different elements of the company's marketing system (consumers, distributors, competitors, and so forth) and have attempted to define how these elements interact.

If a company already has a well-articulated set of decision rules as to what constitutes an "exception," it would not be difficult to build an automated exception reporting system. Such a system could be developed, for instance, for the marketing manager who says, "I always like to know about all situations in which sales, profits, or market share are running 4% or more behind plan. Furthermore, in any exceptional cases I also require the following diagnostic information: prices, distribution levels, advertising, and consumer attitudes."

The problem is, as has been well documented in a Marketing Science Institute study,[2] that many marketing managers, particularly those at the operating level, do not use explicit planning and control systems. They do not make their decision rules and exception criteria explicit. In short, they are not equipped to contribute to the development of a sophisticated MIS, nor are they comfortable with it once it is operating. Though related to research information, their decisions often are highly intuitive. The problem seems less severe at higher management levels, partly because top management control systems are more explicitly articulated than those at the operating level.

System-manager balance. It is important that a balance be maintained between management sophistication and MIS sophistication. As a company upgrades the latter, so must it raise the former.

In a "steady state" (before anyone tinkers with the marketing system) there usually seems to be a correspondence between management sophistication and information quality. Managers usually get the quality of information they ask for. Though they may complain of a lack of good information and blame one or more of the information supplying departments, questioning often reveals that in most cases they have not been asking for better information in any specific way.

If, as we have suggested, the two "quality levels" are roughly in balance, what happens when only the level of information quality is raised significantly? Our prediction is that this would not lead to better decisions. In fact, the reverse may be true, as the result of the confusion and resentment generated by the manager's inability to deal with the more sophisticated information.

Information quality can be upgraded much more rapidly than management quality. It is easy to throw the management system out of balance by installing a sophisticated MIS, but there seems to be little point in doing so. A more positive approach is to develop a master plan for improving the system, but make the improvements gradually—say, over several years. Marketing control systems like Schenley's or IBM's, described earlier, are easier to develop and use than those like the pharmaceutical company's simulation-based planning system. So a company might first install a marketing control system and subsequently, as managers gained experience in using it, develop advanced planning systems.

[2]D. J. Luck and Patrick J. Robinson, *Promotional Decision Making* (New York, McGraw-Hill Book Company, Inc., 1964).

"Complete" systems

While an attempt to develop a highly sophisticated "total" marketing system at the outset has a high probability of failure, it *is* desirable to build a complete subsystem at one time—even if it is only a part of what will eventually be the company's total system. To illustrate:

A company develops a first-rate exception reporting system that will quickly present "exceptional" sales results to the marketing manager. Very likely he will be faced with more problems than ever before, because of the system's ability to monitor large amounts of detailed information. It will be difficult (and dangerous), however, for the manager to act on this information. Before he can take intelligent action, he must also know whether the deviations from plan are the result of deviations in sales effort, of unusual competitive activities, or of other factors. To be complete, therefore, the system must also include a diagnostic procedure.

"Macro" specifications

Apart from decisions on the general characteristics of the system to be used, the company must determine the overall or "macro" MIS specifications. Besides the type of system to be developed, the most important considerations are the nature of the data bank, the form and the method of data display and presentation, and computer selection.

We should, however, underscore here the necessity of ensuring the participation in these decisions not only of top management but also of the line managers. In most cases we have studied, and in all of the least successful instances, the marketing systems developers have failed to involve line managers in the process of developing macro specifications. In many cases where systems developers have made the effort, they have found it difficult to elicit the views of busy line managers in the brief periods available in typical interviews or meetings. The systems developers subsequently present the managers with a fait accompli—which may or may not work.

A more effective approach is to involve the managers in an extended session, lasting days if necessary, in which a consensus on overall MIS specifications can be reached. In these sessions the group should develop flow charts of the "system"—or total environment in which the company operates—and designate critical decision points, identify the information they require for planning and controlling marketing (or other management) activities, and make cost/benefit analyses of alternative designs before agreeing on one design. This approach not only helps ensure a system that is keyed to management's needs, but also allows management to defer a decision on the size of the MIS development budget until it has assessed the alternative systems.

"Micro" data bank. Perhaps the most essential element in upgrading a system is a bank or file based on disaggregated or "micro" data. These are data recorded and stored in the lowest level of aggregation and detail—such as the size, price, time, and location of a single purchase of a product.

As Professor Arnold E. Amstutz of M.I.T. has commented:

At the heart of every successful information system is a disaggregated data file. . . . As new inputs are received they are maintained along with existing data rather than replacing or being combined with existing information. . . . The existence of a disaggregated data file facilitates system evaluation. . . . In the first stages of system development it is simply impossible to anticipate the direction of later advancement. Aggregate data files may preclude highly profitable system modification. The disaggregated data file provides the flexibility which is the prerequisite of intelligent system evolution.[3]

In designing the data bank it is important to provide for common denominators in different sets of data, so that the correlation and analysis potential of the MIS can be realized. This means that such elements as the geographic, time, and responsibility boundaries of different types of data must be compatible to permit meaningful comparisons.

A disaggregated data bank gives the system the flexibility required for future upgrading. The alternative is to try to anticipate all possible future uses of the system and to agree on aggregated units (like aggregating all package sizes of a brand), aggregated time periods (a week, month, or quarter), and aggregated geographical areas (sales territories or regions).

Management must weigh the greater cost of a disaggregated data bank against the possibility that future conditions or new insights may call for analyses which are precluded because the data have been aggregated. Since most people who have participated in MIS development admit that they are unable to foresee all important management information needs, and since most current systems are likely to evolve to increasing stages of sophistication, the prudent decision would be to develop a disaggregated data bank—*if* the company can afford it.

Presentation and format. Developing a sophisticated MIS involves resolving the matters of what information should be presented, how it should be presented, and to whom.

One important aspect of this question is the degree of executive-system interaction desired. At the extreme of "distance," executives receive information in the form of regular reports. With somewhat closer but not complete interaction, the manager can make special requests for information from the data bank. At the extreme of "closeness," the manager can obtain almost instantaneous computer response with a time-sharing or on-line system. Consider Schenley's experience:

Schenley has installed a video display and retrieval system. Of interest is the fact that the new system carries little new information; indeed, the same data were generated previously in the form of computer print-out. The information in paper form, however, was too voluminous and unwieldy to use. What the

---

[3]"The Marketing Executive and Management Information Systems," in *Science, Technology and Marketing*, 1966 Fall Conference Proceedings of the American Marketing Association, p. 76.

new retrieval and presentation system has achieved is simply to make data much more usable for management.

On-line systems such as Schenley's have a tremendous advantage in speed of access to information. Critics of these systems argue that managers do not need to know what happened as of the close of business yesterday.[4] This may be true. But there are benefits in being able to receive split-second responses. A manager's willingness to formulate questions and get data on which to base decisions may depend on the ease and speed with which he can retrieve answers from the computer. Although it is too early to tell whether the cost of this capability can be justified, large companies should seriously consider experimenting with this type of system.

Computer selection. The computer requirement for a company's MIS will, of course, depend on the system's performance specifications and the decisions management has made on each of the preceding design problems. While technical help is necessary in the decisions on equipment, management has the responsibility for making certain that the hardware chosen will meet the MIS needs and specifications at the time of installation, which may be some years away. In this respect, managers should recognize that they probably will learn many new ways to use the computer, such as new marketing planning, control, decision, and research applications, given some experience with an improved MIS. So even with the most careful planning, demands for computer capacity are likely to expand faster than anticipated.

Cost & value

It is difficult to generalize about how much an MIS will cost—or how much it will be worth. Usually there is not a large increase in data gathering costs, since many companies now have available to them much of the raw data required. Cost increases result from data storage and transforming the raw data into useful information. It is extremely difficult to determine MIS development costs, since many companies lack accounting arrangements, like interdepartmental billing, which allow them to keep track of the total cost of the manpower contributing to the program.

On a "best estimate" basis, we are aware of simple or partial systems which have cost only a few thousand dollars. At the other extreme, one complex marketing system we know of must have cost several million dollars. A large company with sales in the $500 million range should expect to invest several hundred thousand dollars (plus equipment charges) to develop a relatively sophisticated, computer-based MIS. And development costs will not end there, since after the first stage is operational, it is probable that management will want to upgrade the system continually.

If top executives authorize expenditures of this magnitude, they are likely to want a justification of the value of the system. Usually, computer-based

[4]See John Dearden, "Myth of Real-Time Management Information," HBR May–June 1966, p. 123.

information systems, such as those used for accounting, have been justified mainly on the ground that they reduce personnel and other administrative costs. Few advanced marketing information systems could be justified on the basis of cost reduction.

However, that test alone is not appropriate for an MIS. The main purpose of an MIS is to help the marketing manager make more profitable decisions, not to reduce data handling and paperwork costs. So an MIS should be evaluated in terms of its estimated effects on marketing efficiency.

Determining how much an MIS could increase marketing effectiveness is not an easy task. The involvement of management in developing overall specifications should help in making an estimate, however imprecise, of system benefits. In addition, the decision on a budget for MIS development need not be made in a single giant step. Rather, it is possible to attain system sophistication in discrete increments, involving a series of smaller budgeting decisions and cost/benefit evaluations.

CONCLUSION

Marketing men in many of the large corporations we studied are almost uniformly enthusiastic about the promise of the computer-based, advanced MIS. Relatively few such systems are now operating, however, and many companies have had indifferent success in deriving benefits from them.

In the more successful companies, the following patterns have been evident:

● The development of the MIS has been viewed as a management responsibility, including both top management and operating line management.

● Formal organizational lines have been drawn to provide leadership in use of the technique—usually including the appointment of a high-level information coordinator or "prime contractor" who develops plans and coordinates the efforts of the departments involved.

● The prime contractor reports to the user group, such as the marketing department, rather than to the central systems group.

● Line managers participate in developing overall specifications for the MIS.

● The sophistication of the system is balanced with that of the managers who use it.

● Systems development typically proceeds in manageable stages, rather than in attempts to develop "total" systems at once.

● The system is based on a disaggregated data bank which allows managers to retrieve analyses in the form they want without having to specify all their information needs in advance.

● Investments in systems development and operation are justified not on the basis of cost reduction, which is often irrelevant with the MIS, but on an estimate of the system's ability to help managers make more profitable marketing decisions.

It is evident that a good deal of faith is required to make substantial invest-ments in the MIS—whose benefits by and large are still unproven. Yet more and more companies are demonstrating their faith. And some of the pioneers already claim their faith is justified.

READING 11

HOW NOT TO DO RESEARCH*†

Robert Ferber

How-to publications are popular today, especially with the reputed publica-tion of *Brain Surgery Self-Taught*. Though it isn't likely that anything as sophis-ticated will happen in marketing research, marketing researchers should try to prepare material of equal value for their profession. Any marketing re-searcher, no matter what his experience or sophistication, with little effort can get himself relieved of arduous research.

Since the following ten rules have not been put into equation form (the style of countless dissertations), they should be easy to follow. Still, it may take time to master these rules, but with practice the average researcher should quickly become adept:

1. Begin the study before formulating a clear purpose or objective. Thus you will more likely confuse everybody, including yourself. If by accident the study has already been simply and definitively formulated, introduce extra-neous issues and incidental questions to confuse the issue.

2. Do not prepare an operational plan or a budget so you can remain flexi-ble, handle problems as they arise, and pester people for advice and money continuously. Following a policy of restricted optimization allows more in-tellectual challenge; what does it matter if the study goes a few thousand dollars in the red or takes extra months?

3. Start the empirical work or data collection before specifying a hypothesis or theoretical basis. A theory or set of hypotheses can always be put together to fit almost any results. If there is a demand for hypotheses—research direc-tors or clients will occasionally try to be pseudo-scientific—use the null hypothesis ploy and simply assert that no relationship exists. Why should you always specify negative price elasticities anyway?

4. If you are conducting a survey, carefully phrase the questions so they will give the expected answers. If you are conducting an experiment, tell the subjects what you are testing so they will clearly grasp the study's meaning and your intent. To be sure of getting the desired answers don't conduct a

*Reprinted from *The Journal of Marketing Research*, published by the American Marketing Asso-ciation, vol. 5, no. 1, p. 104.
†The views expressed here are hardly likely to reflect those of the publisher or the editorial board.

pretest. Also, by avoiding a pretest you will save money and probably won't . be bothered by having to rework questions simply because some silly respondents cannot answer them. You can easily infer from their other answers what they would have said had they understood the questions.

5. On mail surveys, don't bother to follow up the nonrespondents. You can always assume nonrespondents would have given the same answers as respondents, and if you should be wrong, nobody will probably find out anyway.

6. In analyzing the data, don't bother to make significance tests. If people will not accept your word on the reliability of the data, too bad. Any results are meaningful in *some* sense, so with a little rationalization you can have a truly significant piece of work.

7. To test whether a particular characteristic, say, education of family head, influences a variable such as consumer purchases, use bivariate comparisons. By disregarding other possibly relevant variables, you will surely find that the particular characteristic is a major influencing factor, as you had predicted.

7a. However, if you should do a multivariate analysis, mention the results only as an afterthought and base the conclusions on the bivariate comparisons. The comparisons are easier to understand, and you can avoid dealing with troublesome interaction effects or the possibility that some of the variables are not significant after you convince everybody of their importance.

8. If the data are to be analyzed by computer, let the programmer decide what kinds of analyses are easiest for him, then twist your study design so the objectives fit that kind of output. This way, the computer will have time to rest its tired transistors, and the programmers will be free to spend more time on new and powerful ways of playing tic-tac-toe.

9. In writing the report, be brief and vague when discussing the study's details and methods. The more information you give, the more embarrassing the questions you might be asked, and the more likely that mistakes will be found. To ensure your work cannot be checked and your mistakes discovered, be especially careful not to give the base figures for percentage distribution.

10. After you have bought your boss enough drinks so that he enthusiastically approves your report, send it to a journal editor indicating that you are magnanimously allowing him to choose which parts he wishes to publish. To impress him with the work's importance, set a deadline of ten days for acceptance threatening that you will send the manuscript elsewhere.

Undoubtedly more rules could be suggested since the misuse of technical methods or the behavioral sciences has hardly been touched. But, even these few rules should be enough to indicate a rich field for creative researchers.

PART
TWO

THE MARKET

Selling to the "hottest market ever" will require the marketer to understand the dynamics of the market. Bieda and Kassarjian provide us with additional dimensions on the concept of market segmentation. Albert Haring sheds light on the credit phenomena and Professor Lazer reminds the marketer that models play an important role in understanding marketing.

Zaltman brings to focus marketing interface with the behavioral sciences. Lee Adler reminds us that the marketer can "cash in on the cop out." Professor Wasson makes a note of the fact that the marketer must look at the consumer in terms of multiple dimensions. Income class in the trillion-dollar economy is not enough. Kelly and Egan suggest that the consumer decision-making process has many dimensions and that the marketer had better, for example, gain insight into husband-and-wife interaction in the decision-making process. Professor Evans presents a behavioral model for segmentation of the market in terms of social class and stage in the family life cycle. Professor Webster points out that the industrial buyer is also a human in the final selection, "Industrial Buying Behavior: A State-of-the-Art Appraisal."

READING 12

AN OVERVIEW OF MARKET SEGMENTATION*

John C. Bieda and Harold H. Kassarjian

Not unlike the fad of Motivation Research in the post World War II period, the concept of market segmentation has produced a phenomenal proliferation of articles, studies and papers in the past decade. The concept, itself, was first clearly articulated by Wendell Smith in a 1956 *Journal of Marketing* article,[1] a paper that by now has become a classic. And perhaps this should be so, for market segmentation has permeated the thinking of theorists, researchers and managers perhaps more than any of the other fashions and fads that marketing has passed through. Until very recently the controversial nature of the issue has been not whether or not segmentation leads to meaningful analysis as much as on what basis to segment.

To the earlier marketing manager, the natural segments of population were related to the socio-economic and demographic variables found in U.S. Census of Population. From these variables one could distill out *social class*, the ultimate conglomerate in the determination of consumer behavior in the view of many. But the field was not to be left to the census analysts alone; for soon after, personality variables such as gregariousness, authoritarianism,

*Reprinted from *Marketing in a Changing World*, Bernard A. Morin, ed. (Chicago, American Marketing Association, 1969), pp. 249–253
[1]Wendell Smith, "Product Differentiation and Market Segmentation as Alternative Marketing Strategies," *Journal of Marketing*, Vol. 21 (July 1956), pp. 3–8.

inferiority, risk taking and self esteem were to make their impact; and finally such concepts as usage rate, brand loyalty, channel loyalty, advertising susceptibility and even price sensitivity were to make their debut.

The usefulness of any given technique for segmentation, of course, is the ultimate one of applicability. "In other words, a crucial criterion for determining the desirability of segmenting a market along any particular dimension is whether the different sub-markets have different elasticities. . . ."[2] The determination of this criterion, according to Kotler,[3] depends upon several conditions.

The first of these is measurability, ". . . the degree to which information exists or is obtainable on various buyers' characteristics. Unfortunately many suggestive characteristics are not susceptible to easy measurement." The size of each segment that purchases toothpaste because of health fears, dislike of dentists, sex appeal, or because of habitual patterns inculcated by parents is difficult to measure.

A second condition is that of *accessibility*, the degree to which any given segment can be differentially reached. Unfortunately those starved for self-esteem, the hypochondriacal types, or heavy users of toothpaste do not co-operate by differentially exposing themselves to specific media, purchasing from different outlets or necessarily being willing to pay different prices.

Kotler's final condition is that of *substantiality*, the degree to which the segments are large enough to be worth sub-dividing for separate marketing activity.

TWO APPROACHES TO SEGMENTATION

As one reviews the literature on marketing segmentation, two approaches seem to emerge. On the one hand, the researcher starts with an existing product. The function of the researcher is to study the customers of that generic product to determine if there are differences between buyers of different brands. In this case the particular segment of the market that the brands are aimed at is determined empirically. Once such information is gleaned, better marketing decisions presumably are made, and perhaps further product differentiation is possible.

A great deal of the commercial research is undoubtedly of this sort answering such questions as, "Who is our market? and how can we better reach them?"

Evan's now often quoted study on the psychological and objective factors related to Ford and Chevrolet owners is an example of this type of approach. Starting with owners of Fords and Chevrolets he collected demographic and personality data and by the use of discriminant analysis attempted to predict

[2] Ronald E. Frank, "Market Segmentation Research: Findings and Implications," in Frank M. Bass, Charles W. King, and Edgar A. Pessemier (eds.), *Application of the Sciences in Marketing Management*, New York: John Wiley & Sons, 1968.
[3] Philip Kotler, *Marketing Management*, Englewood Cliffs, N. J.: Prentice-Hall, 1967.

the buyers of each make of automobile. His results parenthetically indicated that demographic variables did a better job of predicting brand choice than did the personality variables.[4]

The second type of segmentation research approaches the problem from the opposite direction. The researcher starts with pre-conceived notions of what the critical segmentation variables are—social class, personality, cultural variables, age and sex. Members of each group or segment are one way or another isolated, and product usage, brand and channel loyalty, or media exposure data, are then collected and analyzed. The question the researcher asks is of the sort, "How do young marrieds differ from older persons?" or "What products do southerners use as compared with northerners?" Rainwater's study on the Workingman's Wife is an example of this approach. He collected masses of data on the behavior of working class and middle class housewives relating to their purchasing activities, attitudes, and so on, and made a number of significant comparisons.[5]

Another example of the pre-categorized approach to segmentation is Joel Cohen's study relating purchasing behavior to personality characteristics. Based on Karen Horney's tripartite conceptions of compliant, detached and aggressive styles of life, Cohen developed a questionnaire and attempted to divide his sample into these three groups of persons. Next he searched for and found some differences between groups on brand preference, usage rates and media exposure.[6]

The following overview of the literature in market segmentation includes further examples of both approaches.

AN OVERVIEW OF RESEARCH FINDINGS

Demographic characteristics

That demographic variables are a useful method of segmentation has become almost axiomatic in marketing, and yet the research evidence is not at all clear. Evans, in his study on Ford and Chevrolet owners concludes, "The linear discriminant function of demographic variables is not a sufficiently powerful predictor to be of much practical use. . . . [They] . . . point more to the similarity of Ford and Chevrolet owners than to any means of discrimination between them. Analysis of several other objective factors also leads to the same conclusion.[7]

On grocery store products, the Advertising Research Foundation study in 1964 compared toilet tissue purchasing behavior with 15 socio-economic characteristics. The predictive efficiency of the characteristics was virtually

---

[4]Franklin B. Evans. "Psychological and Objective Factors in the Prediction of Brand Choice," *Journal of Business*, Vol. 32 (Oct. 1959), pp. 340–369.
[5]Lee Rainwater, Richard P. Coleman and Gerald Handel, *Workingman's Wife*, New York: Oceanna Publications, 1959.
[6]Joel B. Cohen, "An Interpersonal Orientation to the Study of Consumer Behavior," *Journal of Marketing Research*, Vol. 4, (August 1967), pp. 270–278.
[7]Same reference as Footnote 4.

nil.[8] Koponen, using the same J. Walter Thompson panel data but on beer, coffee and tea, found very similar results,[9] while Frank, Massy and Boyd using the Chicago Tribune panel data compared 57 product categories ranging from food to household products with demographic characteristics. The results were again similar with a very small portion of the variance being accounted for in the regression analyses.[10] Unfortunately, study after study throws doubt upon the direct usefulness of demographic characteristics as a predictor for product purchase.

Of course, this is not to deny that sanitary napkins are primarily purchased by women, razor blades by men, the influence of the purchase of sugar coated breakfast cereals by children, and canned boiled peanuts in brine primarily by Southerners. But nevertheless, other than very specific products aimed directly at a specific group, the empirical evidence seems to indicate that demographic measures, outside of education, are not an accurate predictor of consumer behavior.[11]

Social class

Perhaps some of the most extensive work on market segmentation has been done in the area of social class.[12] Some differences do seem to emerge in spending patterns, product preferences and shopping habits. Martineau for example found some clear preferences between the lower and middle classes for types of retail stores.[13] Glick and Levy found preference differences in television programs with the middle classes preferring current events, drama and audience participation shows while the lower classes preferred soap operas, westerns and quiz shows. However the degree of overlap is so great that a statistical prediction would be most difficult.[14]

Further, many of the social class studies are now several years old. By the 1970's what we will mean by lower class is perhaps not an income-occupation-education type of differentiation but more specifically Negroes, Indians and Mexican-Americans. Whether there is such a thing as a Negro market that is in fact different from the white market is still a controversial and not sufficiently researched issue. However, our expectation is that no such market exists. In any case, because of more exposure to the mass media consumption behavior differences between classes probably are disappearing.

[8]Ingrid Hildegaard and Lester Krueger, "Are There Customer Types?" as quoted in same reference as Footnote 2.

[9]Arthur Koponen. "Personality Characteristics of Purchasers," *Journal of Advertising Research*, Vol. 1 (Sept. 1960) 6–12.

[10]As quoted in same reference as footnote 2.

[11]Education taken as a uni-variate measure does seem to hold up as a segmentation variable as indicated in several studies and cannot as easily be brushed aside as most other demographic measures.

[12]e.g., James M. Carman, *The Application of Social Class in Market Segmentation*, Berkeley: Research Program in Marketing, Graduate School of Business Administration, 1965.

[13]Pierre D. Martineau, "Social Classes and Spending Behavior," *Journal of Marketing*, Vol. 23 (October 1958) 121–130.

[14]Ira O. Glick and Sidney Levy, *Living with Television*, New York: Aldine Publishing Co., 1962.

Personality

Personality studies have been similarly disappointing. Westfall was able to find differences between convertible owners and sedans but the relationships were weak.[15] Kamen found no evidence to ascertain the consistency of food preferences among personality groups.[16] Koponen in the study mentioned above using J. Walter Thompson data found some minimal differences between smokers and non-smokers on such variables as sex, aggression, achievement, dominance and compliance. However the percentage of variance accounted for both by personality variables and demographic variables combined was less than 12%.[17] Brody and Cunningham on reanalysis of the same data indicated that the personality variables measured by the Edwards Personality Preference Scale on both men and women heads of households accounted for a mere 15% of the variance.[18] Tucker and Painter, similarly, found significant but very weak relationships between measures such as responsibility, emotional stability, sociability and ascendency and product preference. Among the products studied personality variables only differentiated between users of deodorants and cigarettes.[19]

Gruen found no relationship between product preference and inner- and other- direction[20] and Kassarjian could not find differences in media exposure between inner and other-directed subjects.[21]

To sum up the literature, personality as a variable has not been a useful mode of market segmentation. Perhaps it is too much to expect the forces of personality to be powerful enough to differentially produce the purchase of Colgate Toothpaste over Crest or Gillette razor blades over Personna. Also it is possible that marketing has not yet found the right variables to measure, having no personality instruments of its own.

Buyer characteristics

Finally turning to buyer characteristics such as brand loyalty and usage rate, the findings are not dissimilar. For example, Frank and Massy found no significant difference in elasticity between brand loyal and non-brand loyal buyers.[22] Although Twedt did find that heavy and light users can be moderately well distinguished on the basis of their different demographic characteristics,

[15]Ralph Westfall. "Psychological Factors in Predicting Product Choice," *Journal of Marketing*, Vol. 26 (April 1962) pp. 34–40.
[16]Joseph M. Kamen, "Personality and Food Preferences," *Journal of Advertising Research*, Vol. 4 (Sept. 1964), pp. 29–32.
[17]Same reference as footnote 10.
[18]Robert P. Brody & Scott M. Cunningham, "Personality Variables and the Consumer Decision Process," *Journal of Marketing Research*, Vol. 5 (Feb. 1968), pp. 50–57.
[19]William T. Tucker and John J. Painter, "Personality and Product Use," *Journal of Applied Psychology*, Vol. 45 (1961), pp. 325–329.
[20]W. Gruen, "Preference for New Products and Its Relationship to Different Measures of Conformity," *Journal of Applied Psychology*, Vol. 44 (1960), pp. 361–366.
[21]Harold H. Kassarjian, "Social Character and Differential Preference for Mass Communication," *Journal of Marketing Research*, Vol. 2 (May 1965), pp. 146–153.
[22]Ronald E. Frank and William Massy, "Market Segmentation and the Effectiveness of a Brand's Price and Dealing Policies," *Journal of Business* (April 1965), pp. 188–200.

his findings, at best, indicated that the relationships are relatively modest.[23] Again using the J. Walter Thompson panel data, Massy, Frank and Lodahl indicated that heavy and light buying households had virtually identical demographic and psychological characteristics.[24] To continue, Farley could not segment the brand loyal customer,[25] and Frank and Boyd could not differentiate between the private label and manufacturer brand customers.[26] And finally Cunningham found little relationship between rate of purchase and brand loyalty.[27] However Brody and Cunningham found in a two brand discriminant analysis they were able to correctly identify 80% of brand choices.[28]

In general, the consistency of the results tends to indicate that the research to date in market segmentation has either been unsuccessful or if a relationship is shown, quite weak.

Turning back to Kotler's criterion for market segmentation, measurability, accessibility, and substantiality, it is clear that at least some of these conditions have not been met to date. In those cases where segmentation variables are measurable they do not seem to be related to purchasing characteristics. Or, even if the relationship is verified, too often the second condition, *accessibility*, is not a simple matter. Unfortunately media exposure, channel loyalty and purchase rate are not differentiated along the same variables as purchase behavior. To the everlasting frustration of the segmentation specialist, readers of *Argosy Magazine* and *True Experience* too often buy Cadillacs, while upper income professionals and businessmen too often shop at Macy's or Gimbel's in New York.

Perhaps then, the usual modes of segmentation are not sufficient. For example, Yankelovich argues that the analysis of various product markets should be made on the basis of several modes: patterns of usage, values derived from usage, preferences, aesthetics, and buying attitudes and motivations.[29] This view is enticing. Perhaps there are sufficiently substantial groupings of people who on a multi-variate set of dimensions can be considered a market segment. Unfortunately, Yankelovich does not present us with a method for such an analysis.

PROSPECTS

Although the results, to date, from studies on market segmentation have not been very encouraging, we might speculate on why so much of the research has been negative when the theory seems so logical and sound on an a priori

[23]Dik W. Twedt, "How Important to Marketing Strategy is the Heavy User," *Journal of Marketing*, (January, 1964), pp. 71–72.
[24]As quoted in same reference as Footnote 2.
[25]John Farley, "Brand Loyalty and the Economics of Information," *Journal of Business*, Vol. 37, (October, 1964), pp. 370–381.
[26]Ronald Frank and Harper Boyd, Jr., "Are Private-Brand Prone Food Customers Really Different," *Journal of Advertising Research*, Vol. 5 (December 1965), pp. 27–35.
[27]Ross M. Cunningham, "Brand Loyalty—What, Where, How Much?" *Harvard Business Review*, Vol. 34 (Jan.–Feb., 1956), pp. 127–137.
[28]Brody and Cunningham, *op. cit.*
[29]The conclusion is stated by Norman L. Barnett, "Beyond Market Segmentation," *Harvard Business Review*, Vol. 47 (Jan.–Feb., 1969).

basis. Perhaps the major problem of past research is that in an effort to segment markets we have lost sight of the basic premise of the theory: that different people have different needs and at different times these needs may change. Hence, a company's marketing program will have different elasticities when directed to groups of people where the needs in each group are relatively homogeneous and when the needs between groups are relatively heterogeneous.

Consider for a moment the methodological logic of the past research. First, the researcher has arbitrarily selected a group of products or brands that *he* thinks are serving the same market. Then data on purchase behavior is collected for analysis. The analysis consists of using demographic, socio-economic, and psychological variables as independent variables in either a regression or discriminant analysis. The objective is to find out if buyers of different brands are related in any way to the independent variables. If a strong relationship is found a circular argument is used to establish cause and effect, i.e., because the person jointly had the characteristic and bought the product and because the person would not have bought the product unless he needed it, therefore, the characteristic must be the cause of the need for the product. But we never bother to extrastatistically establish the cause and effect relationship. We might ask at this point (1) what kinds of assumptions are made when this type of analysis is carried out and (2) are the assumptions realistic or are other assumptions more plausible?

First, it is assumed that because people have bought the same brand, they have bought it for the same reason, i.e., the same need, desire, tension. The alternative assumption that people buy the same product for different reasons seems more realistic. For example, one family might buy one brand of potato chips because the kids like ridges in them. Another family might buy the same brand because ridged potato chips do not break quite as easily as straight potato chips when served with a dip.

Second, it is assumed that all people perceive the same set of brands to be alternatives from which to choose. Some recent evidence would tend to indicate that this assumption may not be justified. Green, Carmone, and Fox[30] have shown that television programs were clustered differently, on the basis of similarity, by three groups of people. This would tend to support an alternative hypothesis that all consumers do not perceive the same set of products as competing with one another.

Third, it is assumed that each person has the same set of alternatives (brands) available from which to choose to satisfy his needs. But it is common knowledge to every housewife that all stores do not carry the same brands, therefore this assumption does not seem to be justified.

Fourth, it is assumed that people with the same set of characteristics, the same values of the independent variables, have the same needs, wants, and desires. This assumption may be reasonable; however there has been little, if any, systematic research to justify making this assumption on an a priori basis.

One final problem with past studies centers on the complete lack of inte-

[30]Green, Paul E., Frank J. Carmone, and Leo B. Fox, "Television Programme Similarities: An Application of Subjective Clustering," *Journal of the Market Research Society*, Vol. 22 (January 1969), pp. 70–90.

gration into the segmentation analysis of information on the marketing mixes of the products and brands under study. This omission may have contributed to past negative findings if one or both of the following situations occurred.

Situation 1. Suppose that two brands, A and B, were essentially appealing to one set of needs and two other brands, C and D, were essentially appealing to another set of needs. If information on the marketing strategies of the four brands were not incorporated prior to using regression or discriminant analysis then the buyers of each of the brands would be considered a separate group, e.g., we would have a four way discriminant analysis. This being the case, the regression or discriminant function would not be able to distinguish between the buyers of brands A and B nor between the buyers of brands C and D. In this situation we would probably conclude that the results were negative because we could not predict which brand consumers would buy based on the independent variables.

Situation 2. Suppose that one brand was appealing to several segments using different marketing mixes for each segment. If this were the case then we would expect to find the brand satisfying a unique set of needs for buyers in each of the segments. When one or more companies follow this practice a discriminant or regression analysis would not be able to identify purchasers for the different brands because the buyers for each brand are aggregated even though they may belong in different market segments.

A next logical question is: What might we do to obtain more meaningful results on the subject? We would suggest attacking the problem as follows:

1. Determine what products or brands appeal to which set of needs, wants, and desires by the following two-stage procedures. First, apply multivariate analytical techniques to similarity data, i.e., that data obtained by asking the consumers what products or brands they consider similar; then determine homogeneous groups (=clusters) of consumers that perceive the market in a similar manner, i.e., that see the same set of products as being similar. Second, for each of the homogeneous groups again use multivariate techniques to cluster products that are perceived to be similar. Then find out what basic set of needs are being met by each cluster of products. The works of Barnette and Stefflre,[31] Green, Carmone, and Robinson,[32] and Green, Carmone, and Fox[33] are significant contributions in this direction.

2. At this point it is proposed that preference data from the consumers be incorporated into the analysis, i.e., the data obtained by asking the consumer which product(s) he prefers. The preference data, in conjunction with the similarity data provides a method of determining an ideal point for *each* individual in the homogeneous group obtained in the previous analysis. The ideal point for an individual would represent a product whose characteristics would

[31]Norman L. Barnette and Volney J. Stefflre, "An Empirical Approach to the Development of New Products," Unpublished manuscript, 1967.

[32]Green, Paul E., Frank J. Carmone, and Patrick J. Robinson, *Analysis of Marketing Behavior Using Nonmetric Scaling and Related Techniques*, Technical Monograph (Interim), Marketing Science Institute, March 1968.

[33]Same reference as Footnote 30.

be most preferred by the individual.[34] The ideal point for an individual would also serve an additional function as a reference point for determining how closely other sets of needs, represented by the clusters of products, match the needs of the individual. The degree to which the individual's needs and the needs being served by any cluster of products coincide should be an inverse function of the distance of the cluster to the ideal point, i.e., the more similar the two sets of needs the shorter the distance between that cluster and the individual's ideal point. Finally we should cluster the ideal points within each of the homogeneous groups. It would then be appropriate to determine if certain characteristics could meaningfully describe the consumers in each of these groups. This information would, of course, be used in determining future strategy for marketing to these segments.

It should be noted that the current approach takes into account differences in individuals' needs whereas previous work in this area has aggregated individuals over the entire market making it impossible to identify how different products or even the same product is related to individuals' differing needs.

The advantage of this approach is two-fold: first, we can study the basic needs of the consumers as they are currently being served by the market and, in doing so, we make no restrictions on the number or interdependence of the needs each brand can service; second, we can incorporate information on the marketing programs of the brands under study to determine the differential elasticities for each brand in each of the sub-markets.

SUMMARY

In summary, although the concept of market segmentation has captured the imagination of marketers, the results of studies to date have not been very encouraging. Univariate studies on demographic, objective and psychological factors related to consumer behavior have on the whole leaned towards indicating that product choice cannot be predicted from these types of variables.

However, in recent months a series of multivariate studies have emerged that indicate a real potential for a better understanding of the concept of market segmentation.

READING 13

CONSUMER CREDIT AND THE AFFLUENT SOCIETY*

Albert Haring

At the end of 1968, the total amount of consumer credit outstanding was 113 billion dollars of which approximately 90 billion was installment credit. The

[34]Same reference as Footnote 30.
*Reprinted from *Marketing Involvement in Society and the Economy*, Philip R. McDonald, ed. (Chicago, American Marketing Association, 1969), pp. 7–9.

total is an understatement because the figures do not include loans made by life insurance companies to their policy holders. Most level premium life insurance policies require the insurance company to loan the insured an amount close to the policy reserve at a stated rate of interest with no obligation on the part of the insured to repay the principal as long as the stipulated interest and the premium are paid. Whenever the going rate of interest substantially exceeds the rates stipulated in life insurance policies, loans against such policies rise substantially. Although this trend has been reported during the last year, no quantitative evaluation is easily available.

The size of installment credit and its influence on the economy may be better understood as the installment credit extended during 1968 is examined. This amounted to 97 billion dollars.[1] When non-installment credit is considered, charge accounts and service credit might be assumed to have an average 60 days outstanding or a turn-over of six while single payment loans might be assumed to have a twelve months duration. Based upon these assumptions, the 23 billion dollars of non-installment credit would represent an additional $94 billion of credit extended during 1968. Totaling these categories gives 191 billion, a figure representing approximately 56 percent of total retail trade. This is a very significant factor in the current economy.

During 1968, there was considerable inflation (4.9 percent) and a 7½ percent income surtax. Consumer disposable income rose 7.8 percent while savings decreased from 7.5 percent of disposable personal income in the second quarter of 1968 to 6.3 percent in the third quarter, 6.8 percent in the fourth quarter, and 6.1 percent in the first quarter of 1969. This was accompanied by an increase of $11 billion in total consumer credit of which $9 billion was in the installment field. These trends continued during early 1969. The net result was that the consumer was able to adjust to inflation, the income surtax, and to restrictive monetary policy without decreasing standards of living or unit purchases of merchandise for at least one year.

As of late June, 1969, consumer expenditures and plans to purchase appear to be slowing down. In the short run, the affluent consumer of today has the power to counteract government fiscal and monetary policy by adjusting savings and using credit. Business may play a part in this. By increasing the credit stretch, monthly payments may be kept constant in spite of rising prices. Additionally, the cost of money (interest) is only a small part of the cost of installment credit (finance charge). Many credit grantors in the revolving credit field have not even changed their rates. Only in the case of home purchasing on long term mortgages, did the pinch of higher interest rates affect consumers almost immediately.

Developments of the last year suggest strongly that if national fiscal and monetary policy are essential to control inflation and the economy, some additional tool must be used which has a more forceful and faster impact on consumers.

[1]Data presented based on material from the Federal Reserve Bulletins and Economic Indicators unless otherwise footnoted.

The proliferation of credit cards and systems

During recent years, national and regional credit systems have developed dramatically. The bank credit cards have received the most attention and, possibly, have been promoted the most aggressively. In addition, almost all large general merchandising systems, such as Sears, have instituted credit systems which can be used in all retail outlets of the organization. Moreover, brand or patronage credit operations, such as the oil companies, have tied in with motel groups and other retail outlets.

The credit systems have increased in number, the goods and services which can be purchased through their use has increased, and the geographic coverage has expanded. Some systems provide for securing cash as well as goods and services, while cash lenders of various types tend to provide identification for customers which can be used in any of their offices.

Except for supermarkets, and there has been some credit experimentation in this area also, the consumer who is well equipped with credit identification can virtually live in a credit world. With the improved incomes of most American families, plus a reasonable payment record, two-thirds of United States families undoubtedly can, if they wish, equip themselves with credit cards and other credit identification so that they could almost live and travel without cash. And more and more families appear to be tending towards this route. In fact, the credit life has become socially acceptable.

Choice of payment plan and credit limits

Almost all of the modernized credit plans permit partial payment at the discretion of the user. Charges are usually totalled for a month and the consumer is billed; if the bill is paid in full within thirty days, there is commonly no finance charge (cash advances are the normal exception); a minimum payment of 10 percent but not under $10, is usually prescribed with the unpaid balance rebilled a month later with a monthly finance charge of $1\frac{1}{2}$ percent. There may or may not be an agreed upon limit which the carried balance and new charges may not exceed. Plans vary in detail but the credit grantor only prescribes the most liberal arrangement which he is willing to accept; within the limits so set, the method and amount of payment rest with the consumer.

With the regional and/or national coverage of the major credit systems —banks, general merchandise, oil, cash lenders, entertainment and general purpose (such as American Express)—a credit limit, if one is set, is very difficult to enforce. Each credit card or system wants all of the consumer's business and usually establishes a credit limit which will make this possible. Then, if the consumer with ten credit cards or similar identification splurges, collection problems arise. This problem is not new and has always been significant in large cities with several big department and general merchandise stores. Today, the whole situation has been complicated by the increase in the number of credit systems and their greater geographic coverage. In practice, for the short run, business may have actually delegated to the consumer the function of setting his own credit limit.

Naturally, the question arises: has business delegated too much power and responsibility to the consumer as modern credit systems have evolved?

The credit rating of the consumer

In a credit economy, the consumer who has a poor rating or evaluation is in trouble. Under the new credit systems, there are problems in this area.

Under a bank card system, the consumer is completely liable for the amount of the purchase, regardless of whether the merchandise performs as represented or warranted. Under any credit system, this is true, although the customer can create more pressure on the seller when a local merchant extends the credit and where title is retained by the local merchant. Once the credit is passed on to a financial agency, or the central office of a credit system, this contact is lost. Failure to pay leads to a derogatory report to credit agencies and the loss of the specific credit card or similar identification. Business law and consumer understanding differ in this area.

Historically, merchandise departments of large stores have frequently failed to communicate to the credit department when merchandise trouble develops. Now the situation is worse. Also, in the past, a consumer could not in many cases find out what was wrong with his credit record from a credit agency. In some way, the consumer must be able to get his side of a derogatory story on the credit agency records. Here are some of the information reporting problems which require solving:

1. How can the consumer get information about his own credit record . . . and his side of a story on the record?

2. In the case of lawsuits and similar legal actions, should the credit agency record the result of the case as well as its initiation?

3. When should old information be dropped from the record? How often should data be brought up to date?

4. Who should be able to secure credit data? Personal data? Only firms from whom the consumer requests credit? Government agencies? Employers? And what should be available to each group?

5. Is there conflicting interest which is detrimental to the public when a credit data collection agency has a collection department?

Low-income market installment credit

In 1968, the Federal Trade Commission investigated sales practices of retailers selling consumer durables—furniture, major appliances, home furnishing, televisions, etc.—in the District of Columbia and published an "Economic Report on Installment Credit and Retail Sales Practices of District of Columbia Retailers." Scattered excerpts from this report are pertinent:

Low-income market retailers used installment credit in 93 percent of their sales. The comparable figure for general market retailers was 27 percent.

On the average, goods purchased for $100 at wholesale sold for $255 in the low-income market stores, compared with $159 in general market stores. For example, the wholesale cost of a portable TV set was about $109 to both a low-income market and a general market retailer. The general market retailer sold the set for $129.95, whereas the low-income market retailer charged $219.95 for the same set.

Despite their substantially higher prices, net profit on sales for low-income market retailers was only slightly higher and net profit return on net worth was considerably lower when compared to general market retailers.

When calculated on an effective annual rate basis, finance charges of general market retailers varied between 11 percent and 29 percent, averaging 21 percent when contracts were assigned and 19 percent when retailers financed their own contracts. Finance charges by low-income market retailers imposing such charges ranged between 11 and 33 percent per annum, averaging 25 percent on contracts assigned to finance companies and 23 percent on contracts the retailers held themselves.

In all probability, the increased prices charged by low-income market retailers were due substantially to installment credit costs which were not easily included in the finance charges because of legal and competitive reasons. Consumers living in low-income markets see the more attractive prices and more favorable terms available to groups with better economic status; naturally, they are unhappy about the situation. These marketing and credit problems need a better solution.

SUMMARY AND CONCLUSIONS

Consumer credit is sufficiently large and flexible today to have a major influence upon the effectiveness of monetary and fiscal policy. In addition, consumer credit is expanding rapidly in a manner which gives the consumer maximum freedom and the credit grantor minimum control. The very importance of credit in the life of the average American makes credit data collection practices take on a public interest. Likewise, marketing and credit costs to low-income markets appear too high and are under question.

The so-called Truth-in-Lending Bill has recently become law. The Uniform Consumer Credit Code has been introduced in a number of state legislatures. Hearings concerning credit bureau problems have been held. Today's consumer credit problems need more clarification with the hope that improved business practice can minimize the need for legislation and regulation. This is particularly true since projections of further expansion of consumer credit appear on the horizon—financing all home equipment including soft goods under the home mortgage, funding the cost of advanced education, handling credit on a lifetime insurance basis. Here, the thought is to clarify present problems so that they can be, hopefully, solved before those of the future add even more complexity to the situation.

READING 14

THE ROLE OF MODELS IN MARKETING*

William Lazer

Behavioral sciences and quantitative methods are both in the forefront in the current development and extension of marketing knowledge. It is no mere coincidence that both make frequent reference to two concepts: *models* and *systems*. Certainly models and systems have become powerful interpretive tools.[1]

Models and systems have relevance to such significant marketing problems as: (1) developing marketing concepts and enriching the marketing language by introducing terms that reflect an operational viewpoint and orientation; (2) providing new methods and perspectives for problem-solving; (3) conducting marketing research and designing experiments; (4) developing marketing theories; (5) measuring the effectiveness of marketing programs.

Although they may not be recognized as such, marketing models are fairly widely applied by both practitioners and academicians. The use of analogies, constructs, verbal descriptions of systems, "idealizations," and graphic representations are quite widespread in marketing. For example, pricing models, physical distribution models, models of marketing institutions, and advertising models are useful marketing tools.

DEFINITION OF MARKETING MODELS

A model is simply the perception or diagramming of a complex or a system. In marketing, it involves translating perceived marketing relationships into constructs, symbols, and perhaps mathematical terms. For example, an internally consistent set of statements concerning wholesaling, advertising, merchandising, or pricing comprises a model. It relates in a logical manner certain constructs or axioms that are envisaged.

Models are really the bases for marketing theories, since they are the axioms or assumptions on which marketing theories are founded. They furnish the underlying realities for theory construction. Where the perceived relationships are expressed in mathematical terms, we have a mathematical model. In this sense, any consistent set of mathematical statements about some aspect of marketing can be regarded as a model.

All marketing models are based on suppositions or assumptions. These assumptions do not correspond exactly with the real marketing world. Usually they are employed to simplify an existing marketing situation. Therefore, models cannot depict marketing activities exactly. Moreover, no matter how precise mathematical models may be, they do not correct themselves for false assumptions.

*Reprinted from *The Journal of Marketing,* published by the American Marketing Association, vol. 26, no. 2, April, 1962, pp. 9–14.
[1] Paul Meadows, "Models, Systems and Science," *American Sociological Review.* Vol. 22 (February, 1957) pp. 3–9, at p. 3.

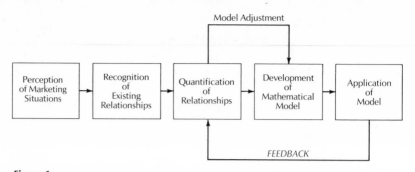

Figure 1
Model building by abstraction

MODEL BUILDING

There are two approaches to the construction of marketing models: *abstraction* and *realization*.[2]

In abstraction, a real world situation is perceived and it is mapped into a model. If it is mapped into a mathematical system, a mathematical model results. This is illustrated by Figure 1.

In abstraction, the model builder must perceive of a marketing situation in a way that permits him to recognize the relationships between a number of variables. For example, he may perceive of relationships between transportation costs, customer satisfaction, and the location of distribution centers; the number of sales calls and resulting sales and profits; the allocation of advertising expenditures and the achievement of favorable consumer response.

Based on this, the model builder will become aware of logical conceptual relationships which he is able to state fairly succinctly and clearly. These relationships may then be quantified through the use of available records and data, experiments, or simulations. The basis for the establishment of a mathematical model is obtained.

Once the mathematical model is determined, it may be applied in "the real world." Feedback will result which will provide the basis for a further alteration of the quantification of the conceptual relationships perceived. It will lead to a refinement and improvement in the mathematical model.

As an example of model building by abstraction, consider the construction of a model representing consumer response to company advertising expenditures.[3] Through observation, analysis of relevant data, and experience, the model builder may recognize that with little or no advertising expenditures consumer purchases of a product are very small. Then it may appear that, as expenditures increase over a certain range, purchase responses increase quite sharply. While response increases even further with additional advertising

[2]See C. H. Coombs, H. Raiffa, and R. M. Thrall, "Some Views On Mathematical Models and Measurement Theory," in R. M. Thrall, C. H. Coombs, and R. L. Davis, editors, *Decision Processes* (New York: John Wiley and Sons, Inc., 1954), pp. 20–21.
[3]A. P. Zentler and Dorothy Ryde, "An Optimal Geographical Distribution of Publicity Expenditure In A Private Organization," *Management Science*, Vol. 2 (July, 1956), pp. 337–352.

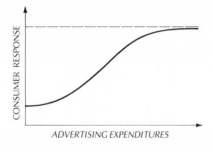

Figure 2

Relationship of consumer response to advertising expenditures

expenditures, it is noted that eventually it tapers off and tends toward some limit.

The resulting model may be depicted graphically as in Figure 2. Through research these relationships may be quantified and expressed in terms of mathematical formulas. A model is thus developed which represents the relationships existing between advertising expenditures and consumer response. Such a model has been constructed, and with further mathematical refinements was used to determine the optimum allocation of advertising expenditures.[4] The model also proved to be useful in developing advertising-response curves, analyzing the impact of time lags in advertising effect, evaluating the interaction of competing promotional effort and estimating the impact of varying promotional resources.

Model building by realization

In realization, the process of model building is reversed. The model builder starts with a consideration of a logically consistent conceptual system. Then some aspect of the real world can be viewed as the model of the system. It is a process of going from the logical system to the real world.[5] This is portrayed in Figure 3.

Model building by realization may be illustrated by considering the mathematical model known as Markov process. This process is a model that is useful in the study of complex business systems. It studies the present state of a marketing system and what has happened through some transition time. For example, it can be of help in studying the users and nonusers of a product (the present state of the system), and what has happened as advertising is applied over a period (the state transitions). It is a theoretical, logically consistent, and abstract model.

Starting with this model, the model builder may perceive that such marketing situations as the use of advertising to switch brand loyalties of consumers, or to change consumers from the state of nonusers to users, deal with the current state of a system and the transition of the system through time. There-

---

[4] Same reference as footnote 3.
[5] Same reference as footnote 2, p. 21.

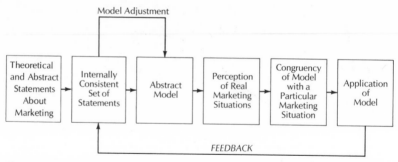

Figure 3
Model building by realization

fore, he may use the Markov process to study the effects of advertising impact. As experience from application of the model is developed, feedback will result and the model can be adjusted. In using this procedure, the model builder has gone from a logical mathematical system to the world of marketing.

Herniter and Magee and also Maffei have discussed the application of Markov process models.[6] Their research indicates that such models are extremely useful in determining the choice of promotional policy for maximizing profits in the long run; in specifying the kinds of experimentation required to measure the impact of promotional effort; and in calculating cost and revenue changes resulting from the use of alternative marketing strategies over time.

KINDS OF MARKETING MODELS

It is difficult to classify marketing models, since there are many dimensions and distinguishing characteristics that may be used as criteria for classification.

Mathematicians, for instance, might classify marketing models according to the type of equations used. They could distinguish among algebraic, difference-equation, differential-equation, and mixed-difference and differential equation models.[7] Physical models can be distinguished from abstract models. Loose verbal models may be contrasted with precise mathematical models. Models that take into consideration changes in factors through time are referred to as dynamic models and are distinguished from static models. Deterministic models are differentiated from stochastic models (models in which some of the variables are random factors and cannot be completely determined). Micro-marketing and macro-marketing models exist, as do linear and non-linear models. Perhaps one of the most meaningful distinctions from a marketing point of view is that of goal models and systems models.

[6]Jerome Herniter and John F. Magee, "Customer Behavior As A Markov Process," *Operations Research*, Vol. 9 (January–February, 1961), pp. 105–122; Richard B. Maffei, "Brand Preferences and Simple Markov Processes," *Operations Research*, Vol. 8 (March–April, 1960), pp. 210–218.
[7]This breakdown is taken from an unpublished paper prepared by Dr. Paul Craig, at the Institute of Basic Mathematics for application to business, sponsored by the Ford Foundation at Harvard University during 1959–1960. The actual classification of models was suggested by Dr. Samuel Goldberg.

Systems models and goal models

A distinction has been made in the behavioral-science literature between *systems models* and *goal models*.[8]

In marketing, a goal model or end-means model starts with a marketing task to be achieved. For instance, it focuses on the marketing objectives and the uses of company resources to achieve them as efficiently as possible. It is the achievement of marketing goals, and not necessarily corporate goals, that becomes important.

The goal model does not lend itself readily to a representation of a multifunctional unit. The marketing department is not viewed as being comprised of a number of different departments with possible conflicting goals, but rather as one over-all unit with a major goal. The implication here is that if we increase the marketing means, we thereby increase our effectiveness in achieving marketing goals. In this model, moreover, the effectiveness of the marketing department is measured by the devotion to the achievement of marketing goals. Although the goal model is useful, it is Utopian and unrealistic.

In the systems model, the starting point is not a goal. The starting point is the model of a total functioning system, for example, the marketing department. It is the model of a marketing unit capable of achieving goals. The systems model recognizes that there can be many conflicting objectives within an organization and that concessions must be made. In this model, the multifunctional units involved in achieving marketing goals are recognized. This model also considers that some means must be allocated to non-goal directed effort, such as the resources necessary to maintain the marketing organization. Given certain marketing conditions and resources, the main consideration is—how can they be programed to achieve the optimum position for the total business system?

The systems model is the superior model for marketing management. It is the model that the operations researcher uses when he perceives of a business as an over-all system of action when he plans the optimal use of resources. The systems approach to the study of marketing is appearing in the literature and should result in a better understanding of the existing interrelationships among marketing elements, a clearer grasp of marketing behavior, and a more effective allocation of marketing resources.[9]

Models and marketing theory

The terms "models" and "theories" are often used interchangeably. An interesting and useful distinction for marketing can be drawn from an idea

---

[8] Amitai Etzioni, "Two Approaches to Organizational Analysis: A Critique and A Suggestion," *Administrative Science Quarterly*, Vol. 5 (September, 1960), pp. 257–278, at p. 258.

[9] See Wroe Alderson, *Marketing Decisions and Executive Action*, (Homewood, Illinois: Richard D. Irwin, Inc., 1957); William Lazer and Eugene J. Kelley, "Interdisciplinary Contributions to Marketing Management," (Bureau of Business and Economic Research, Michigan State University, 1959); William Lazer, "Transportation Management: A Systems Approach," *Distribution Age*, Vol. 59 (September, 1960), pp. 33–35; John F. Magee, "Operations Research in Making Marketing Decisions," *Journal of Marketing*, Vol. 25 (October, 1960), pp. 18–24.

expressed by Coombs, Raiffa, and Thrall: "A model is not itself a theory; it is only an available or possible or potential theory until a segment of the real world has been mapped into it. Then the model becomes a theory about the real world."[10]

As a theory, a marketing model can be accepted or rejected on the basis of how well it actually works. The actual model itself, however, is "right or wrong" (internally consistent) on logical grounds only.

One can distinguish between models and theories by considering marketing research techniques. A stipulated technique for marketing measurement may be called a model. For example, the forecasting technique known as exponential smoothing, or forecasting by exponentially weighted moving averages, has proved to be a useful forecasting model.[11] As a model, it need only be internally consistent. It is a potential marketing theory.

When data are actually measured by the exponential smoothing technique and are mapped into the model, then the model becomes a theory about the marketing data. The resulting theory may be a good one or a poor one.

The relationship among marketing models, theories, and hypotheses now follows directly. Within a theoretical framework, we are able to test certain hypotheses. The assumptions of a marketing model itself, however, need not be subjected to tests, whereas hypotheses should be tested. It should be noted that assumptions in one model may be hypotheses in another.

USE OF MODELS IN MARKETING

Five major uses for models in marketing can be suggested.

1. *Marketing models provide a frame of reference for solving marketing problems.* They suggest fruitful lines of inquiry and existing information gaps. Marketing models do this by playing a descriptive role. The descriptive model does not go beyond presenting a representation or picture of some aspect of marketing activity. However, it serves an extremely important function in the extension of marketing thought. The use of flow diagrams in depicting existing relationships or in developing a logical computer program is an example of the use of descriptive models.

2. *Marketing models may play an explicative role, and as such they are suggestive and flexible.* Such models are more than simple metaphors; they attempt to explain relationships and reactions. The marketing scientist not only is interested in describing marketing phenomena and examining them, but he desires to explain existing relationships and frame of references. For example, "switching models" often attempt to explain the relationships between advertising and brand loyalty.[12]

3. *Marketing models are useful aids in making predictions.* For instance, in answer to the question why models should be used, Bross explains that the

---

[10]Same reference as footnote 2, pp. 25–26.
[11]Peter R. Winters, "Forecasting Sales by Exponentially Weighted Moving Averages," *Management Science*, Vol. 6 (April, 1960), pp. 324–342.
[12]Same reference as in footnote 9.

real answer to this question is that the procedure has been followed in the development of the most successful predicting systems so far produced, the predicting systems used in science.[13] Marketing practitioners and scientists wish to predict and consequently employ various types of forecasting models and inventory models. These models become more than just an explanation and a representation of an existing situation. They become means of presenting future reality.

4. *Marketing models can be useful in theory construction.* Formulators of marketing models may hypothesize about various aspects of marketing as they might exist. Thereby, we have "reality" as it is hypothesized. Simulation, for example, which really involves experimentation on models, can lead to valuable insights into marketing theory. In the same vein, an ideal may be developed as a model. Although the ideal may not be achieved, it provides a useful vehicle for extending knowledge.

5. *Marketing models may stimulate the generation of hypotheses which can then be verified and tested.* Thereby, it furthers the application of the scientific method in marketing research and the extension of marketing knowledge.

Benefits of mathematical models

Why should marketing scientists and practitioners utilize mathematical models rather than other kinds of models?[14] Perhaps the most important reasons are four:

1. *The translation of a model from a verbal to a mathematical form makes for greater clarification of existing relationships and interactions.* It is a rigorous and demanding task; and conceptual clarity and operational definitions are often achieved. The models developed may also become more generally applicable.

2. *Mathematical models promote greater ease of communication.* Within business administration and related subject-matter areas, there is the difficulty of cross-communication because of the terminology used by specialized disciplines. Through the use of mathematical models, all of the disciplines may be reduced to a common mathematical language which may reveal interrelationships and pertinence of research findings not previously known.

3. *Mathematical models tend to be more objective, while verbal constructs lean heavily on intuition and rationalizations.* Scientific marketing can be advanced through the application of objective mathematical analysis.

4. *Analyses that are not feasible through verbal models may be advanced through mathematical models.* Mathematics provides powerful tools for marketing academicians and practitioners. Mathematical models lend themselves to analysis and manipulation. In the manipulation of verbal models, the inter-relationships and logic are easily lost.

---

[13]Irwin D. J. Bross, *Design for Decisions* (New York: The Macmillan Company, 1953), p. 169.
[14]Paul Craig, same reference as footnote 7.

CONCLUDING OBSERVATIONS

The usefulness of a marketing model is a function of the level of generalization the model achieves, and the degree of reality it portrays. Symbolization is used in model building to achieve greater internal consistency and more correspondence with reality. The greater the level of symbolization, and the fewer the restrictions, the more adequate and more generally applicable is the model.

For example, it is true that linear-programing models are more abstract, more general, and more valuable than are mere descriptive models representing a factory and warehousing complex. However, it may well be that the linear-programing model is by no means more widely used.

All marketing models are based on simplifications and abstractions. Only by making assumptions is a model molded to fit reality. Sometimes the reality beyond the boundaries of the model, however, is much greater than the reality within the boundaries. The model then becomes severely limited by the assumptions on which it is based.

To be effective, marketing models should be plausible, solvable, and based on realistic assumptions. The current level of model building in marketing is not yet a sophisticated one. It cannot compare favorably with the level of model building in the physical or biological sciences. As the discipline of marketing matures, however, it will use an increasing number of models and will develop more complex models that have broader application.

READING 15

MARKETING INFERENCE IN THE BEHAVIORAL SCIENCES*

Gerald Zaltman

The area of the behavioral sciences and marketing has received extensive treatment in the literature.[1] Generally, publications dealing with this subject have made contributions by demonstrating that the behavioral sciences can be applied to marketing, and by outlining some of the substantive behavioral areas which have marketing applicability. However, there is something noticeably lacking in marketing accounts of behavioral science use. There has been virtually no discussion of the process of scientific inference which enables one to apply theories and findings from the behavioral sciences to marketing problems.

*Reprinted from *The Journal of Marketing*, published by the American Marketing Association, vol. 34, no. 3, July 1970, pp. 27–32.
[1]For example, John A. Howard, *Marketing: Executive and Buyer Behavior* (New York: Columbia University Press, 1963); Gerald Zaltman, *Marketing: Contributions from the Behavioral Sciences* (New York: Harcourt, Brace & World, 1965); Francesco M. Nicosia, *Consumer Decision Processes* (Englewood Cliffs, New Jersey: Prentice-Hall, 1966); Steuart H. Britt, *Consumer Behavior and the Behavioral Sciences* (New York: John Wiley & Sons, Inc., 1967); Harper W. Boyd, Jr. and Sidney Levy, *Promotion: A Behavioral View* (Englewood Cliffs, N.J.: Prentice-Hall, 1967); James Engel et al., *Consumer Behavior* (New York: Holt, Rinehart & Winston, Inc., 1968); and Rom J. Markin, *The Psychology of Consumer Behavior* (Englewood Cliffs, N.J.: Prentice-Hall, 1969).

This article explores the process of scientific inference involved in bridging marketing and the behavioral sciences, and highlights two important obstacles in this process. The author begins with a brief discussion of definitions and reasons for using the behavioral sciences.

MARKETING AND THE BEHAVIORAL SCIENCES

"Marketing is the analyzing, organizing, planning and controlling of the firm's customer-impinging resources, policies and activities with a view to satisfying the needs and wants of chosen customer groups at a profit."[2] This definition identifies the consumer as both the *starting point* in the marketing process and the *pivotal point* around which various resources must be structured. Thus, an understanding of consumer needs and behavior is a crucial requirement for efficient and effective marketing. The behavioral sciences offer a set of concepts relating to these needs and responses. The following statement can serve as a working definition of the behavioral sciences: Behavioral science consists of the critical, systematic study of the causes, manifestations, and consequences of human activity. Thus, the task facing the marketing man is to derive from these behavioral concepts various market analyses, plans, and controls which will guide the structuring of the firm's resources, policies, and activities around the consumer.

REASONS FOR A BEHAVIORAL SCIENCE APPROACH IN MARKETING

Profit maximization

There are at least four reasons for being concerned with behavioral analyses of market phenomena. The first and most commonly articulated reason is that the proper utilization of behavioral science concepts and techniques is necessary for the achievement of the firm's goals. The understanding of relevant social and psychological processes operating among potential consumers enables the firm to adapt its product, distribution, and promotional strategies to those social-psychological processes. If the marketing manager properly understands those processes, and correctly and skillfully translates that understanding into marketing strategy, his chances for success are increased considerably. In addition to helping us understand consumer response mechanisms, the behavioral sciences also offer insight into sales force management, dealer relations, industrial procurement, sales forecasting, and executive decision making.

Promoting general welfare

The second reason for studying behavioral sciences within a marketing framework is that this activity, when properly pursued, promotes general public

[2]Philip Kotler, *Marketing Management* (Englewood Cliffs, N.J.: Prentice-Hall, 1967), p. 12.

welfare. Concepts and techniques in the behavioral sciences can be important tools in improving the general satisfaction of the consuming public. These tools can help the marketer to identify the nature and origin of consumer wants and the appropriate product response to those wants. Successful goods and services are those which perform needed physical, psychological or socio-logical functions for individuals who buy and consume them. (An individual is better off when more of these functions are satisfied. The efficiency by which this satisfaction is accomplished is also important to the individual and to the consuming public.) The larger the number of satisfied individuals the better off is that portion of the consuming public.

Consumer education

The third reason to be concerned with marketing and the behavioral sciences is that a better understanding of the social and psychological causes, mani-festations, and consequences of consumer behavior provides a necessary first step for remedial consumer education programs among the educationally and economically deprived. Various behavioral concepts can be used to diagnose problems facing consumers in dealing with family budgeting, credit use, comparative shopping, and so on. These concepts may also provide guidelines for solutions to these problems.

Improved behavioral science

The fourth reason for a behavioral approach to marketing concerns not the improvement of marketing strategy, but rather the improvement of concepts and techniques in the behavioral sciences. Not only are the behavioral sci-ences capable of making contributions to marketing, but marketing also has contributions to make to the various behavioral sciences. Researchers and practitioners in these areas are slowly recognizing this interrelationship. The marketing contribution may occur at both a theoretical and a practical level:

● *Theoretical Contributions.* The larger the number of different situations and kinds of implications that can be correctly derived from a behavioral theory, the more credible or reliable is that theory. Marketing contexts offer increased opportunities for the testing of existing theories of human behavior. They also offer a new opportunity for the abstraction of new behavioral theories.

● *Practical Contributions.* In addition to common theoretical concerns, there are also common practical or implemental concerns between market-ing and the behavioral sciences. It is quite possible that eventually marketing will contribute more to other disciplines than it may receive. The marketing manager, public health official, social worker, U.S. congressman, agricultural extension agent, and Peace Corps worker among innumerable others have several things in common. All are concerned with promoting the acceptance or continued use of a good or service among some specified group. They must do this under conditions of limited resources and competing influences from which they must differentiate their own ideas, products, or services. All are faced with the common task of understanding relevant wants of particular groups and developing an appropriate offering and strategy in communicating with the public. Marketing, more than other social action professions, appears to have developed a more systematic approach to the study of its activities. Marketing concepts such as product differentiation, service offerings, competitive strategies, promotion, and distribution are tools which enable the change agent to better utilize his knowledge of human-behavior to bring about the desired changes. Traditional marketing techniques are thus bridging mechanisms between the simple possession of knowledge and the socially useful implementation of what knowledge allows.

UTILIZING BEHAVIORAL CONCEPTS

Deriving useful information

To be truly useful tools, behavioral concepts must be operationalized in a marketing context; they must be expressed in terms of marketing-oriented variables which are causally and meaningfully related. Thus, "How are empirical marketing statements derived from the original behavioral theory and/or assumptions?" The remainder of this paper will focus on this question. The discussion does not take into account how relevant behavioral concepts and hypotheses are *located* and *identified*. This question is beyond the scope of this paper.

Behavioral scientists have been somewhat negligent in studying behavior in the marketplace. As a consequence, the marketing relevance is not always clear relative to techniques utilized by behavioral scientists. It may be useful to explore a "thinking methodology" that might contribute to an understanding of *how* the behavioral sciences are applied to marketing problems.

Scientific inference

As marketers engage in the application, testing, and refining of theories they are also engaging in a process common to all sciences, scientific inference or induction.[3] The consensus is that the logic of scientific inference is essentially the same regardless of context. However, inherent differences among disciplines cause the refinement and application of scientific inference processes to vary from discipline to discipline.

The steps involved in scientific inference in marketing are discussed below and represented in Figure 1. (The two "gaps" in this figure are discussed later.) It should be noted that each step is logically inferred from the previous step.

[3]There are some very good discussions of scientific inference in the literature. For example, Arthur Stinchombe, *Constructing Social Theories* (New York: Harcourt, Brace & World, 1968); Hubert Blalock, *Theory Construction* (Englewood Cliffs, N.J.: Prentice-Hall, 1969); Abraham Kaplan, *The Conduct of Inquiry* (San Francisco: Chandler Publishing Co., 1964); Ernest Nagel, *The Structure of Science* (New York: Harcourt, Brace & World, 1961).

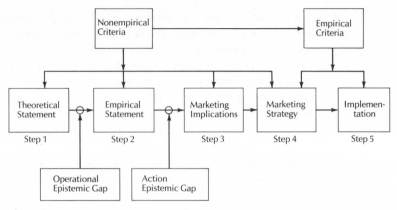

Figure 1
Scientific marketing inference

Step 1. *Theoretical Statement.* The starting point in the process of scientific inference is a theoretical statement describing a relationship between two or more phenomena. The relationship will generally contain an implied causal connection between phenomena.

Step 2. *Empirical Statement.* The theoretical statement will logically imply an empirical statement; therefore, the second step is to derive this empirical statement. The empirical statement should contain operational definitions of the concepts or phenomena contained in the theoretical statement. Operationalization is achieved by setting up variables related to one another in certain specific ways; e.g., co-variance and causal direction.

Step 3. *Marketing Implications.* Step 3 is to derive the marketing implications of the empirical statement. In effect, this step asks, "So what?" It is concerned with stating the appropriate marketing conditions given different possible states of the variables contained in the empirical statement.

Step 4. *Marketing Strategy.* This step is concerned with formulating marketing strategies which constitute management's response to the different possible marketing conditions specified in Step 3.

Step 5. *Implementation.* The final step consists of the implementation of the indicated strategies by manipulating the relevant marketing decision variables. (A marketing decision variable is simply, "any factor under the control of the firm which may be used to stimulate company sales."[4])

Each step must be monitored and modified as necessary. During stages one through four various nonempirical criteria can be applied. A full discussion of these criteria is beyond the scope of this paper. Empirical criteria may be of several forms which in turn have many subcategories.[5] The criteria may

---

[4] Same reference as footnote 2, p. 264.
[5] See especially, Mario Bundge, *Scientific Research* (Heidelberg, Germany: Springer-Verlag Berlin, 1967), Vol. I & II; Robert Dubin, *Theory Building* (New York: The Free Press, 1969); Kaplan, same reference as footnote 3; Bernard S. Phillips, *Social Research* (New York: Macmillan Co., 1966).

take on a (1) formal dimension (e.g., internal consistency and strength); (2) semantical dimension (e.g., linguistic exactness, conceptual unity); (3) epistemological dimension (e.g., external consistency, inclusiveness); (4) methodological dimension (e.g., testability); and (5) metaphysical dimension (e.g., worldview compatibility). These nonempirical criteria help set the stage for the empirical criteria to be applied at steps four and five. Experience in each step may result, through a process of induction, in a modification of the preceding stage.

ILLUSTRATIONS

Partial example

It may be useful to present two examples of scientific inference in marketing. The first example is incomplete and is presented only to facilitate the discussion of the second example.

The author begins with the following theoretical statement: *People are more attracted to others whose opinions are similar to their own.* There are two causally related phenomena or concepts (attractiveness and opinion similarity) in this statement. Both concepts are variables since they are capable of taking on different values. The implied causal relationship is that perceived opinion similarity leads to attractiveness. The next step is to ask whether this statement logically implies an empirical marketing statement. It does. A derived empirical statement would be: *Consumers are more attracted to salesmen whose opinions are perceived similar to their own.*

In this instance specific social roles, those of consumer and salesman, were substituted for the very general individuals (i.e., "people" and "others") mentioned in the theoretical proposition. However, the empirical statement may not be true. The theoretical statement may accurately describe what happens in politics between voters and office seekers or what happens in the formation of social cliques in a university dormitory; however, it does not necessarily describe what happens between consumers and salesmen. At this stage in the process, nonempirical criteria, mentioned earlier, can be applied to both the theoretical and empirical statements. If the two statements successfully meet the various criteria, then they can be subjected to an empirical test in a relatively straightforward manner. The nonempirical criteria help remove statements which are difficult or impossible to test empirically.

Implementing and testing the proposition requires defining a specific selling situation. Consumers in this situation would be questioned about (1) the extent to which they liked the salesman; (2) the extent to which they felt they shared common opinions or beliefs with the salesman; and (3) whether or not a sale was consummated. The researcher may find that the higher the perceived opinion similarity, the greater the social attractiveness of the salesman. Alternatively, it would also be possible to conduct an experiment in which customers and salesmen were matched on relevant variables and the results noted. Then customers and salesmen could be deliberately mismatched, and the result again could be noted and compared with the results of the matched pairs. Given this validation of the empirical statement, certain strategies become evident in assigning salesmen to cover geographical areas characterized by homogeneity in opinions or general outlook.

Complete example

The following steps in the inference process are discussed below:

Step one. Consider a somewhat more meaningful theoretical proposition: *"An individual may be attracted to others because associating with them is intrinsically gratifying or because the association furnishes extrinsic benefits for him."*[6]

Intrinsic rewards received from others include social approval by one's peers, or the feeling of security brought about by being with people whose opinions or values are like one's own. Intrinsic rewards are highly subjective; extrinsic rewards are more objective. Alternative sources of extrinsic rewards are easier to compare than in the case of intrinsic rewards. Advice and material assistance are examples of extrinsic rewards other people provide. The individual receiving either or both of these rewards may, in turn, provide the other person with intrinsic and/or extrinsic gratification. In this case an exchange relationship comes into existence. For convenience in this example, this relationship will be viewed through the eyes of just one party. An assumption is made that a sale is a function of attraction.

The theoretical statement above identifies three variables: intrinsic gratification, extrinsic gratification, and attractiveness. The statement indicates that attractiveness is a result of, or is dependent upon, one or both of the other two variables.

Step two. The second step is to derive an empirical statement describing the functioning of the theoretical proposition in a marketing context. The empirical statement might be as follows: *A consumer may be attracted to a salesman because the salesman is perceived to be supportive of the consumer's value system—the intrinsic reward—or because the salesman provides needed material assistance—the extrinsic reward.*

Step three. The implications of the empirical statement are shown in Figure 2 which depicts four selling situations. The ideal situation exists when the consumer receives both high intrinsic rewards (he believes the salesman holds views similar to his own on important matters) and high extrinsic rewards (the product is perceived to be of good quality). The likelihood of a sale is high when the consumer finds the salesman personally attractive and the product or service the salesman represents appealing. By reverse analogy, the situation in Cell 4 is bleak; neither the salesman nor his product provides the consumer with any satisfaction.

Cells 2 and 3 represent rather interesting states. Consumers in these two cells might be in a state of cognitive inconsistency or imbalance. The resulting cognitive strain toward consistency could cause consumers to move

[6]Peter Blau, *Exchange and Power in Social Life* (New York: John Wiley & Sons, Inc., 1964), p. 58.

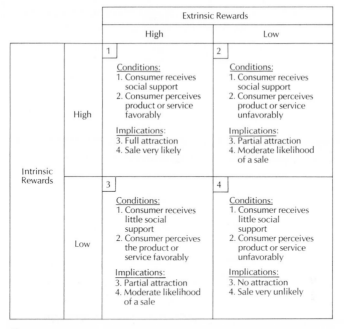

Figure 2
Reward conditions and market implications

toward either Cell 1 or Cell 4 depending on the relative magnitude of the intrinsic and extrinsic rewards.

It is the task of promotional efforts to shift consumers in Cells 2 and 3 to Cell 1. Because of their possible cognitive imbalance and consequent strain toward consistency, consumers in these cells would probably respond to promotional efforts; they are already disposed toward change. Consumers in Cell 4 may display the greatest sales resistance.

Step four. At this point it becomes necessary to outline the appropriate strategy or strategies.

Assume a sales manager with limited resources has obtained data describing the relative importance consumers place on intrinsic and extrinsic rewards. Because of his limited resources, the manager may do only one of two things: (1) He may attempt to increase the intrinsic appeal of the selling situation for the consumer. This could be accomplished by identifying consumer groups on the basis of sociopsychological variables, and by recruiting or reassigning salesmen so that there is a greater matching between salesman and consumer on those variables. (2) He may use his resources to increase the extrinsic appeal of the selling situation through an advertising campaign stressing the advantages of the particular product, or by a training program giving salesmen more knowledge about customer needs and uses for the product.

In analyzing the data, the manager will be concerned with (1) the frequency with which consumers fall into each of the four cells in Figure 2; (2) which of the two situations, Cells 2 or 3, has the largest number of consumers; and (3) the frequency of sales among consumers in each cell.

Step five. The final step is to implement the appropriate strategy. Before doing this on a large scale, however, it may be very desirable to test the implications of both steps four and five through test marketing, survey research, controlled laboratory experiments, simulation, or other suitable techniques.

EPISTEMIC GAPS

Operational level gap

Let us take another look at the inference steps. They began with a theoretical statement containing at least two related concepts and from this an empirical marketing hypothesis was deduced. The marketing statement contained what are sometimes termed "operations" which are empirical measures of theoretical concepts. The relationship between a theoretical concept (such as literacy) and its empirical operation (functional literacy scores) is described as an *epistemic relationship*. It is important that this relationship have an isomorphic quality: the concept and its operation should be similar in form and substance. Isomorphism means that there is a point-for-point correspondence between the theoretical and operational systems. "In a very real sense no theoretically defined concepts can be directly translated into operations nor can theoretical propositions be tested empirically."[7] Hence, the epistemic gap in Figure 1. The operation must be an accurate reflection of its theoretical counterpart. *Perhaps one of the greatest obstacles inhibiting the effective application of the behavioral sciences to marketing problems is that this very important quality of isomorphism can only be determined intuitively.* The researcher cannot obtain measures of association to test for this quality since the initial concept exists at a theoretical level while its operation exists at an empirical level. This language gap between theory and research is present in most scientific research.

Action level gap

An additional language gap exists. After deriving an empirical statement it became necessary to outline its marketing implications and formulate marketing strategies. The author used the social exchange theory framework, and was able to describe four selling situations. Once again, however, an intuitive intellectual judgment is being made. The first such judgment concerned the gap between a concept and its operation, where the so-called operation was judged to be an adequate reflection of the theoretical concept. The new intuitive intellectual judgment concerns the gap between an empirical hypothesis and its strategic implications. The implications exist on an action level whereas the empirical statement occupies a research level.

Figure 3 summarizes two important gaps between behavioral theory and ultimate marketing—the operational research epistemic gap and the action

[7]Hubert Blalock, *Causal Inference in Nonexperimental Research* (Chapel Hill: University of North Carolina Press, 1964), especially Ch. 1.

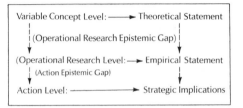

Figure 3
*Levels of abstraction and epistemic relationships
in applying concepts to marketing*

epistemic gap. The two gaps are inherent and can only be bridged by assuming isomorphism between levels. This involves intuitive intellectual judgments. The quality of these judgments constitute the major boundaries defining the limits of behavioral science's applicability to marketing.

CONCLUSION

The application of behavioral concepts to marketing problems is by no means straightforward. The value and applicability of the behavioral sciences in marketing are dependent upon two intuitive intellectual judgments represented in this paper by the operational research epistemic gap and action epistemic gap. However, by being aware of these gaps and by following a series of steps—the scientific marketing inference process—some of the inherent problems in using the behavioral sciences can be made more manageable.

READING 16

CASHING-IN ON THE COP-OUT: CULTURAL CHANGE AND MARKETING POTENTIAL*

Lee Adler

Late one night in March, 1967, three disconsolate young men were sipping coffee and pondering their futures. They had had enough of conventional middle-class values, nine-to-five jobs, and wearing ties. They wanted to drop out. They discussed going to Morocco, living in a commune in Pennsylvania, and other hippie life styles. But how to earn a minimum of "bread" to finance their departure from the larger society? Aware of the mod clothing revolution, the young men decided to go it one better by opening a really "funky" clothing store for both sexes. They rented a loft on Lexington Avenue in New York, bought some surplus World War I U.S. Army jackets for 50 cents apiece, and opened for business.

*Reprinted by permission from *Business Horizons*, February 1970, pp. 19–30.

Today, three years later, The Different Drummer is running at an annual sales volume of over $1,500,000. The firm has expanded its square footage some fourfold. It has created a national franchise plan; the first four stores are now open. It is receiving weekly inquiries from retail chains and textile firms as to its interest in being acquired. There is personal irony in this story for Todd Merer, president and former criminal lawyer, and his two associates, erstwhile schoolteacher and importer, respectively, for instead of dropping out they find they have really dropped in. They experience all the pressures of any other business management. They work long hours and, inevitably, they are drawn into the vortex of conventional commercial life.

The story of The Different Drummer holds a profound message for marketing. The message is that the moral, social, and cultural value system changes occurring today entail the most sweeping and grave consequences for every sector of the marketing front—strategy formulation, new product development, advertising, distribution, and marketing research. These consequences can be problems or they can be opportunities, depending on whether marketers are alert to what is happening in their environments, and what they do about it.

Several difficulties complicate assessment of the situation. One is the common tendency to link serious, deeply rooted change to the generation gap and to equate it with fads and fashions. Sooner or later, it is assumed, these changes will go the way of the green eyeshade and the hula hoop, and things will be as before. A second difficulty lies in the very nature of these changes: they are elusive and hard to define, and their practical effects are often indirect. A third obstacle lies in the nature of the marketing executive. He is likely to become resentful and unyielding in the face of shifting values, rather than acknowledging and capitalizing on them. Young folks may just have something when they decide not to trust anyone over 30.

On the other hand, we should not go to the opposite extreme and regard the current scene as altogether unique. Values always ride a pendulum. Hedonism gives way to Puritanism and, in the fullness of time, hedonism returns. American society has assimilated many changes similar to today's. The emancipation of woman, for example, had countless effects on marketing. Better education allowed them to join the work force, and they were able to add to disposable income. Smoking became acceptable. Fashions were modified. In the 1920's, for instance, our attitudes toward modesty changed, thereby destroying the market for veils.

An army of social psychologists, economists, political scientists, educators, religious leaders, and journalists is chronicling the texture and weave of American life. I will not pretend to duplicate their efforts, but it will be useful to trace briefly the origin, development, and expressions of value change as a foundation for considering their significance for marketing.

OVERVIEW: YESTERDAY AND TODAY

Consideration of some of the basic beliefs that activated the nineteenth century will help to provide perspective on what is happening to our culture in the late twentieth century: mankind will reach the millenium through hard work; progress comes through free enterprise and individual effort; competence sets the only limit to a man's upward mobility in a mobile society; education is eminently worthwhile, for it frees the sons of the working class and resuscitates the immigrant; and accumulation of material goods is a noble endeavor.

In addition, families were large, which provided a sense of belonging and security; life styles were influenced by Puritanism, which took a basically dour attitude toward pleasure, and the Protestant ethic, which emphasized hard work, productivity, and problem-solving; and life for most people was difficult and focussed primarily on satisfying creature needs.

The twentieth century view of the character of the nineteenth century American is partly true and partly myth, but it is of value to us for the counterpart it provides with our current self-image. Some of the principal characteristics of the nineteenth century figure were self-reliance, an unquestioning belief in his self-virtue, a profound sense of purpose, optimism, and a feeling of personal power.

We all recognize the one fundamental force that is generating the shifts in today's society: high technology, as seen in electronic communications media, the computer, automation, and nuclear power. The effects of these technological advances are awesomely widespread. They include an explosion in the mass media; an information revolution; extraordinary affluence, which is related to, produces, and is in turn affected by a rising education level, enhanced tastes, and a sharpening of the critical faculty; a sharp increase in urban disintegration; life in the shadow of a nuclear holocaust; a marked improvement in technology's power to reshape man and his environment (the promise of artificial organs, manipulation of the weather, underseas life, and so on); a velocity of change so great as to constitute a difference in kind rather than merely of degree; an enormously more intricate society; and increasingly intense confrontations between conflicting viewpoints.

These forces, interacting among each other, are generating greater acceptance of modifications in basic values. To repeat, these are *not* just changes among the lunatic fringe, minority groups, or the alienated. I would classify the following factors as particularly vital:

A questioning of materialistic pursuits at the peak of our affluence
Increasing pressure for social justice
A decline in respect for authority and the law
A belief in the rightness of militancy and confrontation
A love of novelty
A passion for style and format paralleled by a loss of interest in content.

These social convulsions stimulate each other to further convulsions, phenomena that include dropping out, psychic malaise, estrangement from institutional authority, social protest, minority group uprisings, role reversals (for example, the old emulating the young), new communications modes, greater assertion of individuality, increased use of drugs, a sharp rise in violence, and greater sexual freedom.

THE NEW CONSUMER

This social upheaval is molding a new American consumer. Because society is in transition, it is impossible to define this consumer precisely; indeed, one of his characteristics is a permanent state of change. We can, however, discern some of his salient qualities. These qualities are most often associated with the young, but they are also to be found among the young in spirit. For one thing, those who have the new state of mind do not change when they reach their thirtieth birthdays. Moreover, the typical reexamination of life's basic purpose, meaning, and direction that psychologists report among people in their forties is resulting in the acceptance of these newer values among the middle-aged. In addition, the near-veneration with which the larger society treats the young promotes the adoption of their views by the older half of the population.

I would list the following as crucial consumer characteristics and behavioral traits from a marketing standpoint:

A more keenly etched sense of self

More cynicism, disbelief, and questioning

Complex needs for self-definition, purpose, love, esteem, a sense of belonging, and esthetic satisfaction

Greater intelligence, sharper wit

Lessened inhibition

A passion for personal involvement

Jaded capacity to receive

Responsiveness to multimedia presentations

Susceptibility to apparent paradox

Tolerance for individual deviations from traditional standards of behavior, dress, and taste

A greater sense of community among the young as a separate subculture, which cuts across social and economic class lines

Emphasis on immediate short-term gratifications, and an associated discounting of the future in terms of planning and saving

An acceptance of, if not positive liking for, impermanence.

IMPLICATIONS FOR MARKETING

The effects of these dramatic changes color the whole spectrum of marketing. Some factors bear on over-all marketing strategy; other implications affect individual line-and-staff functions.

For example, market segmentation in terms of customer wants and needs has been increasingly accepted as a strategy superior to producer segmentation or demographic segmentation. Now the growing tendency to cater to individual tastes, supported by a hedonistic philosophy and the disposable income to finance it, is inevitably leading to ever greater market segmentation. If the product design policy of The Different Drummer was carried to its logical extreme, no two garments would be alike.

The growing concern for social justice and for protecting the individual in an ever more crowded, impersonal, and intricate world has become the foundation for a countervailing force: the consumer movement. The Food and Drug Administration and other regulatory bodies have adopted tougher government controls. Ralph Nader has attacked, successively, the automotive industry, tire manufacturers, excessive fat in frankfurters, and inadequacies in baby foods. Note that he attracts an army of college graduates as zealous as crusaders to help his cause: young people who are not rushing to find executive trainee slots in industry. Even housewives have picketed supermarkets to protest high prices.

Increasingly, industry itself is yielding to these values. "The modern definition of corporate social responsibility," said Robert J. Keith, board chairman, Pillsbury Company, at the 1968 annual meeting, "holds us to larger and more positive standards. In today's world, we are expected to make significant contributions to nothing less than the quality of life, and to do so in the context of growing expectation of quality" (*Advertising Age* [Sept. 16, 1968], p. 1).

After a study of the psychology and sociology of American women, Pillsbury announced that it would "change its approach to product development to meet the needs of this generation," modify existing products, and communicate differently.

The old ideas of Ann Pillsbury will disappear and a new direct relationship with consumers will emerge. And our advertising will be developed with their interests and tastes specifically in mind. . . . we will search for some media systems of our own through which to provide these homemakers with the type of knowledge they require. The research will extend our work in publishing to more than recipe books. It means our labels will contain new and different types of information than we now display.

In a related development, there is new respect for the black man as a consumer, expressed by the rising number of advertising agencies, marketing research programs, and media devoted to the black segment of our population. This awareness has introduced black manikins in store windows, Afro styling, and changes in product design.

The role of style reflects growing sophistication, a refinement of esthetic sensitivity, and a desire for self-enhancement. Style now means not just the cut of a garment or the color of a slip cover, but style of life as well, whether it be casual or elegant, offbeat bohemian or formal and proper. Whatever the style is, it tends to be carried out in a unified way—in apparel, home furnishings, books, entertainment, and food. And it seeks to be gracious and positive. This is leading to smarter styling: to product lines linked by a "look" expressed in color, design, and pattern; to integrated department store merchandising of products that are used together (for example, cooking and tablewares for gourmet dining such as chafing dishes, serving trays, and ice buckets, items formerly scattered in at least three different departments).

Implications for marketing intelligence

A logical point of departure in analyzing the impact of cultural change on marketing is the marketing intelligence function, for it bears the responsibility of identifying, measuring, interpreting, and reporting on what is going on in the larger society. I am deliberately using the term "marketing intelligence" rather than "marketing research" because the former embraces a broader scope using all the tools and methods available, whereas marketing research is often linked with a narrow, mechanical recording of the past. Indeed, the very breadth and speed of social and cultural developments is hastening the growth of marketing intelligence systems.

One of the principal specifics of this evaluation is the emergence of environmental scanning as a discipline for analyzing and weighing the future impact of change. Using both secondary and primary sources of data, scanning systems—like radar—examine the environment on a periodic if not continuous basis. The marketing intelligence man is not content to study only the current market of his company or client; he analyzes the total environment using the disciplines of the social anthropologist, politician, priest, economist, and psychologist. He has also learned to examine the effect of value system evolution on neighboring and distant industries, both here and abroad, and to integrate raw facts from a wide variety of sources in anticipating competitive forays, newly emerging hazards, or unexplored opportunities.

Deeply concerned with the implications of electronic media for journalism, a Chicago newspaper conducted an in-depth study. The investigation, utilizing detailed personal interviews of readers and nonreaders, established that most people no longer rely on newspapers for a straightforward presentation of the news; this they get from television. Rather, they now look to the newspaper for background orientation, analysis, and interpretation. As a result, to be responsive to the needs of its readers, the paper revised its editorial content and direction, as well as its format, and sharply reversed the slump in its circulation.

In another instance, the environmental scanning unit of a major consumer goods producer examined the possible effects of the changing quality of urban life on their business. After trying many correlations they found one of considerable significance: once urban congestion passed a certain point, there was a sharp rise in demand for the company's disposable packages and a decline in demand for reusable containers. Corresponding shifts occurred in preferences for the firm's package sizes. These findings, as measured in terms of population density, led to changes in the packaging mix, in distribution policies, and in local advertising content. In turn, this created better relationships with the company's retailers, fostered a happier selling climate for the sales force and, ultimately, contributed to an improved sales picture in the largest metropolitan areas.

In the mid-1960's, Paul Young, the junior wear buyer at J. C. Penney Company, assessed both U.S. and foreign developments and noted the trend toward mod apparel among teen-age girls in England. He sensed its potential appeal in the United States for young people anxious to express their individuality, to declare symbolic war on their elders, and to wear "badges" that would permit in-group members to recognize each other. He left Penney and set up Paraphernalia, with the backing of Puritan Sportswear. He brought over Mary Quant from England and in October, 1965, opened the first outlet with dancing girls in the windows. Paraphernalia is now a franchise organization of some sixty-five stores nationwide with retail sales of some $4,600,000 a year.

One of the general consequences of the weakened hold of the hair-shirt mentality of Puritanism is a desire for greater comfort. As a society, we are increasingly coming to feel that it is not sinful to be comfortable. This, in turn, is leading to improved design in everything from furniture to can openers to women's undergarments.

In my opinion, the acceleration of value changes also calls for a new look at qualitative research methods. What are the tensions and conflicts deep within the consumer as he hurdles the tremendous psychological gulfs separating conformity from individuality, the concept of original sin from a life of pleasure, a belief that only work is moral from the enjoyment of huge amounts of leisure time? How do we capture the inner thoughts of persons struggling to find life's meaning and to define the proper mission of the individual—now that it is no longer simply earning one's daily bread, and now that the entire middle class is becoming a class of philosophers? What are the consequences of these interior monologues on consumer behavior?

Psychological research in particular merits reexamination for its potential, in the hands of sensitive, perceptive practitioners, for detecting the often subtle shifts in values and attitudes that are not as discernible by quantitative methods. (This is not to reject the latter but rather to suggest the more widespread use of a tandem approach.)

A famous motivation research study of the early 1950's found that women felt guilty about using cake mixes because they did not contribute much to the success of the cake. They felt they were somehow cheating their families. A study completed in mid-1969 for a group of food and appliance manufacturers has found that now women want to get out of the kitchen as quickly as possible. Their desire to feed their families well has not lessened, but they are prepared to trust manufacturers of convenience foods and see no reason to take twenty minutes to do what can be done as well in two. These, and related findings in women's fundamental attitudes toward being in the kitchen, appliances, foods, their role as food preparers and servers have sweeping consequences for new product development, appliance design, kitchen layout, and in what marketers say about these products to make them harmonize with these new values.

A deeper probing of the motivations underlying the nonconformist revolution in apparel suggests a powerful role for escapism. Strikingly different clothes permit role playing or "disguising" of self. It is this urge that also explains the sharp growth of sales of wigs and falls for women and even for weekend beards and sideburns for men.

Implications for developing new products and services

The obvious imperative for marketers wishing to be attuned to the times is to audit their current and proposed lines of products and services and to build in satisfaction of the complex needs and desires of the new consumer. The entire financial services industry is an example of an industry that has redesigned its offerings to appeal to the new consumer. The industry realized that most consumers are trapped between two poles. On the one hand, they seek immediate gratification and resist postponement of pleasure; on the other, they are aware of the need to provide for future financial requirements. The second need is sharpened by the intensified importance society attaches to education and by a somewhat newer value, the desire to retire early and to enjoy retirement.

Having identified these values through ongoing marketing research, sponsored by the Institute of Life Insurance, the life insurance industry has retailored its offerings. Over and above the basic death benefit, life insurance policies now stress the plus values of providing for the education of children, for retirement, and "rainy day" savings. To help provide adequate retirement funds, insurance is being marketed increasingly in packages with equities such as mutual funds.

The over-all direction of the systems approach to financial services is toward family financial planning and the sale of services to fulfill those plans. The ultimate vision is of a package that would include: forecasting income over the life-span of the household based on education and occupation; budgeting expenditures and savings against current and anticipated income; scheduling the acquisition of major items (house, car, boat, or second home) and planning for major expenditures (foreign travel, for example); planning investments, including amount, kind, timing, and risk; retirement planning; and estate planning. The extension of these plans would involve budget worksheets and normative data; continuing counsel on the budget as well as on the use of credit, tax factors, insurance coverages, accounting, and banking services; receipt and disbursement of funds; and arrangements for mortgage financing or loans.

In addition to insurance companies, the commercial banks, savings banks and finance companies are all taking steps in this direction. Chemical Bank introduced its Money Minder service in 1969. By coding each check issued, the customer is able to obtain a monthly and year-to-date report on expenditures by expense category. The system provides budget control and handy data for tax computations. The AIMS Group is a New York-based financial counseling firm specializing in the needs of upper-income men, which recommends and arranges for real estate investments, tax shelter purchases such as oil exploration participations, insurance, estate planning, and related services. A financial field "conglomerate" is planning to sell packages consisting of executive loans and investment in undeveloped real estate and insurance.

An interesting offshoot in the financial services area reflects still another cultural trend: the growing appreciation for things esthetic. To capitalize on this development, a New York organization is setting up a fine arts mutual fund, which will operate exactly like other mutual funds except that paintings and sculpture will replace stocks and bonds. A committee of experts—museum curators, critics, and dealers—will make the selections and counsel on price. Owners of shares in the funds will have to agree to a substantial minimum investment and to a phased deferment of sales of shares, if required, to prevent forced sales of holdings. Lest the fund be accused of utter crassness, shareholders will enjoy the art in their offices or homes on a rotating basis while awaiting long-term capital appreciation.

The art world itself, where it used to take a generation, if not a century, for major movements to evolve, has undergone a transformation. Art vogues have changed from abstract expressionism to pop art, to op art, to minimal, process, and concept art, all within a dozen years and at an accelerating velocity. "Everyone is famous for fifteen minutes," said Andy Warhol.

The love of novelty and style and a swift pace of change are turning an improbable array of products into fashion items. Utilitarian objects like cooking pots now blossom in fashion colors and patterns and, with teak handles, are now elegant enough to serve from. Lathes and milling machines are now not only functional but attractively designed.

Significant role reversals create a market for new clothing items. Sexual differences, for example, are being obliterated in terms of mutual responsibilities, mores, and behavior; hence, we see long-haired males using more toiletries and even cosmetics such as body lotions, moisturizers, and skin conditioners. They are willing to wear "female-styled" clothes such as shirts with ruffles or garments in bright colors made of velvets, velours, and voile, while females sport bell-bottomed slacks, boots, and buckskin jackets. We see his-and-hers matched outfits, and pastel-colored shoes have appeared in such men's shoe chains as French Shriner and Florsheim.

Another development is that the concept of impermanence is more acceptable in our society. The Puritan ethic forbade wastefulness; one did not, for example, discard things until they were thoroughly worn out. Today, however, assisted by technological advances in newer materials and fabrication methods, and by affluence, the disposables "industry" (its state is too primeval, diffuse, and chaotic for it to be a proper industry) is undergoing a boom of vast proportions. One segment of the field, the market for nonwoven fabrics, is expected to soar from an estimated $400,000,000 in sales in 1966 to over $1,300,000,000 in 1975. When Scott Paper Company first offered paper dresses in 1966 as a promotion at $1.25 each, the firm, to its astonishment, sold over 500,000 units. Nonwoven fabrics are now used in a myriad of products—surgeon's gowns, operating room drapes, bath mats, wipes, panties, tablecloths, work uniforms, bed underpads, diapers, coasters, bartenders' and waiters' jackets, rainwear, and so on.

The desire for social equality and the effort to integrate minority groups into the larger society has had an impact on marketing. Afro-styled clothing is featured in many stores, and "soul food"—ham hocks, candied yams, collard greens, and black-eyed peas—may be ordered in some good restaurants, and even in a popular-priced food chain, Horn & Hardart. It does not seem unreasonable to forecast that food manufacturers will soon have packaged and frozen soul food on supermarket shelves alongside Chinese, Mexican, and Italian specialties.

Implications for distribution

To reach the markets created by value system changes, the marketer may be able to use established channels, but it is possible that he will have to hack his own route to market. For example, Paraphernalia began to sell its women's apparel to department stores to expand distribution quickly beyond its first owned store. But the firm found that department stores were unsatisfactory because their impersonal vastness created the wrong ambiance. What young people wanted was their own exclusive buying environment. This prompted Paraphernalia to refine its own retail concepts to provide an intimate, friendly setting, featuring the posters, rock-and-roll music, and lights favored by its target segment—young women who wanted a place to socialize where few aged ladies over 30 would venture.

The Different Drummer has gone even further, violating many of the rules of retailing in the process. They opened for business in a second-story loft; they dared to go uptown rather than to their "natural" location in Greenwich Village. They hired inexperienced ghetto teen-agers as salespeople. Their staff is a haven for drop-outs, including the son of an ambassador and the daughter of a millionaire investment banker. Characteristic of their unique tone is the preamble to their proposal addressed to prospective franchisees:

"If a man doesn't keep pace with his companion, perhaps it is because he hears the sound of a different drummer."—Henry Thoreau

In the complex and tension-filled atmosphere of modern society, existing within Thoreau's meaning may often be wishful thinking. To be able to do so and at the same time gain material rewards, is not always the easiest of things. For us, The Different Drummer has become such an oasis. Will it be yours?

The tempo of the times and the demand for ease and convenience are supporting the phenomenal growth of the "fast food" business. International Industries, Beverly Hills, is one of many examples. The company sold its first International House of Pancakes franchise in 1960. It soon recognized that its real marketing future lay not in pancakes but in franchising systems. In the succeeding nine years, the company grew to a network of franchised fast food outlets, including Copper Penny Restaurants, Orange Julius of America, Will Wright Ice Cream Shoppes, and the Original House of Pies.

The remarkable renaissance of boutiques is a result of the search for ways to reach the new consumer with new types of goods. Within department stores, the boutique tends to cluster goods around a "look," specific usage occasions, or a theme. It is this approach that has led to gourmet shops, patio-living boutiques, "unisex" shops, and similar reorganizations of traditional retailing patterns. Independent boutiques are mushrooming as well; the Paper-hanger in Washington, which deals only in paper fabric products, is a good example. On the industrial front, the perfection of nonwoven disposables is stimulating changes in established modes of distribution. The roles, product lines, and competitive positions of industrial launderers, linen supply houses, wholesale paper merchants and rag dealers are in the process of transition as they compete for the market for paper wipes, towels, and work clothes.

The emergence of new markets has required the creation of entirely new distribution patterns. National Student Marketing Corporation is registering extraordinary volume gains with its unique ways of promoting, selling, and moving goods to students who arrange for and publicize the showing of such "campy" films as W. C. Fields and Laurel and Hardy. Special commercials of equally campy tone and fiercely honest content are interspersed between the films, and samples of sales literature are distributed. The goods advertised can be purchased at the film shows, college bookstores, from the campus representatives, or by mail order.

Implications for advertising and promotion

The implications of the new values are clear for advertising. The under-30 generation loathes sham and hypocrisy; they respect the truth; they resent excesses of earnestness; and they cannot abide pomposity. "Tell it like it is" is the touchstone.

This attitude has generated a new communications mode, the put-on, which bears on the effectiveness of marketing communications. While the put-on superficially resembles practical jokes, irony, and hoax, it is really none of these. The put-on is actually a product of the credibility gap, the inability to accept what is seen as pretentious, dishonest mouthings of vested interests. In effect, the put-on is a vague, ambiguous, hostile, oblique communication in which we cannot be sure of what the speaker really means unless one is really "where it's happening, baby."

Communicating memorably and persuasively with the new consumer clearly calls for new approaches in copy and art. Successful advertising and promotion include indirect, allusive, low key appeals; shorter messages; more experimentation with nonlinear presentations of information (cool, ambiguous, involving); more wit, honesty, verve, self-deprecation, irreverence (but not irrelevance); crisp, contemporary design in formats, packages, physical facilities; greater utilization of mixed media, especially audio-visual modes; blending of the real and the absurd; faster pace; and cautious use of the more ephemeral elements of today's under-thirties subculture (rock-and-roll music, psychedelic art, and high color).

A magazine advertisement prepared by McCann-Erickson, Inc., for General Motors Opel Kadett is one example of the new advertising. A provocative-looking young girl stands next to the car; the headline reads, "Buick introduces automobiles to light your fire." To those familiar with a rock-and-roll group known as The Doors and their song, "Light My Fire," the sexual metaphor is overt. McCann-Erickson researched the headline among over-thirties. It was found to be "not offensive" to those who knew what it meant and, obviously, would not offend those who did not know what it meant. The significance of this should not be overlooked: it seems possible to segment messages even in mass media in ways not previously feasible.

Ten years ago, most product advertising consisted of fairly straightforward, sometimes ponderous, presentations of product features. Five years ago, product sell had become grimly fanciful; Alka-Seltzer's television commercials, for example, showed a stomach tortured by excessive consumption. In contrast, a recent Alka-Seltzer commercial prepared by Jack Tinker & Partners reflects the characteristics of today's advertising in its campy tone and fast cuts. The commercial lightly takes advantage of the rebellious spirit of the day and resentment of authority by showing a prison dining room demonstration against bad food. Most of the time is used to show the convicts banging their tin cups on the tables. Not a word is spoken until the end of the spot, when the convicts begin to chant, "Alka-Seltzer! Alka'Seltzer! Alka-Seltzer!"

The International Coffee Organization reaches its prime target—young people, 17 to 25—through youth-oriented radio stations, college magazines, and the college editions of magazines. The advertising, prepared also by McCann-Erickson, is low key and amiable, full of allusions to the concerns of young people. One magazine ad, for instance, shows a hirsute rock-and-roll group. In the background an M.P. has his hand on the drummer's shoulder. The headline asks, "Another group is after your drummer?" Visually, this ad would immediately "turn off" the older generation—so much so that they might even miss the point, the concern that young people have about going into the army.

The radio spots for this advertiser capitalize on the absurd and the irreverent. The copy approach enables the agency to offer real facts about brewing a good cup of coffee and, by being self-deprecating, catches listeners off-guard, thereby allowing the message to get through. Here is a typical 60-second spot:

He: *You know, Karen, I used to think you were really a freaky girl—learning how to yodel, running off to Tibet for Labor Day weekend.*
She: *Everybody has their little outs, Walter.*
He: *But you were such a homebody making this coffee—measuring just the right amounts of coffee and water.*
She: *There is only one correct grind for every coffee-maker.*
He: *Karen, I think underneath that chrome leotard you're probably a very sweet girl. I mean, you made a full three-quarter pot for just the two of us.*
She: *One must make at least three-quarters of a pot, Walter, or coffee has no soul.*
He: *But what really got me was your insisting on cold water to start the brewing.*
She: *Any guru can tell you good coffee has to start with cold water.*
He: *Karen, the coffee is really delicious. Could you stop standing on your head long enough to have some with me?*
Announcer: *It makes you think. And things happen over it. So next time you have something to think about or talk over, do it over a cup of coffee, the Think Drink.*

The poster craze of the late 1960's illustrates the new attitude toward advertising, the blending of art and advertising in one medium, how companies (even big, staid ones) can capitalize on this movement, and the appeal of disposability. The trend began with the success of giant blow-ups of Humphrey Bogart, W. C. Fields, and other pop culture heroes. The vivid, psychedelic posters became art objects. Subsequently, commercial posters were republished, and campy commercial posters were hung in the home. General

Motors published a Day-Glo poster of a wild bird for the Pontiac Firebird; Humble Oil Company incorporated its tiger into a poster captioned "I need you now." Alka-Seltzer pokes gentle fun at American food tastes with a poster showing a hamburger on a bed of ketchup-drenched French fries and a caption printed red, white, and blue, reading simply, "Alka-Seltzer."

These are only a handful of examples of hundreds. Before switching to its new theme, the Coca-Cola Company had asked prominent personalities and rock-and-roll groups to take the basic music of "Things Go Better with Coke" and score and sing it in their own style and beat and even in their own words. Fifty-three versions of the basic commercial were created; ten years ago, or even five years ago, this would have been heresy. Self-deprecation abounds in advertising; in one superb example, Benson & Hedges cigarettes poke fun at their extra length. Vignettes and fast cuts are popular, reflecting the enormously successful mode of "Laugh-In."

Emerging attitudes also permit the advertising of newer product categories. The new openness about sex, the stress on individual decisions (as opposed to being told what to do by the church), the social value of being able to "do more" for fewer children—all of these factors underlie the acceptance of birth control products and their advertisement in reputable women's magazines and mass magazines. Similarly, the new climate has made it possible to promote vaginal spray deodorants not only in print but on television. This product category is growing so fast one can hardly count the individual brands; together they have created an estimated $15 million market in two years.

Implications for packaging

No sector of the marketing front is unaffected by the impact of the cultural revolution; packaging, too, should be reexamined in the light of value change. Flexnit Company, New York, for example, completed a research study on packaging concepts that one would not even have dared to do ten years ago. The objective of the study was to determine how far the company could go in presenting nudity in its girdle and brassiere packages. Flexnit found that in today's climate they could go as far as they liked in depicting unclad women so long as nudity was logically a part of the situation (for example, a woman stepping out of the shower and starting to dress) and not erotic in intent. The only other limitations were to stop short of showing hair and to avoid showing women in unnatural or awkward poses. Incidentally, nudity seems to be more acceptable in the Midwest and South than in the Northeast.

Implications for corporate policies

The rising tide of social outrage; the deepening concern with truth in advertising, in lending, in packaging; the push for greater assurance of beneficial products, notably in cigarettes and drugs; the desire to help the downtrodden —all of these pressures act on the corporation to accept more social responsibility. The key point for our thesis, apart from the obvious moral issue involved, is that making a contribution to the larger society is not necessarily the opposite of profit making. As a matter of fact, today's values create new marketing opportunities. Put in its most cynical form, the formula would read: today's altruism is tomorrow's self-interest.

Many of these programs are in housing and finance. To make a dent in the urgent problems of housing in ghettos, Celanese Corporation and American Standard, Inc., recently joined in a variant of the so-called "turnkey" approach. The two firms organized Construction for Progress, Inc., and in a gentlemen's agreement with New York City's Housing Authority, erected a six-story, 66-family, low-income apartment building in East Harlem. The private developer was able to put up the building in only 40 percent of the time that the official body, hampered by many bureaucratic restrictions, would have needed. Upon completion, the Housing Authority bought the building for $1,200,000, giving the developer a return of between 3 percent and 4 percent on his investment.

In a comparable arrangement, the New York Bank for Savings and the Bowery Savings Bank jointly initiated a series of turnkey rehabilitations of new housing projects in Harlem. The New York Bank for Savings is also one of the leaders in supplying mortgage money for industrial plants being built in the Flatlands industrial park in Brooklyn to create job opportunities in nearby ghetto areas. Aluminum Company of America, through a subsidiary, Alcoa Properties, Inc., now owns and operates eleven urban development projects in seven cities. Two offshoots are building turnkey, low-rent projects in Monroe, Mich., and Pittsburgh.

There are other ways of being a useful corporate citizen. Xerox Corporation has sponsored a series of television shows dealing honestly with controversial social issues. Clairol is training underprivileged black girls in Washington as beauty parlor operators. Mind, Inc., a subsidiary of CPC International, Inc., has developed programmed learning techniques to provide minimum reading, writing, arithmetic, and typing skills to enhance the employability of the underprivileged.

PRACTICAL APPLICATIONS

What should a marketer do about the kinds of social, moral, cultural, and psychological value system changes that have been discussed? How can he identify practically and act on changes that are relevant to his business?

One industry is tracking cultural and social change and then applying its lessons to all aspects of marketing. The Motion Picture Association commissioned a large national probability sample study of movie-goers, utilizing both quantitative and qualitative information-gathering approaches. The study confirmed the appropriateness of product changes to meet the tastes of the changing market. In particular, movies treating such lively topics as sexual freedom and individuality in a bold, honest, open manner are well accepted by the key market segment—younger people. The industry, having the right product, seeks the right distribution channels: intimate theaters in suburban shopping centers and in university towns, and quasi-art theaters.

Similarly, the industry is remodeling its promotional strategies. The traditional ballyhoo, the claims of "colossal," "gigantic," and "stupendous" are yielding to subtler copy. Concurrently, there has been an increase in the use of specialized media: for example, student newspapers, surfacing "under-ground" publications such as *The Village Voice* in New York, and the college editions of magazines like *Time*.

For some marketers, adapting to the times is a simple process. Salada discovered that younger people regard tea as a weak beverage enjoyed only by little old ladies. To reverse this image, Salada developed a new spot television campaign. One ID opens with a close-up of a grandmother's face, wrinkled and bespectacled. The next frame gives a full view of her—attired in black leather jacket and pants and leaning against a motorcycle.

In other cases, cross-currents in our social climate pose grave moral and practical problems for marketers. Aware of the increase in violent crime, a major manufacturer, for instance, designed a nonlethal cigarette lighter-like device for personal self-defense. The device would spray a Mace-like gas and a nonwashable dye, and would include a siren to summon the police. But negative considerations intruded, and the firm commissioned a qualitative research study using focused group interviews with various demographic segments, including whites and blacks, to test the product concept. The firm decided not to market it for several reasons. Arming the population might aggravate rather than ease social tensions and escalate verbal arguments. Finally, they realized that the promotion to sell the device would have to appeal to fear, and they were opposed to this as a copy platform.

The value changes now taking place in our society should not be dismissed as ephemeral, nor should they be ignored by all but social psychologists. Rather, marketers should be aware of their profound implications for product development, for selling and distribution methods, and for advertising and promotional approaches. Assessment of these changes may lead to a defensive program, at the least, and the more aggressive firm will recognize a vast potential in the wants of the new consumer motivated by different values.

Margaret Mead has observed that today's adults are like the immigrants of several generations ago. They are unfamiliar with current mores and behavior patterns and they cannot understand the language, for they have not grown up in a universe of television, cybernetics, space travel, and the new math. But as marketers, today's adults are going to have to learn the new language; if they don't, they may get left behind.

READING 17

IS IT TIME TO QUIT THINKING OF INCOME CLASSES?*

Chester R. Wasson

Pierre Martineau pointed out that social class is not income class in a widely reprinted article in the *Journal of Marketing* nearly a decade ago.[1] Despite the

*Reprinted from *The Journal of Marketing*, published by the American Marketing Association, vol. 33, no. 2, April 1969, pp. 54–57.
[1] Pierre Martineau, "Social Classes and Spending Behavior," *Journal of Marketing*, Vol. 23 (October, 1958), pp. 121–130.

wide notice this article attracted, marketing texts and many marketing people still treat income level as synonymous with social class and as a sound guide to spending patterns. At the time Martineau had to base his argument on relatively fragmentary data. Today definitive proof exists that his thesis is correct. The tabulations of the Bureau of Labor Statistics 1960–61 Survey of Consumer Expenditures show clearly that the pattern of expenditure allocation has little relation to the income level and that effective market segmentation is primarily a result of such social class indicators as occupational classification and other measures of culture like region, locality, and stage in the family life cycle. Whatever validity income classification ever had was due to a very rough and now disappearing correlation with occupational status.

The *Chicago Tribune* studies of spending of the 1950s, on which Martineau based his thesis, were designed with the aid of W. Lloyd Warner and built on sociological analyses of Warner and his associates.[2] All of them showed that in any given community social class was the basic determinant of the cultural patterns and, therefore, of the pattern of expenditure priorities. Social class was defined originally on the basis of the relative prestige accorded a family by its neighbors, and it was established that the same ranking would be achieved by a rating scale calculated from occupation, source of income, and type of housing—the system used in the *Tribune* studies.

As a practical matter, however, such a multi-factor measure can be costly to use, and little of the available data that must be used in marketing can be so tabulated. All that is usually available are single factor classifications by income, occupation, or occasionally such other social-class-related factors as educational level and housing. The tendency has been to settle on the use of income.

Income level was doubtless a fairly good approximation of social class when the housewife neither had nor sought many employment opportunities outside of the home and when manual labor was, relative to the demand, plentiful. Neither is the case today. Relatively large numbers of blue collar families, whose social status is manifestly well below that of white collar families in general, earn more income than substantial numbers of white collar families and even some professionals. Income reporting is never reliable, as anyone who has ever gathered family budget reports is aware, and its meaning changes over time with changes in the value of money, with changes in the composition of the family, and, for middle-class occupations, with promotions.

The occupational classification, by contrast, is not only related to the family's position in the social hierarchy, but, perhaps more important, is the main basis for it. Not only is occupation of the head one of Warner's three basic indicators, but it is also the main source of income (another indicator) for most families. It is very closely correlated with type of housing and neighborhood as well, of course, as with educational level. It also has the virtue of seldom changing during the life cycle of the family, being easily and reliably identifiable, and of always indicating the same general social station. Further-

[2] See, for example, W. Lloyd Warner and Paul Lunt, *Social Life of a Modern Community* (New Haven, Conn.: Yale University Press, 1941).

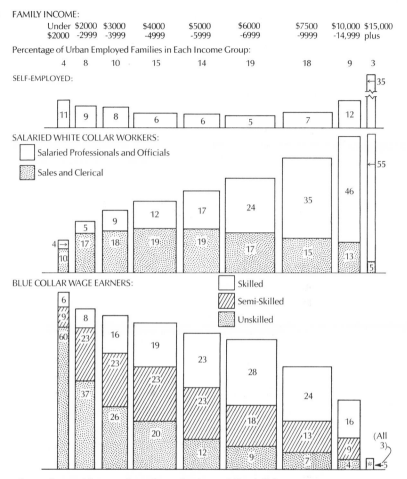

Source: *Survey of Consumer Expenditures*, Supplement 2, Part A, BLS
Report 237-38, July, 1964, U. S. Department of Labor.

Figure 1

*How occupational classes cut across income groups: The percentage distribution
of occupational classes within each income group, urban employed families, U.S.A.,
1960-61*

more, most published studies rest on data which permit occupational classification, and much of it is so tabulated—including the BLS studies. As ordinarily handled, it has one flaw: all of the self-employed are grouped together
whether they are rag-pickers or free-lance stock market analysts. As Figure 1
indicates, the self-employed do not constitute a homogeneous classification.
The income distribution is clearly U-shaped. For the rest, we can clearly distinguish the upper middle class in the category of salaried professionals and
managers, the lower middle class in the group designated as sales and clerical.
The three lower classes are easily recognized in the categories of skilled
workers, semiskilled wage earners, and unskilled wage earners, respectively.

As Figure 1 indicates, the correlation between occupational class and income level is not close. Every income level separately tabulated in the BLS 1960–61 study contained a substantial proportion of families in every class from top to bottom of the occupational scale. And as Table 1 demonstrates graphically, it is occupational class, not income, which determines the proportion of spending allocated to some of the most important categories. (The inter-occupational class comparisons made in this table were limited to incomes between $4,000 and $10,000 because these were the groups which contained substantial numbers of every occupational level and relative comparability of family size, with at least 370 families in every cell in the sample. The tabulated results in the other classifications were consistent with those in the groups depicted.) For example, a government survey indicated that food expenditures have a higher priority the further we go down the occupational scale, and that the middle class white collar workers value housing and quality of neighborhood more highly than do blue collar workers in the same income class.[3] Expenditures for education and reading also have a clear class bias, on the upward side.

When occupational class is held constant, on the other hand, there is no clear relationship between expenditure allocations and income. Although the aggregate tabulation for all occupations indicates some decline in the percentage allotted to food as we go from one income class to a higher one, white collar employees show a level percentage regardless of income, and salaried professionals a possible tendency to increase. Skilled worker families exhibit no clear tendency one way or another, and the two lowest occupational classes tend to exhibit a negative income elasticity of expenditure for food.

The pattern of differences in expenditure allocations are both too consistent and too large to be due to mere chance variation or sampling error. Therefore, it is difficult to perceive any logic in combining such disparate data into single income classifications.

Of course, occupation is not the sole cultural factor segmenting markets. Regional differences in needs are recognized even in the BLS standard budgets. But needs alone are not the full story. The tabulations hint at added real differences in taste and spending priorities which would come as no surprise to experienced marketers or to sociologists familiar with differing regional attitudes. The South, for example, has a total average income level about 10% below that of any other region, but the urban workers there spend a significantly lower proportion of the available income on food than in any other region and a much higher proportion on personal care items. Within-region differences between large cities exhibit interesting disparities which would repay analysis of the BLS computer tapes. The author has analyzed these and some other differences, as shown in the final tabulation, in more detail than there is room for in this paper.[4] Table 2 shows the adaptation of the data to the family life cycle concept the author was able to develop from the BLS tabulations.

[3] *Survey of Consumer Expenditures*, Supplement 2, Part A, BLS Report 237-8 (Washington, D.C.: U.S. Department of Labor, July, 1964).
[4] Chester R. Wasson, Frederick D. Sturdivant, and David H. McConaughy, *Competition and Human Behavior* (New York: Appleton-Century-Crofts, 1968), pp. 52–54 and 114–142; Chester R. Wasson and David H. McConaughy, *Buying Behavior and Marketing Decisions* (New York: Appleton-Century-Crofts, 1969), Chapter 9.

Table 1

Average percentage of total expenditure allocated to selected categories by the major occupational classes at the same income levels, urban employed families, United States, 1960–61

Occupation of Head	Food				Shelter				Education and Reading			
	Income Group ($000)				Income Group ($000)				Income Group ($000)			
	4-4.9	5-5.9	6-7.4	7.5-9.9	4-4.9	5-5.9	6-7.4	7.5-9.9	4-4.9	5-5.9	6-7.4	7.5-9.9
White Collar:												
Professionals	21	23	23	23	16	17	16	14	2.5	2.2	2.1	2.2
Clerical, etc.	24	24	24	24	16	15	14	13	1.7	1.7	1.8	2.0
Blue Collar:												
Skilled	25	26	24	25	14	13	12	11	1.3	1.4	1.5	2.0
Semi-skilled	27	26	26	25	14	13	12	11	1.1	1.4	1.7	1.5
Unskilled	28	27	25	24	14	13	13	11	1.2	1.5	1.9	1.7

Source: Survey of Consumer Expenditures, Supplement 2, Part A, BLS Report 237-8, July, 1964, U.S. Dept. of Labor.

Table 2
Percentage of total expenditure allocated to selected classes of items by families in different stages of the family life cycle, urban United States, 1961

Stage of the Family Life Cycle	Average Age of Head	Percentage of Total Expenditure Which Is Devoted to:						
		Meals Away From Home	Clothing	Recreation	Education and Reading	Transportation	Home Furnishings and Equipment	Medical Care
Young single adults ("Single consumers under 25 years of age")	22	7	14	6	3.3	18	3	3
Early married couples (Husband-wife families with oldest child less than 1 year)	27	5	8	4	1.3	16	10	8
Older Husband-Wife Families with Children:								
Oldest child under 6	29	4	9	4	1.4	16	7	7
Oldest child 6-17	40	5	11	5	1.9	14	5	6
Oldest child 18 or more	52	5	12	4	4.0	17	4	6
Empty nest 2-person families (2-person families 55-64)	60	5	9	3	1.3	16	5	8
Retirees (2-person families 65-74)	69	4	7	3	1.2	14	4	10

Source: BLS Report 237-38, Supplement 2, Part A, July 1964.

This analysis does not mean that income is unimportant, of course. It still obviously limits how much can be spent, given the culturally determined patterns of priorities. The artisan with a family income of $6,000 per year in 1961 would not spend as much for shelter as the $6,000 professional, but the $8,500 artisan would; he might even be a neighbor. Obviously, the 24% of his total spending which goes for food is much less for the clerk with a $4,000 income than the same 24% for the clerk earning $8,000. But the income amount does not influence the distribution of that expenditure, only the amount which can be spent, given the sub-cultural pattern.

These BLS data make clear, as no previously available information has, that market segmentation is influenced strongly by a complex of cultural influences, of which occupation and the other elements of social class are important components. Study of the BLS data alone would be of considerable value to many kinds of firms, and the tapes giving the original data are available for those who wish them. Beyond this, however, they demonstrate the need to look at our marketing studies in terms of occupation first, and only then at income level.

READING 18

HUSBAND AND WIFE INTERACTION IN A CONSUMER DECISION PROCESS*

Robert F. Kelly and Michael B. Egan

INTRODUCTION

The extent and character of interaction between husband and wife appear to represent an extremely important dimension of the decision process for many major household purchases. Nowhere is this more likely to be true than in the purchase of a home, which constitutes the major social and economic commitment for most families in North America.

This paper explores several concepts related to husband-wife interaction; relates those concepts to the house purchase decision process; and, through the results of an exploratory field study, examines the relationships between identifiable household types and interaction patterns, and between interaction patterns and purchase decision outcomes.

Interaction most probably will embrace more than husband and wife in any greater-than-two-member household. It is believed, however, that husband and wife represent the dominant sources of influence in most major household purchasing decisions and, because of the role structures established in most families, the influence of other family members is likely to be expressed indirectly through the husband or wife anyway. Therefore, this paper is confined to an examination of husband-wife interaction patterns.

*Reprinted from *Marketing Involvement in Society and the Economy*, Philip R. McDonald, ed. (Chicago, American Marketing Association, 1969), pp. 250–258.

HUSBAND-WIFE INTERACTION

A family builds a system of values over a considerable period of time and, generally, has great interest in preserving group solidarity and continuity.[1] As a means to that end, family groups establish systems of authority, influence, and values the end result of which is that some decision areas are considered the prerogative of one spouse and some the other.[2] The roles established for husband (provider, protector, maintenance man) and wife (mistress, housekeeper, child rearer) are, quite naturally, the prime determinants of whom is granted what prerogatives.

In any complex decision process, such as that preceding the purchase of a home, there are a host of decision points that must be passed preliminary to the ultimate purchase decision (e.g., the decision to seek a home, how much the family can afford to pay, location constraints). The decision specialties (prerogatives) of both spouses are involved at many of those decision points. Inevitably, differences in values and preferences will lead each spouse to seek a different decision outcome. Where differences are involved, some decision outcomes are husband-dominated, some wife-dominated, and some joint. Interaction (i.e., interpersonal communication of all sorts) is the means by which influence of one spouse is brought to bear on a decision outcome in which the other spouse has an interest. One would hypothesize that the spouse originating the greatest proportion of interaction at a given decision point is most likely to dominate that decision outcome. Where joint decisions are reached, one suspects that the amount of interaction originating with either spouse is approximately equal and the absolute volume of interpersonal communication is likely to be greater than in a dominated or partially-dominated decision.

Since some decision outcomes are husband-dominated or wife-dominated in a manner consistent with the wishes of *both* spouses, dominance, per se, may not jeopardize family solidarity and may not reduce the probabilities of a positive overall purchase decision. Consequently, some form of evaluation of decisions involving both husband and wife beyond the presence or absence of dominance appears desirable. In the field study described in this paper, the concepts *convergence* and *divergence* are employed as a means of developing better understanding of the nature and significance of both joint and dominated decision outcomes. The terms are defined operationally as follows:

Convergence: explicit agreement between husband and wife both on the rationale and the outcome of a decision (excludes mere acquiescence).

Divergence: disagreement, explicit or implicit, between husband and wife on the rationale or outcome of a decision.

Convergence and divergence are seen as an integral part of any multi-person

[1] R. F. Bales and T. Parsons, *Family Socialization and Interaction Processes*, The Free Press, New York, 1955.
[2] See N. Foote (Ed.), *Consumer Behavior: Household Decision Making*, New York University Press, 1961; D. Starch and Staff, *Male vs. Female: Influence on the Purchase of Selected Products*, Greenwich, Conn., Fawcett Pubs., 1958; and Martin Zober, "Determinants of Husband-Wife Buying Roles," in *Consumer Behavior and the Behavioral Sciences*, S. Britt (Ed.), New York, Wiley, 1966, pp. 224–225.

decision process and the extent to which each is present may determine both the nature and, in some instances, the presence or absence of a decision outcome. One would hypothesize that convergence is most likely to occur in joint decisions while, conversely, divergence seems most likely where a partially-dominated or dominated decision outcome results.

In summary, the nature of interaction between husband and wife in a house-purchasing decision process may be expressed in terms of convergence and divergence at various decision points preliminary to an overall purchase decision. Convergence and divergence, in turn, are likely a function of the degree of dominance exercised by either spouse at any given decision point. In the following section, consideration will be given to the conditions under which dominance may be present in a decision.

Dominance as a factor in husband-wife decisions

In order for dominance to exist at any given decision point in a complex decision process there must be (1) desire and ability on the part of one marriage partner to dominate the other, and (2) a willingness on the part of the other partner to accept that attempt at dominance; both are necessary conditions for dominance, neither is a sufficient condition.

Morgan[3] and Komarovsky[4] both employed the term "dominance" in their explorations of interaction patterns in multi-person decision units, although neither of them attempted to define nor extend the term. David Heer[5] uses the term "dominance" in connection with the family power structure and this is also the sense that Rose Coser[6] uses it. Finally, Blood and Wolfe[7] came closest to the concept of dominance as it is used in this paper. They do, in fact, speak of male and female dominance, partial dominance by either male or female, and joint decisions; but they suggest that any of these forms of dominance are determined by decision-making ability, while we maintain that dominance may stem from several factors in addition to decision-making ability.

Figure 1 provides an indication of some possible determinants of dominance. The figure is based upon schemes presented by Morgan and Komarovsky, but depart from them in at least one important respect. What Komarovsky describes as "degree of preference for a product" and Morgan as "strength of own pre-Preference for 'A' per se," are contained within what shall be termed here as "desire to dominate a given decision area." In some instances desire to dominate may be a personality trait. However, it appears reasonable to assume that desire to dominate more often reflects a strong preference on the part of a husband or wife for a given decision outcome.

[3]J. N. Morgan, "A Review of Recent Research on Consumer Behavior," in Lincoln Clark (Ed.), *Consumer Behavior*, Vol. III, Harper & Row, pp. 93–108.
[4]Mirra Komarovsky, "Family Buying Decisions: Who Makes Them, Who Influences Them?", *Printer's Ink*, September 19, 1958, pp. 22–28.
[5]D. M. Heer, "The Measurement and Bases of Family Power," *Marriage and Family Living*, 25 (May 1963), pp. 133–139.
[6]Rose L. Coser, (Ed.), *The Family: Its Structure and Functions*, New York, St. Martin's Press, 1964.
[7]R. O. Blood, and D. M. Wolfe, *Husbands and Wives: The Dynamics of Married Living*, New York, The Free Press, 1960.

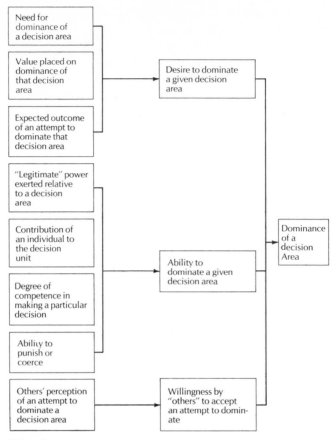

Figure 1

Factors contributing to dominance in husband-wife interactions

Referring again to Figure 1, *need for dominance (or power)* may spring from some or all of the following:

1. The personality traits, inherited or learned of an individual,[8]

2. The degree of power exerted outside the decision unit,[9]

3. The degree of satisfaction with the present power structure within the decision unit.[10]

[8]See Morgan *op. cit.* (J. Douglas, et al., *Human Behavior in Marketing*, Columbus, Ohio, Charles E. Merrill, 1967; F. M. Nicosia, *Consumer Decision Processes*, New Jersey, Prentice-Hall, 1966, p. 57; R. P. Brody, and S. M. Cunningham, "Personality Variables and the Consumer Decision Process," *Journal of Marketing Research*, February, 1968, p. 22ff; E. Grubb, and H. L. Grathwohl, "Consumer Self-Concept, Symbolism, and Market Behavior," *Journal of Marketing*, October, 1967, pp. 141–166; E. Goffman, *The Presentation of Self in Everyday Life*, New York, Doubleday, Anchor, 1959; and T. Parsons, and E. A. Shils (Eds.) *Towards a General Theory of Action*, Cambridge, Mass., Harvard University Press, 1951, pp. 110–158.

[9]See Elizabeth Bott, "Urban Families: Conjugal Roles and Social Networks," *Human Relations* 8 (1955), pp. 345–384. Heer *op. cit.* pp. 65–67 and Coser, *loc. cit.*

[10]D. M. Wolfe, "Power and Authority in The Family," in *Studies in Social Power*, D. Cartwright (Ed.), Ann Arbor, Research Center for Group Dynamics, 1958, pp. 98–116.

The *value placed on an attempt to dominate* a given decision unit may depend upon:

1. The value an individual assigns to his life style;[11]

2. The value assigned to ethnic traditions, religious convictions,[12] and family traditions and values;

3. The number of roles occupied by one within the family unit, and the expectations assigned to those roles by the individual;[13]

4. The value placed on family cohesion;[14]

5. The individual's levels of aspiration;[15]

6. The value placed by an individual on his experience in a given decision situation;[16]

7. An individual's level of acceptance of social values;[17] and

8. The degree of inertia of an individual.[18]

The *expected outcome* of an attempt to dominate may be a function of:

1. The desire and ability of other family members to dominate;

2. The experience of an individual with respect to (1) above;

3. Personality traits of the individual;

4. The pattern and degree of role definition within the family unit; and

5. External support perceived by the individual.[19]

In summary, a *desire to dominate* may be, at one extreme, a function of the personality of an individual, while at the other, it may be based on the roles and role expectations association with that individual within the family unit.

Referring again to Figure 1, one's *ability to dominate* a decision area depends upon one's legitimate power within a family unit; contributions to the

---

[11]See Starch, *op. cit.*, p. 98 and F. Elkin, *The Family in Canada*, Ottawa, Canadian Conference on the Family, 1964.
[12]Blood and Wolfe, *op. cit.*, p. 33.
[13]See G. Zaliman, *Marketing, Contributions from Behavioral Sciences*, New York, Harcourt, Brace, and World, 1965; E. H. Wolgast, "Do Husbands or Wives Make the Purchasing Decisions?", *Journal of Marketing* (October 1958), pp. 151–158; Bott, *op. cit.*, p. 360 ff; W. F. Kenkel, and D. K. Hoffman, "Real and Conceived Roles in Family Decision Making," *Marriage and the Family*, 18, No. 4, (November 1956), pp. 140–143; Elkin, *op. cit.*, pp. 94–105; Parson and Bales, op. cit., p. 259 ff; Douglas, *op. cit.*, pp. 62–64; Coser, *op. cit.*, pp. 16–24; Blood and Wolfe, *op. cit.*, pp. 202–204.
[14]Morgan, *op. cit.*, p. 9 and Komarovsky, *loc. cit.*
[15]*Ibid.*, p. 24, and Douglas, *op. cit.*, pp. 58–62.
[16]Wolgast, *loc. cit.*; W. F. Kenkel, *The Family in Perspective*, New York: Appleton-Century-Croft, (1960); Heer, *op. cit.*, p. 193 ff; Wolfe, *op. cit.*, pp. 101–102; Blood and Wolfe, *op. cit.*, pp. 30–36.
[17]Bott, *op. cit.*, p. 358 and Heer, *op. cit.*, p. 66.
[18]Storch, *loc. cit.*
[19]Wolfe, *op. cit.*, p. 113; Bott, *op. cit.*, p. 360 ff; Heer, *op. cit.*, p. 139.

family; competence, generally and specifically, to make decisions; and ability to punish or coerce.

One's *legitimate power* within a family unit is likely to depend upon:

1. The relative strength of roles established within a family unit;[20]

2. The external support given to the roles played;[21] and

3. Ethnic and family origins.[22]
area; and

One's *contribution* to a family unit is a function of:

1. Level of individual wealth and/or income applied to family funds;

2. Level of social contribution to a family;

3. Level of intellectual contribution; and

4. That individual's ability to communicate within the family unit.

One's *degree of competence* in making decisions affecting the well-being of a family may depend upon:

1. Experience relative to a particular decision area; and

2. Personality traits.

There appear to be two major schools of thought concerning one's ability to dominate family decisions. One, represented by Parsons and Bales, Zaltman, Bott, Kenkel, and others, suggests that ability to dominate is largely a function of the roles one plays within a decision unit. The other, which includes Blood and Wolfe, Hoffman, Strodtbeck, and Heer, believes that ability to dominate is more a function of the resources one contributes to one's family. "Resources," in the sense the second school uses the term, refers primarily to tangible resources (e.g., through earned income). While agreeing with the principle of the second school (we also agree with the first), we would argue that resources need not be tangible. That is, child care may be as much a family resource as a paycheck. Thus, in our judgment, roles and resources are closely interrelated and each provides a basis for dominance in certain family decisions.

A final determinant of ability to dominate a decision area is one's *ability to punish or coerce* other members of one's family. This depends upon:

1. Personality traits of the individual;

2. External support;

[20]See footnote 13.
[21]See footnote 13 and Blood and Wolfe, *op. cit.,* pp. 84–109.
[22]Komarovsky, *op. cit.,* p. 255 ff.

3. Degree of control over family resources;

4. Degree of dominance exercised over other decision areas affecting one's family; and

5. Disparities within the family—e.g., relative strength of personality, relative educational attainment, relative communicating ability.

Willingness of other family members to accept an attempt at dominance by a given family member is ultimately a function of the "others" perception of that attempt. Since acquiescence was specifically excluded from our definition of convergence, one must assume that before dominance and convergence can exist simultaneously there must be a deliberate acknowledgement on the part of other family members that one member has superior ability or right to dominate a decision area. Also, one must assume an absence of desire by other family members to dominate the area in question, whatever the abilities or rights of the various family members may be in that area. Hence, convergence *and* dominance may exist in any given situation, although a more likely event is that there will neither be a complete lack of desire by other family members to influence a decision outcome nor a complete acknowledgement of any one member's superior ability to totally dominate that decision by the remaining members of the family. Consequently, it appears there will exist some degree of divergence in virtually every decision situation the outcome of which the family as a whole considers important.

HUSBAND-WIFE INTERACTION IN THE HOUSE-PURCHASE DECISION PROCESS

In the preceding section, husband-wife interaction was considered in the abstract. This section provides a description of the house purchase process based on recent work on house purchasing by a number of different researchers, and on personal interviews over the past two years by the senior author.

A family becomes aware of a need for housing either because they have no alternative housing or because the housing they occupy at that time is perceived as not adequately meeting the family's needs. In either event, the initial stages of the house-purchase process are characterized by a *decision to search* for a home. Preliminary to or in conjunction with that decision, a great deal of interaction occurs between husband and wife. Each spouse begins with some set of desired house attributes that, in their individual judgment, will satisfy the family's housing needs while remaining within the resource constraints they see as appropriate to their circumstances. Through interaction, some of the differences between husband and wife are identified and reconciled. Also, role assignments (or reaffirmation of acknowledged roles) associated with the house-purchase decision process are made. If the differences between the desired attribute sets of husband and wife are great, and some degree of reconciliation is not achieved, the purchase decision process may end before it has really gotten underway. More likely, however, the husband and wife will have come to share points of view on many home features over a significant period of living together, in which case the process will continue.

In any event, some differences in perception are likely to persist (many differences will not be identified until active search provides an appropriate stimulus), and the stage is set at various decision points for attempts by husband or wife to press for a decision outcome consistent with their individual point of view. Using the terminology introduced in the preceding section, attempts at dominance (and convergence/divergence patterns) may be anticipated.

Search[23]

House search is an information-seeking and information-processing activity designed to match a set of desired house attributes with some set of available house attributes from the market place. Most house purchasing studies suggest that women are the principal searchers and screeners, bringing to their husband's attention only those houses reasonably well-matched with what the family is seeking. Implicit in this pattern is a profound opportunity for wife dominance. It is also possible, however, that the wife may serve as the husband's search agent, the latter having already exercised dominance over those decision areas that mattered to him. The husband-dominated-wife-search was suggested by a number of interviews conducted by the authors.

A number of studies suggest that the extent to which husbands enter into active house searching with their wives is a function of the family life cycle. The earlier in the life cycle, the more likely the husband will be an active searcher. It is also possible that husbands will be assigned the searcher role exclusively. This is most likely to occur when he precedes the remainder of his family to a new geographic location.[24]

The period of search coincides with a highly dynamic stage of the house purchase decision process. During this period:

1. House features are identified that were not an explicit part of either spouse's initial desired attribute set;

2. Attributes are rejected that were originally considered desirable (or they are downgraded on the hierarchy of desired house features); and

3. Interaction between husband and wife is at a high rate to produce the results cited in (1) and (2) above—provoked in large measure, by an evaluation of houses actually available in the market place—and characterized by convergence/divergence-dominance patterns as feature is considered.

Thus, the set of desired house attributes undergoes continual revision as a function of both:

1. What is actually available in the market place; and

2. Interaction (and effective attempts at dominance) between husband and

[23]For a detailed description of consumer search see R. F. Kelly, "The Search Component of the Consumer Decision Process—A Theoretical Examination," in R. L. King (Ed.), *Marketing and the New Science of Planning*, AMA, (1968).
[24]W. Snaith and R. Lorwy, *Project Home*, The Project Home Committees, New York, (1967).

wife at many decision points (i.e., where decisions must be made concerning specific house features or terms of sale or purchase strategies).

Each house seen as a possible match to that sought by the family provokes renewed interaction and serves to better define what is and what is not acceptable to the family.

Some families require a great deal of time to come to the stage where a purchase decision occurs; others require very little time. A very short search phase is most likely when:

1. Time is a critical constraint in the search process—
   (a) There is a pronounced sellers' market—houses that even vaguely match with what is being sought are rare and [when] seen are perceived by the husband and wife as being likely to be purchased by someone in a short time after coming on the market; or
   (b) the family has no acceptable shelter alternative (i.e., their status quo on housing is not a feasible alternative).
2. A great deal of alteration and reconciliation of diverse views has been achieved prior to the active search phase—
   (a) The family has had previous experience in house searching roles and preferences are well defined and accepted by both husband and wife;
   (b) The market was well-known to the family before active search began; or
   (c) The husband or wife is highly dominant—very little conciliation is attempted, interaction is at a minimum—decisions are made *for* rather than *by* the family.

Whatever the time period involved, during search most of the major decision points in the overall decision process are passed. The outcome of the search phase provides the basic information inputs for the final phase of the decision process, the purchase decision.

The purchase decision

The purchase decision phase of the house purchase process involves an evaluation by a family of those housing alternatives (including the status quo, for many families) identified during search that are most like that the family is seeking. Where more than one alternative is being considered, an explicit hierarchy of desired attributes will be developed as a means of choosing between those alternatives. It is also likely that some form of cost-benefit analysis will be used to decide between less-expensive, less-well-matched houses and more-expensive, better-matched houses. Finally, some families will be considering only less-than-satisfactory matches with their desired attribute set, in which case they must decide between accepting one of those available alternatives and reverting back to search. Thus, the purchase decision phase may result in:

1. A satisfactory match and a positive purchase decision—an actual purchase will be attempted;

2. A less-than-desired match—the family is unwilling to search further and the status quo is not an acceptable housing alternative—a positive purchase decision is made;

3. A less-than-satisfactory match—the family is willing to pay in terms of time and continued uncertainty for additional search—a negative purchase decision results; and

4. A less-than-satisfactory match—the family perceives chances of finding a satisfactory house, even through additional search, to be quite low—the status quo is identified as the "most satisfactory" alternative—the purchase decision is negative.

The purchase decision phase is the period where struggles for dominance are ultimately resolved. If some minimum level of convergence has not been achieved by this time in most decision areas, it appears likely that a family's purchase decision outcome will be negative, no matter how well the housing alternative under consideration matches the desired attribute set of one or the other of the marriage partners.

Husband-wife interaction in the house purchase decision process

The description of the house purchase decision process on the preceding pages suggests a structure and a sequence that greatly oversimplifies the behavior of families seeking homes. Some families search for homes off and on over many years without ever making a positive purchase decision. This may occur because of unrealistic and unmodified market expectations; because of a relatively high degree of satisfaction with the status quo; because divergence between husband and wife persists and neither spouse can successfully dominate enough decision areas to provoke a positive purchase decision; and, finally, because house search is an end in itself to some families.

Purchase decisions with a negative outcome are often made on an almost casual basis by either spouse with no explicit interruption in the family research process. The searcher learns a house is for sale, goes to inspect it, and eliminates that house from further consideration without ever leaving his or her car. This usually occurs where it is obvious that one or two house attributes high on the hierarchy of desirability for that family are lacking.

Some families participate in or influence a final purchase decision very little. All the members in a given household may be acquiescent. Dominance at critical decision areas may, in such instances, come from outside the immediate household in the person of an aggressive and forceful salesman or an extra-household family member. Or, alternatively, a family may have serious time or resource constraints. Finally, to some families, a house is not an important component in their mode of life. Shelter is obtained by such families in a casual and offhand manner by following some line-of-least-resistance purchase strategy. Whatever the reasons for non-participation, families that do not control their own house selection are unlikely to engage in significant interaction and dominance patterns will not emerge.

No attempt has thus far been made to differentiate between families on the basis of their patterns of interaction. Yet it does seem likely that a number of factors may contribute to regularities among families on convergence/divergence dimensions as a function of role assignments and role expectations in those households. Among those factors are:

1. *Life-cycle*—according to a number of studies, convergence (and an absence of attempts at dominance) is likely to be highest immediately after marriage and decline thereafter, at least until late middle age.[25]

2. *Life-style*—values held by a family concerning the importance and character of a house as an instrument for living a certain type of life are likely to influence the nature of interaction patterns in that family. The more important a home is perceived to be, the more likely that individual family members will have well-defined house preferences—the stronger one's preferences for specific decision outcomes, the more likely that attempts at dominance will be observed.

3. *Ethnicity/cultural factors*—Different cultures contribute differently defined family role structures and decision prerogatives. The more rigidly roles are defined within a family unit, the less likely interaction will occur and the more likely that dominance will be exercised at various decision points in the house-purchase decision process.

4. *Disparities between husband and wife*—A number of differences such as degree of educational attainment; economic and/or social origin; and present contributions to family well-being may result in both divergence and differential abilities to dominate at various decision points in the house-purchase decision process.

The following section discusses the results of an exploratory field study designed to identify relationships between family characteristics (such as those just cited) and husband-wife interaction patterns, and between specific patterns of husband-wife interaction and house-purchase decision outcomes.

THE FIELD STUDY

The exploratory field study described below is one of a series directed by one of the authors preliminary to a major field investigation of the consumer decision process associated with house purchasing. Its purposes were to:

1. Identify recent home purchasers;

2. Distinguish between purchasers on the basis of life-cycle and selected socio-economic dimension;

3. Determine the degree of role definition within respondent households and the perceptions of each spouse with respect to the defined roles for both house search and the house-purchase decisions;

[25] *Ibid.*

4. Determine the perceptions of husbands and of wives, attribute by attribute, towards the house just purchased and towards some "ideal" home and, indirectly, gain some understanding of both dominance and convergence/divergence patterns in the respondent households; and

5. Test the field procedures and the field instrument described below.

PROCEDURES

A questionnaire comprised of five sections was developed. Section 1 was designed to acquire information on the house search and house buying processes (i.e., search strategy, the degree and nature of task segregation). Section 2 and Section 3 were constructed to obtain respondent perceptions towards their own home and towards some "ideal" home, respectively. Section 4 was concerned with family activities, its purpose was to identify features of respondent life-styles. And Stage 5 contained questions concerning the socio-economic character of husband and of wife before marriage, and of the family up to the time of the interview.

The questionnaires just described were administered in households in the Vancouver, B.C. metropolitan area (population approximately one million) in January and February of 1969. All respondents had purchased their homes within three months of the interview date. Purchase prices of respondent houses were between $18,000 and $40,000, the middle income price range in the Vancouver area. Recent purchasers were selected because they seemed most likely to retain information on their house search experience and they were unlikely to have formulated a "family attitude" on various features of their homes. The middle range of house purchasers was selected because it was large and because we wanted to avoid wide variations in income classes. No attempt was made to apply formal sample selections procedures—respondents were approached and appointments arranged for as they were brought to our attention.

Husbands *and* wives in each household were interviewed separately but simultaneously by a three-person team of interviewers. This procedure was employed to avoid overt interaction between spouses during the interview. We hoped to get separate perceptions from husband and wife towards each of many house attributes and life activities. Each set of interviews required thirty minutes, on the average, to complete.

The procedure just described rests on an assumption counter to that at least implicitly accepted by several observers[26] namely, that husband and wife do hold separate perceptions regarding both role structures and life style. Wolfe *et al* interviewed wives only, which seems patently inappropriate in an examination of interaction patterns.

Limitations

Only sixty-four acceptable husband and wife interviews were obtained. Consequently, numerical comparisons are of very little significance and no

[26]Wolfe, *loc. cit.*, Blood and Wolfe, *loc. cit.*; and Komarovsky, *loc. cit.*

great credence can be placed on any of the individual findings. Furthermore, it became apparent very early in the field phase of the study that the home purchasers of Vancouver tend to be at about the same stage in the life cycle —with pre-school or pre-adolescent children. Thus, our attempts to compare convergence/divergence and dominance patterns of families at different stages in the life-cycle were pretty well frustrated. The major limitation of the study, of course, is that no direct means has been provided for determining the degree, or the nature, of interaction between husband and wife; one must draw inferences from information on perceptual differences.

The findings

Despite the small group of respondents, it is apparent from our interviews that differences in perceptions between husbands and wives do exist with respect to both decision areas and decision role assignments. The fact that such differences were identified in a small group of respondents provides incentive to conduct a large-scale field study employing proper sampling procedures.

1. *The house-purchase process.* Nearly two-thirds of the families interviewed indicated that the decision to begin searching for a house was reached jointly. Of the remaining families, the wife was more often dominant than the husband. This finding is consistent with expectations and emphasizes the significant impact one occupying the role of homemaker may have on the life situation of all family members.

Husbands were more often active searchers than wives. This finding is contrary to those of most studies of house purchasing behavior. It is possible that the high concentration of respondent households with small children —and with tied-down young mothers—accounts for the disproportionate number of husband-searchers.

Most families indicated a degree of urgency was associated with their house search activities. This is confirmed by other information obtained from respondents to the effect that nearly all the families purchased homes within three months after arriving at a search decision. Furthermore, there was apparently little bargaining. Over half the families made an offer on only one house (the one they actually purchased), and this offer came after inspecting the house once or twice at most. Also, they tended to pay on the "high side" of what they had intended to pay upon entering the market. To the extent that urgency was a factor, one would expect less struggling over individual decision areas and less interaction over the process as a whole. The fact that the number of houses inspected ranged up to fifty per family during a one to three month search period is also indicative of some fairly perfunctory purchase decision processes.

2. *Husband-wife perceptions regarding their recently-purchased home.* In response to questions concerning the location of their new homes, husband and wife were agreed that their home was convenient for most things. Differences in perception between husband and wife were revealed, however, on

matters of location convenience relative to place of husbands' work and to shops. One suspects perceptual differences in this instance are a direct result of role segregation. And, for this reason, house location is a decision area where one may expect attempts at dominance by both spouses. There is an intervening variable that obviously conditioned many house location decisions: convenience relative to child-associated activities (e.g., schools, parks). It was obvious that both husband and wife were willing to compromise their own location preferences to accommodate their children's needs. Given her "Mother" role, the wife may have an edge in ability to dominate where both children and divergence are present.

While hobby space, garage space, and storage space were often noted as being inadequate, husband and wife had very similar perceptions about space allocation in their home. There were differences in perception regarding how easy the house was to run (guess who thought it more and who less easy to run); how easy the house was to clean; how easy the garden was to maintain; and how adequate the house was for all of the parents' needs. Each difference would appear to be a function of task segregation, and each suggests an area of possible divergence during the decision-making process.

Two areas where there appeared to be rather complete agreement in perception between husband and wife were aesthetics and the nature of the neighborhood in which their new house was situated. Since both factors are likely related to social class phenomena, and since there were virtually no significant husband-wife social class disparities, we do not consider these findings surprising.

3. *Husband-wife perceptions regarding an ideal home.* The degree of agreement between husband's and wife's perceptions on what a home *should be* was nearly as high as those associated with their present home. Differences were identified with respect to location relative to amenities and services; the costs of financing a home; the type of neighborhood in which the family should live; and the symbolic functions of a home. These findings are consistent with both our own expectations and other recent research on house-purchasing.

A procedural note

Differences in husband-wife perception were identified by asking each spouse to agree, partially agree, or disagree with a series of statements applied to their actual and to their ideal home. Where a husband-wife pair responded in precisely the same manner to a given statement (e.g., "This house was in good condition when we bought it."), they were awarded two points; if they were one response apart (e.g., one "agreed" while the other "partially agreed") they were awarded one point; and spouses who were two responses apart (i.e., one "fully agreed," the other "disagreed"), were given no points. Weighted averages were then derived for each statement and for a series of statements related to a given decision area based on the degree of agreement among all husband-wife pairs. Table 1 provides an example of how this data was summarized.

Table 1

Perception locational convenience aspects of present homes

Factors	Degree of Agreement (max. 21.3)	Agreement Rank
City center	13.7	5
Work	9.7	10
Shops	11.3	8
Relatives	15.3	3
Theatres	13.7	5
Church	13.0	7
Recreational facilities	11.3	8
Friends	15.3	3
Schools	17.0	2
"Most things"	18.3	1

4. *Task segregation in respondent households.* Table 2 contains a summary of the results on family task and role segregation as perceived by husbands and wives. To the extent that task segregation was identified, it followed the classic instrumental-expressive dichotomy. Instrumental tasks specifically identified with the husband included budgeting, keeping the cheque book, and gardening. The wife was seen as a specialist in household tasks and home decorating. While major expenditure decisions were considered by many families to be made jointly, husbands either dominated or partially dominated in 23 cases as compared to only 2 for wives. These findings suggest that there is significant task segregation between husbands and wives across a variety of decision areas. It is what one would intuitively expect, of course, but it does provide additional support to the conceptual framework underlying our exploratory study.

Table 2

Amount task segregation in respondent families

Decision Area	Husband Only	Wife Only	Husband Mainly	Wife Mainly	Both Equally
Major expenditures	9	1	14	1	38
Family budgeting	18	2	11	7	26
Holiday decisions	5	0	10	2	47
Children's education	1	2	1	6	45
Home decorating	2	4	4	22	32
Gardening	4	4	21	11	23
Household tasks	0	22	1	31	11
Evenings out	2	1	8	6	45
Savings	6	1	12	14	29
Cheque book	11	2	24	6	21

Table 3

Degree of participation in family leisure-time activities

Activity	Alone	Together	Never
Dining out	2	52	7
Hobbies	29	22	9
Movies	2	50	5
Community activities	15	12	34
Sports	19	24	18
Shopping	19	39	4
Watching television	12	46	4
Visiting relatives	3	57	2
Holidays	1	61	3
Church going	6	32	24
Visiting friends	2	57	2
Extra education	33	2	26
Club activities	10	18	32
Entertaining	1	58	3

5. *Family activities.* Table 3 provides information on a range of activities husband and wife might share, or pursue independently. Information concerning those activities shared by husband and wife in any given household may provide a clue as to the overall life-style of that family—also to the nature of a set of interaction patterns that, according to several studies at Cornell, have significant impact on house-purchase decision outcomes.[27] Unfortunately, the data gathered in the field study did not provide sufficiently detailed information to draw even the most tentative conclusions about the links between life-style, interaction patterns, and decision outcomes. A family-by-family breakdown of shared and independent leisure-time activities reveals that in most families, most activities that family pursues are shared; there are some families where very few activities are shared; and virtually no families in between.

CONCLUSIONS

Differences in perceptions towards houses do exist between husbands and wives. Where such differences exist, it is likely that husband and wife will

[27]G. Reyer, *Houses are for People*, Cornell University Press, Ithaca, (1955); "Home Selection and Home Management," *Marriage and Family Living* 17, (May 1955), pp. 143–151; *Housing and Personal Values*, Cornell University Agricultural Station, Memoir 364, Ithaca, (July 1959).

seek different outcomes at various decision points in the house-purchase decision process. Attempts at dominance will occur, and the degree of success either spouse has in those attempts will be a function of role assignments and values within that household.

The exploratory field study was not an adequate means to examine the linkage between various family types, interaction patterns, and decision outcome. At best, the study provided evidence that perceptual differences and task segregation exist among respondent families. A more comprehensive field study is clearly needed before any conclusions of operational significance can be drawn. The literature in the field and the exploratory study both suggest that additional study is warranted.

READING 19

A BEHAVIORAL MODEL FOR MARKET SEGMENTATION*

Richard H. Evans

The market for a firm consists of all the present and potential buyers of the firm's products or services. In order to adjust and adapt to the market, components of the marketing mix—such as price advertising, personal selling, transportation, and so forth—a firm may employ the strategy of market segmentation. In this strategy, the total heterogeneous market is delineated and divided into relatively homogeneous sub-markets or meaningful buyer groups.[1] In broad terms, such a strategy can assist the firm in achieving an optimum marketing mix, which in turn can lead to a better allocation of resources and to objective fulfillment.

The purpose of this article is to discuss a behavioral model[2] (see Figure I) that may be used in the market segmentation strategy of a firm. In the model, two constructs[3]—social class and life cycle—are employed simultaneously to segment the market and delineate the patterns of consumer behavior. In this article three aspects of consumer behavior—product cognizance, family decision-making, and sources of information—are discussed. Utilization of this model and research approach by the firm would be a step toward "scientific" decisions in marketing management. The decisions would be "scientific" in the sense that the tools of a behavioral science would be used in a precise, systematic, and objective manner. Thus, the manager would be

*Reprinted by permission from *The University of Washington Business Review*, Autumn, 1968, pp. 55–72.
[1]Philip Kotler, *Marketing Management: Analysis, Planning and Control* (Englewood Cliffs, New Jersey: Prentice-Hall, Inc., 1967), p. 43.
[2]Norman R. Smith, "Developing Pattern of Consumer Behavior," *Business Developments* (Eugene Ore.: University of Oregon, 1963), p. 27.
[3]Simply stated, constructs are categories that are developed by combining selected variables. See Julius P. Gould and William L. Kolb, *A Dictionary of the Social Sciences* (Glencoe, Ill.: The Free Press, 1964), p. 134.

getting away from the general descriptive and intuitive data that are often used as a basis for marketing decisions.

1. DEFINITIONS

Social class denotes "all those individuals (or families) who possess within the framework of some society or community relatively the same amounts of power, income, wealth or prestige or some loosely formulated combination of these elements."[4] In order to delineate the term social class for research purposes, W. Lloyd Warner's classification of occupation, source of income, housing type, and dwelling area[5] was used. Three social class levels were employed on the vertical axis in the construction of the model (Figure I).

Life cycle means, essentially, "an idealized construct representing the important stages in the life of an ordinary family."[6] The system of life cycle stages, devised by Lansing and Morgan[7] and Lansing and Kish[8] in their consumer studies, is used in this study in an abbreviated form. Specifically, four life cycle stages are utilized on the horizontal axis—young married, no children; young married with children; older married with children; and older married, no children—with older married referring to those over 45 years of age.

A family may go through various stages in life—from marriage to child rearing stages, to the postparental period, to the retirement period, and finally to a dissolvement of the marriage due to the death of one of the partners. This cycle is essentially biological in nature, but it has social implications and it is in a sense predictable, as each family goes through the same life processes. The "standard package" of the families in each life cycle stage varies as the families progress through the various life cycle stages.

The respondents in the survey were segmented by social class level and family life cycle stage, and then analyzed simultaneously in terms of a matrix or model as shown in Figure I. A few comments should be given with respect to the dissecting lines in the model. The dissecting lines are not really parallel to each other. The "young married, no children" families are likely to be larger in number in the upper-middle class families because the lower class families in this life cycle usually have children soon after they are married. The lower class wife often wants to assume the mother role as soon as possible after marriage. The "older married with children" families are likely to be large in number in the upper-middle class because of the desire of these families to have children later in life, in part as a result of "planned" children. Therefore, in both of these stages—"young married, no children"

[4]Gould and Kolb, *op. cit.,* p. 648

[5]W. Lloyd Warner, *Social Class in America* (New York: Harper and Row, 1960), p. 123.

[6]John B. Lansing and James N. Morgan, "Consumer Finances Over the Life Cycle," *Consumer Behavior,* Vol. II; *The Life Cycle and Consumer Behavior,* Lincoln H. Clark, ed. (New York University Press, 1955), p. 36.

[7]Lansing and Morgan, *op. cit.,* pp. 36–51.

[8]John B. Lansing and Leslie Kish, "Family Life Cycle as an Independent Variable," *American Sociological Review,* XXII (October 1957), p. 512.

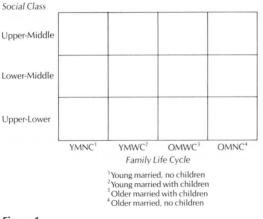

Social Class

Family Life Cycle

[1] Young married, no children
[2] Young married with children
[3] Older married with children
[4] Older married, no children

Figure 1
The behavioral model

and "older married with children"—the vertical sections would be narrower at the bottom than at the top of the model. There is likely to be some movement from the lower social class to the middle social class; therefore, the dissecting lines of the model should be wider apart at the right side (older married stage) than at the left side (young married stage) of the model for the middle social class.

The model, however, is applicable and valuable as problems and issues develop in each stage of the life cycle and the appropriate solution to these problems and issues is often determined by the social class placement of the family.[9] Also, the model is of value and somewhat unique in that it considers the respondents on a family basis rather than as individuals,[10] and it examines the interviewees simultaneously in terms of two constructs.

II. HYPOTHESES

In a study conducted by the author, the behavioral model that has just been described produced some useful tentative hypotheses (see Table 1). These hypotheses, which describe various buyer groups, are outlined below.

● Product cognizance varies in terms of social class.

● The middle class tends to have a relatively high level of product cognizance, while the lower class tends to have a relatively low level of product cognizance.

● Product cognizance varies in terms of stage in the family life cycle for specific social classes.

● Product cognizance in the upper-middle social class is similar throughout the life cycle.

[9]Smith, *op. cit.*, p. 26.
[10]Arthur J. Kover, "Models of Man as Defined by Marketing Research," *Journal of Marketing Research*, IV (May 1967), p. 130.

● Product cognizance in the lower-middle and the upper-lower social classes is not similar throughout the life cycle.

● Family decision-making varies in terms of social class.

● The upper-middle social class tends to make decisions in a syncretic manner throughout the family life cycle.

● The lower-middle social class tends to make decisions in a syncretic and partially syncretic manner throughout the family life cycle.

● The upper-lower social class tends to make decisions in a syncretic, partially syncretic, and autonomic manner throughout the family life cycle.

● Sources of information vary in terms of social class.

● The upper-middle social class tends to consider formal association friends, business friends, and periodicals as sources of information.

● The lower-middle social class tends to consider a few formal association friends, a few business friends, periodicals, extended family members, and neighborhood friends as sources of information.

● The upper-lower social class tends to consider mainly extended family members, neighborhood friends and periodicals as sources of information.

III. THE EXPLORATORY STUDY

In order to investigate, test the model, and verify the hypotheses, an exploratory study, utilizing a judgment sample of 136 families, was conducted by the author. The sample data were collected during the summer months of 1965 from the adjoining cities of Springfield and Eugene in western Oregon. The respondents in the sample were determined by first selecting specific areas that were classified on the basis of two social class variables, house type and dwelling area. Each area within the two cities was sampled to ensure representation in the study. A sample collected in this fashion, given the resources available, allows for an optimum amount of validity. Validity refers to "whether the test measures the quality it is supposed to measure under sufficiently natural conditions."[11] If the study data had not been sampled on a stratified basis in terms of the social class variable, then, given the means available, the respondents would not have been distributed adequately, and consequently, the consumer behavior patterns would have been more difficult to interpret.

The type of personal interview employed was a semi-structured, or focused interview.[12] This form of interviewing allowed the author to probe into the answers and to elicit the attitudes and values of the respondents. The interviewees in the sample were the wives in the families.

The questions in the interview were essentially of the open-ended type.

[11]Darrel B. Lucas and Steuart H. Britt, *Measuring Advertising Effectiveness* (New York: McGraw-Hill Book Company, 1963), p. 39.
[12]Robert K. Merton, Marjorie Fiske, and Patricia L. Kendall, *The Focused Interview* (Glencoe, Ill.: The Free Press, 1956), pp. 3–4.

This question design was chosen because the author wanted the respondents to reveal their true feelings and opinions, with respect to the subject, and to feel free and not limited when replying to the questions. The questions on consumer behavior were asked in terms of selected products. On family decision-making, the respondents were asked the following kinds of questions: "Who makes the decisions in your family with respect to the selected products?" "What role do you and each of your family members play in the decision-making process?" "Who do you think should be concerned with housing materials in your family from a decision-making viewpoint—the husband or the wife—and why?" In terms of product cognizance and sources of information, the respondents were, for example, asked: "What is the difference between hardwood plywood paneling and hardboard paneling?" "What sources of information influenced you most in your purchase decision?"

Products utilized in this study were all related to one industry—housing materials. Specifically, eight interior housing materials—hardwood flooring, carpeting, tile, linoleum, paint, wallpaper, hardwood plywood paneling, and hardboard paneling—were selected for analysis.

It should be mentioned that the study does have a number of limitations. The limitations essentially center around the sample design, the interview method, the two constructs, and the behavioral model. These limitations, however, do not really reduce the value of the study. In an exploratory study, the research design may be flexible. As Wasson states: The "purpose of exploratory research is not measurement per se, but insights and ideas about the formulation and design of later, more definitive research. The applicable designs are therefore the more flexible ones, that make maximum use of available data and summarized experience."[13] It follows, then, that in this exploratory study the pattern of consumer behavior in the model should be interpreted heuristically rather than demonstratively.

IV. THE RESULTS

The purpose of an exploratory study is "to gain familiarity with a phenomenon or to achieve new insights into it, often in order to formulate a more precise research problem or to develop hypotheses."[14] In this study, the author was particularly concerned with developing new insights and hypotheses on patterns of consumer behavior. The results of the study were in turn analyzed and developed into the 13 hypotheses previously listed.

Three paradigms of consumer behavior—product cognizance (product information), family decision-making, and sources of information—are analyzed in terms of the behavioral model.

Product cognizance

To determine a family's relative product cognizance level, three levels of product cognizance were utilized—knowledgeable, familiar, and un-

[13]Chester R. Wasson, *The Strategy of Marketing Research* (New York: Appleton-Century-Crofts, 1964), p. 108.
[14]Claire Selltiz et. al., *Research Methods in Social Relations*, rev. ed. (New York: Holt, Rinehart, and Winston, 1963), pp. 42–43.

familiar. The *knowledgeable* level indicates that a family could identify different products and mention many of the technical details of the products, the *familiar* level indicates that a family could identify some products and mention a few of the technical details of the products, and the *unfamiliar* level indicates that a family could basically not identify different products nor discuss any of the technical details.

As shown in Table 1, cognizance of families with respect to selected products varied within the behavioral model. The upper-middle social class families tended to have a level of product cognizance that concentrated on the knowledgeable and familiar levels throughout the stages of the family life cycle. The lower-middle social class families, on the other hand, have a mixed level of product cognizance throughout the stages of the family life cycle. In the "young married, no children" stage of the family life cycle, families have, essentially, familiar and unfamiliar levels of product cognizance; in the "young married with children" stage in the family life cycle, the families have all three levels of product cognizance—knowledgeable, familiar and unfamiliar; in the "older married with children" stage, families tend to have a product cognizance that includes, essentially, the knowledgeable and familiar levels. Then, in the "older married, no children" stage, the level of product cognizance is basically the unfamiliar level, except in some stages in which the level of product cognizance tends to rise to the familiar level.

Family decision-making

Decision-making in families, with respect to product selection, may be described as syncretic,[15] partially syncretic, and autonomic,[16] as shown in Table 1. *Syncretic decision-making* generally means joint decision-making and *partially syncretic decision-making* means that some decisions are made on a joint basis and some decisions are made by either the husband or the wife. *Autonomic decision-making* means that approximately an equal number of separate decisions are made by each marriage partner. The upper-middle social class families made decisions in, essentially, a syncretic manner throughout the selected stages of the family life cycle, whereas, the lower-middle social class families made decisions in a syncretic manner in the "young married, no children," "young married with children," and "older married with children" stages, but made decisions in a partially syncretic manner in the "older married, no children" stage of the family life cycle. The upper-lower social class families, however, made decisions in a syncretic manner in the "young married, no children" stage of the family life cycle, in a partially syncretic manner in the "young married with children" and "older married with children" stages, and an autonomic manner in the "older married, no children" stage of the family life cycle.

---

[15]Mirra Komarovsky, *Blue-Collar Marriage* (New York: Random House, 1964), p. 223 and Robert O. Blood and Donald M. Wolfe, *Husbands and Wives* (Glencoe, Ill.: The Free Press, 1960), p. 23.
[16]*Ibid.*

Table 1

*Paradigms of consumer behavior (percentage of families)**

Social Class					Consumer Behavior
					Product Cognizance
	50	35	54	55	Knowledgeable
	50	47	36	33	Familiar
	0	17	9	11	Unfamiliar
					Family Decision-Making
	100	90	90	77	Syncretic
	0	10	10	23	Autonomic
Upper-Middle					
					Sources of Information
	100	83	90	77	Periodicals
	80	66	64	89	Formal Association Friends
	60	66	91	90	Business Friends
	20	5	0	22	Extended Family Members
	20	31	36	11	Neighborhood Friends
					Product Cognizance
	14	31	40	8	Knowledgeable
	57	38	50	58	Familiar
	28	31	10	33	Unfamiliar
					Family Decision-Making
	100	85	80	31	Syncretic
	0	15	20	69	Autonomic
Lower-Middle					
					Source of Information
	86	93	90	92	Periodicals
	0	21	30	54	Formal Association Friends
	14	71	70	61	Business Friends
	57	57	20	30	Extended Family Members
	43	50	30	15	Neighborhood Friends
					Product Cognizance
	0	12	0	0	Knowledgeable
	22	19	50	19	Familiar
	78	68	50	81	Unfamiliar
					Family Decision-Making
	100	44	59	6	Syncretic
	0	56	41	94	Autonomic
Upper-Lower					
					Sources of Information
	22	69	86	58	Periodicals
	0	6	14	0	Formal Association Friends
	0	12	0	0	Business Friends
	100	56	71	70	Extended Family Members
	0	63	59	53	Neighborhood Friends
	YMNC[1]	**YMWC**[2]	**OMWC**[3]	**OMNC**[4]	

Family Life Cycle
[1]*Young married, no children*
[2]*Young married with children*
[3]*Older married with children*
[4]*Older married, no children*
**The percentage figures are approximations.*

Sources of information

The terms periodicals, formal association friends, business friends, extended family members, and neighborhood friends, employed in Table 1, should be defined before the interrelationships of the terms are analyzed. *Periodicals,* in this article, refer to the regular mass media publications. *Formal association friends* are friends that a family has through associations that have "definite rules of entrance, membership and exit."[17] *Business friends,* as used in this article, refers to friends that a family has in the business environment. *Extended family members* are the "nuclear family plus lineal and collateral kinsmen."[18] The last concept, *neighborhood friends,* includes those friends that are in a close proximity to the home or in the neighborhood. As shown in Table 1, the upper-middle social class families have mainly three sources of information—periodicals, formal association friends, and business friends. The lower-middle social class families, in general, receive some information from essentially all five sources—periodicals, a few formal association and business friends, extended family members, and neighborhood friends. The lower social class respondents, on the other hand, essentially receive information from periodicals, extended family members, and neighborhood friends.

V. DISCUSSION OF RESULTS

The simultaneous use of social class and life cycle may, in part, explain the consumer behavior patterns. In this exploratory study, five characteristics—social mobility, family income, role of the wife, occupation of the husband, and marital relations—were examined in terms of the two constructs (social class and life cycle), to determine whether there were relationships between the two constructs and product cognizance, family decision-making, and sources of information. This type of information is invaluable, as the market must be both described and explained in order to develop and optimize a firm's market segmentation program.

In this part of the article the behavioral variables of the two constructs are discussed. The discussion includes both a literature review and an analysis of the findings in the study relative to the above five consumer characteristics (shown in summary form in Figure 2), and the three patterns of consumer behavior. In this section of the article the author attempts to explain why patterns of consumer behavior exist. Some of the comments may appear conjectural.

Social mobility aspiration

The study indicated that each social class level and life cycle stage has a different level of aspiration for social mobility, and that, hypothetically, there could be a relationship between social mobility aspiration, product cognizance, and sources of information.

Findings similar to those of the present study, relative to the social class

---

[17]W. Lloyd Warner, *American Life* (Chicago: University of Chicago Press, 1962), p. 227.
[18]Robert F. Winch, *The Modern Family* (New York: Holt, Rinehart, and Winston, 1964), p. 13.

Consumers		Family life cycle stages	
Social classes	Behavioral variables	Young married	Older married
Middle class	Social mobility aspiration	High	High
	Family income	High	Higher
	Role of the wife	Companion	Companion
	Occupation of the husband	Managerial	Managerial
	Marital relations	Good	Good
	Education	University	University, high school
Lower class	Social mobility aspiration	Low	Low, downward
	Family income	Low	Low, decreasing
	Role of the wife	Companion, mother	Housewife, mother
	Occupation of the husband	Semi-skilled	Semi-skilled
	Marital relations	Poor	poor, decreasing
	Education	High school	High school, elementary school

Figure 2

A summary of behavioral variables in terms of social class levels and family life cycle stages

concept and the social mobility variable, have been discussed by authors such as Coleman,[19] Kahl,[20] Davis,[21] Merrill,[22] Davis and Havighurst,[23] Rosen,[24] Hyman,[25] and Komarovsky.[26] Rosen, for example, stated: ". . . social classes in American society are characterized by a dissimilar concern with achievement, particularly as it is expressed in the striving for status through social mobility"[27] and ". . . that members of the middle class tend to have considerably higher need achievement scores than individuals in the lower social strata."[28]

The findings of this study agreed with much of the literature on the subject, indicating that there is a relationship between the aspiration level for mobility and social class.

Education and social mobility. One of the prerequisites, generally speaking, for social mobility is general education. The upper-middle social class families who were found in this exploratory study to have high levels of aspiration

[19]Richard P. Coleman, "The Significance of Social Stratification in Selling," *Marketing: A Maturing Discipline* ed. Martin L. Bell (Proceedings of the Winter Conference of the American Marketing Association, December 28–30, 1960), pp. 159–160.

[20]Joseph A. Kahl, *The American Class Structure* (New York: Holt, Rinehart, and Winston, 1964), pp. 201–203.

[21]Allison Davis, *Psychology of the Child in the Middle Class* (Pittsburgh: University of Pittsburgh Press, 1960), p. 4.

[22]Francis E. Merrill, *Society and Culture* (Englewood Cliffs, N.J.: Prentice-Hall, 1961), pp. 300–320.

[23]Allison Davis and Robert J. Havighurst, "Social Class and Color Differences in Child Rearing," *American Sociological Review,* XI (December 1946), p. 707.

[24]Bernard C. Rosen, "The Achievement Syndrome: A Psychocultural Dimension of Social Stratification," *American Sociological Review,* XXI (April 1956), pp. 204–210.

[25]Herbert H. Hyman, "The Value Systems of Different Classes: A Social Psychological Contribution to the Analysis of Stratification," *Class, Status, and Power,* Reinhart Bendix and Seymour M. Lipset, eds. (Glencoe, Ill.: The Free Press, 1953), pp. 427–429.

[26]Mirra Komarovsky, *Blue-Collar Marriage, op. cit.,* pp. 286–287.

[27]Rosen, *op. cit.,* p. 204.

[28]*Ibid.,* p. 206.

for social mobility also had relatively strong values with respect to general education. Davis said of the upper-middle social class families that they emphasize ". . . long and arduous education, development of complex processes of business, industry, government, church, and education. . . ."[29] The lower-middle social class families on the other hand, also place a value on learning, but the strong desire that is present in the upper-middle social class families does not exist in the lower-middle social class. To some, however, there is a desire to learn, and as Mayer points out "many are discontented with their status, and therefore, highly value self-improvement, attending lectures and reading books and magazines in the hope of making a better place for themselves or at least for their children."[30] The present study indicated that the upper-lower social class families did not place a high value on general education. Some parents in this class thought their children should have more education than they did, but generally speaking, numerous respondents in the sample appeared to think that education and learning was out of their reach and capabilities—they seemed downtrodden and mystified with respect to learning. Hyman made several statements in this regard: "To put it simply, the lower class individual doesn't want as much success, knows he couldn't get it even if he wanted to, and doesn't want what might help him get success,"[31] "ability may also be retarded by lack of individual striving to obtain whatever training in turn is instrumental to economic advancement."[32] Chinoy, also, stated with respect to automobile workers, that they had limited aspirations and pessimism with regard to opportunity.[33] The aspiration level for social mobility and one of its prerequisites—education and learning—appeared, in this study, to have a correlative relationship with social class and product cognizance in respect to the selected products. The higher the level of aspiration for social mobility, the stronger the desire to be knowledgeable with respect to the environment, and consequently, the higher the level of product cognizance. The upper-middle social class families, as compared to the upper-lower social class families, want to be socially mobile, or, at least to maintain their social position, therefore, they become cognizant with regard to subjects that might affect their social mobility.

Family life cycle and social mobility. The aspiration level for social mobility can also be considered in terms of the stages in the family life cycle.[34] Albrecht stated: "Upward mobility in a lifetime characterized the upper and both middle classes, while downward mobility centered in the two lower classes."[35] The level of product cognizance remained constant through the life stages in the upper-middle social class, and correlatively, the level of

[29]Allison Davis, "Socialization and Adolescent Personality," *Readings in Social Psychology,* T. M. Newcomb et al., eds. (New York: Holt, Rinehart, and Winston, Inc., 1947), p. 149.

[30]Kurt B. Mayer, *Class and Society* (New York: Random House, 1955), p. 38.

[31]Hyman, *op. cit.,* p. 427.

[32]*Ibid.,* p. 429.

[33]Ely Chinoy, "The Tradition of Opportunity and the Aspiration of Automobile Workers," *The American Journal of Sociology,* LXII (March 1952), p. 459.

[34]Robert O. Blood and Donald M. Wolfe, *Husbands and Wives* (Glencoe, Ill.: The Free Press, 1960), pp. 86–98.

[35]Ruth Albrecht, "Social Class in Old Age," *Social Forces,* XXIX (May 1951), p. 405.

aspiration for social mobility also remained relatively vigorous through the stages of the life cycle in this social class. In the lower-middle social class and the upper-lower social class, however, there appeared a decrease in the level of product cognizance after the "older married with children" stage of the family life cycle had been reached, and congruently, a decrease in the level of desire for social mobility. The families in these two social classes in the "older married, no children" stage of the family life cycle did not expect to rise in the status hierarchy, because of their age, education, income, and health, and consequently they appeared to have a relatively low interest in the selected products.

Periodicals and social mobility. In the exploratory study, the respondents were asked what periodicals (magazines) they purchased relative to the products in question. The relationship between the aspiration level for social mobility variable and the type of periodicals selected is such that families with a higher mobility aspiration level usually selected periodicals that illustrated upper status products (products that have an upper-middle social class and above image, that are expensive, and that are of a certain style). The families with the high mobility aspirations are striving for higher or a more secure social position and they want to be identified with a higher or high social class; therefore, they purchase, as a source of information, periodicals that illustrate the higher status materials. It follows, therefore, that in this study the families with the high social mobility aspirations were the upper-middle social class families, and correspondingly, they are the families that purchase periodicals with upper status product illustrations.

At the lower end of the social class scale in this study are the upper-lower social class families. These families, as stated previously, are not so social mobility conscious, and many realize that they will never reach a social position that will encourage them to purchase upper status products. Therefore, as they realize their mobility position, they purchase periodicals that illustrate materials that are more within their budget range, value system, and mobility realization level. In other words, they purchase periodicals that illustrate lower status products (products that have a lower-middle social class and below image, that are relatively inexpensive, and that are of a certain mass-consumption and modern style).

Another reason periodicals were utilized as a source of information is that they assisted the families in maintaining and/or increasing their level of social status. For example, by analyzing the products illustrated in the shelter periodicals (magazines that are concerned with interior housing materials such as furniture, flooring, and wall products, and with home horticultural activities), the upper-lower social class families could determine what was being used by all social classes and what was being used by mainly upper-lower social class families. In other words, the shelter periodicals were being used as mediums of social class reinforcement and as mediums for social mobility assistance.

Shelter periodicals are read by upper-lower social class families to maintain their social class level, while in the lower-middle social class families, and, to a greater extent, in the upper-middle social class families, the reasons for reading shelter periodicals are both to maintain social status and to obtain ideas or concepts useful in terms of social mobility.

Personal influence and social mobility. The level of aspiration for social mobility also affects the type of persons that the families consulted as sources of information. The upper-lower social class families, with their low level of aspiration for social mobility, primarily consulted extended family members and a few neighbors. The lower-middle social class families, who, in the main, had an average level of aspiration for social mobility, consulted a few formal association and business friends, a few relatives, and a few neighbors, but the upper-middle social class families who had a strong desire for social mobility consulted mainly a large number of formal association and business friends. The upper-middle social class families, in particular, anxious for social mobility, wanted to make sure that their selection of products was identified with their present status level or a higher status level. Therefore, because of this strong desire for social mobility, the upper-middle social class families consulted, for information, a wide array of sources in the segment of formal association and business friends which would, in turn, reinforce the families' position in the social hierarchy, or, in terms of the actual selection of products, provide a consensual validation.

Family income

The level of income, although not a criterion used to determine social class, usually increases as social class level increases. In this study, the upper-middle social class families have the highest income, followed by the lower-middle social class families with a lower income, and finally the upper-lower social class family with the lowest income. Coleman, in an article entitled "The Significance of Social Stratification in Selling," illustrated a similar pattern of income distribution. In this article, Coleman stated:

In the middle of each class income range are its "average" members, families who are neither underprivileged nor overprivileged by the standards of their class. You might think of this as the Upper-Middle class family between $12,000 and $20,000 a year, the Lower-Middle family in the $7,000-$9,000 range and the Upper-Lower family near $6,000 per annum.[36]

Level of income and periodicals. The level of income, as related to social class and life cycle, appears to affect the type of periodicals read by a family, the patterns of family decision-making, and the levels of product cognizance. The upper-lower social class families have a relatively low income, and therefore have little to spend above their daily necessities and "mass consumption" products required in the home. These families usually cannot afford to purchase expensive and upper status products illustrated in the upper class shelter periodicals. They do, at times, read these periodicals in the hope that they might obtain an idea and be able to use the products illustrated, but this is

[36]Coleman, *op. cit.*, p. 165.

rarely the case—the products are just too expensive. The survey indicated that the upper-lower social class families prefer shelter and family periodicals that illustrate the less expensive and lower status products.

The upper-middle social class families, on the other hand, did not indicate the same feelings as the upper-lower social class families with respect to shelter periodicals that illustrated expensive products. The upper-middle social class families read these periodicals and gave no indication that they were at all aggravated by the cost or status characteristics of the illustrated products.

Levels of income and decision-making. Social class differences in decision making could also conceivably be attributed to income levels of families in each social class. As Blood and Wolfe state:

High-status husbands are more apt to handle the money and bills. The reason for this appears to be that there is a larger increment of money involved beyond the level of daily necessities. Such husbands are also making a major investment when it comes to choice of a house, whereas for low-status families one flat is about as good as another.[37]

and as Rainwater, Coleman, and Handel state:

The working class housewife is typically the chief purchasing agent of her family, and she is more likely than her middle class counterpart to have major financial control. In some cases, the woman handles practically all the purchases, simply relieving her husband of his weekly pay check and disbursing it as she finds necessary. More often she is the family accountant and purchasing agent, but discusses the matters with her husband. Less often, is there the clear sharing of money management and shared responsibility most characteristic of the middle class family. As has been pointed out, this is probably partly due to the more complex financial management necessary for the middle style of life. To a large extent, it is probably also due to the working class husband's preference for avoiding household worries, his desire to earn the money but let the wife worry about how it is spent.[38]

Komarovsky also confirms these patterns as she states:

The dominant role of the lower-class wife is apparently not only in "keeping track of money and bills" but with regard to each item. The relative proportion of "wife only" answers decreases consistently with rise in income for all items.[39]

Basically, the same trends were found in this study, and these same patterns could be applied to decision-making with respect to the selected products.

---

[37]Blood and Wolfe, *op. cit.,* p. 33.

[38]Lee Rainwater, R. P. Coleman, and R. Handel, *Workingman's Wife* (New York: Macfadden-Bartell Corp., 1962), p. 164.

[39]Mirra Komarovsky, "Class Differences in Family Decision-Making on Expenditures," *Household Decision-Making,* Nelson M. Foote, ed. (New York: New York University Press, 1961), p. 263.

Related to income, then, why does the pattern shown in Table 1 exist in decision-making? The answer lies, in part, in the amount of income above the subsistence level and in the values of the different social classes.

In upper-lower social class families, the housewife has little income above the subsistence level. In order to purchase the products in question, the housewife must consider how much money to set aside each month or what to go without if a purchase is to be consummated. The value system of this class is such that the husband, through disinterest, expects the wife to be familiar with the symbolic and utilitarian functions of the selected products.

On the other hand, the upper-middle social class families, and, to a lesser extent, the lower-middle social class families, have more income above the subsistence level and their financial management is more complex than that of the upper-lower social class families. Income and financial management are not the only aspects that should be considered, since the middle classes have a different value system than the lower classes. The upper-lower social class homes are basically not status symbols; moreover, the husbands are not particularly interested with the inside "look" of the homes. In the upper-middle social class homes, and, to a lesser extent, in the lower-middle social class homes the emphasis is on the home as a status symbol. The husband and wife operate jointly to create the desired image—both are concerned with the inside symbolic and utilitarian functions of the home.

In short, the upper-lower social class families have less income above the subsistence level and disinterest on the part of the husband, thereby leaving the decision-making, with respect to certain products, mainly to the wife. However, in the upper-middle social class families and, to a lesser extent, in the lower-middle social class families, there is more to spend above the subsistence level, complex financial management, and image considerations, causing the decision making by both marriage partners.

Levels of income and product cognizance. Product cognizance may also be related to the level of income in each social class. As there is a relatively large amount of income above the subsistence level for the upper-middle social class families, there is more opportunity to select and analyze products —price, relatively speaking, is not a crucial selective criterion. However, in the lower-middle social class, and, to a greater extent, in the lower class, there is less income above the subsistence level and consequently less opportunity for these families to select and analyze housing products. The families in these two social classes, and in particular the upper-lower social class families, purchase what they can afford with price being, essentially, the major criterion for selection. The upper-lower social class families, and, to some extent, the lower-middle social class families compare mainly price, while the upper-middle social class families compare price, quality, product effect, and different products when they make purchasing decisions.

Decrease in the level of product cognizance after the "older married with children" stage in the family life cycle in the lower-middle and upper-lower social class families may result, in part, from the decrease in income that may occur in this stage of the family life cycle. Older people, and, in some cases, families in the "older married with children" stage of the family life cycle may face, as Albrecht says, a ". . . loss of status; loss of income from work; meager pensions; heavy drain on resources to meet increasing needs for physical care; rising cost of living, and other factors leading to loss of economic security."[40] Therefore, families in this stage in the family life cycle, because of the low and decreasing amount of income above the subsistence level, take little interest in different types of products and their various attributes.

Upper-middle social class families, on the other hand, have a constant level of product cognizance throughout the stages of the family life cycle. They have sufficient amount of income above the subsistence level at each stage in the family life cycle.

The above comments concerning income and social class, however, must be analyzed further to prevent misinterpretation. It should be pointed out that the families in the study had similar patterns of consumer behavior within each social class, regardless of total income. When income is approximately the same for each social class, the families or respondents still behaved in a manner typical of their social class.[41] The upper-lower, lower-middle, and upper-middle social class families with equal incomes had patterns segmented in terms of social class levels.

Role of the wife

Patterns in consumer behavior may be attributed, in part, to the role of the housewife in each social class. Role is discussed by Linton in his book, *The Study of Man*. Linton states that "a role represents the dynamic aspect of a status. The individual is socially assigned to a status and occupies it with relation to other statuses. When he puts the rights and duties which constitute the status into effect, he is performing a role."[42]

The study indicated that housewives in each social class had basically different roles.

Housewives in the upper-lower social class families are, essentially, home- and family-oriented. The study indicated that they were not particularly interested in obtaining many friends outside the family or becoming active social members in the community. They were content with their family members, their relatives, and a few close neighborhood friends. Hollingshead and Rainwater, Coleman, and Handel express the same view with respect to the role of the upper-lower social class housewife when they state, respectively, that:

The wife and mother's role in the community is encompassed by domestic duties. She is judged by the way she keeps her house, dresses her children and manages the family budget. The community does not expect these women to join the Women's Club or other social organizations and they are discriminated against if they have ambitions along this line. The men

[40]Albrecht, *op. cit.*, p. 400.
[41]For a discussion on this subject see Richard P. Coleman, "The Significance of Social Stratification in Selling," *Marketing and the Behavioral Sciences*, Perry Bliss, ed., 2nd edition (Barton: Allyn and Bacon, Inc., 1967), pp. 184–187.
[42]Ralph Linton, *The Study of Man* (New York: Appleton-Century-Crofts, 1936), p. 114.

are judged by how well they provide and by their moral actions, not by their business or organizational contacts.[43]

and "She believes that her family, her husband and her home should come first in her attentions—and that clubs should only occupy her time after these obligations have been fulfilled."[44]

On the other hand, the lower-middle social class housewives and the upper-middle social class housewives are not so family and home conscious. To be sure, they are interested in the family and the home, but they are also interested in making social contacts and friends in the community. The middle-class housewife wants to divert some of her activities from the family and home, as Rainwater, Coleman, and Handel state: "It is this kind of diversion —mental stimulation, personal improvement, or widened social acquaintanceship—that motivates middle class women to seek involvement in associational apparatus."[45] The middle class housewife, then, wants to make many acquaintances in the community. This is especially true of the upper-middle social class housewife who feels particularly strong about being socially active and accepted in the community.

In terms of sources of information in the upper-lower social class families, because the housewife is basically home-centered and family-oriented, she mainly associates with family members, relatives, and a few close neighborhood friends. In the lower-middle social class families, the housewife is relatively home- and family-centered, but also has an interest in some community activities. Consequently, the family's friends are a mixture of relations, neighbors, formal association friends, and business friends. The upper-middle social class family housewives, on the other hand, play the role of companions to their husbands—they are companions in the home and socially. As Kirkpatrick says:

The privileges pertaining to this role include pleasures shared with the husband, a more romantic emotional activity, and chivalrous attentions. On the other hand, it implies as obligations the preservation of beauty under the penalty of marital insecurity, the rendering of ego and erotic satisfaction to the husband, the cultivation of social contacts advantageous to him. . . .[46]

The housewife, almost as much as the husband, takes an active part in numerous community social activities, and consequently, in part because of this role of the housewife, the upper-middle social class families consult formal association and business friends when seeking information.

The role of the spouse in the family also tends to influence family decision-making patterns with respect to selected products. In other words, because of the domestic role of the housewife in the upper-lower social class, decisions

---

[43]August B. Hollingshead, "Selected Characteristics of Classes in a Middle Western Community," *American Sociological Review*, XII (August 1947), p. 387.

[44]Rainwater, Coleman, and Handel, *op. cit.*, p. 123.

[45]Rainwater, Coleman, and Handel, *op. cit.*, p. 130.

[46]Clifford Kirkpatrick, *The Family as Process and Institution* (New York: Ronald Press Co., 1963), p. 168.

are by and large made on a partially syncretic and autonomic basis, with the housewife being dominant in the decision. The role of the upper-middle social class housewife, and, to a slightly lesser extent, the role of the lower-middle social class housewife is basically one of companionship. Therefore, housewives in these two classes, generally speaking, make most decisions mutually or syncretically with their husbands.

In summary, role behavior as a variable of the constructs in the model tends to influence sources of information and types of family decision-making.

Occupation of the husband

The occupation of the husband is another variable that may assist in explaining the different types and number of friends that families in each social class have and consult for information on various products. The occupation of the husband varies in each social class. Husbands in the upper-middle social class basically must mix socially if they want to maintain their social positions. As Blood and Wolfe state with respect to high-status occupations, "off-hours contact with work mates pays off financially and promotion-wise at their occupational level. . . ."[47] and as Kahl states, "a career man is always concerned about his public behavior and reputation. His network of contacts is important. He cares what others think about him."[48] On the other hand, the lower-middle, and, to a greater extent, the upper-lower social class families are basically not affected by external contact, and consequently they associate with only a limited number of people.

Thus there is a correlation between occupation and type and number of friends. The type and number of friends determines, to an extent, the type and number of families consulted for information on various subjects. Upper-middle social class families, because of the husband's occupation, interact socially and have many friends, and obtain their information on products from formal association and business friends. Lower-middle social class families are basically intermediate, but the upper-lower social class families, because of the husband's occupation, in part, do not interact socially to a large extent. Consequently, they obtain information mainly from relatives and a few neighbors.

Marital relations

Another behavioral characteristic, marital relations, may be considered in explaining family decision-making patterns in terms of the two constructs (life cycle and social class). *Marital relations* is a general term that includes, for the purposes of this study, marital satisfaction, husband interaction, and companionship.

In terms of family life cycle stages, a dichotomy developed between the upper-middle social class families and the upper-lower social class families

---

[47]Blood and Wolfe, *op. cit.*, p. 169.
[48]Kahl, *op. cit.*, p. 195.

with respect to marital relations (see Table 2). The upper-middle social class families continued to have good marital relations throughout the stages of the family life cycle, and made syncretic decisions, but the upper-lower social class families, after the "young married, no children" stage in the family life cycle, developed relatively poor marital relations and partially syncretic and autonomic decisions. The lower-middle social class families, on the other hand, had good marital relations and thus syncretic decisions, up to the "older married, no children" stage in the family life cycle; then, at this stage, decreased marital relations prevailed and partially syncretic decisions became dominant.[49]

Turning now to social class, it was found in the survey that the upper-middle social class housewives spoke more favorably of their husbands than the upper-lower social class housewives. This is not to say that the upper-lower social class housewives spoke derogatively about their husbands, but subjectively, there appeared to be a relaxed, proud tone or manner when the upper-middle social class housewives discussed or mentioned their husbands. The upper-lower social class housewives seemed to speak of their husbands in a less affectionate manner. This relationship could result from the harsher aspects of life which plague the upper-lower social class families and the fact that upper-middle social class housewives participated with their husbands in social and recreational events, whereas the upper-lower social class housewives had relatively little social activity with their husbands.

On this same subject, Blood and Wolfe and N. Hurvity had some findings and comments. Blood and Wolfe stated that "in general, high-status wives share their troubles more often but also more discriminatingly,"[50] "talking and doing things with the husband tends to be characteristic of high-status people, whereas low-status wives more often confess that they take out their feelings angrily or aggressively against their husbands,"[51] and "in general, co-educational leisure-time patterns characterized high-status marriages whereas sex-segregated patterns are found especially in low-blue-collar marriages."[52]

Hurvity, when studying lower class families, found that:

There are few companionship activities in which the spouses participate together. Most of the husband's free time is taken up with doing his chores and repair work about the house, tinkering with the auto, building models, cleaning and repairing guns or fishing materials, and so forth; and the wife, when she is not busy with the children, is involved with her household chores.[53]

It may be concluded that upper-middle social class and lower-middle social class families have better marital relations, and correlatively employ syncretic decision-making, while upper-lower social class families have poorer marital

---

[49]For a discussion pertaining to this subject, see Blood and Wolfe, *op. cit.*, pp. 159–265.
[50]*Ibid.*, p. 195.
[51]*Ibid.*, p. 186.
[52]*Ibid.*, p. 169.
[53]Nathan Hurvity, "Marital Strain in the Blue-Collar Family," *Blue-Collar World*, Arthur B. Shostak and William Gomberg, ed. (Englewood Cliffs, N.J.: Prentice-Hall, 1964), p. 99.

relations and consequently show partially syncretic and autonomic decision-making. In the "young married, no children" stage in the family life cycle, families in all social classes have good marital relations and make decisions syncretically. In the "older married, no children" stage in the life cycle, on the other hand, families have good marital relations and employ syncretic decision-making in the upper-middle social class; medium marital relations and partially syncretic decision-making in the lower-middle social class; and poor marital relations and autonomic decision-making in the lower class.

VI. CONCLUSION

After reading the above material on the paradigms of consumer behavior and possible reasons for the paradigms in terms of the behavioral model, two questions may come into focus—(1) how can a firm determine whether the segmentation variables of social class and life cycle are usable; and (2) what is the value of market segmentation to the firm?

To answer the first questions regarding the feasibility of the two constructs, we may consider the three criteria of measurability, accessibility, and substantiality.[54] *Measurability* refers to the problem of whether or not the market can be delineated, or to the problem of whether the characteristics of the market are determinable. *Accessibility* refers to whether or not selected market segmentation variables can be effectively utilized by the firm. *Substantiality* is the degree to which the chosen market segmentation constructs can be profitably cultivated by the firm. The constructs in this model can be measured and utilized profitably by the firm, given the correct total operating environment. Simultaneous use of the two constructs, social class and life cycle, in the form of a model does appear to meet the above criteria. However, the value of an actual application depends on market characteristics and deployment of the marketing mix.

The value of market segmentation to the firm is manifold, but, essentially, market segmentation contributes to the synchronization of the marketing mix with the consumer; to an expansion of the product mix in relation to the market; to penetration of the market in depth; to a focused form of promotion; to the delineation of different demand curves; to a higher dollar sales value; and to greater product loyalty because of the tailoring of the product to fit the market. These values of market segmentation are, of course, not without their limitations, such as increased marketing costs.

This behavioral model is useful not only in delineating patterns of consumer behavior, but also in explaining possible reasons for the patterns of behavior. Description and explanation or market delineation and purchase motivation of consumers are concomitantly necessary if one is going to develop an effective market segmentation program.[55] Once a market is described and explained, problem solving and decision-making become more "scientific." The result is better marketing management.

[54]Philip Kotler, *Marketing Management: Analysis, Planning and Control* (Englewood Cliffs, N.J.: Prentice-Hall, Inc., 1967), p. 45.
[55]Thomas A. Staudt and Donald A. Taylor, *A Managerial Introduction to Marketing* (Englewood Cliffs, N.J.: Prentice-Hall, Inc., 1965), pp. 18–19.

READING 20

INDUSTRIAL BUYING BEHAVIOR:
A STATE-OF-THE-ART APPRAISAL*

Frederick E. Webster, Jr.

Professional marketing people with an interest in either industrial marketing or buyer behavior are often struck by the relative lack of attention to the particular problems of industrial buying behavior. The industrial marketing manager (or the teacher of industrial marketing) often finds himself wishing that he knew more about industrial buying behavior as the basis for marketing strategy decisions. Every strategy decision depends, at least implicitly, upon a prediction of market response, and such predictions are based upon "models" (sets of assumptions about important variables and the relationships among them) of buyer behavior. Likewise, the industrial market research specialist, looking for information that will be useful in the development of marketing strategy, finds that he is operating with relatively little information about such important questions as the locus of buying responsibility and the nature of the buying decision process within potential customer organizations.

Like other students of buyer behavior, the industrial marketing researcher must be frustrated by the fact that most of the potentially relevant literature on buyer behavior has a lop-sided emphasis upon the behavior of individual consumers and households, and more specifically upon the purchase of frequently-purchased packaged goods such as coffee, cigarettes, and beer. Less well understood are such areas of consumer behavior as the decision to purchase furniture or major appliances, although automobiles have received a fair share of the attention. One could tentatively generalize that students of consumer behavior have shown more interest for products which are bought and sold on the basis of imagery, relationship to self-concept and life style, and other "psychosocial" considerations, and less interest in purchases where product performance and functional considerations predominate in the decision process. One important distinction between consumer and industrial buyer behavior is that industrial purchasing typically finds functional considerations predominating, especially in non-routine purchase decisions. This is one major reason why the literature on buyer behavior has only passing interest for the student of industrial marketing.

The purpose of this paper is to assess the current state-of-the-art in research on industrial buying behavior. To direct the discussion, the first part of the paper will suggest why factual and conceptual knowledge of buyer behavior is of value to the industrial marketing strategist and researcher. Next, we shall review briefly the major work that has been accomplished in the study of industrial buying behavior. Then an "ideal" statement of the requirements for moving forward will be made. This will be followed by an analysis of some of the reasons why progress in the study of industrial buyer behavior has been slow and a suggestion on how the situation can be improved.

*Reprinted from *Marketing in a Changing World*, Bernard A. Morin, ed. (Chicago, American Marketing Association, 1969), pp. 254–260.

USES OF BEHAVIORAL MODELS

It is often said that "there is nothing so useful as a good theory" and it is that viewpoint which motivates the so-called "scientific" approach to marketing management. Those who are concerned with the development of new knowledge in marketing, whether their primary tools are the concepts of behavioral science or the analytical techniques of mathematics and statistics, share with the marketing manager an orientation that is ultimately pragmatic. When all is said and done, the objective is to provide a basis for decision making that leads to an improvement in profitability and a more efficient utilization of marketing resources to achieve the strategic objectives guiding the firm.

Modern marketing managers realize that their decision making can be no better than the information upon which it is based and the analytical framework available for interpreting that information. It is the function of industrial marketing research to gather such information as will be valuable to the decision maker in his planning and controlling responsibilities. There is now available a set of analytical tools, provided by Bayesian decision theory, for determining the optimum amount of information to collect as a function of the cost and reliability of information-gathering procedures, the manager's degree of uncertainty, and the amount at stake.[1]

Such analysis avoids the basic question of *what* information to gather, however. That important function of determining what variables are most likely to be critical in a given decision situation and of specifying the possible relationships among them is the function of the behavioral model. This line of reasoning is reflected in the organization of many marketing management courses in business schools today. An introduction to the basic concepts of marketing management and strategy is followed by an examination of buyer behavior, with this material designed to pave the way for consideration of methods for collecting and analyzing market information as the basis for management decision making.

Behavioral concepts provide the analytical structure within which the researcher and the strategist can determine what information should be gathered. These concepts also provide a framework for interpreting the results of research and can suggest those relationships among variables that are likely to be most significant in a given situation.[2] Kornhauser and Lazarsfeld called these "master techniques," useful in planning, organizing, and controlling research and in interpreting findings, as distinguished from "servant techniques" that have use in the actual collection and assembling of facts.[3]

Although Kornhauser and Lazarsfeld were writing almost thirty-five years ago, their analysis seems surprisingly current when one looks at industrial marketing research, for they noted that "attention has focused disproportionately upon the servent techniques—upon the details of gathering and

[1] Frank M. Bass, "Marketing Research Expenditures—A Decision Model," *Journal of Business*, Vol. 36 (January 1963), pp. 77–90.

[2] Frederick E. Webster, Jr., "The Behavioral Sciences and the Marketing Manager," *Washington Business Review*, Vol. 1 (October 1966), pp. 25–35.

[3] Arthur Kornhauser and Paul F. Lazarsfeld, "The Analysis of Consumer Actions," *The Techniques of Market Research from the Standpoint of a Psychologist*, (New York: American Management Association, 1935), reprinted in Ralph Day, *Marketing Models: Quantitative and Behavioral*, (Scranton, Pa.: International Textbook Company, 1964), pp. 13–26.

tabulating bits of information."[4] They also stressed the similarity among the master techniques of the engineer—his mathematical and physical principles; the master techniques of the physician—from physiology, bacteriology, and pathology; and the knowledge of human behavior which could provide the master techniques for the marketing· researcher. One more quotation from their paper will show the importance these early scholars in marketing research attached to behavioral models:

We suggest simply that a systematic view of how people's market behavior is motivated, how buying decisions are arrived at, constitutes a valuable aid in finding one's way around midst the thousand and one questions of specific procedures and interpretations in market research.

This need for a psychological view grows out of the very nature of market research. *For that research is aimed predominantly at knowledge by means of which to forecast and control consumer behavior.* [Italics in original.][5]

This line of reasoning has been more thoroughly accepted by consumer goods marketers than by industrial market planners and researchers. If one attempts to systematically review the available knowledge on industrial buying behavior, he finds few published sources of a scholarly nature. There is a wider literature in the so-called "trade press," but this consists mostly of case studies with little or no opportunity to generalize to other classes of industrial buying. Let us consider more thoroughly the nature of available knowledge on industrial buying behavior and then suggest some reasons for this state of affairs.

CURRENT KNOWLEDGE

There are relatively few academic researchers working in the industrial buying behavior area. The most significant result in recent years was the publication of the Marketing Science Institute study, which was based on observation of buying decisions in three companies.[6] This rather limited data base was supplemented by analysis of a fourth company's buying decisions with special attention to the question of "source loyalty."[7] Levitt's study of the influence of company reputation and salesman presentations on industrial buying decisions was equally significant, and there have been other small-scale studies of communication effects in an industrial marketing context.[8,9,10] Earlier case

---

[4]*Ibid.*, p. 13.
[5]*Ibid.*, p. 14
[6]P. J. Robinson, C. W. Faris, and Y. Wind, *Industrial Buying and Creative Marketing,* (Boston: Allyn & Bacon, Inc., 1967).
[7]Yoram Wind, "Industrial Buying Behavior: Source Loyalty in the Purchase of Industrial Components," unpublished PhD dissertation, Graduate School of Business, Stanford University, 1966.
[8]Theodord Levitt, *Industrial Purchasing Behavior: A Study of Communications Effects,* (Boston: Division of Research, Graduate School of Business Administration, Harvard University, 1965).
[9]Frederick E. Webster, Jr., "On the Applicability of Communication Theory to Industrial Markets," *Journal of Marketing Research,* Vol. 5 (November 1968), pp. 426–28.
[10]Frederick E. Webster, Jr., "Word-of-Mouth and Opinion Leadership in Industrial Markets," in Robert L. King (ed.), *Marketing and the New Science of Planning,* (Chicago: American Marketing Association, 1968), pp. 455–59.

studies of industrial buying have not been followed by a more systematic analysis of industrial buying decisions.[11,12] The present author's attempt to construct a generalized model of industrial buying behavior was frustrated by the basic complexity of the process and led to a conclusion that each of the several stages of the buying process—problem recognition, search, evaluation of alternatives, and choice—could best be attacked individually.[13]

Related to studies in the area of communication in industrial markets have been some recent efforts to explore the diffusion of innovations in industrial markets. While some of this work has appeared in the marketing literature,[14,15] it has primarily been the province of the economist with the result that the implications for marketing strategy are seldom obvious.[16] An ongoing research project under the direction of Richard Cardozo had supported the hypothesis that some concepts from consumer behavior, such as perceived risk, may be useful in studying industrial buying decisions and in segmenting the industrial market.[17] More extensive research is needed to test these and other concepts for their applicability to industrial markets.

What does all this sum to? Most of the studies referred to are exploratory in nature. The principal methodology has been the unstructured interview, and self-reporting, with the usual problems of bias and general lack of rigor. While these are necessary first steps, they add up to something less than a reasonably comprehensive theory of industrial buyer behavior.

A review of these several studies would support the following generalizations which seem to summarize very roughly the current state of our knowledge of industrial buying behavior. Each of these generalizations should be regarded as an hypothesis for further testing.

1. Industrial buying decision making is an organizational process involving several individuals and several roles including users, influencers, deciders, and buyers.

2. The professional buyer, the purchasing agent, is often not the most important factor in the decision process, although he may exercise considerable influence as a "gatekeeper" controlling the flow of information into the buying organization.

3. There are classes of buying decisions which can be defined by position on a continuum from simple and routine decisions (habitual behavior and

[11]E. Raymond Corey, *Industrial Marketing: Cases and Concepts*, (Englewood Cliffs, N.J.: Prentice-Hall, Inc., 1962).

[12]D. H. Thain, C. B. Johnston, D. S. R. Leighton, *How Industry Buys*, a study sponsored by the Business Newspapers Association of Canada and the Toronto, Hamilton, and Montreal Chapters of National Industrial Advertisers Association, 1959.

[13]Frederick E. Webster, Jr., "Modeling the Industrial Buying Process," *Journal of Marketing Research*, Vol. 2 (November 1965), pp. 370–76.

[14]Urban B. Ozanne and Gilbert A. Churchill, Jr., "Adoption Research: Information Sources in the Industrial Purchasing Decision," in King, *op. cit.*, pp. 352–59.

[15]Frederick E. Webster, Jr., "New Product Adoption in Industrial Markets: A Framework for Analysis," *Journal of Marketing*, forthcoming.

[16]For a good review of this work, see Edwin Mansfield, *Industrial Research and Technological Innovation: An Econometric Analysis* (New York: W. W. Norton & Co., Inc., 1968), and Edwin Mansfield, *The Economics of Technological Change*, (New York: W. W. Norton & Co., 1968).

[17]Richard N. Cardozo, "Segmenting the Industrial Market," in King, *op. cit.*, pp. 433–40.

automatic reordering) to complex decision making characterized by large amounts of money and significant change from previous practice.

4. There are stages in the buying decision process from initial awareness through to final buying action, and the behavior of individuals and of the buying group as a whole is significantly different according to the stage of the buying decision. One way of describing these stages is awareness, interest, trial, and full-scale use, although there are other classifications of equal validity.

5. Buyers' reliance upon and preferences for information sources vary according to the stage in the buying decision process and in relationship to other factors (such as class of buying decision and degree of perceived risk) that are not well defined.

6. Industrial buying decision makers are motivated by a combination of individual needs and organizational needs. While it is wrong to characterize industrial buying decisions as completely "rational" or "non-emotional" it is probably true that industrial buying decisions are motivated by economic considerations and the search for a relative advantage over competitors.

7. Procedures for gathering information and identifying alternative courses of action are "simple-minded" in that there is a tendency to rely upon the familiar and to try sources that have been worked before.

8. Individual decision makers in industrial buying situations show responses to communication similar to those that have been found in other areas of communication research. These responses include the existence of source effect and the processes of selective attention, perception, and retention.

While these findings certainly do not exhaust all that is known about industrial buying behavior and probably do injustice to research results of which the author is unaware, they do give a flavor for the current state-of-the-art in the study of industrial buying behavior. It is obvious from this brief review of current research that investigators tend to agree that industrial buying behavior can best be viewed as a form of decision making (a viewpoint recently gaining strong support concerning consumer buying behavior) and that industrial buying behavior is a combination of individual and organizational processes.

There are several major shortcomings within the available knowledge that must be corrected before we can treat this body of knowledge as having the status of a "theory" or as a generalizable "model" applicable to a majority of industrial buying decisions. The first major shortcoming is that virtually none of these studies has been replicated. Indeed, few of them have been reported in a form that would permit replication. As noted earlier, a major problem is the reliance upon more-or-less unstructured interviews as the primary source of data and the subjective interpretation of these data.

A second major shortcoming is the fact that most of these studies have not been well-planned in the sense of having a clearly stated hypothesis, a careful plan for the collection of data, and unambiguous criteria for accepting or rejecting the hypothesis according to rigorous analysis of the data. As stated above, these studies have been "exploratory" in nature, which is the same as saying they have not met the criteria of "scientific" research.

A third problem with this body of research is the lack of a consistent model or view of the world which integrates and inter-relates the findings of one study with another and leads to a consistent and developing body of knowledge. Finally, it is worth drawing attention again to the basic fact that the number of studies (as compared to consumer behavior and as compared to the basic importance of industrial marketing in our economy) is very, very small. These studies have virtually all been done by academicians, and the vast majority have not had either the financial or moral support of a business organization actually interested in using the results. By way of contrast, studies of consumer behavior have often been conducted by an alliance of business and academic organizations, and the quality has been improved as a result. There is a positive probability that students of industrial buying behavior have been talking to themselves and have missed some fundamental points. The other side of this coin is the fact that industrial marketers have neither contributed significantly to this research nor have they derived the benefits of "master techniques" for planning research or frameworks for designing marketing strategy that such studies could provide.

REQUIREMENTS FOR PROGRESS

These remarks have identified at least three requirements for improving the study of industrial buying behavior. First, there is need for more research on industrial buying behavior. Second, there is need for not just more but better data on industrial buying behavior. We need a source of data other than *post facto* self-conscious answers to a series of questions about a vaguely defined decision procedure and information acquisition and evaluation process. Third, we need a model—an explicit framework general enough to include several, if not all, classes of buying decisions but specific and explicit enough to be non-trivial. This model should have sufficient appeal to enough researchers to serve as a coordinator and guide to their efforts so that each could borrow from and build upon the work of others.

In a moment, the discussion will return to the question of what is required if the study of industrial buying behavior is to progress. The need for a "scientific approach" to the study of industrial buying behavior will be stressed and related back to the use of this knowledge by market planners and researchers. First, it will be instructive to consider some possible explanations for the fact that the study of industrial buying behavior has not kept pace with the study of consumer behavior. This analysis of reasons for our slow progress may reveal some opportunities for improving our performance.

REASONS FOR SLOW PROGRESS

Why have there been so few studies of industrial buying behavior? Why has there been less collaboration between industrial marketing managers and the academician? Why is there no generally accepted way of looking at, or "model" of, industrial buying behavior? The answer to these questions may be suggested by consideration of four factors: (1) the attitudes of industrial marketers; (2) the nature of industrial buying decisions; (3) the state of the researcher's conceptual knowledge, and (4) current attitudes and fashions among academic researchers in marketing. From this analysis may emerge an idea on how to move forward in the study of industrial buying behavior.

Industrial marketers' attitudes

One reason for slow progress is the negative attitudes of industrial marketers to research on buying behavior, and their frequent unwillingness to encourage such studies or to supply information. There is an unflattering stereotype of the industrial marketing manager that may explain these attitudes in part. It has four major components. First, he is much more likely than his consumer goods counterpart to have spent a considerable part of his career in field sales. He knows how complex industrial buying decisions are and how unique each buyer tends to be. Furthermore, he knows that personal selling is his most important marketing activity and that the most significant element of his marketing strategy is the strategy which each salesman develops with each customer. Generalizations about the market or about industrial buyers' behavior are likely to raise his eyebrows and his suspicions. He wants to look at specific buying situations and specific customers.

The second distinguishing feature of the industrial marketing manager is what is usually called "product orientation." Especially if he was trained in the engineering and physical sciences—as so many industrial marketing managers have been, he will be more oriented to "things" and less oriented toward people than his consumer goods counterpart. This characteristic product- and technology-orientation seems to pervade industrial marketing organizations. It has taken industrial marketers a lot longer than the consumer marketers to adopt the customer-oriented marketing concept. However, the last decade's diversification trend has resulted in increased competitive pressures which are inevitably concentrating more management attention on the marketplace.

There are reasons for the industrial marketer's characteristic concentration on specific buying situations. Industrial marketing is much more in the nature of a one-to-one relationship than consumer marketing. Industrial marketers have always been customer-oriented, with an emphasis on the needs of specific, individual customers and less on the "market" consisting of all potential customers. That's how business gets done in industrial marketing—one-to-one. Solving customers' problems is the name of the game and winning requires a current, dynamic, and developing technological capability and a marketing team fully informed and able to develop those solutions.

While a desire to keep things in perspective suggests a warning that we are talking about differences of degree, not of kind, it is true that industrial marketing *is* different from consumer marketing. Industrial marketers sell specific problem solutions to a relatively small number of customers on an individual basis. Consumer marketers sell general solutions to a mass market. In most industrial buying, economic and technological considerations predominate. In consumer marketing emphasis shifts to the psychosocial consequences of product use and appeals are often based on the reactions of other people to one's purchase decisions rather than the performance of the product itself. This may help explain why consumer marketers have been more interested in the application of behavioral sciences.

The third part of this stereotype of the industrial marketer is his *unhealthy* respect for his competitors. He would be flattered if his competitors were as afraid of what *he* would do with a piece of *their* information. There are no obvious reasons for this fear. Perhaps a legitimate concern for the confidential nature of technical information gets generalized to all facts. At any rate, industrial marketers have been afraid to share information with marketing scholars and competitive considerations are among the most frequent reasons given.

The fourth part of the stereotype is an overconcern with immediate results and short-term accomplishments. (There is an ugly similarity between the academician who publishes a work before he is really satisfied with it, in the pressures of his "publish or perish" world and the businessman who commits his time and energy to projects that will improve this year's performance —and bonus and chances for promotion.) The industrial marketer is quick to ask the academic researcher "What's in it for me?," which is often interpreted as anti-intellectualism. For the researcher to honestly answer "very little" is clearly ruled out by the expectations which each has for the other. When he begins to talk in terms of "better understanding of the decision processes and patterns of influence which characterize your markets" and "contribution to knowledge," the academician is well on his way to turning off the industrial marketer's interest.

To summarize this view of the industrial marketer's attitudes toward his work and toward research on marketing, his thinking (conditioned by his field sales experience) tends to emphasize specific customers, products, and technology, competitive secrecy, and immediate results. None of these viewpoints is consistent with cooperation, or even interest, in scholarly studies of industrial buying behavior. This expresses itself in three negative ways: (1) the industrial marketer is unlikely to have initiated any studies of buyer behavior within his own company; (2) if such studies have been conducted, the data may be confidential; and (3) he is unwilling to commit resources to a proposed attempt to gather such information.

The complexity of industrial buying decisions

The attitudes of the industrial marketer alone certainly do not explain the lack of knowledge about industrial buying behavior. These attitudes have a strong basis in the very nature of industrial buying decisions. They are more complex than consumer buying decisions on several dimensions and they are therefore "richer" in terms of the amount of data required to describe them. It is hard to generalize about *the* industrial buying process across all types of customers and products. The industrial marketer's pessimism about the validity of generalization is well founded. The scholar may look as naive to him as he looks anti-intellectual to the scholar.

A quick look at some of the major sources of complexity in industrial buying decisions is also informative in identifying *what* we don't know about them. First, there are multiple buying roles in industrial buying decisions. These include users, influencers, gatekeepers, purchasers, and deciders. One individual may play two or more roles and within a given customer organization the roles are likely to vary from one situation to the next. They certainly vary from one customer to the next.

Second, there are frequently long time lags between effort and response, more so than in consumer goods marketing. As a result, it is difficult to trace the effects of changes in the quality or level of marketing effort. It is harder to do experiments and to develop knowledge about how industrial buyers respond to marketing effort. (Conversely, the relatively small time lag between effort and result has favored study of frequently-purchased consumer products.)

Third, each buying organization is different. Its problems are different because its objectives, its resources, its people, and its abilities are different from other industrial customers. And, these differences are critical in determining the nature and result of buying decisions. Of course, individuals and households are also significantly different from each other. In the consumer case, however, we have theory to explain the influence of these differences —income, social class, personality, reference group, demographics— on preference and decision making. In industrial marketing we have not even developed means of classifying important differences among buyers, let alone a theory for explaining how those differences influence decision making.

Fourth, technology is a source of complexity in industrial marketing. Technical complexity means that buying decisions take longer, require more information, require longer evaluation, and involve more uncertainty about product performance. Theories of individual risk-taking and information processing can be (and are being) applied to the analysis of consumer decision making in the light of uncertainty about product performance.[18] Only two investigators, however, seem to have attempted to relate these concepts to industrial buying decision making.[19] Also, the behavioral theory of the firm offers possibilities for investigating the riskiness of technical complexity.[20] In this case, the available theory is way ahead of the available data on specific industrial buying decisions. Likewise, communication theory has made a significant contribution to our understanding of the individual consumer's decision-making process but significant modifications in the theory are required before it can productively be applied to industrial marketing. Among

[18]Donald F. Cox (ed.), *Risk-Taking and Information Handling in Consumer Behavior* (Boston: Division of Research, Graduate School of Business Administration, Harvard University, 1967).
[19]See the work of Levitt, *op. cit.*, and Cardozo, *op. cit.*
[20]Richard M. Cyert and James G. March, *A Behavioral Theory of the Firm* (Englewood Cliffs, N.J.: Prentice-Hall, Inc., 1963).

other things, the basic fact that industrial buying is *economic* decision making needs to be integrated.

The state of conceptual knowledge

The fact that industrial buying decisions are complex therefore leads directly to the need to appraise the adequacy of concepts about buyer behavior that have been developed primarily in the analysis of individual consumers' behavior. A casual review of the literature of buyer behavior will reveal two facts of major importance. First, there are many models of buyer behavior but there is no really coherent theory.[21] Second, available models and knowledge pertain to a rather narrow, albeit important, class of purchases: frequently purchased, relatively inexpensive consumer packaged goods. Coffee marketers have made by far the most significant contribution to the study of buyer behavior.

Several years ago, Professor Massy and I argued that a scientific approach must be adopted by researchers in marketing and the behavioral sciences and quantitative analysis must work together if they are to develop a sound body of knowledge in marketing.[22] A body of conceptual knowledge—it was argued then and it can be argued now in the specific case of industrial marketing —can develop and grow only if a *scientific approach* is followed in developing that knowledge. The scientific approach has four hallmarks. First, objective and systematic procedures are followed in collecting and analyzing the data. Second, measuring instruments and procedures used have known properties. Third, results are presented in a form which permits objective analysis after the fact, which is to say that results are reproducible. Finally, the procedures and the results are public and alternative explanations for observed phenomena are evaluated objectively.

Only if a scientific approach, as defined above, is followed, do we get a growing and evolving body of knowledge with each study building upon and adding to the sum total of knowledge. Without this base, each researcher must "reinvent the wheel" and depend only upon his own limited knowledge base. In contrast to the objective, systematic, and "public" nature of the scientific approach, knowledge of industrial buyers has been developed on a piecemeal, case study approach using subjective procedures for data collection and analysis. Interpretation of study results has depended heavily on the analyst's judgment and intuition with virtually no possibility of determining the reliability of the reported results. Results of studies conducted by companies are seldom reported in a public fashion.

As a consequence, there is no body of knowledge warranting the label "theory" (or even a "general model") of industrial buying behavior. At best we have some specific models of a descriptive nature and these are few in number. The result is less efficiency in industrial marketing research and a real blind spot in the development of marketing science.

---

[21]For a reasonably complete review of the literature that specifically looks at the state of theory see Jagdish N. Sheth, "A Review of Buyer Behavior," *Management Science*, Vol. XIII, (August, 1967).
[22]William F. Massy and Frederick E. Webster, Jr., "Model-Building in Marketing Research," *Journal of Marketing Research*, Vol. 1 (May 1964), pp. 9–13.

Current academic research fashions

In a hard-fought battle for academic respectability, business school researchers in many areas have latched onto one of the most visible aspects of the scientific method—statistical analysis—and have shucked off such suspect methods as open-ended interviews, judgment samples, and the subjective (and sometimes creative) interpretation of results. It seems at times as if the main criterion for evaluating research today is the amount of computer time consumed by the project.

The most frequently reported (and easiest to get accepted in the journals) kind of academic research is the statistical analysis of consumer panel data and at least half of the articles in the past five years fit that definition. In the late 1950's, there was some concern about the quality of consumer panel data but once the researchers found out how easy it was to publish the results of such studies, they stopped asking such embarassing questions. As a result, marketing scholars are sooner or later going to have to use some other data to validate models developed from analysis of panel data. They will have to chink-up the cracks in this important foundation of buyer behavior theory.

A second result of this emphasis on statistical analysis and aggregate data is that the study of industrial buyer behavior has been virtually ignored. Industrial marketing researchers have nothing like the data base available to students of consumer behavior. Furthermore, the kinds of phenomena around which the study of consumer behavior has been organized (brand loyalty, store loyalty, brand switching, deal-proneness, etc.) are most important for low-dollar-value, frequently purchased products. While there may be an analogy in the more routine aspects of industrial purchasing, these are certainly not the most interesting aspects of buying in industrial markets. As a result, the transferability of these research findings has been very limited.

NEEDED: INFORMATION AND ANALYSIS

It is important to note that scholars don't "invent" knowledge. They can do little in the absence of good data. Given the data, gathered according to appropriate procedures, they can apply their conceptual knowledge and analytical techniques to produce new insights into the phenomena being studied and to move that body of knowledge forward.

In the study of industrial buying behavior, the fundamental problem at the moment seems to be an almost complete lack of objective data. It is in the businessman's and the scholar's best interests to work together to develop a body of data on industrial buying behavior. The businessman has access to the information needed by the scholar. Such cooperation will also assure that the knowledge being pursued by the scholar will have ultimate usefulness for the business community. The manager can also provide important insights into the nature of industrial buying decision making that can be a useful guide in the development of better descriptive theory. The scholar also needs to state his case clearly to his academic colleagues and to create increased acceptance within the academic community for the kind of data required to describe and analyze the behavioral and economic complexities of industrial buying behavior.

While students of industrial buying behavior have certainly not exhausted the possibilities for modifying consumer-oriented theory to fit the peculiarities of industrial buying behavior, my opinion is that a more fruitful approach will be to attempt to develop a reasonably comprehensive and generalizable model of industrial buying behavior (which, I believe, will be a decision process model). This model will serve to integrate research in many areas and to point the direction for studies with a higher probability of contributing to knowledge of industrial buying.

Within the industrial marketing profession we need cooperative efforts between businessmen and academicians to gather together the available information and to push forward the study of industrial buying behavior. A major contribution could result if industrial marketing researchers would make a stronger effort to get their study results published (after suitable lags to protect confidential information, or with disguised data, for example). Given the major contribution which knowledge of industrial buying behavior could make to the planning of market research studies (the "master techniques" mentioned earlier), it doesn't make much sense for the businessman to depend completely upon the scholar to develop this knowledge for him. Furthermore, the marketing scholar cannot operate effectively without the cooperation and stimulation of the interested businessman.

SUMMARY

To summarize, industrial buying behavior has not received the attention it deserves as a potential contributor to efficiency in industrial marketing planning and research. The study of buyer behavior has emphasized a particular aspect of consumer buying—frequently-purchased packaged goods and the resulting theory has very limited usefulness in understanding industrial buying behavior. Both businessmen's attitudes toward research and academician's limited conceptual tool-kit have hindered progress.

Progress will come to the extent that we can develop a better data base on industrial buying behavior. Also needed is a generalizable model of industrial buying behavior that will recognize the variability of buying situations across decisions of varying complexity and among companies and industries. At a minimum, this model should recognize that industrial buying is a decision process involving both individual and organizational processes and that there are multiple roles in the decision making process. An important step in the direction of providing more data could be accomplished if industrial marketing researchers would make available for publication those studies of industrial buying which could pass the tests of the "scientific approach" and would therefore be capable of contributing to the basic knowledge of industrial buying behavior which we are seeking.

PART
THREE

THE PRODUCT

The marketing manager's mission is to manage his firm's marketing mix. This and the following three parts of this book provide additional knowledge bearing on marketing-mix management. This part covers product aspects.

Customers do not purchase products and services, they purchase *solutions* to their consumption problems. Product symbolic dimensions, fashion as a product characteristic, and a product's visual design are probed—and the consumer does place a *value* on these aspects. White, Wasson, and Mertes provide a resourceful discussion on these points.

READING 21

NEW PRODUCT DIFFERENTIATION: PHYSICAL & SYMBOLIC DIMENSIONS*

Irving S. White

In an earlier forum, I discussed the problems of marketing new products in an economy where most, if not all, of the basic physical needs of consumers are more than amply satisfied. I posed the question: How do marketers maintain their competitive position in a world where almost every known utility has been achieved by existing products? The answer I supplied at that time contained a rather stringent emphasis on the understanding of the consumer experience, that is, the cultural and psychological background of consumers, so that marketers could differentiate products along *symbolic* dimensions —by the very values which are relevant in differentiating the consumers themselves. The phrase "psychographic or psychological segmentation" has since come into its own. Few sophisticated marketers are unaware today that the value system of consumers (or "life style") is a critical instrument in the differentiation of new products in the marketplace. "Product values", I have continually stressed, are attributes of products which affect the self-enhancement of consumers and represent a new product's reason for being, and especially its reason for being *different* than other products of the same generic class. The example of two identically designed homes, equal in price, placed in two different ethnic neighborhoods, illustrates simply the function of how a customer value system serves to segment the market along choices that transcend the physical properties of the product. A product must not only satisfy the utilitarian orientation of the consumer but must enhance his sense of how he lives.

Since my early observations and first references to symbolic segmentation,[1] the relationship of product as a clear, physical and symbolic expression of value and product as a means of facilitating consumer segmentation has become even more emphatic as the base of the diffusion process in marketing.

*Reprinted from *Marketing in a Changing World*, Bernard A. Morin, ed. (Chicago, American Marketing Association, 1969), pp. 99–103.
[1] Irving S. White, "The Functions of Advertising In Our Culture," *Journal of Marketing*, July, 1959.

Products must have role-clarity to achieve a position. There can be no question now that *ambiguous* products, that is, products that have fluidity in their function and image, cannot achieve a broad diffusion in the mass market because of the possibility that they might appeal to many consumers in variant ways. In a multi-media electronic age, a product either achieves a *perceptual unity* fairly quickly or it becomes a source of confusion. A beer can no longer appeal both to the working classes because of its "appeal to the old gang", for example, at the same time that it is appealing as a device for party sociability to the upper middle class family. Despite the early attempts to defend ambiguity in brand values of products as a means of broadening the consumer market—and that original University of Chicago study on the images of automobiles remains one of my favorite strawmen—it has become more and more evident that market segmentation is one involving a relatively clear co-relationship between *perceived* product benefits and actual consumer life-style needs which are physical and/or symbolic.[2]

I would like to refine some of my own experiences—and, of course, that of Creative Research Associates—with respect to new products and how they are differentiated so that they become factors in the segmentation of consumers into purchase-prone sectors.

With increased exposure to the full scope of new product marketing, I have tended to develop a healthier respect for the physical realities of new products and for the appreciation of these simple physical dimensions by consumers. When a consumer experiences newness, the novelty of a functional quality cannot be under-emphasized. My psychological antennae are still out for the uncovering of the *deeper* appreciation of the value of the product, but I no longer feel I must use them at all times and particularly not when the explanations for a new product's success are concretely obvious. For example, a new razor blade that lasts three times the life of its predecessor need be only that to its purchaser. An improved physical property has carved out a new segment of those shavers who want longevity in their blades. That seems simple. Must we social scientists persist in pushing for a higher more abstract role of a symbolic "value" in such a new product's success? Is the segmentation of consumers created by a *physical* difference in a new product inferior to a segmentation by a *symbolic* difference in a product?

This very question in the marketing of new products poses a problem in American marketing that is analogous and runs parallel to the controversy now becoming central to theorists and practitioners in psychotherapeutic method.

On the one hand, we have the *behaviorists* in psychology who say that deep generic or historic forces within the individual—that is, the elements of experience which produce deep-rooted symbolic meanings in behavior—are not important in the observation and guidance of human behavior. For these psychologists, only changing of the external here-and-now environment; the concrete changes in specific behaviors and actions—will change the long-

---

[2] Joseph Newman, J. Wiley & Sons, "The Perception of Value in Products", *On Knowing the Consumer*, 1966.

term character of the individual. By concentrating on teaching new physical behaviors, behaviorists report success in their patients, including helping drug addicts kick the habit, converting homosexuals to heterosexuality, even giving psychopaths some elementary conscience, symptoms considered by others to have been incurable. For the symbolic school of "depth" or dynamic psychologists, behavioral change can come only when the deeper symbolism of the aberrant behavior is ferreted out and understood.

That analogy to the problem of achieving effective market segmentation by new products is a critical one if we are to understand the roles of physical and symbolic dimensions in the differentiation by consumers of new products.

The psychologist, or social scientist in general, has contributed an important corrective in pointing out that new product differentiation may derive not only from physical innovations but from consumer experiences or values, the symbolic benefits. I have previously observed that "perhaps 80 per cent of all consumption in America today is a symbolic ritual where the consumer is gratified not in any utilitarian fashion but in the transcendent expression of a value-system."[3]

This is still true today, but we pose a new problem. Must the consumer *experience* the symbolic value of a new product, and is not the experience by consumers of a new—or different—*physical* dimension in products enough to help him differentiate it from others along lines of benefit to him *without* having to consciously attach "higher" values to the new product?

As in the general controversy among psychologists, we are asking if it is necessary for the consumer to know and understand the symbolic values in order to act upon the perception of concrete stimuli in a product. If not, why must advertisers bother with the creation of elaborate creative methods for the communication of symbolic differences? Why then don't we tell our R&D personnel to establish "product differences" in the laboratory which present even minute product advantages in a most concrete way?

The fact of new product differentiation is that both a physical difference or a symbolic difference can produce a consumer response. The consumer market may indeed be organized along the lines of

a. *physical benefit segmentation*—those to whom specific product advantages represent the critical difference for purchase, and

b. psychological, or *symbolic segmentation*—those to whom a new life-style value, usually made explicit in the communications surrounding the physical product, represent the critical difference for purchase. (We will defer a third model for later discussion.)

Examples of the first—physical benefit segmentation—are numerous: the filter tip cigarette which traps more tar, appealing to the tar-conscious consumer, the photocopy machine that turns out copies in three-quarters the time of its closest competitor, appealing to the efficient consumers, the power-

[3] Irving S. White, "Marketing in an Economy of Abundance", *Food Product Development*, February–March, 1968.

ful sensory impact of a new toothpaste, appealing to those who want a fresh feeling in mouth. All of these physical dimensions are capable of yielding consumers segments which convert such product differences into purchase acts without their conscious translation into life-style or self-expressive *symbolic* benefits. Examples of the second—*symbolic benefit segmentation*—are also numerous: The youthful, energetic spirit of the Continental Airlines image differentiates its passengers sharply from the passengers attracted to the conservative affluent image of TWA. Winston cigarettes differ in their symbolic appeal from Marlboro cigarettes; Time magazine differs from Newsweek. None of the above mentioned products have symbolic benefits which are *obvious* correlates of actual product-rooted benefits. Yet, here too, we clearly find divisions among consumers who point to differences *they* perceive in the products. These consumers belong to a "symbolic benefit segment" because they are essentially aware—at least marginally—of the role of symbolic value in their choice of the product. Ask the woman shopping at Saks Fifth Avenue or Bergdorf Goodman if she would prefer "an identical coat" with a Macy label for less money. Her refusal would illustrate clearly the meaning of *symbolic segmentation.*

CRA's ten years' work on this problem suggests that each of the two types of consumer segments do not necessarily consist of the same consumers across the board of all product categories. For example, the cigarette smoker who happens to be "symbol prone" in his discrimination among cigarettes may differentiate products on the basis of purely physical benefits in other product categories, as in a choice to buy Campbell's instead of Heinz's vegetable soup because it is less spicy, let us say. Thus, we can only loosely talk about *consumers* as "symbolic benefit prone" or "physical benefit prone", because we are aware that the same consumer may differ in his benefit criteria from one product category to another. Yet, we may indeed talk about products as having symbolic and/or physical benefits affecting correlate segments which perceive these differences.

Having made an initial distinction between symbolic benefit segmentation and physical benefit segmentation, it now falls on our shoulders to indicate the practical implications for the differentiation and diffusion of *new products inherent in this scheme.*

If we can create a new product diffusion model which categorizes products as optionally capable of benefit segmentation through the agency of *perceived physical values, perceived symbolic values,* or a mixture of both values, we will have contributed at least some practical understanding of the development and communication of new products.

The following applied observations are offered here not as a closed-end system, but as an example of the frame-of-reference that each new product marketer must generate for himself and to his satisfaction if he is to follow through with consistency in his development program. Cultural differences, changes over time in technology, and intra-psychic fluidity—that is, consumers who act with one personality-system in one product area and as another personality-system in another product category—all these fluctuating variables, serve to make an across-the-board theoretical benefit model difficult if not impossible.

We'll now take a crack at an applied system of product benefit differentiation: Let us determine whether we can develop a scheme for new products which may be *categorized* by the character or quality of the *benefit value* that should ideally be perceived by consumers if they are to be effectively segmented into purchase sectors or sub-markets. What product-types are best diffused through an emphasis on *physical benefit* differentiation, and what product-types are best diffused through an emphasis on *symbolic benefit* differentiation? Moreover, what product conditions would *demand* an explicit co-participation of physical with symbolic benefits—that is, a perceived relationship between the two—if effective differentiation is to be made by consumers?

It is at this point that we must introduce a theoretical distinction between two product roles in the lines of consumers, a distinction which is valid only to the extent that life can be separated into dichotomous zones such as "rational" and "irrational", "self" and "other", "utility" and "luxury", and so on. There *is* some practicality, however, in compartmentalizing for *emphasis* purposes in understanding new product development and communication so that the marketer and advertising man may have a clear vantage point for relating to their target markets.

The initial distinction that we may make is between "*expressive* products" and "*utility* products". Expressive products are those whose very use constitutes an *act* of identification for the consumer—that is, each product purchase and/or use constitutes a public or private communication to both self and community of the *individuality* of the consumer. These are the products which say, "I *am* the consumer" or where the consumer says, "I am the product." We shall provide examples shortly. "Utility products" are those which are primarily to be *used* (often literally "consumed") with a minimum ancillary communication—publicly or privately—about one's individuality. One might say that "expressive products" tend to be defined and treated in our culture as *personalities or character-traits* while "utility products" tend to be treated as *things*.

A list of "expressive products" would include such items as: cigarettes, cosmetics, furniture, clothing, art, automobiles, beer and whiskies, and numerous special-taste foods from desserts to gourmet entrees.

A list of "utility products" would include such items as: breads, milk, seasonings of a conventional type, canned foods, and most inexpensive products which are often capable of being sold with an unknown in-house store brand.

This dichotomy is often elusive and difficult to make, and the marketer must provide his own emphasis in definition. It is true that a manufacturer of salt may want to believe that *his* salt is indeed a "self-expressive" purchase of unique import to the consumer, or conversely, a cosmetic manufacturer may want to sell an unbranded line of eye make-up on the assumption that "it's all the same" to the lady and why not pass on the money saved on brand advertising to the consumer? Of course, these inversions cited here are extreme cases; yet we must realize that the product dichotomy suggested is a judgmental one, involving *emphasis* rather than total distinction. It offers us a working scheme for blueprinting a marketing program that strives for consumer segmentation through the anticipated use of *physical benefits* of sym-

bolic benefits as the emphasis in effecting product differentiation and ultimately consumer segmentation.

Thus, two axioms in new product marketing may be stated as follows:

*In the diffusion of "self-expressive" new products, emphasis should be
made in communication on the symbolic dimensions of value which are
to be attached to the over-all brand or uniquely to the product itself, even
if there are specific physical product advantages available.*
*Conversely in the diffusion of new "utility products", it is evident that
differentiation must be made on the basis of an emphasis on physical benefits, including cost, even if symbolic benefits may be meaningfully made.*

In the first case, the diffusion of "self-expressive" products, the success
stories of those products that have emphasized symbolic benefit perception
are too numerous to detail. They must include "Marlboro", Colombian coffee,
Coca-Cola, and many others.

On the other side, the "utility products" that have successfully segmented
their consumers on the basis of *physical benefit* perception are equally abundant. They must include most of the successful detergents which have stressed
new ingredients, the new packaging of Morton's salt, the improved razor
blades and shaving equipment, and numerous others.

However, any thoughtful examination of the previous axiom of new product
differentiation must raise at least two questions: First, how does the marketer
know how to classify those products that appear to fall into a vast hinterland
between "utility" and "self-expression"? Second, how *much* emphasis should
be made on one type of benefit over another, *even* when a marketer has presumably clarified the role of his product as being *primarily utilitarian* or *primarily symbolic* in its potential advantage over competitors?

In asking these questions—which may be the most critical questions in the
problem of physical versus symbolic dimensions of benefit—I reveal the
psychologists' true aversion to dichotomies and to atomized systems. I also
reveal the role of devil's advocate in suggesting that the attributes of new
products may be easily separated into physical and symbolic ones, into body
values and soul values.

The answer to these questions lies in a *third model* of differentiation which
is perhaps the most realistic, the most deep-rooted from the point of view of
the consumer's capacity to discriminate among product cues, and the most
creatively challenging from the marketer's point-of-view. This third model
—or set of axioms—is indicated when several conditions exist:

1. When an "expensive" product category has diffused into a homogeneous
image so that the consumer's ability to discriminate basic *physical benefits*
among the available products has become impaired. Examples of this condition are many. Here are a few:

    a. When many cigarette brands attempted to differentiate themselves
positively through a "filter trap" derby concerning which brands trap more
tar.
    b. When compact cars attempted differentiation through a stress on greater
degrees of economy or efficiency.

c. When hairspray brands tried to be superior through a claim of more holding power or "body".

All of the above expressive products failed to enable the consumer to differentiate on the basis of the physical attributes of the competitive products.

2. When a "utility" product category has diffused into a homogeneous image so that the consumer's ability to discriminate basic *symbolic benefits* among the available products has become impaired. Examples of this type of diffusion are many. Here are a few:
   a. When the margarine brands each appealed to the "smart housewife" as the "can't-tell-the-difference butter substitute"
   b. When all toothpastes attempted differentiation through a promise to *produce* "winning smiles"
   c. When detergents concentrated on a promise of "magic whiteness in a flash"

The above examples indicate how consumers seeking basic differentiation in a utility product category find it difficult to discriminate on the basis of the promised *symbolic benefits*.

3. When a product category is *ambiguous* in its essential benefit: Is it a "utility product" or an "expressive product"? For instance, the question: "Is it differentiated primarily by physical benefit or by symbolic benefit?" cannot be answered with assurance by the marketer (or when the marketer does not *want* to dichotomize in this fashion). Examples of this market condition are many and include many cases among the products cited earlier. For example, facial and bath soap, facial tissues, feminine hygienic products, ballpoint pens, and others, are notoriously difficult to dichotomize into "expressive" and "utility" products. In most of these cases, an argument can be made for stressing either physical benefit segmentation or symbolic benefit segmentation in the market-place.

Where the above perceptual conditions exist, the objective for the marketer is to achieve *out of both sets of benefits dimensions a clear, differentiated, and integrated image for his product.* To do this, the *manufacturer* and *communicator* functions must become carefully inter-related so that a co-participation of *physical* with *symbolic* benefits are perceived by the consumer. This is the third model of benefit segmentation, where the so-called product advantage is related to the social or psychological value of the consumer, where physicality is *attached* to *identity*.

When co-participation of benefits—*or gestalt benefit perception*—happens in a product category where previously homogeneity has reigned, chances have increased for effective product differentiation. The breakthrough of "Virginia Slims"—the integrated dimensions of delicateness and length with femininity—is one example of benefit co-participation. The introduction of a European beer for sophisticated drinkers highlighted by a new bottle design is another. The introduction of a line for "weight watchers" for those people who symbolically want to be in better control of their bodies and lives with each product packaged uniquely and in special forms is another. The innovation of "bucket seats" in compact, economy cars coupled with an appeal to less affluent sporty types, namely, the young and the white collar workers, is yet another example of breaking through the barrier of perceptual homogeneity with a co-participating set of benefits.

Let us now summarize our applied program to aid in the innovation and differentiation of products using the scheme of expressive products (or symbolic benefit segmentation) and utility products (or physical benefit segmentation): Three new product differentiation models have been cited. They are:

1. Where *physical benefit* is stressed in the innovation of *utility* products. We shall call this "PB" segmentation.
2. Where *symbolic benefit* is stressed in the innovation of *expressive* products. We shall call this "SB" segmentation.
3. Where *symbolic benefit relates to, or participates equally with, physical benefit* in the innovation of products in the product categories which:
   a. are ambiguous in their benefit role
   b. have been homogeneous in their competitive presentation: We shall call this "S-PB" segmentation.

In the final analysis, it is the contention of this researcher that while the first two new product differentiating models may lead to a reasonably effective segmentation, the long term effect will be a fragmented or partial segment, appealing to those special consumers who are either uniquely "symbol benefit prone" in a given category, or uniquely "product benefit prone" in a given category. Such segmentation may prove to be less stable and more fragmentary than one where the product is innovated on the *basis* of a *total* or *gestalt* differentiation, produced by a co-participation of physical and symbolic benefits. Time and complexity preclude a comprehensive "how-to-do-it" kit for marketers and advertisers. I ask forgiveness for merely provoking rather than delving into solutions. If I merely have raised a few questions, I would consider this paper to have been productive.

Finally, I would like to summarize my modified position about new product diffusion and consumer segmentation—a position that was perhaps more extremely "psychological" up to recently, but which now re-synthesizes the symbolic with the physical values in products:

The proper generation of new products and reformulation of old products must begin with an awareness of the values in the consumer society. The product which is successful is that which has an underlying "concept" directing it to a segment of the market which seeks the expression of that value. To uncover important values which are not currently expressed by products often represents as much of an innovation for a company as the development of a laboratory method for making a product less expensively or for adding new features.

It must be said that a product's acceptability can be best enhanced by the integration of symbolic values with product traits. Thus, Product X can be fully experienced by consumers only if they are *oriented* toward experiencing the physical values inherent in the product. A product without a symbolic concept is like selling a house in terms of its rooms and footage without reference to the community in which it is found.

This is a country rich in its variety and abundance of experience, replete with regional and class differences, made up of numerous ethnic, occupational, and social groupings. No single product can appeal to all Americans, and similarly no singular product quality can build a market. What industry must do is to go out and observe, through its social scientifically oriented marketers, the various life-styles and their associated values and to "attach" these values to related concrete product improvements.

READING 22

HOW PREDICTABLE ARE FASHION AND OTHER PRODUCT LIFE CYCLES?*

Chester R. Wasson

No aspect of marketing is so uncertain as the acceptance of new products, particularly those with a fashion element. Yet product introduction and fashion itself are such basic necessities for continued success that the gamble must be taken repeatedly. Clearly, a sound means of forecasting the onset of any popularity wave is needed, of predicting its course, and of recognizing the earliest symptoms of a forthcoming decline. Market planning needs a fundamental explanatory theory of the fashion cycle which would explain the clearly observable, ceaseless fluctuations and their subsequent course. The explanation can be sound only if based on known tendencies of human behavior and on the way human motives, both innate and socially conditioned, cause people to react to the kind of stimulus called a new product. To be useful the theory also must indicate at the minimum the general direction of the next fluctuation and detect the timing of at least the first signs of a new swing.

The thesis of this paper is that already a suitable framework exists for such a theory. It can be drawn from the documented results of product acceptance research when interpreted in the light of human reaction to product offerings and the social psychology of perception and motivation. Furthermore, the theory is at least testable for some kinds of products and corresponds with the results of some proprietary research, unfortunately not published. If valid, this theory is the direct antithesis of the popular myth of "created" fashion.

THE MYTH OF CREATED FASHION

That fashion is a synthetic creation of the seller is an idea so entrenched that even marketing professionals are often blind to the observably low batting

*Reprinted from *The Journal of Marketing*, published by the American Marketing Association, vol. 32, no. 3, July, 1968, pp. 36–43.

average of those who attempt such "creation." Even within the area of women's apparel, the fact most obvious to those who follow the news of new offerings is the diversity of their direction and the large numbers of "dictated" designs which fall by the wayside after every Paris showing. However, fashion is not limited to women's apparel, nor confined to matters of commercial exploitation.

There are fashions in politics and in business decision methods as marked as the documented cycles in styles of clothing and architecture.[1] A colleague once demonstrated similar cycles in religious interest in a study of church publications, and followers of the stock market are aware of the constantly changing identity of the "glamor" stocks. Whether on the dance floor, in the dress shop, or in the business conference room, the "in" thing changes with the calendar.

No seller can afford to ignore the state of the fashion cycle. Chrysler's misreading of the trend in taste caused real trouble for the firm on at least three occasions: with the 1934 Airflow Chrysler and DeSoto, with the unpopular early 1950s designs, and with the "lean look" models of 1962. Ford's later correct reading of the trend gave the firm the well-publicized triumph of the Mustang introduction. In fact, even a superficial knowledge of the successes and failures of design introduction which dot the history of every major auto maker should long ago have convinced everyone that human behavior is not subject to the easy manipulation assumed by the created-fashions myth. The acceptance of a fashion is but one aspect of the process of new product acceptance and rests on the same principles of individual and social behavior.

FASHION, PRODUCT ACCEPTANCE, AND HUMAN BEHAVIOR

Both fashions and fads are, of course, successful new product introductions. The distinction between the two is generally defined on an *ex post facto* basis —on the nature of their acceptance cycle. Fashions are generally thought to have an initially slower rise to popularity, a plateau of continuing popularity lacking in most fads, and a slow, rather than abrupt decline typical of the fad. (See Figures 1A and 1B). The acceptance cycle of a fashion is thus considered the same as the accepted theoretical course of the normal product life cycle (Figure 1A). Such an empirical after-the-fact basis for distinction, however, deprives any theory of most of its potential utility. It cannot be used for rational market planning. To be useful the theory must distinguish fads from other new products *in advance* on the basis of measurable product attributes, which explain why a market development period might be unnecessary and why acceptance disappears at the very peak of the market. If such an explanation is possible, it should be possible to identify and predict in advance another class of products: a class which requires little or nothing in the way of early market development, but rises in an active growth market from the moment of introduction and then remains popular for long periods. (See Figure 1C). Those who have observed any fashion-oriented market will also recognize

[1] Chester R. Wasson, *The Strategy of Marketing Research* (New York: Appleton-Century-Crofts, 1964), pp. 67–77.

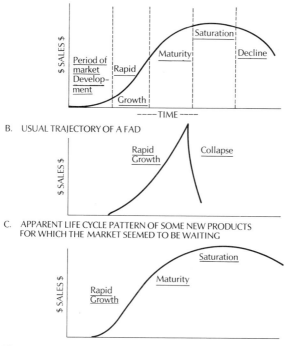

A. THE THEORETICAL NORMAL LIFE CYCLE OF A FASHION
OR OTHER NEW PRODUCT

B. USUAL TRAJECTORY OF A FAD

C. APPARENT LIFE CYCLE PATTERN OF SOME NEW PRODUCTS
FOR WHICH THE MARKET SEEMED TO BE WAITING

Figure 1

Three types of product life cycles

the need to explain another related phenomenon with the same theory—the *classic*—the style which is never out of style for its market segment and is rarely the "rage."

To be really useful for product planning, a product acceptance theory should be based on known tendencies of individual and social behavior and encompass in a single model an explanation of:

1. Why and how any new product gains acceptance, and why about half of the seemingly well-screened and well-researched products fail.[2]

2. Why some products must pass through a slowly accelerating period of market development of some length before sales catch fire whereas others zoom to early popularity from the start.

3. Why some products succeed in attainment of a relatively solid niche in the culture, why the popularity of others tends to fluctuate, and why the popularity of fads collapses at their very sales peak.

4. How and why classics exist in a fashion environment.

---

[2] *Management of New Products* (Chicago: Booz, Allen & Hamilton, 1960).

The behavioral basis for such an explanation starts with the managerial economics view of a product as a compromise bundle of attributes perceived by buyers as an inseparable set of sources of satisfaction and also of some off-setting dissatisfactions for times for a set of desires.[3] To gain the satisfactions, the buyer must pay some price—he must sacrifice some measure of time, money, and/or effort. Whether he moves toward possession of this offering depends on his personal evaluation of the net gain in satisfaction its possession will bring.

Expressed in these terms, an operant psychologist would recognize the purchase as an *approach-avoidance* reaction. Satisfactions sought cause the buyer to approach the offering and seek its possession. The offering, however, includes a repelling force—the avoidance factors of the various prices exacted to obtain those satisfactions. Part of the price is monetary, part is search effort, and an important part can be the compromise enforced by the nature of product design—the denial of satisfaction for some of the elements in the desire-set whose appeasement is sought.

Product compromise and the hierarchy of motives

The buyer usually seeks the simultaneous satisfaction of a set of several motivating desires in making a purchase. In practice, the product offering can seldom satisfy all at the same time and must strike some compromise in the kind and degree of satisfactions offered. Any offering will thus satisfy some buyers well, others partially; and some, perhaps not all, may even yield negative satisfaction for still others. The dress may be bought for physical warmth, figure enhancement, and freedom from restriction at the same time—attributes which cannot be equally well satisfied in the same design. The successful physician may long for the qualities of a prestige car but desire something sufficiently inconspicuous to avoid offending patients at billing time. Thus, the buyer must normally compromise between the ideal set of satisfactions sought and the reality of product design potentials. Nearly every purchase involves some compromise. This is evidenced by the fact that few, if any, products are immune to the inroads of differentiated offerings. Motivational compromise holds the key to an understanding of fashion oscillation when viewed as an extension of the knowledge of the hierarchical nature of motives and their dynamic character.

The intensity of any one desire varies over time within an individual, and, at any given moment, some motives gain priority over others. Even such basic motives as hunger and appetite dominate only until satisfied. As the meal is consumed, the drive to eat is extinguished and some other drive assumes top priority. This second drive was already inherently present before the meal but was not evoked until the hunger was appeased. The hierarchical nature of the

[3]Edward H. Chamberlin, *Theory of Monopolistic Competition*, 8th edition (Cambridge, Mass.: Harvard University Press, 1962), Appendix F, pp. 275–281; Chester R. Wasson, *The Economics of Managerial Decision* (New York: Appleton-Century-Crofts, 1965), pp. 55–87; and Chester R. Wasson, Frederick D. Sturdivant, and David McConaughy, *Competition and Human Behavior* (New York: Appleton-Century-Crofts, 1968), pp. 4–25.

motivating drives has long been recognized.[4] Individuals respond most actively to those stimuli that promise satisfaction of those most highly valued drives which are at the moment least well satisfied and at the same time felt to be important. Every satisfactory purchase thus becomes in time the initiator of a search for a somewhat different offering to satisfy newly felt drives. Thus, this continual restructuring of the motivational hierarchy gives the basis for a model explaining fashion oscillation and furnishes a framework for prediction of its new direction:

The popularity of design attributes in a given utility-bundle will oscillate because no one design can encompass in full measure all of the attributes in the desire-set. The oscillation will tend to be polar, swinging from one extreme to the opposite, because the satisfaction-yield span of any one design will extinguish the very drives which led to its adoption and bring to the fore those drives least well fulfilled by the design.

Consider the example of the automobile design problem (Figure 2) and the oscillations of popular approval between the large and massive and the compact, relatively economical. The 1955 designs fulfilled all of the drives associated with massive appearance and power. In developing these designs, the automobile industry had to leave some other drives less well satisfied—for example, low cost of ownership and maintenance and such ease-of-use aspects as parking and roadability. Once most drivers had acquired the highly ornamented mammoths they desired, attention began to focus on the drivers whose satisfaction had been neglected, and size became an avoidance factor for many. Buyers became attracted by models offering high gasoline mileage, low physical and temporal depreciation, and ease of parking and handling. The sales of foreign makes which offered such attributes in abundance began a climb, and slowed down only when Detroit developed its own compacts in 1960. But the fickle customer, having a free choice of offerings giving most of what he desired, began to yearn again for the attributes associated with size, and the cycle restarted. By 1965, he was buying "compact" models almost as large as the 1955 "big" cars.

However, the composition of the desire-set varies so much from one person to another that the explanation needs one further element to account for the completeness of most new-fashion adoption and the rapidity of its spread. That element is furnished by that human drive for social approval—the desire to be "in the swim." The result is an almost universal tendency toward overadoption. Overadoption is painfully apparent with every extreme swing in the feminine fashion silhouette—the bandy-legged adopted mini-skirts which could only reveal physical deficiencies of the wearer. Overadoption became quite obvious in business management when organizations replaced an effective $300-a-month clerk with a $3,000-per-month computer which often did the clerk's job less efficiently. Overadoption has been documented in the studies of rural sociologists who found farmers adopting machinery which

[4]A. H. Maslow, "A Dynamic Theory of Human Motivation," *Psychological Review*, Vol. 50 (March, 1963), pp. 370–396.

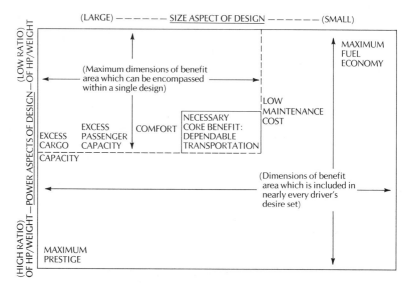
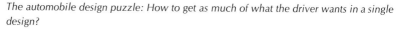

Figure 2

The automobile design puzzle: How to get as much of what the driver wants in a single design?

was uneconomic for their scale of operation.[5] The desire for social approval thus speeds adoption, but at the price of leading many to overadoption—to adoption of offerings which do not satisfy their desires well. The result is a considerable market segment which quickly develops an avoidance reaction to the fashion and triggers a decline from the peak.

The three principles of product acceptance—inherent purchase compromise, the changing hierarchy of motivation, and the tendency toward overadoption—furnish a necessary and sufficient explanation of the swings of fashion. However, they leave unexplained the existence of the classic—the style whose changes are minimal, but which remains always in the range of the acceptable. No theory of fashion can be adequate which omits an explanation of the classic and its appeal to a minority market which does not conform to major swings of fashion.

THE CLASSIC

The changeless, always acceptable classic is found in every recognized area of fashion. A woman can always feel comfortable in a tailored suit with a skirt line close to the knees. In automobiles, designs similar to the postwar Loewy-designed Studebaker still find a ready market around the world. The values placed by buyers on some security issues respond little to the gyrations of the bulk of those listed on the Big Board. Beige and off-white colors always sell well in automobiles and house paints. Such classics occasionally become the reigning fashion, but seldom are they "the rage."

[5] Everett Rogers, *The Diffusion of Innovations* (New York: The Free Press, 1962), pp. 142–145.

What makes a classic? Observation seems to indicate that all classics are midpoint compromises and their buyers either have a special kind of personality or are prospects seeking only a few of the core attributes in the bundle for sale. The classic automobile design is neither starkly spartan nor highly ornamented; it is roomy but not gargantuan. The classic color is not found in the "hot" red end of the spectrum nor at the icy blue extreme; it is moderately pleasing but not conspicuous. The classic gives some measure of satisfaction to nearly all of the desire-set of drives, and probably does so at the expense of complete satisfaction of any drives except those at the core of product's physical functions. The classic buyer, then, has to be a person seeking only the core function attributes (such as convenient transportation in a Volkswagen) or one who recognizes that compromise is necessary in any case and who has chosen a compromise least likely to develop over time. He most certainly must be an individual who does not value highly the satisfaction of the drive for new experience. Such a consumer is a poor prospect for any fad, but may well be an excellent early-market customer for innovations of major functional import which others would be slow to accept, since he feels little need for complete conformity. If so, he is important in the early adoption of those products which are slow to catch on at first. Certainly, the differences in the speed of acceptance of various kinds of offerings is one of the most obvious puzzles of new product introduction which must be explained.

DIFFERENCES IN THE EARLY ACCEPTANCE PATTERN AND THEIR EXPLANATION

As already indicated, some products follow the standard conceptual curve of the product life cycle, but others, particularly fads, leap-frog the early market development phase of this curve with a rocket-like ascent to popularity. Clearly, the marketing mix must differ with the kind of sales acceleration likely to be experienced. Also, different levels of resource commitment are needed for the product which undergoes an extended period of slowly developing sales and those which attain their market potential early. When black-and-white television became a commercial reality, even fly-by-night electronic firms could get a profitable market share, and those who knew how to build on their early success could and did carve out a permanent market niche. Waiting out the ten long years until color television sales hit the growth phase, however, required the resources of an RCA.

A great many pairs of seeming anomalies can be cited from every kind of marketing operation. Soluble coffee existed for over a generation before World War II; and even when wartime developments brought its price down, six years were needed to develop the market potential. Frozen orange juice, another wartime beneficiary, rose from scratch to peak market in three years, as fast as facilities could be developed. The astonishing benefits of hybrid corn yields were not sufficient to get more than 6% of the farmers interested during the first six years on the market, although little else is planted today. However, another farm improvement—2-4-D and related insecticides were so avidly sought by farmers upon their release after the war that they became a real threat to health. Some textbooks take years to gain acceptance of the approach championed, yet Samuelson's *Economics* rose to quick dominance of the elementary course in colleges.

The anomaly disappears when we examine the value an adopter perceives in any product new or otherwise. To the purchaser, a product is only one element in the use-system which is the real source of the satisfaction of the desire-set. Products deliver their potential satisfactions only in the context of some established set of procedural habits organized around their use. Seed corn yields the sought-after crop only when procured, planted, cultivated, harvested and stored in a carefully planned and well-learned system of habitual practices. Television yields entertainment only when manipulated and viewed in another set of habit patterns.

The development of most habit patterns is a painful—or at least annoying —process for most of us. The extinction of one habit system leading to a satisfactory result and its replacement of another is even more so, as anyone who has gone from a three-speed manual automobile shift to a four-speed can testify. The degree to which a product offering involves habit pattern relearning will thus slow down its adoption. Conversely, innovative products which can simply replace old ones using the same set of procedures, or the same set simplified, should gain ready acceptance.

Good examples of products fitting neatly into existing procedures are the new insecticides, black-and-white television, and frozen orange juice. The new insecticides were applied by the same spray methods, with a similar timing, as the ones they displaced. They simply delivered a noticeably higher level of satisfaction—greater kill over a broader spectrum of pests. Black-and-white television entertained in the same way the movies did, by sitting and viewing a picture, but it avoided many nuisance steps—additional cost for every show, problems of travel, parking and getting tickets, and finding a desired seat position. Black-and-white television, too, simply delivered more value in the same system. (Eventually, of course, adoption of TV changed family living patterns. But such pattern changes were not a pre-condition for adoption.) Frozen orange juice fitted into kitchens long used to canned goods; the fact that it was frozen fitted into established perceptions of frozen foods being the equivalents of fresh ones. These products required no substantial learning of new habits or relearning of old. By contrast, hybrid seed corn, color television, and instant coffee all involved learning of some sort.

Any new offering can pose the problem of one or more of three kinds of learning:

1. Learning of a new sequence of motor habits (as in changing over from a three-speed shift to a four-speed, or from a wringer to an automatic washer);

2. Learning to perceive new benefits as valuable and thus worth paying for (as in learning to appreciate the cornering qualities offered by the small sports car);

3. Learning to perceive one's role in the use of the product as of less importance (as in the acceptance of an automatic transmission).

The acceptance of the use of hybrid seed required the learning of both a new sequential element and of the perception of relative value. Before its adoption, the farmer usually saved some of the better quality of the previous year's crop and replanted it. The use of hybrid seed meant the complete disposal of the crop and the repurchase of seed each year. (The farm journals of the period ran many an article warning farmers not to replant seed from hybrid crops.) Moreover, the seed he bought cost several times as much per bushel as the farmer received for the crop he sold. This resulted in a real value-perception problem.

The acceptance of color television in 1955 required no change in motor or other use-habits, but did involve a substantial change in value perception. It required seeing that the mere addition of color to the picture was worth hundreds of dollars—at a time when Technicolor movies had never achieved use in more than a minority of films. Color also deprived the viewer of the satisfaction of closure—the supplying of missing details himself. Psychologically, successful closure heightened the satisfaction gained, and has probably always been an element of successful entertainment. The double-meaning joke gets its whole point from the use of closure.

Soluble coffee certainly simplified the brewing process and required little in the way of motor learning. Once wartime experience had reduced its cost, any problem disappeared. But soluble coffee downgraded the homemaker's role; it required her to see her role in relation to mealmaking as less important. Coffee brewing is susceptible to individual skill, and many housewives pride themselves on their coffee. Acceptance of soluble coffee required admission that the housewife's kitchen role was less vital to family happiness than it had been. Is it any coincidence that the use of soluble increased with the growing acceptance of the housewife as a major contributor to the family's *outside* income?

The overnight successes of radically new products like Samuelson's *Economics* are explainable as examples of products filling a missing link in an already developed system. They are products for which the market has been waiting. Economists began to pay increasing attention to the macro aspect of economic theory in the early 1930s. By 1946, when Samuelson's first edition was published, many economists were orienting their courses entirely in this direction. Since no satisfactory texts were available, a well-done text, as Samuelson's was, could hardly help but succeed. Rubber tractor tires provide a similar example. Mechanized farming became well established on the better-managed farms, but the steel-tired tractors compacted the soil, could not be run over paved roads, and did not always furnish the desired traction. Once a satisfactory tire was developed, the steel-wheeled tractor disappeared overnight. The supermarket was also a missing link in a developing food shopping and storing system. The automobile had widened the shopping range of the family; the need to park it called for a single stop. In addition, ownership of mechanical refrigerators was wide enough to eliminate the daily shopping trip. All that was needed was the foresight of a few independent entrepreneurs. Even though such missing link products do require learning of elements not required by the products they displace, the learning process is complete by the time of their introduction.

The rate of early-adoption acceleration is thus seen as contingent on the degree of learning required to accept and properly use any new offering. Both learning-content and attribute-compromise analyses are feasible, rendering the proposed model of product adoption speed and of fashion fluctuation subject to test and confirmation.

THE EVIDENCE OF TESTABILITY

A model is valid if it has utility for prediction. The main recommendation for the proposed model is its testability—parts of it rather easily—and the fact that it is in harmony with some known successful proprietary unpublished private research predictions. Three kinds of evidence as to its validity can be cited:

1. Such known proprietary research clearly demonstrates that taste and fashion are predictable ahead of promotion and sales, and even in advance of design, on the basis of analysis of consumer reaction.

2. It is possible to cite at least a few examples of situations in which a simple learning-content analysis would have greatly improved otherwise extensive research on product acceptance.

3. Some limited observation and research has proved successful in prediction of a fashion cycle.

Sensing the trend in taste ahead of introduction

A sizable body of proprietary research has established the fact that rather simple, carefully administered checks of consumer reaction can reveal in advance which of an equally-promoted group of designs will succeed and which will fail. Dilman M. K. Smith[6] has sketched some of the results of successful Opinion Research studies in this area, some going back over three decades. The author of this article himself was able to develop a very simple ahead-of-the-season measure of relative demand in a line of dresses over 20 years ago —a test still in routine use by the employer for whom he developed it. A research director for a maker of permanent waves was able to alert his firm to a change in hair style tastes months before the change began to show up in beauty parlors and thus permitted a successful effort to buttress the firm's market position. Even more relevant was an unpublished Opinion Research triumph: the development of a new, instantly successful rug weave based on a revelation of an unsatisfactory consumer compromise. When research showed that housewives liked the texture of velvet rugs but were repelled by such a weave's tendency to show tracks, the firm advised a client to find a velvet weave which was trackless. After considerable prodding, designers came up with the sculptured wilton, which took off on a typical fast growth curve when introduced.

Unfortunately, understanding of consumer product acceptance has not

---

[6] Dilman M. K. Smith, *How to Avoid Mistakes When Introducing New Products* (New York: Vantage Press, 1964).

gained much from this private research, since only fragments of a minor part could land in footnotable publications. The rest remains hidden in the files of those who pay for it and confined to conversations among a few research analysts. Confirmation of the learning content aspect of the proposed model, fortunately, does not always require access to any confidential data.

Learning content and prediction

The author has shown at length[7] elsewhere that use-systems learning requirements can be determined easily by means of simple comparison of flow diagrams—one diagram for the current means of obtaining the satisfaction desired and one for the system which would be the setting for use of the new product. Such a comparison quickly reveals both the advantages and the avoidance factors involved in adoption of the new. One need read only the preparation instructions on a pouch of dehydrated soup to discover why this thoroughly-researched product was a market failure which cost Campbell's alone some $10,000,000 in unsuccessful promotion,[8] according to news stories. The flow diagrams reveal a tremendous time-and-effort price disadvantage for the dehydrated product relative to the canned concentrate. It should have been clear that the housewife would not pay such a price for the kinds of satisfactions expected from soup in the American diet pattern. It may well be much of the failure of carefully investigated new products traces to the failure to investigate the learning-content requirements and the preparation-time price.

Perceptual-learning and value-learning requirements do not yield to as simple an analytical device as the flow chart, of course, but they are certainly possible to discover with currently available research techniques. And this singular aspect of the proposed model is manifestly testable against past history. Prediction of fashion oscillations is not so clearly testable against the past.

Checking fashion oscillation predictability

Almost any hypothetical model must start with some classification and observation of past experience. But any model involving as many complex factors as the one proposed for fashion oscillation cannot be safely checked against history alone. This is true particularly when few observations from that past contain any substantial evidence of the psychological motives that buyers hope to appease with their adoptions. Most such observations have to be limited to studies in the fluctuations among physically measurable attributes which may or may not be the relevant items involved. The result can be a number of plausible but different explanations, each of which can be rationalized as fitting if the classifications and other data are carefully chosen. An acceptable theory must give more than a plausible explanation of past events:

[7]Chester R. Wasson, Frederick D. Sturdivant, and David McConaughy, *Competition and Human Behavior* (New York: Appleton-Century-Crofts, 1968), pp. 83–91.
[8]"Campbell's Drops Red Kettle Line," *Advertising Age* (August 29, 1966), p. 3.

it must have pragmatic validity, be capable of predicting the future in some meaningful manner.

In this respect, the author can cite only a single documented successful prediction although he has attempted several others, unpublished, which have borne or are bearing fruit. As noted earlier, the author, writing in 1961 (for publication in 1964), traced the history of the swings in research fashion and noted that the current wave was at the peak of the recurrent mathematical emphasis. A swing to behavioral models and techniques was predicted. At the time of the analysis, the *Business Periodicals Index*[9] listed only two articles under "Innovation," neither of them in marketing journals and neither of them on research into the process. Concurrently, one of the marketing publications turned down Lionberger's *Adoption of New Ideas and Practices* as "not germane to the interests of" its readers. By 1965, both the Detroit and New York chapters of the AMA were holding New Products conferences, and "diffusion theory" is now the current shibboleth.

One such prediction success, or any number of them, does not constitute the final test of validity, however. A sound theory in any field must dig beneath any coincidence between its predictions and subsequent events to explain why the events can be expected to occur in the manner observed. A sound theory must have construct validity, be based on behavioral constructs which themselves are capable of test and confirmation or modification. The theory offered above is just such a theory. It is possible to test it pragmatically —to make predictions as to the next direction of a fashion swing or as to the speed of adoption of a projected new product and then to observe the objective events. But this theory also postulates a specific behavioral mechanism as responsible for the observed patterns, a mechanism fairly well established in behavioral knowledge and subject to test itself. What is being proposed is thus no mere attempt to invent plausible behavioral labels to explain known observations. Rather, it starts from a series of established behavioral constructs derived independently of the kind of data to which they are being applied, and attempts to see if their implications fit the phenomena of fashion and product acceptance. This theory thus offers a framework for research into product acceptance in general as well as formulating an improvement for the practical problem of new product screening and testing.

CONCLUSION

Not only fashion, but product acceptance in general is far more predictable than is generally thought, providing we make full use of the basic concepts of a product as a compromise bundle of desire attributes, demand as a desire set based on social conditioning, and motives as existing in a dynamic hierarchy and constantly restructured in the very process of their appeasement. These concepts alone are adequate to explain both the existence of a constant oscillation in fashions and the directions these oscillations take. Fads are explainable within the framework of this model as products which satisfy solely a single utility-drive for new experience; thus they pose neither a learning

[9]*Business Periodicals Index* (New York: The H. W. Wilson Co., July, 1961–June, 1962), p. 378.

requirement nor have much value once their newness has gone. The speed of adoption of products of any kind depends on the amount of required learning of three types: use-systems learning, value perception learning, and role-perception learning. All are researchable and describable in objective terms in advance.

READING 23

VISUAL DESIGN AND THE MARKETING MANAGER*

John E. Mertes

The modern marketer is basically concerned with the dynamics of change in all its ramifications as it concerns the consumer. Visual design is only one aspect of his total task. In the past, marketing decisions have been made primarily by rule-of-thumb methods. Today's marketers are searching for criteria to use as more valid guides in making executive decisions. The search is gradually leading them toward the development of marketing theory and principles to be used for guidance in the planning, execution, and control of marketing activities.

The historical development of styles outside the sphere of business activity may provide the marketer with meaningful insights. This avenue of approach is beneficial, because the principles developed from a study of the history of visual design can be objectively focused on the marketing task, and the criteria developed can be accurately tested in the crucible of the marketplace.

The concepts applicable to the marketing task, as deduced from the history of styles, fall into two broad categories.

- The dynamics of change and its influence from the consumer's standpoint.

- The dynamics of change and its influence from the designer's standpoint.

Principles derived from both categories can serve the marketing manager in his decision making and can also provide a springboard for analyzing various marketing activities from a design viewpoint.

One of the marketer's product-planning tasks is to develop products with an appearance more satisfying to the consumer. A close correlation between producer criteria and consumer criteria is necessary if the product is to receive acceptance in the market.

The appearance aspect

The history of styles as applied to utilitarian objects provides some insight into the appearance aspect of product planning. Within each cultural epoch, there have appeared a multitude of styles executed in terms of the available technology and materials. For example, the styles developed for the chair have been numerous.

At any given time, however, many of the chair designs were not accepted. The motivations of the designer or maker in such instances did not coincide with those of the buyer or consumer. To mesh this divergence, the services of the industrial designer evolved. Unlike the pure designer, the industrial designer gives basic consideration to market potentials in the visual design of a product. Unlike the analytical and exact approach of the engineer, his perception of the problem and its solution is more expressive of both the technological and consumer factors. His services correlate the artistic, production, and marketing aspects in developing a successful product. Thus, the planning of a product for the market on the basis of certain consumer design criteria will result in a product with a higher degree of consumer acceptance in the marketplace.

The design cycle

The pattern of visual design creativity. The first basic criterion that can be used by the marketer is the pattern of visual design change. When one traces the history of the evolving styles of utilitarian objects, a distinct pattern or cycle of design change emerges.

The endless variety of visual designs developed through history indicates that man's interest in any given form is transitory. This desire for change was as evident in earlier cultural epochs as it is in our contemporary civilization. From primitive civilizations to the contemporary scene, change in product design has been a continuous cultural phenomenon, resulting from the use of new materials, new techniques, and altered conditions of living.

What is the pattern of visual design change? The evidence suggests that the first styles originated in pure form—that man was primarily concerned with symmetry.[1] Weltfish supports this contention in a definitive study of primitive art: "Naturalistic art, the form of art some people thought was first, is only 20,000 years old, but long before that time symmetry, which is one of the important essentials of art, had been achieved by man in the course of his work."[2]

In each of the epochs of Western culture, man returned to pure form in his visual designs. The Greek, the Roman, the Gothic, the Renaissance, and now the modern period all started from a reinterpretation of the design of objects in pure form.

Pure form

The stage of pure form is not static. Pure form develops evolutionally from an experimental beginning through various stages until an ultimate expression

[1] See H. Read, *Art and Industry* (New York: Harcourt, Brace and Co., 1935), p. 119.
[2] G. Weltfish, *The Origins of Art* (Indianapolis: Bobbs-Merrill Company, 1953), pp. 10–21. Weltfish uses symmetry as a synonym for pure form.

is reached in terms of an object's function and the materials and techniques used. In primitive civilizations this was true. According to Weltfish, "One of the earliest tools we find in the French caves is the *coup de poing,* or hand hammer . . . if our time reckoning is right, it took man nearly one hundred thousand years to perfect this sculptured form."[3] In each of the cultural epochs of Western civilization this progression toward an ultimate design solution was observed in the presentation of styles. Even today, we can observe such ultimate form in many familiar items, such as a spoon, a hand hammer, and a saw.

Many utilitarian objects, once developed, do not proceed beyond this stage, except perhaps for color differentiation. When an ultimate form is reached, the form becomes static. It is at this point that ornamentation is applied to the product, continuing the cultural phenomenon of change.

In the stage of pure form, the textural quality of the material used, such as the grain of the wood or the polished sheen of the metal, is the only decoration. From this stage, man has shown an increasing concern with variations in an object's structure, shape, and ornamentation. In other words, ultimate form did not completely satisfy man's psychological or emotional needs since man is instinctively picture-making. According to Mumford, a contemporary observer of the American scene, "the arts represent a specifically human need, and they rest on a trait quite unique to man: the capacity for symbolism."[4] Therefore, to satisfy himself sensorially, man added visual symbols or ornamentation to his products. For example, when the Spiro Mound Indian applied decoration to both his utilitarian and magical objects, he was expressing this basic necessity. On this subject, Hamlin has made a further comment: "The human need that made the Greeks decorate cups and vases still exists, despite all the changes in economic conditions and means of manufacturing."[5]

As color is applied to a product's design, a gradual evolution in ornamentation begins which finally develops through flamboyancy to a point where both shape and structure are disguised to such an extent that the basic form cannot be visually identified. An object so designed is very elaborate, the result of an overuse of applied chromatic and representative ornamentation.

When the need for embellishment is first felt, nonrepresentative structural ornament is used to emphasize the object's form, such as incised lines scribed on a vase by the pottery maker's tool. Next, sculptural ornament is applied to the form of the object. Sculptural ornament then goes through the following evolutionary stages: *the geometric* and *the stylized,* after which change in ornamentations reverses in direction until the stage of pure form is again reached. The cycle pattern for both form and ornamentation which emerges from this analysis of styles in visual design is visualized in Figure 1.

Reflection on the pattern of visual design change indicates that the cycle, though continuous, develops cumulatively. The various styles are the result of specific design innovations. As each style is created, it becomes source

[3]*Ibid.,* pp. 19–21.
[4]L. Mumford, *Art and Techniques* (New York: Columbia University Press, 1952), p. 17.
[5]T. Hamlin, *Architecture: An Art for All Men* (New York: Columbia University Press, 1947), p. 169.

Form Ornamentation

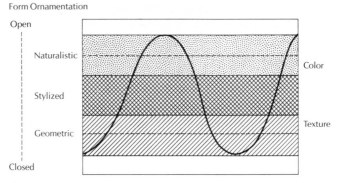

Figure 1

The design cycle (a visualization of the evolution of form and ornamentation in product design. The shape of the curve does not proportionately reflect time.)

material for the creation of new styles. From the resultant storehouse of ideas, an endless number of new combinations is possible. The growth of form and ornamentation gradually refines the initial design concepts until absolute interpretations occur. The various designs developed for the chair are illustrative of this growth.

Analyzing trends

The visual design cycle is useful from a product-planning standpoint as it provides the marketing manager with an insight for the analysis of trends in the creation of visual designs. The time period involved in this evolution varies in length. Prior to the Age of Salesmanship and Advertising, the progress from stage to stage was slow. Even so, each succeeding past epoch has completed the cycle at a faster tempo. And at the present time, the contemporary period, the acceleration has further increased. Within the last thirty years, the development of new materials and mass production techniques has resulted in a re-emphasis of pure form. In recent years, emphasis has been on the textural qualities of the material, pure or primitive color, and geometric ornamentation. One comment predicts that the stage of open form may be reached soon:

Inasmuch as, in the past, a baroque expression has always written the final chapter to what started as a rebellious movement in art, architecture, or design, it follows that we too may witness in the next 25 years the full-blown efflorescence and ultimate decadence of the present modern movement.[6]

Thus, the marketer, by introspective study of consumer acceptance trends of visual design patterns, possesses a tool for analysis that should result in a better interpretation of the types of designs acceptable to today's sophisticated shopper. Yet it must be remembered that as invention and improved com-

[6]A. Auerbach, "Modern . . . From Where to Where," *Interiors*, CXII:12 (July 1953), 42h.

munication have shortened the time lapse between design stages, use of the demand-creation tools by the marketer has accelerated product acceptance in terms of design. This realization suggests the next question for analysis—a consideration of the cultural lag in terms of design.

Consumer acceptance

The lag in the acceptance of visual design. Although the development of visual designs within the cycle is based upon man's transitory interest in any given design form, the acceptance of a change is paradoxically impeded by his customs and mores. Many designs may be created that are not currently accepted; many may be ahead of their time. From a marketing standpoint, a currently acceptable design is one that coincides with the consumer's current taste.

The Eames chair

This problem of consumer acceptance is well illustrated in the following comments by Edward S. Evans, who first offered the unusual Eames molded plywood furniture to the consumer market:

A multitude of new product designs have gone before the public and have been refused acceptance. Many of these products still retain their inherent utility and are still exceptionally well designed products. But they are ahead of their time. The public is not ready for them. So the manufacturer must be certain that his products conform to present public taste—no matter what the increased advantage of the new design may be. . . . The American man-in-the-street has the last word. If he will not buy—if the product is too new for him—then the manufacturer must build products that will suit the man-in-the-street's demands.[7]

Ogburn, the eminent sociologist, has observed that there is resistance to change in the sense of the new: "Cultural forms may persist apparently because it is easier to use an existing form than it is to create a new one."[8]

To facilitate consumer acceptance it is usually necessary for the marketing manager to adapt "breakthrough" products in the guise of past or current styles. In this manner, consumer resistances are gradually offset, with the result that the cultural lag as described by Ogburn is not so serious as to delay the marketing of products of differentiated design.

Two types of design

Qualitative and quantitative visual designs. The dynamic change apparent in the visual design cycle and the cultural lag attendant to such change sug-

[7] E. S. Evans, Jr., "The Manufacturers' Position," *Good Design is Your Business* (Buffalo, New York: Albright Art Gallery, 1947), p. 28.
[8] W. F. Ogburn, *Social Change with Respect to Culture and Original Nature* (new ed.; New York: Viking Press, 1950), p. 159.

gest that the marketer should classify visual designs into two broad types: *qualitative designs* and *quantitative designs*. Products of qualitative design are new and completely differentiated, limited in market, of intellectual appeal, and of greater risk for the marketer. Products designed in a familiar guise are quantitative, appeal to a broader market, and incur less risk for the business organization.

Thus, it behooves the marketing management of business organizations to study the trend in design creation and acceptance. To do so, objective observation, research, and tests of varying types for tentative exploration should be made to determine consumer reactions to designs not only in the sense of increasing interest in the new but also in the lagging interest in the old. Once a favorable trend exists for a given design, the use of sales promotion, advertising, and salesmanship can accelerate acceptance to such a degree that mass production of the design becomes feasible. As interest lags, the older designs may then be eliminated from the manufacturer's line.

The force of ennui

Consumer choice and visual design change. Criteria useful to the marketer can also be deduced from the historical study of styles by determining the reasons for design change. Basically, *the reasons stem from the consumer's act of choice, induced primarily by ennui and emulation.*

When man was both form-giver, maker, and user of utilitarian objects, their total entity was his responsibility. In choosing a form which pleased and satisfied him, he developed a valid esthetic appreciation for good design. But when the Industrial Revolution divorced him from both the design and execution of the product, his customary avenue of creative expression was partially blocked. Fortunately, the creative act of choice, or sense of discrimination, inherent in man because his environment has never been uniform, still remains to be exercised in the marketplace.

The world around man is not uniform; therefore appreciation through discrimination is innate. Perhaps nature has been too thorough a teacher. The variations between the seasons, the continuously changing panorama of the clouds in the sky, and the passing of the moon into its phases are but a few of nature's manifestations that have convinced man that both change and variety are within his compass.

Or perhaps the nonperfectibility of nature has left its imprint on his mind. No two of nature's "products" are identical. Not even the miscibility of wheat can disguise the fact that there are differences in each grain. Moreover, nature has provided innumerable "styles" of its "products." Flowers grow as orchids and gardenias on one hand and as black-eyed Susans and sunflowers on the other. Amid such profusion, man has developed an acute sense of discrimination within the framework of his own experiences and education. The many styles that have been created in the past are a reflection of man's sense of discernment; today he may exercise his discrimination in selecting from the products available in the marketplace those that reflect his taste.

But what prompts man's choice in the marketplace? He is influenced by ennui or emulation or both. Consumers, in making their selections from among the available products, do so in a paradoxical manner. Although each consumer wants to be like everyone else within his social group, he also wants to feel that he is different. This feeling, assuming freedom of choice, is expressed in the market by his purchasing through a period of voluntary regimentation, followed by a breaking away from the sameness of things. The consumer tends to possess an inherent dissatisfaction at some point through time with those styles which formerly gratified him. Such dissatisfaction stems from either the ennui influence or the emulation influence. The ennui force[9] is based on the fact that people become bored with that which they have; that is, they react defensively to the sameness of things. The emulation force, first popularized by Veblen, is based on "the stimulus of an invidious comparison which prompts us (the consumers) to outdo those with whom we are in the habit of classing ourselves."[10]

Ennui, or man's dissatisfaction with things as they are, is first expressed in the visual design of objects. According to Wolfflin,

The history of forms never stands still. There are times of accelerated impulse and times of slow imaginative activity, but even then an ornament continually repeated will gradually alter its physiognomy. Nothing retains its effect. What seems living today is not quite completely living tomorrow. This process is not only to be explained negatively by the theory of palling interest and a consequent necessity of a stimulation of interest, but positively also by the fact that form lives on, begetting, and every style calls to a new one.[11]

In the same sense, the customer, in making selections in the market, responds to the ennui influence. Thus, to the marketing executive it is important to recognize this influence that induces the consumer toward purchases of quantitative designs.

A better mouse trap

The emulation influence is expressed by man in his ceaseless attempt to create designs superior to those already in existence, usually through the restatement of an object's function in terms of new materials and techniques. Similarly, the consumer, in selecting from among the available designs, is tempted by the new and novel for purposes of marginal differentiation.[12] Few consumers make such purchases originally, but those innovators who do lead the way for others to follow.[13] Thus, emulation influences the consumer to purchase qualitative rather than quantitative designs.

[9] See G. Kubler, *The Shape of Time* (New Haven: Yale University Press, 1962), p. 79.
[10] T. Veblen, *The Theory of the Leisure Class* (reprint; New York: Random House, 1934), p. 103. Words in parentheses inserted by author.
[11] H. Wolfflin, *Principles of Art History* (reprint of 7th ed.; New York: Dover Publications, Inc., 1929), p. 230.
[12] David Reisman with Reuel Denney and Nathan Glazer, *The Lonely Crowd: a Study of the Changing American Character* (New Haven: Yale University Press, 1950), pp. 46–47.
[13] Everett M. Rogers, *Diffusion of Innovation* (New York: Free Press of Glencoe, 1962), pp. 168–192.

The act of choice under conditions of modern marketing can be exercised only when an adequate number of both qualitative and quantitative designs are available. And even though man is no longer the artist and maker, as he was in the Age of Handicraft, he still has choice as an avenue of creative expression. The assembling of the component furnishings in decorating a room reflects the discriminatory taste of the buyer; such selection is an act of choice which permits him to express his individual preferences with the same psychic satisfaction as when he was the artist and maker in the Age of Handicraft.

The marketing manager must carefully develop a sufficient variety of differentiated designs, depending upon the motives to which he desires to appeal, to permit a degree of discernment by the purchaser. Some critics, in referring to the Age of the Industrial Revolution as one of standardization, make the point that standardized, mass-produced objects do not permit man to exercise fully his sense of discrimination. But such criticism is hardly valid. There is an evolution toward similarity in products at any given time, in the same manner that designs expressed in given materials and processes point toward an ultimate solution in terms of form. But just as a breaking away from tradition in the creation of visual designs occurs, the customer also shifts away gradually from customary acceptance patterns.

Many critics have lost sight of the fact that, since the Industrial Revolution is reaching a point of full-flowering, there actually exists a greater degree of frequency in design differentiation in mass-produced items than in any of the handicraft products. This is not difficult to perceive, although many social commentators fail to realize that within the cultural sphere of handicraft societies from the primitive to the more advanced there existed far more regimentation of design than in the current American economy. For example, the Windsor chair and the Cape Cod cottage are mute evidence of this fact in our American culture.

The manager's role

From the foregoing discussion, the marketing manager's task is twofold:

● He seeks answers as to the increasing or decreasing consumer acceptance of given quantitative designs.

● He accumulates information as to the future trends for experimental or qualitative designs.

In analyzing the design activities of the contemporary designer, three considerations are pertinent to modern marketing management:

1. The method followed by designers in solving visual design problems.

2. The concept of design integration advanced by designers.

3. The design criteria used for design integration.

Each of these concepts initially resulted from design activities far afield from basic business activities.

Approaches to the solution of visual design problems. In analyzing the development of visual designs since the beginning of the Industrial Revolution, those produced by the machine evolved from mental concepts rather than from actual physical effort as expended by the craftsman. To derive his ideas for developing visual innovations, the designer may employ either of two approaches:

- *The creative approach.*
- *The eclectic approach.*

When using *the creative approach* the designer attempts to develop new and novel visual design solutions from an integration of his knowledge of prior designs, his awareness of new materials and processes, and his interpretation of current living conditions. The Aalto chair in which the designer applied the cantilever principle, as first developed by Mies van der Rohe with the use of steel tubing, is illustrative of the creative approach. Through a combination of prior knowledge with an adaptation of a new material, a contemporary design was developed. Aalto's chair led the way to the Eames chair, in which the new element was a modern process for molding plywood. Creative visual designs evolve and are not separate and distinct within themselves.

Some of the visual designs that develop from the creative approach seem strange in form when compared to existing ones. Quite often they are ahead of their time and, from a marketing standpoint, unusable at the time of their creation. While the consumer may gradually accept some of them, he will reject others for a variety of reasons, among which two are important from a marketing standpoint: *a prohibitively high price or an unfamiliar appearance.* Since the designer who utilizes the creative approach usually thinks in terms of "design for design's sake," he is not primarily concerned with the marketing implications of the product. His is the viewpoint of the "design purist." And on the basis of modern design criteria, his designs possess qualitative characteristics superior to the quantitative characteristics of those developed through the eclectic approach.

In utilizing the creative approach for developing designs to be machine-produced, the designer has three methods at his disposal which he may use singly or in any combination: *the derivative, the functional, and the inventive.*

The derivative method is used when the designer either intuitively or intentionally derives his concepts from current sources similar to his own field. Throughout the past cultural epochs, the endeavors of the architects and the fine artists profoundly influenced the design of utilitarian objects. Along with new styles of architecture, new furnishings were designed for purposes of harmony. As revolutionary styles of expression, such as Expressionism, Futurism, and Non-Objectivism, arose in the field of art, their overtones appeared in the visual design of many everyday products. For instance, the influence of Piet Mondrian, the Dutch painter, spread into the fields of architecture, furniture, furnishings, and advertising design and typography.

The functional method is used when the designer approaches his problem by a restatement of the function of the product in terms of available materials and processes. As indicated in the history of styles, there are various facets to the solution of the problem when this method is used. The visual designs so developed often proceed from intensive research. In conceiving the storage wall, an architect made innumerable measurements of objects stored in the home, such as typewriters, card tables, and folding chairs, to determine the most logical space relationships. As another example, an industrial designer created a design for an electric iron by studying the ironing habits of the housewife before attempting to improve the design. From his research he learned of three major disadvantages in using an ordinary iron: its weight, the effort involved in lifting it, and the fatigue arising from pushing it back and forth. The designer solved these problems and functionally improved the iron by:

- Reducing the weight of the iron,

- Providing a bulge on the side of the iron whereby it could be turned on its side rather than lifted and placed on a stand, and

- Giving the back of the sole plate an oval shape for less moving resistance.

The inventive method is used when the designer develops a completely new design concept in terms of the product's shape and structure. Such a design possesses novel form, which has usually proceeded from a restatement of the design problem in terms of an integration of new materials and/or new techniques of manufacture. The Mies van der Rohe chair, which combined the cantilever principle with the resiliency of bent tubing, was a solution by this method. A current illustration consists of the projected designs which use plastics in conjunction with the automation process.

When using *the eclectic approach* the designer, through retrospective search, adapts past styles or variations of contemporary styles to currently produced objects. He interprets his problem in terms of those designs of the past which are familiar to the customer or of those contemporary ones which are receiving increasing consumer acceptance in the market. Quite often his design develops from the standpoint of "design change for the sake of change." Basically, his contribution is but an interpretation of trends in customer acceptance—an interpretation which is often the result of business policy. Illustrative of the use of this approach are the reproduction and re-introduction of a Shaker breakfront for the seasonal market showings and the adaptation of the streamlined shape to incongruous objects. As contrasted with the innovations resulting from the use of the creative approach, these changes are quantitative rather than qualitative.

Thus, design innovation results from technological or psychological change. In either instance, prior designs are being destroyed as the innovations are developed. Such design development is continuous. George Nelson, in commenting on the process of design, suggests a concept of "creative destruction":

Evolution and revolution, creation and destruction are different names for the same thing. We use one or the other depending on our choice of a frame of reference. The designer who fails to realize this lacks one of the basic tools of his trade.[14]

The qualitative and quantitative designs just discussed are thus developed in the first instance by the creative approach and in the second by the eclectic approach. The designs resulting from the creative approach are much less conducive to successful exploitation by the marketer. Qualitative designs incur greater risk and are relatively limited in customer acceptance as they possess intellectual connotations; appreciation for them occurs through specific education or re-education of the buying public. Quantitative designs, because they are related to the familiar, are more easily presentable; they already possess a high degree of acceptability. Qualitative designs are for the future rather than for today's market. The task of the marketing manager, if past history is an indicator, can only be to speed up the realization that the future is here by judgmental promotional timing in conjunction with the educational influences of books, the press, and museum exhibitions.

Design integration and marketing. During the Renaissance, the artist was concerned with artistic endeavor in every phase of living. A Leonardo da Vinci or Brunelleschi integrated all of the arts in their buildings and other works. During the modern period, a cognizance of the desirability of such an approach to contemporary living is seen in the precepts developed by the work of certain architects and urban planners. The work of the firm of Morris, Marshall and Faulkner in nineteenth-century England re-emphasized the concept of the use of the artist as a coordinator during the beginning stage of the Industrial Revolution. Resistance to machine manufacture at that time, however, delayed the universal acceptance of the idea by designers and manufacturers. Later, Horta in 1893 and Van de Velde in 1894–95 restated the idea in two houses designed in the Art Nouveau motif. Frank Lloyd Wright carried the idea further in his early work and was possibly the first to adapt this organic approach to commercial activities. Wright designed not only the structure, but also the furniture, lamps, dishes, and identifying monogram for the Midway Gardens in 1931. Finally, the De Stijl group (1917) and the Bauhaus (1919) applied the concept to a civilization in which the machine was recognized as the necessary impetus. Proceeding from a product designed specifically for machine manufacture, they extended their efforts into interior design, graphic design, and exhibit and display design—or into every business activity where a problem of visual design existed. Using this point of departure, the Bauhaus then extended the design philosophy to the community as a whole.

Areas of applicability

Theoretically, from a marketing standpoint, visual integration would be applicable in business to every visual area which has an influence and impact on the consumer. *Directly, areas of applicability would be:*

[14]G. Nelson, "Problems of Design: Ends and Means," *Interiors*, May 1948, p. 85.

1. From a merchandising standpoint, the visual design of the product and its package.

2. From an advertising standpoint, space and television advertising.

3. From a sales promotion standpoint, sales literature, customer literature, labeling, dealer promotions, merchandise presentations, including window, interior, and point-of-purchase displays and exhibits.

Indirectly, with overtones of public relations, the *applicable areas of visual impact and influence would be*:

1. The company structures, such as plant, warehouse, offices, showrooms, dealer stores, and transportation equipment.

2. Company forms, such as letterheads, order blanks, and billing forms.

To achieve visual design integration, the business organization may adopt two broad policies, singly or in combination.

● The first is the policy of coordinating the business activities of the concern with the contemporary taste connotations of modern design such as that followed by CIBA, Abbott Laboratories, or the Container Corporation of America.

● The second is the policy of visual graphic arts coordination for the purpose of corporate identity as implemented by the Weyerhaeuser Company.

In the first instance, the company can, for example, more fully promote progressiveness by the result of its action. The visual design coordinator would be given the responsibility for the coordinated use of design in the current idiom; his influence in such an organizational context would be all-pervasive throughout the company. The creation of a corporate image connoting progressiveness would be the visual communicator's responsibility. Such an approach is especially appropriate when a product's style and fashion are the concern of the company.

In the second instance, the visual design director would coordinate visual impressions on the company's customers through the use of standardized logotype and prototype building designs, using these devices wherever they were promotionally applicable. By providing a frame of instant recognition, the company could better sell itself as an institution. Using an identity program, the many corporate visual expressions are received by the consumer as accumulated impressions—a favorable corporate image.

These two concepts suggest ideas which are of benefit to the business organization. Although the conceptualizations stem from the work of the designer in other areas, design integration merits adoption by modern marketing managers from an over-all marketing standpoint.

CONCLUSIONS

As products are planned to be more indicative of our evolving industrial society, the task of the marketing manager becomes one of demand creation through the use of advertising, sales promotion, and salesmanship to supplement the other educational influences which shape the taste of the consumer.

However, this discussion has been more specifically based on the styles developed by the initiative of the maker and the designer. The marketing manager's task has been to seek an adequate compromise between producers' criteria and consumers' criteria in an effort to plan and develop a product which would have a degree of consumer acceptance in the marketplace. In the past, the visual design compromise leaned in the direction of the maker; today, the pendulum has swung toward the user. Some may view this concern with the consumer aspect of appearance design as the easy way out and would stress technological change as the only reason for product change. Perhaps the approach may seem less challenging as less risk is involved in visual solutions.

Until now, a corollary of mass production was the development of a product for mass consumption in a populous, national market. During the last two decades, this market has been fragmented into such segments as the leisure and intellectual markets. All of this thrusts the consumer approach upon the marketing manager if the risk is to be minimized in reaching visual design decisions.

Also, the effective use of a proper blend of a company's promotional tools has only recently been brought into proper focus by the marketing concept. Contemporary communication theory has indicated the importance attached to a company's piercing of the noise screen. Another tenet, that the promotional activities of a concern cannot create a want has forced marketing management to seek guidance from the consumer in reaching product planning decisions.

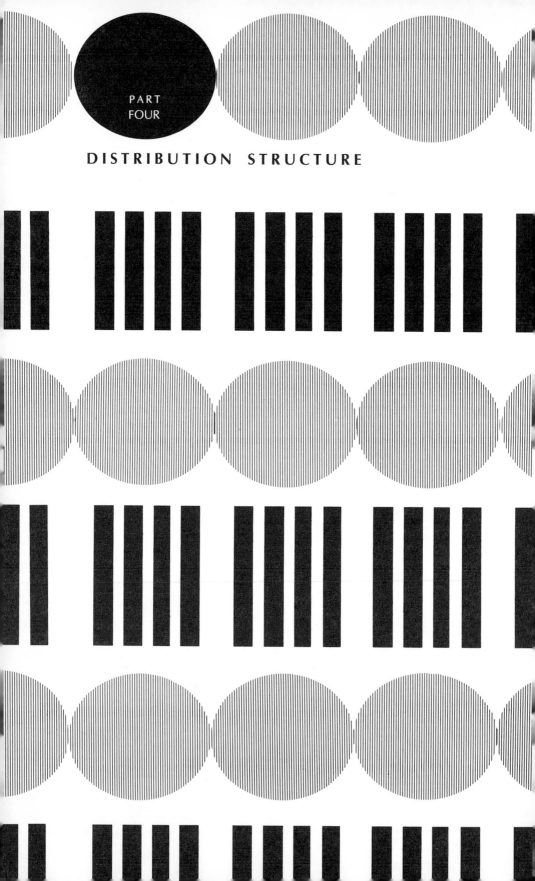

PART
FOUR

DISTRIBUTION STRUCTURE

The most visible institution in the distribution structure is the retailer. Taylor assesses the retail landscape by examining some consumer buying trends and relating them to retailing institutions. This article will give us greater appreciation of "change" and the pressures brought to bear on the retailer by consumer behavior. Professor Davidson's "Changes in Distribution Institutions" provides additional insight into *future* possible changes in retail institutions during the 1970's.

Wholesaling in the distribution structure will take on new importance in the next decade. Richard S. Lopata's "Faster Pace In Wholesaling" evaluates this dimension. Stern's article on "The Concept of Channel Control" provides additional dimensions on conflict and cooperation in marketing channels. Dommermuth and Andersen argue that the channel should be treated as a *functional system* rather than an institutional sequence. The final selection in Part 4, "Physical Distribution Development, Current Status, and Potential", puts into focus what some have called the "forgotten frontier" in marketing.

READING 24

THE REVOLUTION IN RETAILING*

Jack L. Taylor, Jr.

Retailing is undergoing a revolution, and there is little agreement about the cause or the probable outcome. Your eyes have surely given you ample evidence of the dynamic character of American retailing in recent years. In your home town or neighborhood, you must have seen the opening of one or more large supermarkets, or the conversion of a hardware or drugstore to some degree of self service. You or your family have probably made some purchase at a discount house, or at the department store that has resorted to discount pricing in some of its departments as a defense against the competing discount houses.

There is a good chance that you have visited one or more of the new suburban shopping centers. Perhaps your family is one of the countless thousands that now use telephone order service or one of the big mail order houses.

UPHEAVAL IN MARKETING

No individual can possibly experience first hand, however, all the developments in the retailing field, since many are directed at special consumer

*Reprinted by permission from *Credit and Financial Management*, December 1964, pp. 32–40.

groups and interests. For a comprehensive picture of these new retailing developments, a student of retailing must read, both extensively and intensively, the wide variety of trade journals and business publications available.

The whole field of marketing is in ferment. New styles of selling are being tested. New types of stores, different from any that America has known in the past, are being opened. New methods—such as air freight—are being found to distribute the tremendous variety of products that flow from the nations mills and factories.

Behind this upheaval in selling are basic changes in the way we Americans live, work, and play—changes undreamed of a few years ago. The signs are apparent on every hand—in the sprawling shopping centers, in the big neighborhood supermarkets, in the redevelopment of blighted downtown areas.

Here are some of the things that you can expect:

1. Shopping centers, already a familiar sight on the fringes of our big cities all over the country, will get bigger and fancier as more and more people move to the suburban neighborhoods.

2. Drive-in specialty stores, each selling a different type of goods—such as shoes, clothes, hardware, garden supplies, hi-fi and stereo equipment—dot the highways increasingly, to serve the overwhelming number of people who shop by auto.

3. Serve-yourself systems will be used increasingly in all sorts of stores—because customers like the idea, and because it helps cut the cost of operation. In Washington, D.C., a new self-service store sells lumber, wallpaper, hardware and other building supplies. In Wichita, Kansas, an apparel chain has opened the tenth of its suburban self-service clothing stores.

4. Supermarkets will continue to grow in size and to offer additional non-food items. These concerns will come to resemble the department stores, with sections for drugs, home appliances, and other household needs.

5. Department stores will meet increasing competition by trying new selling techniques: they will offer more self-service, wider selection of merchandise and many will open branch stores in outlying areas.

6. Discount houses, selling furniture, housewares and appliances at cut rates, will make further inroads in the retailing field. What the discounters will face is a different type of competition from the regular retailers, who are cutting prices and offering specialized services to customers.

7. Gasoline stations and garages will get bigger as more cars crowd the road. There will be a wider use of credit cards for buying gas and oil. Many filling stations will relocate as the network of expressways and access highways spreads. By 1975 motorists will burn up the roads at the rate of 820 billion miles a year—against 770 billion today. Now there are 22 cars for every mile of road. In 1941 there were 11.4. In short, road building will not be able to keep up with the number of cars on the road in the years ahead.

8. Downtown stores, hard hit by competition from merchants in the suburbs, will step up their efforts to revive dwindling business. There will be new moves to renovate outmoded store buildings, and to provide more downtown parking space. More than 100 cities are now working on plans to convert the crowded downtown streets into spacious pedestrian ways, banishing autos to the edge of the central shopping area.

PATTERN FOR THE FUTURE

The pattern for shopping centers of the future is already evident in today's planned and strategically located shopping centers. A decade ago, only a handful of these centers dotted the countryside. Now there are over 2,500. By 1975, estimates show there will be as many as 8,500.

Many of the new stores being opened today are in shopping centers. They account for 50% of the new grocery stores, 77% of the drug stores, and 85% of the shoe stores. Traditional dividing lines of retailing will break down even more than in the past. The old-time corner drugstore has given way to the gleaming self-service mart that sells not only prescriptions and health goods, but electrical appliances, cameras, sporting goods, and stationery. Variety stores—the familiar 5 & 10's—offer TV sets, lawn furniture, and other price items far out of the 10¢ range.

Gasoline stations now account for more total retail volume than do the nation's department stores. Some are adding new products such as power lawn mowers and garden tools. Others are going for neighborhood canvassing to get new customers. In St. Louis, an oil company will serve your car while you park outside the grocery store—portable gasoline pumps and an underground network of pipelines do the job. You pay for the gas and oil with your groceries at the store's checkout counter.

Automatic selling in coin-operated vending machines, an industry already grossing more than $2 billion a year, is likely to become more widespread in the future. There are more than 3 million robot salesmen in the country today, vending everything from hot lunches to fishing worms. Machines dispense 16% of all cigarettes, 21% of all candy and 30% of the soft drinks sold throughout the U.S. A newly invented device for changing dollar bills and ten dollar bills into coins, which I understand is already on the market, is expected to spur the growth of the automatic vending machines.

One retailer sums up the trend toward diversification this way:

What we are seeing in retailing today is a game of musical chairs. We storekeepers are clamoring to decide who is going to sell what products. At the same time we are battling with every other sort of enterprise—auto dealers, vacation and travel agencies, insurance men, and the entertainment field—for a bigger share of the consumer dollar.

When you look behind the trends in retailing today you will find these major influences at work:

1. America's shifting population has upset traditional ways of shopping. As people have moved to the suburbs, stores have had to follow. Growth on the

fringes of the big city has been six times as great as within the city limits in recent years. The exodus to suburbia has been responsible for the building of the regional shopping center with anywhere from a dozen to eighty stores and with parking space for thousands of cars.

2. People are busier. They want to get things done fast. The old time department store, laid out so that people would happen upon merchandise they might buy, is no longer considered sound engineering.

3. In recent years, more married women are working than ever before. Employment has increased, particularly among women over 35, who were once the bulk of shoppers in the downtown stores.

4. More husbands and wives are shopping together either in the evening or on weekends. Many shopping centers stay open six days a week. Some of these stores do up to 70% of their volume at night. There is a developing trend—resisted strongly by most retailers—toward keeping suburban stores and supermarkets open on Sundays.

5. The U.S. population is becoming an increasingly mobile one. More than 75% of all families own autos; many families have two. These people want to shop more where they can find a place to park. Convenience for the shopper often outweighs lower prices as a factor in deciding where they'll do their buying.

Let me now turn to some specific trends that will affect credit managers directly or indirectly. The first is what is called the "rental rampage." Let me start by asking, "Is the American consumer switching from pride of possession to pride of being without?" Some crystal-ball gazers predict that by the end of the twentieth century, consumers will be less interested in owning and more interested in using. On the subject, Ferdinand M. Mauser, professor of marketing at Wayne State University, says in the *Harvard Business Review*:

People in a busy, rapidly-moving, affluent society increasingly realize that they are not interested in things per se, but rather in their use in a convenient, worry-free manner.

One implication is clear. The affluent citizen of the next century will be oriented to buying time rather than products. He will take the myriads of sophisticated products at his disposal for granted. His chief concern will be to provide himself with free time in which he can conveniently use products that function to conserve time for leisure and pleasure. It is scarcity which creates value. Hence, as scarcity of product disappears, the scarcity of time ascends the value scale.

One of the implications of Professor Mauser's theory is that merchandise will be sold so that a family income is doled out in committed amounts. Lending some credence to the prediction of an ultimate switch from product owning to product leasing is the growing rage to rent as a marketing phenomena. Some marketing authorities predict increased sales on credit of all types of consumer goods and the prospect that more people will rent hard goods instead of buying them outright. Last year, for example, more than 15 million consumers rented automobiles. There is a rapid growth in long-term leasing of automobiles, trucks and trailers.

THE TREND TO RENTING

In the future, says a former vice president of R. H. Macy and Company, major appliances—stoves, refrigerators and TV sets—may be distributed on a rental basis. The homeowner will turn in the old model every year or so for a new one paying monthly rental in the meantime.

Today's consumers can rent practically anything that isn't used up in one sitting. The more they find that is rentable, the more they want, from bridal gowns to wheel chairs. In the 1950's rent-a-car service became available. In the early 60's, rental arrangements were established for a wide variety of consumer goods.

Some of the renting of specialty items, in both hard and soft goods, will burst the confines of the small, local operator; for the consumer usually gets what he wants—even if what he wants means a totally new concept in marketing for the company that didn't contemplate that renting would ever be one of its concerns.

Here is a practical list of rental categories for department stores: babies' needs, men's wear, tools, appliances, sporting goods, automobiles, gardening tools, sick room needs, party equipment, women's apparel, wigs, and photographic equipment.

WIDE DIVERSIFICATION

Renting is just the beginning. Notice the trend toward wide diversification. Until recently, Hertz confined its operation to vehicles. The company has now opened in New York (and a handful of other cities) the first of its Hertz Rent-All operations. The operation will rent literally hundreds of items for entertaining, for the sickroom, and for health and reducing. If it is successful, you can expect similar establishments from coast to coast.

Montgomery Ward recently announced that it would go into the rental business. The giant mail order house will rent, of all things, formal clothes. However, there is nothing new about renting formal wear. For generations a number of small businesses, and some in metropolitan areas not so small, have made a good thing of catering to the average man who can't or won't invest a sizable sum in cut-aways or evening clothes to be worn only once and shut in the closet. Sears Roebuck is also in the same picture. Singer has been in renting for years.

Culture is also for rent. New Yorkers can rent paintings based on the assessed value of the art work. A painting valued at $200 costs a minimum rental of $5 a month. A painting valued at $4,000 rents for a maximum fee of $80 a month. If the customer decides to buy the particular art work, the rental paid is applied to the purchase price of the painting.

EDP FOR STORES

But renting is not the only new phenomenon. One of the long-term goals of the electronic industry is complete electronic data processing systems for stores. Such systems will begin at the point of sale and ultimately provide complete information instantaneously on every step of the retail transaction.

Also significant is the trend toward retail giantism. Mr. E. B. Wiess (of Doyle, Dane, Bernbach, New York) has established an outstanding reputation in the field of retailing for his predictions of merchandising trends—self service, shopping centers, highway retailing, discount centers, and giant retailing, to name just a few. He has this to say about giantism:

In 1922 a food broker sales organization had to cover 300,000 outlets to achieve 80% distribution. In 1962 some 50,000 food stores provide the same distribution, and some 1,500 buying offices provide the prime target for the food producer seeking to achieve or maintain 80% distribution. Some 20 years ago, in what may have been one of the first studies of retail concentration, I established the fact that at the time some 400 retail giants controlled about 50% of the nation's total of retail volume in their major merchandising category. 20 years later, two things have happened: the figure is now down to about 100 retail giants who control 50% of the total retail volume in the major merchandising category. The number and variety of these merchandise categories have increased substantially.

The trend towards retail giantism shows every indication of picking up additional momentum. Probably by 1970, about 40 giant retail organizations will control 50 to 60% of the nation's total retail volume in practically all major merchandise classifications. Of course, this will change the credit problem for wholesalers and others who sell to retailers since they will have fewer companies to deal with.

INCREASED CONVENIENCE

Another factor in retailing is the trend toward convenience. I think a personal experience will clarify this point.

Last Christmas, my wife wanted to buy toys for the children. She went downtown on what finally turned into a three-hour excursion. She went to five department stores, three variety stores, and two 5-and-10 stores and came home three hours later in a terrible mood, since she had not found anything for the children. Trying to keep peace in the family, I suggested that we pick up the Montgomery Ward and Sears Roebuck catalogs and "shop" for the toys via catalog. This we did, made a phone call to the store to place our order and picked up our completed order the following day, just eighteen blocks from our home. Convenient? Yes. Problem solved? Yes, indeed! Selection of merchandise? Excellent. Price? Lower than other leading department stores.

I think Professor Mauser has a point. We do value our time. It is worth something to us. Therefore, I think the significant element in retailing today is the trend back to the phone and catalog order house, if for no other reason than the convenience and saving of time.

INFLUENCE ON CREDIT

The modern credit executive cannot afford to keep up to date only on the latest *credit* techniques; overall trends in retailing substantially influence the standing of individual retailers. The executive must know the newest developments in the field and whether his customer is keeping abreast of them. One who ignores these trends—to renting, to shopping centers, to mail order buying, and the like—risks losing substantial business to more informed competitors. Thus trends in retailing must influence the credit executive in making truly informed decisions on the extension of credit.

READING 25

CHANGES IN DISTRIBUTIVE INSTITUTIONS*

William R. Davidson

The purpose of this article is to indicate briefly the major changes to be expected in the distribution industries during the first half of the 1970s. Some of the major implications of these changes from the standpoint of business strategy and research will be identified. The distributive structure of the economy is defined to include retailing, service, and wholesaling establishments, plus the distribution activities of manufacturers and other form-utility producers as well as the product-acquisition activities of consumers. It is important to consider both the manufacturer and the consumer as active participants in the distribution process, in an era characterized by increasing vertical integration and enlarged willingness to shift marketing functions among or between the traditional channel of distribution levels.

CHANGES IN THE DISTRIBUTIVE STRUCTURE

It is not possible to deal with all anticipated changes in a comprehensive manner or to support points of view with documentation within the scope of this article. Consequently, attention is focused upon a few major interrelated institutional changes. The discussion will be somewhat oversimplified for purposes of emphasizing the major thrusts within a complex and dynamic distribution environment. Moreover, attention is restricted primarily to the distributive structure for consumer goods, although many of the changes here discussed have a counterpart in industrial marketing.

The following changes were selected for discussion:

1. Rapid growth of vertical marketing systems.

2. Intensification of intertype competition.

3. Increasing polarity of retail trade.

*Reprinted from *The Journal of Marketing*, published by the American Marketing Association, January 1970, vol. 34, no. 1, pp. 7–10.

4. Acceleration of institutional life cycles.

5. The emergence of the "free-form" corporation as a major competitive reality in distribution.

6. The expansion of nonstore retailing.

Each of these changes represents a trend the direction of which is already evident. These trends are expected to accelerate and intensify in the early 1970s. The major impact of these trends will be upon the range of strategies which can be successfully implemented by firms within the distributive structure.

GROWTH OF VERTICAL MARKETING SYSTEMS

Conventional marketing systems are being rapidly displaced by *vertically organized marketing systems* as the dominant distribution mechanism in the economy. Conventional channels are those fragmented networks in which loosely aligned and relatively autonomous manufacturers, wholesalers, and retailers have customarily bargained aggressively with each other, established trade relationships on an individual transaction basis, severed business relationships arbitrarily with impunity, and otherwise behaved independently.

Vertical marketing systems, by way of contrast, consist of networks of horizontally coordinated and vertically aligned establishments which are managed as a system. Establishments at each level operate at an optimum scale so that marketing functions within the system are performed at the most advantageous level or position.

The recent rapid and expected continued growth of vertical marketing systems is evident by the performance of three major types of distributive systems with high vertical programming potential—corporate, contractual, and administered systems.

Corporate systems may be regarded as roughly synonymous with integrated chain store systems, although the impetus for vertical programming may come from companies primarily regarded as retailers (e.g., Sears, Roebuck & Company), or manufacturers (e.g., company-owned stores in the self supply network of Firestone Tire & Rubber Company), or wholesalers, some of whom have company-owned stores and are integrated into manufacturing. Chains of 11 or more store units, which accounted for a relatively stable one-fifth of total retail sales between 1929 and 1958, exhibited a renaissance of growth in the 1960s and now account for some 30% of all retailing, with a continuously accelerating growth rate evident.

Contractual systems include three sub-types—wholesaler-sponsored voluntary chains, retailer-cooperative organizations, and franchising organizations. Each sub-type involves voluntary but contractual integration of retail store or service units with other supply units at an antecedent channel level. There are no official data on the aggregate importance of such systems. A recent trade-by-trade analysis by the author and his associates suggests that 35 to 40% of all retail trade is accounted for by some form of voluntary chain, cooperative, or franchising organization. This includes old organizational forms such as automobile dealer franchises and the I.G.A. type of food store voluntary, and very new organizations such as Ethan Allen furniture franchise stores of the Baumritter Corporation. Other new forms are the various convenience food stores and fast food franchise operations.

Contractual systems, like chain store organizations, are not new. However, their recent and expected future rapid growth rate *plus* the increasing sophistication of vertical programming are of major interest. Once characterized primarily by goals of economy in the form of buying power and low operating expense rations, such operations have moved into an era of complete management systems, achieving high market impact through the rationalization and clarification of the total firm product-service offer.

The third type of vertical system, *administered*, pertains to a line or classification of merchandise rather than to a complete store operation. While historically many examples of close store-vendor relationships existed, there is current intensification of such relationships by means of vendor-developed *comprehensive programs* for distribution through the entire channel. Of interest are retail merchandising programs developed by O. M. Scott and Sons Company in lawn products, by Villager in young women's apparel, by Magnavox Company in the home entertainment field, and by Kraftco Corp. in the supermarket dairy case. There are no data of any overall significance for administered systems of this type. However, proprietary studies conducted by the author and his associates for a group of leading firms in the general merchandising field clearly indicate that such vertically coordinated programs are growing rapidly.

INTENSIFICATION OF INTERTYPE COMPETITION

All channel levels are characterized by increasing competition of an intertype character. A phenomenon known in the early 1950s as *scrambled merchandising* has surpassed all early expectations predicted for it. Owing to increased fragmentation or segmentation of the consumer market, a wide variety of establishment types find it increasingly feasible to abandon "line of trade" conventions and to offer a variety of products that may be purchased by consumers to which that type of firm has market access. It is estimated that as many as 450,000 retail establishments (about one-fourth of all retail stores) are involved to some degree in selling tires, batteries, or other automotive parts, supplies, or accessories. As many as 200,000 outlets are believed to be involved to some degree in marketing housewares.

This accelerated trend means that wholesale distributors and manufacturers who wish to achieve a significant total market share will find it increasingly necessary to develop multiple marketing programs designed to meet the economic goals and operating characteristics of specific outlet types. It also demonstrates the diminishing analytical significance of conventional Census of Business classifications (e.g., drugstores, hardware stores, and jewelry stores).

INCREASED POLARITY OF RETAIL TRADE

Retail trade is becoming increasingly polarized at two extremes. On the one hand are mass-merchandising operations that have successfully implemented supermarket approaches. This group includes the general merchandise types of discount or promotional department stores, and also the more specialized establishments with a large mass appeal. Examples are the 70,000 square foot stores of Central Hardware Company of St. Louis, the home modernization stores of the Wickes Corporation and Lowe's Companies, Inc., and the large mass appeal drug store such as Super X, a relatively new division of The Kroger Company. Super X has developed into the third largest U.S. drug chain since its first store opening in 1961. At the other pole are highly specialized boutique types of stores which carry a deep assortment of a very specialized line, often limited to a concept or a "look," as opposed to commodity types. Illustrative examples are Villager specialty shops which feature only a well-coordinated assortment of classic sportswear items, and the Ethan Allen stores of Baumritter which sell only Early American style furniture and coordinated furnishings. Such shops tend to be strong on services and are often distinguished by the provision of consumption advice as opposed to conventional selling approaches.

At both poles, establishments tend to be organized into vertical marketing systems upon the achievement of scale. Between the poles are conventional and often nonprogrammed single-line stores of the family apparel, hardware, drug, and jewelry types. For these stores and their supply systems, the polarization is suggestive of increased obsolescence and profit difficulties in the 1970s.

ACCELERATION OF INSTITUTIONAL LIFE CYCLES

Institutions, like products, may be regarded as having life cycles which consist of stages such as inception, rapid early growth, maturity, and decline. The time required to reach a mature stage is constantly diminishing. Conventional department stores, as an institutional type, achieved a mature position over the span of about three-quarters of a century. The more standardized variety store reached maturity within half a century. Supermarkets achieved the same within little more than a quarter of a century. Fast food service chains and franchising organizations will have achieved maturity in little more than one decade.

Further acceleration of institutional life cycles is to be expected. There will be an attendant massive impact upon existing institutional forms. The reasons include a variety of total vertical marketing systems models, a growing number of entrepreneurs and managers with interorganizational administrative skills, and a stock market that will instantly fund on a large scale any promising new concept.

THE "FREE-FORM" CORPORATION IN DISTRIBUTION

Distribution industries, once characterized by institutions which specialized by channel level and by kind of business classifications, are feeling the accelerated impact of the emergence of the free-form distribution corporation as a major competitive reality. Free-form corporations are in part a response to other changes previously discussed, especially intertype competition and the polarity of trade, and in part a perceived opportunity to redefine business purpose so as to better utilize corporate resources and distinctive competences.

The J. C. Penney Company, Inc. is now an example of a free-form corporation. Ten to fifteen years ago, Penney's was a chain of small town, limited service, general merchandise stores. It has now evolved to an aggressive free-form operation consisting of full-scale urban Penney department stores, Penney auto and truck service centers, Treasure Island discount stores, the Thrifty Drug Company chain, a large catalog sales division, a financial subsidiary for accounts receivable funding, a life insurance marketing program, and European stores through an equity interest in Sarma S.A., a Belgian company with 100 stores and 270 franchised units. Another outstanding and prophetic example is the Dayton-Hudson Corporation formed in 1969 by the merger of two of the best known department store companies (Dayton's of Minneapolis and Hudson's of Detroit). This corporation also operates Diamonds department stores (Phoenix); Lipman's department stores (Portland, Ore.); Target Stores, Inc., a prominent general merchandise discount chain; Lechmere's, a Boston area hard lines mass merchandiser; two chains of specialty book stores; several jewelry store operations; and real estate subsidiaries engaged in shopping centers and other land development activities.

The number of corporations with a new-found willingness to go anywhere and do anything in distribution will have increasing competitive impact. This development is likely to enlarge markedly concentration ratios at all levels of distribution. Moreover, such corporate approaches are often perceived as strategic ways of avoiding the decline phase of the institutional life cycle.

GROWTH OF NONSTORE RETAILING

In an increasingly affluent society which is ever more oriented to education, leisure, and recreation, it may be expected that functions performed by consumers in the product acquisition process will be somewhat reshuffled with important benefits accruing to various forms of nonstore retailing and the distribution networks that supply nonstore operations. Many housewives will have a lower relative preference for "shopping," especially for routine categories of consumption, than for other demands upon or optional uses of time.

This trend is expected to benefit at-home selling, illustrated by the growth of Avon Products, Inc., with 1968 sales of $558.6 million, an increase of 59% since 1965. Catalogue selling is also expected to expand. Penney's adventuresome entry into this field and the expanded use of seasonal catalogues by all manner of regular store retailers illustrate the growth of catalogue selling. Marketing through the mail is presumably increasing as illustrated by single-item and short catalogue promotions. Examples are product selling promotions by major oil companies and banks to credit card customers, credit card companies, magazines, and other firms not basically in the business of operating stores. The consumer's desire for time and place utility is increasing the range of products available through vending machines as well as the number and types of vending locations. The development of electronic devices is making new approaches possible to at-home shopping for staples which can be supplied by routinized order processing and delivery from central distribution warehouses.

Many new concepts involving nonconventional forms are expected to emerge partly as the contribution of entrepreneurs and also as a new dimension of the mature corporation which has been reprogrammed for project management approaches under the free-form pattern.

RESEARCH IMPLICATIONS

None of the major trends selected for emphasis in the preceding sections is readily traceable through Census of Business benchmark data, other conventional wholesale trade series, or annual statistical series of trade associations. Hence, one research problem of considerable magnitude is merely one of measurement. Beyond that, there are research challenges of managerial significance to ascertain improved methods of managing interorganizational relationships, to devise sophisticated management systems which will provide information that will help managers understand and optimize total system relationships, and to explore ways in which product life cycle concepts can be better applied to institutions. In the realm of social concern, it is essential to study more comprehensively the impact of these developments upon consumer choice, the state of competition, and the need for modifications in public policy, especially antitrust.

Among the methodologies that are expected to receive major emphasis in the pursuit of these research objectives are (1) empirical economic studies of competitive conditions and market performance; (2) computer simulation models to evaluate total systems performance under varying conditions; (3) behavioral analyses of concepts of power and conflict in channel relationships; and (4) the utilization of laboratory methods in the refinement of such behavioral concepts, with a view to better understanding their utilization in total system marketing.

READING 26

FASTER PACE IN WHOLESALING*

Richard S. Lopata

Although the wholesaling industry represents a major segment of the U.S. economy, it is little understood as an area, poorly defined, and considered by

*Reprinted by permission from *Harvard Business Review*, vol. 47, no. 4, July–August, 1969, Copyright 1969 by the President and Fellows of Harvard College; all rights reserved. pp. 130–143. *Author's note*: I am particularly indebted to my colleagues, William P. Hall, Charles H. Koenig, William E. Oddy, Roger M. Peterson, Richard E. Petersen, and F. Lee H. Wendell, who have contributed editorial evaluations and suggestions.

many to be dying or even dead. This paradox is reflected directly in the general literature of management, which contains little about wholesaling despite the fact that a majority of our large companies have a stake in it. Graduate schools of business also seem to neglect wholesaling; witness the fact that the number of courses they offer which deal with it can be counted on the fingers of one hand. Business schools, university extensions, the American Management Association, and many other organizations very frequently sponsor seminars on manufacturing, for instance, and yet devote no attention to wholesaling. Why? I suspect that for many people the answer to this question would be, "Well, there's really nothing much *to* wholesaling these days —it's a declining business function." Nothing could be more mistaken.

Today wholesaling is a big, growing industry that is changing rapidly and significantly. In this article I want to put wholesaling in a better and more realistic perspective, and especially to show how it is changing, and must continue to change, in response to the challenges of our present-day economy.

WHOLESALERS TODAY

First of all, who are the wholesalers? Today there are some 185,000 independent merchant wholesalers. Altogether they generated almost $220 billion in revenues in 1968. They are a highly diverse group—i.e., big, small, profitable, unprofitable, satiated, hungry, smart, dumb, conservative, and change-seeking. E. B. Weiss has described the new wholesaling milieu as a "scrambled" world in which there are wholesalers who manufacture, wholesalers who retail, and wholesalers who are uncertain whether they are producers, wholesalers, jobbers, retailers, financiers, or whatever.

In a number of ways, the wholesaler feels the impact of constant changes and innovations in the whole marketplace. Technological advances, product line proliferation, changing retail structures, and social adjustments are only a few of the real problems that complicate his life. Each improved product passing through the wholesale level generates a new demand for investments in warehouse space, market analysis, and sales training, and for myriad adjustments in the wholesaler's information systems. Each major retailing shift designed to satisfy customer needs obliges him to adjust his selling patterns, to review the customer service levels, to study product assortments, and to revise his strategies.

He must also deal with the growing aspirations of his once-content employees, the changing values of the available labor pool, and the increasing demands of the community for social service. The typical wholesaler faces such challenges with each new day—often without the resources of the larger manufacturing organizations that sell to and through him. If one still regards today's wholesaler as that traditional, unsophisticated middleman of the past, he must wonder how the wholesaler has survived at all—let alone grown strong—in our complicated social and economic system.

In the course of professional contacts, and in studies and seminars conducted over the past two decades with thousands of wholesalers and their suppliers, my colleagues and I have drawn certain conclusions that may help to explain the survival and growth of today's independent wholesaler and to forecast his future.

Functions & characteristics

An initial problem in discussing wholesaling is the matter of definition. Webster defines the wholesaler as "a merchant middleman who sells chiefly to retailers, other merchants, or industrial, institutional, and commercial users mainly for resale or business use." This is somewhat vague for my present purposes, and I should like to narrow down the definition of the wholesaler. The wholesaler is one who:

1. Purchases goods from manufacturers for his own account (as distinguished from the agent, who typically does not purchase for his own account) and resells them to other businesses.

2. Operates one or more warehouses in which he receives and takes title to goods, stores them, and later reships them. (In some cases, he may have goods shipped directly by the manufacturer to the customer, so the goods do not actually pass through his warehouse. Still, a good part, and usually all, of the goods which the wholesaler handles do, in fact, pass through his warehouse.)

The wholesaler's customer group varies according to his product mix. For example, there is one broad class of wholesalers who sell to retailers such diverse commodities as food, drugs, tobacco, hardware, dry goods, and appliances. Another class sells such items as food, paper products, medical goods and supplies, and so on, to restaurants and institutions. A third class sells building materials to builders and contractors. A fourth class sells manufacturing supplies such as tools, chemicals, abrasives, and so on, to manufacturers. In the complex automotive parts aftermarket, there are even warehouse distributors who sell only to other jobbers—i.e., wholesalers who sell to retail outlets.

Finally, we may classify wholesalers in terms of ownership. The wholesaling function can be performed by "manufacturers' branches" or by retail chains. The branches are captive wholesaling operations owned and operated by a manufacturer; this practice is common in electrical supplies (e.g., Westinghouse Electric Supply Company and General Electric Supply Company), and in plumbing (e.g., Crane Supply Company and Amstan-American Standard). Captive branch operations are also common among truck manufacturers, full-line farm-equipment manufacturers, and the large producers of major appliances. In the retail food field, A&P, Kroger, and other chains operate warehouse systems which do, in fact, perform a wholesaling function.

Here I shall be mainly concerned with the *merchant* wholesaler as described by the Department of Commerce. The merchant wholesaling house may be privately or publicly owned, but in either case it stands in the market as a distinctive, independent enterprise. According to the Department's definition, the merchant wholesaler is primarily engaged in buying and selling in the domestic market. More specifically, he buys and sells merchandise on his own account; sells principally to retailers or to industrial, commercial, or professional users; usually carries stocks; assembles in large lots and generally redistributes in small quantities, usually through salesmen; extends credit to customers; makes deliveries; services merchandise sold; and renders advice to the trade.

While the entire wholesaling category includes factory branches, petroleum bulk stations, merchandise agents, brokers, and so on, the merchant wholesaling category excludes such operations.

PERIOD OF GROWTH

In 1939, merchant wholesaler sales amounted to $23.6 billion, or 41% of all wholesaling as defined by the Department of Commerce. By 1963, the volume had increased almost sevenfold, to $157.4 billion, or 42% of total wholesaling activity. In the 1960's, however, the merchant wholesalers have *really* come on strong—in 1968 their sales were about $220 billion, as shown in *Exhibit 1*.

As one can see from this exhibit, merchant wholesaling volume grew at an annual rate of 7.1% between 1963 and 1968; this compares favorably with the 7.9% growth rate of the gross national product for the same period. Growth in the two largest segments (durable and nondurable goods) was at least 7%, while the "Miscellaneous" category decreased to 4.2%. The decrease in this category may be due in part to the fact that farm products (a major segment) have been increasingly recategorized as part of the food manufacturing system. *Exhibit 1* also shows that from 1963 to 1968 the wholesaling volume increased very substantially.

Why this remarkable growth instead of the deterioration that some have predicted? Not all the credit can be given to a "new breed" of wholesaler, as has been suggested. Some credit—perhaps the lion's share—must go to manufacturers. In numerous commodity lines, manufacturers have evaluated distribution alternatives, tried them out, and later abandoned these attempts to

Exhibit 1

Sales of U.S. merchant wholesalers, 1954–1968

	Sales (in billions of dollars)				Compounded annual growth rate	
	1954	1958	1963	1968	1954–1963	1963–1968
Durable goods	$ 39.9	$ 50.9	$ 67.4	$ 98.1	6.0%	7.8%
Nondurable goods	43.2	49.7	61.6	86.6	4.0	7.0
Miscellaneous products	18.2	21.4	28.4	35.2	5.1	4.2
Total	$101.3	$122.0	$157.4	$219.9	5.0%	7.1%
GNP	$364.8	$447.3	$589.2	$860.6	5.5%	7.9%

Sources: U.S. Census of Business, Wholesale Trade—Summary Statistics and Monthly Wholesale Trade Reports; and Office of Business Economics, U.S. Department of Commerce, Gross National Product or Expenditure.

"eliminate the middleman." They have learned, albeit at substantial tuition fees, that they can eliminate the middleman, but they cannot eliminate the economic *function* of wholesaling.

There are four good reasons why this is so:

1. The wholesaler has continuity in and intimacy with the market.

2. He has a more acute understanding of the costs of holding and handling inventory, in which, after all, he has a major capital commitment.

3. He can concentrate his managerial talent on localized marketing strategies without the distractions of manufacturing problems.

4. He has the important advantage of local entrepreneurship.

One hypothesis suggested to explain the rapid expansion of wholesaling is that independent wholesalers are growing in strength through the default of the manufacturers. That is, manufacturers, preoccupied with return on investment, prefer to allocate scarce resources to research and production rather than to distribution, which they know has historically delivered a much lower return. Manufacturers also frequently view entry into wholesaling as an added burden on their already beleaguered management teams. Finally, and more tangibly, there remains the fear of some manufacturers that the federal government may attack their expansion into distribution operations. A case in point is the vigorous government attack on paper manufacturers' acquisitions of paper distributing organizations.

For most manufacturers, experience proves the value of a strong, independent wholesale network. In many instances, such a network has resulted in the lowest possible total distribution cost—which is of course the manufacturers' real goal in this area.

Wholesalers have thus survived and even thrived in the modern economy. The types of wholesalers, of both durable and nondurable goods, have changed significantly and continue to change, as have the numbers of wholesalers engaged in handling particular commodity lines and combinations of lines. Let's look more closely at some of these shifts.

Exhibit 2 shows the sales growth of merchant wholesalers in the nondurable goods area for the period 1954–1968. Unfortunately, the figures by themselves do not satisfactorily reflect certain important changes in the composition of the wholesaling group, although they do reflect some of the dynamics that have been at work. Comparing the compounded growth for the two periods, 1954–1963 and 1963–1968, gives one a rough indication of where some of the major changes have occurred:

● Grocery wholesalers grew more rapidly in the 1963–1968 period than in 1954–1963 because of the strengthening of the voluntary and cooperative organizations that have so successfully withstood the inroads of the food chains.

● The tobacco jobbers grew at a slower rate in 1963–1968, probably because many of them were absorbed into wholesale grocery operations during

Exhibit 2

Sales of selected nondurable goods by U.S. merchant wholesale groups, 1954–1968

	Sales (in billions of dollars)				Compounded annual growth rate	
	1954	*1958*	*1963*	*1968*	*1954–1963*	*1963–1968*
Groceries and related products	$22.2	$25.3	$30.9	$44.1	3.7%	7.4%
Beer, wine, distilled alcoholic beverages	5.7	6.6	8.2	11.1	4.1	6.3
Drugs, chemicals, allied products	3.4	4.6	6.0	8.8	6.7	8.0
Tobacco, tobacco products	3.2	3.7	4.7	5.6	4.4	4.0
Dry goods, apparel	5.7	5.9	7.1	10.3	2.5	7.7
Paper and paper products	3.0	3.6	4.7	6.7	5.0	7.3
Total	$43.2	$49.7	$61.6	$86.6	4.0%	7.0%

Source: U.S. Census of Business, Wholesale Trade—Summary Statistics and Monthly Wholesale Trade Reports.

this period. An increase in direct-vending operations and the controversy surrounding the effects of smoking on health also contributed to this slowdown.

● Of the categories shown, the dry-goods and apparel category increased at the slowest rate in 1954–1963 (2.5%) and at the highest rate in 1963–1968 (7.7%). One explanation for this upward shift is that in the later period there were broadened opportunities in lower-cost imported items, accompanied by broadened consumer and retailer acceptance of such imports. Significantly, the wholesalers in this area acted aggressively in shifting from the domestic to the foreign sources to exploit the new opportunities and the changes in consumer buying habits.

Durable-goods wholesalers

Exhibit 3 shows us some noteworthy shifts in the durable-goods merchant wholesalers. For example, the growth rate of the "hardware, plumbing, and heating" category expanded in 1963–1968, while the "lumber, construction materials" category remained about the same. How could this have been, since both are closely related to construction activity? Part of the explanation for the low growth rate in construction materials is that the large building materials manufacturers increased their direct distribution to builders. Also, the chains (like Wickes and Sears) increased their share of the building-materials market, and the construction of single-family dwellings was sluggish. In contrast, the marked growth in hardware, plumbing, and heating is largely due to better exploitation of the industrial and home-improvement markets.

Some segments of wholesaling have followed changes in the marketplace, and some have even introduced improvements, while others have failed to respond to market shifts. As in other business forms, the wholesaler who survives and grows must remain flexible. He must be astute enough to cope with

Exhibit 3

Sales of selected durable goods by U.S. merchant wholesale groups, 1954–1968

	Sales (in billions of dollars)				Compounded annual growth rate	
	1954	1958	1963	1968	1954–1963	1963–1968
Auto equipment, motor vehicles	$ 4.0	$ 7.2	$10.3	$16.8	10.5%	10.1%
Electrical goods	6.3	8.0	9.9	15.0	5.1	8.6
Furniture, home furnishings	2.1	2.5	3.4	5.0	5.5	8.0
Hardware, plumbing and heating supplies	4.9	6.0	6.8	9.8	3.7	7.4
Lumber, construction materials	6.6	6.3	8.7	10.4	3.0	3.7
Machinery, equipment and supplies	9.4	12.4	16.9	25.4	6.5	8.4
Metals, minerals	4.2	5.6	7.9	11.0	7.4	7.0
Scrap, waste materials	2.4	2.9	3.5	4.7	4.3	6.1
Total	$39.9	$50.9	$67.4	$98.1	6.1%	7.8%

Source: U.S. Census of Business, Wholesale Trade—Summary Statistics and Monthly Wholesale Trade Reports.

the encroachment of manufacturers, as the electrical distributors appear to have done. He must also cope with the encroachment of retailers. To this extent, the food wholesalers appear to have been more successful than have their building-materials counterparts.

The growth of wholesaling is a complex phenomenon; and, as my remarks thus far have indicated, a major source of this complexity is the great variety of conditions peculiar to each commodity. Nevertheless the wholesaler has indeed foiled the prophets of doom of the 1940's. The percentages shown for the 1963–1968 period are substantially higher, in almost all cases, than the percentages for 1954–1963.

Some coming shifts

On balance, then, the independent wholesaler remains a vital and significant part of our economic system. So long as there are men willing to take on the risks, problems, and specialized functions of handling and selling a changing variety of goods to changing markets, there will be a large, vital, and independently operated wholesaler-distributor sector in the U.S. economy.

The wholesaler's success will depend on his response to the manufacturers and retail chains that want to absorb his function and on his ability to adapt and apply new concepts and techniques. Just as the manufacturers' strategies change with technological, political, and social developments, so must those of the merchant wholesalers.

It is possible to identify some commodity wholesalers who will pass from the scene. Others will swiftly shift to new commodities. Some will build regional or national networks of warehouses along single commodity lines, as have the paper merchants, electrical supply companies, and automotive parts distributors. Others will form tighter wholesale-retail franchised groups, such as Super Valu, Ace Hardware, Butler Brothers, and Western Auto. Still others will become multicommodity super-marketing systems, with all the accoutrements of sophisticated marketing technology. As a matter of fact, such wholesalers as these already exist; a prime example is Foremost-McKesson, whose sales of over $1 billion in 1967 included the wholesaling of drugs, grocery products, liquor, and health and beauty aids.

CHANGE IN ATTITUDE

Many wholesalers have stopped regarding themselves as strictly warehousing or break-bulk points in the distribution complex, and have begun to stimulate and respond to their markets on their own. This new marketing posture requires that the wholesaler dissect his available markets to determine which segments are potentially the most profitable and exploitable ones. In some instances, he has shifted selling emphasis from traditional markets to new ones. For example:

● Many electrical and electronics distributors have directed a new sales effort in recent years to industrial and commercial markets, to supplement their established electrical-contractor market.

● The progressive plumbing house has expanded its market from nearly complete reliance on master plumbers and craftsmen to include industrial accounts as well.

● Many grocery wholesalers, both the voluntary food groups and those independents who still exist, have added a sales effort geared to the growing institutional market, including hotels, airlines, restaurants, hospitals, and schools.

Interestingly, the 1967 business census shows that merchant wholesaler sales for the first time are divided about equally between retailers (or resellers) and business and industrial users.

Market analysis is strongly influencing the type and variety of merchandise and commodity lines handled by the wholesaler. One effect is that the wholesaler is now increasingly sensitive in his selection of product lines, and tends to review and adjust his product range in response to the needs of his various market segments. At the same time, however, he is more cautious than before; he carefully weighs the cost of entry into new markets against the cost of satisfying new needs of established markets.

It is true that some independent wholesalers (as well as some manufacturers with captive wholesale networks) have inflated opinions as to the depth, breadth, and flexibility of their organizations. That is, after a few successes in adjusting their products to existing market segments, they tend to feel that they can serve *any* market segment. They take the highly optimistic stance that a *real* wholesaler can handle any product for any market, that "all it takes is some managerial skill."

But successful wholesaling is founded on the service satisfactions of proximity, broad product assortments, and rapid response to the needs of local retailers, contractors, and other customers. Wholesaling organizations by nature must count as their most important resource their intimate knowledge of the product and service requirements of a particular market segment. In the sense that manufacturers can best rely on their know-how for *producing* for selected markets, wholesalers can best rely on their know-how for *servicing* selected markets. Venturing beyond the available knowledge and skill requires significant investments of time and money, and instant success is by no means guaranteed.

The point to be emphasized here is that long-run truth must arise from short-run reality. The cost of multiple short-run adjustments to exotic market segments is real and high. A line of building materials *can* be added to the ordinary lines handled by a paper merchant, for example, but the attendant traumas militate against any significant increase in short-run profit.

BASIC TRENDS

This conglomerate-type expansion is not the most significant kind of change that is taking place in wholesaling patterns today. The more important developments lie closer to the traditional operations of wholesaling; and within the current swirl of changing patterns one can distinguish several major trends that are shaping the future of wholesale distribution.

Increased integration

Historically, the goods-producing and distribution area of the economy has been separated into four distinct levels—manufacturing, wholesaling, retailing, and consuming. This structure of levels is becoming blurred. Because of wholesale-retail franchising, conglomeration, and joint venturing, *vertical* and *horizontal* marketing systems are emerging. In some of these systems the merchant wholesaler holds a pivotal position. Consider the following examples:

- J. M. Jones Company of Champaign/Urbana, Illinois, is an IGA wholesale grocer. It dominates its Central Illinois grocery market through its *owned* and member stores. Indeed, the total national IGA wholesale network operates more stores than its competitor, A&P.

- Allied Farm Equipment Company of Chicago, a basic distributor of short lines of farm equipment, manufactures over 200 items for its network of branches in the United States and Canada.

- Midas International, which originated as an automotive warehouser-distributor, today both *buys* and *manufactures* items for its franchised network of over 500 Midas Muffler and Brake Shops.

- Distronics Corporation is a joint venture of six plumbing and heating wholesalers which provides them with real-time, on-line, random-access computer services. At any distance up to 1,200 miles, a member wholesaler is able to make use of a central computer on a joint basis with his fellow venturers.

Additional examples can be found in drug, hardware, furniture, appliance, and other commodity groups. Most interestingly, and certainly significantly, these systems seem to have evolved through creative entrepreneurship rather than as a result of studied corporate effort. If this is true, then the trend is quite likely to continue as the merchant wholesaler (who is essentially an entrepreneur) becomes more sophisticated and searches for new opportunities.

More "aggressive" service

As newer technologies develop, new marketing systems evolve, and more sophisticated financial concepts come into use, the merchant wholesalers are adjusting their service emphasis. For example:

● Among industrial equipment and supply distributors, service and merchandising efforts are being tailored in the light of both OEM (i.e., original equipment manufacture) and MRO (maintenance and repair operations) activities. To provide better service for its industrial customers, Englewood Electric Supply Company of Chicago has shifted its emphasis from personal-contact sales to programmed reordering via Data Phone.

● A number of wholesale druggists now handle the retail druggist's customer account records. This "service" is really a device to "tie" the retailer more closely to one wholesaler.

● In the grocery field, credit extension used to be a prime function of the wholesaler. Today almost all wholesale grocery products flow into retail stores on a cash basis, for all intents and purposes. Here service has shifted from credit extension to merchandising support, inventory management counseling, and profit analysis on behalf of the retailer.

These changes suggest the vigor with which the wholesaler is searching for competitive advantage and his willingness to break with traditional methods. Such action, I might say, is hardly in keeping with the view of the wholesaler as a sterile anachronism.

Pricing and credit

The wholesaler has been critically reviewing pricing and credit policies, and he has made numerous changes. First, he has examined his prices in terms of the internal costs both to himself and to his customer. He has found, for example, that pricing arrangements such as system contracting ordinarily result in lower cost and better service for the customer than do older and more conventional pricing methods. Today's merchant wholesaler is likely to regard the improvement in service as a decisive advantage of system contracting, even given the fact that the selling price resulting from it may frequently be higher or lower than the current price in the open market. In fact, a number of wholesaler-distributors have been successful in switching customers from direct account buying by persuading them that "our price may be higher, from time to time, but remember—your internal possession costs will be lower because of our improved service."

He is also reviewing credit policies and revising them to take advantage of sophisticated financial methods. For example, a major electrical and electronics distributor in Canada has revised his credit operations and policies to emphasize two modern concepts: (a) a concept of accounts receivable management which includes the use of probability assessments of trade-category risks, and (b) control by importance and exception. This revision led him to reduce the term of credit from 60 days to 40 days, a step that released a substantial amount of capital which he put to much more profitable use in building inventory and exploring his markets.

Wholesalers will continue to experiment with new approaches to pricing and credit. One evidence of this is that it is not unusual to find a wholesaler applying only direct costs to a special sale as a means of competitive pricing, ignoring traditional gross-margin requirements. Also, it is not unusual to find a wholesaler requesting an "extra 5%" from a supplier for a special deal and then giving the customer an extra 7%! This trend reflects the restlessness and inquisitiveness of modern wholesaling management.

Regional coverage

One can cite numerous new approaches to regional coverage. Thus, subsidiary branches and "twigs" with limited, fast-moving inventories, but with ready access to the central warehouse, are sprouting all over the map. This new pattern is well established among plumbing, heating, and cooling distributors, and wholesalers of electrical parts and equipment are adopting it as rapidly as they can identify which items move fastest and where. Indeed, the 1963 census showed that the branch-operating wholesalers, who represent about 7% of all merchant wholesalers, accounted for approximately 36% of total merchant wholesaler volume.

Of particular interest is a leapfrogging strategy of market penetration that some wholesalers are now following. Instead of an "oil slick" type of expansion, these wholesalers are trying "backfire" tactics: they are reaching out as far as 1,000 miles from headquarters to establish operations which hopefully will spread back to the home base. These new operations have been started both by missionary effort and through acquisition. This closing of distance is bound to increase as communication and physical-distribution techniques advance.

Organizational form & size

The trend toward larger corporate organizations through public financing, merger, and acquisition is pervading the economy, and it is particularly notable in the wholesaling area. The Bureau of the Census reports the following facts about the composition of the merchant wholesaling group:

	1958	1963
Sole proprietorships	**31.0%**	**27.5%**
Partnerships	**15.3%**	**10.6%**
Corporations	**52.6%**	**61.3%**
Cooperatives and other forms	**1.1%**	**0.6%**
Total number of merchant wholesalers	**190,000**	**209,000**

Furthermore, in 1958 Moody's *Industrial Manual* listed 70 wholesale distributors and jobbers; but by 1967 the listing had risen to 129, an increase of nearly 85% in only nine years.

These data indicate a definite shift from proprietorships and partnerships to the corporate form—the traditional, family-owned operations are declining in numbers, and the publicly held wholesaling corporations are increasing. There is every reason to expect this trend to continue, inasmuch as the formalized corporate structure enhances the ability to grow.

In our continued contact with wholesalers, my colleagues and I have also noted their mounting interest in setting values on their equity and their willingness to loosen their hold on ownership through public issues and employee stock plans. Tax laws have undoubtedly stimulated this open-mindedness, and in this sense have exerted a highly beneficial influence. Public ownership brings more capital resources and, at the same time, brings pressure on management to use more sophisticated management techniques. It also spurs a search for opportunities to automate in such areas as information systems, materials handling, order selection and processing, and delivery operations.

The Census Bureau also reports that, according to sales volume figures, merchant wholesalers are growing in size. Between 1958 and 1963, there was a 7% increase in the number of merchant wholesale establishments with less than $1 million in annual sales, a 27% increase in establishments with $1 million to $5 million in sales, and a 41% increase in establishments with sales in excess of $5 million a year.

Still, of some 209,000 establishments owned by 185,000 merchant wholesalers in 1968, only about 1,400 were generating over $10 million in annual sales. A Dun & Bradstreet listing of wholesalers by location, sales, and employee size shows that approximately 4,000 merchant wholesalers presently generate more than $5 million in sales.

Evidently, the wholesaler-distributor is changing his corporate form and growing in size. This trend, along with other trends already noted, shows that wholesaling is responsive to its environment and that it can effectively adapt to the pressures for lower-cost distribution from both suppliers and customers.

THE CHALLENGES

The wholesalers must continue to interpret these pressures and respond and adapt to them. There is considerable evidence that the wholesalers realize this. They have, for example, converted their trade associations into centers for researching present and future problems of distribution and educating their members about them. They have also pooled their efforts in order to gain from their collective experience.

At the center of the pool is the National Association of Wholesalers, a federation of over 58 commodity-line organizations. It offers a comprehensive education and development program for all types of wholesalers. Its leadership has both followed and been spurred on by the individual commodity associations.

The NAW and many of the member associations have developed dynamic leadership in their full-time staff and in the individual wholesale houses. This leadership recognizes its own stake in pulling the industry behind it, but it must battle ignorance, inefficiency, sloth, and the practices of certain kinds of marginal operators who undermine the advancement of the industry as a whole.[1]

A second source of innovative leadership is the manufacturing sector. The wholesaler-distributor and his supplying manufacturer share a common goal: to reduce the cost of distribution while (a) obtaining sufficient profit for adequate return on investment and (b) paying for innovation necessary to ensure growth of the enterprise. The manufacturer, with his larger resources, has a strong motive for helping the wholesaler develop an operational network that can meet these challenges, and in fact many manufacturers have come forward to offer useful assistance. The wholesaler is basically an entrepreneurial personality, and frequently has plowed ahead on his own; but he is the first to acknowledge the important contribution that the manufacturing sector has made to improving financial, promotional, sales, and inventory management within wholesaling.

Inventory management

Judging from various surveys and trade discussions, the wholesaler's major problem is inventory control and management. One might expect this, since inventory comprises the main part of a wholesaler's assets and the number of different items kept in stock can be very large indeed. Beyond that, however, our economy has annually generated a monumental number of new products, particularly in the past few years. As companies further increase their R&D expenditures on new-product development, the inventory problem of wholesalers will grow more and more acute.

Product proliferation is most apparent in the grocery area, where the number of new-product introductions has been matched, and even exceeded, by the number of modifications in the size and packaging of older product lines. Similar product expansions are taking place in the automotive parts, electronic equipment and components, building materials, plumbing, heating, air conditioning, electrical, industrial papers, and numerous other lines. Today, for example, the automotive distributor carries about 70,000 identifiable items, as compared with 40,000 only ten years ago. Each item must be identified, labeled, handled, stacked, controlled, picked, packed, shipped, and invoiced —a very considerable job.

[1] See Louis E. Newman, "Diseases That Make Whole Industries Sick," HBR March–April 1961, p. 87.

The sheer number of inventoried items presents an immense and unending problem for individual wholesalers. How much of what should he carry in stock, and when? One of the wholesaler's reactions has been to demand that manufacturers reduce the size and variety of the lines they offer. Another is "cherry picking" of lines.

These reactions are based on the wholesaler's realization that a full and complete line is often not the most profitable one. The practice of carrying every item in a commodity line in stock at all times is fast disappearing, and the practice of maintaining only 80%–95% coverage is becoming increasingly common.

Manufacturers are also becoming increasingly sensitive to line profitability. American Standard, for example, recently reduced its line of brass fittings by more than 30%, much to the relief of many of its network members.

To come to grips with the inventory management problem, some wholesalers are selecting items and setting stock levels according to patterns of item demand and item movement. One way of doing this is to group all items on an "ABC" basis for analysis. In an article in *Sales/Marketing Today*, William P. Hall describes the case of one farm-equipment wholesaler who started to apply the ABC concept to his inventory analysis in 1963.[2] By 1967 he had achieved a much more profitable stock configuration. *Exhibit 4* gives some of the relevant figures. Note that in 1963, B- and C-items accounted for 82% of his volume. His strategy was to shift concentration to A- and B-items by:

● Dropping many supply items in the C-category and steering sales efforts toward the higher-priced lines, with larger dollar volume.

● Aiming promotion and preseason selling campaigns directly at higher-value lines.

● Retraining salesmen as equipment demonstrators, and discouraging them from merely "taking small orders."

By 1967, he had achieved significant results. Although the number of C-items (23) was the same in 1967 as it had been in 1963, the dollar volume in this category dropped from 36% to 20% over the four years. At the same time, the dollar volume of A-items grew from $267,000 in 1963 to a healthy $859,000 in 1967, when it represented 41% of sales. Sales of A- and B-items accounted for 80% of his total sales volume.

Another significant element of inventory management is inventory carrying cost. Studies indicate that the annual cost of possession ranges from 20% to 35% of the average cost of inventory. Thus a wholesaler with a $500,000 inventory should not ordinarily tolerate cost of $100,000 to $175,000, say, for carrying slow-moving or unsalable items. If he finds himself in this kind of situation, the wholesaler should remember that *turnover is the name of the game*. If his $500,000 inventory turns twice, his per-dollar carrying cost is 10¢ to 17.5¢. With ten turns, his per-dollar cost drops to 2¢ to 3.5¢.

As I have suggested, the wholesaler is beginning to obtain assistance and

---

[2] "The ABC Principle in Management," November 1968, p. 15.

Exhibit 4

Comparison of a farm-equipment wholesaler's sales, grouped by product category, in 1963 and 1967

		1963			1967		
Category	Annual sales per line	Number of lines	Total dollar volume	Percent of total sales	Number of lines	Total dollar volume	Percent of total sales
C	$0–$49,000	23	$532,000	36%⎫	23	$425,000	20%
B	$50,000–$199,000	5	$695,000	46%⎬ 82%	8	$819,000	39%⎫ 80%
A	$200,000 and over	1	$267,000	18%	3	$859,000	41%⎭

advice on new approaches to inventory control and management from his suppliers. To an increasing extent he expects to benefit from his suppliers' overall knowledge of market requirements. Some progressive manufacturers who recognize these needs are even conducting educational programs for the wholesalers who distribute their products. For example:

● The UCON Refrigerants Division of Union Carbide has held many successful seminars for its network members over a period of some years. In 1968, Union Carbide researched, developed, and conducted extensive seminars in inventory management for its wholesalers. The two-day program included specially prepared materials, work sheets, checklists, and illustrations of inventory control systems that covered the entire typical inventory of a wholesaler, not just his inventory of refrigerant items.

Unfortunately, however, the wholesalers who really practice modern inventory management techniques and strategies are few in number. Although it is true that every wholesaler has some sort of inventory control system, integrated systems of selling, buying, and financing are still quite rare.

Sales management

Wholesalers have been sales-oriented, traditionally, but as a group they have not really caught on yet to modern, professional, systematic techniques of selling and promotion. Much of their sales effort has been personal selling by individual salesmen. Some exceptional wholesaler-distributors are demonstrating real imagination in this area, of course: for instance, wholesale druggists are utilizing in-house telephone sales techniques to support the efforts of their more highly specialized personal salesmen. These personal salesmen limit their calls to key accounts, specialized customers, and prospects that show high potential. In fact, some drug wholesalers are taking 80% of their orders over the telephone.

Automatic reordering is another innovation that has been adopted to capture repeat sales and achieve lower costs. It is being used in electronics, plumbing, hospital supplies, and numerous other commodity lines. Since the automated approach frees salesmen from routine reordering tasks, it provides them with more time for specialized customer counseling and creative selling. In a number of cases, the use of "cash and carry" and catalog selling has substantially reduced the size of the wholesaler's sales force.

Wholesalers who operate multibranch companies are beginning to concentrate their big selling efforts on their customers' top management. They use their individual branches and twigs primarily to provide routine delivery service and to introduce product variations at the buyer level. This pattern indicates a trend toward divorcing the selling function from the product-handling function at the local level.

Personal salesmen in the wholesale area are also striving for deeper understanding of their customers' businesses. In particular, they are learning to help customers identify opportunities to reduce cost—for example:

● An electronics distributor in Ann Arbor analyzed the stockkeeping methods of one of his industrial customers and recommended revised delivery schedules, prearranged items, packs suitable for assembly line use, and standardized item identification. The customer was able to reduce the possession costs on his stock by 15% of its average value.

Unfortunately—once again—most wholesale selling is still conducted on a highly personal basis by relatively untrained and unsophisticated salesmen who call only on well-established customers. Still, wholesalers recognize the need for more systematic and sophisticated sales efforts, a need which is being satisfied in part by the National Association of Wholesalers.

The NAW began conducting sales management seminars and workshops in 1947. Paul Courtney, Executive Vice President of NAW, estimates that in the past five years more than 1,250 wholesaler-distributor houses have participated in one or more of these, and another 4,500 have participated in other programs. Individual commodity associations have also established more specialized sales training programs to help wholesalers field systematic, technically sound selling forces.

Aggressive manufacturers who have important stakes in their distributor networks have also increased their efforts to provide wholesaler managers with educational support through their field representatives and, in some cases, through formal training programs.

Promotion management

Manufacturers are also assisting their wholesalers with dealer shows, trade shows, advertising direct-mail promotion, and catalog preparation. Certain wholesalers, however, have rejected supplier assistance in this area in favor of proprietary programs that emphasize house identification. The wholesaler who elects this course is usually attempting to identify himself as *the* source for certain high-quality product lines, rather than as simply a "Brand X" wholesaler. This approach has been adopted by quite a number of wholesalers who deal in musical instruments and in the plumbing and heating and cooling lines. For example:

● The David Wexler Company of Chicago is a well-known merchant of musical merchandise. A relatively unknown item gains prestige and an aura of special value just by being listed in its catalog—witness the fact that customers have testified, "If an item is found in the Wexler catalog, it must be good."

The wholesaler faces not only product expansion, but a concomitant *promotion* expansion on the part of his suppliers. He is thus placed in the position of a "promotional censor," who is literally forced to sift and screen the promotional items and concepts that are directed into his local market. He often bases such screening on a purely subjective set of criteria. *Exhibit 5* indicates that this censorship is very extensive. The figures in this exhibit were de-

Exhibit 5

Comparison of wholesale promotions offered and those actually accepted by 400 wholesalers in 1966

Commodity line	Average annual number of promotions . . .		Percent accepted
	offered to each wholesaler	accepted by each wholesaler	
Electrical	56	8	14.3%
Plumbing, heating and cooling	36	8	22.2
Drug	3,700	390	10.5
Food, candy, and tobacco	244	39	16.0

veloped from a survey of 400 wholesalers I conducted in 1966 in conjunction with the National Association of Wholesalers.

Despite what I should call intense promotional effort by the suppliers, these wholesalers screened out between 78% and 90% of all promotions offered to them. In fact, the highest number of offerings met the lowest percentage of acceptance. The wholesalers who participated in the survey indicated that they support a promotion if:

● It is well structured to generate sales and profit.

● It is offered by a supplier who has cultivated a good relationship with the wholesaler.

● The supplier's salesman is properly trained and communicative.

● The promotion incorporates sound forward planning.

● It is "tailored," at least to some extent, to the individual wholesaler or his market.

● It reflects recognition of the wholesaler's handling costs and promotion budget.

While most wholesalers are not promotionally sophisticated, they are becoming increasingly selective about promotions:

● The progressive wholesaler usually develops an overall promotional strategy and then seeks out promotions that mesh well with this strategy in terms of timing and objectives.

● He is learning how to *use* supplier promotion programs for his own advantage, and is no longer content merely to be used *by* the supplier in his promotion activity.

• He is becoming more active in designing his own promotions.

Alert suppliers are nurturing and supporting such creativity on the part of the wholesaler; they find this cooperative approach less costly and more productive than the system of outright wholesaler censorship. By cooperating in this area, the supplier finds that he can sometimes ride along on the wholesaler's own promotion efforts at little or no additional cost to himself.

There are many dramatic examples of excellent sales and promotional programs conducted by wholesalers, particularly the larger corporate ones. Yet it appears that most wholesalers practice the basic functions of selling and promotion on a haphazard basis, with few controls and with insufficient energy. Their opportunities for upgrading such activities are enormous, and even the most elementary improvements can be highly profitable.

Financial planning & management

Because he is traditionally sales-oriented, the wholesaler has tended to leave finances to manage themselves. I have observed, though, that the old saw, "If it's good for sales, let's do it," appears to be giving way to "What's the profit impact?"

Many factors are pressuring the wholesaler into paying more attention to the principles of good financial management—increased competition, increasingly complex tax-reporting requirements, and his growing engagement with computerized information and control systems, to name a few. The manufacturer has long recognized that good information systems, good budgeting, and good accounting are fundamental to the control of his own complex operations; the wholesaler is beginning to recognize this as well.

The NAW has responded to this recognition with seminars on financial planning and management, and other trade associations are offering a number of outstanding programs for their memberships. The Central Supply Association (plumbing and heating products) has organized a five-day seminar for executives which covers these topics:

• The business executive in a changing world.

• Corporate goals and objectives.

• Long-range plans and policies.

• Formal and informal organization.

• Management information systems.

• Management succession.

• Communication networks.

• Automation and the use of computers.

- Management sciences, such as operations research.

- The use of financial ratios.

- Credit and financial management.

Manufacturers naturally recognize their own advantage in encouraging the managements of distributor networks to learn more about financial management. General Electric, Union Carbide, and Steelcase are only a few of the suppliers with training programs in this area.

PROFITS

Despite a lack of financial sophistication, wholesaling profits have been good in recent years, sometimes much better than the published figures reveal. During one series of seminars, my colleagues and I asked 80 wholesalers to calculate their rate of return, using their most accurate data and *eliminating assets related to nonbusiness activities*, which we suspected to be a distorting factor in many of the published financial reports. After such adjustment, the median rate was 17%, which is very close to the median reported by Dun & Bradstreet for all manufacturer groups. This experiment added substance to our belief.

For years wholesaling has been portrayed as the classic low-return, high-volume "sad sack" of the business world. This is inaccurate. *Exhibit 6* compares the rates of return on tangible net worth of selected manufacturers with those of their related wholesalers. The figures show that while the wholesaler's return is generally lower than the manufacturer's, in several cases it is actually a little higher.

Our experience leads us to believe that wholesalers are beginning to appreciate ROI concepts. In particular, most of them recognize two vital conditions for gaining ground in their businesses:

1. A rate of capital turnover that permits a relatively high level of activity with a relatively low capital base. (In practice, they frequently achieve this by reducing accounts receivable and inventory per dollar of sales. In their efforts to improve their capital turnover, wholesalers have begun to adopt such modern controls as cash-flow budgeting, a relatively recent development for this group.)

2. Good capital leverage based on a relatively high ratio of debt to equity. (Quite a number of wholesalers have overcome their native conservatism about debt, and are willing to take advantage of the services that investment banking offers them.)

On the other hand, we see ample evidence that the great majority of wholesalers are unsophisticated in financial matters. Too often they leave budgeting, financial analysis, and elementary planning to their bookkeeper or the local accounting firm. Indeed, such widespread financial ignorance lends

Exhibit 6

Profits of selected U.S. merchant-wholesalers and manufacturers, 1966 and 1967

	Net profit on tangible net worth[a]			
1. Durable goods	*Merchant wholesalers*		*Manufacturers*	
	1966	*1967*	*1966*	*1967*
Auto parts and accessories	7.56%	6.85%	14.60%	11.05%
Electrical parts and supplies	10.83	8.65	14.89	14.83
Furniture and home furnishings	8.20	8.90	10.94[b]	7.87[c]
Hardware	6.56	3.87	12.15[d]	9.51[e]
Plumbing and heating supplies	7.97	6.23	8.51	8.41
Lumber and building materials	6.84	6.73	9.76[f]	7.55[g]
Metals and minerals	10.30	8.33	9.90[h]	9.23[i]

Notes: [a] *Median percentages, after taxes.*
[b] *Furniture.*
[c] *Wood and upholstered household furniture.*
[d] *Hardware and tools.*
[e] *Cutlery, hand tools, and general hardware.*
[f] *Average of concrete, gypsum, and plaster products and lumber.*

[g] *Average of concrete, gypsum, and plaster products, and sawmills and planning mills.*
[h] *Integrated iron and steel operations.*
[i] *Iron and steel foundries.*

	Net profit on tangible net worth[a]			
2. Nondurable goods	*Merchant wholesalers*		*Manufacturers*	
	1966	*1967*	*1966*	*1967*
Groceries	7.83%	6.42%	10.53%[b]	11.25%[c]
Wines and liquors	7.68	7.40	10.38[d]	7.48[d]
Drugs and drug sundries	9.16	6.50	14.93	10.38
Chemical and allied products	12.93	7.43	10.01[c]	8.35[e]
Apparel and accessories	6.82	6.72	9.22	7.83
Paper	8.61	6.92	10.17	8.50

Notes: [a] *Median percentages, after taxes.*
[b] *Fruits and vegetable canners.*
[c] *Canned and preserved fruits, vegetables, and seafoods.*

[d] *Malt liquors.*
[e] *Average of agricultural and industrial chemicals.*

Source: *Dun & Bradstreet, Inc., Key Business Ratios in 125 Lines, 1966 and 1967.*

support to the observation that wholesaling is a "wholesome" business in which money can be made in spite of the lack of management sophistication. This may once have been the case, but I doubt that it is so any longer—for wholesaling, or any other major area of our present economy.

CONCLUSION

Like the rest of the economy, wholesaling is in a state of rapid change. The dynamics of the business world have hit some commodity lines and some kinds of wholesalers harder than others, but I believe that all have been affected. It is difficult to assess the violence and rapidity of change in this industry because of certain factors that blur visibility. Low-volume operations, for example, and family- or privately-controlled operations account for a substantial portion of the wholesaling volume, and one cannot usually obtain reliable statistics about such operations. Also, of course, wholesale-distribution networks owned or controlled by manufacturers account for another sizable chunk of the volume, and one cannot always separate the progress of these operations from that of their parents.

Despite the poor visibility, however, one can see that a growing number of wholesale operations are using modern business techniques and concepts. Since wholesalers view themselves as entrepreneurs and as profit-oriented businessmen, there is reason to believe that they will not restrict their activities to wholesaling alone. Indeed, they appear quite willing to develop marketing systems, some of which include manufacturing and retailing operations, using their wholesale houses as operational focal points.

On the negative side, a number of wholesalers are still tied to traditional forms and methods of operations, accepting the newer management techniques only slowly if at all. So far, the less sophisticated wholesaler seems to be surviving; in so doing, he demonstrates the intense need in our economy for the continued services of this resilient entrepreneur. It is questionable, however, whether the future will continue to allow easy entry into wholesaling or permit the inefficiencies of naive management. In the light of continuing pressures for lower-cost distribution, more complex marketing systems, and advancing management technologies, the only courses open to the myopic wholesaler are to close shop, sell out, or shape up.

In general, however, wholesalers seem determined to participate in our expanding economy. To an increasing extent, they are educating themselves and demonstrating a willingness to invest in newer systems and techniques. They are seeking and listening to the counsel of their more sophisticated suppliers, and they are cooperating with them on common problems.

As wholesalers continue to build their management strength and learn to handle the risks inherent in change, I am confident that they will maintain pace with the economy, prosper within it, and add value to it. The outcome, hopefully, will be a much more effective and efficient distribution structure in our economy.

READING 27

THE CONCEPT OF CHANNEL CONTROL*

Louis W. Stern

Channel control is used here to signify the ability of one member of a marketing channel for a given product (or brand) to stipulate marketing policies to

*Reprinted from *The Journal of Retailing*, published by The Institute of Retail Management, New York University, Summer 1967, pp. 14–20.

other channel members. For example, in a simple channel where a buyer interacts directly with a seller, the party gaining control in the bargaining process either through the use of sheer economic power, political or legal means, superior knowledge, more subtle promotional aids or other methods, obtains a major advantage in all aspects of their relationship. When marketing policies may be stipulated by any one party, this may have a marked influence on the efficiencies of both. Their goals may not be totally compatible; therefore, by complying with the dictates of buyers, for example, sellers may frequently be forced to alter their methods of operation in a manner that is not often profitable for them.

The exercise of channel control can, of course, vary widely. At one extreme are situations of channel tyranny in which one channel member insists on compliance to policies and practices from other members that he believes are in his best interests but which may not be in theirs. At the other extreme are situations of benevolent channel leadership in which the most powerful member is able to manage the channel so that overall channel performance can be increased.[1]

Buyers or sellers rarely achieve complete control over the marketing activities of their channel opposites. One group or member may, however, exercise the balance of channel power. This latter factor provides the means by which the "victors" in the vertical conflict are able to stipulate marketing policies to the vanquished. It is also likely that the extent of control achieved by a channel member may vary with the type of vertical conflict involved. For example, the seller may establish the price discount schedule for various quantities, but the buyer still determines (within the constraints of the seller's policy) the quantity actually purchased, which may or may not be the most profitable from the standpoint of the seller. In addition, there may also be an ephemeral quality to channel control.

CONTROL IN A HIGHLY CONCENTRATED INDUSTRY

In situations where a few sellers or buyers share the vast majority of the market for a given product, the existence (and emergence) of channel control is, frequently, blatant. An historical example of such control is afforded by the activities of automobile manufacturers relative to automobile dealers. Other examples can be found in numerous highly concentrated industries.

Concerning the distribution of automobiles, Ridgeway has made the following observations: (1) An automobile manufacturer is in a strategic position to try to bring order and uniformity to the marketing channel for his products, because he occupies a centralized position within it. (2) "Manufacturers seek to control the activities and operation of the dealers individually and collectively." (The term "control" refers to "the ability of the manufacturer to have the dealer operate for the benefit of the system.") (3) The manufacturer with his suppliers and/or dealers comprise a system, and "this system is in compe-

[1]Bruce Mallen describes various channel relationships as approaching either autocracy, democracy, or anarchy in "Conflict and Cooperation in Marketing Channels," *Reflections on Progress in Marketing*, L. George Smith, editor (Chicago, Ill.: American Marketing Association, 1965), pp. 65–85.

tition with similar systems in the economy. In order for the system to operate effectively as an integrated whole, there must be some administration of the system as a whole, not merely administration of the separate organizations within that system."[2]

If, as Ridgeway appears to suggest, the marketing channels for automobiles can be "controlled" by manufacturers so that the final result of their inter-organizational management is desirable from the standpoint of all parties involved, then such a situation would approximate that of benevolent channel leadership. There is, unfortunately, no tangible evidence that this optimum situation has been reached. In fact, there is some historical evidence that indicates that automobile manufacturers have exercised despotic control within the channel to achieve their short-run objectives.

In the years immediately following World War II, dealers were able to increase sales yearly. During this period, manufacturers became intensely interested in achieving even higher rates of growth than the dealers were supplying. As a result, dealers were placed under tight franchise agreements and were assigned sales quotas that were designed to permit the manufacturers to realize maximum operating economies as well as to increase their overall growth rates. Dealers were forced to pay for shipments on delivery and then were expected to sell all the cars shipped by the plants. Dealers were also held to pricing and servicing standards set by the factory and were assessed part of the national advertising costs. If a dealer disagreed with these policy stipulations, he was disenfranchised. The manufacturers maintained this form of control until the middle 1950's, when the market for new automobiles slumped drastically. At that time, the dealers found it impossible to sell all of the automobiles being shipped and began to revolt against the inequities imposed by the manufacturers.[3]

There is no certainty that the remedial measures taken by manufacturers as a result of the "revolt" have eradicated the form of control existing during the decade after World War II. Ridgeway's conclusions cited previously apparently refer to an idealized situation that would, no doubt, be satisfactory to all channel members. It is unlikely, however, that the form of control has changed radically enough in the past ten years to bring the industry full circle from channel tyranny to benevolent channel leadership.

CONTROL IN A BILATERALLY COMPETITIVE INDUSTRY

In order to illustrate the potentially wide applicability of the concept (and study of) channel control, it is useful to isolate situations where control is theoretically not supposed to exist, and then examine whether it does exist. In this sense, the wood household furniture industry provides a meaningful example.

[2]Valentine P. Ridgeway, "Administration of Manufacturer-Dealer Systems," *Explorations in Retailing*, Stanley C. Hollander, ed. (East Lansing, Mich.: Michigan State University, Bureau of Business and Economic Research, 1959), pp. 250 and 256.

[3]The dealer revolt was well publicized. A description of it can be found in the following issues of *Business Week*: February 4, 1956 (p. 29); March 3, 1956 (p. 104); March 23, 1957 (p. 65); February 2, 1957 (p. 25); and April 6, 1957 (p. 173).

The wood household furniture industry (including both manufacturers and retailers in the term "industry") is bilaterally competitive. In other words, the industry is characterized by low degrees of market concentration on both the manufacturing and retailing levels in the channel of distribution.[4] Channel control in the hands of either retailers or manufacturers should be nonexistent or, at best, weak, because according to economic theory, the operation of open market forces should dictate the basic modes of doing business and thus should militate against the establishment of control in any one level of the channel. But control does, in actuality, exist in the wood household furniture industry; it resides at the retail level because furniture retailers have gained the greatest influence over the final sale of the products of the industry.

The fact of this control is illustrated in retailers' buying methods. Many of the manufacturers' marketing practices have been stipulated by, administered by, and/or enacted to placate furniture retailers, even though some of these policies and practices work to the detriment of manufacturers. As evidence of this bargaining phenomenon, a few examples of retail buying methods are enumerated below.

Buying at furniture markets. Furniture markets are manufacturers' exhibits held periodically in the major manufacturing and retailing centers. At the markets manufacturers set up product displays, and in certain locations they maintain these displays throughout the entire year at considerable expense even though the markets, which usually last about one week, are held only two to four times each year. They are closed to the public, and sales are made only to retail stores and wholesale buyers. For example, between 500 and 1,000 manufacturers exhibit at the Chicago Furniture Mart. In terms of dollar volume, 75 percent of the industry is represented. It is estimated that approximately 25,000 to 30,000 representatives of retail stores visit this mart during the two market periods (January and July).

The furniture markets have been strongly supported by furniture retailers and generally disliked by furniture manufacturers. The reason for this attitude difference is that, at any given market, a buyer has an opportunity to inspect the products of a large number of manufacturers and to make detailed comparisons of competitive prices. Thus, a shrewd buyer can literally play off one manufacturer against another in the space of a few minutes within the same building. Manufacturers do complete a considerable volume of sales during the markets, but they have continually deplored their adverse bargaining positions and have sought ways to eliminate the markets for this and other reasons. Buyer insistence, however, has been a casual factor in influencing

---

[4]Some of the material appearing in this article was developed by the author for Arthur D. Little, Inc., as part of a program of technical assistance for the Federal Republic of Nigeria, sponsored by the United States Agency for International Development, and appeared in the report *The Nigerian Wooden Furniture Industry.* For a detailed description of competition in the furniture industry, see Kenneth R. Davis, *Furniture Marketing: Product, Price, and Promotional Policies of Manufacturers* (Chapel Hill, N.C.: University of North Carolina Press, 1957). A parallel to the wood household furniture industry can be found by reading Bain's description of the ladies' dress industry. See Joe S. Bain, *Pricing, Distribution, and Employment* (New York: Henry Holt and Company, 1948), pp. 249–50.

the manufacturers' policies with regard to market attendance and to continuation of them.

Sold-order buying. There is a trend in the furniture industry toward purchase on what is called a "sold-order" basis. Under this system, retailers carry minimum inventories and limit this inventory to floor samples. Upon sale at retail, the store notifies the manufacturer to ship a new suite either to the customer directly or to the store. This places a tremendous inventory burden on the manufacturer and increases his delivery costs, as well as creating a relatively long waiting period for ultimate consumers prior to delivery.

Exclusives. Retailers continually press for "exclusives" and generally are successful in achieving them. The greater the number of exclusives a manufacturer must sell, the shorter his production runs of any one suite and thus the higher his costs.

Cumulative quantity discounts. Cumulative quantity discounts are more common than noncumulative quantity discounts in the furniture industry. Cumulative discounts favor the buyer and often work to the disadvantage of the seller, because goods may be shipped in small lots at a number of times, thus involving higher billing, packing, transporting, and collecting costs. In fact, the cumulative discount is offered largely as a means of encouraging concentration of purchases and rewarding customers for their patronage.

Attitude toward brands. Furniture retailers look askance at manufacturers' attempts to establish strong brand identity, especially where the manufacturers may have wide distribution in their particular locale. The reason for this is that retailers know that consumers will shop for furniture and, if brand identity is established, will compare price from store to store on the same advertised suite. The consumer may also become highly confident in his choice prior to entering a store, thus limiting a furniture salesman's selling latitude. "Switching" by sales personnel from low-margin to high-margin items within the store is common practice.

The feelings of retailers toward brands is often extremely heated; in some cases, retailers have been known to burn off brands and remove manufacturers' labels on floor samples. Furniture manufacturers have again acquiesced to retailers' demands with the result that the level of national (manufacturer to consumer) advertising has remained at a very low level, relative to other nonconcentrated consumer durable industries.

RETAILER CHANNEL CONTROL IN THE FURNITURE INDUSTRY

Furniture retailers have appeared to gain control over marketing policies within the channel because both consumers and manufacturers apparently abdicate their bargaining powers to them. When purchasing wood household furniture, the average consumer is inadequately prepared to judge quality and thereby to compare prices among similar suites. Furniture is a shopping good, and the intelligent consumer should, therefore, make her selection on the basis of a comparison of quality, price, and style. Because of a lack of information about various furniture pieces, the consumer must rely primarily on style when making her purchase decision. But any style is available in all price ranges; style piracy is very common among furniture manufacturers. The retailers can, quite easily, convince consumers of the worth of various grades of furniture as long as the style is satisfactory. This sales influence forms the core of retailers' competitive strategy and the means by which control in the channel is secured.

On the other hand, most furniture manufacturers are not astute merchandisers and promoters. Selling methods are often archaic when compared with the methods used by marketers of other consumer durables. Even though most individual manufacturers may not have the financial strength to engage in large national advertising or promotion campaigns, for example, they have, in concert, formed a well-financed furniture manufacturers association that could influence consumer buying habits through institutional advertising. They have not, however, chosen to attempt to influence the ultimate sale by engaging in such advertising. Because style is a subjective element in the shopping task, a consumer who can determine quality may become an intelligent shopper. With the absence of shopping intelligence, the consumer must rely heavily on the retailers for product information. This reliance permits retailers to influence greatly the purchase decision and thereby gain channel power.[5]

ECONOMIC THEORY AND CHANNEL CONTROL

In cases of vertical conflict, the locus of channel control is frequently related to the types of markets in which both sellers and buyers compete. In an excellent discussion, Heflebower has described the bargaining relationships between supplying and distributing industries when these industries compete in markets characterized as oligopolistic and competitive.[6] Despite some of Heflebower's negative conclusions regarding the appropriateness of bilateral oligopoly theory for explaining the emergence of channel power among mass distributors, it is possible to attempt to make some modifications of his findings in order to show their applicability to the concept of channel control.[7]

Buyers or sellers operating in oligopolistic markets can frequently gain channel control when dealing with sellers or buyers operating in more com-

[5]Investigations by the National Commission on Food Marketing indicated that situations of channel control may be found within specific segments of the food industry. For example, see *Studies of Organization and Competition in Grocery Manufacturing*, Technical Study No. 6, National Commission on Food Marketing, 1966, prepared for the Commission by the author. For documented examples of channel control in a variety of industries, see Valentine P. Ridgeway, *op. cit.*; Joseph C. Palamountain, Jr., *The Politics of Distribution* (Cambridge, Mass.: Harvard University Press, 1955); Ralph Cassady, Jr., and Wylie L. Jones, *The Changing Competitive Structure in the Wholesale Grocery Trade* (Berkeley and Los Angeles, Calif.: University of California Press, 1949); and Bruce Mallen, *op. cit.*
[6]See Richard B. Heflebower, "Mass Distribution: A Phase of Bilateral Oligopoly or of Competition?", *Explorations in Retailing, op. cit.*, pp. 193–204. The situation whereby "competitive-like suppliers" sell to "competitive-like distributive trades" is mentioned but not discussed by Heflebower.
[7]*Ibid.*, pp. 201–3.

petitive markets. One theoretical reason to explain the emergence of channel control in these situations is that oligopolists have, to some extent, stabilized competition among themselves. They interact under the constraints of a rather well-defined oligopolistic rationale while actors in a theoretically more competitive environment cannot rely on such a rationale to maintain some semblance of market stability. The latter have, almost by definition, less information about competitors, and even if there were an opportunity for more competitive commonality, deviants would always be willing and ready to spoil the tranquility of the market. Another theoretical reason, among others, that might explain the emergence of channel control is the ability of oligopolists to utilize relatively large profits, gained through joint maximization, in developing strong consumer loyalties to their products or brands.

In addition, the theory of countervailing power can be extended to a theory of reaction to control. When a group of sellers, for example, "enjoys a measure of monopoly power and is reaping a measure of monopoly return as a result," and when that power can be exploited by large buyers,[8] the process of such exploitation is a factor signifying a shift in control.

For example, through an increased emphasis on private labels, retailers have found an opportunity to share the gains of manufacturers' market and channel power, especially with regard to physically undifferentiated (or highly similar) items within a given product category. Retailers have used private labels as impressive bargaining levers in their negotiations with manufacturers. The implied threat by retailers to "push" their private labels at the expense of manufacturers' brands through the manipulation of shelf space, prices, and promotion has created the need for new and more retailer-oriented (oftentimes stipulated) marketing policies on the part of manufacturers in order to forestall possibly disastrous consequences for their own brands. In many cases, manufacturers have been too slow in developing these policies, and retailers have, therefore, placed even more emphasis on private labels.[9] As retail markets have become more concentrated, the locus of control has begun to shift away from manufacturers, and the private label phenomenon has been an important vehicle influencing the shift.[10]

In sum, if, in a number of industries, control and, concomitantly, the balance of bargaining power are centralized in one organization within a system of interrelated organizations, e.g., a marketing channel, the application of existing economic theory should provide a means by which the location of control can be determined. On the other hand, a weakness in economic theory is that it too often concentrates on price manipulation as the main determinant in bargaining situations. An important contribution of marketing studies to economic theory has been the discovery that, in most situations, price manipulation is only one element in the mix of competitive methods available to firms and that even if price is stabilized, control can be established

---

[8]See John K. Galbraith, *American Capitalism* (Boston, Mass.: Houghton Mifflin Company, 1956), pp. 111–12.
[9]Additional thoughts relating to the effects of increased private label activity may be found in Louis W. Stern, "The New World of Private Brands," *California Management Review*, VIII, No. 3 (Spring 1966), pp. 43–50.
[10]See Richard B. Heflebower, *op. cit.*

and maintained through the manipulation of other elements, as is apparent in the case of the wood household furniture industry cited previously.

READING 28

DISTRIBUTION SYSTEMS—FIRMS, FUNCTIONS, AND EFFICIENCIES*

William P. Dommermuth and R. Clifton Andersen

A marketing institution acquires its particular designation of retailer, commission merchant, food broker, and so forth because of what it does—the functions it performs. Because institutions are more visible than their functions, however, a common reaction evoked by the term *channel of distribution* is visualization of a sequence of institutions, generally of middlemen rather than a sequence of functions in a systems framework.

Elaborate and sophisticated analyses of distribution channels as institutional sequences have been developed, some complete with intricate notational designations.[1] While these may be of some usefulness in understanding marketing channels, we argue that an approach which treats a channel as a *functional system* rather than an *institutional sequence* is of greater value in generating new ideas about the dynamics of channel structure, efficiency, and profitability.

While such an approach does not "eliminate the middleman," it subordinates his existence as an institution to his existence as a system functionary.

A marketing channel can then be defined as a particular or unique system of functional performances. The institutions which participate are incidental; what is critical is the system design through which functions can be best performed.

In implementing a systems approach to marketing channels, it is helpful to ignore the customary institutional designations—wholesaler, retailer, and so on. Discarding these terms has more than mere symbolic value. It encourages speculation about mixtures of functional delegations which do not currently exist because no appropriate institutions currently exist. This, in turn, opens the field for analysis of why they do not exist, whether they should, and if they eventually might. In short, it points the way toward new opportunities.

What is a marketing function? Even the most cursory search of marketing literature will reveal that it is easy to find many different answers. It also is obvious that marketing scholars have for many years employed the concept of functions as a basis for organizing and analyzing marketing activities. Most of the differences in classifying activities into certain functions are rather minor, and derive from the analytical objective of the particular writer.

*Reprinted from *MSU Business Topics*, published by The Graduate School of Business Administration, Michigan State University, vol. 17, no. 2 (Spring 1969), pp. 51–56.
[1]See, for example, Ralph E. Breyer, "Some Observations on Structural Form in the Growth of Marketing Channels," in Reavis Cox, Wroe Alderson, and Stanley J. Shapiro (eds.), *Theory in Marketing* (Homewood, Illinois: Richard D. Irwin, Inc., 1964), pp. 163–75.

With this in mind, we have selected a concept of marketing, and from it a particular view of marketing functions which, we believe, best implements our analytical objectives. While other functional approaches could be applied to this presentation, they would add much to the complexity, little to the meaning.

Our starting point is McInnes' "A Conceptual Approach to Marketing."[2] The market is viewed as "the gap which separates producer and consumer." Marketing, then, becomes "any activity which actualizes the potential market relationship between the makers and users of economic goods and services." The major types of separation inherent in this view are spatial separation, separation in time, perceptional separation, separation of ownership, and separation of values.

We posit four functional areas as being of primary relevance in closing the gaps between makers and users.[3] The particular system through which these functions are combined, integrated, and allocated among various firms comprises a marketing channel.

Transportation deals with spatial separation and includes all activities directly concerned with moving goods from the place of production to the place of sale or such other place as may be designated by the user.

Inventory deals with temporal separation and includes those activities directly concerned with holding goods between the time of production and the time of sale or such other time as may be designated by the user.

Promotion deals with perceptional separation and includes all activities directly concerned with providing information, including persuasive information, regarding the nature of goods and services and their relationship to the potential user's perceived needs.

Transaction deals with separation of ownership and values. It includes all activities directly concerned with active negotiation and transfer of title.

All of these functions are interrelated and, in practice, promotion and transaction are often so closely interwoven as to be difficult to distinguish. All of these functions involve a number of component activities. Some component activities, most notably administration, coordination, financing, and risk-bearing pervade all four functions. Users could, and sometimes do, take the initiative in functional performance, but typically this initiative is taken by the *producer*, a term not necessarily meaning the manufacturer. The producer has the choice of either performing the functions himself or delegating part or all of the performance to other firms. In either event, he must consider both cost of performance and his resources and capabilities.

If we assume that the producer aims at profit maximization, it follows that he will always seek to minimize cost of input requirements for any given level of output. This requires determination of the most efficient available system of functional performance.

---

[2]William McInnes, "A Conceptual Approach to Marketing," Cox, Alderson, and Shapiro (eds.), *op. cit.*, pp. 51–67.

[3]While we have drawn certain basic notions of marketing and the nature of its activities from the McInnes article, our functional classifications differ from those presented by him. This is because we have chosen to group activities into rather broad categories to prevent the analysis from becoming unnecessarily complex.

FIRMS, FUNCTIONS, AND EFFICIENCIES

Within the system there are four possible alternatives to lower costs through improved efficiency. These alternatives can be designated as:

1. Intrafunctional—intrafirm

2. Intrafunctional—interfirm

3. Interfunctional—intrafirm

4. Interfunctional—interfirm

Intrafunctional—intrafirm efficiency occurs when a firm is able to lower the cost of performing a particular function while holding output constant. As an example, an appliance manufacturer might introduce an improved type of materials handling equipment into his warehouse, changing his average cost curve from *(IN)* to *(IN$_1$)*, as shown in Figure 1, and lowering his cost per unit of input for the inventory function from *XA* to *XB*.

Intrafunctional—interfirm efficiency occurs when a lower cost can be achieved by delegating the performance of a function, or some portion of it, to another firm. The second firm's ability to perform the function at a lower cost typically stems from specialization and from economies of scale.

For example, if our appliance manufacturer finds an intermediary operating on a cost curve exactly the same as his own *(IN$_1$)*, but able to combine performance of the manufacturer's inventory function with an equal quantity of performance for another manufacturer, then cost of functional performance moves to the right and down along the cost curve. The average cost per unit of input drops.

However, because the intermediary is a specialist, with special skills, plant, and equipment, it is likely that he will enjoy an even more favorable cost curve than *(IN$_1$)*. In this event, intrafunctional—interfirm efficiency will lower cost per unit of input even further.

Interfunctional efficiency occurs when increased total expenditure for performance of one function results in a more than offsetting decrease in the total cost of another function.

The activities encompassed by the term *physical distribution* probably have received the most attention in this connection, especially the combination of the transportation and inventory functions.

As an example, a firm might substitute air freight for surface transport, thereby raising the level of its cost curve for transportation. However, because of reduced delivery time, the firm now can operate with less total inventory, reducing the input requirement for inventory. While total cost of transportation is increased, inventory costs are decreased by a greater amount. Since decrease in total inventory cost is greater than increase in total transportation cost, there is a gain through interfunctional efficiency.

Like intrafunctional efficiencies, interfunctional efficiencies may be either intrafirm or interfirm. In either case, one expects they would be more difficult to implement. In the interfunctional—intrafirm situation, departmental lines

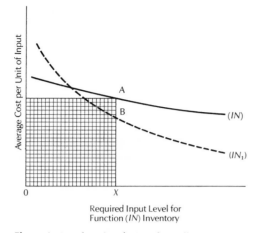

Figure 1 *Intrafunctional - intrafirm efficiency*

of authority may obstruct acceptance. In the interfunctional—interfirm situation, cooperation and agreement between completely independent units may require the hand of a skillful negotiator.

FUNCTIONS, MIDDLEMEN, AND INSTITUTIONS

We have discussed a few of the ways in which intrafunctional and interfunctional efficiencies might be achieved on either an intrafirm or interfirm basis. We believe the list is sufficiently illustrative, though by no means exhaustive.

The issue of importance is this: at one and the same time such analysis demonstrates why middlemen exist, and also why it is misleading to concentrate upon them in analyzing channels.

The two characteristics possessed in common by all middlemen are the following: they are independent of the producer, and they handle all or part of the transaction function. Sometimes they are delegated other functions, sometimes they are not. An independent firm which handles one or more functions, but not the transaction function, is designated as a facilitating agency, and generally relegated to some mysterious limbo outside the channel. Examples include advertising agencies, storage warehouses, and transportation companies.

Even among middlemen concentration tends to center upon merchant middlemen, those who not only participate in transaction but take title to goods. Admittedly, transaction is probably the most basic and sensitive function. After all, this is the area in which the sale is finally consummated. Admittedly as well, transfer of title has as its corollary transfer of control. For these reasons the producer might show a more than casual interest in middlemen, particularly merchant middlemen. However, they are still only actual or potential parts of a channel system. They are not a system per se.

IN	IN	IN	IN	IN		T	T	T	T	T		L	L	L	L	L		P	P	P	P	P
IN	IN	IN	IN	IN		T	T	T	T	T		L	L	L	L	L		P	P	P	P	P
IN	IN	IN	IN	IN		T	T	T	T	T		L	L	L	L	L		P	P	P	P	P
IN	IN	IN	IN	IN		T	T	T	T	T		L	L	L	L	L		P	P	P	P	P
IN	IN	IN	IN	IN		T	T	T	T	T		L	L	L	L	L		P	P	P	P	P

INVENTORY   TRANSPORTATION   TRANSACTION   PROMOTION

Figure 2*

Systems one - four

CHANNELS AS FUNCTIONAL SYSTEMS

We turn now to a brief of how a distribution channel might look if depicted as a system of functional inputs designed to achieve a given level of output. Then we shall speculate upon a few variations in channel design which might be envisioned if consideration of institutions were subordinated to consideration of functions.

The system's objective is to maximize the surplus of output over expenditure for inputs. System output is defined as total revenue from sales and represented graphically (in Figures 2 and 3) by all of the area within the outside boundary lines. Surplus is indicated by the blank squares in each graph. Lettered squares represent expenditures for the indicated required functional inputs. To simplify the illustration, manufacturing inputs are disregarded, although in practice of course they are very much a part of a larger, total system.

Four systems will be described, with reference to Figure 2. Each represents an alternative channel choice available to a producer at a given point in time. That is, we might assume a manufacturer planning a marketing channel system for his product involving the performance of transportation (T), inventory *(IN)*, transaction *(L)*, and promotion *(P)* functions. His concern is total input expense relative to total output revenue for each system.

We begin with System One, a hypothetical starting point, where it is assumed that the total system input of 100 units of expenditure is required to produce a system output of 115 units of revenue, and that input expense is equal for the four functions. The surplus then is 15 units.

We can now speculate upon an alternative, System Two, which introduces the opportunity for interfunctional—intrafirm efficiency, a trade-off between the inventory and transportation functions. Let us assume that the transportation function cost increases from 25 to 30 units, but inventory cost is reduced by 10 units. The system now shows a surplus of 20 units of revenue output over expense input, with all functions still performed by the producer.

Suppose a second organization participates, thereby introducing opportunities for intrafunctional—interfirm efficiency. In this new alignment, System Three, the second firm absorbs a part of the inventory function and a part of the transaction function. We will hypothesize that, by delegating a portion of the transaction function to an intermediary, it is possible to decrease expense of functional input requirements by five units. This occurs because the intermediary handles other products and its average transaction cost is there-

*Figure 2 contains a total of 115 squares; each of the four input function groups contains 25 squares; surplus is represented by the 15 blank squares.

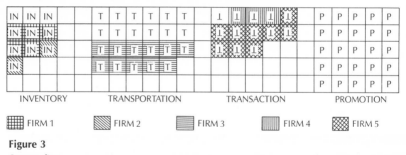

Figure 3
System five

fore lower than that of the producer. Its participation as an inventory handler, in and of itself, adds nothing to system efficiency, but is required to enable improved performance of the transaction function. The surplus in System Three is 25 units.

We can now envision System Four in which a third firm enters the channel. Because of this third firm's specialized capabilities and scale of operations, inventory input cost is reduced from 15 to 12. The saving benefits the total system. Again because of specialization and scale, this additional firm cuts transportation input expense from 30 to 24, and transaction input expense from 20 to 15. The system surplus is now 39 units.

At this point it might be appropriate to ask, "Why not call the second firm a retailer and the third firm a wholesaler and admit we have been talking about middlemen all the time?"

The difference is that when the system is presented in the present fashion, some revealing features appear that go beyond mere recognition of middlemen utility.

For one thing it can be observed that the delegation of functions in groups is not inescapable *unless the functions happen to be inseparable.*

Suppose we found it was possible and more efficient to delegate each of the functions to different firms at each stage of delegation. Suppose that by doing so, one unit of input expense is saved at each point. The result is System Five, shown in Figure 3. From a functional point of view it does precisely the same thing as Systems One through Four but does it much more efficiently. It might be difficult to develop an appropriate institutional designation for some firms participating in our theoretical System Five. It might prove even more difficult to find existing firms available to perform functions in this fashion in the real world.

But it might also be a better system, and to say that a type of firm does not exist is not to say that it should not exist or will not exist.

SOME COMMENTS AND CONCLUSIONS

We have assumed output as a predetermined, presumably optimal constant. In practice, determination of what total output should be is interwoven with the question of effecting changes in cost of input requirements. Given an elastic demand curve, for example, we would expect the reduction of input costs demonstrated in Systems One through Five to reduce marginal cost and bring about a lowering of price to the user with a consequent increase in total revenue output. This in turn means revised cost factors for inputs.

Systems graphs, such as those depicted in Figures 2 and 3, are, of course, expository rather than analytical devices. Actual analysis and application presupposes a fairly accurate knowledge of cost relationships as shown previously in Figure 1. While even the most advanced methods of accounting and estimation are likely to make such knowledge available on only a limited basis, electronic data processing and other developments in business intelligence-gathering mechanisms are constantly improving a firm's ability to acquire more accurate cost information and to use it more effectively. Profit maximization is a theoretical principle. In the real world its derivative is profit improvement. On this basis, distribution cost analysis on functional rather than institutional lines seems both applicable and sensible given present techniques.

The availability of appropriate institutions for optimal functional delegations is probably a greater hindrance to radical changes in the design of distribution channels than is the lack of cost data. It could be argued that the producer, again usually the manufacturer, probably would not be able to find or create such institutions even after determining the best systems alignment from a functional cost point of view.

The ability of producers, particularly large firms, to influence the creation of new institutional forms is probably under-estimated. In some industries, channel structure is clearly producer-dominated. Control and change at the retail level are probably most difficult to implement, since the shopping desires and store loyalties of ultimate consumers are involved. Even here, however, we see occasional evidence of producer dominance, as witness the automobile and gasoline industries.

But the notion of market channels as system-centered rather than institution-centered is of as much, if not more, importance to institutional strategists as it is to producers. Some of the most pronounced changes in distribution patterns —supermarkets and discount houses, for example—have been initiated by entrepreneurs specializing in the performance of marketing functions.

A look at functional system graphs might suggest certain possibilities for the reassessment of functional alignments to facilitating agencies as well as to middlemen. If a railroad or truck line looked beyond its function as an inter-city transportation agency, might it find that it was partly a distribution agency capable of coupling transportation with inventory maintenance? Might a grocery wholesaler decide that he could function more profitably by divesting himself of transaction and promotion, specializing in transportation and inventory, extending beyond groceries and handling diverse lines of merchandise?

In summary, ridding channel analysis of its traditional institutional orientation makes it possible to speculate more meaningful about institutions themselves. New types of marketing firms will continue to develop in relationship to the performance of functions, typically offering an opportunity for improving the input/output ratio of a channel. Systems orientation holds the promise of expediting the development of such firms because its emphasis on functions is less likely to limit one's outlook to the status quo.

READING 29

PHYSICAL DISTRIBUTION DEVELOPMENT, CURRENT STATUS, AND POTENTIAL*

Donald J. Bowersox

During the past two decades the discipline of physical distribution has evolved as a major facet of business administration.[1] The objectives of this article are: to highlight some major developments which have served as catalytic forces to the emerging field, to provide a synthesis of contemporary physical distribution thought, and to offer a brief diagnosis of some areas providing research opportunities.

A DECADE OF CRYSTALLIZATION

Physical distribution consists of those business activities concerned with transporting finished inventory and/or raw material assortments so they arrive at the designated place, when needed, and in usable condition. Economists have long recognized this process as a vital aspect of value added through the distribution process. However, in the typical commercial enterprise and within the study of business administration, the overall process of physical distribution has traditionally received fragmentary and most often secondary consideration. The concept of integrated physical distribution emerged during the 1950s. The following quote from a 1954 speech of the late Professor Paul D. Converse provides a general appraisal of physical distribution as recently as fifteen years ago.[2]

In the study of marketing and the operation of marketing departments and businesses a great deal more attention is paid to buying and selling than to physical handling. In fact the physical handling of goods seems to be pretty much overlooked by sales executives, advertising men and market researchers. . . . problems of physical distribution are too often brushed aside as matters of little importance. I have for many years been reading business and economics magazines. Such publications over the years have devoted relatively little space to physical distribution.

*Reprinted from *The Journal of Marketing,* published by the American Marketing Association, vol. 33, no. 1 (January 1969), pp. 63–70.
[1]Other common titles used to describe what is here called Physical Distribution are Business Logistics, Logistics of Distribution, and Materials Management.
[2]Paul D. Converse, "The Other Half of Marketing," *Twenty-Sixth Boston Conference on Distribution,* Boston Conference on Distribution (Boston, Massachusetts, 1954), p. 22.

A logical explanation for the neglect and subsequent late development of physical distribution can be attributed to at least two major factors.[3] First, prior to the time that computers emerged from infancy and before applied analytical tools were generally at the disposal of business, there was no reason to believe that an overall attack on physical distribution activities would accomplish improved performance. The 1950s were destined to witness a major change in traditional orientation since neither computers nor quantitative techniques were to be denied the fertility of physical distribution applications.

A second major factor contributing to a reexamination of traditional viewpoints was the prevailing economic climate. The prolonged profit squeeze of the early 1950s, highlighted by the recession of 1958, created an environment conducive to the development of new cost control systems. Integrated physical distribution provided a productive arena for new methods of cost reduction.

Thus, technology and need abruptly changed during the 1950s. After a great many years of relative obscurity, the period from 1956 to 1965 was to become the decade during which the integrated physical distribution concept would crystallize. An interpretation of the literature reveals that the physical distribution concept congealed as the product of four significant developments. Each is briefly discussed in this section. A synthesis is provided in the next section.

The notion of total cost

In 1956 a specialized study of air freight economics provided a major new orientation to physical distribution costing.[4] The study, while explaining the economic justification for high cost air transport, introduced the concept of total cost analysis. Total cost was developed as a measure of all expenditures required to accomplish a firm's physical distribution mission. The authors illustrated that high freight rates required for air transport could be more than justified by trade-offs in reduced inventory possession and warehouse operation costs.

The concept of total cost, while basic in logic, had not been previously applied to physical distribution economics. Probably because of the economic climate of the times, the immediate reaction was a flurry of attention to physical distribution problems. Subsequent refinements provided a comprehensive treatment of physical distribution cost characteristics and related functional analysis of available trade-offs.[5]

---

[3]For an expanded treatment see Donald J. Bowersox, Edward J. Smykay, and Bernard J. LaLonde, *Physical Distribution Management: Logistics Problems of the Firm*, Revised Edition (New York: The Macmillan Company, 1968), pp. 8–15.

[4]Howard T. Lewis, James W. Culliton, and Jack D. Steel, *The Role of Air Freight in Physical Distribution* (Boston, Mass.: Division of Research, Graduate School of Business Administration, Harvard University, 1956).

[5]In particular see: Marvin Flaks, "Total Cost Approach to Physical Distribution," *Business Management*, Vol. 24 (August, 1963), pp. 55–61, and Raymond LeKashman and John F. Stolle, "The Total Cost Approach to Distribution," *Business Horizons*, Vol. 8 (Winter, 1965), pp. 33–46.

Application of the systems concept

It is difficult to trace the exact origins of the systems approach to problem solving. However, the notion of total integrated effort toward the accomplishment of predetermined goals rapidly found a home in physical distribution analysis. The systems concept provided a research posture, and total cost analysis offered a method of evaluating among alternative system configurations.

The first general articles directed to the subject of physical distribution relied heavily on systems technology.[6] In particular, it became apparent that the great deficiency of the traditional viewpoint was the prevailing practice of treating the many physical distribution activity centers as isolated performance areas. The result was a failure to capture the benefits obtainable only from integrated control.

When viewed from a systems viewpoint, integrated physical distribution creates a new requirement for compromise between traditional business activities. For example, manufacturing traditionally desires long production runs and lowest procurement cost, while physical distribution raises questions concerning the total cost commitment of these practices. Finance, traditionally favorable to low inventories, may force a physical distribution system to adjust components in a less than satisfactory total cost arrangement. With respect to marketing, traditional preferences for finished goods inventory staging and broad assortments in forward markets often stand in conflict to economies offered through total system evaluation.

The basic belief that integrated system performance can and most often will produce an end result greater than possible from non-coordinated performance rapidly became a primary focal point in development of the physical distribution concept. The logic of systems technology offered a regimented way to penetrate the traditional viewpoint.

Beyond cost

By the early 1960s the horizons of the emerging field of physical distribution began to expand. Peter Drucker stimulated top management's attention to the emerging new dimension of business administration.[7] During this period, emphasis began to shift toward a more penetrating appraisal of the improved customer service capabilities gained as a result of a highly integrated physical distribution system. Another 1962 article which made a major impact was authored by Professor Lazer; it served to provide a synthesis of developments between physical distribution and managerial marketing.[8] Lazer and Drucker

---

[6]For example see: Harvey N. Shycon and Richard B. Maffei, "Simulation—Tool for Better Distribution," *Harvard Business Review*, Vol. 38 (November–December, 1960), pp. 65–75; Donald D. Parker, "Improved Efficiency and Reduced Cost In Marketing," *Journal of Marketing*, Vol. 26 (April, 1962), pp. 15–21; J. L. Heskett, "Ferment in Marketing's Oldest Area," *Journal of Marketing*, Vol. 26 (October, 1962), pp. 40–45; and, John F. Magee, "The Logistics of Distribution," *Harvard Business Review*, Vol. 40 (July–August, 1962), pp. 89–101.

[7]Peter Drucker, "The Economy's Dark Continent," *Fortune*, Vol. 72 (April, 1962), pp. 103–104.

[8]William Lazer, "Distribution and The Marketing Mix," *Transportation and Distribution Management*, Vol. 2 (December, 1962), pp. 12–17.

thus made a particularly noteworthy contribution by adding new posture to the field of physical distribution. Attention was now directed to issues of demand cultivation and to the overall importance of physical distribution to corporate vitality on other than a purely cost orientation that dominated earlier treatments.[9]

Physical distribution now came into focus as representing a balanced effort between product delivery capabilities and related system alternatives. Given a programed level of service, several alternative systems might be capable of accomplishing the stated goals but at various levels of total cost expenditure.

Emphasis upon temporal relations and physical commitments in a channel context

An additional development in physical distribution thinking relates to the dynamic elements of channel management. The majority of physical distribution systems have been studied from the vantage point of vertically integrated organizations. A more useful viewpoint is that physical distribution activities and related responsibilities seldom terminate when product ownership transfer occurs. Many significant costs of physical distribution are experienced between firms linked together in cooperative vertical marketing systems. The interface of two or more individual firm physical distribution systems may well lead to excessive cost generation and customer service impairment for the total channel. Even under conditions of system compatibility, the total cost of physical distribution for the channel may rapidly accumulate as a result of efforts duplicated by various firms within the total channel.

A more realistic approach to channel-wide physical distribution performance evolved from an evaluation of information lags and product assortment commitments inherent in channel organizations. In 1958, Jay Forrester provided a new view of business operations. In terms of physical product flow, the Forrester treatment dramatically illustrated the impact of information dynamics upon fluctuations in inventory accumulations.[10] The impact of time delays had been generally neglected among early treatments of physical distribution in deference to a primary emphasis upon spatial relationships. During more recent years a more balanced approach considering the interrelated impact of spatial and temporal relationships has emerged.

With respect to product assortment commitments, it is now generally accepted that the strategies available to a single firm or a cooperative vertical marketing system are directly related to the quantity of inventory nodes contained within the system. A great deal of the impetus in this direction resulted from the classical work of the late Professor Alderson.[11] The functional approach that he provided served to revive, expand, and update the contribu-

---

[9]For an outstanding review of the customer service impact of physical distribution see Wendell M. Steward, "Key to Improved Volume and Profits," *Journal of Marketing*, Vol. 29 (January, 1965), pp. 65–70.

[10]Jay W. Forrester, "Industrial Dynamics," *Harvard Business Review*, Vol. 36 (July–August, 1958), pp. 37–66.

[11]Wroe Alderson, *Marketing Behavior and Executive Action* (Homewood, Ill.: Richard D. Irwin, Inc., 1957).

tions of early marketing scholars concerning the risk and degree of commitment involved in physical supply.[12]

PHYSICAL DISTRIBUTION 1969: A SYNTHESIS

Thus, by 1965 management was afforded a rather segmented—but theoretically sound—approach to the development of physical distribution planning. The years since 1965 have been characterized by a refinement in basic concepts and development of greater precision in tools of analysis. While 1961 saw the first book devoted to the subject of physical distribution, today a wide variety of text and reading collections are available.[13] Currently, four trade journals are exclusively devoted to practical applications in physical distribution, and articles frequently appear in leading academic journals.[14] The field is represented by an active professional association, the National Council of Physical Distribution. The physical distribution course has become a common offering among many leading business schools. Thus, the flurry of attention that Professor Converse saw as a critical need in 1954 has by 1969 become a reality. In this section contributions regarding physical distribution noted earlier are synthesized.

At the individual firm level

For the most part, physical distribution is viewed in a micro context wherein attention is directed to the managerial aspects of a single firm's integrated system. To this extent, physical distribution management can be defined as that responsibility to design and administer corporate systems to control the flow of raw materials and finished inventories.[15] This systems orientation stands in direct contrast to the traditional approach of treating the many activities integral to physical distribution on a separate or diffused basis.

The main strength of physical distribution seems foremost to evolve from the development of techniques and concepts for treating the range of inherent functions on an integrated basis. Systems technology provides the framework for studying alternative system designs and evaluating feasible system arrangements on a total cost basis. High speed computers provide the tool required to evaluate complex system designs plus to keep track of the multitude of details engaged in geographically dispersed physical distribution operations.

In a strategic context, the central or focal point of physical distribution is the corporate commitment to inventory. Individual products are properly

---

[12]In particular see Percival White, *Scientific Marketing Management* (New York: Harper and Brothers, 1927), and Fred E. Clark, *Readings in Marketing* (New York: The Macmillan Company, 1924), Chapter 15.

[13]The initial book in the field was: Edward W. Smykay, Donald J. Bowersox, and Frank H. Mossman, *Physical Distribution Management* (New York: The Macmillan Co., 1961).

[14]The four trade journals exclusively devoted to physical distribution are: *Transportation and Distribution Management, Handling and Shipping Illustrated, Distribution Manager,* and *Traffic Management.*

[15]Same reference as footnote 13, p. 3.

viewed as a combination of form, time, place, and possession utilities. The product has little value until form is placed in a temporal and spatial context which will provide the opportunity to enjoy the physical and psychological attributes related to possession. If a firm does not consistently meet the requirements of time and place closure, it has nothing to sell. On the other hand, if a firm does not *efficiently* meet the requirements of time and place closure, profits and return-on-investment are placed in jeopardy. Excessive inventory stockpiles can compensate for errors in basic system design and may even overcome poor administration of physical distribution activities. The proper objective in inventory commitment is to deploy the minimum quantities consistent with specified delivery capabilities and management's willingness to underwrite total cost expenditures.

To achieve these managerially specified goals the inventory allocation must be integrated within a system of facility locations, transportation capability, and a communications network. The capacity of such a system is measured in terms of the dual standards of total cost and customer service.

Managers should keep in mind that excessive commitments to high levels of customer service can be extremely expensive. System attributes of fast and consistent customer service both have related costs. The higher each of these qualities of performance, the greater will be the required cost. In fact, individual physical distribution studies support the conclusion that physical distribution cost and related improvement in customer service have a nonproportional relationship.[16] Each additional unit of customer service capability requires a greater incremental expenditure. For example, a firm that strives to support a service standard of overnight delivery at 95% consistency may confront nearly double the total cost of implementing a program of second-morning delivery with 90% consistency.[17]

The typical firm must seek that balance between reasonable customer service and realistic cost expenditures which will achieve managerial goals. Two factors concerning the cost-service relationship are significant. First, seldom will such a balanced relationship result in the lowest possible total cost physical distribution system. Second, in terms of the temporal aspects of customer service, consistency of delivery can be expected to be viewed among customers who buy for purposes of resale as a greater virtue than pure speed of delivery. This premium upon delivery consistency is directly related to available techniques of inventory control. While sophisticated forecasting techniques and more rapid order transmitting systems have improved the ability to predict sales during leadtime and thereby reduce safety stocks, inconsistency in delivery has the net result of introducing the need to apply probabilistic methods to the delivery time portion of the order cycles. Unlike sales patterns, consistency in delivery performance can be controlled. Among buyers of substitute products it is reasonable to assume that preference will be afforded those sellers who can promise and provide consistency in delivery, if other factors are equal.

---

[16]Same reference as footnote 13, pp. 314–321.
[17]Same reference as footnote 13.

Beyond the firm

Today increased attention must be given to the rapidly advancing extension of physical distribution subject matter to the broader issues of channels and to the emerging concerns of macro-distribution.

Early treatments of physical distribution seemed to rely upon assumed vertical integration for the conception and development of total cost systems. The more realistic viewpoint is that physical distribution operations and responsibilities seldom terminate when ownership transfer occurs. Many significant costs of physical distribution occur between firms linked together in a marketing channel. The interface of two or more physical distribution systems operated by individual firms may well lead to excessive cost generation and customer service impairment. Even under conditions of system compatibility the total cost of physical distribution for the channel may rapidly accumulate as a result of efforts duplicated by various firms within the total channel. The net result of duplication may well be a weakening of overall competitive posture of the total channel.[18]

Two facets of viewing physical distribution performance on a channel-wide basis illustrate the nature of issues that arise. First, when product flow is viewed on a cooperative channel basis, it is interesting to observe that individual enterprises having the greatest impact upon channel performance often enjoy the smallest risk in total channel destiny. For example, negligent and sporadic performance by a common carrier may well negate consistent service capabilities for the channel with little or no corresponding penalty to the carrier. Consequently, the range of intermediary specialists must be expanded beyond the traditional institutions of marketing to include all influential parties. The performance of these low risk specialists must be calibrated in terms of impact on total channel effort.

Second, there appears to be no justification to support the traditional assumption that an outstanding network of marketing intermediaries will have the requisite capability to achieve efficient physical distribution performance. Differentiated marketing to a wide variety of market segments may have the inherent weakness of forcing small shipment diseconomies and related disadvantages in physical flow. The specialized institutions proficient in performing marketing functions may be different from those most capable of outstanding physical distribution support.

The development of multi-firm physical distribution channels raises a need for careful review of traditional concepts of marketing channels. The social justification for intermediaries has always appeared questionable and has led to the widespread promulgation that the elimination of middlemen will

[18]For some representative treatments dealing with physical flow in marketing channels see: Louis P. Bucklin, "Postponement Speculation and the Structure of Distribution Channels," *Journal of Marketing Research*, Vol. 3 (February, 1965), pp. 26–31; J. L. Heskett, "Costing and Coordinating External and Internal Logistics Activities," unpublished paper presented before joint seminar, The Railway Systems Management Association and The Transportation Research Forum (Chicago, Ill.: October 6, 1964); and Donald J. Bowersox, "Changing Channels in the Physical Distribution of Finished Goods," in Peter D. Bennett, editor, *Marketing and Economic Development*, Proceedings American Marketing Association (Chicago, Ill.: American Marketing Association, 1965), pp. 711–721.

result in increased marketing efficiency. However, middlemen appear to have increased in numbers and importance.[19] Perhaps reevaluation of the transaction generating and physical distribution support functions of middlemen will yield significant returns toward a more general understanding of marketing channels.

Beyond questions of channel structure, dynamics, and efficiency remain a series of interesting broader issues. For this article, suffice it to acknowledge that applications of systems technology hold significant potential toward greater precision in policy formulation to guide public resource allocation. Issues of a macro-distribution nature seem on the verge of greater attention when one considers the degree of population congestion predicted for this nation during the years ahead. Our aggregate capability to perform physical distribution activities under the demands of expanding city-state and revitalized urban centers will, to a great degree, rest upon well-planned public transit and carrier networks.

SOME ISSUES FOR RESEARCH

A rapidly expanding field such as physical distribution naturally offers a vast array of potential research topics. This final section outlines some areas and issues that appear most germane to subject matter expansion during the immediate future.

Some remaining questions of cost

As noted earlier, a great deal of initial concern with physical distribution was cost orientated. Emphasis was placed upon finding ways to reduce prevailing physical distribution costs. However, many questions regarding cost remain unanswered. The most pressing issues can be divided in terms of aggregate expenditures in the economy and in terms of deficiencies in managerial accounting.

What are the true aggregate costs of physical distribution in the United States? Does physical distribution really account for one half of total marketing costs? Is relative cost increasing or decreasing as a result of renewed interest in the physical distribution process? What are the prospects for improved aggregate performance in the economy during the decades ahead? The above questions highlight the current lack of data regarding the magnitude of national expenditures on physical distribution effort.

At the individual firm and channel level, traditional accounting does not generally provide the necessary information for physical distribution decision making. While considerable effort has been made to isolate and classify cost accounts, managerial accounting models to guide decisions concerning alternative system designs at various throughput volumes remain deficient.[20]

[19]Reavis Cox, *Distribution In A High-Level Economy*, (Englewood Cliffs, N.J.: Prentice-Hall, Inc., 1965), p. 51.

[20]For an expanded development of costs related to distribution see: L. Gayle Rayburn, "Setting Standards for Distribution Costs," *Management Services*, Vol. 4 (March–April, 1967), pp. 42–52.

Some of the following questions require more detailed answers. Are adequate cost accounting procedures and understanding of account structures available to perform true total cost analysis? How do current costing techniques stand up to the problems of total channel design analysis? Should there be standards for physical distribution performance, and, if so, what should they be? What standards exist for measuring comparative channel performance when viewed on the basis of multi-firm involvement? Finally, do current concepts of regulation and corporate taxation restrict realization of potential benefits available to cooperative vertical channel marketing systems?

During the years ahead a renewed interest can be expected in the financial affairs of physical distribution. Accounting will take a back seat in favor of the development of managerial decision models. For example, a problem common to industry, but not solved in reported research, is the question of measuring buyer performance. How can the traditional viewpoint of the open-to-buy be reconciled to the overall cost trade-offs acknowledged from physical distribution systems analysis?

The questions could go on, since they flow far easier than answers. The fact of the matter seems to support the conclusion that the state of the art in applied distribution costing has not significantly improved despite wide acclaim for the theory of total cost analysis.

The channel—a research media

The time now seems right for the distribution channel to be subjected to comprehensive research.

The dichotomy between textbook descriptions and real-world experience regarding channels has often been noted. The research questions which evolve from channel issues extend beyond the exclusive domains of physical distribution. However, penetrating answers to the following questions will require research steeped in a physical distribution orientation.

Does ample opportunity for specialization exist to justify separation of physical distribution and marketing activities in terms of channel structure? What techniques of leadership or other persuasive forces can and should be applied to encourage greater channel efficiency? To what degree are alternative methods of channel integration preferable from a social viewpoint? Have middlemen, in fact, been decreasing in numbers and importance? If so, what type or classification has been eliminated? Is there a disproportionate degree of change between those intermediaries engaged in physical distribution as contrasted to those who perform traditional marketing functions? What opportunities exist for experimental analysis of channel design prior to resource commitment?

The channel appears to have been one of the most elusive of marketing subjects. Therefore, channel subjects offer rich research opportunities. The functions of physical distribution extend far into channel domains. In the years ahead, we can expect significant returns from channel-orientated physical distribution research.

The international arena

Perhaps the most significant thing that can be said about international physical distribution is that it is currently nonexistent in terms of the literature. Beyond some elaborate statements regarding documentation and some attention to container standards, little has been written about international product flow.

Little doubt exists that industrialized economies are now moving toward worldwide markets. Accordingly, individual firms are now becoming multinational in scope of operations. With few exceptions, international efforts have concentrated upon marketing and manufacturing competence with lesser attention to logistical operations. While traditional notions of comparative economic advantage have diminished and restrictive trade barriers can be anticipated to lower with the passing of time, little can be done to alter the natural geo-reference arrangement of international markets. What countries will emerge as vital new commercial forces as a result of superior geographical proximity in time and distance to international mass markets? Will free ports be a major concern to the formulation of new world commercial powers? Does Hawaii, for example, possess an inherent competitive advantage from a logistical viewpoint that will render the islands the commercial center of the Pacific?

While many hold that marketing is properly a feature of highly developed economies, physical distribution may be a major factor toward helping emerging nations become tomorrow's mass markets. Extensive research into international physical distribution capability and opportunities may well constitute a profitable national as well as individual firm investment.

Issues of time in physical distribution system design

As noted earlier, the impact of interfirm information flows upon physical distribution channel performance has received increased attention during recent years. However, in reviewing available material one gets the feeling that a great deal remains to be discovered concerning the many ramifications of time relationships upon physical distribution performance and system design.[21] For the most part to date, inventory models have been temporal in orientation, whereas location models have been spatial in perspective.[22] A realistic view of a physical distribution system is that the network consists of one or more storage points interconnected by a series of transportation linkages. Thus, integration of the temporal aspects of inventory must be accomplished in terms of the geography of location. A major deficiency of existing quantitative models available to guide physical distribution system design is the inability to accomplish spatial and temporal integration.

[21]For expanded elaboration of this deficiency see: J. L. Heskett, "Spatial and Temporal Aspects of Physical Distribution," in Peter D. Bennett, editor, *Marketing and Economic Development*, Proceedings American Marketing Association (Chicago, Ill.: American Marketing Association, 1965), pp. 679–687.

[22]For two exceptions see: Donald J. Bowersox, *Food Distribution Center Location: Technique and Procedure* (East Lansing, Michigan: Bureau of Business and Economic Research, Michigan State University, 1962), and Ronald H. Ballou, "Dynamic Warehouse Location Analysis," *Journal of Marketing Research*, Vol. 5 (August, 1968), pp. 271–276.

To elaborate, consider alternative treatment of transportation capability in location and inventory models. Most locational models seek a solution to the number and geographic arrangement of network facilities by minimizing the transportation expenditure in relation to facility operating costs. Inventory is normally assumed at a specified level (average inventory) in order to estimate possession costs. In locational models transportation costs are normally assumed linear or near linear as a function of distance. Accordingly, alternative transport methods are evaluated on a total cost basis using cost-per-ton mile. This is a spatial measure of transport capability.

The relevant concept in inventory models that embraces transportation is the order cycle. The order cycle is defined as the total elapsed time from initial purchase commitment until the arrival of goods or materials. One significant aspect of order cycle is transit time between two specific locations (buyer and seller). Transportation is now, considered in terms of elapsed time to transverse a specified geographical distance with at best passing attention to the question of cost-per-ton mile.

At the extremes, one could conclude that the fastest mode of transport would always be favorable to inventory solutions while the lowest total cost movement would always be favored in location solutions. Such extremes do not materialize as a result of common sense applications. Average inventory in transit is evaluated and costed in the selection among alternatives in location solutions, thereby reducing some element of error. Conversely, the fixed location network assumed for inventory models normally specifies the transportation method to be employed as a function of size of shipment. However, complete integration of time and space is lacking.

The research questions which unfold from an integration of temporal and spatial factors may well lead to a new level of understanding regarding the dynamics of physical flow. At this junction, it appears likely that the entire field may well move toward more dynamic modeling in an effort to integrate inventory and locational considerations.

Some final issues

The list of potential research questions could continue far beyond the intent of this article. However, a few additional areas which appear worthy of consideration are listed in these final paragraphs.

As with any emerging field, physical distribution currently suffers from a lack of standardized definitions and vocabulary. The overall field would gain significantly from a clear definition of subject matter and issues.

The question of organization must be treated in a more comprehensive manner than thus far accomplished. Initially, it appeared physical distribution should be part of a firm's marketing operation. However, it is hard to justify the contribution marketing can make to the logistical support of manufacturing operations. Likewise, wouldn't the overall strength of marketing be improved if it could contract for a specified level of customer service without the accompanying problems of operational performance?

The impact of total information systems is currently being felt in all dimensions of traditional corporate structure. Mass information systems need data coding systems to perform accurate and relevant analysis of operation. This overall subject appears so important to future corporate vitality that considerable study from the viewpoint of the physical distribution operation appears justifiable. Of course, once again, this subject extends beyond the strict domains of physical distribution.

A final subject worthy of concern is the relationship between current business practice and the theoretical development of physical distribution subject matter. Initially, business seemed to lead the way for increased attention to the general field of physical distribution. However, this gap was soon closed by research in academic circles. The situation now seems to support the generalization that practical applications have not fully capitalized upon academic contributions. The burden of responsibility to disseminate research findings rests with the academic community.

CONCLUSION

The purpose of this article was to review the where been, where now, and where going of physical distribution. While a few short years ago physical distribution was relegated a rather passive role in the study and practice of business administration, forces of the past decade have caused a marked reversal. The long-range contribution of physical distribution to a better understanding of business and toward an improvement in the quality of commercial performance remains to be judged with the passing of time. It appears certain the course of future events will be significantly altered by the quality and comprehensiveness of physical distribution research efforts. It is difficult to draw an analogy to any previous area of inquiry that held forth the opportunity for improvement in current business operations offered by physical distribution. At this juncture in time, the future of this new and vital dimension of business study appears bright indeed.

PART
FIVE

THE PRICE SYSTEM

The price of a good or service requires the price setter to consider not only cost, but also supply and demand, the psychology of price, the law, and other behavioral dimensions.

The first selection, "The Perplexing Problem of Pricing," points out the nature of the pricing problem. Next, Bill Darden's article "An Operational Approach to Product Pricing" provides a formal vehicle to harness the judgment, experience, and intuition of businessmen. Brown and Oxenfeldt evaluate the relationship between costs and prices. Another consideration is marginal cost pricing. "Airlines Take the Marginal Route" illustrates how an airline uses marginal cost pricing. Joel Dean's classic article, "Pricing a New Product," presents three pricing objectives which must be achieved, the choice of pricing strategy, and what you should look at in setting a price for a new product.

Products and services pricing is also important in the industrial market. Professor Corey discusses "A Concept of Pricing Strategy," and considers the pricing process. The law can influence price. Professor Werner's review discusses some recent United States Supreme Court decisions and how they affect price. Among the cases and laws reviewed are the Borden case and Section Two of the Robinson-Patman Act.

The final selection, "The Concept of Price Limits and Psychophysical Measurement: A Laboratory Experiment," is an example of the type of price research which is being conducted today. This paper explores the notion that buyers have ranges of acceptable prices (prices they would be willing to pay) for contemplated purchases, and reports on the methodology and the results of an experiment.

READING 30

THE PERPLEXING PROBLEM OF PRICING*

Grey Matter

THE PERPLEXING PROBLEM OF PRICING

Few areas of marketing are so confounding and beset by doubts, uncertainties and fears as *pricing*. Yet few offer such substantial rewards *to the innovative thinker today*.

Students of pricing theories, economists and practical marketers agree that too often the *emotional approach* to price decisions outweighs *rationally* calculated strategy based on fact.

This may well be the reason that while product development, packaging, distribution patterns, advertising, merchandising and selling have been subject to constant changes, pricing policies (with a few exceptions) have long

*Reprinted from *Grey Matter*, published by Grey Advertising, Inc., vol. 37, no. 12 (December 1966).

been *strait-jacketed* by outworn traditions within industries, by rigid bonds of old-line retailing, and, as some authorities hold, by extremes of fear and prudence, often within the same company.

To add to management's perplexity, price policies are increasingly subject to *political and economic pressures*.

Professor William H. Peterson, writing in the Harvard Business Review, summarized the problems involved:

Pricing policy must somehow touch base with such economic factors as foreign competition, competition of substitute products, industry competition (including price leadership), yield on investment, average cost and marginal cost, product demand, quality and other selling features of the product and condition of the market.

Further, pricing policy must weigh important governmental or legal elements; Congressional concern over administered prices; the not always consistent anti-trust policies on pricing of the Justice Department, the Federal Trade Commission, the courts, and the anti-trust statutes themselves; and public relations, i.e., the impact of a price advance or cut on public opinion, government, the press, the business community, the company's employees, its unions, customers and suppliers.

MORE PERPLEXITIES

If all these variables were not enough to bedevil a decision-maker blessed with most enviable acumen, he must also cope with shifting patterns of *distribution*, an overwhelming proliferation of *new products*, expansion of product lines *within a company*, and intra-company brand competition as well as the rising tide of vertical and conglomerate *mergers*.

Here we shall attempt to isolate a few aspects of pricing policy which, from our vantage point in the market place, demand *special attention* from marketing executives.

It is increasingly clear that consumers respond to the *value* inherent in the product for them, rather than to *price* alone. More marketers need to learn to think in these terms. They need to recognize that price (or *value*) segmentation of the market is just as real as geographic, economic or psychographic segmentation.

For many alert marketers this has meant trading up. But for many others it has meant lowering prices—or covering *several different price segments in the same product field*.

Hence, you see Ford recognizing price segmentation in the sports car field by following up its successful Mustang, Detroit's first popular-priced sports car, with Cougar in the medium-priced range—both underneath the pioneering Thunderbird at the top of the line.

The old retail adage to the contrary, *lowering prices does not inevitably expand sales*. There are some product categories which are not susceptible to price marketing; others where it would be suicidal from a profit—or psychological point of view. But there are many categories where lowering prices is the *only* way to increase the total market.

Example: Scott recognizes that there is *more than one price segment* to be served in napkins by bringing out its line of Scott family napkins underneath the Scottkin brand.

It is becoming more and more apparent that if you want consumers to respond to price segmentation at the top, *you must also give them the same opportunity at the bottom.*

Flexibility and a *willingness to challenge and change* prevailing pricing practices is the hallmark of the astute marketer in this critical area.

THE NEED TO KNOW ECONOMICS OF DISTRIBUTION

1. Being thoroughly steeped in the *economics* of their distributor's operations is becoming a more critical element in the equipment of today's marketing executives because of the onrushing *"information revolution."* No question but the computer will develop new *facts,* new *strategies* and new *principles* of price merchandising at retail which will deeply affect manufacturers' specific pricing strategy.

2. Promotions, couponing, cents-off as elements in price merchandising will undergo closer scrutiny, study and analysis, particularly by *manufacturers.* The share of the cost of a cents-off deal which the retailer will be asked to pay is *sure to undergo considerable change.*

3. Psychological retail prices will come in for deeper study by *manufacturers.* Electronic data processing will shed more light on the difference in sales impact on the consumer between 98¢ and 99¢ and between 99¢ and $1 and between $4.95 and a $5 bill. Obviously, a retailer can get 2% *more gross* on a dollar item than on a brand selling for 98¢, if the cost is the same.

Some innovative retailers have already splintered age-old notions about psychological prices. But ingrown concepts are usually so *deeply rooted* that they must be blasted out to permit *new ideas* to enter.

THE ROLE OF ADVERTISING IN PRICING POLICIES

No discussion of pricing as a marketing tool would be complete without calling attention to the increasing concentration of government agencies on *advertising as a cause of higher prices.*

The whole history of the influence of advertising in *stimulating demand, spurring competition* and *ultimately bringing down the cost of goods in terms of real value* is ignored or unknown to many influentials in our governments.

Remember the report of the Senate anti-trust and monopoly committee some 8 years ago in which the automobile industry was charged with *administered pricing* and the public was informed that advertising adds at least $100 to the cost of each car?

This notion is echoed from time to time on the campus as well as in Congress and on rostrums all over the country.

It has even jumped to England, where the British Government's Monopoly Commission last April recommended that Kodak Ltd. reduce its prices for color and film processing.

More recently, British officials even went as far as to advocate a law *limiting the percentage a company may spend for advertising* so as to keep prices down.

There are also indications that here the FTC will expand its regulatory action to the *entire area of price reductions*.

Unquestionably, this will mean more headaches to marketing and advertising executives involved in pricing. Yes, marketers will have to keep a sharp eye on government agencies when setting price policy.

SOME CONCLUSIONS

The problem of pricing to the consumer is a compound of *conflicts, complexities* and *confusion* caused by the tremendous number of variables which confront the decision-makers in our fast-moving markets.

However, some general conclusions about pricing may be drawn:

1. Pricing policies must be *freed* from *ingrown* ideas and time-worn traditions. Price must be related to the *product's value*—psychological or otherwise—in the mind of the consumer in the target price segment.

2. Pricing philosophies must be continually and *realistically reviewed* and overhauled in the light of *changing consumer attitudes*, the *revolution in retail distribution*, the *emergence of the computer*, as well as changes in *manufacturers' own distribution philosophies*.

3. The list price became a *fiction* in a vast number of industries. Therefore, *new guides to retail pricing* must be constantly framed by manufacturers to help retailers.

4. Above all, more research (lots more) is needed

to determine under what conditions *presence* or *absence* of prices in ads is a *help* or a *deterrent* to the *selling power* of advertising.

to *demonstrate* to retailers the profitability of strongly pre-sold products, in keeping with the changing concepts of "how to make a profit while pricing for volume."

to find out whether a company's (or the industry's) pricing philosophy is based on factors which *no longer exist*.

to study the cause and effect relationship of fluctuating prices to volume and profit.

to assess the validity of psychological prices in today's and tomorrow's market place.

READING 31

AN OPERATIONAL APPROACH TO PRODUCT PRICING*

Bill Darden

The best brains in the business and academic worlds labor to provide the product pricer with a repertoire of sophisticated techniques and approaches, and he continues pricing products in his usual manner. While the economist expounds use of concepts of demand and marginal analysis, the pricer uses experience, intuition, and cost-plus. While the statistician calls for probability and payoff tables, the pricer uses experience, intuition, and cost-plus. While the professional expounds the use of price elasticity and cross-elasticity concepts, the pricer again uses experience, intuition, and cost-plus.

OBSTACLES TO OPTIMAL PRODUCT PRICING

Why does the pricer persist in this "irrational" behavior? This question seems to evoke answers from academicians and professionals that are as "irrational" as the pricer's behavior. Actually, the answers are simpler than presupposed and are all in the form of obstacles to "optimal" pricing. Some of these obstacles are:

1. The pricer does not have the time, nor the interest, to read and digest the latest literature on pricing, even if it were directly applicable in practice, which it is not.

2. In many cases the objectives of the pricer may be quite different from the objectives assumed in the literature for arriving at optimal guides to action.

3. The typical pricer usually has many product lines, and in each product line he may have many products. Thus, the time that he may allot to pricing each product may be very small.

4. Also, while the pricer recognizes that many products are substitutes or complementary to each other, he has no way to quantify or measure these effects properly.

5. The product pricer also has problems in determining competitor reactions to price strategies. The direction and degree of *price* reactions is a prime trouble area.

6. Again, the pricer does not have the methods, time, or money to measure demand curves or other consumer response curves properly. From experience, intuition, and judgment he must make hypotheses about future decision relationships. Future positive feedback increases the belief in these hypotheses, while negative feedback decreases the belief in these hypotheses. With negative feedback, the pricer begins to investigate his "key" hypotheses, sequentially, and these may be revised.

*Reprinted from *The Journal of Marketing*, published by the American Marketing Association vol. 32, no. 2 (April 1968), pp. 29–33.

The above "obstacles" do not begin to show the difficulties of the "complete" pricer. The "complete" pricer must deal with all the myriad combinations of price, advertising, sales promotion, personal selling, place, and product. Heuristically, he must hypothesize about the degree to which competitors will react to his price change and in what form this reaction will occur. The product pricer must "guess"—on the basis of his present hypotheses—what blend of marketing decisions will go best with a given price, and he must in turn determine what effect the given price will have on the sales of other products in the product line (both in the short run and in the long run). To continue with the latter thought, the product pricer must coordinate pricing policy with channel decisions, product decisions, and promotion decisions. *This coordination must take place through time*, not only at a point in time (as economic analysis often assumes).

It is not surprising, then, that the product pricer cannot predict the quantity demanded for a given price during a given period. However, it is probable that the product pricer does use an implicit, informal method of determining a sales volume range for a given price. Thus, it is believed that most product pricers *do* consider more than cost and turnover in pricing. It is hypothesized in this paper that many pricers use experience and intuition to arrive operationally at hypotheses which serve as a basis for price making. The purpose of this paper, then, is to formalize, heuristically, an operational approach to pricing, given the beliefs of the pricer.

PROFIT VARIANCE AND PRICE LIMITS

The central concept of the proposed pricing approach is exemplified in Figure 1. Assuming some given price, P_1, the breakeven chart in Figure 1 can be easily produced. The typical marketing executive will determine the most likely quantity demanded at P_1—in this case, Q_M. Now the marketing student determines the most likely profit at Q_M, as well as the breakeven quantity, Q_B. This approach is likely to be repeated for several prices, yielding respective profit and breakeven quantities for each price. Actually, the marketer is using repetitive breakeven analysis to feel out demand.

In addition, the marketer may determine optimal advertising and sales promotion for each price, which in turn also affects the profit and breakeven quantities received for each price. It is also recognized that the final most likely price is that which reflects judgments about competitive reactions.

Now the price investigator can estimate for a given price a pessimistic quantity demanded and an optimistic quantity demanded. These estimates are Q_P and Q_O, respectively, for price P_1 in Figure 1. Thus the pricing specialist has three sales volume estimates at a given price, P_1: a most likely estimate (Q_M), a pessimistic estimate (Q_P), and an optimistic estimate (Q_O).

Rationale and uses of quantity estimates

In the Program Evaluation and Review Technique, commonly called PERT, the planner is faced with the problem of estimating times required for accomplishing particular activities. In order to draw upon the judgment and experience of the superintendent or foreman in charge of completing the activity, and at the same time eliminate bias, the planner asks for three time estimates. These time estimates include an optimistic estimate, a pessimistic estimate, and a most likely estimate. In the cases of optimistic and pessimistic estimations, the planner counsels the estimator to choose times that have a chance of 1 in 100 of occurring. The rationale behind this counsel is that such estimates can be used to approximately fit a beta probability density function to the time occurrence of the given activity.

The same rationale lies behind the estimations of Q_P, Q_M, and Q_O at P_1 in Figure 1. The marketer is unsure what future volume will be generated by the projected marketing mix (including, of course, the price, P_1). For example, the degrees to which competitors may react, the change in marketing environment, and changes in company implementation effectiveness are all subject to varying degrees of change. However, using the three quantity estimates and assuming a beta probability distribution, the price-maker can determine a sales volume which stands a 50-50 chance of occurring. This volume will be called "largest expected volume" and is denoted by Q_E. Borrowing from PERT network analysis, the following formula yields an approximation of Q_E, using the three quantity estimates:

$$Q_E = \frac{Q_P + 4Q_M + Q_O}{6} \tag{1}$$

An important characteristic of this approach is the flexibility of the beta distribution. It allows the volume estimator to make the extreme volume estimates asymmetrical around the most likely volume, if he so chooses. Thus, the probability distribution fitted to the volume estimates may be positively skewed, negatively skewed, or symetrically distributed.

Variance of the sales volume

In addition to yielding the "largest expected volume" for a given price, this "operational approach" produces a good estimate of the volume variance. Using again the volume estimates at P_1, the marketer can compute this approximate variance with Equation 2 shown below:

$$\sigma^2 = \frac{(Q_O - Q_P)^2}{36} \tag{2}$$

Price range and the "operational approach"

The major strength of the "operational approach" lies in its ability to draw on the experience and judgment of marketing specialists in the firm. The knowledge in regard to competitor reactions, market changes, consumer behavior, and company implementation effectiveness should to a great degree be reflected in the estimates of volume at a given price. Using a repetitive approach, the same analysis can be made for several prices.

Specifically, the pricer wishes to determine some upper and lower limits for prices that must be investigated. Figure 2 shows a special type of demand

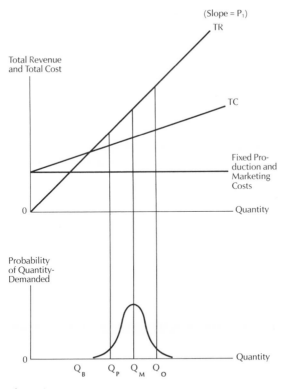

Figure 1
*At a given price (P_1), the use of three volume
estimates to fit a beta probability distribution.*

curve (or curves). This demand curve actually represents three demand curves:
the first (D_O) indicates optimistic quantity estimates at various prices; the second (D_M) shows most likely sales volume at all prices; and the third (D_P)
shows pessimistic estimates. These three curves generate three total revenue
curves in Figure 2: the optimistic revenue curve, the most likely revenue
curve, and the pessimistic revenue curve.

The marketer begins at a high price level, decreasing the price until at a
given price (in this case P_1) the pessimistic quantity estimate generates only
enough revenue to just break even (BEP_1). At a higher price P_{1+}, the volume
Q_{P1-} will not cover costs and at a lower price P_{1-}, the volume Q_{P1+} will generate profits. The price (P_1) which accompanies Q_{P1} becomes the upper price
limit, ensuring the firm that it will do better than break even over 99% of the
time at this price.

In order to establish a lower price limit, in Figure 2, the marketer lowers the
price past P_1 until a price is reached which allows the pessimistic revenue
curve to break even again (BEP_2). At P_2, such a situation occurs and this price,
again, will generate profits 99% of the time.

The marketer has now "bracketed" the feasible prices available to him.
This price range may be so small that the respective quantity estimates of the

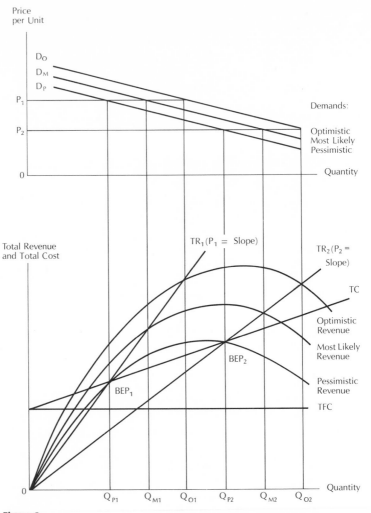

Figure 2

Determination of feasible price range through the interaction of pessimistic, most likely, and optimistic demands with cost curves.

two extreme prices may overlap; however, this seems unlikely in most cases.

The price range determined above provides a very conservative price zone for analysis. Actually, there are other criteria which provide a wider range of prices for investigation. For example, the product pricer could determine the upper and lower price limits on the basis of the largest expected quantity estimates. The probability of breaking even using this criterion (at either price limit) drops from .99 to .50. Another criterion, the most likely quantity estimate, provides a compromise, most likely guide, and, depending upon the individual industry and market, may prove the most feasible criterion for most firms.

After the upper price limit ($P_1 = P_U$) and the lower price limit ($P_2 = P_L$) have been determined, the firm may wish to find the largest expected quantities and the quantity variances at each price limit. From this information, the largest expected profit can be determined at both P_U and P_L as shown below.

$$Q_{E1} = \frac{Q_{P1} + 4Q_{M1} + Q_{01}}{6}$$

Expected Profit = $PR_E = Q_{E1} (P_U) - TFC - (V)Q_{E1}$

Where V = Average Variable Cost
$\qquad$ TFC = Total Fixed Cost

Now the same information can be determined at the lower end of the price bracket.

Implications for pricing strategy

The "operational approach" provides the product pricer with a formal vehicle to summarize and integrate his various hypotheses into a clear picture of economical alternatives. Some considerations for the pricer are:

1. The quantity estimates for the upper price limit and the lower price limit may overlap. For example, the upper limit may have an optimistic quantity estimate of 500,000 units, while the lower price limit may have a pessimistic quantity estimate of 499,000.

2. While Figure 2 assumes that costs remain constant in determining the upper and lower price limits, this assumption is not necessary. Thus, the pricer can change marketing blends to optimize some given objective at each price without changing the usefulness of the operational approach.

3. The use of three quantity estimates for a given price *does not* require that pricing specialists within a firm reach complete agreement as to forecasted sales. Thus, the difficult problem of "consensus" in pricing is largely overcome.

4. Once the product pricer has "bracketed in" the upper and lower price limits, he can use a sequential approach to test the expected profitability of intermediate prices.

5. The product pricer can not only compute and compare expected largest profits, but he can also compute and compare quantity and profit variances at various prices. There is no guarantee that quantity variances will be similar at different prices; therefore, a product pricer may be willing to accept a lower expected largest profit at some price in exchange for a much smaller variance (in other words, the pricer may be willing to trade off expected profit for a greater degree of certainty).

CONCLUSION

In general, the product pricer must use experience, intuition, and cost to price products. The pricer cannot wholly rely on sophisticated techniques and theory for optimal pricing of products. If it can be accepted that product pricers must rely on "operational" techniques for pricing then it would appear that one of the principal tasks of the marketing academician is the exploration of these approaches. Thus, major contributions can be made to marketing by providing marketing management with operational approaches which allow the executive to efficiently use his hypotheses about the decision situation. Bayesian decision theory is one move in this direction; however, the complexity of its methodology, as well as the problem of determining subjective probabilities for the various alternative outcomes of a given price strategy, prohibit its use by most product pricers.

This paper presents an operational approach to pricing that takes into consideration the above complexities and provides a formal vehicle to quantify the pricing hypotheses of businessmen. The approach involves no change in thinking. However, the methodology does allow use of a sequential approach and probability theory.

READING 32

SHOULD PRICES DEPEND ON COSTS?*

F. E. Brown and A. R. Oxenfeldt

Must consumers pay the cost of advertising? Is a large company with a costly Research and Development program able to match the prices charged by competitors that have no such expense? Is it generally sound business to add a reserve for contingencies in setting price? Do high profits for business mean a misallocation of resources? Are the rights of a businessman to a fair profit subordinate to the rights of the consumer to reasonable prices? All of these questions refer to pricing practices and, directly or indirectly, to the relationship between costs and prices.

The proper relationship between costs and prices has been discussed for many years and from many viewpoints. There are three principal sources for the confusion that exists with respect to this question. First is the fact that the different viewpoints have not been identified or maintained consistently within a discussion. Second is a failure to note in sufficient detail the huge disparity among different types of costs. Any discussion that seeks to treat all costs as a single category is doomed to failure. The third source of confusion is a failure to recognize that both costs and demand are and should be factors in pricing, and both are likely to change concurrently. Any attempt to discuss the relationship between costs and prices is thoroughly booby trapped with these three issues, and this article will no doubt fall prey to them also. But this identification of the booby traps should aid the reader even if it does not insure that writers will avoid them.

*Reprinted from *MSU Business Topics*, published by the Graduate School of Business Administration, vol. 16, no. 4 (Autumn 1968), pp. 73–77.

THE DIFFERENT VIEWPOINTS

The several viewpoints used in discussing the effect of changes in costs on changes in prices should be made explicit. The chief viewpoints adopted are those of the: (1) academic economists whose interests are mainly resource allocation and long-run prices, (2) individual businessmen whose interests are presumably long-run private profits, and (3) government representatives whose interests are public welfare and compliance with existing legislation. Beyond these diverse viewpoints, the connection between costs and prices can be approached *descriptively*—providing a picture of what actually happens; or it can be treated *normatively*—explaining what should be done. All of these viewpoints and approaches are legitimate and worthy; to shift from one to another without notice is not.

The matrix in Figure 1 suggests the six alternative approaches that might be made to the subject. This article concentrates on what businessmen should do about price when their costs are changed (cell five), but it touches on the others. Even for cell five, the discussion is far from complete.

Cost objectives—reservation price

When a firm makes outlays or its employees devote effort to a particular task, it does so in its own business interest. That should mean that the outlays or efforts are expected to increase sales, permit a higher price, reduce other costs, or some combination of the three.[1] If such benefits were not expected, the outlay could not be justified. The price effect of adding new costs presumably would vary, depending on which of these three motivations generated the change.

If new costs can bring about any one of these three developments, an analysis of the nature of costs should reveal some rather basic differences among items that are similarly classified as "costs." Such an analysis must focus on a more general objective of the business firm and then must determine differences in the ways various types of costs contribute to that general objective. The general objective of the firm is an improvement in the profit position.

A profit position is improved, by definition, when incremental costs are less than incremental revenue.[2] With this as a start, it becomes necessary for the businessman to determine the incremental cost associated with any change in his operations. Unless the change in revenue is equal to or greater than that change, the contemplated change would be unwise.

The term "reservation cost" or "reservation price" is associated with the expected change in costs. The businessman should view that amount as a floor or minimum that must be covered by his new price. Three frequently overlooked properties of reservation cost should be stressed. (1) The base

---

[1] Costs may also be incurred to prevent the reverse of these developments; namely to prevent sales decline, lower prices, or increase in other costs.

[2] The present value of each, the time distribution of inflow and outflow, magnitude of investment, and degree of risk can be introduced in order to make this underlying definition more sophisticated. Since these additions would not change the conclusions of the article, they will not be incorporated in the principal discussion.

	Economists	Business	Government
Descriptive	1	2	3
Normative	4	5	6

Figure 1

Alternative approaches to the connection between cost and prices

against which the comparison is to be made is *not* present or past operations, but the results for a future period—given a continuation of present methods. (2) It is an expectancy concept and thus ex ante, not ex post—for both the continuation of present methods and the introduction of the change. (3) Properly construed, it refers to unit costs, not total costs even though unit costs are calculated by dividing expected total costs by the expected number of units associated with those costs.

The difference between total costs and unit costs is one of the main stumbling blocks to an understanding of reservation costs. The total incremental cost must be covered by total incremental revenue, and total costs typically rise when additional services or promotional efforts are added by a seller. If quantity increases, per unit costs need not rise but could decline. This rather obvious statement requires examples in order to see its relevance in practical business decisions.

The following categories of costs, more than others, bear an uncertain relationship to reservation price: promotional costs, products redesign, and administrative costs in one category; and R and D, contingencies, and reinvestment in a second category. The conclusions reached with respect to the first are much different from those reached for the second.

ADVERTISING

We have all heard the argument that advertising lowers prices by making possible the economies of large-scale production. Thus, certain costs might actually *reduce* reservation price. Despite the argument that advertising brings lower prices, one does not encounter the seeming corollary that a seller should charge less for his product simply because he is increasing his outlays for advertising. Advertising costs may be incurred for any of the three reasons listed earlier (increased sales, increased price, or a reduction in other costs). The effect on reservation price will differ, depending on the objective.

If the objective of advertising is increased volume and it is realized, *total costs* would increase by the outlays for advertising, plus increments in other costs that vary with volume. But the increased total costs would be spread over a larger number of units. If the increase in volume is large, reservation price may be lower. Clearly higher *total* advertising costs need not mean higher prices. Thus, the effect of advertising on reservation price depends on its effect on the demand schedule in the specific case.

If a firm instituted advertising in the belief that it would be able to command a higher price as a result, the firm would naturally be expected to charge a higher price. As developed in the preceding paragraph, the firm's reservation price need not be higher. An effective advertising program raises demand and permits the seller to raise prices if he so chooses. An increase in the price charged by the seller may be a sound profit-optimizing strategy, particularly if the product has an inelastic demand with respect to price, even if reservation price were lower. This outcome, a very common one, offends the spokesman for the public who sees no change in the product, but a higher price to the consumer. (Note that the latter statement represents a shift in viewpoint.)

The third possibility, that added advertising costs are incurred in order to reduce some other costs, stresses changes in the marketing mix. The costs that may be reduced range from other promotional costs to personal selling to services and product features. The result could be either lower total costs or lower unit costs or both—but, of course could also mean higher costs.

Advertising is illustrative of a whole group of promotional costs; namely, those that do not vary directly with number of units. Raffles, demonstrations, store remodeling, and customer services fall in this group; and their effects would be similar to that of advertising. They may be viewed as a type of fixed costs, and their effect on reservation prices depends on the change in quantity of sales generated by them.

COSTS THAT VARY

A second group of promotional costs are those that do vary directly with the volume of sales. They include premiums, trading stamps, and other extras that are tied directly to sales. This group requires a separate analysis.

The giving of premiums or stamps is a programmed cost and may represent an attempt to realize any of the three objectives enumerated for adding costs. Our own studies[3] of prices charged by stamp and non-stamp food stores indicate that stores giving stamps are extremely heterogeneous in price levels and merchandising strategies, as are those that do not give stamps. In this situation, one would expect that the role performed by stamps would differ.

Some stores may substitute stamps for other promotional costs—or possibly for services or nonpromotional costs. If these stores employ stamps in order to reduce costs, their reservation price may be lower than their current offering price. "May be" lower because one must know the effect of stamps on demand and quantity in order to determine per unit figures. The seller does eliminate some of the uncertainty in establishing reservation price when he substitutes a variable cost for a fixed cost, but demand changes cannot be ignored.

If premiums or stamps are incremental costs adopted in order to increase volume, changes in demand are even more significant for price decisions. A change in level of activity, produced by the new promotions, means that fixed costs are now spread over more units. It also raises the possibility of lower marginal costs for even the variable costs. Reservation price might well be lower in this case even though total costs are increased.

The possibility that the businessman may choose higher prices rather than increased volume should not be ignored. In this event the increased costs would be spread over the same number of units; both offering price and reservation price would then be higher.

[3]A total of sixty-three food stores in Greensboro, North Carolina; Havertown, Pennsylvania; New York, New York; St. Louis, Missouri; and San Francisco, California, were studied by means of an eighty item market basket.

The promotional expenses considered in the preceding sections are illustrative of all potential strategies for the businessman. Each separate action is fundamentally in one category or the other; either it calls for fixed expenditures which do not depend on volume or it calls for variable expenditures whose total magnitude does depend on the level of operations. Installation of a computer, hiring of a new typist, reorganization of the administrative staff, and modernization of the plant layout all fall into the first category. A new package design, use of new raw material in the product, and an extra coat of paint are in the second group.

The similarities between the two types should also be noted. The three possible motivations apply to each type and to all of the examples cited. The underlying motive is higher profit, which may be produced by cutting other costs, by permitting a higher price, or by raising unit sales. A second similarity is that each alternative will influence other costs and the demand for the product—in the long run, if not the short. It is this second point, the influence of new costs on other costs *and* on demand, that is frequently ignored in pronouncements concerning the relationship between costs and prices.

The determination of reservation price in each instance requires three estimates: the total costs uniquely associated with the new activity, the number of units that would be demanded under the revised operation, and any changes in existing costs that would accompany the change. The total change produced by these factors must then be reduced to a per unit figure: reservation price.

Since reservation price and quantity are interdependent, each contemplated action has several reservation prices. If 100,000 units will be sold, reservation price is one figure; if 125,000 will be sold, reservation price is lower. But whether 100,000 or 125,000 will be sold depends on the offering price of the seller. Therefore, the seller must estimate several points of the demand schedule and attempt to optimize his strategy.

Reserves for contingencies

The asking price established by many manufacturers includes an item for "contingencies." Their inclusion makes price significantly higher than it would be otherwise. The contingencies, thus, have the same effect on reservation prices as do any other estimated costs.

We would not argue that decision makers could avoid uncertainty, but uncertainty brings both pleasant and unpleasant surprises. There is no a priori reason to believe that management's estimates will be either too high or too low. If estimation errors cancel, on the average, there would be no need to include contingencies in computing reservation price.[4]

The inclusion of contingencies in pricing decisions, like that of most incremental costs, apparently rests on the mistaken assumption that "one can get his money back if he adds his costs to his price." This view overlooks the

---

[4]Contingencies and uncertainties do play a role in reservation price but in quite a different manner. The rational decision maker will require a higher expected return on risky investments than on those with less risk.

fact that one may make less profit at high prices than at low prices. If high prices would be more profitable, firms could charge them and should—but because of convictions about demand rather than rationalizations based on irrelevant costs.

R AND D COSTS

Many large firms claim to be unable to meet the competition of their small rivals, at least on certain items. They claim their small rivals have smaller overhead costs and are not compelled to engage in costly research and development work. Some of these firms contemplate the dropping of some items even though their small competitors enjoy an attractive profit on them.

It is more than a paradox—it is a plain error—that activities such as research and development, various specialized administrative services, and others are a source of disadvantage to large firms. Surely these activities should not and would not be undertaken if they yield no profit. The difficulty stems from the fact that these costs frequently represent investments in potential *future* endeavors of the firm; their costs should not be charged against *current* products. However, current practice (perhaps motivated by tax considerations) finds accountants charging those costs against existing products. Thus, reservation prices are raised without any logical reason. The practice can also create an appearance of unprofitability when the reality is otherwise.

REINVESTMENT COSTS

Several major industries have argued that a firm should add to its price an amount that will permit investment in technologically improved plant and equipment. Such arguments have been advanced as a defense against public censure or worse, especially by highly visible firms that announced price increases. Typically this position has been taken as a justification for price increases during periods of inflation.

This line of argument is curious on several grounds. First, the notion that a private firm must justify its price demands is incompatible with the ethos of capitalism; but it is wholly consistent with the facts of modern business life. Even hard-headed businessmen resent suppliers that "take advantage of shortage situations" to raise prices—even though they may do precisely the same thing themselves. Thus, "cost-plus pricing" is a widely held moral standard even though it is generally incompatible with private gain and possibly with social benefit.

Of course, the notion that customers should finance investment in new facilities also represents a major shift in the rationale underlying capitalism —and is no less a departure when applied to research and development as in the last section. One would presume that investment would be provided by investors rather than by customers. Beyond this, the attempt to include reinvestment needs in reservation price could easily lead to unprofitable pricing decisions from the businessman's standpoint.

CONCLUSIONS

General conclusions with respect to the relationship between changes in costs and changes in prices are extremely limited. Higher costs may mean higher prices, but they do not *necessarily* mean higher prices. Reservation price, the minimum price required to cover new costs, is dependent upon the total demand under the revised operation and the effect of that revision on existing costs in addition to the new costs. Beyond this, the fact that reservation price is more sensitive to changes in demand when the new costs are fixed costs rather than variable costs is of great significance.

The fact that higher costs, in some instances, should lead to higher prices need not be detrimental to the consumer. The obvious point that higher costs may produce a better product or add valuable services is often ignored in our discussions. The consumer may secure a better buy at the higher price than was available at the lower price before the changes were introduced.

Finally, current practice frequently leads firms to allocate investment costs for future activity to current products. These products do not benefit from the costs, and inclusion of the costs in prices for current products is not justified in terms of profit maximization or social welfare.

READING 33

AIRLINE TAKES THE MARGINAL ROUTE*

Business Week

Continental Air Lines, Inc., last year filled only half the available seats on its Boeing 707 jet flights, a record some 15 percentage points worse than the national average.

By eliminating just a few runs—less than 5%—Continental could have raised its average load considerably. Some of its flights frequently carry as few as 30 passengers on the 120-seat plane. But the improved load factor would have meant reduced profits.

For Continental bolsters its corporate profits by deliberately running extra flights that aren't expected to do more than return their out-of-pocket costs —plus a little profit. Such marginal flights are an integral part of the over-all operating philosophy that has brought small, Denver-based Continental —tenth among the 11 trunk carriers—through the bumpy postwar period with only one loss year.

Chief contribution. This philosophy leans heavily on marginal analysis. And the line leans heavily on Chris F. Whelan, vice-president in charge of economic planning, to translate marginalism into hard, dollars-and-cents decisions (see box, below).

*Reprinted from *Business Week*, April 20, 1963, with the kind permission of the publisher, Copyright 1963, McGraw-Hill, Inc.

Marginal analysis in a nutshell

Problem: **Shall Continental run an extra daily flight from City X to City Y?**

The facts: **Fully-allocated costs of this flight**   **$4,500**
           Out-of-pocket costs of this flight   **$2,000**
           Flight should gross   **$3,100**

Decision: **Run the flight. It will add $1,100 to net profit—because it will add $3,100 to revenues and only $2,000 to costs. Overhead and other costs, totaling $2,500 [$4,500 minus $2,000], would be incurred whether the flight is run or not. Therefore, fully-allocated or "average" costs of $4,500 are not relevant to this business decision. It's the out-of-pocket or "marginal" costs that count.**

Getting management to accept and apply the marginal concept probably is the chief contribution any economist can make to his company. Put most simply, marginalists maintain that a company should undertake any activity that adds more to revenues than it does to costs—and not limit itself to those activities whose returns equal average or "fully allocated" costs.

The approach, of course, can be applied to virtually any business, not just to air transportation. It can be used in consumer finance, for instance, where the question may be whether to make more loans—including more bad loans —if this will increase net profit. Similarly, in advertising, the decision may rest on how much extra business a dollar's worth of additional advertising will bring in, rather than pegging the advertising budget to a percentage of sales —and, in insurance, where setting high interest rates to discourage policy loans may actually damage profits by causing policyholders to borrow elsewhere.

Communication. Whelan finds all such cases wholly analogous to his run of problems, where he seeks to keep his company's eye trained on the big objective: net profit.

He is a genially gruff, shirt-sleeves kind of airline veteran, who resembles more a sales-manager type than an economist. This facet of his personality helps him "sell" ideas internally that might otherwise be brushed off as merely theoretical or too abstruse.

Last summer, Whelan politely chewed out a group of operational researchers at an international conference in Rome for being incomprehensible. "You have failed to educate the users of your talents to the potential you offer," he said. "Your studies, analyses, and reports are couched in tables that sales, operations, and maintenance personnel cannot comprehend."

Full-time job. Whelan's work is a concrete example of the truth in a crack by Prof. Sidney Alexander of MIT—formerly economist for Columbia Broadcasting System—that the economist who understands marginal analysis has a "full-time job in undoing the work of the accountant." This is so, Alexander holds, because the practices of accountants—and of most businesses—are permeated with cost allocation directed at average, rather than marginal, costs.

In any complex business, there's likely to be a big difference between the costs of each company activity as it's carried on the accounting books and the marginal or "true" costs that can determine whether or not the activity should be undertaken.

The difficulty comes in applying the simple "textbook" marginal concept to specific decisions. If the economist is unwilling to make some bold simplifications, the job of determining "true" marginal costs may be highly complex, time-wasting, and too expensive. But even a rough application of marginal principles may come closer to the right answer for business decision-makers than an analysis based on precise average-cost data.

Proving that this is so demands economists who can break the crust of corporate habits and show concretely why the typical manager's response —that nobody ever made a profit without meeting all costs—is misleading and can reduce profits. To be sure, the whole business cannot make a profit unless average costs are met; but covering average costs should not determine whether any particular activity should be undertaken. For this would unduly restrict corporate decisions and cause managements to forgo opportunities for extra gains.

Approach. Management overhead at Continental is pared to the bone, so Whelan often is thrown such diverse problems as soothing a ruffled city council or planning the specifications for the plane the line will want to fly in 1970. But the biggest slice of his time goes to schedule planning—and it is here that the marginal concept comes most sharply into focus.

Whelan's approach is this: He considers that the bulk of his scheduled flights have to return at least their fully allocated costs. Overhead, depreciation, insurance are very real expenses and must be covered. The out-of-pocket approach comes into play, says Whelan, only after the line's basic schedule has been set.

"Then you go a step farther," he says, and see if adding more flights will contribute to the corporate net. Similarly, if he's thinking of dropping a flight with a disappointing record, he puts it under the marginal microscope: "If your revenues are going to be more than your out-of-pocket costs, you should keep the flight on."

By "out-of-pocket costs" Whelan means just that: the actual dollars that Continental has to pay out to run a flight. He gets the figure not by applying hypothetical equations but by circulating a proposed schedule to every operating department concerned and finding out just what extra expenses it will entail. If a ground crew already on duty can service the plane, the flight isn't charged a penny of their salary expense. There may even be some costs eliminated in running the flight; they won't need men to roll the plane to a hangar, for instance, if it flies on to another stop.

Most of these extra flights, of course, are run at off-beat hours, mainly late at night. At times, though, Continental discovers that the hours aren't so unpopular after all. A pair of night coach flights on the Houston-San Antonio-

El Paso-Phoenix-Los Angeles leg, added on a marginal basis, have turned out to be so successful that they are now more than covering fully allocated costs.

Alternative. Whelan uses an alternative cost analysis closely allied with the marginal concept in drawing up schedules. For instance, on his 11:11 p.m. flight from Colorado Springs to Denver and a 5:20 a.m. flight the other way, Continental uses Viscounts that, though they carry some cargo, often go without a single passenger. But the net cost of these flights is less than would be the rent for overnight hangar space for the Viscount at Colorado Springs.

And there's more than one absolute-loss flight scheduled solely to bring passengers to a connecting Continental long-haul flight; even when the loss on the feeder service is considered a cost on the long-haul service, the line makes a net profit on the trip.

Continental's data handling system produces weekly reports on each flight, with revenues measured against both out-of-pocket and fully allocated costs. Whelan uses these to give each flight a careful analysis at least once a quarter. But those added on a marginal basis get the fine-tooth-comb treatment monthly.

The business on these flights tends to be useful as a leading indicator, Whelan finds, since the off-peak traffic is more than normally sensitive to economic trends and will fall off sooner than that on the popular-hour flights. When he sees the night coach flights turning in consistently poor showings, it's a clue to lower his projections for the rest of the schedule.

Unorthodox. There are times, though, when the decisions dictated by the most expert marginal analysis seem silly at best, and downright costly at worst. For example, Continental will have two planes converging at the same time on Municipal Airport in Kansas City, when the new schedules take effect.

This is expensive because, normally, Continental doesn't have the facilities in K.C. to service two planes at once; the line will have to lease an extra fuel truck and hire three new hands—at a total monthly cost of $1,800.

But, when Whelan started pushing around proposed departure times in other cities to avoid the double landing, it began to look as though passengers switching to competitive flights leaving at choicer hours, would lose Continental $10,000 worth of business each month. The two flights will be on the ground in K.C. at the same time.

Full work week. This kind of scheduling takes some 35% of Whelan's time. The rest of his average work week breaks down this way: 25% for developing near-term, point-to-point traffic forecasts on which schedules are based; 20% in analyzing rates—Whelan expects to turn into a quasi-lawyer to plead Continental's viewpoint before the Civil Aeronautics Board; 20% on long-range forecasts and the where-should-we-go kind of planning that determines both which routes the line goes after and which it tries to shed. (Whelan's odd jobs in promotion, public relations, and general management don't fit into that time allotment; he says they "get stuck on around the side.")

The same recent week he was working on the data for his Kansas City double-landing problem, for instance, he was completing projections for the rest of 1963 so that other departments could use them for budget making, and was scrutinizing actions by Trans World Airlines, Inc., and Braniff Airways, Inc. TWA had asked CAB approval for special excursion fares from Eastern cities to Pacific Coast terminals; Whelan decided the plan worked out much the same as the economy fare on Continental's three-class service, so will neither oppose nor match the excursion deal. Braniff had just doubled its order—to 12—for British Aircraft Corp.'s 111 jets. Whelan was trying to figure out where they were likely to use the small planes, and what effect they would have on Continental's share of competing routes in Texas and Oklahoma.

At the same time, Whelan was meeting with officials of Frontier Airlines and Trans-Texas, coordinating the CAB-ordered takeover by the feeder lines of 14 stops Continental is now serving with leased DC-3s.

And he was struggling, too, with a knotty problem in consumer economics: He was trying to sell his home on Denver's Cherry Vale Drive and buy one in Los Angeles, where Continental will move its headquarters this summer.

READING 34

PRICING A NEW PRODUCT*

Joel Dean

New product pricing is important in two ways: it affects the amount of the product that will be sold; and it determines the amount of revenue that will be received for a given quantity of sales. If you set your price too high you will be likely to make too few sales to permit you to cover your overhead. If you set your price too low you may not be able to cover out-of-pocket costs and may face bankruptcy.

WHAT IS DIFFERENT ABOUT NEW PRODUCTS?

New products that are novel require a different pricing treatment than old products because they are distinctive; no one else sells quite the same thing. This distinctiveness is usually only temporary, however. As your product catches on, your competitors will try to take away your market by bringing out imitative substitutes. The speed with which your product loses its uniqueness will depend on a number of factors. Among these factors are the total sales potential, the investment required for rivals to manufacture and distribute the product, the strength of patent protection, and the alertness and power of competitors.

Although this process of competitive imitation is almost inevitable, the company that introduces the new product can use price as a means of slowing the speed of competitive imitation. Finding the "right" price is not easy,

*Reprinted by permission from *The Controller* (now *The Financial Executive*) vol. 23, no. 4, April 1955, pp. 163–165.

however. New products are hard to price correctly. This is true both because past experience is no sure guide as to how the market will react to any given price, and because competing products are usually significantly different in nature or quality.

In setting a price on a new product you will want to have three objectives in mind: (1) getting the product accepted, (2) maintaining your market in the face of growing competition, (3) producing profits. Your pricing policy cannot be said to be successful unless you can achieve all three of these objectives.

WHAT ARE YOUR CHOICES AS TO POLICY?

Broadly speaking, the strategy in pricing a new product comes down to a choice between (1) "skimming" pricing, and (2) "penetration" pricing. There are a number of intermediate positions, but the issues are made clearer when the two extremes are compared.

Skimming pricing. For products that represent a drastic departure from accepted ways of performing a service or filling a demand, a strategy of high prices coupled with large promotional expenditures in the early stages of market development (and lower prices at later stages) has frequently proven successful. This is known as a skimming price policy.

There are four main reasons why this kind of skimming price policy is attractive for new and distinctive products: *First*, the quantity of the product that you can sell is likely to be less affected by price in the early stages than it will be when the product is full-grown and imitation has had time to take effect. This is the period when pure salesmanship can have the greatest effect on sales. *Second*, a skimming price policy takes the cream of the market at a high price before attempting to penetrate the more price-sensitive sections of the market. This means that you can get more money from those who don't care how much they pay, while building up experience to hit the big mass market with tempting prices. *Third*, this can be a way to feel out the demand. It is frequently easier to start out with a high "refusal" price and reduce it later on when the facts of product demand make themselves known than it is to set a low price initially and then boost the price to cover unforeseen costs or exploit a popular product. *Fourth*, high prices will frequently produce a greater dollar volume of sales in the early stages of market development than a policy of low initial prices. If this is the case, skimming pricing will provide you with funds for financing expansion into the big-volume sectors of your market.

A skimming-price policy is not always the answer to your problem, however. High initial prices may safeguard profits during the early stages of product introduction, but they may also prevent quick sales to the many buyers upon whom you must rely to give you a mass market. The alternative is to use low prices as an entering wedge to get into mass markets early. This is known as penetration pricing.

Penetration pricing. This approach is likely to be desirable under the following conditions: *First*, when the quantity of product sold is highly sensitive to price, even in the early stages of introduction. *Second*, when you can achieve substantial economies in unit cost and effectiveness of manufactur-ing and distributing the product by operating at large volumes. *Third*, when your product is faced by threats of strong potential competition, very soon after introduction. *Fourth*, when there is no "elite" market—that is, a body of buyers who are willing to pay a much higher price in order to obtain the latest and best.

The decision to price so as to penetrate a broad market can be made at any stage in the product's life cycle, but you should be sure to examine this pricing strategy before your new product is marketed at all. This possibility certainly should be explored as soon as your product has established an elite market. Sometimes a product can be rescued from a premature death by adoption of a penetration price policy after the cream of the market has been skimmed.

The ease and speed with which competitors can bring out substitute prod-ucts is probably the most important single consideration in your choice be-tween skimming and penetration pricing at the time you introduce your new product. For products whose market potential looks big, a policy of low initial prices ("stay-out pricing") makes sense, because the big multiple-product manufacturers are attracted by mass markets. If you set your price low enough to begin with, your large competitor may not feel it worth his while to make a big production and distribution investment for slim profit margins. In any event, you should appraise the competitive situation very carefully for each new product before you decide on your pricing strategy.

WHAT SHOULD YOU LOOK AT IN SETTING A PRICE?

When you have decided on your basic pricing strategy you can turn to the task of putting a dollars-and-cents price tag on your new product. In order to do this you should look at at least five important factors: (1) potential and prob-able demand for your product, (2) cost of making and selling the product, (3) market targets, (4) promotional strategy, and (5) suitable channels of dis-tribution.

DEMAND

The first step in estimating market demand is to find out whether or not the product will sell at all—assuming that the price is set within the competitive range. That is, you should find out whether or not this product fulfills a real need, and whether enough potential customers are dissatisfied with their present means of filling that need. To do this, you should make some estimate of the total potential market for the new product and all its competing sub-stitutes and then estimate the portion of this potential that your product is likely to get.

Next, you should determine the competitive range of price. This will be easier when substitutes are relatively close or when customers are familiar with the cost and quality of substitutes and act rationally on the basis of performance.

The next step is to try to guess the probable sales volume at two or three possible prices within the price range. The best way to do this is by controlled experiments; next best is by a close estimation of buyers' alternatives in the light of market preference.

Finally, you should consider the possibility of retaliation by manufacturers of displaced substitutes. If your new product hits any one of your competitors hard enough, you may be faced with price retaliation. The limit to this price cutting is set by the out-of-pocket cost of the price-cutting competitors. Therefore, some knowledge of the out-of-pocket cost of making competing products will be helpful in estimating the probable effects of a particular price.

COSTS

Before going ahead with your new product, you should estimate its effect on your investment, your costs, and your profits. First you should estimate the added investment necessary to manufacture and distribute the new product. This investment estimate should include estimates of increased working capital that will be required at various sales volumes. Then you should estimate the added costs of manufacturing and selling the product at various possible sales volumes. The way to estimate costs is to calculate what your total costs would be with and without the new product; the difference should be assigned to the new product. Allocations of overheads that you are already incurring should not be assigned to the new product because they will be the same whether or not you go ahead with the addition to your product line.

In building up your two sets of cost and investment figures—one showing the situation *without* the new product, and the other showing the contrasting situation *with* the new product added to your line—be sure to take into account *all* pertinent items. It often happens that companies which lose money on new products have run into trouble because of unanticipated costs or investment requirements which have absorbed most of or all the profits realizable from the new idea.

New product costs may be segregated into half a dozen main categories: direct labor, materials and supplies for production, components purchased outside, special equipment (such as jigs, dies, fixtures and other tools), plant overhead, and sales expenses.

Direct labor. Methods of estimating direct labor may be built up in one of three ways: (1) You can compare each operation on each component with accumulated historical data, from your files, on similar operations for similar components, (2) you can develop a mockup of the proposed work-place layout and actually time an operator who performs a series of manufacturing operations, simulated as accurately as possible, (3) you can apply one of several systems of predetermined, basic-motion times which are currently available from private sources.

Make certain, however, that you include any added time used for setup work, or needed to take the item from its transportation container, perform the operations, and return the item again to its transportation container. When the total direct labor time is determined multiply it by the appropriate labor rates.

Materials and supplies for production. In developing reliable cost figures for materials and supplies make a methodical list of all requirements. Having listed everything in an organized fashion, you can enter the specifications and costs on a manufactured-component estimate form. Remember to include any extra costs which may be incurred as a result of requirements for particular length, widths, qualities, or degrees of finish. Allowances for scrap should also be made as accurately as possible and corrected by applying a salvage factor if the scrap can be sold or reused.

Components purchased outside. Place your specification for parts purchased from other concerns with more than one reliable supplier and get competitive bids for the work. But in addition to price considerations be sure to give proper weight to the reputation and qualification of each potential producer. Moreover, if you use a substantial volume of purchased parts you may want to use a "plus" factor above the cost of the components themselves to cover your expenses involved in receiving, storing, and handling the items.

Special equipment. Take careful precautions against making a faulty analysis of your expense and investment in special jigs, dies, fixtures, and other tools which you will need to produce the new product. To avoid trouble in this area make a table showing all cases where special equipment will be needed. The actual estimating of the costs of such equipment is best done by a qualified tool shop—your own if you have one or an outside organization. Here again, competitive bidding is an excellent protection on price. Do not include costs of routine inspection, service, and repair; these are properly charged to plant overhead.

Plant overhead. The overhead item may be estimated as a given percentage of direct labor, machine utilization, or some other factor determined by your accountants to be the most sensible basis. In this way you can allocate satisfactorily charges for administration and supervision, for occupancy, and for indirect service related to producing the new product. Overhead allocations may be set up for a department, a production center, or even, in some cases, for a particular machine. In calculating plant overhead make certain that in setting up your cost controls, your accountants have not overlooked any proper indirect special charges which will have to be incurred because of the new product.

Sales expenses. Your estimates of sales revenue at various potential volumes can now be compared with your estimates of added costs at those volumes. The difference will be the added profits of introducing the new product. Although the costs themselves probably should not be used as a basis for setting price, you should not go into any venture that will not produce for you a rate-of-return on the added investment required that is adequate to compensate for the added risk and still be at least as high as the return you could get by investing your money elsewhere. If no price that you set will provide enough revenue to produce an adequate profit over your added costs, then you should either drop the venture, try to cut costs, or wait for a more favorable time to introduce the product.

MARKETING TARGETS

Assuming that the estimates of market demand and of cost and investment have been made and that the profit picture looks sufficiently rosy, you are now in a position to set up some basic goals and programs. A decision must first be made about market targets—that is, what market share or sales volume should be aimed at? Among other factors, you should probably consider what effect it will have upon investment requirements, whether or not your existing organization can handle the new product, how it fits in with the rest of your present product line, and so forth. These decisions should be made after a cold-blooded survey of the nature of your new product and of your company's organization and manufacturing and distributive facilities.

PROMOTION

Closely related to the question of market targets is the design of promotional strategy. As an innovator, you must not only sell your product, but frequently you must also make people recognize their need for this kind of product. Your problem here is to determine the best way of "creating a market." You must determine the nature of the market and the type of appeal that will sell the product and secure prompt acceptance by potential buyers. And you should also estimate how much it will cost you to achieve this goal.

CHANNELS OF DISTRIBUTION

Frequently, there is some latitude in your choice of channels of distribution. This choice should be consistent with your strategy for initial pricing and for promotional outlays. Penetration pricing and explosive promotion calls for distribution channels that promptly make the product broadly available. Otherwise you waste advertising or stymie mass-market pricing. Distribution policy also concerns the role you wish the dealer to play in pushing your product, the margins you must pay him to introduce this action and the amount of protection of territory and of inventory required to do so.

YOUR DECISION

These are the factors you should look at in setting a price. Estimating these factors shrewdly and objectively requires specialized training and experience. Good estimates will make your pricing more realistic and successful. But pricing cannot be established by formula. Combining these factors into a pricing policy requires judgment. In the last analysis you must pull all the estimates of the experts together and arrive at your own decision. You will want to make sure that the pricing analysis is guided by sound principles and that the activities of your specialists are all geared toward the same end—devising a sound, effective marketing and promotional program in conjunction with a price that will meet your objectives of market acceptance, competitive strength, and profits.

READING 35

A CONCEPT OF PRICING STRATEGY*

E. Raymond Corey

An English Shakespearean scholar once wrote, "The worth of a thing is what it will bring."[1] This simple truth sums up some vast complexities on the subject of pricing, and serves as a useful point of departure.

Pricing is the art of translating into quantitative terms (dollars and cents) the *value* of the *product* to customers at a point in *time*.

In this context, the concept of "value" is quite subjective. It is the value which the customer himself recognizes. It includes easily quantified elements such as the cost saving that may be realized by buying a new machine with which to replace an old one. It includes intangible benefits such as the pride of ownership that may be associated with the possession of modern equipment, attractive in appearance and efficient in operation.

It may be that the *potential* worth of a product to the customer is much greater than the value he *currently* recognizes. He may not, for example, fully comprehend all of the ways in which he can use the product. He may not visualize the extent to which differences, functional and other, between one product and another can be translated into lower costs, higher sales volume, or new market opportunities in his business. Probably, then, the most important function of a marketing program is to help the potential customer develop clearly his own subjective measure of value of the product.

In the definition of pricing, "product" ought probably to be construed in its broadest sense. The purchaser of a turret lathe, for example, not only buys the machine tool itself, but also the repair and maintenance service the seller provides. The original equipment manufacturer who buys components, such as motors, may put value on the motor manufacturer's brand name because of its potential usefulness to him in promoting the equipment he in turn makes. A user of steel may value his relationship with his supplier as a factor that might help him to obtain sufficient quantities of steel during periods of short supply. All these elements, tangible and intangible, are part of the "product package" to the customer and have "value" to him.

The value which one customer group may associate with the product will differ from its value to other customer groups that use the product in different

*Reprinted from E. Raymond Corey, *Industrial Marketing*, Englewood Cliffs, N.J., Prentice-Hall, Inc., 1962, pp. 215–234.
[1] J. O. Halliwell-Phillips, *Dictionary of Archaic and Provincial Words* (London: John Russell Smith, 1847), Vol. II, p. 864.

ways. Finally, for any one customer group, the value of the product is likely to change with time, since customer needs and product use patterns change.

In making pricing decisions, what factors should the industrial marketer take into consideration? There are at least four areas that need to be examined. These are: (1) the nature and extent of customer demand; (2) the actions of competitors; (3) costs of making and selling the product; and (4) the company's basic objectives of marketing this and related products in the line. These four areas are considered in detail below. The final section of this introduction deals with questions of over-all pricing strategy and of the *process* of establishing and changing prices.

CUSTOMER DEMAND

If the value of a product varies from one group of customers to another, the analysis of customer demand, as in product planning, should begin with the identification and analysis of these several groups. Potential customers, then, may be classified according to their use of the product and its value to them.

A customer classification scheme helps answer two important questions relevant to pricing: what sales volume is likely to be generated at different price levels? Also, what opportunities might there be of charging different prices for the product to different customer groups, and what are the competitive advantages of doing so?

Volume-price relationships

The relationship between the various price levels at which a product might be sold, and the expected sales volume at each price level, can be expressed by means of a "demand curve." A demand curve describes the "price elasticity" of a product, or the rate at which sales volume is expected to change with changes in the price.[2]

A demand curve is really an estimate of a relationship, quite rough at best, and not something describing historic fact. For practical purposes, then, pricing decisions cannot be made scientifically by estimating a demand curve for a product and setting its price at that point at which the price-volume relationship is such as to yield the maximum profit.

Nevertheless, pricing decisions are based either implicitly or explicitly on certain assumptions with regard to the potential volume of sales available at different price levels. Therefore, price elasticity is a useful *concept* both in thinking about setting prices at the outset and also in analyzing, on a continuing basis, market reactions to price changes.

How should the industrial marketer go about predicting at the outset what volumes of some new product will be sold at what price levels? Given a system of customer classification, it will be useful to list for each customer cate-

[2]For descriptions of price elasticity, see: Joel Dean, *Managerial Economics* (Englewood Cliffs, New Jersey: Prentice-Hall, Inc., 1951), pp. 161–163. Harry L. Hansen, *Marketing: Text, Cases and Readings* (Homewood, Illinois: Richard D. Irwin, Inc., 1956), pp. 582–586. Paul A. Samuelson, *Economics* (5th ed; New York: McGraw-Hill Book Company, Inc., 1961), pp. 411–430.

gory, the products with which the new product will compete and which it might conceivably replace. Working with these categories, it is useful to ask, for each one, what would the price of the new product have to be to replace the product now used for this application? Adding together the potential volumes to be realized in different use categories, with each successive price reduction, provides a measure of price-volume relationships. These relationships can be described in the form of a conventional demand curve.

To illustrate this concept, we might consider the effect of price on the demand for aluminum in three of its many markets—aircraft, household wrap and containers. Used as "skin" material in making aircraft, aluminum is unique because of its light weight relative to its strength, its ductility, and its corrosion properties. Even at much higher prices than those for which aluminum is now sold, it would still be in great demand for making airframes.

At current prices, aluminum competes effectively with wax paper and certain plastic materials as a household wrap. Because it is considerably higher in price than wax paper, however, it can claim those segments or use categories in the household wrap market in which its unique properties have value for consumers. Aluminum foil has certain folding characteristics, insulating qualities, and moisture-vapor transmission characteristics which make it particularly good for many wrapping applications. It would be expected, however, that if aluminum foil could be significantly lowered in price relative to wax paper and plastic wrapping materials, it would be substituted for these materials in an increasing number of household uses.

Aluminum also has a place in the container market. It is used primarily to make trays for baked goods. Its use in making cans has only been attempted for a very limited number of applications. Aluminum is not likely to enjoy a major share of this market until its price is lower relative to the price of tinplate (or unless tinplate is in short supply). If the basic price of aluminum could be lowered by perhaps 10 to 25 per cent, and if the price of tinplate remained fixed, a vast market might then become available for the newer material.

When there are several producers of a product, as is usually the case, there is the problem of working from estimates of *total* demand to an estimate of the demand for an *individual* supplier's output of that product. Estimating demand for the individual supplier is perhaps even more difficult than calculating total demand. But there are at least three relevant considerations. If the product in question fits into a line of related items, it may be hypothesized that total demand for it will be roughly split among competitors in proportion to their existing market shares in these related lines. Another consideration is timing. The share of market which an innovating company retains in the long run depends importantly on how aggressively and effectively it enters the market and how much time it has to establish its position with customers before competitors enter. Finally, the demand for an individual supplier's output of the product will be related to the promotional effort he expends. While there is no formula, then, for calculating one firm's share of market for a product, useful benchmarks are his market share for related products, the lead he has on competitors, and the resources he is willing to commit to market development.

Factors affecting volume other than price

In appraising the effect of price changes on volume, it is important to recognize that there are many factors which influence sales volume in addition to price and to take these factors into consideration in making pricing decisions. First, of course, the industrial buyer's demand for a product is most frequently determined by his own level of production and sales. Hence, the demand for industrial goods is said to be a "derived demand"; that is, it depends ultimately on the level of demand for the products which these goods are used to make. Under these circumstances, reductions in price on an industrial product may actually be accompanied by falling volume levels, if the customers' volume of business is declining at the same time.

Again, demand for the product, and the extent to which lower prices will increase volume, are dependent upon potential buyers' familiarity with the product and its use. Lowering price may obviously have little effect on sales volume if other considerations stand in the way of its use by potential customers. The point may be illustrated by the case involving the development of a market for aluminum sleeve bearings by the Aluminum Company of America. In this instance, the possibility existed of pricing aluminum bearings at a figure significantly lower than the conventional bearings which they would replace. Aluminum bearings cost much less to make. Nevertheless, it is unlikely that low price would have expanded sales volume greatly in the early years. Engine builders were unfamiliar with the performance of the new bearings and were unwilling to experiment with their use in large and costly diesel engines.

The effect of price change on volume, further, is likely to depend on how significant an element of the buyer's cost is the price of the product. When it is a large element of cost, small reductions in price may result in heavy buying.

The degree of sensitivity of price-volume relationships will be affected by the sensitivity of the buyer to other purchasing considerations. He may be particularly sensitive to the product's brand reputation and, thus, to the level of advertising, or to the availability of product service, or to fast delivery, or to the effectiveness of the supplier's technical and field sales effort. Each of these things, along with price, is describable in terms of elasticity. Advertising elasticity, for example, may be described in terms of the relationship between sales volume and the level of advertising.

There is a strong tendency, as markets grow and as products gain in acceptance and use, for sensitivity to price to increase relative to other purchasing factors. As buyers develop continuing needs for the product in their operations, as competing suppliers are able to offer products of equivalent quality and develop well-rounded marketing programs, purchasing decisions will hinge increasingly on price considerations.

Other important considerations, then, in addition to price strongly affect sales volume. These include the "derived demand" factor, the buyer's familiarity with the product, and the buyer's sensitivity to purchasing considerations such as brand name, service, delivery and the field sales program. Because of these considerations, price changes frequently do not result in a direct and proportional change in sales volume.

Price differentiation among customer groups

Probably industrial marketers could maximize profits if they were able, like the peddler in a Persian market, to set a whole series of prices on a product, charging each customer exactly what he would be willing to pay. Aluminum producers as a group might maximize profits if they charged a high basic price to aircraft manufacturers, a lower price for aluminum used in household foil and a still lower price for aluminum to be used for making cans. But legal considerations as well as the ease with which products can move across market segments make it impossible to go to this extreme.

However, it is quite usual for manufacturers to vary prices by giving distributors functional discounts, by setting different prices in different geographic areas, and by granting quantity discounts. Thus, distributors may be given a lower price than ultimate customers, the difference usually being explained as compensation for certain services rendered by the distributor such as carrying inventory, extending credit, and servicing the product. This difference is referred to as a "functional discount."

Buyers geographically located near certain designated "basing points" may be quoted lower prices because of transportation cost and industry practice. Quoting different prices in different geographic areas has been the subject of prolonged and involved legal debate. The topic has been well covered in other sources.[3]

Buyers of large quantities may be quoted a lower price than purchasers of small lots. The amount of a quantity discount is usually intended to be the equivalent of manufacturing and marketing cost savings which the seller realizes through making quantity shipments. In fact, the Robinson-Patman Act,[4] which deals with price discrimination, requires that quantity discounts be explainable in terms of cost savings to the manufacturer, if the competition among buyers of the product may be affected by the fact that some of these buyers paid a higher price than others.

In actual practice, however, both functional and quantity discounts[5] are exceedingly difficult to account for either in terms of the value of functions performed, on the one hand, or in terms of cost savings on the other. Nevertheless, there is still a strong tendency to treat distributors and users, and large quantity buyers and small quantity buyers, as distinct market segments, and

---

[3]Hansen, *op. cit.*, pp. 636–649. Ralph S. Alexander, James S. Cross, and Ross M. Cunningham, *Industrial Marketing* (Homewood, Illinois: Richard D. Irwin, Inc., 1956), pp. 324–341. Dean, *op. cit.*, pp. 541–547.

[4]For a thorough discussion of the Robinson-Patman Act, see Hansen, *op. cit.*, pp. 610–626.

[5]For a discussion of price discounts, see: Dean, *op. cit.*, pp. 501–541. John A. Howard, *Marketing Management* (Homewood, Illinois: Richard D. Irwin, Inc., 1957), pp. 311–316. Hansen, *op. cit.*, pp. 601–606.

to vary the prices charged to these different groups. Probably, however, price differences in many cases reflect the realities of competitive conditions in these different market segments. Sometimes, then, OEM's receive the greatest discount; sometimes it is the jobber or distributor who enjoys the greatest discount off list price.

As with all attempts to charge different prices for a product in different market segments, price discount structures tend to break down and the general price level to fall to that level represented by the lowest price. Customers who may have enjoyed large quantity discounts in the past may continue to take these discounts in paying bills even though purchasing small amounts of the product. Small competitors may compete by quoting carload prices for less than carload quantities. Finally, the customer group receiving the lowest price may sell the product to members of another customer group at less than the price this latter group would have to pay the original supplier if buying directly from him.

In addition to using geographic, functional and quantity price differences, industrial marketers may try in other ways to differentiate among customer groups in pricing their products. Relatively minor differences may be made in the form or color of a product, in packaging, and in brand name to disguise the fact that the same basic product is being sold at different prices in different market segments. A manufacturer might label some of his output as "seconds" or "off-grade" and charge a lower price than for "first-grade." Physical differences may be minor between "first-grade" and "off-grade"—and perhaps in some cases, non-existent.

Also, prices may be varied according to the channels used. A paper manufacturer, for example, may set a certain price on a grade of paper he sells to his regular distributors, and sell excess quantities of this grade at "spot" market prices to other wholesalers on a job lot basis.

To conclude, if we regard the "product" in terms of a range of uses or applications, and in terms, too, of the product service that goes with it—delivery, brand reputation, and relations with a source of supply—we can say first that this "package" will differ in value from one customer group to another. Customers, then, may be usefully classified according to what they have in common as buyers and users of the product, and these groups analyzed in terms of the factors which determine their respective demand levels for the product. How sensitive, it should be asked, will volume be to price changes for each of these groups at any point in time—and how sensitive is volume to other buying considerations? Price elasticity is likely to vary from one market segment to another.

The discussion to this point has been concerned with one of four areas for consideration in making pricing decisions. The other three—*competition, costs* and *pricing objectives*—need to be studied. Then it will be useful to examine in our discussion of the *pricing process* the way in which the analysis of these four areas in each instance leads to the final selection of a specific price for a product at a point in time.

COMPETITION

Competition frequently establishes the upper limit to what Joel Dean has called "the range of discretion" in pricing.[6] This is the range within which the seller may, as a practical matter, set his price. To exceed the price at which competitors offer identical, or closely similar, products is to risk serious loss of market share.

The degree of freedom which a seller has to price his product above his competitors' prices will normally depend on the extent to which he can differentiate it in the mind of the buyer. This differentiation can be tangible or intangible. That is, the product may differ from competitors' in its quality or in some other physical dimension which enhances its value in use. Or, it may be differentiated in terms of services provided by the seller, or even in terms of the salesman's reputation with the customer, or in terms of the financing which the seller offers the purchaser. If the value to the customer of these points of difference can be accurately gauged, they can often be translated into price premiums.

In any case, direct competitors must be taken into account. It may be useful for purposes of this discussion to consider, first, what determines competitors' reactions to price cuts and, second, what determines their response to price increases.

Competitors' reactions to price reductions

Price reductions on relatively undifferentiated products are most often met immediately by all suppliers, with little resultant shift in market share. But this is not always the case, and, therefore, it is useful to examine the factors which determine competitive response.

A major factor is the competitor's *costs*. If his costs are relatively high, he may be deterred from meeting prices which eliminate his profit, and he may try to hold market position by aggressive promotional efforts. In the short run, he may meet competitive prices if he can cover his out-of-pocket costs, but if he does not cover his fixed overhead, he cannot continue in business for long.

Knowledge of competitors' costs, then, can be exceedingly useful. These costs can sometimes be estimated by studying the published statements of competing suppliers. Frequently, costs to manufacture a particular product can be estimated by engineers who take apart one unit of the product and calculate its cost of manufacture piece by piece. In process industries, like chemicals, metals and petroleum, manufacturing costs can be estimated if the particular process is known. Having the lowest cost process is a factor of major competitive significance in process industries.

Further, it may be useful in certain cases to know what costing practices and policies are observed by competitors. For example, in large decentralized companies, it is often the practice to transfer semifinished goods and com-

[6]Dean, *op. cit.*, p. 413.

ponents between departments at market prices. The receiving department's costs are likely, then, to be higher than if it were charged simply with the supplying department's manufacturing costs. Again, such information is useful to have in appraising competitors' cost positions.

A second major factor is the *speed* with which competitors can react to price competition. Generally, they can react immediately. But when a price reduction is accompanied, and made possible, by a change in the method of production or in the design of the product, competitors may need time to introduce similar changes. Under these circumstances, the immediate impact of the price change on sales volume for the company initiating the price cut may be quite great. Then a critical question in the pricing decision may be how long it will take competitors to set up new facilities, or redesign the product, or do whatever is required to enable them to meet the new low price. A related question is whether competitors have both the financial resources, and the willingness, to operate at a loss while product and process changes are being made.

Third, competitors may be deterred from meeting price moves if by so doing they run into conflict with other existing commitments or interests. It may be that a substantial reduction in price on one group or class of products disrupts the consistency and harmony of prices in the total line of products. Then it may be that meeting the price reduction will bring the product in question into sharp internal competition with somewhat similar products in the line. For example, the result of reducing the price of a "quality" line may be that it replaces the "standard" line. Reducing the price of one size of a product without corresponding price changes in the whole line may cause that size to draw sales volume from both larger and smaller units.

A fourth major factor affecting reactions to price moves is the relative sales volumes of various competitors. A small supplier may often be able to quote a slightly lower price than his large competitor without fear of his price being met. If large competitors meet the low price, the absolute loss in total revenue for each may far exceed the value of the small amount of business they protect by so doing. For at least five years after World War II, the large and growing market for polystyrene was shared by four large plastics manufacturers. Then another small firm, a company which originally was in the plastics molding business and purchased from these four, began to make polystyrene. For several years this supplier's price was 1 or 2 cents a pound under the price set by the major companies. Because his volume of business was relatively small, major polystyrene producers apparently did not consider it worthwhile to meet his price. The new supplier's sales volume increased rapidly, therefore, and by the time the major suppliers did elect to meet his price, the newcomer reportedly had overtaken one of these firms to become the fourth largest supplier.

Such a situation is not unusual. In many industries, small suppliers can "snipe" at the business of their large competitors, through low price, with the expectation of enjoying a temporary price advantage. It is simply too costly for the large supplier to reduce his price on his total output in order to protect his business in one small segment of his market.

Large companies often sense other kinds of deterrents in pricing vis-à-vis their small competitors. Large suppliers may feel that their pricing practices are more subject to public scrutiny than those of their small competitors and that they are more vulnerable to legal entanglements. They may adhere steadfastly, then, to published price lists at times when they suspect small competitors are offering direct or indirect price concessions.

A sixth consideration is the level of capacity at which competitors are operating and the size of their order backlog. If a competitor's shop is full and enough business has been booked to keep his plant running at full capacity for a year or more, he has little to gain by meeting current price reductions. The level of competitors' backlogs is often an important consideration in bidding on large contracts. If companies which might normally provide strong competition already have a lot of business on hand, the bidding may not be so keen. The successful bid is likely to be higher than if all competitors were operating at low levels and were anxious to have any new business that may be available.

Competitors' responses to price increases

On the other side of the coin, it is often critically important to know what competitors' reactions are likely to be to a price *increase*. If one supplier initiates an increase and others do not follow, he risks losing sales to his competitors.

Willingness on the part of other companies to follow will depend generally on three factors: a belief that demand conditions are such that a general price increase will not reduce the *total* size of the market; a feeling that all other major suppliers share this belief and have a strong desire to increase prices; and often a sense of faith that the supplier initiating the price increase has acted intelligently and in the best interests of all producers as a group.

This last consideration serves to introduce the concept of price leadership. In some industries and for some products, price increases are initiated typically by one or two supplying firms. These same firms, however, may not typically initiate price cuts although they may formalize a generally deteriorating price situation by publicly announcing lower price schedules.

A price leader may or may not be self-appointed—and often is not. A price leader often emerges because his competitors watch him closely and exhibit a willingness to follow his moves. No agreement, tacit or otherwise, is needed for the existence of price leaders and price followers.

Very often the price leader is the largest supplier. He has more at stake than his competitors, and they are likely to reason that he, in particular, has a vital interest in general price conditions in the market for the product. Hence, he is likely, in the opinion of his competitors, to act wisely and in the best interests of the *total* industry.

The price leader may be regarded favorably among his competitors for his wisdom, his foresight and his good reputation with customers. Each successful price increase which he initiates serves to strengthen his leadership position; two or three unsuccessful moves may cause the industry to search elsewhere for leadership. To be successful, a price increase should be accepted by customers, followed by competitors and should not result in loss of volume. The price leader must continually analyze to the extent possible such factors as general market demand, the cost positions of all significant suppliers, and the availability of supply of raw materials. These considerations, and price leadership in action, are examined specifically in the Seneca Paper Company case.

Pricing and poker

It may be said that there is a poker-playing flavor to pricing decisions. In pricing, as in poker, it is critically important to anticipate accurately, and in the absence of complete information, what competitors' responses are likely to be to any given move. These expectations become determining factors in making pricing decisions; they also provide the basis for planning subsequent price moves. It seldom suffices to make a single move in pricing. As in poker, or in any game, the successful competitor is one who plans a sequence of moves based on his assumptions regarding his opponents' reactions.

To pursue further the poker-playing analogy, companies, like people, have personalities. They often exhibit certain characteristic kinds of behavior in pricing situations. It is helpful, indeed, to know these behavior patterns and to understand for each major competitor the background considerations which shape these patterns.

COST CONSIDERATIONS

If competitive prices demark an upper limit to the "range of discretion" in pricing, manufacturing costs form something of a limit on the bottom end of the range. Cost seems like such a solid benchmark in pricing that, in many instances, manufacturers set prices by calculating unit cost and adding a percentage profit (say 10 per cent).

A supplier may practice "cost-plus" pricing if he finds the benchmark of customer value difficult to gauge. He may derive some sense of security from thinking that if his costs are as low as his competitors' costs, he may be relatively free from the threats of competitive price cutting. This feeling is based, of course, on certain assumptions regarding competitors' costs but, more critically, it is based on the assumption that competitors will behave "rationally," that is, that competitors will not attempt to increase market share at the sacrifice of a "normal" profit.

Such assumptions are tenuous at best. Moreover, the "cost-plus" approach to pricing may be followed at great sacrifices in profits if prices are set below customer value levels.

While the "cost-plus" approach is open to criticism, it is still important in pricing to use cost data as a lower-limit reference point. A great deal of judgment is required, however, to estimate costs usefully for pricing purposes. Unit costs are not fixed and immutable. They fluctuate with volume; they vary with time; and they are subject to different interpretations depending on what cost factors are included or excluded.

Incremental versus full costs

In the short run, choices have to be made frequently between incremental cost or full cost in establishing a cost benchmark for pricing purposes. *Incremental costs* are the direct costs of material, labor and supervision that are incurred if a certain order is taken, costs that otherwise would not be incurred. Full costs include these direct costs as well as an assigned portion of manufacturing, selling, and administrative overhead, including depreciation. These overheads are, of course, expenses that are incurred whether the order is taken or not and will not be affected by the decision.

There is a tendency in a going business, operating below capacity, to accept orders that will cover incremental costs and make a *contribution* to overhead. Such action is often competitively sound in the short run but may be hazardous for the long run if *all* pricing is based on incremental costs.

In his study of *Product Policies of Nonintegrated New England Paper Companies*, Professor Stuart U. Rich describes a "marginal approach" to pricing, which recognizes the realities of using incremental cost as a primary short-run reference point, but which provides for covering full costs in over-all product line pricing. While his discussion has particular reference to the paper industry, the marginal approach can be usefully applied in other industries.

Costs tend to set the lower limits of product prices, and since they vary with volume they also influence the amount produced. The costs referred to here are those directly attributable to the product in question, that is, those which would be avoided if the product were dropped. It is these costs, rather than full costs including overhead allocations, which set the floor on prices, at least in the short run. In the long run, taking the product line as a whole, full costs must be recovered and a profit earned in order for the firm to stay in business. This means that the price structure for the entire product line should be set so as to maximize the difference between total revenue and total cost. Let us see how this might be done by using the marginal approach to pricing.

In using the marginal approach to pricing, a company tries to secure from each product the greatest possible marginal contribution to common overhead and profit. As noted above, the "marginal contribution" of a member of the product line can be defined as the difference between the price received and the cost directly attributable to the product in question. This approach may require some rethinking about what the significant costs are in setting individual prices. Many businessmen in the paper industry as elsewhere try to adhere to full cost pricing. This means that they estimate the total costs of a product, including overhead allocations, and add a margin of some kind for profit. This method tends to ignore the realities of demand and competition as well as the arbitrary nature of many allocated costs. A better approach would be to price each product according to the demand and competitive situation in the market where it is sold.

As an aid to maximizing the revenue secured from the total product line, it may be useful to classify its various members according to their contribution as follows:

1) products which contribute more than their pro rata share toward overheads after direct costs are covered;

2) products which just cover their pro rata share;

3) products which contribute more than incremental costs but do not cover their pro rata share;

4) products which fail to cover the costs saveable by their elimination.

With such a classification in mind, management would then be in a better position to study ways of strengthening the performance of its total product line. Pricing decisions on individual products in the four categories listed above would be made in the light of demand and competitive conditions facing each grade category. This means that some products, such as new specialty grades, may be priced to yield a very high margin of profit, while others, such as certain highly competitive standard lines, may have to show an actual loss. By retaining these marginal grades to "keep the machines running" and to help absorb fixed overhead costs, management may be able to maximize the total profits from all its lines. A few items which make no contribution may have to be kept to round out the line offered.[7]

Predicting future costs

Estimates of costs for pricing may vary significantly depending upon assumptions regarding the period of time involved and the amount of business in question. If the supplier has had little or no previous experience in making the product and if the contract involves a large number of identical units of the product, he may be able to reduce his unit costs as he gains production experience. He will then find it useful for pricing purposes to make predictions as to how his costs are likely to behave over a certain number of units of output.

Many manufacturers have used the "learning curve" as a device for estimating future costs. If the work involved is unlike work previously performed in his shop, a manufacturer may anticipate a fairly steep learning curve experience. That is, his costs will fall relatively rapidly with each production lot. If the novelty of the work is not so great, cost reductions may not be so dramatic. Based primarily on his judgment, then, regarding the newness of the work, the manufacturer selects a curve having a certain slope to describe his expectations regarding future unit costs. He may, for example, elect an 80 per cent learning curve. This means that, with each doubling of production volume, costs are expected to be reduced by 20 per cent. If 1,000 units cost a dollar each to make, 2,000 units will cost eighty cents each, and 4,000 units will cost sixty-four cents each to manufacture.[8]

Under these circumstances, estimates of average unit costs for all units will be determined mainly by estimates of how many units, in all, the manufac-

[7]Stuart U. Rich, *Product Policies of Nonintegrated New England Paper Companies.* DBA thesis, Harvard University, Graduate School of Business Administration, June 1960.

[8]For a description of the use of learning curves, see Robert N. Anthony, *Management Accounting, Text and Cases* (Homewood, Illinois: Richard D. Irwin, Inc., 1960), pp. 528–530.

turer expects to make and sell. He may elect, in calculating unit costs, just to base his figures on an order which is immediately available to him, or he may reason that if he completes this order successfully, a large amount of further business will come his way. He may then decide to base his unit cost calculations on his estimate of immediate, plus future, business to arrive at a lower unit cost calculation than otherwise. An initial price based on such a cost estimate may place the manufacturer in a strong competitive position in bidding for the initial piece of business. But such pricing can be risky. If future business does not actually materialize, the manufacturer may easily incur a loss in this venture. The strategy of taking an initial order at a short-run loss in anticipation of recouping the loss on subsequent orders is sometimes referred to colloquially as "buying into the business."

The question of "what cost is," then, is far more complex than may usually be supposed. The selection of a cost basis for pricing purposes involves making some difficult managerial judgments involving the company's short- and long-run strategy and its basic policies of doing business.

PRICING OBJECTIVES

If considerations in the areas of customer value, cost, and competition are accurately analyzed, and prices set accordingly, the resulting price-volume-cost relationships should yield maximum profit. There are a number of considerations, however, which may lead a firm to select a price which may not maximize profits on the product over a given time period. These factors are (1) uncertainty regarding the accuracy of the analysis, (2) the effect on customer relations of a price move, (3) the impact on volume and profits yielded by some other products in the line, and (4) legal considerations.

Uncertainty

An element of considerable conservatism is usually found in pricing actions. Objective analysis may, for example, suggest the desirability of pricing a product at a level significantly below or above that of certain competing products with the expectation of achieving high volume and/or profits. The risks may appear to be too great, however, in view of the uncertainties involved and the low degree of confidence management has in the pricing analysis. The issue is then resolved by setting the price at or very near the price levels for directly competing products.

There are, of course, great uncertainties involved in any estimate of price-volume-cost relationships. Competitors may behave differently than was expected. The product may not enjoy the widespread customer acceptance which was predicted. Actual manufacturing and selling costs may exceed even very conservative estimates.

It is important to note that the willingness to take risks under conditions of uncertainty will vary considerably from one situation to another, and from one company to another. One company's management may gamble on the accuracy of its analysis in an effort to make the largest possible profits. Another may settle for modest gains, hoping that if it follows a conservative pricing approach, competitors will not react sharply. The choice may depend on the company's financial resources and its ability to withstand a loss. It may actually depend, too, on the personal motivations of the individual or individuals in the company responsible for making the pricing decision, and on how much they personally can gain or lose in the venture.

Probably businessmen would gain from being somewhat less conservative in pricing and somewhat more experimental. The inflexibility in pricing that characterizes the behavior of many companies can be costly in terms of lost profit opportunities. Dynamic and imaginative pricing can result in increased sales volume and profits, and carefully designed price experimentation can be used to probe the potential that exists.

Customer relations

An important background consideration, working against short-run profit maximization in pricing, is the maintaining of good relations with customers. Because of this consideration, price changes may be made less frequently than if suppliers took advantage of every surge in demand by charging "what the traffic will bear." There is a strong feeling on the part of sellers that price changes have to be justified to buyers in a way that imputes "fairness." Often this means that sellers explain price increases to buyers and to the general public in terms of increases they (the sellers) have sustained in their own costs. Presumably such an explanation serves to adjust the measure of value of the product in the customer's mind and to make him willing to pay the higher price.

Professor M. A. Adelman reported in an article written in 1958, "I have been teaching economics for ten years, and have had a standing offer in all that time of a prize to the student who will find a public announcement of a price increase which does not blame it all on higher costs, particularly labor costs." [9]

Price moves are often timed to coincide with the introduction of product improvements. In explaining the price increase, then, management may suggest that the amount of the increase is to be equated with the increased usefulness and value of the product to the customer.

This desire on the part of company managements to rationalize price increases by linking them either to cost increases or product improvements is not to be underestimated as a factor in pricing. Company executives dealing with the public and field salesmen dealing with customers are likely to be sensitive to charges of "jacking up" the price. They are not likely to explain price increases on a product by saying simply, "The demand for it is increasing and we thought we could get more for it!"

Impact on other products

Suppliers may refrain from maximizing profit on one product, if doing so results in loss of sales and profits on another. Some new product may be de-

[9] M. A. Adelman, "Pricing by Manufacturers." *Proceedings, Conference of Marketing Teachers from Far Western States*, p. 148 (University of California, Berkeley, September 8, 9, and 10, 1958).

veloped, for example, which can easily replace an existing product made by the same supplier, in certain uses. The supplier may elect not to make the old product obsolete, together with the facilities used to make it, by immediately pricing the new product below the old. He may, instead, gradually replace one with the other through a pricing policy which lets him make the transition over a period of time.

Legal considerations

Finally, legal considerations ought to be included, for the sake of completeness, in any list of factors which serve to modify the objective of profit maximization in pricing. This aspect of pricing, however, is thoroughly covered in other references. It will only be mentioned, since it is not in keeping with the purpose of this discussion to treat the subject in detail.

Out of concern for the antitrust laws, manufacturers are wary of charging one customer or group of customers more than another, even though one will pay more than another. Furthermore, the antitrust laws provide important deterrents to pricing in a way that drives some competitors out of business and leaves a few suppliers in an oligopolistic position. Therefore, in many corporations, recommended price decisions are scrutinized by lawyers and may be modified if, in their judgment, such pricing has antitrust implications.

THE PRICING PROCESS

Because pricing decisions are based on estimates and predictions and because so many uncertainties attend actions in this area, an effective approach to pricing is likely to be an approach which allows for periodic adjustments. A price is a quantitative expression of what the buyer *thinks* the seller will pay for the product, and it assumes a certain level of sales volume. This judgment will often need to be revised as it is tested in the market place.

Professor Adelman makes this comment:

The basic point of this paper is that a price is determined in a market, and that a market is a system of information on cost and demand, a set of signals which the business firm must learn to read as best he can. Market information is extremely imperfect, coming as it does in bits and pieces, full context usually missing, permitting wide latitude in interpretation, and, therefore, offering considerable premiums to those who can read the signals just a little better, or can enforce their reactions a little more effectively. The range of uncertainty, and the degree of freedom of choice, or compulsion to choose, is very wide from market to market, and even within the same firm from product to product. For the choice in favor of one price or product mix or method rather than another is only the beginning of the pricing process. The next step is to see how far wrong the original decision was. The market is a feedback and corrective information system as well as an original information system.[10]

---

[10] *Ibid.*, pp. 147–148.

Competitive effectiveness in pricing depends significantly on the amount and quality of information used as the basis for making price decisions. Reports on what prices competitors are charging, and on whether lost business is to be attributed to price or to some other factors, are facts of great significance to pricing. Then as price changes come along, it is useful to analyze the reactions of customers and competitors to each one so that the next price may be made with less uncertainty than the last. Such analysis is facilitated if historical records are kept of price changes, of who initiated these changes, of other changes in the product or in the marketing program which were made concurrently, and of the apparent effect on sales volume.

Steps to secure reliable and detailed information through the field sales force and through trade channels are well worth taking. However, information which comes through field sales may tend to exaggerate price considerations. Field sales representatives, concerned as they are primarily with sales *volume*, may show an inclination to attribute poor performance to competitors' pricing practices, and often to report suspected undercover price concessions. Such a tendency may require some discounting in the interpretation of the data.

The development of good information is one prerequisite of effective pricing; another is a long-range sense of objective. In a particular case, the objective may be stated in terms of volume and profit goals, or in terms of market position. It should be formulated on the basis of some judgments, however crude, as to what total volume is possible at different price points over a broad range of prices. It should be established, too, on the basis of judgments as to how manufacturing costs are likely to behave for different levels of output. Then as further market information and cost data become available, these estimates can be refined.

If volume and profit objectives are determined, then pricing decisions may be regarded as positive moves in the direction of achieving these objectives. Pricing then has a point of focus, a sense of purpose.

SUMMARY

Pricing is the art of translating into quantitative terms the value of the product to customers at a point in time. In this context, the concept of value is quite subjective, and the worth of the product may vary considerably from one customer group to another.

In making pricing decisions it is useful to consider (1) the nature and extent of customer demand; (2) competitors' actions; (3) manufacturing and marketing costs; and (4) the company's pricing objectives.

Analysis of *customer demand* in the market place might well begin by classifying potential customers into groups according to the nature of the markets they serve, the potential uses they have for the product, their size and their geographic location. Such a classification scheme may provide a basis first for estimating what potential sales volume exists for a new product at different price levels. The products with which the new product competes in each market segment can be listed and the volumes of these products going to these market segments may be estimated. A series of judgments as to the prices at which the new product can drive competing products out of these market segments then provides basic data for estimating price-volume relationships for the new product.

A customer classification scheme is essential if different prices are to be charged to different classes of customers. Theoretically, a manufacturer might maximize his profits by setting a whole series of prices on a product and charging each customer group exactly what it will pay. But there are severe practical limitations, legal and other, to doing so.

However, manufacturers often do differentiate between distributors and user customers (through functional discounts), and between buyers of large amounts and small (through quantity discounts). In many instances they will also charge different prices in different geographic areas. Finally, efforts are sometimes made to charge different prices to different customer groups by making minor variations in the form of the product.

Two observations may be made regarding price differentiation schemes. First, there is a strong tendency for these prices to reflect competitive conditions in the market segments rather than cost differences to the manufacturer. Second, there is a strong tendency for these price structures to deteriorate so that the lowest price becomes the general market price.

While customer value is a basic reference point in pricing, *competition* tends to set an upper limit in the industrial marketer's "range of price discretion." Usually he can charge no more than his competitors. In addition, if he wishes to make a price move he will need to anticipate what the reactions of his competitors will be.

Most often, competitors will meet price cuts rather than suffer a loss in revenue. Under certain conditions, however, they may be deterred from doing so. If the new price is below competitors' out-of-pocket costs, they may not follow. If meeting the price cut would hurt their sales of another product or reduce their sales of the same product to another market segment, they may be deterred from reducing price. In addition, if the firm which cuts the price has only a small sales volume, larger competitors may be unwilling to meet the cut and thereby lose a large amount of revenue.

Price increases, too, need to be weighed in the light of the likely reactions of competitors. If they do not follow the increase, the firm initiating the price move may risk a substantial loss in sales volume. In many industries, however, competing firms recognize a "price leader" and look to him to initiate price increases when market demand conditions are favorable. The price leader is often, but not always, the firm with the largest market share. He may be accorded a leadership position by the industry because of his broad concern for the "health" of the industry in which he has such a large stake and because of his record for using good judgment in his price moves.

Cost considerations tend to set a lower limit to the range of price discretion. "Cost-plus" pricing leaves much to be desired, and pricing according to customer value will, in the long run, be more profitable. Nevertheless, costs need to be carefully analyzed for pricing purposes.

Cost analysis requires great judgment. Unit costs fluctuate with volume and vary over time. They are subject to differing interpretations depending on what cost factors are taken into account. Choices need to be made, for example, between using full cost or incremental cost; between using current costs or anticipated future costs. In highly competitive industries prices tend to be driven down by competition to the level of incremental costs. Hence, it often becomes realistic to take incremental cost as the lower limit and to price for maximum contribution to overhead and profit.

A fourth factor influencing price determination is the company's *basic objectives*. While a company will tend always to maximize short-run profits, it may be deterred from doing so because of certain long-run considerations. One such consideration is the company's relations with its customers. Customers may be irritated by arbitrary price increases. For this reason, industrial marketers seem more willing to increase prices when this action can be explained to customers in terms of increased costs or in terms of product improvements.

Another deterrent to maximizing short-run profit on some product is the possible impact of doing so on the profitability of related products in the line. Another deterrent has to do with legal vulnerability; a price move may tend to discriminate among competing customers or it may threaten to drive small competitors out of business, leaving the company open to antitrust action. Finally, managements sometimes price conservatively to avoid attracting competitors into the business.

The last part of this chapter considered the *pricing process*. An effective approach to pricing allows for periodic price adjustments, and is based on the intelligent analysis of historical data on price-volume relationships in the industry. Price moves should be followed up carefully and data gathered on their apparent effect on sales and on competitors' behavior. Then further moves may be planned intelligently.

Finally, pricing action might usefully be oriented toward certain well-defined long-range objectives, regarding market share, volume, and profit. Pricing then has a sense of purpose and ceases to be just an erratic response to competitive pressures.

READING 36

MARKETING AND THE UNITED STATES SUPREME COURT, 1965-1968*

Ray O. Werner

A review of the decisions of the 1964 Supreme Court term predicted that future Courts would "impel marketers to accept new organizational and operational forms."[1] The thesis of this current study of the Supreme Court

*Reprinted from *The Journal of Marketing*, published by the American Marketing Association, vol. 33, no. 1 (January 1969), pp. 16-23.
[1]Ray O. Werner, "Marketing and the United States Supreme Court," *Journal of Marketing*, Vol. 31 (January, 1967), pp. 4-8.

terms of 1965, 1966, and 1967 is simple—the prediction made over two years ago has been verified. As a prediction of things yet to come, it is still valid.

Now, as in that earlier analysis, the premise is that a major component of the environment in which business must function is a legal one. Courts resolve specific controversies, but their dispositive pronouncements reveal to the alert marketer the bounds within which he may act. Courts, despite some vapid disavowals by imperceptive legalists, do "make law."

During the most recent three terms of the Supreme Court, major decisions altered the legal environment of marketing in three areas. First, the permissible operational practices of contemporary marketing were significantly modified. Second, the organizational structures which business might adopt were sharply altered. Third, certain aspects of regulatory procedure were changed.

OPERATIONAL CONSTRAINTS RESULTING FROM THE COURT'S DECISIONS

Price discrimination and product identity

Complete autonomy in pricing policy has not been accorded business for many years, but recent Court decisions have further abridged the existing freedom to act. Foremost among the decisions limiting autonomy in pricing was the *Borden* case.[2]

The *Borden* case arose from a charge that Borden sold milk at two different prices in violation of Section 2(a) of the Robinson-Patman Act prohibiting price discrimination among buyers of a product of "like grade and quality." Part of the milk Borden produced was marketed under the Borden label; the other part, physically and chemically identical with the Borden labeled milk, was packaged for marketing under a customer's private label. Borden's price for its own brand of milk was higher than the price it charged private customers for private branded milk.

The Supreme Court mistakenly reduced economic reality to objectively quantifiable terms and supported the Federal Trade Commission finding that physical identity was alone relevant in determining likeness of grade and quality of products. Yet the Court ignored the obvious fact that quality definitionally cannot be divorced from the non-quantifiable. It dismissed brand names and labels in the consumer evaluation of similarity of product quality, tersely declaring that "the *economic factors* inherent in brand names and national advertising should not be considered in the *jurisdictional inquiry* under the 'like grade and quality' test." (Italics added.)

Justice Stewart, with whom Justice Harlan joined in familiar dissent, replied pointedly that product differentiation forced retail price differentials on the private-brand milk. He then added—to no avail—that "[t]his simple market fact no more than reflects the obvious economic reality that consumer preferences can and do create significant commercial distortions between otherwise similar products." Commercial reality notwithstanding, the Court has spoken —products, if they are physically identical are from the point of law (if not economic reality) economically identical. As they affect products of "like

[2]*Federal Trade Commission v. Borden Co.*, 383 U.S. 637 (1966).

grade and quality," price differences will be considered *prima facie* evidence of price discriminations in violation of the Robinson-Patman Act.

The *Borden* case raises the question: What other consequences may be inferred from the Court's analysis? First, may a marketer of a nationally known premium product reduce his price to the level of competitive non-premium products? In past decisions, Section 2(b) of the Robinson-Patman Act which allows a firm to *meet* in good faith the equally low price of a competitor has been interpreted as preventing such a reduction. It was held that such a reduction represented an "undercutting" of the competitive price.[3] The Court, confronted with this apparent contradiction between its present decision and that of past Federal Trade Commission positions chose to avoid the issue declaring: "We need not resolve these contrary positions. The issue we have here relates to Section 2(a), not to Section 2(b), and we think the Commission resolved it correctly. The Section 2(b) cases are not now before us and we do not venture to decide them." In short, owing to the Court's propensity for truncating what economically is indivisible, business is left in absolute obscurity about what it legally may do.

Faced with the situation in which different prices are illegal and in which identical prices are suspect, the question remains of what a marketer can do. Clearly, of course, he can give up the production of the private label product. Such an action, however, has economic ramifications in terms of growing concentration that is at once apparent and undesirable in its reduction of the variety of goods from which the consumer may choose. Alternatively—but not realistically—producers may abandon production of their own premium products upon which so much marketing effort has been lavished, and direct their total productive effort to the private brand market.

The *Utah Pie* case[4] also involved pricing policies held violative of Section 2(a) of the Robinson-Patman Act. In that case, Utah Pie, a Salt Lake City bakery with over 66% of the market, experienced a market challenge in which the Continental and Carnation companies cut prices of their pies in the Salt Lake City area. They did not, however, meet the low prices of Utah Pie; they simply cut their prices sharply below those prevailing in other national markets in which they sold. In some instances, they cut their prices below the level of direct costs plus a reasonable allowance for overhead. However, Utah's volume of sales rose, and it retained 45% of the market while its net income expanded.

The Court, however, held that price discrimination had occurred even though the evidence did not support the presumption that Carnation and Continental were contemplating an "immediate destructive impact" of their pricing actions. Since it could be inferred that "a drastically declining price structure" resulted from "continued or sporadic price discrimination," the Court found Continental and Carnation's pricing policy illegal.

Surprisingly, the Court chose in this case to insulate a dominant (though not nationally known) firm, Utah Pie, from the rigors of price competition as

---

[3]See *Gerber Products Co. v. Beech-Nut Life Savers Co.*, 160 F. Supp. 916 (D.C. S. N.Y., 1968) cited by Borden in its brief.
[4]*Utah Pie Co. v. Continental Baking Co. et al.*, 386 U.S. 685 (1967).

pejoratively labeled in the majority opinion's language. Certainly no marketer should conclude that predatory pricing below cost is likely to be condoned by any important United States court. What marketers of national scope should also note is the likelihood that to engage in price reductions in a local market not met by similar reductions elsewhere is to risk unfavorable legal action. Adherence to uniformity of prices with all its attendant and dubious economic consequences seems a safer rule than does discretionary and variable pricing in submarkets.

In the *Albrecht* case[5] the Supreme Court reinforced its long-standing stricture that all price fixing, be it the fixing of minimum or maximum prices, is per se illegal, although some interesting nuances characterized the case. In this case, the essence of the offense was the *St. Louis Post Dispatch's* cancellation of a distributor's exclusive territory because the distributor exceeded the maximum newspaper prices established by the publishing company.

The publisher's argument, rejected by the Court, was that its fixing of maximum prices was designed to protect its readers from illegitimate price control conferred upon the distributor by his power over an exclusive and monopolistic market. The Court refused to tolerate price fixing even if it "blunts the pernicious consequences of another distribution practice." Even the pointed retort of three dissenting justices that the consequences of the majority's holding "stands the Sherman Act on its head" does no more than focus on the reemerging truth: no matter what the justification, the Supreme Court is adamant in its view that there are no legal price fixing activities.

A fourth case involving pricing practices under Section 5 of the Federal Trade Commission Act was the *Mary Carter Paint* case.[6] Mary Carter had long advertised that a "free" can of paint would be given to a buyer of a can of equal quantity and quality. The FTC had issued "Guides Against Deceptive Pricing" and despite Mary Carter's attempt to conform to those Guides the FTC found that the "free" offer violated the Guides.

The Court accepted the FTC's analysis that Mary Carter was selling two cans of paint since it quite naturally had no history of selling single cans of paint. Instead, the FTC held that Mary Carter was allocating the price of two cans of paint to one can and then calling the other can "free." Mary Carter's offer to demonstrate that the grade and quality of a single can of its paint was chemically and physically the "equal or superior to the leading paints that sell at the same per-can price level without giving bonus cans" was, ironically, summarily rejected.

Consumers may wonder along with marketers about the protection they are afforded by the contradictory attitude of the FTC and the Court toward the specifically verifiable composition of products pursued too zealously in the *Borden* case and forsaken so quickly in the *Mary Carter* case. Marketers may wonder, too, to what extent the second-unit-free pricing plan has been effectively restricted by the Court's narrow interpretation of the FTC's Pricing Guides.

---

[5]*Lester J. Albrecht v. The Herald Co.*, 88 S. Ct. 869 (1968).
[6]*Federal Trade Commission v. Mary Carter Paint Co.*, 382 U.S. 46 (1965).

Discounters, franchises, and channels of distribution

The *General Motors* case,[7] although characterized by the Court as a "classic conspiracy" in restraint of trade, presents the question of whether a marketer may foreclose his product to distribution by discount houses and referral services.

General Motors relied on the "location clause" in its Dealer Selling Agreements "which prohibits a franchised dealer from moving to or establishing 'a new or different location, branch sales office, branch service station or place of business . . . without the prior written approval of Chevrolet.'" Contending that the establishment of selling arrangements with discounters constituted an added sales office violating the location clause, General Motors in concert with individual Chevrolet dealers in the Los Angeles area, undertook "joint, collaborative action . . . to eliminate a class of competitors by terminating business dealings between them and a minority of Chevrolet dealers and to deprive franchised dealers of their freedom to deal through discounters if they so choose."

The Court did not deal with the question of most concern to marketers —could the franchises of offending dealers have been legally canceled for distributing the product through discount houses without authorization? If done unilaterally by the franchisor, perhaps they can. However, the tone of the Court's decision casts some doubt on the probability of an affirmative response. What is certain, however, is that a "joint, collaborative action" reinforced by threats, cajolery, and economic coercion is clearly not a permissible method of enforcing a contractual franchise provision.

Franchise provisions were also involved in the *Brown Shoe* case of 1966.[8] Section 5 of the Federal Trade Commission Act was invoked against Brown Shoe's Franchise Store Agreement. Retail shoe stores that accepted the Agreement (some by written contracts; others without executing the agreement formally) contracted to restrict their purchase of shoes for resale to Brown lines and to refrain from "purchasing, stocking, or reselling shoes manufactured by competitors of Brown." In return, dealers who accepted the agreement received valuable services (including merchandising records, architectural plans, field representative services, and the right to participate in a low-rate group insurance plan).

The Court held that the franchise agreement was an unfair method of competition with incipient power to restrain trade. The FTC was held to have the power to prevent such potentially deleterious trade practices that remove the freedom of purchasers to buy in the open market. Outright proof of the violation of the relevant provisions of Section 3 of the Clayton Act and Section 1 of the Sherman Act was not required. Marketers can conclude, however, that exclusive franchises limiting a participator's access to competitors will now be more vulnerable under Section 5 of the FTC Act than under provisions of other previously applicable antitrust laws.

---

[7]*United States v. General Motors Corp. et al.*, 384 U.S. 127 (1966).
[8]*Federal Trade Commission v. Brown Shoe Co., Inc.*, 384 U.S. 316 (1966).

Wholesalers, attempting to divide the Oklahoma retail liquor market territorially and by brands, were sternly reproached by the Court.[9] Lower courts discovered the market division but excused it in an argument reminiscent of the "original package" doctrine once common in the Constitutional commerce clause controversies. These courts contended that the offense was not actionable since the liquor involved ceased to be in interstate commerce after it had halted its journey from the distillers and resided in the wholesalers' warehouses. The Court, in a *per curiam* opinion, disagreed brusquely; the territorial market division substantially *affected* interstate commerce and hence was prohibited by the Sherman Act. Once more marketers could discover the impatience of the Court with specious and archaic evasions of responsibility masquerading under the guise of immunity from the commerce clause.

State liquor price regulation as adopted by New York indicated the extent of possible pricing regulations the Supreme Court would approve.[10] New York requires that wholesalers file monthly price schedules with the State Liquor Authority affirming that the bottle and case liquor prices in New York are "no higher than the lowest price" of sales made elsewhere in the United States during the previous month. The Court found that this regulation was not unconstitutionally vague and that it was a legitimate pricing regulation not unlike that adopted by liquor monopoly states. The decision, hardly a surprising one, is suggestive of the extent to which state regulation of pricing may now legally be extended.

The conclusion marketers can draw from this series of cases seems clear. Pricing autonomy continues to be circumscribed by Court action. While some of the limitations on business action have become so common that they are accepted, some are novel and onerous. In the realm of the discriminatory pricing of products of chemical and physical identity, the marketer cannot be certain of the position of the Court, which can best be characterized as unsettled. In other realms, however, it seems clear that the best rule to follow is one of great caution.

Direct-buying retailing and promotional allowances

Promotional allowances under Section 2(d) of the Robinson-Patman Act received lengthy Supreme Court consideration in the *Fred Meyer* case.[11] The Federal Trade Commission alleged that Section 2(d), which requires that allowances be offered on proportionally equal terms to all customers competing in the distribution of any product, had been violated by Meyer. Meyer, who engaged in an annual advertising promotion, had secured valuable concessions (coupon-page advertising grants and free replacement of some advertised goods) from some of its suppliers from whom it bought directly.

[9]*Burke v. Ford,* 88 S. Ct. 443 (1967).
[10]*Joseph E. Seagram & Sons, Inc., et al. v. Hostetter, Chairman, New York State Liquor Authority, et al.,* 384 U.S. 35 (1966).
[11]*Federal Trade Commission v. Fred Meyer Inc., et al.,* 88 S. Ct. 904 (1968).

On the other hand, some of Meyer's competitors purchased from wholesalers who had purchased from the same suppliers as Meyer; these competitors of Meyer did not receive advertising allowances on those purchases.

The Supreme Court in a far-reaching 6-2 decision held that those retail competitors of Meyer who purchased not from the suppliers of Meyer but from wholesalers were nevertheless competing for customers with Meyer. Hence the suppliers from whom Meyer purchased directly were obligated to offer these competitors of Meyer allowances proportionally equal to those Meyer received.

Suppliers are faced with a particularly difficult problem by the *Meyer* decision. Either they must devise appropriate methods to assure that wholesalers with whom they deal will extend allowances to buyers of products of the suppliers, or else they must abandon the promotional allowances heretofore offered exclusively to direct purchasers. Neither alternative is desirable. Suppliers will quite naturally regret the loss of the competitive device the promotional allowance afforded in competing for large purchasers. They will find the alternative of policing the wholesalers an undesirable, if not impossible, burden. Perhaps creative marketing will find new methods of extending promotional allowances in those cases in which direct-buying customers compete with firms which buy only indirectly. What is more likely is that certain types of advertising allowances will be substantially eliminated from the marketing repertoire by the *Meyer* decision.

Territorial allocations systems

Use of territorial allocations systems received extensive Court analysis in the companion *Sealy* and *Schwinn* cases.[12] When the Court completed its examination, territorial allocations systems were suspect as a legitimate marketing device, although some conditions of acceptability did emerge.

The *Sealy* and *Schwinn* cases did not present identical issues. In the *Sealy* case the Sealy licensees who agreed not to sell products outside an exclusive, designated area were found to be the actual owners of the licensing company. As owners who controlled the daily operations of the licensing firm, the licensees were found to have engaged in a horizontal territorial limitation involving "an aggregation of trade restraints" (primarily price fixing and policing actions) violating Section 1 of the Sherman Act.

Justice Harlan, in familiar dissent, found the invocation of the *per se* rule against the Sealy arrangement questionable. His view was that the rule of reason should have been applied; under it he would have found the Sealy licensing program a non-contrived one legitimately used for lawful purposes. Justice Harlan could find nothing automatically illegal in Sealy's operational arrangements, although close scrutiny of such arrangements was considered necessary.

The Schwinn territorial allocations plan provided that Schwinn's wholesale

---

[12]*United States v. Sealy, Inc.*, 388 U.S. 350 (1967); *United States v. Arnold, Schwinn & Co., et al.*, 388 U.S. 365 (1967).

distributors would sell only to franchised dealers in specific territories. Clearly, in this case, Schwinn's restrictions were vertical, not horizontal, and they were not burdened by unlawful price fixing. Schwinn, in the face of declining sales and profits, merely responded to competitive merchandising pressures. The issue before the Court, however, was not whether sound business reasons motivated Schwinn, but whether "the effect upon competition in the market-place [was] substantially adverse."

The Court's decision contained two key points. First, if Schwinn retained "all indicia of ownership, including title, dominion and risk, and so long as the dealers in question are indistinguishable in function from agents or sales-men," territorial restrictions were, absent of price-fixing activities, held to be legal. Second, if distributors actually purchased the product from Schwinn, then no "condition, agreement or understanding limiting the . . . freedom as to where and to whom it will resell the product" could legally be imposed. In reaching its conclusion the Court chose not to consider a Government plea for "a standard of presumptive illegality" which apparently would find a *prima facie case* against a firm if it could be shown simply that the product had been "distributed by means of arrangements for territorial exclusivity and restricted retail and wholesale customers."

Several conclusions emerge from this elaboration by the Court of territorial and customer restrictions. First, the *Schwinn* case clearly points the way for a supplier to impose successful territorial restrictions—the retention of "title, dominion, and risk" without allied price-fixing activities. Second, organiza-tion subterfuges, even innocently devised, will constitute a basis for attacking territorial limitations. Territorial restrictions are, in short, even less secure than they appeared to be prior to the *Schwinn* and *Sealy* cases.

ORGANIZATIONAL IMPACT OF THE COURT'S DECISIONS

The Supreme Court's impact on marketing has not been limited to business operations. Marked organizational consequences follow from the analyses of the Court; merger decisions have been crucial in determining the pattern of growth of enterprises. These decisions have had an impact not only in retail-ing, but also in banking, railroading, manufacturing, and even agricultural cooperative marketing. Generally it can be concluded that, despite its protes-tations to the contrary, the Court looks with disfavor on growth by mergers; such a disapproval is mirrored in Justice Stewart's tart remark: "The sole con-sistency that I can find is that in [anti-merger] litigation, the Government always wins."

The merger of the Pabst and Blatz breweries demonstrates the Court's pro-pensity for interpretations limiting mergers.[13] The legal battle was joined on the issue of whether the merger of Pabst and Blatz might tend to reduce com-petition in the "relevant market."

The Government identified three markets it considered relevant—a single-state market, a three-state market, and a national market. As the scope of the

---

[13]*United States v. Pabst Brewing Co. et al.*, 384 U.S. 546 (1966).

market was increased, the amount of concentration the merger would produce decreased. In an emphatic statement the Court resolved the issue: Section 7 of the Clayton Act, under which the action was developed, merely provides that the Government show substantial lessening of competition "*in any section of the country*." If the requisite anti-competitive effect follows "somewhere" in the United States, the anti-merger law is violated and the Government is now given *carte blanche* to search for the appropriate area.

In the *Von's Grocery* case,[14] the merger of two successful grocery chains was effected in the Los Angeles area. The market area had been one characterized by a steady decline in the number of stores; small firms had, to an extent, been absorbed by larger ones. The majority opinion of Justice Black, equating competition with "a large number of small competitors," held the merger violated Section 7 of the Clayton Act. Again the barbed dissent of Justices Stewart and Harlan appeared describing the majority opinion as "a simple exercise in sums" which argued that "the degree of competition is invariably proportional to the number of competitors."

The extent to which the majority opinion examined the economic structure of the Los Angeles grocery market is startlingly compressed. In the colorful language of the dissenting justices, the opinion is "hardly more than a requiem for the so-called 'Mom and Pop' grocery stores that are now economically and technologically obsolete in many parts of the country." No consideration was given to the extent to which symmetry and turnover among leading grocery firms reduced the potentially evil effects of the changing composition of the market. No consideration was given to the ease of entry of new stores into the market as manifested by new firms actually formed during the relevant period. No consideration was given to the extent that marketing patterns of the consumers indicated that the merged stores represented a market extension merger rather than a horizontal merger. Simply put, the merger somewhere in the United States had occurred coincidentally with growing concentration. The conclusion of the majority was thus demonstrated: the merger represented almost a *per se* threat to competitors—if not necessarily to viable competition itself—and was to be prevented.

Disapproval of conglomerate mergers also occurred. In the *Procter & Gamble* case,[15] the Court held that Procter's "product extension merger" with Clorox, the major producer of household liquid bleach, violated the anti-merger laws. Procter, a dominant oligopolist, would have been a "powerful acquiring firm" replacing a dominant but smaller firm in a single industry. The Court reasoned that such an acquisition would reduce potential competition by the other firms in the industry and would discourage the entry of new firms (including entry by Procter itself). Potential economies could not justify the acquisition no matter what the source of the economies. Competition was to be preserved without regard for potentially offsetting public gain resulting from the merger.

Justice Harlan in a separate concurrence focused on some of the neglected

[14]*United States v. Von's Grocery Co., et al.*, 384 U.S. 270 (1966).
[15]*Federal Trade Commission v. Procter & Gamble Co.*, 386 U.S. 568 (1967).

though important aspects of the case. Refined economic analysis, in Justice Harlan's view, was difficult but necessary, and he undertook a detailed weighing of the competitive elements of the merger. What Justice Harlan along with modern marketers notes is that market behavior may not be as destructive of economic rivalry as an overemphasized market structure test may imply. Small competitors producing a competitive but unadvertised product might set an "effective ceiling on the market price through the mechanism of an acceptable differential." Alternatively, economies achieved by innovation undertaken by one large producer may be matched by other firms with the benefits of competition flowing to the consumer in lower prices. In short, mere market structure tests do not resolve the issue that is of key relevance in marketing operations—the extending of lower prices to the consumer. Justice Harlan noted that the Court failed to weigh properly the issue of the economies of the marketing process of a merged organization. However, he argued that although the evidence introduced by the Federal Trade Commission "overstated and oversimplified" advertising as a legitimate device to achieve economy in marketing, the decision was a legally defensible one.

The increasing importance of conglomerate mergers indicates the primary significance of the decision. In virtually no instance will a major producer be secure in acquiring a firm in a related industry. In almost every case the replacement of a firm by a powerful oligopolist will render the field less attractive for potential entrants. In short, virtually every case involving a conglomerate merger will be vulnerable to the Court's logic: the movement toward concentration must be condemned. In passing, it is not irrelevant to note that there is a degree of relatedness between Procter's basic household products and that of Clorox. Hence this case does not involve a "pure" conglomerate merger in the sense that joining of the acquired and acquiring firms cannot affect the degree of actual competition in the market of either. It does, however, represent the most nearly conglomerate merger the Court has yet evaluated.

Mergers in banking, in the natural gas industry, and in railroading were also examined by the Court.[16] The Court's basic position in cases involving banking was simple: exceptions to the coverage of the antitrust prohibitions on mergers contained in the Bank Merger Act of 1966 required the merging banks to demonstrate that "considerations of community convenience and need outweighed any anticompetitive effects of the merger." So, too, in railroading in the *Seaboard Air Line Railroad* case.[17] The Interstate Commerce Commission may approve a railway merger otherwise violative of Section 7 of the Clayton Act if the merger is "consistent with the public interest." In the natural gas industry, the divestiture proceeding examined in the *El Paso Natu-*

---

[16]*United States v. First City National Bank of Houston et al.*, 386 U.S. 361 (1967); *United States v. Marshall and Ilsley Bank Stock Corp. et al.*, 387 U.S. 238 (1967); *United States v. Third National Bank in Nashville et al.*, 88 S. Ct. 882 (1968). A fourth banking decision in *First Security National Bank & Trust Co. of Lexington et al. v. United States*, 382 U.S. 34 (1965), set aside a lower court's contempt of court conviction based erroneously on a bank's delay in submitting a divestiture decree consistent with an earlier Supreme Court order.

[17]*Seaboard Air Line Railroad Co. et al. v. United States et al.*, 382 U.S. 154 (1965).

ral Gas case[18] by the Court outlined "guidelines" for an appropriate decree in which the status quo as it existed prior to the illegal merger was, insofar as possible, recreated in the public interest.

Important as the merger decisions of the Court may be, the decision in the reappearing *United Shoe Machinery* case[19] comprehends potential and far-reaching consequences. The *United Shoe Machinery* case dates from a 1953 action charging the company with a violation of Section 2 of the Sherman Act. After protracted hearings, United was found guilty of attempting to monopolize and a decree designed to create a competitive market was drawn. As a part of the decree, a provision was adopted that after ten years either party could petition to modify the decree.

In January, 1965, the federal government found the share of the market controlled by United so great that it was felt a non-competitive structure still predominated. The Government asked that a new decree be drafted. Specifically, it asked that United be required to submit a proposal to divide itself into two viable, fully competitive companies. The Supreme Court, on appeal from the district court's denial of the government's petition, supported the government's basic position: the initial decree was not effective and further remedial action was warranted.

What the *United Shoe Machinery* case portends seems momentous. American marketing must be aware of the revitalization of decrees issued to reduce market power. Even if a significant reduction in the *degree* of market power does occur, its persistence may remain a basis for continued action against a firm. The key, if this case be appropriately accepted as a landmark, is the numbers game: does the percentage of market control appear to be continuing at too high a level to satisfy those empowered with supervision? This is not to suggest mere caprice will dominate either the supervisory agency or the reviewing judiciary's evaluation. Instead it suggests that the power to revise decrees such as is contained in the *United Shoe Machinery* case is of great significance to modern marketers.

The *Grinnell* case[20] presented a unique issue arising under Sections 1 and 2 of the Sherman Act. Monopoly power was inferred from Grinnell's control of 87% of the relevant market; several allegedly competitive services were excluded when the market was defined as that of insurance-company-accredited central station alarm services. By the very limited definition which the Court noted was akin to that embodied in Section 7 of the Clayton Act, the market was delimited in such a way that a verdict that Grinnell violated the Sherman Act was assured. Thus, under the monopolization provisions of Sections 1 and 2 of the Sherman Act, as under the merger provisions of Section 7 of the Clayton Act, the business structure was modified by a decree of dissolution which the Court said might appropriately be buttressed by relief allowing the Government to require reports, to examine documents, and to interview company personnel.

---

[18]*Cascade Natural Gas Corp. v. El Paso Natural Gas Co. et al.,* 386 U.S. 129 (1967).
[19]*United States v. United Shoe Machinery Corp.,* 88 S. Ct. 1496 (1968).
[20]*United States v. Grinnell Corp. et al.,* 384 U.S. 563 (1966).

In the final case exerting a marked impact on the organization of marketing, the Supreme Court examined the citrus cooperative, Sunkist Growers.[21] Sunkist believed that under the provisions of the Capper-Volstead Agricultural Producers' Associations Act, it was immunized from the provisions of Section 1 of the Sherman Act. However, the Supreme Court noted that 15% of the Sunkist members were associations that processed fruit for producers. The Capper-Volstead Act is limited to *producers* of agricultural products; the inclusion of the processors in the organization destroyed Sunkist's immunity from the antitrust acts which it would otherwise have had. The Court was sharply divided on what might be salvaged of the Sunkist organization; what is significant here is the extent to which marketing must once more adjust organizationally to the findings of the Court.

REGULATORY PROCEDURE ASPECTS OF SUPREME COURT DECISIONS

Even though those decisions bearing directly on marketing organization and operations seem of primary importance to business, a number of cases affecting the procedure of regulation should not be ignored. Regulatory decisions, onerous or favorable, are a function of the ways decisions are made and of the institutions by which they are made. The Supreme Court, vitally concerned with legal and administrative processes, has exerted a marked impact on the "how" of contemporary marketing regulation.

The Supreme Court has approved the Federal Trade Commission's occasional practice of issuing cease-and-desist orders with the concurrence of a majority of a quorum of the Commission rather than a majority of the full Commission.[22] Thus FTC orders are binding if only two of three members present adopt them; this accords with the common law rule that if the enabling statute is silent (especially where administrative agencies are involved), then a majority of a quorum suffices for purposes of decision.

The Federal Trade Commission was also granted broader powers by the decision in the *Dean Foods* case.[23] A merger involving Dean Foods was challenged by the FTC and although disapproved, no formal cease-and-desist order was issued. Subsequently Dean Foods indicated it would proceed with the merger; the FTC asked that under provisions of the All Writs Act, the court of appeals prevent the consummation of the merger. The Commission contended that effective remedial action would prove impossible if consummation did occur. The Court, by a 5-4 vote with Justice Fortas rendering an exhaustive dissent, upheld the power of a court of appeals to support the FTC even in the absence of a formal action by the Commission. Expeditious support of FTC action by courts of appeals thus becomes possible by this device previously not available to the Commission.

In an allied procedural decision[24] the Court held that a court of appeals lacked the power to reverse an FTC denial of a firm's request that an order be

---

[21]*Case-Swayne Co. v. Sunkist Growers, Inc.*, 88 S. Ct. 528 (1967).

[22]*Federal Trade Commission v. Flotill Products, Inc.*, 88 S. Ct. 401 (1967).

[23]*Federal Trade Commission v. Dean Foods Co. et al.*, 384 U.S. 497 (1966).

[24]*Federal Trade Commission v. Universal-Rundle Corp.*, 387 U.S. 244 (1967).

stayed. Only if a "patent abuse of discretion" by the FTC can be demonstrated, does an appelate court have the power erroneously invoked in the *Universal-Rundle* case.

Nor did the Supreme Court find that orders entered before the Finality Act of 1959 became effective were unenforceable. In the *Jantzen* case,[25] the more than 400 outstanding cease-and-desist orders were held enforceable under provisions of Section 11 of the Clayton Act.

The Court also dealt with orders issued under provisions of the Federal Food, Drug, and Cosmetic Act and its amendments. In a liberalizing opinion, the Court established the conditions under which preenforcement review of regulations issued by the Commissioner of Food and Drugs may occur. In a series of three cases,[26] the general guides emerge. If regulations are self-executing and if their impact on business is both very burdensome (entailing heavy financial burdens, extensive operational changes, and potential loss of good will) and if the penalties for non-compliance are severe, then courts may accord pre-enforcement review of the regulations.

Other procedural decisions of the Court are important but they bear less directly on the daily legal environment of marketing.[27] However, one case involving the powers of local government is noteworthy.[28] The decision may prove to be of doubtful practical significance, but the Court has held that under the Fourth Amendment inspection of private commercial premises by an administrative agent requires, if demanded, a suitable warrant. Clearly such a requirement will not long deter an earnest inspector; the warrant will be forthcoming. What does emerge from the welter of apparently contradictory opinion is the legitimate and expanding concern of the Court for the protection of the rights of business.

A NEW LOOK

The Supreme Court is a unique amalgam of an idiosyncratic structure, a cherished tradition, and strong personages. It brings powerful opinions to bear on contemporary and controversial issues springing from the vital events of daily life. Its resolution of those controversies creates an environment to which modern decision making must adjust even while the adjustments are frequently accompanied by anguished wails protesting to Heaven the injustice of it all.

Glances backward have shown how profoundly the legal environment of

[25]*Federal Trade Commission v. Jantzen, Inc.*, 386 U.S. 228 (1967).

[26]*Abbott Laboratories et al. v. Gardner, Secretary of Health, Education, and Welfare, et al.*, 387 U.S. 136 (1967); *Toilet Goods Association, Inc. et al. v. Gardner, Secretary of Health, Education, and Welfare, et al.*, 387 U.S. 158 (1967); *Gardner, Secretary of Health, Education, and Welfare, et al. v. Toilet Goods Association, Inc. et al.*, 387 U.S. 167 (1967).

[27]*Swift & Co., Inc. et al. v. Wickham, Commissioner of Agriculture & Markets of New York*, 382 U.S. 111 (1967); *Leh et al. v. General Petroleum Corp. et al.*, 382 U.S. 54 (1965); *Carnation Co. v. Pacific Westbound Conference et al.*, 383 U.S. 213 (1966); *Federal Maritime Commission et al. v. Aktiebolaget, et al.*, 88 S. Ct. 1008 (1968); *Federal Maritime Commission et al. v. Aktiebolaget Svenska Amerika Linien et al.; American Society of Travel Agents, Inc. v. Aktiebolaget Svenska Amerika Linien et al.*, 88 S. Ct. 1005 (1968).

[28]*See v. City of Seattle*, 387 U.S. 541 (1967).

business has been modified. Subtly, in the past three terms of the Court, the boundaries of marketing operations, organizational forms, and procedural methods have been altered. Usually, though not always, those boundaries of autonomous marketing decisions have been narrowed; adaptable marketers have adjusted to the new limits on their scope of action. Adjustments may have served to restrain sound growth of individual business and of the general economy but adaptability has nevertheless prevailed.

Glances forward, insofar as they can perceptively be made, yield no visions of revolutionary changes in either the role or attitude of the Court or of modern marketer's adjustment to it. In a sense, a look to the future in all likelihood represents one more verification of the cold and chiseled prophecy above the entrance to the National Archives: "The Past is Prologue."

READING 37

THE CONCEPT OF PRICE LIMITS AND PSYCHOPHYSICAL MEASUREMENT: A LABORATORY EXPERIMENT*

Kent B. Monroe and M. Venkatesan

INTRODUCTION

Price theory generally assumes that price enters into the determination of buyer choice because price serves as an indicator of cost to the buyer. And when the buyer knows the prices of all goods, he is in a position to optimally allocate his budget to maximize his utility. However, buyers really do not have complete and accurate information about the utility received from a set of products, nor the prices of these products. Yet, buyers somehow acquire sufficient information about products and about the satisfaction received from these products to decide which products to purchase with a given budget.

Some information is acquired through the promotional efforts of the seller; other information is acquired through experience—of others or of the purchaser. Even so, the buyer is uncertain whether the anticipated purchase will provide the desired level of satisfaction. Lacking complete information about the utility associated with the product, the buyer attempts to assess the product on the basis of known information. That is, he attempts to assess the quality of the product—the reliability of the product providing the desired level of satisfaction.

Except in rare circumstances, one piece of information always available to the buyer is the product's price. If over time there is a positive correspondence between price and the level of satisfaction acquired from the purchase, it seems reasonable to use price as a criterion to assess product quality.

Because other pieces of information about anticipated purchases are not always known (or at least known less frequently than price), the buyer cannot

*Reprinted from *Marketing Involvement in Society and the Economy*, Philip R. McDonald, ed. (Chicago: American Marketing Association, 1969), pp. 345–350.

be sure other possible criteria to assess quality will always be available. And even if other information is available, the buyer may not know its degree of completeness and reliability since this information is not always available. In addition, information not always available may introduce uncertainty about the ability to make correct predictions about product quality.

RELATED RESEARCH ON PRICE

An understanding of why price affects buyer choice depends upon a determination of how buyers actually perceive the price of a product.[1] Beginning with Tibor Scitovsky's paper on the relationship between price and imputed quality, several studies have been conducted that provide some insight into this problem.[2]

Leavitt experimented with choice situations for four products in the 50 cent to $1.00 range.[3] In this experiment, Leavitt's subjects

1. Indicated they would often choose the higher-priced brand when price was the only differential information;

2. Were more ready to make the higher-price choice for products believed to be different in quality;

3. Showed a tendency to select the higher-priced brand when the price difference was large.

These findings suggest price may have more than one meaning for a buyer.

Tull, Boring, and Gonsior explored Leavitt's experimental method to determine if his findings could be replicated.[4] Choosing from three lettered and differentially priced brands, each subject "purchased" a brand of each of four inexpensive products. This experiment supported Leavitt's findings in that the respondents tended to choose the higher-priced brands of similar products.

Gabor and Granger in a series of studies explored the issue of price as an indicator of quality.[5] However, instead of simulating purchase decisions, they sought to establish housewives' opinions of acceptable price ranges for various products. Their research was based on the hypothesis that a buyer has two price limits in mind: an upper limit above which the product would be judged too expensive; and a lower limit below which the quality of the product would be suspect. Gabor and Granger also concluded that price reveals

---

[1]Perception is defined as the link between the actual reception of energy through the sense organs and such mental processes as judgment, reasoning, and memory. It is the process by which an actor gives meaning to the raw material provided by the external world.

[2]Tibor Scitovsky, "Some Consequences of the Habit of Judging Quality by Price," *The Review of Economic Studies*, 12, (32), 1944–45.

[3]Harold J. Leavitt, "A Note on Some Experimental Findings About the Meaning of Price," *Journal of Business*, 27, July, 1954, pp. 205–210.

[4]D. S. Tull, R. A. Boring, and M. H. Gonsior, "A Note on the Relationship of Price and Imputed Quality," *Journal of Business*, 37, April, 1964, pp. 186–191.

[5]Andre Gabor, and C. W. J. Granger, "On the Price Consciousness of Consumers," *Applied Statistics*, November, 1961, pp. 170–180; "Price Sensitivity of the Consumer," *Journal of Advertising Research*, December, 1964, pp. 40–44; "Price as an Indicator of Quality: Report on an Inquiry," *Economica*, February, 1966, pp. 43–70.

not only the cost of the product to the buyer, but provides the buyer some measure of the value of the contemplated purchase.

McConnell experimentally tested the hypothesis that the price of a product or brand was a determinant of quality perception.[6] Using a homogeneous product (beer), and three lettered brand names, he found the highest priced brand was perceived as being a better quality product. His study supports the conclusion previously cited that price is a determinant of the buyer's perception of a product.

In a study dealing with social categorization as a function of latitude of acceptance and series range, Carolyn Sherif found that there were lower and upper price limits (valued series).[7]

CONCEPT OF PRICE LIMITS

These studies indicate the buyer's subjective perceptions of price may include a range of acceptable prices for a given product. That is, a buyer may have upper and lower price limits for a product. If the product price is below the lower limit, the product is perceived to be "too cheap"; and if the price is above the upper limit, the product is perceived to be "too expensive."

This concept of price limits raises a question about the previously accepted shape of the theoretical demand curve for a product. Demand curves may not be invariably negatively sloped. If a buyer has both a lower-price limit and an upper-price limit for a contemplated purchase, it is unlikely he would be disposed to purchase the product if the price were above his upper limit or below his lower limit.

PSYCHOPHYSICS AND THE PRICE LIMIT CONCEPT

The price limit concept

The hypothesis that a buyer has two price limits in mind for a contemplated purchase has foundation in the theories of psychophysics.[8] It has been established that every human sensory process has an upper and lower limit of responsiveness to a stimulus. If we consider price to be a demand stimulus, then a *priori* there are upper and lower price limits for a contemplated purchase. The extent to which these price limits prevail is not known. Our interest is to be able to determine how given values of the stimulus (price) affect the willingness to buy (response).

This experimental research is an exploratory investigation of the price limit concept for different products. The Gabor and Granger study cited earlier is the only reported study concerned with the price limit concept. However, their study suffers from the same pitfalls that befall survey methodology. Moreover, our study is aimed also at exploring the appropriateness and

---

[6]J. Douglas McConnell, "Effect of Pricing on Perception of Product Quality," *Journal of Applied Psychology*, 52, No. 4, 1968, pp. 331–334.

[7]Carolyn W. Sherif, "Social Categorization as a Function of Latitude of Acceptance and Series Range," *Journal of Abnormal and Social Psychology*, 67, 1963, pp. 148–156.

[8]Psychophysics is the study of relationships between sensory attributes and physical objects.

validity of psychophysical methods for investigating pricing perception phenomena.

Experimental methods of psychophysics

Because the experimental procedure is adapted from psychophysics, a brief review of psychophysical methodology is appropriate.

The notion of a limit or threshold is one of the most common measurements used in psychophysics. As has been implied in the previous section, a threshold or limit is a point, or region, on a scale where a response shifts from positive to negative, or negative to positive, as the case may be.

One approach to threshold measurement is *the method of limits*. In this method, a subject is presented with a series of stimuli, each stimulus differing by a small magnitude from the preceding stimulus, and his response to each stimulus in the series is recorded. For example, to determine the threshold for pitch, the experimenter can increase the frequency of sound waves in small steps, and the subject will report when he hears a tone. If an ascending series is used, the initial stimulus intensity of the series is presented at a value the subject will not detect and, on each succeeding trial, the experimenter increases the intensity of the stimulus by a constant small amount until the subject detects the presence of the stimulus and gives a positive response. If a descending series is used, the initial stimulus intensity of the series is presented at a value the subject will easily detect and, on each succeeding trial, the experimenter decreases the intensity of the stimulus by constant small amounts until the subject can no longer detect the presence of the stimulus and gives a negative response.

There are a number of objections in the practical use of the method of limits. The threshold obtained is influenced by the size of the changes in intensity from step to step, by the rate of change in intensity if the adjustment is continuous, and by the direction of adjustment and whether the series is ascending or descending. In addition, the subject is likely to reverse judgment from positive to negative and back to positive around the threshold region. The possibility of such reversals illustrates an important property of threshold measurement: *response near the threshold is a probabilistic phenomenon.*

Because of this response uncertainty near the threshold, a second experimental method is often used to measure thresholds, *the method of constant stimuli*. There are three steps to this method. First, the method of limits may be used to obtain an approximate region indicating the probable threshold stimulus. The second step is to select a series of stimuli covering the range from a point where the subject will rarely detect the stimulus to a point where he will always detect it. Third, these chosen stimuli are presented many times in a prearranged order and the relative frequency of the occurrence of detection is recorded.

METHODOLOGY

To investigate the concept of price limits, the experimental methodology of psychophysics was utilized. The investigation was conducted in two phases.

The structure of the first phase was similar to the method of limits and the structure of the second phase was similar to the method of constant stimuli. It was necessary to modify these two methods because upon presentation of the price stimulus, the subjects would immediately know the measured intensity of the stimulus, whereas in conventional psychophysical experiments the subjects are not aware of the intensity of the particular stimulus.

Thus, the objectives of the study were to explore experimentally the application of psychophysical methods for testing the price limit concept and to conduct a series of experiments to obtain additional information about the perception of price. A controlled laboratory experiment was designed to test the appropriateness of the methodology and to test the hypothesis that subjects have a range of acceptable prices for a contemplated purchase.

Phase one

To determine the approximate region of the price limits, the first phase of the study was conducted, using students as subjects. Using the criteria of prior product knowledge, price awareness, and prior purchase experience, the following products were chosen: for males; dress shirts, after-shave lotion, three-season sport coats, and electric shavers; for females; blouses, portable hair dryers, liquid shampoo and dress shoes. The subjects were asked to indicate, on a continuous scale, for each product, the set of prices they would consider *acceptable* if buying the given product. As a check on consistency they were also asked to indicate the set of *unacceptable* prices.

The scales were the same for all the products. Each scale had six reference prices as cues to guide the rater in defining the price continuum for each product. The subjects were free to use any portion of the scale including that part of the scale beyond the anchor prices and were free to indicate as many prices as being acceptable or unacceptable as they desired.

A frequency count of the relevant limits of the prices indicated as acceptable and unacceptable provided the basis for determining the range of the series of prices to be used during phase two of the experiment. However, due to the myriad package sizes and product forms for hair shampoo, the female subjects had extreme difficulty in visualizing what the term "standard size" meant, and consequently were not confident in their ratings of this product. To overcome this difficulty, the product hair spray was substituted for liquid hair shampoo during the second phase of the study.

Two hundred males and fifty females, all students at the University of Massachusetts, took part in both of the phases of the experiment. The incentive for participation was a lottery in which the names of ten participants were chosen to receive $10 gift certificates to be redeemed at a local store of their choosing.

It should be noted how the method of limits was adapted for phase one. Instead of presenting the stimuli singly and in serial order, the subjects were presented a rating scale of prices where the prices were shown on a continuum, thereby accomplishing the stimuli presentation requirement of the method of limits. By requesting each subject to indicate the set of acceptable prices, it then was possible to determine for each subject his lower and upper price threshold for each product. The frequency distribution of the lowest and highest acceptable price for each student and each product provided the approximate region of the relevant price threshold to be used in phase two.

Phase two

Design. For phase two, except for the substitution of hair spray for liquid shampoo, the same products were used. In this phase, which was conducted about a month later, new subjects were shown fourteen slides for each product. Each slide consisted of a single price, and each set of price stimuli was concentrated around the lower or higher acceptable price limits determined in the first phase of the study. For each product, there were six treatments: ascending low, descending low, ascending high, descending high, random low, and random high. For each product three treatments, *viz.*, descending low, ascending low, and random low, related to the lower price limit and the three remaining treatments related to the higher price limit. In the descending low and ascending high treatments, the price stimuli started at a price that was clearly acceptable to 90 percent or more of the subjects during phase one. For all serial presentation of the price stimuli, the prices were changed by a constant amount at each step. This constant varied by product. In the random treatment the stimulus sequence was determined randomly, but the prices were identical as in the corresponding serial presentation. Thus, there were 24 treatments for each set of four products.

Each male subject was exposed to two treatments, one for each of two products. The two-product combination was chosen on the basis of one high-priced and one low-priced product. For six groups of male subjects, the products were dress shirts (low price item) and electric shavers (high price item) and for the other six groups the products were after-shave lotion and three-season sport coats. The experimental design is shown in Figure 1.

Each female subject was exposed to four treatments, one for each of the four products. Because of the limited number of female subjects, four of the five groups were exposed to both the random high and random low treatments. The experimental design is shown in Figure 2. All subjects were assigned randomly to the treatments and the treatment sequence for each product also was randomly determined.

Procedure. Subjects as a group were seated in alternate seats in the laboratory. A set of instructions was read to the group explaining the procedure, and they were shown an illustration of what they were going to see and a sample page of the answer sheet. Then a 14-page booklet was given to each subject. On the right-hand side of each page in bold letters was printed SLIDE NO. ——. On the first page was printed SLIDE NO. 1 and consecutively numbered pages ended with SLIDE NO. 14. The subjects were told they would see 14 slides, each one containing a price for the product mentioned on the page. (Each page contained the name of the product prominently, on the top left-hand side.) On each page of the booklet, the subjects were asked (1) to write

Group No.	Dress Shirt	Electric Shaver	Group No.	After-Shave	Sports Coat
1	DL[a]	AH[d]	2	AH	DL
	n = 12	n = 12		n = 12	n = 12
3	AH	DL	4	RL[e]	RH[f]
	n = 14	n = 14		n = 15	n = 15
5	RL	RH	6	DH[b]	AL[c]
	n = 15	n = 15		n = 16	n = 16
7	RH	RL	8	DL	AH
	n = 16	n = 16		n = 17	n = 17
9	DH	AL	10	AL	DH
	n = 13	n = 13		n = 14	n = 14
11	AL	DH	12	RH	RL
	n = 15	n = 15		n = 14	n = 14

[a]DL: Descending Low Prices
[b]DH: Descending High Prices
[c]AL: Ascending Low Prices
[d]AH: Ascending High Prices
[e]RL: Random Low Prices
[f]RH: Random High Prices

Figure 1
Experimental design for male subjects

the price they saw on the slide, (2) to evaluate the price for the given product on a continuous scale, ranging from extremely low to extremely high with five other cues in between, and (3) to indicate whether or not they would be willing to buy that product at that price.

They were told that to keep each price separate, first a slide would appear on the screen reading "Slide Number——" and a few seconds later, the slide with a price in dollars and cents would be shown on the screen. Thus each "price slide" was preceded by a "slide number" slide. The objective of the "slide number" slide was to help the subject complete the page and keep pace with the price slides appearing on the screen. Each slide remained on the screen for approximately 10 seconds. The timing of exposure to each price slide was accomplished by permitting the "volume of paper noise" to serve as a cue for showing the next slide. Thus, in the beginning the slides

Group No.	Blouse	Hair Dryer	Dress Shoes	Hair Spray
15	**DH**[b] n = 9	**AH**[d] n = 9	**AL**[c] n = 9	**RH**[f] **RL**[e] n = 9
16	**DL**[a] n = 10	**DH** n = 10	**AH** n = 10	**AL** n = 10
17	**AH** n = 10	**RH RL** n = 10	**DH** n = 10	**DL** n = 10
18	**RH RL** n = 7	**AL** n = 7	**DL** n = 7	**DH** n = 7
19	**AL** n = 8	**DL** n = 8	**RL RH** n = 8	**AH** n = 8

[a]DL: Descending Low Prices
[b]DH: Descending High Prices
[c]AL: Ascending Low Prices
[d]AH: Ascending High Prices
[e]RL: Random Low Prices
[f]RH: Random High Prices

Figure 2
Experimental design for female subjects

were on the screen longer than at later stages. After the series of 14 slides was completed for a product, the experimenter collected the booklets. Then he explained that the procedure was the same, but that now the subjects would see prices for a different product. This procedure was repeated for the next product. At the end of the showing, the subjects were given a questionnaire asking for their opinions about the study and their understanding of the purpose of the study.

Again, the congruence between the above procedure and the method of constant stimuli should be noted. The results of phase one produced the approximate region of the price limits for each product. The price stimuli were then selected for the appropriate limit region and prearranged orders of stimuli presentation were developed. Finally the price stimuli were presented to the subjects and the "buy" or "not buy" responses were recorded.

RESULTS AND DISCUSSION

Strictly defined, the price threshold or limit, is that separation of two points that yields 50 percent responses of "buy" and 50 percent responses of "do not buy." Using both the linear interpolation process and the normal-graphic

Product	Lower Price Limit		High Price Limit	
	Linear interpolation	Normal-graphic process	Linear interpolation	Normal-graphic process
Blouse	$ 3.58	$ 3.80	$10.87	$ 9.70
Dress shoes	10.50	9.00	19.50	19.10
Hair spray	0.57	0.59	1.88	1.88
Portable hair-dryer	14.99	13.80	24.25	23.50
After-shave lotion	1.62	1.75	3.20	3.38
Dress shirt	3.33	3.25	7.25	6.50
Electric shaver	13.00	13.75	24.90	22.50
Three-season sports coat	23.70	24.75	54.68	41.50

Table 1
Price limits—phase two

process for determining limens, the price limits were obtained as shown in Table 1.

For the product dress shirts, it can be seen from Table 2 that the estimate of the low price limit lies between $3.25 and $3.33. The simplest solution is a linear interpolation between the proportions of 41.5 and 56.1 to find the low price limit LP which would give a proportion of .50. A general formula to fit this problem is

$$LP = \frac{P_L + (P_H - P_L)\,(.50 - p_1)}{p_h - p_1} \tag{1}$$

where P_H is the price immediately higher than the threshold price
P_L is the price immediately lower than the threshold price
p_h is the proportion of subjects responding "buy" for the price immediately higher than the threshold price
p_1 is the proportion of subjects responding "buy" for the price immediately lower than the threshold price.

Or, for the dress shirt, the solution is

$$LP = \$3.25 + \frac{(\$0.13)\,(.085)}{(.146)} = \$3.33 \tag{2}$$

The linear interpolation method is useful as a means of obtaining a quick estimate of the price limits. However, this method is objectionable because it does not use all of the response data. In the example, only two of the proportions were used. Secondly, the assumption the curve is linear between two points is questionable.

The normal-graphic process

To overcome these objections, the normal-graphic process was used to obtain better estimates of the price limits. This method uses normal probability graph

Individual Low-Price Limits[a]	Number Responding (cumulative)	Proportion Responding (cumulative)
$1.38	1	2.4%
1.88	3	7.3
2.12	4	9.8
2.38	8	19.5
2.62	12	29.3
2.88	16	39.0
3.12	17	41.5
3.25	17	41.5
3.38	23	56.1
3.62	24	58.5
3.75	31	75.6
4.25	35	85.4
4.75	36	87.8
5.25	40	97.5
5.75	41	100.0

[a] Each price limit represents the midpoint price between a "yes" and a "no" response by an individual subject. For example, $1.38 is the rounded mid-point between a "no" response at $1.25 and a "yes" response at $1.50. The prices ending in $0.25 were obtained from subjects in high treatments who actually had very narrow ranges of acceptable prices. Thus, these subjects were able to indicate both the lowest and highest acceptable price during a high treatment.

Table 2
Summary data for low-priced threshold dress shirt

paper on which one axis is divided into uneven steps of percentages. The steps are spaced according to the normal distribution function such that when proportions are plotted against stimulus values, the regression is linear.

To obtain the regression line, a least squares regression of the form $z = a + bP$ was fitted to the data. The price limit estimate is then read off the regression line for p equal to 50 percent. Figure 3 illustrates the use of this method of obtaining the high and low price limits for the product dress shirt. Due to space limitations, only this single illustration is provided. However, the results for all eight products were presented in Table 1.

The data clearly confirm the hypothesis that the subjects have lower and higher price limits for products, and that they would apparently be unwilling to consider buying the products outside the price range.

That the final results of this study confirmed the concept of low and high price limits was not surprising. For the data from phase one also confirmed clearly that subjects had a definite range of acceptable prices for the products tested. The methodology of phase two did present a means of obtaining more refined estimates of the low and high price thresholds.

Where price is the only differential information available it is clear the subjects do have a range of acceptable prices that is not bound on the low side by a price of zero. That is, the median lowest acceptable price that subjects were willing to consider paying for any product was greater than zero. This finding is applicable to relatively low-priced products such as hair spray and

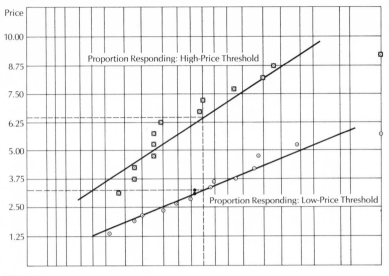

Figure 3

Determinants of low and high price thresholds—dress shirt.

after-shave lotion as well as to relatively high-priced products such as the hair dryer and sport coat. The immediate implication is that the demand curve bends backward at low prices instead of sloping down and to the left as postulated in price theory.

This particular finding has even broader implications for pricing decisions. Specifically, a reduction in price may actually lead to a reduction in demand, particularly if the product is already low priced from the buyers' points of view. Thus, demand for a product, along with such factors as cost and competition, may serve as a constraint as to how low a price should be set. Previously demand was generally considered only as a constraint as to how high a price might be charged.

CONCLUSIONS

It should be recognized this experiment does not incorporate any other information normally available to the buyer except price, such as brand name, visual presentation of the product, frequency of purchase, purchase objective, brand and product familiarity, store environment, or offer situation. Recognizing this limitation, additional pricing experiments are being conducted to determine the effect these variables may have on the subjective perceptions of price. In addition, a refined experimental methodology is being tested.

However, this limitation does not diminish the nature of the results reported here. These results confirm the Gabor and Granger conclusions that buyers have a range of acceptable prices for contemplated purchases. Furthermore, the controlled laboratory experiment diminishes the criticism of the Gabor and Granger study that their method may have used leading questions. Research must now be directed toward finding the determinants of the range of acceptable prices and to validate further the price limit concept.

PART
SIX

PROMOTIONAL ACTIVITIES

The word promotion means advancement in rank or position, furtherance or encouragement, or the act or promoting. Promotion takes on each of these meanings when viewed by the marketer. McNeal sets the stage in his article "Promotion: An Overview." Promotion is used by the marketer to communicate to consumers information about product availability and attributes of products and services, and to convince the consumers to purchase the offering.

The customer buys a solution to a problem, not a product or service. Our next selection, "How System Selling Is Revolutionizing Marketing," develops the concept of system selling. The personal selling function is a "linking pin" between the buyer and seller organization. Cotham's article, "Selecting Salesmen: Approaches and Problems," explores the need for improvement, expansion, and uniformity of effort in research on personal selling. The importance of personal selling is suggested by the fact that in many large companies personal selling expense is the single largest operating expense, often equaling 8 to 15 percent of sales.

Another linking pin between the buyer and seller organization is advertising. Irving S. White explores the function of advertising in our culture. Dik Warren Twedt's essay presents a three-step method for planning new products, for planning product improvement, and for evaluating relative strength of copy claims. Next, Dennis H. Gensch presents a review article on media factors. He points out that qualitative factors influence media selection and attempts to identify and group these factors. The final article is on media management in the 1970s; the Grey Advertising Agency asserts that this is the creative challenge of the next decade.

READING 38

PROMOTION: AN OVERVIEW*

James U. McNeal

The term, promotion, originates from the Latin term, *promovere*, meaning to move forward. From the viewpoint of business practice, the original meaning of promotion has been narrowed to include only communicative activity. Thus, promotion, as discussed here, is any communicative activity whose purpose is to move forward a product, service, or idea in a channel of distribution.

Defining promotion in this manner does not limit its use just to business. Other institutions, such as churches, governments, and schools have assimilated much business behavior including promotion. In fact, some of the most successful promotional efforts have been those of our national and state

*Reprinted from *Readings in Promotion Management,* James U. McNeal, ed. (New York: Appleton-Century-Crofts), 1966, pp. 3–19.

governments. Since this book was developed primarily for use by business and business schools, however, the discussions of promotion will center about business. The principals and concepts involved are nevertheless applicable to any promotional undertaking.

PROMOTION AND MARKETING

Promotion is a tool of marketing. Marketing, as a function of business, has the purpose of interpreting demand and directing those activities, other than production, necessary for profitably satisfying that demand. Promotion is used by marketing to inform consumers (demand) of the availability and attributes of products and services and to convince the consumers to purchase the offering. Thus, promotion is a means of moving forward the offering of a company to intermediate and final consumers.

Figure 1 illustrates the relationship of promotion to marketing.[1] Marketing activity results from and is determined by the overall company objectives. These objectives usually are stated in terms of products and services, e.g., to produce and sell the highest quality, safest, most dependable auto tires. Marketing activities do not actually come to life until the overall company objectives have been translated into overall marketing objectives, e.g., to deliver to car-owners the highest quality, safest, and most dependable auto tire consistent with their desires and the profits of the firm. With these two sets of basic objectives in mind, the marketing unit goes into action by first developing a wide array of data that will permit an adequate understanding of the market to be served by the company and its products. Then a marketing mix is developed. This mix, or system, consists of all the marketing efforts and marketing tools in the correct proportions that are necessary for satisfying the company's consumers and the company's objectives.

Included in the marketing mix are:

1. Price

2. Place (channels of distribution)

3. Product

4. Promotion.

Each of these four general terms describes a sub-mix. *Price* includes pricing policies and objectives and the determination of selling price and middleman discounts. *Place* consists of the type and number of middlemen employed and the means for transporting and storing the offering. *Product* includes the design and assortment of the product and its brand. *Promotion,* the subject matter of this book, consists of those communicative tools needed in order to inform consumers of the firm's offering and persuade them to buy it. Let us examine the promotional mix in more detail.

---

[1]The framework used here is adapted from E. Jerome McCarthy, *Basic Marketing: A Managerial Approach* (Homewood, Ill.: Richard D. Irwin, Inc., 1960).

THE PROMOTIONAL MIX

The concept of promotional mix assumes that there is a variety of means for communicating with consumers and the final selection of them will depend on the jobs assigned to promotion and the environment in which these jobs are to be performed. The concept further assumes, that while certain promotional types may be better suited for some tasks than others, all promotional types are compatible and interchangeable.

Referring to Figure 1 again, it can be seen that the promotional mix is one of the four major parts of the marketing mix. Other significant facts to be observed in Figure 1 about the promotional mix are:

1. Before the promotional mix is developed, overall company and marketing objectives have been set and the potential market for the product has been located and described. Thus, the promotional mix has purpose—the company and marketing objectives—and it is developed with a specific body of potential consumers in mind.

2. The promotional mix is consumer oriented as indicated by the C in the center of the marketing mix illustration. This symbol also means that *all* of the marketing mix elements are consumer oriented. The term, consumer oriented, implies more than just saying that the promotional mix "is developed with a specific body of potential consumers in mind," as was noted above. It implies that all decisions regarding the promotional mix are made with the potential consumers' *satisfaction* as a focal point.

3. There is an integral relationship between the promotional mix and the other three mixes, price, product, and place. Decisions made about the promotional mix will influence, and thus must consider, the other elements of the marketing mix. Likewise, the constituents of the promotional mix must be considered when decisions are made about the remaining elements of the marketing mix.

Elements of the promotional mix

The actual elements of a promotional mix are variable depending on such matters as the tasks assigned to promotion and the environment in which the promotion must operate. Figure 2 is a generalization of the promotional mix just as Figure 1 was a generalization of the marketing mix. It shows that the promotional mix consists of five basic constituents: (1) advertising, (2) packaging, (3) personal selling, (4) publicity, and (5) sales promotion. And all focus upon the consumer. A brief discussion of each of these five elements will give some idea of the possible extent and complexity of the promotional mix.

Advertising. According to the American Marketing Association, advertising may be defined as ". . . any paid form of nonpersonal presentation and promotion of ideas, goods or services by an identified sponsor."[2] While this

---

[2]*Marketing Definitions* (Chicago: American Marketing Association, 1960), p. 9.

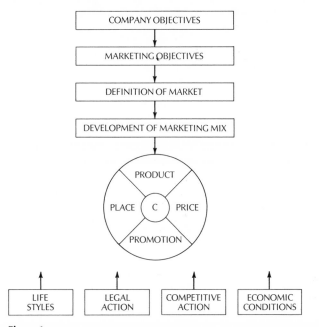

Figure 1

definition has certain weaknesses,[3] it does point out that advertising is *non-personal, paid for*, and has a *sponsor*. It is nonpersonal as contrasted with personal selling; it is paid for by an identified sponsor as contrasted with publicity.

Advertising is further distinguished by the fact that it is employed for promotion to large audiences. In fact, it is often referred to as mass selling. Through the medium of television, for instance, an advertisement may reach 16,000,000 prospective consumers at one time.

A further important characteristic of advertising that usually distinguishes it from personal selling is the high degree of control that can be maintained over its promotional efforts. For example, if an advertisement is supposed to tell potential consumers of five new ways to use an existing product, one can depend on these five ways being listed in the December issue of *McCalls*, or whatever medium is selected. On the other hand, these five new ways of using an existing product are as likely to become four or six in the hands of a personal salesman who has his own feelings about the particular product. It is true that the medium (newspaper, magazine, etc.) for an advertising message is usually in the control of a person other than the advertiser, while the medium (salesman) for a personal selling message is usually within the control of the seller. Typically, though, the lack of control over the advertising medium does not impede control over the advertising message, whereas the control over the personal salesman is rarely adequate enough to insure perfect reproduction of the desired message.[4]

---

[3]The definition easily can be interpreted to include packaging and sales promotion.
[4]This is particularly true of field salesmen. It is less true of retail salesmen who usually operate within visual and audible control.

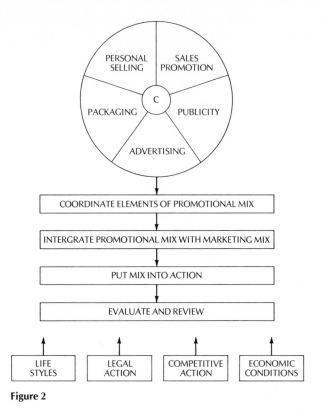

Figure 2

The means through which an advertisement may be presented are countless. The most important according to expenditures are newspapers, direct mail, television, magazines, and radio, in that order. The impact, however, of such media as the programs of football games and outdoor signs may be just as great as that of the above five. Any media that most effectively and efficiently reaches the company's market is, of course, the correct one to use.

The nature of the company's product will determine, to a great extent, the degree to which advertising is employed in the promotional mix. Highly complex products usually do not lend themselves to effective promotion through advertising. While it is possible to develop advertising to explain the complexities, it too often is difficult to get prospective customers to read such. Advertising, in this case, is best used to enhance brand and company image.

Very expensive products (which are often complex) also are not very adaptable to advertising as a basic means of promotion. If for no other reason, it is difficult for advertising to argue against the most common objection to buying: "It costs too much money."

In general, advertising is a good basic promotional tool for low-cost, mass-consumed products. For other types of products, advertising is best used as supporting promotion.

Personal selling. This type of promotion is unique, in as its name suggests, it is presented on a personal basis. Since it is personal, it has the highly desirable characteristic of flexibility.[5] From the standpoint of the nation's business expenditures, it is the most important type of promotion. However, like advertising, its degree of use in the promotional mix is variable and depends on such factors as the nature of the product and its market. One national distributor of tobacco products, for example, uses no personal selling but relies mostly on direct mail advertising to sell its products. At the other extreme, a producer of heavy manufacturing machinery spends more than 98 percent of its promotional budget on personal selling.

Personal selling, as contrasted to advertising, lends itself to the promotion of complex and expensive products. In promoting such products the personal salesman can ascertain what aspects of a complex product are difficult for the prospect to understand and dwell on them in greater detail by employing such visual aids as diagrams and demonstrations. The salesman of expensive products is present to counter objections about high costs if they arise. He can emphasize the durability of the product or its low cost per use by employing various dollar figures.

Personal selling is actually a general term for there is a number of types of salesmen. They range from the cashier at the supermarket to the very aggressive door-to-door salesmen. Some salesmen, usually termed supporting salesmen, do no selling at all in the sense of actually accepting an order for their companies. Again, generalizing, it is usually desirable to have a highly trained, aggressive salesman for complicated and expensive products. A clerk-type salesman is more suitable for selling those less expensive and less costly products that are purchased frequently. Supporting salesmen, or missionary salesmen, may be employed to pave the way for the regular salesman or to aid him in his presentation or other tasks such as installing point-of-purchase displays.

Employing personal salesmanship as the basic element of the promotional mix is a major undertaking. The recruiting, selection and hiring of salesmen usually entail extra personnel for performing these tasks. In addition, the functions of training, compensating, and motivating the salesmen must be planned for. Because of these factors, the costs of presenting a sales message to a prospective customer may be hundreds of times more than the costs of presenting the same message by advertising or some other promotional means.

Packaging. Too often packaging is not given the credit it deserves for its promotional achievements. It is still looked upon by many businessmen as simply something to contain the product and to protect it from spoilage and damage. Certainly, these are two important functions that the package performs, but in many cases, they are no more important than the promotional function.

Packaging has been given the nickname of the "silent salesman"—and for a good reason. In a matter of 5 or 10 seconds it can attract a person's attention, create interest in the packages' contents, and present a sales message that will

---

[5]It is a desirable characteristic because the promotion can be adapted to each particular consumer. This human trait of flexibility, however, is the cause of the imperfect control over personal promotion that was discussed earlier.

convince the prospect to buy. A salesman would have to be a magician to come close to competing with such a performance. It is for just this reason that the package has often replaced the salesman.

The package receives its promotional ability mainly through the properties of color, lettering, and illustrations. In the hands of a professional package designer these factors can be combined into a very effective selling message. Just witness the mouth-watering illustrations on cake mix packages.

Two other significant promotional characteristics of packages are convenience of use and reuseability. Such devices as pour-spouts and zip-openers make the product more convenient to use and create a more favorable attitude toward the product. Packages that can be reused after their contents are consumed, such as jelly jars for drinking glasses, also encourage the sale of products.

The costs of promotion through packaging are difficult to ascertain. Since a package is usually required to protect the product, it would be incorrect to charge total packaging costs to promotion. Only those costs incurred to give the package sales ability should be included in the promotional budget. Thus, of the 20 to 25 billion dollars spent annually for packaging, perhaps no more than 50 percent should be considered promotional expense. At this rate, the average cost of promotion through packaging would be less than that of advertising.

Like other types of promotion, packaging is used more by some industries than others, so packaging costs will vary. As a percentage of manufacturer's selling price, packaging expenses run as low as 1.4 percent for office machines to as high as 50 to 70 percent for soaps and toothpaste.[6]

The importance of the package apparently is being recognized because more decisions regarding packaging are being made by top management. In a study conducted by the Folding Paper Box Association of America of 307 companies in the food industry the following results were obtained regarding the attention given to packaging by top management.[7]

*Who was the most influential in final decisions to use most recent package?**

Sales Manager	30%
Packaging Committee	24
President	18
Production Department	11
Purchasing Agent	9
Advertising Manager	9
Legal Counsel	1
Miscellaneous	19

Figures add to more than 100% because of multiple answers.

[6]McCarthy, op. cit., pp. 365–366.
[7]Ferdinand F. Mauser, Modern Marketing Management (New York: McGraw-Hill Book Company, Inc., 1961), p. 128.

In a number of companies there has evolved a packaging coordinator who is responsible for the major decisions to be made about packaging.[8] He often heads up the packaging committee mentioned in the above table.

Sales promotion. It is unfortunate that a specific type of promotion should be termed sales promotion. The term is misleading and has a general ring to it.[9] Probably a more descriptive term to use would be *supporting promotion.* Sales promotion, nevertheless, is the term used in the business world and it will be used here to refer to any promotion, other than packaging and publicity, that supports and enhances advertising and personal selling activities.

Often it is difficult to distinguish between sales promotion and advertising, or between sales promotion and personal selling. Actually, either the advertising or the sales organization could and often does handle the sales promotion task. But, more and more, sales promotion, like packaging, is gaining an independent status in firms, and specialists are developing in the field.

Sales promotion activities can be categorized on the basis of the markets at whom they are aimed. From this viewpoint, there is sales promotion to (1) consumers, (2) dealers, and (3) the company's own sales force.

1. *Consumer sales promotion.* A good example of consumer sales promotion is sampling, i.e., placing a sample of a product in the hands of potential consumers at no charge. This activity supports both advertising and personal selling. It helps to convince consumers that what advertisements say about the product is true. And it, hopefully, causes consumers to go to the retailer for more, which in turn, makes it easier for manufacturers' salesmen to sell the product to retailers.

Other types of consumer sales promotion by manufacturers include premiums attached to products, contests, and demonstrations. Consumer sales promotion is also practiced by retailers and may range from offering trading stamps to "playing games" with the customers.

2. *Dealer sales promotion.* Producers rely on sales promotion to make selling and advertising to their middlemen more effective. Food retailers are often given premiums, for example, for each case of goods they buy. This promotion is intended to encourage larger orders and repeat orders from the retailer. Trade shows, another type of dealer sales promotion, allow dealers and potential dealers to get a firsthand look at products that have been referred to in the manufacturer's sales and advertising efforts.

Contests, special store fixtures, and signs are also good examples of sales promotion aimed at increasing sales to dealers. One other type of dealer sales promotion that should be mentioned is all of the various specification sheets and data sheets that the manufacturer offers to the dealer. These materials

---

[8]*Ibid.*
[9]Some texts refuse to use the term. See, for example, Edward L. Brink and William T. Kelley, *The Management of Promotion* (Englewood Cliffs, N.J.: Prentice-Hall, Inc., 1963).

make dealers' selling efforts easier and thus support manufacturers' selling efforts that are aimed at the dealers.

3. *Sales force sales promotion.* A significant amount of a company's sales promotional efforts often are aimed at the company's own sales force. The idea behind such activity is, of course, to make the salesmen's efforts more effective.

Sales promotion to the sales force may include contests, premiums, sales portfolios, and visual aids to be used in sales presentations. Even sales meetings designed to spark interest in new products could be considered a sales promotion function.

Publicity. Since both publicity and advertising may appear in the same media and since both are developed to promote a company and its products, it may be difficult to distinguish between the two. Actually, the distinction between publicity and advertising is rather simple according to Wright and Warner. They state:

Publicity is information placed in media because of its newsworthiness; the company benefiting therefrom does not pay for its appearance, nor is the company identified as the source. Advertising, on the other hand, appears in the same media but the sponsor is identified and pays for the privilege of telling his story there.[10]

Thus, publicity is information about a company and its products that appears as a news article in such media as newspapers, magazines, and radio and television broadcasts. An excellent example of publicity is the annual articles that appear in such household magazines as *Life* and *Look* that describe in lengthy and colorful detail the new yearly models of automobiles.

Often the terms publicity and public relations are used interchangeably. While such practice is understandable, it may not be entirely correct. Publicity is a function of public relations. Public relations is the broader term that "connotes the entire being of an organization with respect to its self expression to the world."[11] Public relations is concerned with creating and maintaining a favorable public attitude toward a company, its products, ideas, and personnel. Publicity is only one of a number of ways of performing this task.[12]

Unlike the other types of promotion mentioned here, publicity is rarely placed in the hands of the marketing organization. As a rule, it is located at the top of a business organization, reporting to the president or one of his aides. This situation can cause some difficulty in the coordination of publicity with the other promotional tools.

Probably the greatest asset of publicity lies in people's reactions to it. Because it is viewed as a news item, and not as advertising, it possesses a high

[10]John S. Wright and Daniel S. Warner, *Advertising* (McGraw-Hill Book Company, Inc., 1962), p. 491.
[11]Herbert M. Baus, *Public Relations at Work* (New York: Harper & Brothers, 1948), p. 180.
[12]Other means may include, for example, answering customer inquiries, making adjustments for customer complaints, and granting scholarships to college students.

degree of believability. Because of this value, a company introducing a new product that possesses some unique characteristic usually will make a strong effort to get this characteristic talked about in newscasts, newspapers, and so on. Automobile manufacturers, for example, may present a private preview of new models to newspaper and magazine reporters, hoping that the reporters will observe certain outstanding characteristics and favorably report about them in their respective media.

MULTI-STAGE COORDINATION OF PROMOTION

Rarely does a business employ just one of the five basic types of promotion mentioned here. In fact, the average manufacturer of consumer products probably uses all five types and a variety of each. Since all the promotional tools employed have a common objective, i.e., to promote or move forward goods and services, coordination of them is an obvious necessity.[13]

Coordination of promotional effort occurs at three different stages of the marketing operation. The first stage coordination consists of defining the tasks of each type of promotion, inventorying the tasks to make sure all jobs necessary for achieving the basic promotional objectives are being done, and comparing the tasks of each promotional type to minimize duplication. In this stage the necessary promotional tools are selected and placed in a compatible relationship. The result is the promotional mix that was illustrated in Figure 2.

Second stage coordination of promotion might better be termed *integration*. At this point the promotional mix is integrated with the marketing mix. All the promotional elements are examined in light of such marketing mix elements as pricing practices, product design, and the channels of distribution to be employed. Again, compatibility is sought, and any conflicts between the promotion mix and the other mixes are removed. This often entails a reorganization of the promotion mix. For example, strong reliance on personal salesmanship will not be possible, although it may have been planned, if discount houses are to be the major type of retail outlet. An adjustment in the promotional mix will be necessary. The result of the integration of the various sub-mixes, including the promotional mix, is a sound marketing mix that is illustrated in Figure 1.

In practice, the first and second stages of promotional coordination are performed as a single operation wherever possible. And it is quite possible that some second stage coordination will take place first. Nevertheless, the two steps of coordination must be recognized and accomplished if there is to be effective coexistence among the elements of the marketing mix.

The third stage of promotional coordination occurs in the implementation of the results of the other two stages—when the marketing mix is put into

[13] One might inquire as to the need for a variety of promotional tools since each has the same basic objective. The answer is this: (1) not all promotional tools are equally suitable for the varying conditions (products, markets, competition) under which marketing operates; (2) combinations of promotional tools are usually necessary to meet these conditions; and (3) certain sub-objectives, necessary for meeting the basic objectives, can be performed best only by certain promotional types.

Figure 3

action. Up to this point the operation has been one of modelizing promotional behavior and marketing behavior. Now, the *real* operations begin when the product or service is commercialized. In the execution of the marketing mix a new type of coordination is demanded. It is of a *supervisory* rather than of a planning nature. In this stage the managers of the various promotional elements continually observe and control the promotional operation to make sure that its parts are working in unison as planned. Salesmen, for example, are kept informed about the nature of new advertisements and their time schedule. And all promotional elements are checked to see that they are conveying the same brand image.

For most effective achievement of promotional objectives, all three coordinative stages beg for a single promotional organization that is responsible to the chief marketing executive (see Figure 3). In this organization there is an executive responsible for each major type of promotion. These executives have similar organizational status and work closely together. They, in turn, report to and are coordinated by a chief promotional executive who answers to the chief marketing executive. Such an organization would permit the highest degree of intracoordination and intercoordination of the promotion mix.

The ideal promotion organization illustrated in Figure 3 is highly unlikely to occur, however. As noted earlier, for instance, the publicity function is rarely placed in the marketing department. Also, such an organization as this one would probably be viewed as diminishing the powers of the marketing manager.[14] Last, the complex organizations of today that are oriented to such factors as geography, products, and customers, could, at best, adopt only a modified version of this organization.

EVALUATION OF PROMOTIONAL EFFORT

After the promotion mix is planned and placed into action, it is logical to see if it is doing what it is supposed to do, i.e., achieving certain objectives. The basic objective, of course, is to move merchandise. An evaluation is needed, however, to see how much merchandise is moved at what cost, in what length

[14]Actually, this arrangement would allow the marketing manager more time to act as a coordinator of marketing (with other business functions) and to conduct long-range planning of such matters as sales forecasting, channels of distribution, and future products.

of time, and in what geographic area. This should be a major matter for the promotion manager.

In order to achieve the basic objective, the various promotional elements are given more specific objectives. For example, personal selling may be expected to sell a certain amount of goods per time unit in certain territories while remaining within a certain cost range per sale. A check should be made to see if it, in fact, is doing this.

It is more difficult to determine the amount of sales that are created by advertising. For this reason, the specific objectives of advertising are usually stated in terms other than sales. To change people's attitudes toward a product, for example, might be one of the jobs of advertising. In such a case, people's attitudes can be examined after the advertisements are presented to see if changes have resulted.[15]

Not all evaluation of promotion can be as objective as is suggested above. Determining how well certain sales promotion is supporting personal selling, for example, is a difficult and often subjective task. The promotional value of packaging and publicity is just as difficult to ascertain. To the extent, though, that promotion is given specific tasks to achieve, some measurement of how well it performs them can be determined. All the efforts of coordination would be futile without this measure.

ENVIRONMENT OF PROMOTION

When developing a promotional mix and integrating it into the marketing mix, the promotional manager must give consideration to the environment in which the promotional mix must function. The environment contains forces which can greatly influence the success of promotional effort, and unfortunately, the promotional manager has little control over them. These forces, or at least the major ones, are illustrated in the lower part of both Figures 1 and 2 and consist of (1) life styles, (2) legal action, (3) competitive action, and (4) economic conditions.

Life styles

A life style is a "distinctive or characteristic mode of living, in its aggregative and broadest sense, of a whole society or a segment thereof."[16] Thus we may speak of consumer life styles, family life styles, or even the life styles of specific groups such as a social class or an age group.

A promotional mix is developed in view of certain life styles. These life styles can and do change. Consumer behavior patterns change, family behavior patterns change, and so on. Changes in life styles, even minor ones, usually require changes in the promotional mix.[17] In fact, life styles can change even during the time between the conception of a promotional program and

---

[15]It is assumed that the nature of the people's attitudes were known prior to the advertisements. A before-and-after comparison will test the effectiveness of the advertising effort.

[16]William Lazer, "Life Style Concepts and Marketing," in Stephen A. Greyser (ed.), *Toward Scientific Marketing* (Chicago: American Marketing Association, 1964), p. 130.

[17]Eugene J. Kelley, "Discussion," in Stephen A. Greyser, (ed.), *Toward Scientific Marketing* (Chicago: American Marketing Association, 1964), pp. 164–171.

its introduction. It has been suggested that consumer life styles changed between the conception and introduction of the Edsel automobile.[18]

Legal action

The promotional mix also must be developed in terms of given legal restraints. For example, the package must be designed so as not to be misleading or deceptive, advertising must pass tests for truthfulness, and personal selling messages must not misrepresent the product.

Further, legal restraints, like life styles, change and often necessitate adjustments in the promotional mix. For example, recently the Federal Government introduced the requirement that cigarette manufacturers indicate on their respective packages that cigarettes may be injurious to health. This new law forces each cigarette manufacturer to redesign his package so as to include this notice. It is conceivable that this statement will reduce the promotional effectiveness of the package.

Competitive action

It is a rare company that does not have competitors and their reactions must be anticipated when a promotional program is structured. Competitors may copy a promotional campaign, introduce a countering campaign, or even try to sabotage a campaign. All these competitive actions have the result of reducing the effectiveness of one's promotional efforts.

Unfortunately, it is impossible to accurately forecast competitive action. Consequently, after one introduces a promotional program, changes in it can be expected to be made as competitive action takes form and reduces the effectiveness of the program.

Economic conditions

General economic conditions can influence consumer purchases.[19] Therefore, a level of economic activity must be forecasted for the period in which a promotional program will function. This forecast may be the task of the company or the company may rely on the forecasts of others such as the government or consultants. Rarely is the promotional manager responsible for the forecast.

Once the economic level is ascertained, the promotional mix can be developed. After the promotional program is operating, close observation of economic conditions must continue. Behavior of our country's leaders, troubles with foreign countries, and changes in interest rates are just a few of the factors that may cause economic conditions to change. Another result of such activities may be a change in consumer behavior patterns which would necessitate a change in promotional strategy.

---

[18] See "Annals of Business: The Edsel," *The New Yorker* (Nov. 26, 1960), p. 57 ff. (Dec. 3, 1960), p. 199 ff.
[19] See George Katona, *The Powerful Consumer* (New York: McGraw-Hill Book Company, Inc., 1960).

NEED FOR PROMOTION

Many questions have been raised about the need for promotion and some rather damaging attacks have been made about its existence. Questions about the wastefulness and ethics of promotion have appeared frequently.

There is a difference between attacking the nature of promotion and attacking its existence. There is no question that some promotion is wasteful. But it is not meant to be. Businessmen do not have money to waste. Aside from normal business error, waste in promotion results from a lack of a thorough understanding of the promotional process. As knowledge is gained about promotion, and it is being gained very rapidly, promotional effort will become much more effective.

As for the questions about the ethics of promotion, they also are justified, at least to some extent. Out of millions of businessmen, there are bound to be some who violate ethical borders. The intense competition among businessmen causes the more desperate to turn to questionable practices. And, too, the line between what is ethical and unethical is not a clear one, which may cause some promotion to appear unethical to one person but ethical to another.

The attacks on the existence of promotion are *not* justified. Given our type of economy, promotion is an absolute necessity. A reminder of the nature of our economy and its consumers will explain why.

The nature of our economy

Production in our economy is on a *mass basis*. Mass production requires mass marketing (and, of course, mass consumption). Promotion makes mass marketing possible. Without some technique for notifying millions of people about the availability and attributes of a product, mass production would again become custom production. The fantastic cost advantages of mass production would be lost and the relative costs of products would become very high as they were in the 18th and 19th centuries.

Unlike custom production, mass production is performed *in anticipation of demand*. Once it is believed that consumers will buy a certain product, factories do not wait for orders to accumulate. They begin production on the assumption that output will be sold. A process is needed that will move this output at a rate comparable with production. That process is promotion.

Another feature of our economy that makes promotion necessary is its *oligopolistic nature*. Because of the logic of mass production and mass marketing, most businesses try to gain as many customers as possible. The result of this has been that a small number of companies conduct most of the business in most industries.[20] Typically, the margin of profit per unit at which these companies operate is very small. Thus, a loss by one company of a significant part of its business would cause it to entail serious profit losses.

Usually, too, the few large companies in an industry sell similar products at similar prices. If one company lowers its price significantly, it will capture

[20]Together, these are usually referred to as the "big three," the "big four," and so on. The automobile industry is an excellent example.

a large portion of the customers of the other companies and cause serious profit losses in those companies. Consequently, any price cuts by one company will be matched immediately by the others. The result of a price reduction, then, is that each company ends up selling the same amount as it did prior to the reduction but at a lower price. Due to the lower profit margin per unit, each firm will be making less profit. This situation obviously discourages the use of price as a competitive weapon.

In order to compete, the many firms in oligopolistic markets have turned to promotion. Through advertising, personal selling, and so on, the firms attempt to increase their sales while maintaining stable prices. Firms may depend on other marketing tools, such as product design and channels of distribution, for means of competition. However, these items usually are not as manipulative in a short run as promotion.

The nature of consumers

There are two closely related characteristics of consumers in our economy that make some kind of promotion necessary. First, consumers customarily do not initiate the buyer-seller relationship. It is more practical for a relative few businessmen to come to the consumer rather than millions of consumers going to the businessmen. Thus, businessmen either come to the consumer's door or set up stores where the two may meet. In order for businessmen to assume this leadership, they must employ a variety of promotional tools to inform and serve the large number of customers with which each must deal. It is difficult to imagine consumers traveling to the various factories for their needs. Such a system would be extremely inefficient and time-consuming.

A second characteristic of consumers that begs for promotion is their imperfect knowledge about product offerings. Promotion helps consumers complete their knowledge about where to buy products, their prices, uses, and so on. Just witness the reliance placed on newspaper advertising to determine what movies are playing at the theatres and which supermarkets have special prices on certain goods.

In summary, then, in order to have our type of economy we must have promotion. We can give it some other name or cloak it in Latin terms, but some type of process is needed that will allow a mass production-mass marketing system to operate. Again, that process is promotion.

READING 39

HOW SYSTEMS SELLING IS REVOLUTIONIZING MARKETING*

Business Management

If you haven't given much thought to systems selling, do so right now. It's a marketing method that's already being adopted by some of the nation's more

*Reproduced from *Business Management* (June 1967), vol. 32, no. 3, pp. 60–62.

alert firms, and it promises to gather real momentum in the months ahead.

"Beyond question, systems selling is going to spread, but some companies will go out of business before they grasp it," says I. D. Canton, director of commercial development, International Minerals & Chemical Corp.

Canton's warning is by no means exaggerated. The shift to systems selling turned his firm around and, in one variety or another, is doing much the same for others.

How does systems selling evolve? What is it? What are the risks and the rewards?

The evolution begins the day a company decides to sell solutions to customers' problems instead of selling products. The next stage comes with the realization that, although customers want one answer, most problems cannot be solved by a single product. So the company soon finds itself investigating a whole family of ideas, products and services.

WHAT IT MEANS

Once a firm embraces this total marketing concept, there is no turning back. Systems selling, the next logical step, requires even more of a total company effort than a commitment to the marketing concept, if this is possible. However, pressures from customers, competitors and technology are going to be too great to resist.

A system is simply a combination of parts—tangible or intangible—that work smoothly together to perform a function. Generally, a system consumes one or more of the manufacturer's products, thus assuring him of repeat sales. One example would be a computer system that uses the computer maker's cards or tapes. But even when the system involves none of the manufacturer's consumptible products—for example, a nuclear reactor or power station—the emphasis is always on the interaction of the parts rather than on any one of the individual products.

Each system is custom-built. In trade jargon, its components are interfaced or intermatched so that they will operate compatibly to perform the job the customer wants done. He cares less about the names and reputations of the manufacturers of the various motors and drives in the system, which may come from several makers, than he does about the engineering capability of the supplier to devise a system that will solve his problem.

To the systems supplier, however, the items that make up the system he sells are of prime importance. If he produces most of them himself, he will probably make a greater profit. If he has to buy from other manufacturers to round out the system, he has to select them carefully, because he must guarantee the performance of the system of which they become a part.

Why bother with systems selling? Companies that reversed a losing streak by adopting systems selling see it as the only way to growth.

"If you have the guts to face the changes and challenges and to take the risks, the rewards are great," says William Evans, Carborundum's vice president of marketing.

The investment is spread out over a period of time—sometimes it's only a matter of changing the way the funds for advertising, sales training, or research and development are spent—and the ultimate adjustment, though major, happens gradually. Even firms that deliberately set out to organize for systems marketing take several years to complete the shift.

WHY IT'S GROWING

One of the first and biggest customers looking to buy a total system was the government. During World War II, the Defense Department began awarding contracts to companies with the capability to design, engineer, build and service a complete package or system, instead of buying individual items or subsystems from the lowest bidders. The government still buys a great deal in this way, and the big aircraft manufacturers, General Electric, Westinghouse Electric and the computer manufacturers, who were among the earliest marketers of systems, are still leaders in this type of marketing. It's beginning to take firmer hold in industry because purchasing agents schooled in value analysis and costing are realizing the advantages in turning over responsibility for a complete installation to a single supplier.

Without the computer, however, the concept could not have spread so rapidly nor widely. A system in itself, the computer now often takes on the role of a subsystem when linked to other equipment. The computer also made automatic or stockless purchasing possible, allowing large buyers of MRO (maintenance, repair and operation) supplies to cut down on inventories and reorder automatically under an annual contract, usually at a price advantage. This practice became known as systems contracting.

However, suppliers and distributors selling on contract and using an automated system for distribution added the handy expression "systems selling" to their vocabularies, which muddies the somewhat more pure definition of the term. If we include systems contracting on the basis of popular usage, three main types of systems selling can be distinguished:

● *Product systems.* The purists define systems selling as that which involves both capital goods and consumptibles. To them, the only true system consists of products combined through engineering and design into an operating unit to perform a specific function. Carborundum's system for hot grinding and cutoff of steel, described later in this report, fills the bill. It solves a long standing problem of the steel industry and uses Carborundum's grinding wheels in the process.

● *Systems contracting.* Some suppliers and distributors are concerned only with selling the consumptibles. They do not sell systems, but they may use a system to sell. Beals, McCarthy & Rogers, Inc., an industrial distributor in Buffalo, N.Y., is a good example. Beals does no manufacturing but it offers customers the use of its computer and data transmission system to facilitate ordering, speed up distribution, reduce paper work and cut the costs of acquisition. Customers do not have to buy any communications equipment. They can lease Dataphone service by the month and reorder as often as they wish under a systems contract.

● *Service systems.* Though intangible, a carefully integrated and balanced information system that can help a customer manage his business better can stimulate use of the vendor's products as effectively as a product system. International Minerals & Chemical Corp., Skokie, Ill., both sells a "better management" system and uses a system to sell. It offers customers a computerized scientific farm management service, designed to make more profit for the farmer through proper and balanced use of IMC's fertilizers, nutrients and other agricultural chemicals.

The following case histories of the three types of systems selling illustrate the effects of the approach on organizations adopting it. Like the total marketing concept that it implements, systems selling modifies every aspect of a firm's activities.

New titles and new departments spring up, old ones become obsolete. Research efforts are funneled into developing components for systems in existing markets rather than into dreaming up new products for which a market must be created. There are fewer new product failures, and products that are developed can be distributed by existing salesmen to existing customers, precluding the need to set up a whole new distribution system.

For example, if a successful manufacturer of shoe polish that is sold through shoe repair shops comes out with a new floor polish to be distributed through hardware stores or supermarkets, he is product-oriented. If, however, he decides to introduce a new type of shoe lace that will complement his present product and be sold through the same outlets, he is thinking systems.

The systems approach also simplifies management decisions about acquisitions, licenses and joint ventures. If a company concentrates on acquiring companies and technology that allow it to produce more of the components for the systems it designs and sells, its chances of making successful investments are considerably enhanced. The resulting conglomerate mergers, however, make it increasingly difficult for prospects to predict what type company does what type job.

Westinghouse Electric, for example, got into water desalination in this seemingly roundabout way. Westinghouse manufactured heat transfer equipment. It got involved in water purification for its industrial customers, and this led into water desalination, not exactly what might be expected either from the company name or its previous products. Here's where the company's advertising must keep pace with the change by publicizing the areas of capability a company is developing.

HOW SYSTEMS MARKETERS THINK

Systems-oriented companies concern themselves with such questions as: "Where is such-and-such an industry going?" "What are its problems?" "What do companies in that field want to do that they can't?" "How can we help them?" This quest for truth tends to lead manufacturers into direct selling to users and in some cases can conceivably mean the gradual abandonment of distributors and dealers.

There's no question that the adoption of systems selling will change a company's time-honored ways of doing business. Some marketing positions will evaporate, and new ones will be created in their stead. Advertising emphasis will change. A new program for approaching the market—and specifically, key customers—is vital. As William W. Evans, Carborundum Corp.'s 39-year-old marketing vice president points out, "To succeed at true systems marketing, it is imperative to establish very specific quantified objectives, aimed at specific industries and specific customers within them."

With the emphasis on what customers want to do, however, there is little talk even among salesmen about product or price. Sales presentations reflect analysis and research. Salesmen must learn to anticipate every possible question and to articulate their recommendations clearly.

Success becomes a matter of teamwork. Sales require intricate price and contract negotiations, as well as engineering and technical know-how, and compensation plans have to be changed accordingly. Salesmen are assigned to industries instead of by product and territory, and many of them become specialists in the industries they serve. With the upgrading of the sales force, the role of the national accounts salesman—as missionary and coordinator—becomes clearer and more important.

There's more crossing of divisional lines. A system may use products from four or five different divisions and, if communications are not excellent, the company may not be in systems selling very long.

Since each system is different, there's no chance to test market. Advertising stresses a company's capability rather than its products, and, as this capability becomes recognized customers bring their problems much as they would to a consultant. Systems marketers find that they have fewer customers but sell them more. Some also report that it is easier to attract young people to selling systems than to products because they look upon problem solving as more sophisticated than ringing doorbells. There is still a shortage, however, of people capable of selling systems and there are more purchasing agents eager to shop for systems than there are suppliers willing to adapt to it.

The first company to attack a prospect's major problems definitely has the jump on his competitors. Profits, as the following cases show, can be phenomenal.

1 SOPHISTICATED MANAGEMENT SYSTEM

Ten years ago, International Minerals and Chemical Corp., traditionally miners and refiners of raw chemical fertilizer materials, faced a serious marketing problem. Its major commodities—phosphate and potash—were virtually indistinguishable from those of competitors. It was difficult to achieve individual identity by packaging or advertising, and price-cutting was widespread in the industry.

Then IMC found a new weapon. It decided to concentrate on ways to solve some of its customers' basic problems, instead of cooking up ways to push its products. The result was an information system that provides one of IMC's biggest customers—the farmer—with data that helps him multiply his profits. This shift in marketing philosophy has turned IMC into a real profit maker.

Today, some 1,500 farmers are totally involved with IMC's farm management program. They depend on the company's unique capability to help them build their business. It's not at all unusual for IMC to get a query something like this: "I have an opportunity to buy the 200-acre farm next door. Should I?"

IMC's computer already knows all about this man's present operation—the size of his farm, the type of soil, what crops he has been planting, what yields he is getting, what equipment and personnel he has, as well as the current market prices and weather data for his location. With a little more information about the adjacent farm, the computer will print out an analysis of how the purchase will affect the farmer's present operation and profits.

IMC is using a system to sell a system. "It's a system within a system," says Neal G. Schenet, vice president of IMC's Plant Food Division. And although the system IMC markets—professional farm management—is free and intangible, it leads to the use of the consumptibles that IMC sells and its components are as carefully intermatched as are the drives and motors that make up a product system. The heart of IMC's management system is the computer, since the service involves countless bits of data that must be compiled and analyzed.

The company's goal, which some executives feel is not yet fully realized, is the total commitment of every person in the company to customer service.

Painful birth, healthy child

"Someone has to plant the seeds of an idea and then champion it," says I. D. Canton, director of commercial development, one of those who actively spread the systems gospel both inside and outside IMC. "He has to be able to take scorn and laughter, and to shout enough to make people do things differently, without losing his vision."

The concept that has evolved into a highly sophisticated approach to systems marketing was pioneered at IMC by Vice President Anthony Cascino, a man with a total service philosophy. It began when Cascino was head of the marketing team, simply as a series of programs to help solve the problems of IMC's fertilizer raw material customers. Gradually, the approach spread to other levels of marketing, including the franchised dealers and eventually into direct sales to the farmer and ultimate user of IMC's products.

"And we still have a number of programs or subsystems that have to be welded into the total system," says Canton.

The over-all system for complete customer service became operational seven years ago. "It is no coincidence," President N. C. White told stockholders last year, "that this is the same year that the company began its period of greatest growth."

Net sales in 1966 just missed the $300 million mark, nearly three times what they were in 1960, and net earnings have risen from $7.6 million to $24.6 million, approximately a 20% average annual earnings increase for the seven-year period. Fertilizer and fertilizer materials account for 70% of the total corporate sales, with feed ingredients, industrial chemicals and minerals, and fermentation products making up the balance.

Essentially, what IMC did, after its first analysis of the fertilizer manufacturing industry to which it sells raw materials, was to change the name of the game from "Save Money" to "Make Money."

The fertilizer industry's return on investment was among the lowest in America. IMC reasoned that the customer's problem was not, as he thought, to buy products at the lowest possible price. It was to have those products on hand at his plant at the time he needed them.

IMC set out to become management consultants to its customers in every aspect of their businesses. The first services provided were the usual—manuals specifically for the fertilizer industry, seminars at home and abroad, customer advisory panels, and an offer to send out an executive to consult on his specialty whenever a customer called to ask for help. IMC even leased a fleet of giant railroad hopper cars—it now has more than 4,000 at its disposal—to solve the car shortage problem and to lower its materials customers' costs for getting the raw materials from mine to plant. Then, it began developing special formulas for fertilizer tailored to the peculiarities of different areas and the crops to be grown, and franchised a number of regional independent fertilizer manufacturers to produce these products for sale in their marketing areas. IMC not only sold the raw materials but updated the formulas each year, provided production know-how, marketing and sales training and advertising for the franchisee.

Eventually, IMC got around to analyzing the farmer's operations and what he was really trying to do. Research showed that he, like the industrial buyer, spent too much time trying to buy his supplies cheaply instead of trying to manage his farm better. Everyone sold him products, but no one worried about their interactions or the allocation of the farmer's assets. He could spend $10,000 and still get a poor crop if the seeds, herbicides and fertilizers didn't interact properly or if he used them at the wrong time.

Fresh analysis

IMC's thinking about the farmer went like this: Sellers weren't treating the farmer like an important account because they did business with him on his dining room table. But a cash grain farmer with a 640-acre section buys about $25,000 worth of crop chemicals annually. His net worth in land, machinery and buildings may be as much as $500,000. Clearly, he is a sizable businessman.

One of the key steps in the move to systems selling is a new definition of the customer and the business he is really in. Often he has not identified his own problem correctly. A farmer, for example, may think he needs a new truck when what he really needs is a bigger unloader so that he gets faster turnaround.

"The main contribution you can make," says IMC's Canton, "is a fresh, unbiased analysis of what your customer is really trying to do. There should be someone other than marketers in the group doing the analysis. Otherwise, your analysis is likely to be burdened by as many myths, legends or traditions as your customer's."

The farmer revisited

So IMC took a new look at the farmer to see what he was really doing. It realized that he produces not just food and fiber, but celluloses, carbohydrates, proteins and oils—all processed chemicals. What basic raw materials does he use? Besides seeds, nothing but chemicals—fertilizer, lime and pesticides. Therefore, if he buys basic chemicals and produces processed chemicals, he must be a member of the chemical industry. That insight, says IMC's Canton, broke the log jam.

"As chemical businessmen, we knew how we would buy. We would go to a firm of expert process engineers for a researched, matched and balanced production system—all the products and services needed to do the job—and that is what we could expect the businessman-farmer of the future to do. What IMC had to do was offer a total system for producing a crop, instead of just selling fertilizer."

However, you can't offer a lick and a promise and expect to be successful at systems selling. It takes a lot of planning and cooperation for a company to put at the disposal of customers the combined talents of its technical, marketing, public relations, engineering, personnel and finance people.

In the case of the farmer, there are additional problems. He operates with more uncontrolled variables than any other enterprise in the world. He's at the mercy of rain, hail, frost, insects, weeds, fluctuating world commodity prices and political developments. IMC knew it could not prevent the variables but it could enhance the farmer's chances of behaving successfully in the midst of them if it identified and quantified them.

Secondly, no two farms are alike. Thus, information for every crop had to be individualized according to the farm's size, fertility, soil type, capital availability, farm machinery, management capability and unforeseen local idiosyncracies. And there was a third hurdle: Where would IMC get the agronomists and farm management specialists to sell the systems to the agri-businessman?

IMC found the answers to all three problems in the computer. To construct the model, researchers had to collect an enormous amount of economic and agronomic data and feed it to the computer. Now, when the computer is fed the details of a particular farm's operation and resources, it prints out a series of alternative profit plans. The farmer decides which crops to plant on which fields and what yields to shoot for. The print-out gives details on what kind of fertilizer, insecticides and seeds to use. If all or part of the farm is rented and sharecropped, the computer even breaks down plans into profit goals for landlord and operator.

IMC's system, say company officials, usually helps the farmer generate about 20% more profit than he would normally get. IMC's researchers also developed a mathematical method for forecasting prices. It is far from perfect, but better than the farmer could do. The researchers knew they couldn't control the weather, but they could predict the effects of today's weather on cropping conditions a few months later. Hence, they developed a computer program, Agriclimate, to predict the weather's impact. Every six hours the computer takes the precipitation, temperature and wind data from 200 U.S.

Weather Bureau stations and, already equipped with equations for the soil moisture-holding capacity of each area, it prints out the regional data. This allows IMC to draw up maps of soil temperature and soil moisture conditions east of the Rockies, and advise farmers how to alter their programs to fit local growing conditions.

The first farmer to try IMC's computerized farm management or M.O.R.E. (Mathematically Optimized Resource Employment) Profit Program was Joe Nuytten, Marshall, Minn. In 1962, the computer said that he could make a bigger profit by planting more soybeans than corn. He did and his net profit for the year was up 8% over the previous year.

Then in 1964, the computer correctly predicted a drought in the Midwest at a time when the USDA was predicting a record corn crop. There was a drought, but Nuytten—following the computers advice—had eased up on planting and conserved water, thus cutting his loss.

Each farmer on the M.O.R.E. program gets a new plan each fall, updated to correspond to price trends and weather predictions and government farm programs. They depend upon the computer for advice in making such decisions as: Should I buy or lease additional land? Should I put some former land bank fields into use? Should I try a new crop? Should I delay planting because of the moisture content of the subsoil?

Easier harvest for salesmen

IMC first started promoting better management by selling and training its own salesmen. It called the men together for a hard-hitting and lively sales meeting such as the fertilizer industry had never known. New sales aids were prepared. IMC adopted the use of motion pictures, film strips and portable flip-top projectors, so that the story would always be persuasive, regardless of which salesman made the presentation. Data input and output forms were designed in a simple fashion so that any salesman could collect the information and feed back the answers to the farmer. Dealers get the same company backing and help in the areas they serve as do the company's own sales representatives. Incidentally, company salesmen and dealers maintain mutually exclusive territories.

Once a farmer accepts the program, he is so close to IMC that all the salesman has to do—theoretically, at least—is to ask when the farmer wants the fertilizer delivered. The computer has specified the formula and the amount. All IMC has to do is get it there at the right time for that location's planting schedule.

"Ninety-eight percent of them buy," says Vice President Neal Schenet. "We've gotten many new customers, and it takes less time to get desirable customers than it did when we were concentrating on selling products."

But it's not all roses for the salesman. The ease of closing a sale is more than counter-balanced by his other chores. Collecting information about a farm's operation and getting to the hardcore problem, counseling on the myriad questions that arise, modifying each program as conditions change, and monitoring each customer to see that he follows the program that has been prescribed, means that a salesman can handle only about 25 accounts efficiently.

Salesmen must select prospects carefully. First they study the productivity and potential of the farms within a 30-mile radius of one of IMC's distribution centers. Then, they invite 10 or 15 farmers to a meeting at which the salesman, an agronomist, and sometimes other specialists from headquarters explain the program, tell about the results M.O.R.E. farmers are getting and answer questions. Salesmen seldom talk about products or prices any more. They talk about the participant's problems and the profit-making services that IMC offers him.

Following a meeting with prospects, the salesman makes a date for a depth interview with any farmer who is interested in filling out the forms that provide the input for the computer. Sometimes, when the salesman delivers the suggested program to the farmer, the latter may decide to put only part of his land on the program as a test, converting the balance the next year.

J. Ross Baird, Williamsfield, Illinois, first heard about the M.O.R.E. program from Bryan Spencer, IMC's local sales supervisor, three years ago when the company entered this market area. He was one of 10 farmers who attended the first meeting on computerized planning. After the presentation, Baird decided to put his entire farm into the computer service program. The business includes more than 1,000 acres, with large plantings of corn and alfalfa for feed for 1,200 livestock.

Together, Spencer and Baird completed the data collection forms and IMC's data processing facilities produced the recommendations for the entire acreage. This took about one month—IMC can come up with the answers much faster now—and the early recommendation surprised Baird. Nevertheless, he went along, reducing the alfalfa acreage but increasing fertilization on that crop.

"The extra profits from that alfalfa crop will buy my fertilizer for several years," Baird said at the end of the season.

Salesmen always warn customers that the biggest increment they can possibly expect in one year is 25%. "Once they grasp the program, they aren't disturbed if it doesn't work out quite as well as the computer predicts," says Neal Schenet, vice president of the Plant Food Division. "Their yield is still better than they ever had before. They love the computer and they know it can't be rigged to tell them to order more fertilizer than they need."

The systems approach, typically, has led to a general upgrading of IMC's sales force.

"You can't afford to fire and replace your whole sales force," says Schenet, "but with the computer to extend the salesman's capabilities, we didn't need to. In any reorganization, there are always a few early adaptors, maybe 10% who grasp a new approach and do something fruitful with it. When this moves down to the middle majority, then you've got it made. Those who don't go along, fade away. Hiring criteria change. Eventually, the whole sales force and, finally, the whole company will be committed."

In a company doing systems selling, research and development activities may benefit most. Competent scientific staffs are a necessity but, instead of developing new products that may not sell, R & D efforts are directed toward developing components to improve systems for an existing market. At IMC —where custom-blended fertilizers for individual fields are an old story —scientists are now looking for a way to get plants to use more sun.

Growing corn in the computer

This sort of approach appeals to people like Tom Army, senior research associate, Research and Development Division.

"Who says planting corn in rows is best?" asks Army. "More sun goes between the rows than on the plants. What we want is more corn, not bigger plants. If we can develop a plant with upright leaves, then we can put the plants closer together. Now we get 20,000 plants to an acre, with ears eight or 10 inches long weighing about half a pound each. The total yield is about 143 bushels of corn an acre. But suppose we plant dwarf variety, 150,000 plants to an acre, with three-ounce ears. The ears would be a joke at the county fair, but we'd get a 15-fold increase in the number of ears and a net yield of about 400 bushels per acre."

Other research projects at IMC include improving the digestible proteins in corn instead of increasing the amount of corn, and developing smaller cotton plants that don't need to be sown in rows, now that picking is done by combine instead of by hand. Even blue-sky projects, such as growing feed in test tubes, have relevance and lend an aura of social service to IMC's systems approach.

"We can't put much sophistication into our products, the way technological systems do," says I. D. Canton, director of commercial development, "so we have to build it into our marketing system."

2 THE PRODUCT SYSTEM APPROACH

There's no pulling punches about the upheaval that can be caused by a shift to systems selling. Consider the observation of William W. Evans, marketing vice president of Carborundum Co., Niagara Falls, N.Y.:

Systems development and systems marketing affects people, prerogatives and classical ways of doing business. A good many functions and prerogatives will disappear. People will change jobs and be moved physically. New literature must be printed, new brand names created. Money will have to be spent; at times, large amounts. A new marketing plan is a necessity. But if you have the guts to face the changes, the challenge and the risk, the rewards are great.

Every company that moves into systems selling gobbles its share of aspirins. Carborundum is no exception. But the biggest headaches are over, and the company is busy scanning the industrial field to see which industries might be the best prospects for the systems Carborundum has developed.

Carborundum began tooling up for systems marketing three years ago, in 1964, when President William Wendel decided that the road to growth lay in the total systems approach to marketing. Even earlier, the 75-year-old firm had begun expanding its capability by acquiring machine companies with specialized know-how and manufacturing facilities. It teamed these companies up with its three major abrasive product lines—grain, bonded and coated grinding wheels—until each had its own related machinery line.

"Most customer problems simply can't be solved by one product or one division," William Evans observes. "That's why diversification is so important. Any company that is marketing-oriented has to go to systems selling."

The first target

One of the companies Carborundum acquired was Tysaman Machine Co. in Knoxville, Tenn. Teamed up with the Bonded Abrasives Division, this purchase made Carborundum the only abrasives company with a completely integrated capability in steel conditioning.

In fact, the steel industry was Carborundum's first target. Since the steel industry was making moves toward modernizing, it was a prime prospect for Carborundum's newly developed ability. So, in 1964, the company set up a Bonded Abrasives Research Center separate from the corporate research and development facility.

The center is headed by John Mueller, manager of abrasive systems development. It has a staff of 15 (three engineers and a dozen technicians), occupies 39,000 square feet of floor space, contains $400,000 worth of equipment, and eats up $50,000 worth of steel each year in tests.

The center's purpose is twofold: to provide a showcase for demonstrating Carborundum's capabilities to prospects in an actual production operation setting, and to accustom Carborundum's people to customer's problems.

"If we were going into systems, we had to do things that couldn't be done," says Mueller. "If abrasives couldn't do chipping—removing defects from steel before it is rolled—then we probably couldn't go into systems for carbon steel, because this is an early step in the process."

But Carborundum found that it could be done, by redesigning its grinding wheels and adapting Tysaman's machines. Today, a workman can take off the scale and remove surface defects from a cylinder of steel in one hour and 15 minutes, a job that takes eight hours by older methods. The steel industry's main objection—that grinding would disguise the cracks—proved unfounded; it uncovered them.

While new products and product adaptations are bound to result from the systems approach to a customer's problems, Carborundum had the advantage of knowing what to look for. Its market researchers are convinced that the steel industry is going to convert to continuous casting that will require hot cutoff and hot grinding.

By making an arborless grinding wheel, with a series of small holes instead of a large center opening, the center's researchers were able to increase the running speed of a wheel by 25%. Then they devised a machine to grind hot steel (1800 degrees F.), so that cooling, moving, grinding and reheating could be eliminated. Combining this machine with the arborless grinding wheel, Carborundum was able to more than double the amount of steel that can be removed in an hour and, although steel makers don't want to remove more, they do want to do it faster.

But the industry had to be shown. By the fall of 1964, Carborundum had its new grinding and cutoff system set up at its research center and ready to be shown off. One hundred and fifty representatives of the steel industry were invited to Niagara Falls for a preview, then flown to the Pittsburgh Hilton for a two-day seminar. The conference resulted in a number of leads, one in the Chicago area.

A second conference was held there, followed by numerous private sessions with the prospect's personnel—the industrial engineers, the general manager of operations, the head of quality control and their staffs, and the men who would operate the equipment.

They all had to be sold

The salesman on the account began by organizing teams—for example, a development engineer and a machine man—to go into the prospect's plant with him, to specify the problem, to formulate a plan of attack, to put on further demonstrations. Workmen who, up to now, knew nothing about grinding were taught.

This education and counseling process went on for about eight months. At the end of that time, the salesman knew enough about the customer to write the proposal. (It took another eight months, incidentally, for Tysaman to cus-tom-make the machines and adapt the unit to the customer's space.) The price for the package: $500,000.

A key point was that Carborundum warranted the system's performance —either the removal rate or the abrasive replacement cost or both. This guarantee covers many items the company does not make—motors, gear boxes and other components—but which are included in the over-all system. This has important implications for any company contemplating systems marketing. Since the seller of the system has to guarantee all the parts in it, he'd better be extremely careful in his purchasing. It could cost untold time and money—possibly even the sale itself—if one of the links in the system doesn't hold up.

As soon as the prospect accepted the proposal, his purchasing agent and Carborundum's salesman, with the aid of their legal departments, sat down to draw up the contract.

So far, the customer had paid nothing. The challenge to the marketing department and to the systems salesman in particular is to prevent the prospect from getting all this free counseling and engineering service, then taking part or all of it and going with another supplier. Some companies have found it necessary to charge for the preliminary studies, but suppliers just entering systems selling usually have to take the risk themselves. Carborundum plans to leave it up to its salesmen to sell prospects not only on the system, but on going with Carborundum.

"Follow-up goes on as long as the customer uses our grinding wheels," says Evans. "The salesman is in his plant every week, but if there's trouble, he'll be there within an hour. Second, he has to make sure we keep a big enough back-up stock of grinding wheels in the warehouse nearest the customer's plant."

Nothing unusual, says customer

Even with a number of systems going for him, the salesman can't relax. The customer is under no obligation to buy his grinding wheels from Carborun-dum, even though he may have taken the system. Product manufacturers can build systems that work best with their own supplies, of course, but tie-in agreements requiring the use of their products are illegal. So, in working closely with a customer as a systems man does, he may have a good fix on what the customer is going to use, but no fix on what he's going to buy from Carborundum. That's still the salesman's problem.

And it doesn't look like there's any relief in sight, at least as far as William Evans is concerned. "The greatest changes in the next 10 years will be in the sale of consumptibles," he says. "The introduction of systems contracts, the computer, national accounts and other marketing innovations will become a major way of business life. Thus, the marketing man will be faced with a prob-lem of creating the system, of marketing the system—and then of living with a systems contract to provide the product that's consumed in the process."

Customers tend to take all the "free" services for granted. The purchasing director of the Midwest steel company being served by Carborundum sees nothing very unusual about the systems approach. "We expect all our sup-pliers to offer that kind of service and know-how," he says. "We look to all our vendors to help us lower our costs, through new products, larger orders, packaging or stocking."

This attitude among purchasers who've taken up value analysis and total costing, instead of buying on price alone, is one of the big causes for the spread of systems selling.

Reorganization blues

When a company shifts to systems selling, whether by evolution or by design, as Carborundum did, the emphasis shifts from manufacturing to marketing, from product line to the customer's industry, and the trauma of reorganization is felt throughout the company. New jobs are created, old ones disappear or change. Personnel have to relinquish their "right of ownership" and work as teams, a tough adjustment for both engineers and salesmen. The sales force has to be assigned by industry—to steel, paper, chemicals—and representa-tives from different departments may be called on to make joint presentations to prospects, so that methods of compensation and training have to change. During the reorientation, sometimes a long process, there may be some casualties, although Carborundum's marketing vice president sees no reason why a good man can't adjust to the total company effort.

Of the changes at Carborundum, Evans says: "It wasn't absolutely neces-sary to put consumptibles and capital goods under one management but we think it's better this way. In fact, without the joint research the two groups have done at the center and their cooperation on production problems, we probably wouldn't be in systems selling."

The company does not have a general sales manager. Instead, three group vice presidents—of abrasives, resistant materials and international operations—report directly to President Wendel and, for the first time, Carborundum has a national accounts manager, Peter Judd.

Judd doesn't sell. He does missionary work with Carborundum's major accounts and prospects. He also acts as a coordinator, getting prospects to come into the center for demonstrations or getting salesmen to give customers more attention. Judd has no staff and doesn't expect to, but he's an important factor in systems marketing.

Both public relations and graphic design are marketing functions at Carborundum, with the department heads reporting to the marketing vice president. Advertisements currently play up abrasive systems instead of products.

"This is the direction industrial marketing is going to take," says Evans.

How fast depends partly on customers. When, for example, will the big steel makers take up continuous casting and other modern methods? "They have to be interested," says a Carborundum engineer. "One of our grinders can eliminate several dozen chippers."

This in itself may be as much an obstacle as an advantage, because managers tend to be reluctant to increase productivity too much in one year.

Carborundum—although it has eight proposals out for abrasive systems—isn't sitting on its corporate hands waiting for the revolution in steel. The marketing department is evaluating several other industries—foundries, farm machinery, aerospace, paper—deciding which to assault next. Moreover, it is preparing to take systems selling abroad this year, using the same approach as in the U.S.

Already Carborundum has acquired several foreign companies that build machines using grinding wheels—Rowland in England, Fondermatica in Italy—and it is exploring firms in other countries that might complement its present capability. Representatives from Germany have visited the Bonded Abrasives Research Center at Niagara Falls and this summer Carborundum will hold seminars in Germany, Austria and England.

"We'll be the only company with a systems selling plan for all of Europe," says Evans. "We'll go after the market industry by industry just as we do in the U.S. although the specific actions we'll take will vary from country to country. But the over-all marketing approach is for the whole continent."

3 THE SYSTEMS CONTRACTING APPROACH

At Beals, McCarthy & Rogers, Inc., Buffalo's giant industrial supermarket stocking 25,000 items of hardware, tools and steel stock, systems selling—or more accurately, systems contracting—means using the computer and Dataphone to give customers instant service. Some, like Carborundum in nearby Niagara Falls, get shipment within 24 hours. To plants further away in New

York and Pennsylvania, Beals sends a truck once or twice a week, so that the purchaser knows anything ordered by Friday noon will arrive early Monday morning in time for the first shift.

Beals got into the systems act in 1961 when it was losing both customers and money. Its first Dataphone customer was Sylvania Electric's plant at Towanda, Pa. The purchasing agent was receptive to the suggestion of Frederick Davis, then Beals' director of marketing, that there was a way to save on the cost of acquisition, and together they explored the idea.

Beals was already putting every order on a punch card before processing, so the next step was to have the orders come in on punch cards. Now, the distributor furnishes prepunched color-coded cards to Sylvania, and its other Dataphone customers for every item they buy. Basic information is filled in —in some cases even the amount to be shipped is prepunched—and all the customer does is fill in the optional information and insert the card in his Dataphone. Beals' phone rings, the equipment to which it is connected punches out a card identical to the one the customer has inserted, the computer prints packaging and shipping slips for the item and deducts it from inventory.

This system, in Davis' opinion, captures the best features of verbal and written orders; it is fast and almost without error. All the paper work required is done in five minutes; whereas a telephone order clerk would spend from 15 to 20 minutes handling the same kinds of chores.

A business builder

Since the system was instituted the Sylvania account has grown by leaps and bounds. Not only is the Towanda plant ordering more, but four other Sylvania plants are now transmitting orders by telepunch.

"Any distributor who already has EDP equipment and isn't using it to process orders, should investigate doing so," says Davis.

The statistics tell why. Beals total volume in 1961—its lowest year before the market reorganization that started the gradual shift to Dataphone selling —was only half its 1966 dollar volume. The company has been making a profit since 1964. Although only 38 of its 2,700 customers are currently on systems contracts, they account for 22% of the dollar volume. Last year, the distributor served three times as many customers whose annual purchases ran more than $10,000 as it did in 1961, and the number of accounts whose annual purchases run into six figures, while still low, is five times as many as five years ago.

Not only do Dataphone accounts show the biggest volume increases, but those increases in comparison with the accounts not buying in this fashion are almost unbelievable. A good increase in volume for one of Beals' non-Dataphone accounts is to have it buying three times as much now as in 1961. Several Dataphone accounts, however, are buying several hundred times as much and one is buying 2,000 times its volume of five years ago.

Customer service is the core

Bell Aerosystems in Niagara Falls was buying very little from Beals until the distributor showed how, with Dataphone ordering, Bell could eliminate its central stores, cut down on paper work and free up dollars for other uses. Bell, involved in building rocket engines, moon landing systems and other aerospace equipment uses a lot of small cutting tools. Besides the inventory in central stores, there were tool cribs in each plant. The man in charge of each crib might requisition one-eighth inch drills, for example, from central stores and also reorder from the vendor to forestall running out. Beals simply added to its own inventory, put color-coded cards in each crib, and eliminated the central inventory. The cost to the customer for the system is about 25% of the cost of carrying the inventory.

Each account has its own special program. "This is not regimentation," Davis points out. "Beals doesn't insist on a customer fitting his paper work and billing into any set pattern. There's lots of flexibility in the system. Each customer's pre-punched order cards contain the information he wants on them and some customers by preference get punched cards instead of packing slips with their orders."

Representatives of Corning Glass came to Beals, not to buy but to find out if they could adopt a similar system for internal use. Corning was maintaining a central store room from which all its small plants requisitioned supplies when needed. After studying Beals' operation, Corning put Dataphone in its storerooms and plants to speed up deliveries internally. About a year later, Corning decided to buy its supplies to refill its central stores in the same way, and now gets deliveries from Beals twice a week. Corning's goal was to reduce inventory by 75%. So far, it is down 50%, and Beals and Corning are continuing their joint efforts to make further reductions.

Selling the concept

Most sales of the systems contract type are made on a personal basis. Two years ago, Beals, McCarthy & Rogers set up a separate department to handle Dataphone orders, and now does much of its selling by having the prospect come into the Dataphone center to see how orders are being handled. Robert Krebs, manager of contract and telepunch sales, has a four-man staff and, like the metro sales manager and manager of the outside sales force, reports to the marketing manager.

Whenever, a salesman brings in a promising lead or when a customer's volume of purchases seems to indicate the desirability of converting him to systems contracting, Beals schedules a presentation. Usually, the salesman goes out with Krebs and the director of marketing and sometimes other executives join the sales team. It is well-armed with evidence that costs of acquisition and possession will drop. (See box, page 86.) Several presentations may be necessary to convince the materials manager and controller, as well as the top purchasing personnel, to give the system a try, and three or four months often elapse from the time Beals' representatives make the first call until the first order is transmitted over the Dataphone hookup. Cost to a buyer —even one who doesn't have EDP equipment—is minimal, since he can lease both computer and Dataphone service by the month, without making any large capital outlay.

Salesmen continue to make about the same number of calls on their systems contract customers as on their other accounts, but their time goes into strengthening the customer-supplier relationship rather than in trying to sell an order.

"The salesman has better acceptance in the plant," points out Davis. "He's free to talk to the tool designers, maybe explain a new product, or to work with the shop people in developing new applications or greater efficiency. He can help customers select the right grade of steel or a grinding wheel for a particular job."

A good time to sell a customer on converting is when a new purchasing agent arrives, eager to be a hero and save on the costs of acquisition. Conversely, you can lose a customer that way, too, when the new man wants to do something different from his predecessor, as Beals knows from experience. However, if service is satisfactory, Davis says, it's tough for another distributor—one without Dataphone—to crack the account.

But what will happen to Beals' competitive advantage when all distributors adopt systems contracting and automatic ordering?

"I don't think all distributors ever will," says Davis. "Some don't have the data processing capacity to handle large volume orders immediately, and the small specialty houses will continue to stress specialty items. But I wish more distributors would go into systems selling. It would be easier to sell the concept."

Internal effects

Although its dollar volume has doubled since 1960, Beals, McCarthy & Rogers has only 145 employees, 15 fewer than it had then. Not only does the Dataphone transmit 450 to 500 cards an hour—the number of items that it might take a telephone order taker a whole day to process—but at the same time, it reduces substantially the number and size of telephone orders.

"Distributors will always sell by telephone," says Davis. "Even Dataphone accounts do some buying of special items by phone. But if Beals were to stop using Dataphone today, the company would have to add people and it would probably have difficulty getting enough qualified people to handle the increased volume."

Beals reviews its entire product line weekly. If a customer is not ordering as anticipated, or if the buying pattern changes, this information will be picked up in inventory control and a salesman will check to find out the reason for the change. The computer recomputes lead times and order quantities as usage changes.

Says Davis, "There are no problems unless the electricity goes off."

READING 40

SELECTING SALESMEN: APPROACHES AND PROBLEMS*

James C. Cotham, III

Personal selling research has largely followed two basic approaches. One is the older, traditional view of salesmanship emphasizing the salesman's influence in the transaction. This approach is represented by a voluminous literature. A more recent approach places the salesman in a "personal selling process" situation in which the buyer has been assigned an active role. This emerging methodology puts the sales transaction into a social behavior context with the outcome hinging, in part, on the customer-salesman interaction. The situational environment (firm, product, experiences, attitudes, prior relationships, and so forth) serves as a frame of reference for the actions of both costumer and salesman.

Both approaches are similar in the sense that each seeks to identify and measure relevant determinants of personal selling performance. Moreover, to be other than an intellectual exercise, either approach should ultimately be useful to sales force management by offering operationally feasible personnel tools.

Thus, if personal selling research is to eventually provide a significant managerial payoff, more uniformity of effort is required. It is extremely important that future research improve as well as build on existing designs and data gathering methodologies. While not exhaustive, the purpose here is to provide an overview of a fairly comprehensive representation of prior personal selling research in terms of predictor variables and performance dimensions investigated, general findings, limitations and implications for future research, and sales force management. Because it would unduly complicate the presentation, detailed statistical findings or quantitative data about the psychological test instruments used in past research are not included. Rather, the extensive references cited in this article should provide direction for those seeking more specific information concerning these and other issues related to personal selling research.

In what follows, salesmen's characteristics popularized by sales management literature as behavioral determinants of personal selling performance are categorized for examination into three groups of variables. The first deals with salesmen's cognitive factors, including intelligence and sales aptitude. In the second group, the variables considered are salesmen's life history experiences (application blank items) thought to help shape abilities and response preferences in the selling situation. In the third group the variables consist of measures of personality, social intelligence, and empathy, representing foundations for salesmen's interpersonal responses.

*Reprinted by permission from *MSU Business Topics,* published by the Graduate School of Business Administration, vol. 18, no. 1 (Winter 1970), pp. 64–72.

INTELLIGENCE

While there is no one generally accepted substantive definition of general intelligence, Robert M. Guion suggests that a common thread of meaning links most conceptualizations of the intelligence construct. Thus, from a personal selling research viewpoint, intelligence or mental ability per se is too general a concept to be operationally useful. Because personal selling researchers are confronted with selecting from a number of tests yielding a variety of measures, each thought to be associated with the demands of the sales job, intelligence must be operationally defined as a trait measured by a given instrument.[1]

In personal selling research

In a comprehensive survey of personal selling literature between 1915–1950, Ronald L. Austin found relatively few investigations including intelligence tests as part of the measurement battery. Out of 150 research reports analyzed, only thirty included an intelligence instrument. In response to his findings, Austin drew the following conclusions concerning the relationship of intelligence to personal selling ability:

● The relationship between intelligence, as measured by tests, and sales performance varies with the level of selling.

● In the low grades of selling, a low inverse relationship exists between intelligence and sales ability.

● In sales jobs of average level, there is no measureable relationship between intelligence and sales ability.

● In high level selling jobs, to an undetermined extent, there appears to be a positive relationship between intelligence and success in selling.[2]

A review of O. K. Buros' *Tests in Print* and *The Sixth Mental Measurements Yearbook* (Gryphon Press, 1961, 1965) lends support to Austin's findings by revealing little evidence of recently published sales research using intelligence testing techniques. Moreover, the small amount of available research indicates an association of intelligence to sales performance ranging from a fairly low positive correlation to a nonsignificant relationship.[3]

[1]Robert M. Guion, *Personnel Testing* (New York: McGraw-Hill Book Company, 1965), pp. 231–36.
[2]Ronald L. Austin, "The Selection of Sales Personnel: A Review of Research" (Ed.D. diss., Graduate School of Business, Indiana University, 1954), pp. 128–29. Unfortunately, this discussion did not include operational definitions or specify distinctions between the three levels of sales jobs; therefore, the generalizations drawn have little meaning for the purpose of generating hypotheses.
[3]See, for example, T. W. Harrell, "The Relation of Test Scores to Sales Criteria," *Personnel Psychology* 23 (Spring 1960): 65–69; M. D. Dunnette and W. K. Kirchner, "Psychological Test Differences Between Industrial Salesman and Retail Salesmen," *Journal of Applied Psychology* 45 (April 1960): 121–25; and J. B. Miner, "Personality and Ability Factors in Sales Performance," *Journal of Applied Psychology* 44 (February 1962): 6–13.

Sales performance

As specific intelligence tests useful in the personal selling environment are designed and validated, the traits tapped by the instruments could conceivably become generalized as a managerial tool. However, the inconsistency of existing published research does not warrant much optimism at present.

A major reason for this position is that the nature and extent of the intelligence influence on personal selling behavior remains unclear. For example, in the past, researchers apparently have not been particularly concerned with the anatomy of intelligence-performance relationships. While some studies have validated intelligence tests against a variety of performance criteria, there has been little expressed concern with the actual meaning of these predictors in terms of understanding performance in specific selling situations.

In summary, it would appear that little uniformity exists with the relationship of intelligence to personal selling performance being largely a function of the operational specification of intelligence utilized, criteria measured, and the operating characteristics of the sales organization.

SALES APTITUDE

Guion suggests three major categories of aptitude determinants for any type of work, presumably including personal selling. These categories include: intellectual traits, physical factors (including psychomotor abilities), and the motivational traits of interest, attitude or temperament needed for persistent and attentive effort. Providing two alternative approaches to aptitude analysis within each of the above categories, Guion states that highly specific measures of aptitude may be sought, or aptitude within any one of them may be considered as highly generalized.

While several generalized sales aptitude tests are in print, instruments constructed to focus on highly situational components of personal selling such as major appliances or industrial machinery are not available. Moreover, little can be said about general sales aptitude instruments. Guion reports that while nearly two dozen aptitude tests are available, not enough technical data have been published about any of them to permit serious evaluation.

LIFE HISTORY EXPERIENCES

A major source of sales personnel data has been application blank items. The value of personal life history experiences as well as prior occupational experiences as performance predictors has been put into perspective by William A. Owens and Edwin R. Henry. Evaluating the use of biographical data in industrial psychology, they suggest that it may be possible to use biographical items as a screening device with psychological testing being used "only when more precise information is needed."[4] These writers further indicated that biographical items may in fact become more reliable predictors of performance than psychological tests.

In the same study W. E. Williams warns that the biographical method should not be applied blindly in empirical research. Specifically, he argues that the selection of specific life history items to be investigated should be based on prior hypotheses. This implies that the use of standard application forms is not a sound personnel practice. Rather, the task becomes one of defining the crucial determinants of success in given sales jobs and then finding valid techniques of measuring and interpreting these determinants for use in salesmen selection programs.

While extremely fragmentary, personal selling researchers seeking performance predictors have investigated the biographical approach.[5] In an attempt to determine the validity of background items as a pretest screening device, Harrell found some value in the use of life history items as indicators of potential negative performance. It was suggested in this study that the presence of two negative biographical indicators, rather than relying on only one item, may be a more valid basis for eliminating salesmen at an early stage of the employment process. Researching the usefulness of the application blank in a variety of settings, a number of investigators have experienced only limited success in relating selected personal history items to performance criteria. W. K. Kirchner et al. have found age to be statistically associated with sales effectiveness.

Investigating selection procedures in a retail department store, James N. Mosel identified twelve life history and sociodemographic items which distinguished the performance of two groups of female sales clerks. Further, Mosel and R. R. Wade attempted to identify potential short-term retail department store employees at the time of their employment by studying life history experiences. They concluded that the use of life history items as a predictor of tenure may or may not be valid in different store situations, depending on the items selected for analysis. Similarly, C. H. Rush found that the successful use of personal history items as a success predictor was a function of the type of criterion measure selected for analysis. Finally, due to inconclusive results obtained for several biographical items compared against job performance ratings and sales production ratings, Richard S.

[4]William A. Owens and Edwin R. Henry, *Biological Data in Industrial Psychology: A Review and Evaluation* (published by The Creative Research Institute of the Richardson Foundation, Inc., 1966, pp. 14–15).

[5]See, for example, Donald E. Baier and Robert D. Dugan, "Factors in Sales Success," *Journal of Applied Psychology* 41 (February 1957): 37–40; D. F. Kahn and J. M. Hadley, "Factors Related to Life Insurance Selling," *Journal of Applied Psychology* 33 (April 1949): 132–40; A. K. Kurtz, "Selecting Salesmen by Personal History Items, Methods and Results," *Psychological Bulletin* 36 (June 1939): 528; Wayne K. Kirchner, Carolyn S. McElwain, and Marvin D. Dunnette, "A Note on the Relationship Between Age and Sales Effectiveness," *Journal of Applied Psychology* 44 (April 1960): 92–93. See also James N. Mosel, "Prediction of Department Store Sales Performance from Personal Data," *Journal of Applied Psychology* 36 (February 1952): 8–10. J. N. Mosel and R. R. Wade, "A Weighted Application Blank for Reduction of Turnover in Department Store Sales Clerks," *Personnel Psychology* 4 (Summer 1951): 177–84. C. H. Rush, "A Factorial Study of Sales Criteria," *Personnel Psychology* 6 (Spring 1953): 9–24. Richard S. Schultz, "Test Selected Salesmen Are Successful," *Personnel Journal* 14 (October 1935): 139–42. Cecil L. French, "Correlates of Success in Retail Selling," *American Journal of Sociology* 66 (September 1960): 128–34.

Schultz found little support for using age and length of service as indices of success in selling life insurance.

Cecil L. French attempted to isolate correlates of retail selling success for a group of department store salesmen. Of particular importance here was the finding that there was no apparent difference between high producers and low producers with respect to age, time on the job, and formal education. Further, looking ahead, few high producers intended to stay on the present job until retirement. Moreover, high production was highly correlated with downward occupational mobility and a higher reference group.

Status of biographical items

Empirical personal selling research has not yet determined conclusively the validity of using application blank items as sales performance predictors. Published data have yielded little which could be construed as having widespread operational significance.

In summary, the conflicting results of past research indicate the warning to carefully examine on a firm-by-firm basis potential relationships between application blank items and a variety of performance criteria. Standard application forms containing traditional biographical data thought to be useful in the selection process might, in fact, be misleading and be more harmful than beneficial.

PERSONALITY

Although a widely researched area, personality testing has a history of inconsistent and disappointing results. According to Guion, "one cannot survey the literature on the issue of personality tests in industry without becoming thoroughly disenchanted." Further, "there is no agreement about which kinds of personality . . . measures deserve support and continued use." Austin's survey, for example, identified only self-report instruments (which may be evaluated objectively).

Recent attempts at using projective techniques to get at personality have been reported by J. B. Miner and David Rodgers. Miner suggests that projective data offer insight into the relationship between individual salesmen and their job demands. Using a projective instrument, he found that "a man can be a good salesman for a variety of reasons . . . there is, however, the question of the nature of the cause-effect relationship."[6] In addition to being more costly, due to a variety of difficulties associated with administering and interpreting projective techniques, they are generally less reliable than are objective types of personality instruments.

Prior research indicates that, even though a great deal of confusion exists, conceptually personality testing is a legitimate approach to aiding the development of salesmen selection programs. This is particularly true in selling situations thought to be multi-dimensional in composition and when researchers utilize batteries of tests. In this regard, Austin has suggested that a core of personality variables may exist which contribute to success and failure in a wide variety of sales occupations. Taking a futuristic attitude,

[6]David A. Rodgers, "Personality of the Route Salesmen in a Basic Food Industry," *Journal of Applied Psychology* 43 (August 1959): 235–39; Miner, *Personality and Ability*, p. 11.

he sums up the problem by stating that "an adherence to sound, proven research practices, plus an imaginative, open-minded approach to new suggestions, should permit personality measurements to make a substantial contribution to the solution of sales personnel selection problems."

SOCIAL INTELLIGENCE

The factor of social intelligence has been explored in a number of studies.[7] William Stanton and Richard Buskirk call for more emphasis on social intelligence in selection testing programs. According to these authors, since social intelligence is the facility for dealing with human relationships, beyond a minimum level, abstract intelligence and intellectual achievement are seldom of vital importance in personal selling. Moreover, defining social intelligence as "effectiveness of interpersonal relations," Lee Sechrest and Douglas N. Jackson emphasize that variance in social effectiveness exists "which is beyond that accounted for by academic intelligence and general pleasantness."

Richard W. Husband, in an early literature review, offered the conclusion that prior studies using traditional measures of intelligence, personality, and interest consistently show weak correlations with sales data. The primary reason given by Husband was that selling is largely a social function. This, of course, is in harmony with the current interest in personal selling as a customer-salesman social interaction process.

Research by F. A. Moss et al. has encouraged the view that social intelligence offers an alternative to abstract intelligence as a performance predictor. Similarly, in a sample of petroleum salesmen, Harrell found a significant positive relationship between a social intelligence measure and sales production records.

EMPATHY

Empathy, as it related to personal selling, has been a subject of discussion.[8] Research by Williard A. Kerr and Boris J. Speroff, and also by Francis P.

[7]William J. Stanton and Richard H. Buskirk, *Management of the Sales Force,* rev. ed. (Homewood: Richard D. Irwin, Inc., 1964), p. 261; Lee Sechrest and Douglas N. Jackson, "Social Intelligence and Accuracy of Interpersonal Predictions," *Journal of Personality* 29 (June 1961): 168; Richard W. Husband, "Techniques of Salesmen Selection," *Educational and Psychological Measurements* 9 (Summer 1949): 129–48; F. A. Moss et al., *Examiner Manual for Social Intelligence* (Washington, D. C.: Center for Psychological Services, 1955); Thelma Hunt, "The Measurement of Social Intelligence," *Journal of Applied Psychology* 12 (June 1958): 317–34; and Harrell, *Relation of Test Scores.*

[8]Williard A. Kerr and Boris J. Speroff, "Validation and Evaluation of the Empathy Test," *The Journal of General Psychology* 50 (April 1955): 269–76; Francis P. Tobolski and Williard A. Kerr, "Predictive Value of the Empathy Test in Automobile Salesmanship," *Journal of Applied Psychology* 36 (October 1952): 310–11; Kerr and Speroff, *Empathy Test,* p. 269; Leonard E. Jarrard, "Empathy: The Concept and Industrial Applications," *Personnel Psychology* 9 (Summer 1956): 157–58; G. H. Mead, *Mind, Self, and Society* (Chicago: University of Chicago Press, 1934), p. 366, as reported in Rosalind F. Dymond, "Personality and Empathy," *Journal of Consulting Psychology* 14 (October 1950): 343; A. Koestler, *Insight and Outlook* (New York: Macmillan Company, 1949), p. 360, as reported in Dymond, *Personality and Empathy;* Rosalind F. Dymond, "A Scale for the Measurement of Empathic Ability," *Journal of Consulting Psychology* 13 (April 1944): 127; L. S. Cottrell, "The Analysis of Situational Fields in Social Psychology," *American Sociological Review* 7 (June 1942): 374, as reported in Dymond, *Empathic Ability;* and Ronald Taft, "The Ability to Judge People," *Psychological Bulletin* 52 (January 1955): 3, 1, 20–21.

Tobolski and Kerr suggests that a salesman's emphathic ability may be a valid indicator of performance potential. Kerr and Speroff define empathy as the "ability to put yourself in the other person's position, establish rapport, anticipate his reactions, feelings, and behavior." According to Leonard E. Jarrard, earlier definitions of empathy omitted anticipation (prediction of another person's behavior) as an element and focused only on the "identity" of empathic feelings. Rosalind F. Dymond, drawing on conceptual discussions of the meaning of empathy by Mead and Koestler, stated that empathy "may lead to positive feelings and closer social relations, as when it results in sympathy, but this is not necessarily the case."

Recognizing the existence of individual variation in empathic ability, such as the "ability to transpose oneself into the thinking, feeling, and acting of another," Dymond calls empathy a challenging and important area for further investigation. This apparent interest stems from the fact that the presence of empathy seems to assure more effective communication and understanding in interpersonal situations. Significantly, L. S. Cottrell, in an early analysis of "situational fields" in social psychology, concluded that empathy is basic to all social interaction.

With regard to measuring empathy, Ronald Taft makes an important distinction between empathy and mass-empathy. If a particular test attempts to predict the combined responses of a group of people it is considered a mass-empathy measure. Alternatively, attempted predictions of a certain subject's behavior by a judge who is either an acquaintance of the subject or is given data about him is an empathy test.

A specific approach

In a summary of factors thought to be related to the ability to "judge people," Taft points out that common sense suggests a person possessing good ability to judge (predict behavior of others) should be able to profitably use this ability in situations requiring social skill, such as salesmanship. "While there is some evidence to support this view," Taft states, "there is sufficient evidence to the contrary to force us to seek a more sophisticated attitude.

Assuming that predicting customer behavior is a characteristic of successful personal selling, Taft identifies three main attributes of the ability to judge others. One is having the appropriate norms, such as the judge and the person being judged having similar backgrounds. Another is having the relevant ability for judging others, which perhaps includes some combination of general intelligence and social intelligence as well as the possibility of a factor for handling nonanalytic judgments (intuition). Finally, and most important, according to Taft, is the attribute of motivation. Assuming that the first two attributes are present, Taft argues that if the judge is motivated to make accurate judgments and feels free to be objective, there is a good chance that he will achieve his goal.

Based on this viewpoint, the implications for developing and utilizing empathy measures in personal selling are clear, especially in studies focusing on the sales transaction as a customer-salesman interpersonal interaction.

JOB SATISFACTION AND SALES PERFORMANCE

A sizable literature has developed on the role of motivation in individual work performance. Unfortunately, however, little theoretical or empirical attention has been given to the kinds of influence that "willingness to perform" is likely to have on actual personal selling productivity or efficiency of effort.

Defining the concept

Several attempts have been made in recent years to define *job satisfaction* and *morale,* with both terms being used often and interchangeably in the literature. Operational definitions of morale have been offered by a number of writers with some lack of agreement.[9]

Traditional literature in the sales management field typically uses morale in an effort to describe the mental attitude of salesmen in their work environment. On the other hand, job satisfaction has been used to describe the same phenomenon when researchers with a behavioral science orientation report findings concerning work attitudes and personal selling performance.

Job satisfaction—personal selling research

The sparse amount of empirical research in this area reveals conflicting findings concerning the job satisfaction-personal selling performance relationship.[10] For example, in Pearson's candy route salesmen study, it was found that the most successful salesmen were significantly more satisfied with their employment situation than were the lower rated salesmen. On the other hand, French's study of department store salesmen uncovered no statistical relationships between job satisfaction and high production. Also, a recent investigation into retail major appliance sales groups revealed no evidence that satisfied salesmen were better performers.

Relating satisfaction to personal selling

Apparently the key dimensions of job satisfaction as a measure of morale should be determined at the firm level with the individual salesman rather than the sales force as the focal point. This view emphasizes group morale only to the extent that the operating environment uniformly affects individual performance, and salesmen interact with this environment. If true,

---

[9]See, for example, Irvin Child, "Morale: A Bibliographic Review," *Psychological Bulletin* 38 (June 1941): 393–420; Robert Guion, "Industrial Morale—The Problem of Terminology," *Personnel Psychology* 11 (Spring 1958): 59–61; Victor Vroom, *Work and Motivation* (New York: John Wiley and Sons, Inc., 1964); and Kendrith M. Rowland, "Selected Determinants of Effective Leadership" (D.B.A. diss., Graduate School of Business, Indiana University, 1965), p. 41.

[10]Judson B. Pearson, "Sales Success and Job Satisfaction," *American Sociological Review* 27 (August 1967): 424–27; French, "Success in Retail Selling," p. 129; and James C. Cotham, III, "Job Attitudes and Sales Performance of Major Appliance Salesmen," *Journal of Marketing Research,* November 1968, pp. 370–75.

it would appear logical that, once operating policies are firmly established for a specific operating period, further development of active group goals is in part based on the reaction of salesmen to existing policies. The strength of these goals and the extent of each individual's participation in the further attainment of group goals should be determined by the operating flexibility as well as nature of rewards or sanctions available to each salesman. For example, French found in his study that "high production as measured by sales volume and money earned, seems to depend upon the individual's disposition to violate the group's norms."

Thus, unlike many assembly line work situations, personal selling apparently tends to be less structured, requiring more independent action in completing the task. Since a salesman normally interacts with many customers, each with unique preferences and requirements, he generally adjusts to one of several approaches available to him suitable in a given transaction. In addition, the design of most compensation plans suggests little dependence on other salesmen for task completion. To the extent that a salesman's compensation is either totally or partially based on incentive payments, the impact of morale (job satisfaction) on performance could be unlike that of a work group whose compensation is fixed or dependent on the behavior of others involved in completing the assigned task. In short, because sales positions differ significantly in terms of products sold, customer types with whom interaction occurs, and compensation plans available to salesmen as well as other job components, job satisfaction and personal selling performance must be considered at the present to be essentially a firm-level relationship.

A recent approach to measuring satisfaction

Of importance is the confusion that exists in the measurement of morale concepts.[11] Many techniques and methods have been used to measure morale; however, high inter-correlations do not exist among the various techniques attempted.

Recently, morale has been recognized to be multi-dimensional in nature. Several approaches have been used to isolate the dimensions of job satisfaction as measures of morale with major interest on the *semantic differential* technique developed by Charles Osgood, George Suci, and Perry Tannenbaum. According to these authors:

The semantic differential is essentially a combination of controlled association and scaling procedures. We provide the subject with a concept to be differentiated and a set of bipolar adjectival scales against which to do it, his only task being to indicate, for each item (pairing of a concept with a scale) the direction of his association and its intensity on a seven step scale.[12]

[11]See Raymond Katzell, "Measurement of Morale," *Personnel Psychology* 11 (Spring 1958): 71–78; Rowland, "Effective Leadership," p. 44; and Robert Wherry, "Factor Analysis of Morale Data: Reliability and Validity," *Personel Psychology* 11 (Spring 1958): 78–79.
[12]Charles Osgood, George Suci, and Perry Tannenbaum, *The Measurement of Meaning* (Urbana, Ill.: University of Illinois Press, 1957), p. 20.

William E. Scott has reported the experimental use of a form of the semantic differential in several industrial settings.[13] This approach is conducive to assessing the personal selling situation in terms of numerous relevent job dimensions using factor analysis and other multivariate techniques.

The most basic element of a salesman's job is to sell goods and services. Sales proficiency, from this standpoint, is a quantitative measure. To the extent that customer goodwill is necessary to the continued success of the sales organization, sales proficiency acquires a qualitative dimension.

CRITERION MEASURES

Operationally, the selection of performance criteria in a specific selling situation requires a basic decision. It must be determined whether multiple measures of performance exist for all selling situations in the firm or whether selling performance is a unitary measure which assumes that good and poor salesmen differ on only one performance dimension.

Measurement of performance

Recent research suggests that selling performance is both situational and multidimensional. In a brief review of special problems involving performance measurement, Guion identified several basic criterion issues indicating the need to empirically determine existing relationships by matching crucial jobs to relevant criterion measures. Moreover, Rush, in his analysis of typewriter salesmen, found that sales success was multidimensional and concluded that the use of a broad measure of success seemed undesirable.

While studying interrelationships among various performance criteria, S. E. Seashore, et al. found little support for the concept of overall job performance as a "unidimensional construct."[14] Further, it was proposed "that the use of a single job performance variable as a proxy for total performance is not justified without prior determination of interrelations among the different aspects of performance." Although this study did not specifically deal with selling performance, it indicates the need for personal selling researchers to take into account "systems of causal and conditioning variables."

Other studies focusing on personal selling performance suggest a variety of potential measures.[15] In the past, most studies have dealt primarily with ob-

---

[13]For a review of this initial study, see William E. Scott, "Some Motivational Determinants of Work Behavior," *New Developments in Research and Graduate Education in Business and Economics* (Bloomington: Indiana University, Bureau of Business Research, Graduate School of Business, 1965).

[14]Stanley E. Seashore, Bernard P. Indik, and Basil S. Georgopoulos, "Relationships Among Criteria of Job Performance," *Journal of Applied Psychology* 44 (June 1960): 195–202.

[15]See, for example, Daniel J. Bolanvich and Forrest H. Kirkpatrick, "Measurement and Selection of Salesmen," *Education and Psychological Measurement* 3 (Autumn 1943): 333–39; Edwin G. Flemming and Cecil White Flemming, "A Qualitative Approach to the Problem of Improving Selection of Salesmen by Psychological Tests," *The Journal of Psychology* 21 (January 1946): 127–50; James E. Kennedy, "A General Device Versus More Specific Devices for Selecting Car Salesmen," *Journal of Applied Psychology* 42 (June 1958): 206–09; Miner, *Personality and Ability*; and Rogers, "Route Salesmen." See also E. M. Goldwag, *The Use of Psychological Tests in Selecting Salesmen* (New York: National Sales Executives, 1956), as reported in Guion, *Personnel Testing*, p. 429.

jective measures rather than management ratings. The Goldwag survey, sponsored by the National Sales Executive organization, described "objective" measures used by business firms in measuring salesmen's performance. Included in this survey, in order of frequency of mention, were sales volume, sales volume against quota, number of calls made, gross margin secured, number of demonstrations made, and earnings. Unfortunately, the study did not reveal how successful these measures were.

Toward a theory of job performance

It is evident from prior research that little progress has been made toward creating a complex theory of job performance which takes into account possible multiplicative relationships between selection devices and crucial components of the job. According to William W. Ronan and Erich P. Prien, "Much of the empirical work in the various areas of personnel psychology has been a matter of expedience, motivated by the need for solutions to specific problems rather than by the desire to generate a theoretical framework."[16] This point rings true particularly in today's personal selling management environment.

Personal selling as a social interaction

Kenneth R. Davis and Frederick E. Webster, Jr., summarize the conceptual basis of the currently popular emphasis on personal selling as a customer-seller interaction.[17] This stream of research identifies "social behavior" and "interpersonal interaction" as proxies for underlying performance determinants of both parties to the transaction. Especially important, it appears, are personality characteristics which influence salesman and customer perceptions of each other and ultimately contribute to the sales outcome.

Unfortunately, to date, few interaction studies have attempted to isolate the basic traits of successful salesmen, in "sales process" terms, that could be used in a personnel selection program. The most notable psychological-oriented approach to the sales management problem of fitting the right type of salesmen to the selling situation has been F. B. Evans' exploratory research. Evans found significantly higher correlations between personality attributes of salesmen and customers in successful "dyadic transactions" than were found in unsuccessful "dyads."[18]

In summary, whether the focus is on the traditional view of the salesman's

[16]William W. Ronan and Erich P. Prien, *Toward a Criterion Theory: A Review and Analysis of Research and Opinion* (Creativity Research Institute of the Richardson Foundation, Inc., 1966), p. 2.
[17]Kenneth R. Davis and Frederick E. Webster, Jr., *Sales Force Management* (New York: The Ronald Press Company, 1968), pp. 151–65.
[18]F. B. Evans, "Selling as a Dyadic Relationship—A New Approach," *The American Behavioral Scientist*, May 1963, pp. 76–79. For other promising attempts at explaining customer-salesmen interactions see, for example, R. P. Willett, "Customer-Salesmen Interaction in Appliance Retailing" (Graduate School of Business, Indiana University, 1966); Allan L. Pennington, "Customer-Salesman Bargaining Behavior in Retail Transactions," *Journal of Marketing Research*, August 1968, pp. 255–62; and Stephen J. Miller, "The Social Base of Sales Behavior," *Social Problems* 12 (Summer 1964): 15–24.

behavior or the more modern emphasis on the prospect-salesman inter-personal interaction, the only way to improve the contribution of personal selling in a firm's marketing mix is to locate salesmen with the capacity and willingness to perform given the total selling environment in which they must operate.

CONCLUSIONS—IMPLICATIONS

Published empirical research on personal selling is plentiful though very fragmented and largely outdated. Most studies have focused on salesmen at the manufacturing and wholesale levels with a sizable concentration of effort on life insurance selling. On the other hand, empirical research at the retail level useful to sales management is scanty.

Major problems exist hampering the generalization of most prior studies to selling situations other than the one investigated. For example, there has been a lack of uniformity in the use of predictor variables and criterion mea-sures. Additionally, past research has not identified a common ground for linking salesmen's performance potential in unlike selling situations. More-over, the identification of useful performance measures has in itself been an elusive task.

In short, progress to date has clearly established that sales occupations should not be presumed to be homogenous. Rather, research has indicated the need to recognize differences in various types of selling and to treat major product classifications separately if more accurate performance indices are to be developed. In fact, it may well be that predictors for one type of personal selling work may simply be of little value in a different personal selling setting.

The requirements of a particular job and the specific demands imposed upon a salesman by the firm as well as by customer's characteristics affect-ing his success must be given careful consideration when selecting predictor instruments and other indices to be used in a personnel management pro-gram. No standard classification of sales jobs has been established that would provide the means by which uniform criterion measures could be related to a set of universal performance traits. Furthermore, as evidenced by recent "customer-salesman interaction" studies it is highly unlikely that such a categorization of jobs could be accomplished due to the uniqueness of selling requirements in terms of customer characteristics, firm operating policies, product lines, and bargaining demands.

In conclusion, Flemming and Flemming reported in 1946 that "there is no single composite of qualities, each in specified strength, making up a complex entity called general sales ability."[19] The evidence since 1946 indicates that the same situation exists today. Thus, if anything significant is to come out of either stream of personal selling research, such as an empirical theory of personal selling, future efforts must eventually be co-ordinated in terms of conceptual design and methodology, psychological tests utilized, and performance measures, as well as other information sources with a sales force management payoff.

[19]Flemming and Flemming, "A Qualitative Approach," p. 128.

READING 41

THE FUNCTIONS OF ADVERTISING IN OUR CULTURE*
Irving S. White

The function of advertising in our culture may be characterized in two theoretical ways.

First, there are those who state the theory within the framework of economic laws, asserting that advertising affects knowledge about and demand for a product.

This article attempts to develop a second orientation. It is that the function of advertising is to help to organize and modify the *basic perceptual processes* of the consumer, so that he is guided toward *seeing* and *feeling* a product in a given predictable way.

Advertising as a perceptual process

With the recently formed partnership between the social scientist and the marketing professional, some foundation has been laid for a general reorientation toward understanding this influence as a dynamic process between communicators and perceivers. David Ogilvy and other advertising practitioners have formally incorporated terms such as "brand image" as applied to various advertised products. Journalists such as Martin Mayer have come to see advertising as affecting the "values" of a product.[1]

Yet "images" and "values" have no meaning outside of the experience and outlook of the consumer as a personality and the consumer-market as a social group. Gardner and Levy, influenced by the social psychology of George Herbert Mead, have shown how consumers are swayed toward or against a product because of the way a brand image is perceived.[2] And Martineau's *Motivation in Advertising* is a practical and lucid application of that proposition.[3]

It is a truism that the function of advertising is to inform and sell. But the more basic theoretical question is, how does advertising perform this function?

The variables of consumer experience

Most advertisers would agree that advertising should orient the consumer toward a consistent, and usually pleasurable, relationship with their products. Consistency implies a rather stable organization of meanings and values centering around a product as an "object" in one's life. It is this consistency which gives what is often called "character" to a product or service. Cadillacs, for example, have traditionally meant specific mechanical, aesthetic, and social

---

*Reprinted from *The Journal of Marketing*, published by the American Marketing Association, vol. 22, no. 3 (July 1959), pp. 8–14.
[1]Martin Mayer, *Madison Avenue, U.S.A.* (New York: Harper and Brother, 1958).
[2]Burleigh B. Gardner and Sidney J. Levy, "The Product and the Brand," *Harvard Business Review*, Vol. 33, No. 2 (March–April, 1955), pp. 33–39.
[3]Pierre Martineau, *Motivation in Advertising* (New York: McGraw-Hill Book Company, Inc., 1957).

experiences to their adherents. Buying a Cadillac has often meant success and power to the purchaser, and the conviction that in several years from the time of purchase his car would still connote the same qualities. Pleasure merely means that the consumer derives gratifications out of this object-relationship that motivate him toward repeating and reinforcing the experience.

To structure the experience of the potential consumer along lines of consistent and predictable satisfactions requires an understanding of the total source of meanings, the *whole* interaction between the consumer and the product. For any advertiser, there is a certain amount of realistic humility inherent in the knowledge that advertising is only one of the several sources of stimulation that a product contains for the individual in society. The influences of culture and of private sensations modify and intermingle with the stimuli of advertising to achieve the final pattern of relationship between the seller's product (or ideas and services) and the consumer. What perceptions can advertising influence, and what can it not?

Even to begin to answer this question means an investigation of the structure of the product as an "object" in relationship with the individual. After interviewing hundreds of consumers, utilizing techniques of different levels of penetration, getting at "unconscious" and "conscious" attitudes and needs, three sources of meaning about a product have been isolated.

The first source is the set of meanings stemming from the *cultural definition* of the product. The second source of meaning comes from the consumer's organized set of notions about the brand, that is, the *brand image*. The third source of meaning is from direct *experience with the product*.

CULTURAL DEFINITION OF THE PRODUCT

Social psychology and anthropology have dealt with the problem of objects in culture. That is, how do people come to understand and relate in a socially consistent manner to artifacts that are with them from time of birth?

The concept of "object" implies more than just a unidirectional flow of activity from the manipulator to the manipulated. It also implies a set of stimulations and communications in the reverse direction that guide the actions of the user. This means a dynamic relationship between the artifact and the user, wherein the latter perceives and acts upon the former according to the organized meanings that the culture and its subcultures have formulated for it.

The fact that few objects are naturally and intrinsically what they seem to be has been clearly indicated by such thinkers as George Herbert Mead, Jean Piaget, and Heinz Werner. A child growing up within a society begins by viewing an object in an idiosyncratic, self-centered way, and gradually redefines his relationship to it in terms of the broader, adult society. The acculturated individual internalizes the way the general society view the artifact, and sees the product in a setting of needs and values that control his action and attitudes about it. For example, there is nothing intrinsic in a baseball bat to account for its relationship to its user; a member of a primitive society could easily mistake it for a weapon.

It is perhaps more accurate to think of culture as involving a "climate of valuations" rather than being a thing apart from people. "Climate" implies the possibility for shift, and "valuations" suggests that the climate is made up of ideas, beliefs, feelings, and actions expressed by people. Yet the word "culture" as an abstraction also implies that the whole is greater than the sum of its parts, and that people learn from and conform to the patterns of people as a whole.

Elvis Presley in his early exposure on television and in popular music was responded to by a host of individual teen-agers who reacted to him with their own private senses. As Presley grew as an ideal, teen-agers were no longer free to accept him or reject him simply as individuals. They had to cope with a new level of values—that of the teen-age *society*.

Sometimes the important patterns of behavior and perception are learned from smaller reference groups, as adolescents, for example, respond to popular records. Sometimes learning is funneled through the larger, common culture, as in the singing of "The Star Spangled Banner." Although adults live in the same culture, they do not see a popular hit in the same light as teen-agers. Nor do non-Americans respond to the national anthem in the same way as Americans. An object or an idea differentiates itself along lines of the implied *membership* behind it.

Culture places the product in a social context and imbues it with meanings that set the broadest limitations on how it is experienced. A commercial product becomes culturally defined by the broad history of interaction with its market. In particular, the definition is determined by the social, biological, and psychic needs the product fulfills for its user. Thus, when a product achieves a niche in its cultural context, it is an object which denotes *consistent* (*not* unalterable) and *predictable* behavior within the social structure.

The ballpoint pen, for example, is intrinsically nothing but a complex set of tactile and visual sensations. These sensations are selected and modified by its user, according to the cultural definition of a ballpoint pen, and purposively placed in a social setting. That is, the object becomes perceived by the consumer. The result is that the user experiences a handy, easy-to-use, and relatively inexpensive tool for communicating his thoughts.

Advertising and culture

Cultural influence is obvious when one thinks of how a cigarette in the mouth of a woman may be perceived today as compared to how it was perceived thirty or forty years ago. The above-the-ankle skirt might have indicated many qualities about its wearer during the last century that would be fallacious today.

Advertising must take account of the current values and product-definitions of the society (or subsociety) in which it intends to operate. In other words, advertisers must be aware of the role of the object in the life of the consumer. Likewise, advertisers must understand the limits of these broader cultural definitions before trying to amplify the product into a brand image.

For example, the social values implied by the concept "perfume" are such that its users are necessarily considered feminine. Any attempt by advertising to contradict the strong mores inherent in such a cultural definition might backfire as a commercial enterprise. Advertisers of male cosmetics and other self-indulgent items have discovered that they must carefully conceal the femininity and narcissism involved in colognes.

Culturally, then, the function of advertising is to understand, to reflect, and in most instances to accept the value-structure of society before it can go about its creative task of helping to organize in a consistent, gratifying manner the numerous stimulations a product contains for the potential consumer. Advertising can help to select and reinforce certain values and needs inherent in the role of the product. It can operate within the limits of culture to create new expectations for the consumer.

Occasionally an entire society may entertain negative or distorted notions about a product that may be a result of an unfortunate long-standing history between object and consumer. The potential for a limited, positive redefinition on a societal or subsocietal scale may exist in the case of such products.

The reader may think of numerous examples of products and services, the mere mention of which sends a wave of disdain, fear, disgust, discomfort, and other negative reactions through him. Spinach, dentists, hypodermic needles, and long underwear are examples of "objects" with a positive function subordinated to the unfavorable experiences behind them.

In these cases, advertising can embark on the Herculean task of pointing up new avenues of more pleasurable interaction between the product and the consumer, and reformulate aspects of the cultural definitions of a product class. Of course, true reformulation lies in the response by the consumer society to the communicator's message. If the message is consistent with the society's experiences, an advertising-success story may indeed occur in a social movement toward a product. In such instances, reformulation is based on a pleasure-pain principle that promises to take the consumer from an unsatisfying relationship to a gratifying one.

For example, dental care in the mind of the average American is fraught with annoyance and discomfort, on the one hand, or with special precaution, compulsiveness, and concern on the other. Dental care and dentists are too often associated with a conception of teeth as a set of nuisances which nature ordained shall be in one's mouth. The American Dental Association is trying to reorient the client toward conceiving of his teeth and their care in the positive light of self-grooming and social reward in much the manner of the cosmetic industries.[4]

And when the Tea Bureau suggested that tea is the "hefty, hale, and hearty" drink for the average man, it was attempting to counter the stereotyped notions of effeteness, femininity, and snobbishness culturally attributed to the drink.

If the program of redefinition dramatically and effectively brings a product closer to the experience of the consumer, a new cognitive orientation toward the product will take place. Success in changing a popular concept depends upon how intense and stable, how true to experience, is the cultural tradition concerning products, ideas, or services.

---

[4]"A Motivational Study of Dental Care: A Pilot Investigation," prepared for the American Dental Association by Social Research, Inc., in the *Journal of the American Dental Association*, serialized in Vol. 56 (March, April, May, and June, 1958).

Although advertising can help to reorganize some of the social interaction between a consumer and a product, it must be sensitive enough to these patterns to recognize their intensity and stability. An extremely exotic product, perhaps suitable for a small elite group, cannot be converted into a mundane, mass product *merely* by advertising.

THE BRAND IMAGE AS A SOURCE OF MEANING

The cultural definition of a product is too broad and generalized to allow a consumer to select a brand. It helps to create the initial set of expectations about the product which is then qualified by the second variable in product-consumer interaction, the brand image.

The brand image, as a source of meaning, helps the consumer further to select and organize the stimulations of the product, display, and other communications directed to him. Mead's social psychology suggests that an "image" guides one's actions and attitudes toward the object.[5]

It has been further suggested that the *meaning* of any message is the "change which it produces in the (already existing) image" that an individual harbors about the object in question.[6] This means that the message value of a television commercial, for example, lies in the degree and direction of change in a brand image previously held by the viewer. (Reinforcement of an already existing image implies a change in degree.)

Differences among brand images represent much more than literal product differences. A whole different set of notions and actions are inherent in the name "Lincoln" as compared with the name "Jaguar," despite the fact that each make has at least one or two models that are functionally comparable. It is somewhat difficult to imagine the typical Lincoln owner sitting behind the wheel of the typical Jaguar. The difference in the two images is, therefore, more intricate than the simple differences between the two lines of cars.

Tests of consumer reactions to various products and their advertisements indicate that the brand image may undergo change more quickly than the basic cultural definition of the product. Perception of the brand image is more capable of being influenced than is the perception of the general class of the product. This is logical, as the image is formulated within the limits of a culture.

The changes which took place in the brand images of certain filter cigarettes, for example, were fairly swift once the underlying cultural attitudes about filter cigarettes were modified by broader social influences affecting their definition, such as science, medicine, group hysteria. Marlboro could become a *manly* cigarette rather quickly once society relaxed its notions about who might smoke such a cigarette.

The image of the brand appears to be a relatively stable organization of percepts about a product. Once established, a brand image lends the consistency and predictability in the consumer's relationship with the product which

[5]George Herbert Mead, *Mind, Self, and Society,* edited by Charles W. Morris (Chicago, University of Chicago Press, 1934).

[6]Kenneth E. Boulding, *The Image* (Ann Arbor: University of Michigan Press, 1956), p. 7.

allow him to select and experience those aspects of the product he values. Schweppes quinine water must indeed be a different experience to those who have responded to its image than is that of several other brands. The senses become attuned differently, and the social values inherent in the product-consumer interaction are different from brand to brand.

Advertising and the brand image

The major influence of advertising appears to be felt in the area of consumer perception of the brand. The brand image is the major organizing concept through which the consumer is guided toward perceiving unified patterns of stimulation. This imagery provides the emotional and sensual qualities which distinguish a brand from the general product-class and help the consumer discriminate from brand to brand.

Jello is not just a gelatin dessert, nor are Jello and Royal simply two products united by their common class. For the purchaser of a brand, there is usually a feeling that one has purchased a product distinctly different from another brand. This is probably most obvious in the case of beer and cigarettes.

This is the clue to what is often termed the "irrational" motive of the consumer in purchasing products. Skeptics, classic economists, and behaviorists in market research might demonstrate by blindfold tests how suggestible the average consumer is. They point out that the average consumer cannot distinguish between a Camel or a Philip Morris, or between Schlitz and Miller.

What such a literal understanding of the product-consumer relationship fails to consider is that *the value of a brand and its over-all symbolic effects on the consumer cannot be teased apart by tests oriented toward seeing the product in its barest, utilitarian terms.*

Another way of saying this is that the consumer purchases the brand and its cluster of meanings as much as he purchases the literal product. What Vance Packard calls "hidden persuasion" is probably the reference-group and other symbolic values implied in most social communications.[7]

The function of advertising is to create strong sub-categories of values and needs within the social structure, and to associate these with the product. Consumers may then select those brands whose sets of implied experiences fit into the sub-group with which he identifies.

The *Chicago Tribune* study on cigarettes and smokers clearly indicated that it is as reasonable to talk about the man who smokes Camels, for example, as having a "Camel personality" as it is to say that the brand itself has a personality.[8] It is reasonable because the two are correlates of each other. To the extent that the consumer perceives the brand image in this stable, predictable (and pleasurable) manner, the brand becomes a need-satisfying monopoly rather than a competitor with other brands. The power of the monopoly is dependent on the degree to which the brand is differentiated from other brands and is pleasurable at the same time.

---

[7] Vance Packard, *The Hidden Persuaders* (New York, David McKay Company, Inc., 1957).
[8] *Cigarettes: Their Role and Function, A Study for the Chicago Tribune,* prepared by Social Research, Inc., Chicago, 1953.

If this aspect of the function of advertising is recognized, much of the arrogant and sanctimonious tone in some advertising can be relieved and a positive program of distinctive image development put in its place.

This relationship between the consumer and the brand must be understood by the advertiser in the earliest stages of planning if some measure of control and predictability in one's message is to be realized. If it is believed that facial tissue "A" can appeal to an important part of the market not adequately tapped by facial tissue "B," its advertisers must understand both the expectancies of this market and how advertising might serve to fit in with, reinforce, and organize these sets into a satisfying perceptual whole.

DIRECT EXPERIENCE WITH THE PRODUCT AS A SOURCE OF MEANING

The third perceptual area is that of direct experience, the *use* which classical theory states determines the *utility* of the product and ultimately its demand. By direct experience with a product, a consumer finally gets his "feedback" in terms of social gratifications and primary sensory experiences that the brand image and cultural definitions have set up for him.

In a sense, the consumer is not fully open to his experiences and is not likely to perceive all the stimuli of a product. His own needs, in conjunction with the social conceptions reinforced by the imagery surrounding the product, emphasize certain aspects of direct experience and weed out others.

In some research on the ballpoint pen, for example, consumers were asked to describe their *writing* experiences with three brands of pens. One of these pens is a brand which stresses efficiency and predictability. The second brand emphasizes a general quality of competence, including prestige and status. The third brand focuses on inexpensiveness and dispensability.

Consumers described their experiences with the pens in terms of the generalized brand image, giving evidence of an awareness of how they were oriented toward the product. It is fairly evident that technical product improvements alone, unless they are highly dramatic or extreme, do not radically alter the consumer's previous ideas about the product. Some outside agent must serve to create a new expectation about the product that will allow the consumer to perceive the difference.

Advertising and direct experience with the product

The function of advertising in this third area of consumer perception is to supply the *terms* in which the product is valued. In some ways advertising sets up a "self-fulfilling prophecy." [9] Most researchers are aware that a consumer's reaction to use is channeled in an important way by what he expects to experience. The terms in which the consumer responds to use are, in good part, supplied by advertising. The facets of experience beyond the scope of advertising are the concrete physiological sensations of the consumer.

---

[9]Robert K. Merton, "The Self-Fulfilling Prophecy," in Robert K. Merton, *Social Theory and Social Structure* (Glencoe, The Free Press, 1949).

Nor can broad organizing concepts, such as a cultural definition or a brand image, account for the unpredicted idiosyncrasies of either the consumer or the product. However, by the time the consumer has selected and organized all the communications of the product, he will evaluate the use experience in a fairly patterned manner.

Too often, the advertiser is so close to competitive aspects of his product that he has personally defined it in a manner that is not of optimum value to the consumer. Competition often causes advertisers to "hop on the current bandwagon" of advertising claims and to shout loudly about values that have little positive meaning to the consumer. In the automobile industry, a complex language of power dynamics has been foisted upon the consumer. Is this the optimum language of use available for him? In filter cigarettes, the language of use among certain competitive brands has been the number of filter-traps contained in the cigarette. Is the filter-cigarette smoker aided in getting gratification out of a cigarette by a terminology that concentrates upon the negatives of smoking?

The advertiser might improve his relationship with the consumer if he realized that his characterization of the consumer's use-experience helps the latter selectively perceive out of the product's numerous stimulations. Direct experience with a product is patterned by the communicable language of the product which has been created or reinforced by advertising.

READING 42

HOW TO PLAN NEW PRODUCTS, IMPROVE OLD ONES, AND CREATE BETTER ADVERTISING*

Dik Warren Twedt

The term "brand loyalty" has semantic implications of consumer fidelity and allegiance that are a brand's due, *and no brand has ever had that right.* In our competitive economy, a branded product or service will succeed only to the degree that it offers consumers more total satisfactions than other available brands.

These satisfactions, of course, can be of different kinds—economic, physical, or psychological—but unless a given branded product can legitimately claim that it does a better job (at a given price) than its competitors in providing one or more of these consumer satisfactions, it has not really established its right to be represented in the marketplace. Although this principle has always been true for products in abundant supply, natural selection (and the resulting "survival of the fittest") operates more swiftly today than ever before. There are four major reasons why this is so:

*Reprinted from *The Journal of Marketing* published by the American Marketing Association, vol. 33, no. 1 (January 1969), pp. 53–57.

1. Increasing consumer sophistication resulting from higher educational levels, and changes in income distribution which permit more people to exercise greater brand choice.

2. Exponential proliferation of consumer choice, both within and between product categories.

3. Higher absolute levels of media promotion, and more effective mass advertising.

4. Increased sophistication of retailers (often aided by computerization), which is reflected in quicker decisions about a given brand's viability.

Alert marketing management has recognized these trends and has responded by even greater attempts at product differentiation, thus quickening still further the tempo of competition for the consumer dollar. It would appear that now and in the foreseeable future marketers are caught in a competitive spiral, in which competitive pressures will always be "more than yesterday, but less than tomorrow."

If this is to be the nature of the competitive environment, what is the most appropriate strategy for the individual marketer? The answer is two-fold:

1. to continue to improve present products so that they will maintain or extend their differentiation and

2. to plan new product entries so that maximum differentiation is built in from the very beginning.

A deceptively simple but powerful, three-step method exists to accomplish both objectives. During the past two decades, this method has been applied successfully in new product planning and product improvement for more than a score of major marketers in this country and abroad. Here is how it works. (In the first step, *carpet sweepers*—a mature product category—will be used as an example.)

STEP 1—IDENTIFICATION OF POSSIBLE PRODUCT ATTRIBUTES

Step 1 is a *systematic creative exploration* of all the ways in which (carpet sweepers) can vary. Note that the analysis is not restricted to ways in which carpet sweepers *do* vary, or have varied in the past; we inquire rather into all conceivable ways in which carpet sweepers could be made to vary! This approach owes much to the "brainstorming" technique pioneered by the late Alex Osborn.[1]

As in brainstorming sessions, the small group working on the initial listing of ways in which product attributes can vary should carefully avoid any

---

[1]Alex Osborn, *Applied Imagination: Principles and Producers of Creative Problem Solving* (New York: Charles Scribner & Sons, 1963). For an interesting and somewhat different approach to the same problem, see William J. J. Gordon, *Synectics: The Development of Creative Capacity* (New York: Harper & Row Publishers, 1961).

mutual criticism, or even attempts to prematurely evaluate suggestions. "Hitchhiking" is encouraged, that is, the constructive elaboration of another group member's idea. At this stage, primary emphasis is on sheer quantity of ideas; the objective evaluation comes later. By striving for as long a list of attributes as possible, the chances are greater that more areas of the product domain will be explored.

Obviously there is no magic number at which the listing of possible attributes should stop; listings will vary in length with products of different complexity. But don't stop too soon! In one analysis, more than 80 cigarette attributes were recorded before someone thought to add a key attribute, "flavor."

In an actual application of this method almost 20 years ago, one of the product attributes that an advertising agency group conceived for carpet sweepers was "color." Until that time, carpet sweepers had been available in only two colors, black or dull gray. By introducing a line of pastel "decorator" colors, the Bissell Company was able to reverse a declining sales trend. What might have been considered a minor, non-functional change in an unimportant product attribute, actually resulted in a major change in marketing position.

For new product concepts, the same logic is followed as for mature products. The first step is to list systematically all of the ways in which the product or service can vary. Suppose, for example, that prior to the introduction of aerosol packaging, a marketer of dairy products had wanted to expand his share of the market for high butterfat cream. One of the product attributes that could have been assigned to cream was "greater convenience." From this identification of the opportunity for product differentiation could have come the concept of whipped cream in ready-to-use form.

One of the more obvious product attributes, but one that is seldom fully explored for its differentiation potential, is sheer *size*. The market for a branded product may often be expanded considerably merely by offering a larger range of sizes. Of course the size variations must make sense to consumers; needless proliferation is likely to be confusing to the public and discouraged by Congress.

STEP 2—ASSIGNMENT OF DIFFERENTIATION RATINGS

When the product attribute list is long enough to suggest that most of the possibilities for product differentiation have been considered, it is time to proceed to the second step: an assignment of one of three *differentiation ratings* to each product attribute. For each attribute, a judgment is made as to whether our brand is *superior, equal,* or *inferior* to most competitive brands. As a beginning, this judgment can be based upon informed marketing opinion. Eventually, depending upon the size of the risk involved, it may be appropriate to test the validity of such judgments with consumer research.

In designing a new product, step 2 calls for a series of decisions about what attributes should be built into the product, rather than merely assigning competitive comparison values to attributes of existing products.

Let us suppose that we are members of a group that has been asked to devise a marketing strategy for typewriters to be sold to the home market. We begin with the almost purely theoretical, exhaustive listing of the ways in which typewriters can vary. In step 2, we judge how our present typewriter actually compares with most competitive brands on each attribute listed. An example of a partial listing follows:

Step 1. Listing of Typewriter Attributes	*Step 2. Assignment of Differentiation Ratings. Compared with most competitive brands, our brand is . . .*		
	"Superior" +	*"Equal"* =	*"Inferior"* −
1. Price		=	
2. Portability	+		
3. Esthetic design (geometric)	+		
4. Esthetic design (color)	+		
5. Versatility of use		=	
6. Availability		=	
7. Service guaranty	+		
8. Convenience of cleaning		=	
9. Convenience of replacing ink element		=	
10. Adjustability to different touches			−
11. Convertability to different fonts		=	
12. Ruggedness and so forth			−

If we made competitive judgments objectively, and if we can be reasonably confident of their validity, a preliminary evaluation of the product's marketing future can be made at the end of step 2. If honest self-appraisal turns up no plus marks, but only a few equalities and the balance minuses, it is probably time either to drastically improve the product or retire it.

It is self-evident that not all product attributes are of equal importance to consumers, and also that one golden virtue may compensate for many minor shortcomings. In planning for product differentiation, an attempt should be made to move as many ratings as possible to the left in this three-column analysis—from equalities to pluses, and from minuses to equalities, or even pluses.

It is rarely possible to move all ratings to the first column of plus marks. Some of the attributes in a given product profile require tradeoffs. For example, if a typewriter were clearly superior in attributes 2 through 12 in the listing shown, it is likely that such superiority would be reflected in higher price. Whether non-competitive prices are "inferior" or "superior" product attributes is debatable. The traditional viewpoint that high prices tend to deter sales (which would lead to classification of high price as an "inferior" product attribute) may not be true in our present affluent economy.

STEP 3—TRIVARIANT ANALYSIS

The third step is to determine the relative marketing potency of the attributes identified in step 1 and evaluated in step 2. Originally, this determination was made by simply asking consumers, "How desirable to you is (the attribute in question)?"

In 1951, Dr. Perham Nahl, now with the Leo Burnett Company, and I were working on the advertising campaign of a large manufacturer of canned pet food. It was found that the product attribute "Government inspected" was considered to be highly desirable by purchasers. However, after further investigation, it became clear that advertising based upon this selling idea was not likely to have much impact; people thought this attribute was already true for all brands. (It happens that most brands of canned pet food are *not* Government inspected, but remember that the model deals with attitudes and opinions rather than with matters of fact.)

In addition to *desirability*, then, a product attribute, to provide effective consumer motivation, must have some degree of *exclusivity*. Development of this simple two-dimensional model, with its assumptions that advertising will be more effective if it stresses product attributes that are desirable, and also relatively exclusive to the brand advertised, led us to a search for other dimensions—such as believability, meaningfulness, ego-involvement, and so forth.

The results of our empirical research was "trivariant analysis," in which the position of each product attribute is located on three scales: *desirability, exclusiveness*, and *believability*. A simple mathematical expression of this relationship is:

$$MP = f \ (D) \ (E) \ (B)$$

in which MP (marketing potency, or the extent to which a given product attribute will effectively promote sales) is assumed to be a function of a multiplicative relationship among the three factors—multiplicative because the reduction of any of the three right-hand terms to zero or near zero sharply reduces the attribute's marketing potency.

This general formula is obviously naïvely stated because equal weight is assigned to each of the three factors. It is hardly likely that this is true for all product attributes and all product categories. The model has been useful, however, in determining relative potency of a wide variety of attributes for many categories of products and services.

The basic assumptions are not new. Creative people have known since the beginning of advertising that to interest consumers, advertising must say something desirable about the product. At the same time, it must say something that doesn't automatically apply to any and all brands in the product category. Finally, the statement must be either believable or provable. Tri-

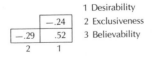

1 Desirability
2 Exclusiveness
3 Believability

variant analysis is simply a convenient way to express these three factors in quantitative terms.

An intercorrelation matrix of the three factors, based upon 105 attributes taken from studies of seven different product categories, suggests that although the factors are not wholly independent, they are worth measuring separately.

These correlation coefficients indicate that if a product attribute was thought to be desirable, there was a slight tendency for it to be thought of as "not exclusive," but there was a moderately strong tendency for consumers to believe the claim. If a product attribute was thought of as "exclusive," consumers had a slight tendency not to believe the claim.

HOW PRODUCT ATTRIBUTES (OR COPY CLAIMS) ARE EVALUATED BY TRIVARIANT ANALYSIS

The mechanics of measuring the three factors are straightforward. Each product attribute is briefly described in a "copy capsule." The copy need not be an unemotional recital of dull fact; it can and often should be an enthusiastic presentation of a single argument as to why the consumer should buy. The test themes or copy paragraphs are typed on 3 × 5 cards. A few examples of such copy capsules are:

A hair spray that lasts through three shampooings
A wrist watch that varies less than two seconds a day
The bourbon that makes even the rocks taste better
A refrigerator with a 10-year guaranty on all moving parts
The first completely nourishing breakfast you don't have to cook
This dog collar flea-proofs your dog for three months in 28 seconds

Unless the basic selling idea depends heavily upon the brand name, it should be tested without the support of the brand name. If the product attribute has high potency, linkage with a well-accepted brand should make it even more acceptable to consumers.

All cards are rated by each respondent on a rating scale for *desirability* of each attribute, then the same cards are shuffled and rated again for *exclusiveness*, and finally for *believability*. A description of each operation follows:

1. Here are a few brief descriptions about some (product category) you might buy. For each description, which number on this scale (refer to scale 1) comes closest to your own opinion? If your opinion comes somewhere in between these numbers, give a number in between that best represents how *desirable* each description is to you personally.

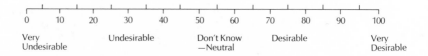

2. Here are the same brief descriptions again. Now this time, please give the

number on this scale (or some number in between) that comes closest to the way you feel about how *exclusive* each description is to you.

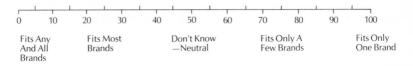

3. Now here is the last scale. Here are the same descriptions again, and this time please give the number on the scale (or some number in between) that comes closest to your own *belief* in the description as it might apply to a particular product.

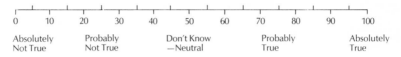

This technique allows a large number of product attributes to be tested, including an advertiser's present copy claims, experimental claims, competitive claims, and even new product concepts not yet fully developed. A computer program is available that yields mean scores and measures of variance for 22 attributes, and that also provides separate scores for such dichotomous variables as light versus heavy users, men versus women, exposure to advertising versus non-exposure, and so on. The program also prints out differences in scores that are significant at the 1% and 5% confidence levels for any dichotomy selected.

Trivariant analysis has an important limitation. Although it is an efficient way to test the probable effectiveness of *factual* claims, it seems less applicable to advertising approaches that depend heavily upon *emotion*, or upon *graphics*. (Copy research has not yet found a way to obtain from consumers their belief in such a theme as "Modess—Because," and it is also rather difficult to establish the desirability of such illustrative devices as the Marlboro tattoo.)

A report is made in the form of a two-dimensional chart (the third factor, believability, is shown in parentheses) that locates the desirability and exclusiveness of each attribute. Figure 1 shows how consumers evaluated different potential attributes of refrigerators, information which was subsequently used in planning specifications for a new line of refrigerators.

After mean scores for each claim are plotted on the desirability and exclusiveness scales (with believability scores shown in parentheses), quadrants 1 through 4 are established by drawing dotted lines so that half the claims fall above the line and half below, and half fall to the left of the vertical line and half to the right. Product attributes in quadrant 1 (upper right-hand of chart) are considered to be relatively desirable, and yet they are not commonplace characteristics of brands already available. They are thus better candidates for developing what Rosser Reeves has called the USP, or Unique Selling Proposition.

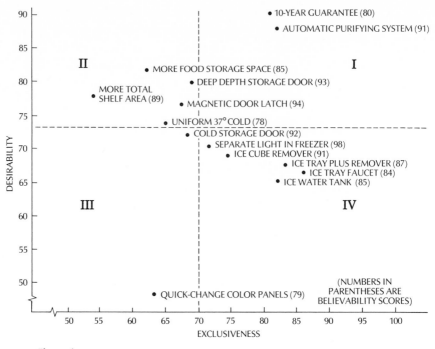

Figure 1

Trivariant analysis: Refrigerators

Believability scores provide an indication of the amount of assurance the consumer requires before he is willing to accept the selling proposition. Low believability scores suggest cognitive dissonance, but they are not always bad, provided there is a way to prove the claim's validity (through such means as demonstration, testimonial, case history, expert witness, and so forth).

These charts have also been useful to creative groups planning advertising copy strategy because they provide diagnostic profiles that suggest ways in which particular copy claims may be strengthened. If, for example, a claim is strong on desirability and exclusiveness but low on believability, the creative objective becomes one of furnishing adequate proof for the claim. Or if a claim happens to be low on desirability, it may be because the claim as stated has not yet made clear how the attribute really benefits the consumer, or it may be because the consumer simply doesn't care.

The three-step approach described here obviously depends greatly upon the quality of operations performed by the smallest but most powerful of all computers—the one located midway between the ears. Much of what has been described requires good, hard thinking. If the thinking has been productive, the methods outlined are likely to be helpful in developing orders of priority for new product planning, for improvement of present products, and for selecting those attributes of advertised products that are most likely to motivate customers to buy. With such working priorities established, the probability is substantially increased that consumers will be better served and that corporate net earnings will be increased.

READING 43

MEDIA FACTORS: A REVIEW ARTICLE*

Dennis H. Gensch

INTRODUCTION

Selection of the most effective television shows, radio programs, magazines, newspapers, and other media vehicles to convey a message to a target population has always been more involved than simply selecting the set of media vehicles with the lowest cost-per-thousand. Other factors to be considered include the editorial climate of the vehicle, its prestige, the visual and/or audio qualities in relation to the requirements of the product message, interactions among vehicles, and the social environment in which the audience reads or views the vehicles. Prior to the sixties these additional factors were combined under the title "experienced judgment." Cost-per-thousand estimates were adjusted by an agency's "experienced judgment," implying that all relevant factors were taken into account in the ultimate media selection.

The development of the computer generated even more data as well as quantitative models to structure and evaluate the data. The quantitative models used the term *media weights* to stand for the "experienced judgment" factors.

Quantitative models using linear programming, dynamic programming, iteration, heuristic programming, and simulation have been designed to select media schedules. These models have been reviewed in the literature [13, pp. 414–24],† and most use media weights. The model *builders* tend to stress the functional relationships postulated in a particular model and go into considerable detail on its unique mathematical properties. It is then left to the model *user* to fill in the blanks and provide the media weights for a model to become operational. Furthermore, there can be little question that the accuracy and usefulness of any of the quantitative models is heavily influenced by the quality of the media weight estimates.

There has also been some discussion of response functions [3, 7, and 21] in the literature. The mapping of responses by all members of the target population to alternative advertising campaigns in *n*-dimensional space forms a response surface. The emphasis of most of the response function articles is on discussion of "search" routines in response surfaces assumed to have particular shapes. The underlying question of identifying the advertising variables and specifying the functional relationships among them that generate the shape of a response surface is usually ignored or assumed away. In order to make practical use of the theoretical concepts developed in the response function literature, it will be necessary to empirically measure the response functions for specific segments of the population. Marc [21] points

*Reprinted from *The Journal of Marketing Research,* published by the American Marketing Association, vol. 8 (May 1970), pp. 216–225.
†Bracketed numbers are keyed to references at the end of this reading.

out that empirical measurement is needed to see if there are general response laws. Until this is done response models have little practical value as a media planning tool. Carpenter [7] states that the interactions of media weights must be understood before a response function can be realistically defined and empirically measured.

In the more descriptive literature on advertising, the importance of qualitative factors in media selection is recognized as an important consideration in practical day-to-day media selection decisions [31, pp. 12–7]. Thus, whether quantitatively, behaviorally, theoretically or applied in their orientation, members of the advertising community consider the qualitative aspects of media selection, the media weights, to be an important consideration in media selection. Significant planning tools are being theoretically developed. These require a more rigorously defined theory, *explaining the contributions of the qualitative media weights,* before these tools can be of practical use to the media planner. Yet, while the *importance* of media weights is well recognized there has been surprisingly little discussion of the media weights themselves.

This article is intended to stimulate a dialogue among advertising researchers by attempting to answer several questions. What are the common sets of media weights? What factors should be considered in determining the value of a specific media weight? What are the ways of measuring the influence of each relevant factor? What research has been done on these factors?

Preliminary analysis can greatly reduce the number of alternatives evaluated by the quantitative model. The media planner can usually specify the types of media that should be considered on the basis of (1) distribution system for product; (2) target population; (3) budget size; and (4) characteristics of the product. For example, it is of limited value to advertise heavily in geographic areas when the product is not sold or where few members of the target population live. Thus for a local or regional product national television and magazines may be excluded from consideration. A product may have characteristics that must be seen to be understood, so radio might be eliminated. Besides eliminating certain types of media from consideration the initial screening can also eliminate specific media vehicles unavailable to the advertiser. There is little sense in evaluating "Family Affair" if it is known that present sponsors plan to continue.

Basic factors

Following this initial screening, the complex problem of picking the best set of media vehicles from acceptable and available choices must be faced. Factors used to adjust a simple cost-per-thousand ranking of vehicles can be grouped into five categories.

1. Target population weights

2. Vehicle appropriateness weights

3. Commercial exposure weights

4. Commercial effectiveness weights

5. Cumulative frequency weights.

In the opinion of this author, weights that attempt to attribute attitude change or sales increases directly to specific commercials are presently of little value to media schedulers. Attitude change is *primarily* a function of the individual's existing set of attitudes, what the copy says, how the copy format presents the message, and the attitudes of people who influence the individual. Media selection may play a small role in attitude change by providing a more or less favorable setting for an advertising message, but attitude change does not appear to be highly responsive to different media schedules. Furthermore, is it realistic to believe a person's attitude has really changed because of *one* advertising exposure? The Schwerin (pre-post) method of measuring attitude changes caused by television commercials on the basis of one exposure has been both criticized and defended as to technique and meaningfulness [5, 11, and 12].

Weights that attribute sales directly to advertising are usually gross oversimplifications of the real world. Purchase decisions are not a sole function of advertising. Many other variables such as product price and quality, availability, actions by competitors, peer group evaluation of product, present cash position, etc., interact with advertising to determine purchase. To ignore the actions of these other variables seems unrealistic.

Media weights may be applied on an aggregate or individual basis. Most of the models use aggregate weights because, first, the algorithms used cannot handle the data on an individual basis, at least not at a computer cost that practitioners are willing to accept, and second, most of the syndicated data come in aggregate form.

The aggregate data on media viewing are usually broken down into a number of demographic and socioeconomic characteristics (e.g., home ownership). The covariance and higher order correlations among the demographic and socioeconomic subgroups are seldom provided by the syndicated services. For the model builder, who is trying to incorporate the interrelationships among marketing variables, the subgroup totals are of little value unless he is provided with some statistics which measure the interrelationships between the subgroups. What usually happens in this situation is that the model builder will simply *assume* an independent relationship between all subgroups.

The purpose of advertising research should be to identify and then measure the interrelationships between the components of the advertising system. To use a weighting system which *a priori* denies the possible interrelationships guarantees that models so formulated will be of little practical value in aiding media schedulers to deal with their problems, probably a major reason why many mathematically sophisticated models have failed to produce useful insights or results.

Individual weights are usually derived from sample information. Here the viewing and reading patterns are recorded *by individual.* All other weights are determined *by individual,* thus preserving the interactions between the variables. Syndicated sources such as W. R. Simmons and Brand Rating Index provide data on an individual basis.

Use of individual weights will lead to more realistic models. The relationships between variables should be measured and functional relationships postulated on the basis of empirical data. Only then will the *consequence* of assuming no interrelationship be known. Only then can one judge if a model's assumption of independence seriously distorts the real world situation. The remainder of this article will discuss media weights on an individual rather than aggregate basis. Each of the five categories listed above will be reviewed, including references to research.

TARGET POPULATION WEIGHTS

The advertiser usually considers certain members of the mass audience to be of greater importance to him than others. Advertising has been designed for and will have greater effect upon a certain subset of the total audience. This target population may be identified and valued on the basis of past purchasing activity, socioeconomic variables, or personality traits.

The target population can sometimes be defined on the basis of a single attribute; for example, denture adhesive advertisers may define their target population as only those people who wear dentures. A simple one or zero value can be attached to each individual in the vehicle's audience. Most target populations are not determined on the basis of only one *attribute.* Many target populations are valued over a one-*variable* spectrum such as past purchase behavior. A canned dog food manufacturer might assign the following weights on the basis of past purchase behavior and dog ownership:

Weight	Category
1.00	**Purchased 30 cans of dog food in the last month**
.60	**Purchased 15 cans**
.40	**Purchased 10 cans**
.20	**Purchased 5 cans**
.10	**Purchased 0 cans but own dog**
.01	**Purchased 0 cans but do not own dog.**

These weights attempt to reflect the purchasing potential as well as the past purchasing record of each individual. It is hoped that light users can be encouraged to increase purchases; thus, weighting is not in direct proportion to past purchases.

Individuals can be identified on the basis of socioeconomic variables, past purchasing, and personality traits. Assuming potential customers are identified by some combination of these variables (for example, where the product in question is a new form of baby food) the potential customer may be defined as female, college educated, with traits of aggressiveness and venturesomeness, with youngest child less than 30 months of age.

To the advertiser, some variables are more important than others; also many variables can be present in various strengths or degrees. Thus, variables must be weighted on both an inter and intra basis. The table shows this weighting scheme for three variables in the baby food example.

The weight indicates the importance of one variable in relation to another. The scale indicates the degree to which the particular individual possesses each variable. The .01 value is used in place of zero so that each individual will have a positive value, which is desirable when combining the individual weights with other systems of weights.

This approach is fine when the variables and weights are known. Unfortunately, the advertiser is usually not sure what the most relevant variables are, much less what their relative importance is. Through research techniques the advertiser can identify these variables and their relative importance. Multiple regression analysis and factor analysis are methods of identifying variables which appear to be significant. One can even get a crude weighting system from these approaches. Multiple discriminant analysis can reduce the multidimensional system with a continuous dependent variable to a multidimensional system in which the dependent variable is dichotomous. In other words, individuals are rated either as potential customers or not. They are weighted one to zero depending on whether they are customers or not. This removes the relative differences in potential.

Another approach is to estimate the relative importance of various individuals to the advertiser. A cluster analysis technique [14, pp. 387–99] could be used to determine the set of variables which seem important. Using cluster analysis or factor analysis as a first step, one could rank order the variables. Then, various nonmetric scaling methods [10, pp. 298–306] could be employed to change the ranking from ordinal (first, second, etc.) into cardinal (1, 2, 3.6, etc.) scales.

Given the information obtained from the methods mentioned above, the advertiser might actually build a model that attempts to explain interactions among the relevant variables mentioned above. Based upon this approach, each individual in the target population could be weighted in terms of his probable response to the ad and his purchase potential.

VEHICLE APPROPRIATENESS WEIGHTS

Most professional advertising experts have taken the position that media vehicles are much more than passive conductors of messages. There is an interrelationship between the vehicle and the advertising message it delivers to an audience. This vehicle "rub-off" effect can make substantial negative or positive contributions to the advertising effectiveness of the message. Alfred Politz verbalized this attitude in his introduction to the well-publicized *Reader's Digest-Saturday Evening Post* exposure study [25].

Exposure is entirely the responsibility of the medium, though the medium's function goes beyond that—into the mood it creates in its readers, viewers, or listeners, their confidence in the medium and other benefits the medium delivers for its advertising content. These other benefits are not measured in this study, which confines itself to exposure.

Individual weighting system, baby food

Individual	Variable 1 College Education			Variable 2 Child < 30 months			Variable 3 Aggressiveness			Individual's Value Weight			
	Weight	Scale	V1	Weight	Scale	V2	Weight	Scale	V3	V1	V2	V3	Weight
1	3	1.00	3.00	10	1.00	10	5	.20	1.0	3.00	10	1.0	30.0
2	3	.01	.03	10	1.00	10	5	.80	4.0	.03	10	4.0	1.2
3	3	1.00	3.00	10	.01	.1	5	.50	2.5	3.00	.1	2.5	.75
4	3	.50	1.50	10	.01	.1	5	.60	3.0	1.50	.1	3.0	.45

This belief that vehicles have carry-over effects which influence the effectiveness of their ads has been documented in studies related to magazines, radio, and television.

Winick used paired comparison methods in testing how the same advertisement might be perceived in the context of two different magazines. Magazines X and Y were directly competitive. In Magazine X the advertisements were significantly *better liked* (chi-square = 22.6, $p < .01$), *more believable* (chi-square = 73, $p < .01$) and *better recalled* (chi-square = 6.3, p between .01 and .02). From this and further research Winick concluded [36, p. 28]: "Where advertising is placed—its vehicle—affects recall of its message, rating of its sponsor, and return of its coupon." A 1957 radio study concluded [23]:

Listeners pay more attention to these CBS Radio stations than to the leading independents. Listeners distinguish between stations—regard these CBS Radio stations more favorably than the leading independents. Listeners believe these CBS Radio stations more than the leading independents —both their programs and their advertising. It seems it's a matter of authority.

Television studies conducted in Britain and the United States indicate that programs affect the audiences' response to commercials. Nuttall of the London Press Exchange observed [24, p. 25]:

We also establish that the interest of viewers in the programs they watched considerably affected their attention to commercials. This was reflected both in the lower levels of activity during commercials of viewers to programs of high interest relative to programs of low interest, and also in the greater ability of these viewers to correctly identify advertisements that had appeared.

Barclay, Doubs, and McMurtrey concluded that, during the daytime, certain programs had a more positive effect on commercials [2, p. 46]:

In the daytime serial programs generated somewhat more recall and, especially, attentiveness than other specific program types. Situation comedies fared least well. At night major program types differed relatively little.

Research by Crane [9, pp. 15–8] tends to support this conclusion. He observed that women were significantly more affected than men by the media vehicle in making judgments about commercials.

Once it is accepted that the media vehicle affects advertising effectiveness, the media schedule must weight the number of exposures generated per vehicle by the factors that make one exposure in Vehicle A more effective than one exposure in Vehicle B. Here are some factors that may affect the media vehicle appropriateness weight:

1. Editorial climate

2. Product fit

3. Technical capabilities

4. Competitive advertising strategy

5. Target population receptiveness

6. Product distribution system.

These variables do not necessarily affect each advertising message. As products, target populations, and advertising messages differ, various factors can influence the appropriateness of each media vehicle. It is up to the media scheduler to decide the relevance and importance of each factor in relation to his particular advertising message.

The effect of any stimulus is influenced by the environment in which it is presented. Thus the *editorial climate* or environment can produce a more or less suitable setting for the advertisement. Some of the authority or believability of the publication affects the advertisement. Generally readers select magazines, newspapers, television news and discussion shows that reinforce their present views. For this reason editorial climate is usually considered a positive factor, as it puts the reader in an accepting frame of mind. The editorial climate is primarily associated with the general "honesty," "authority," "timeliness," and "believability" of the vehicle in handling political and social issues.

Some vehicles are assumed to have more knowledge and authority on certain products. For example, a power drill manufacturer might prefer that a reader see his ad in *Popular Mechanics* rather than *Playboy*. A manufacturer of men's slacks might feel *Playboy* is viewed as having more knowledge and expertise on men's fashions than *Popular Mechanics*. This is one way of fitting the product to the available vehicles.

Vehicles may be more fitting for a particular product because of their "mood" or "prestige." Products that have built an exclusive quality image such as brands of women's perfumes or men's colognes may use "status consciousness" as an appeal. High prestige magazines such as the *New Yorker* may be preferred as advertising vehicles to high circulation mass media, for otherwise it might appear that the product was recommended for everyone.

Technical capabilities such as quality of paper, brightness of color, and quality of sound vary from one media vehicle to another, making some vehicles more suitable for certain types of copy format.

Competitive strategy considerations may make some media vehicles more desirable than others. If the competition is spending heavily on prime time television, a decision may be made to go very lightly in this area and instead try to dominate the magazines reaching the target audience. It is also important to consider how different the product's appeal, copy, and format are from the type of ads anticipated to be in the same issue. Uniqueness or difference enables an ad to stand out and be remembered. This author, while working for an advertising agency, was involved in tests to determine the degree to which color affected the attitude rating and recall score of an ad. It was interesting to note that if one black-and-white ad was inserted near the end of a sequence of 20 all-color ads, it received good attitude ratings and excellent recall scores. The same black-and-white ad viewed in a sequence of 10 color and 10 black-and-white ads ranked below average in attitude ratings and recall scores.

The *social context* in which a media vehicle is viewed or read can make a difference. Some advertisements might want to reach the entire family as a group. Thus evening television would be more desirable than daytime television, magazines, or newspapers, where exposure is more likely to be on an individual basis. On the other hand, an advertiser might wish to reach the housewife when she is relaxed, suggesting that television programs should be weighted in relation to the time of day at which they are on.

Certain programs are thought to fit various products and target audiences. Depth interviews reported by Campbell-Ewald [6] suggest men's products are best advertised on Westerns, whereas food products do best on situation comedies. Schwerin [26] reports food commercials fit well with situation comedies but do poorly in a mystery, adventure, or Western context. Analgesics do well both in adult Westerns and situation comedies. A problem with this type of research is that viewers do not always put programs into the same general categories as do the researchers.

Distribution systems for many products are not uniform throughout the country. Therefore, vehicles with the highest ratings or circulation in areas where the product has the strongest distribution should receive higher weights. Sometimes it is also desirable to give higher weights to the media vehicles that wholesalers and retailers in the distribution system feel are particularly good. This does not mean that the distributors' favorite vehicles are superior to others, but it might be of value to have the retailer feel the manufacturer is doing the best job he can in supporting the product.

COMMERCIAL EXPOSURE WEIGHTS

There are really two separate systems of commercial weights. The first set attempts to predict the number of commercial exposures, given the number of vehicle exposures. The second set is more concerned with perception of the ad, once exposure has occurred.

The concepts of exposure and perception are really quite different. An exposure is simply the opportunity to perceive. Perception means that some cognitive action has been taken by the individual. Although exposure and perception are clearly two different concepts, they are often treated as one in weighting systems used both by advertising models and by media research studies. These concepts will be kept separate, first discussing the probability that an individual will be exposed to the advertising message given exposure to the media vehicle.

A number of studies have focused on the attention individuals give to television commercials. Nuttall [24, p. 24] found that for British housewives the proportion reported as program viewers who were in fact not present in the viewing room during part of the commercial varied from 34% to 19%, with an average of 24%.

Viewers' Attention

Not in room	**24%**
In room but not sitting down	**10%**
Viewing plus other activity	**35%**
Viewing only	**30%**
	100% (99)

Of the housewives classified as viewers of the program, only about 30% were solely viewing during the commercial, with the remainder engaged in some other activity as well, not necessarily even in the same room.

The same study indicates that the pattern of viewing changes throughout the evening. The proportion of women program viewers absent from the room during commercials grew from 13% in the early evening to 28% by peak time; it then fell again to 17% in the latter part of the evening. The proportion of men viewers absent from the room during the commercials was somewhat smaller than that of housewives, falling from about 20% at 7 p.m. to about 10% by 8:30 p.m. One of the conclusions from this study was that a considerably larger number of people are absent during breaks than during programs. This, of course, has implications for spot vs. program-sponsored television.

Research findings in the U.S. are quite similar to the British findings. A study conducted by Barclay, Doub, and McMurtrey [2, p. 44] reports "in 49% of the network-tuned homes, the housewife reported being in the room at commercial exposure time." Steiner [28, pp. 272–304] reported that only 14% of the in-home audience watches all, or almost all, of an average network commercial.

According to Wheatley, the "island" commercial (one surrounded by program context) receives more attention than a "clutter" commercial [35, pp. 199–202], one which occurs near the beginning or end of a program, closely preceded or followed by spot commercials, station identification, public service announcements, etc.

Steiner found that while the proportion of people actually getting up and leaving the room more than doubled for 60 and 120-second spots, compared to 20-second spots, as the length of the commercial increased, interestingly, the percentage of people who paid *full* attention to it increased. Steiner explained that the longer a commercial, the more likely it is to follow programming rather than another commercial. As commercials' length increases from 20 to 120 seconds, full attention preceding them climbs from 51.8% to 80.3%. Since it is easier to maintain a viewer's attention than to reattract this attention once lost, it probably does make some difference if a commercial follows programming rather than another commercial.

Measuring print exposure

The three methods of measuring print exposure without regard to perception are glue-sealed issues (an individual must break a thin glue seal in order to look at each page), fingerprint tests, and eye-camera tests. While glue sealed issues and fingerprint tests clearly show the exact pages examined by a reader, they do not guarantee that the small ads on the page were observed. Camera tests reveal the exact pattern a viewer's eye traced over a page. These three tests are not regularly used because they are costly and time-consuming for the information they provide. The laboratory environment with the eye camera, in which the subject must hold his head in fixed rigid position to enable the camera to stay focused on his eye while he reads the ads, is unnatural and creates a viewing pattern quite different from the pattern the subject would follow if he were casually browsing through the magazine in his home.

COMMERCIAL PERCEPTION WEIGHTS

Given exposure to a commercial message, what is the probability that an individual will consciously perceive the message? People can have open eyes in front of a television set without really seeing or hearing what is being advertised. They are thinking about something else; their minds are not consciously open to the product message. Thus a set of commercial weights to predict perception is often used in conjunction with commercial exposure weights.

The methods most commonly used to measure perception are recall and recognition. In recognition tests, a subject is shown a magazine and asked if he can pick out the ads he recognizes from a previous reading. Unaided recall asks him to list these ads. Aided recall gives the subject clues as to what the advertisements were. Both of these tests measure not only if the subject *actually perceived* the ad but also if the subject *consciously remembers* what he perceived, in which vehicle he perceived the ad, and when he perceived it.

Therefore, when interpreting findings such as Greenberg and Garfinkle's observation that illustrations substantially increase recall scores [14, pp. 30–5], is this because the illustrations increase depth of perception or because they are easier to remember than printed copy?

The following four variables are most often used to predict the probability of perception of print advertisements: (1) length of ad, (2) use of color, (3) position of ad, and (4) thickness of issue.

What advantages do various page sizes have? Troldahl and Jones [30, pp. 23–7] looked at four factors affecting the probability that a newspaper ad is "seen." Page size and type of product advertised were found to be highly significant, explaining 60% of readership variation. Page size alone explained 40%. The other two factors—ratio of illustration size to copy space and number of items included—had little effect on whether or not the tested ads were "seen." Dr. Daniel Starch, who has conducted continuing studies of newspaper reading since 1932, reports that [34, p. 49]:

Readership as a rule is directly proportional to the size of the advertisement with this exception: a full page attracts not quite twice as many readers as a half-page ad, and a two-page ad attracts not quite twice as many readers as a full page. Also, spectacular, or multi-page advertisements will attract a smaller total reader audience than the same number of pages issued as separate one-page ads at suitable intervals.

To provide a simple heuristic rule for use in mathematical models, functional relationships between page size and exposures have been suggested. The best known of these relationships is the "square root" rule, first used by Lee and Burkhardt [18, pp. 113–22] in their heuristic model for advertising media selection. The concept is that the change in attention is equal to the square root of the multiple by which one changes the page size (if 100 people observe a ¼-page ad, 200 people are expected to observe a full-page ad). There is little reported research to validate this rule. Most researchers take the position that a strict functional relationship between attention and any one of the several variables affecting exposure without regard for the influences of the other variables is convenient but naive. Alan Donnahoe, Executive Vice President, *Richmond Times-Dispatch* and *News Leader*, has used Starch data and the "square root law" to calculate reading at various linage levels by men and by women for each of 20 different product categories. He concludes [34, p. 48]:

Just as products differ in innate interest, so do they also differ in incremental gain in readership with increase in ad size. . . . In the case of alcoholic beverages, for example, doubling the space size produces an average gain of 30 per cent in men readers and 14 per cent in women readers. In beer advertising, the comparable gains are 47 and 106 per cent. If a choice is to be made between large-space advertising and small-space times greater frequency, these data suggest that a beer manufacturer should select the former and a liquor distiller the latter alternative.

The conclusion that relative page size affects the exposure probability in a positive but not directly proportional ratio is supported by most of the research on magazine page size. Daniel Starch reports [33, p. 69]:

Detailed results of three years' study based upon inquiries from 8,200 advertisements in national magazines disclosed that if returns from full pages were pegged at 100, half-page advertisements "bring returns equal to around 60, and quarter pages produce returns equal to around 33."

In a 1957 study by the J. Walter Thompson agency, page size was reported to affect exposure probabilities more than the use of color, [29, p. 1]:

In terms of cost against added readership, four-color spreads are not so efficient as pages. They generally add about 50 per cent more readership at double the cost . . . since female ad-noting for a page is usually higher than male, spreads increase female readership on the average by only one-third.

Next to page size, the variable most often considered is use of color. Assael, Kofron, and Burgi [1, pp. 20–6] analyzed 1,379 advertisements in *Iron Age* by a multiple regression technique which included an iterative heuristic to form subgroups. They found the key characteristics in order of importance, to be 3 or 4-color, inserts, coated stock, spread, color with illustrations, and bleed pages.

The position of the ad within the vehicle has been studied from time to time.

Covers and turnout spreads clearly give higher exposures than other pages. The evidence on left vs. right-hand exposure seems inconclusive. The top is generally felt to be superior to the bottom of a page for a fractional page ad. While the buyer can specify cover and spreads (by paying a premium), he usually has little control over the left vs. right or top vs. bottom positioning of his ad. The publisher usually decides this relatively independently.

The thickness of the vehicle has some effect upon the exposure. Starch attempted to estimate this effect by counting the number of inquiries generated by each advertisement. His conclusion was that: "Within the range up to 200 pages, the effect of thickness of issue is moderate. For larger issues, the decline in inquiries becomes more rapid" [27, p. 38].

The conclusion seems reasonable that as the size of the vehicle increases there is a point at which readers will no longer read each page. However, the method of using inquiries to measure exposure or perception is questionable. Some types of ads clearly do not lead to inquiries, nor are they intended to. Readers of specific vehicles may have different degrees of willingness to make inquiries. Thus, the inquiry counting could be measuring different target populations' propensity to inquire rather than exposure.

Unpublished surveys by a number of advertising agencies come to the same conclusion. As magazine page count passes the 175-page mark, a sharp decline in the recognition scores per advertisement begins. This conclusion, too, should be taken with caution; it could be explained by the fact that some survey respondents get tired of the interview and start to plead ignorance of ads in order to terminate the interview.

The result for newspapers is much the same. Carter [8, pp. 39–41] reported that in a newspaper study, ads in thin issues received higher recall scores and reading time per page decreased as the number of pages increased.

Anyone wishing to determine commercial exposure weights from the type of regression analysis used in most of the research mentioned above should be aware of two major limitations. First, there is clear evidence of considerable *interaction* among these variables. Assael, Kofron, and Burgi reported that having over half-page of illustrated area was the most important independent variable predicting recognition of an advertisement when all were four-color. Yet the half-page illustration ranked as only the fifth most important when the ads were all black and white. The Gestalt psychologist would argue that the probability of exposure and depth of perception are not determined by adding up component weights of the advertisement; rather the ad must be viewed in its entirety and in the environment in which it is expected to appear before a meaningful commercial exposure weight can be assigned. The key factor determining the probability of commercial exposure may be its uniqueness in relation to the others carried by the media vehicle.

Second, there is research to indicate that the probability of advertising exposure is determined by the product being advertised, rather than by aspects of ad format. Those interested in specific products will search out these messages regardless of whether the message is presented in full page, 4-color or ¼-page, black and white. Buchanan [4, pp. 9–15] reports that interest in the product significantly affects recall of magazine ads, but not television commercials. Wells [32, pp. 2–9] reports that men's like-dislike rating of television commercials was primarily determined by product rather than program context and commercial type. Troldahl and Jones [30] found the product advertised to be significant in predicting rating scores.

Thus it would seem that weighting advertisements on the basis of particular advertisement features may provide a starting point, but judgment must be used in adjusting these weights to fit the product being advertised and in estimating the ad's uniqueness in relation to the expected environment of competing advertisements.

The Gallup-Robinson Report and the Starch Advertisement Readership Report are syndicated sources providing current data on the perception of an individual print ad. The latter employs a recognition method; after an individual indicates he has read a particular issue, the interviewer pages through the issue with him and estimates his degree of perception and memory for each ad in the issue. Readers are placed into four categories:

Non-reader
  One who did not remember having previously seen the advertisement in the issue being studied
"Noted" reader
  One who remembered having previously seen the advertisement in the issue being studied
"Seen-associated" reader
  One who not only "noted" the advertisement but also saw or read some part of it which clearly indicates the brand or advertiser
"Read most" reader
  One who read half or more of the written material in the ad.

Users of these data should be aware of the limitations of the Starch study. Sample sizes are small, ranging from 100 to 150 per sex per issue. Chance variations in sampling could be expected to cause variations of over 20 points at the .01 level of significance, thus making it risky to rate one advertisement over another on the basis of these numbers. Also, there is the carryover effect of national advertisements seen in other magazines and media vehicles. It is difficult for people to remember in exactly which issue they saw a well-known ad. In defense of Starch, in 1955 the Committee on Printed Advertising Rating Methods (PARM) of the Advertising Research Foundation duplicated both the Starch and Gallup and Robinson studies for one issue of *Life* magazine. The independent and extensive research conducted by PARM indicated that both Starch and Gallup and Robinson provided reasonably accurate results [20, pp. 9–20].

There is no syndicated service that rates the levels of perception for individual television commercials shown to United States audiences. Advertising agencies often check perception levels for specific commercials using telephone interviews and aided recall techniques. These studies are conducted for specific clients and usually are not published.

CUMULATIVE FREQUENCY WEIGHTS

Does the nineteenth exposure to the same ad have the same effect on the viewer as the first? Most advertising professionals would answer no, yet they would be hard pressed to indicate what the precise relationship is. Very little empirical research has been performed in measuring the cumulative effect of advertising. An example of a weighted frequency distribution is given in the following table:

Frequency	Frequency weight
1	.30
2	.40
3	.50
4	.80
5	1.00
6	1.00
7	.90
8	.80
9	.80
10	.80

The exposures are all weighted in relation to the number of exposures the advertiser judges necessary for the particular product message and target population under consideration. In this example, the rationale for weighting is that the first three exposures by themselves will tend to be lost in the swirl of competing messages and stimuli. The fifth and sixth exposures are the ones that register with the individuals. The seventh to tenth exposures repeat and remind individuals of the message. This weighting system would call for a campaign aimed at exposing most of the individuals at least six times. In terms of *estimated effectiveness* per dollar it appears better to deviate on the high side than on the low side.

The objectives of *repetition* and *coverage* are the dominant variables in estimating the weighted frequency distribution. These are modified by five other factors, discussed later.

Zielske supervised and published a study on this topic at Foote, Cone and Belding in 1959, and little has been published since. In his study [37, pp. 239–43] two groups of randomly selected women were mailed an advertisement for an ingredient food product. The first group received an ad every week for 13 weeks; the second received an ad every four weeks, for one year. Recall of the advertising was measured by telephone interviewing throughout the year. The results of this campaign are shown in the figure. The curve for thirteen exposures at four-week intervals has a saw-toothed shape, since there was forgetting of the advertising between exposures in this schedule. Actually, there is also some forgetting between exposures in the weekly schedule, but one week was the smallest unit of time measured in the study.

If recall is accepted as a valid criterion for measuring advertising effectiveness, it is clear that the relative value of the thirteenth exposure in relation to the first is dependent on the time between exposures. Also, advertising is

RECALL EXPOSURES

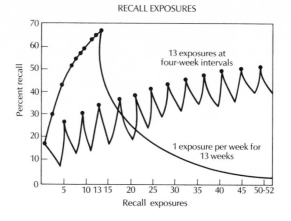

Recall exposures

quickly forgotten if the consumer is not continuously exposed, and as the number of exposures increases, the rate at which the ad is forgotten decreases. These conclusions are consistent with the psychological literature on learning theory, which says that the recall rate for a given advertisement may be affected by: (1) clarity of organization, (2) present interest in product, (3) present attitude set, (4) memory differences, and (5) personality differences in relation to copy appeal.

The qualities of advertising copy that most significantly affect the speed at which an ad will be learned and remembered are *meaningfulness* and *organization*. Advertisers and copy writers may talk in terms of *attractiveness*, but research presently being conducted by this author indicates that if a person perceives an ad as meaningful, he tends also to rate the ad as attractive.

Meaningfulness is a function of the receiver as well as copy, whereas organization is a direct function of copy only. Information theory suggests that meaningful or well organized material is learned more rapidly because it requires learning less. Miller and Selfridge [22, pp. 176–85] point out that when the material is not organized, one has to learn both the pattern (or organization) and the content, but when the material is well organized, one merely fits new information into a known pattern. Clarity of organization is probably more important in advertisement learning than in other learning situations (e.g., classroom). Most adults do not make a strong, conscious effort to learn commercials, and if the message is unclear or disorganized, they tend to disregard the ad and move to some other stimuli attracting their attention. Krugman [17, pp. 349–56] calls this process "learning without involvement."

What factors influence an individual's perception of meaningfulness? One factor is his present interest in the advertised product, usually highest in two groups. One group is those who feel the product could satisfy their needs and look to ads for information and encouragement as a prelude to possible purchase. The second group is recent purchasers of the product who seek reassurance that they have purchased the correct brand and/or that purchase was a highly desirable act, as noted in dissonance theory.

Messages sympathetic to one's set of attitudes are learned more quickly than those that challenge it. Levine and Murphy [19, pp. 507–17] have demonstrated that in experiments involving two types of prose material, one consistent and the other inconsistent with the subject's own attitudes, it takes longer to learn the latter, and it is more rapidly forgotten. People seem consciously or subconsciously to screen out messages that would lead to the tensions of resolving internal doubts and conflicts. The more a given attitude is integrated into one's value system and self-perception, the more difficult it is for conflicting stimuli to penetrate his screening defenses.

If memory tests such as recall and recognition are used, different learning curves can be expected because of the variance in the memory capacities of individuals. Hovland, Janis, and Kelly [16] point out that personality traits will affect the learning response rate for particular types of appeals. They argue that personality factors influence an individual's susceptibility to persuasion or attitude change, and have devised and tested a series of propositions dealing primarily with personality factors related to intelligence, motivation, and emotion. If it is possible to break the target population into subgroups on the basis of these personality traits, it would be interesting to establish a weighted cumulative frequency distribution on the basis of each subgroup's estimated *susceptibility to persuasion* for the particular advertising message being considered.

It is difficult to generate meaningful empirical data on the relative effect of each repetition of the same advertisement. The situation is further complicated when more than one medium is used. Do exposures to the same message on television, radio, newspapers, or magazines have the same effect? If not, should exposures interact and affect the learning and forgetting rates? Subjective judgments are clearly required to assign appropriate weights, because of the *sparseness* of empirical research on the cumulative effectiveness of advertising.

CONCLUSIONS

A number of factors besides cost-per-thousand should be evaluated in selecting media schedules. Most of the recent media research has concentrated on the development of quantitative models to use in combining exposure data and subjective judgments. However, the quality of presently available data shows that it is doubtful if the decision maker has accurate or meaningful *measures* of the variables he wishes to consider in selecting media. Furthermore, there is a lack of empirical research upon which to postulate the functional relationships between variables. Sophisticated models are presently limited by their basic data.

Those interested in response functions need the same type of information in order to determine the probable shape of the response surface for a given set of circumstances. Once it is possible to generate the response surface that corresponds to a real world problem, the search techniques being developed could be applied to practical problems.

Finally, the day-to-day advertising media scheduler is attempting in some heuristic way to take into account the qualitative factors of media schedules that affect a target population's response to a particular advertising message.

For these three groups, it appears the most useful and significant research in the field of advertising media selection, at this time, will be to measure and define the interactions between the key variables.

REFERENCES

1. Henry Assael, John Kofron, and Walter Burgi, "Advertising Performance as a Function of Print Ad Characteristics," *Journal of Advertising Research*, 7 (June 1967), 20–6.

2. William Barclay, Richard Doub, and Lyron McMurtrey, "Recall of TV Commercials by Time and Program Slot," *Journal of Advertising Research*, 5 (June 1965), 41–7.

3. Simon Broadbent and Susanna Segnit, *Response Functions in Media Planning*, London: The London Press Exchange Ltd., 1967.

4. Dobbs I. Buchanan, "How Interest in the Product Affects Recall: Print Ads vs. Commercials," *Journal of Advertising Research*, 4 (March 1964), 9–15.

5. Robert D. Buzzell, Marshall Kolin, and Malcolm P. Murphy, "Television Commercial Test Scores and Short-Term Changes in Market Shares," *Journal of Marketing Research*, 2 (August 1965), 307–13.

6. Campbell-Ewald Company, *The Television Viewer-His Tastes, Interests, and Attitudes* Detroit: Campbell-Ewald Company, 1961.

7. R. C. Carpenter, "Response Functions-Problems and Limitations," *ADMAP*, 4 (March 1968), 136–43.

8. David E. Carter, "Newspaper Advertising Readership: Thick vs. Thin Issues," *Journal of Advertising Research*, 8 (September 1968), 39–41.

9. Lauren Crane, "How Product, Appeal, and Program Affect Attitudes Toward Commercials," *Journal of Advertising Research*, 4 (March 1964), 15–8.

10. J. E. Fothergill and A. S. C. Ehrenberg, "The Schwerin Analysis of Advertising Effectiveness," *Journal of Marketing Research*, 2 (August 1965), 298–306.

11. ———, "Concluding Comments on the Schwerin Analysis of Advertising Effectiveness," *Journal of Marketing Research*, 2 (November 1965), 413–4.

12. Ronald Frank and Paul Green, "Numerical Taxonomy in Marketing Analysis: A Review Article," *Journal of Marketing Research*, 5 (February 1968), 298–306.

13. Dennis H. Gensch, "Computer Models in Advertising Media Selection," *Journal of Marketing Research*, 5 (November 1968), 414–24.

14. Paul Green, Ronald Frank, and Patrick Robinson, "Cluster Analysis in Test Market Selection," *Management Science*, 13 (April 1967), 387–99.

15. Allan Greenberg and Norton Garfinkle, "Visual Material and Recall of Magazine Articles," *Journal of Advertising Research*, 3 (June 1963), 30–5.

16. C. I. Hovland, I. L. Janis, and H. H. Kelley, *Communication and Persuasion: Psychological Studies of Opinion Change*, New Haven: Yale University Press, 1953.

17. Herbert E. Krugman, "The Impact of Television Advertising: Learning Without Involvement," *Public Opinion Quarterly*, 29 (Fall 1965), 349–56.

18. Alec M. Lee and A. J. Burkart, "Some Optimization Problems in Advertising Media Planning," *Operational Research Quarterly*, 11 (September 1960), 113–22.

19. J. M. Levine and G. Murphy, "The Learning and Forgetting of Controversial Material," *Journal of Abnormal and Social Psychology*, 38 (October 1943), 507–17.

20. Darrell B. Lucas, "The ABC's of ARF's PARM," *Journal of Marketing*, 25 (July 1960), 9–20.

21. Marcel Marc, "Beware of the Pitfalls," *ADMAP*, 4 (March 1968), 126–34.

22. G. A. Miller and J. Selfridge, "Verbal Context and the Recall of Meaningful Material," *American Journal of Psychology*, 63 (April 1950), 176–85.

23. Motivation Analysis, Inc., *Mike & Mike—are not alike—Different!* New York: CBS Radio, Inc., 1957.

24. C. G. F. Nuttall, "TV Commercial Audiences in the United Kingdom," *Journal of Advertising Research*, 2 (September 1962), 19–28.

25. Alfred Politz Media Studies, *Ad Page Exposure in Four Magazines*, New York: The Reader's Digest Association, Inc. and The Curtis Publishing Company, 1960.

26. Schwerin Research Corporation, "Program-Commercial Compatibility," *Schwerin Research Corporation Bulletin*, 8 (August 1960), 1–6.

27. Daniel Starch, "How Thickness of Issue, Seasons, Affect Inquiries," *Media/Scope*, 3 (February 1959), 38.

28. G. A. Steiner, "The People Look at Commercials: A Study of Audience Behavior," *Journal of Business*, 39 (April 1966), 272–304.

29. J. Walter Thompson, "Report on Magazines as an Advertising Medium," *Advertising Age*, May 5, 1958, 1.

30. Verling Troldahl and Robert Jones, "Predictors of Newspaper Advertising Readership," *Journal of Advertising Research*, 5 (March 1965), 23–7.

31. William M. Weilbacher, "The Qualitative Values of Advertising Media," *Journal of Advertising Research*, 1 (December 1960), 12–7.

32. William D. Wells, "Recognition, Recall, and Rating Scales," *Journal of Advertising Research*, 4 (September 1964), 2–9.

33. "What is Best Size for a Magazine Ad?" *Media/Scope*, 9 (October 1965), 69.

34. "What is Best Size for a Newspaper Ad?" *Media/Scope*, 9 (July 1965), 48–9.

35. John J. Wheatley, "Influence of Commercial's Length and Position," *Journal of Marketing Research*, 5 (May 1968), 199–202.

36. Charles Winick, "Three Measures of the Advertising Value of Media Content," *Journal of Advertising Research*, 2 (June 1962), 28–33.

37. Hubert A. Zielske, "The Remembering and Forgetting of Advertising," *Journal of Marketing*, 23 (January 1959), 240.

R E A D I N G   4 4

MEDIA MANAGEMENT . . . CREATIVE CHALLENGE OF THE SEVENTIES*

Grey Matter

The accelerating changes which are revolutionizing so many aspects of contemporary life will have a more profound effect on *media strategy* than is realized by most marketers.

Media management must prepare for a generation

— which will increase real *per capita consumption* by almost two-fifths;

— in which the college-trained will become *half again more numerous*;

— the number of *young adults* will grow twice as fast as the total number of people;

— the suburbs will expand *twice as fast* as the urban centers;

— *leisure time* (which is already absorbing more dollars than national defense) will increase phenomenally.

How can media managers prepare to meet the needs of a society in which two-thirds will by 1980 be composed of people whose *formative years* were lived in the affluent postwar era?

Discovering and *evaluating* these trends is a pivotal problem for everyone concerned with planning the media mix which will create the most potent *buying impact* on the advertiser's potential customers.

*Reprinted by permission from *Grey Matter*, published by Grey Advertising, Inc., vol. 40, no. 12 (December 1969), pp. 1–4.

In these pages we offer a digest of a study of some trends which will shape media strategy in the seventies.

EDUCATION AND AFFLUENCE WILL AID MAGAZINES

— Magazines will reap the benefits of the growth of a better-educated and more affluent population.

— Mass books will change their editorial approach to the *why* of events, leaving newspapers, television and radio to the *what*.

— Class publications, particularly those with *special-interest editorial approaches,* will enjoy the greatest growth in the 70's.

— Increased availability of regional and market editions will lead to the use of these vehicles as *alternatives for traditional local media* such as spot television, newspapers, radio, etc.

— The trend in magazines will be toward *new ways* of using space and eventually even to product sampling.

CHANGES IN NIGHT NETWORK TELEVISION

— The seventies will see a greater degree of *sponsorship.*

— Development of *new program types* with special appeals: talk (i.e., Johnny Carson), informational, instructional, cultural.

— New *scheduling techniques* for repeats and originals.

— Advertising of *product categories* rather than specific brands will get more attention as ad costs increase.

— Exploration of new television *commercial lengths,* both longer and shorter.

— Expanded and continuing research on commercial *effectiveness.*

DAY NETWORK TELEVISION WILL BE MORE VULNERABLE

We expect day network to be more *vulnerable* due to:

— *Growth in number of working women* and lesser availability of daytime viewers, particularly among housewives with children 6–17.

— *Higher educational and economic levels* of viewers which may result in a daytime TV audience which is *no longer as responsive* to the same programming as heretofore.

PRESSURE ON SPOT TELEVISION

Spot television will be under *increased pressure* due to a greater amount of clutter resulting from use of the medium for retail and national advertising.
    Efforts will be made to overcome these pressures by:

— Use of local programming to *segment* target audiences.

— Commercials *customized* to local market needs.

— Use of *flights* to a greater extent rather than continuous advertising support.

— *More public programming* supporting needs of local markets.

NEWSPAPERS WILL HOLD THEIR OWN

— Through the use of increased availability of *color and special sections.*

— Because the trend in newspaper consolidation will continue, individual newspapers will be hard-pressed to fulfill *all* the retail needs of local advertisers. Therefore, national advertisers will be forced to use larger space *to fight for visibility.*

— Newspapers will make available suburban editions *locally-edited* to increase circulation in the fast-growing suburban areas and counteract strength of local weeklies.

— Newspapers will trend toward *network-type buys* with single order placement to encourage national usage. Nevertheless, we don't anticipate increased use of one-rate newspapers, such as that available now in Louisville.

RADIO WILL DIVERSIFY MORE

— However, continuing growth in station facilities will mean *dilution of audiences.*

— Diversity of listening choices will cater to growing trend toward listener *selectivity and segmentation.*

— Growing importance of FM stations, which offer more favorable environment for commercials and capture *significant share* of radio audience.

INFLUENCE OF TECHNOLOGICAL CHANGES

Technological changes now on drawing boards can drastically change many of today's media patterns. While technological advancements already visible, and some already available, may produce *major breakthroughs* in the next five years, we believe the possibilities are slight.

The history of color television and CATV, as well as the slow growth patterns of ownership of dishwashers and automatic clothes-dryers indicate that within the average home, *acceptance of technological change is slow,* even where income is available.

But the development of *completely new media* to replace or supplement commercial broadcast and print in the 1980's is a possibility.

One such medium marries two technical phenomena very much currently discussed: *Cable television* and *computers.*

The new medium looks like a cross between a television set and a typewriter. A centrally-located *computer* stores information designed to feed the new system from libraries, newspaper libraries, product information, late-breaking news stories, etc. The revolutionary quality of many technical possibilities is clear.

What will be the role of media and advertising when such new media become available? Only time and our ability to stay abreast of the trends will help us determine *how* advertisers will use them when they burst upon the scene.

WILL NEW MARKETS SPAWN MEDIA CHANGES?

There are many signs pointing in that direction.

Just one example:

The leisure market is the *fastest growing* in this country. It has already exceeded the amount of money this country spends for defense. It has so many aspects that it touches almost every sector of the business world.

Some segments of the leisure market (mobile homes, boats) are getting big enough to be *rich markets* in themselves.

The proliferation of *specialized media* reaching these markets is inevitable. Example: "Invitation to Snowmobiling" annual magazine launched recently.

IN SUMMARY

Demographic, economic, social, political and technological changes are bound to have far-reaching effects on advertising and marketing.

Of necessity, media planning and strategy will be deeply involved.

The role of the media executive is thus expanded. He must become more of an economist, a sociologist and a seer.

Creativity in media management . . . that's the challenging trend of tomorrow.

MARKETING IN SPECIAL FIELDS

During the seventies, the marketing of services will become more decisive. Gilbert Burch, writing in *Fortune,* argues that "the more time we save in making goods, the more time we spend providing services." The second selection is "A Product Life Cycle for International Trade" by Louis T. Wells, Jr. He concludes that an understanding of the international product life cycle may lead to improved policies resulting in increased exports and a reduction in the effectiveness of import competition.

READING 45

THERE'LL BE LESS LEISURE THAN YOU THINK*

Gilbert Burck

Nothing is easier to take for granted in the U.S. than long-term economic growth, and a good many people accordingly take it for granted. The prophets of Automatic Abundance assure us that the economy of the 1970's will grow as effortlessly as crabgrass in a lawn, that technology has solved the classic problem of scarce resources. The big tasks of the 1970's, the A.A.'s aver, will be to distribute production equitably, to improve the physical and spiritual quality of life, and to gain more leisure. They do not go so far as Marx, who predicted that "money-commodity" relationships would sooner or later be abolished—i.e., that things would become so abundant they would be handed out free, "to each according to his need." But many A.A.'s believe that the day is near when people will no longer be condemned to long hours on life's treadmills, and that ambitious labor leaders who are warbling about the four-day and even three-day week are only anticipating the inevitable.

Unfortunately, most of this is nonsense or illusion, or both. The word "affluent," so often used to describe the U.S., is both euphuistic and inaccurate. Granted that the American economy is an engine of production that seems bound to justify the optimistic projections of its expansion, the nation is still far from wealthy. Median family income is about $9,000. Although this represents high living indeed to a subject of the Soviet Union, it is not enough to buy an American family a decent living. As for the "redistribution" about which young revolutionaries talk darkly, it is nonsense double-distilled. If all personal income over $30,000 a year could be redistributed without paralyzing incentives, each family would enjoy only a few hundred dollars more a year. The unhappy fact is that not everybody can yet buy everything he needs, to say nothing of everything he wants. The U.S. is and will remain a "scarcity" economy—one that allocates its limited resources efficiently through the natural feedback system embodied in the profit motive and the market.

*Reprinted by permission from *Fortune,* March 1970, pp. 86–89, 162, 165–166.

Now that improving the quality of life has become national policy, productivity growth is all the more necessary. Controlling pollution, reviving mass transit, rebuilding cities, reducing crime, and providing ample medical care and education will put stupendous additional demands on the nation's resources. Only if our productivity, or output per man-hour, keeps rising at least as fast as it has been, can we do all that we want to do without sacrificing something desirable and important.

The catch is that large and rapid shifts in employment patterns may soon begin to depress the rate of productivity growth. Prices of services will rise inexorably, producing new inflationary stresses. Contrary to all the predictions that automation will throw millions out of work, the scarcest of all resources will be manpower. By 1980 the economy will be able to draw on some 200 billion man-hours a year, up from 165 billion today. But 200 billion man-hours will suffice only if they are employed with increasing efficiency. Meantime the prospect of greatly reducing the hours on life's treadmills remains mainly a prospect. For a long time we'll probably have to work as hard as ever.

AN APPETITE FOR TIME

The basic reason why carefree abundance and leisure are not likely to fall into our laps like ripe fruit may be put very simply. The more time we save in making goods, the more time we spend providing services. The nation's total output can be conveniently divided into the production of goods (manufacturing, mining, farming, and construction), the provision of services (government, trade, finance, and personal services), and "TUC" (transportation, utilities, and communications). During the past twenty years, output of goods has more than doubled, but productivity of the goods industries rose so much that the number of people producing the goods increased only from 28 to 29 million. In the same years the output of TUC much more than doubled, but the number of people rose only a few hundred thousand, to 4,500,000. But behold the services. The number of people providing them increased by no less than 70 percent, from 28 million to nearly 48 million. Thus the services have accounted for nearly all the increase in total employment since 1950.

The trend seems bound to continue. By 1980, when total U.S. output will have increased by at least two-thirds, employment will have increased by nearly 25 percent. The number of people employed in producing goods will very likely rise a couple of million, 6 percent or so above its present level, but it will then be only some 11 percent greater than in 1948. TUC employment will probably rise a few hundred thousand. So service jobs will again account for the overwhelming bulk of the increase in total employment. They will mount to around 65 million (more than 67 million including the armed forces), or about two-thirds of *all* jobs, and nearly as much as total employment in 1958. By 1990 the services may well account for more than 70 percent of all jobs. As if obeying a law of compensation that dooms men to eternal toil, the services are expanding enough to eat up not only the time that, so to speak, is saved in goods production, but also nearly all the time embodied in the yearly additions to the labor force.

The very nature of the services makes them greedy for time. Goods production depends on a wide variety of services—on trade to distribute products, research organizations to help innovate, legal and financial advice to help make policy, government surveys to help gauge markets. As these services become more complex, more and more of them are being supplied by outside specialists. The very efficiency of goods production, moreover, has played a big part in generating a need for government services such as education, highways, and pollution control.

Perhaps the most important reason services devour time so voraciously is that many of them—legal, financial, and medical advice, for example—depend on live performance and personal contact between buyer and seller. Most of the rest, including research, advertising, and management consulting, are valuable precisely to the extent that they embody a lot of specialized, time-consuming personal effort. Unlike power plants, factories, and refineries, which enormously increase their output per employee with expensive labor-saving capital equipment, most services cannot substitute capital for labor on a large scale.

Finally, service workers are probably less efficient than goods workers. According to Victor R. Fuchs of the National Bureau of Economic Research, who is the country's No. 1 expert on services, service workers put in fewer hours a week than goods workers and receive somewhat lower wages per hour. And their quality, measured by such things as level of schooling, has not been improving as much as that of goods workers.

A TASK FOR A FOOLHARDY CALCULATOR

As a result of all this, productivity in the services is increasing, on the average, no more than half as fast as in the rest of the economy. A year and a half ago, in "The Still-Bright Promise of Productivity" (October, 1968), FORTUNE estimated that the productivity of the *private* economy had been rising at a little better than 3 percent. The productivity of goods and TUC combined had been rising at around 4 percent, but the over-all average was brought down by the bare 2 percent for the services. Since then government agencies and others have made detailed projections of the economy for the decade of the Seventies. It now appears that the huge and continuous shift of employment to low-efficiency services will by 1980 result in a small but perceptible falling off in the growth rate of productivity in the private economy. Everything else being equal, that growth rate will decline from more than 3 percent to 2.8 percent; the difference is equal to some $40 billion worth of output a year (at today's prices).

Those official figures, moreover, grossly overestimate productivity growth because they omit government employment from the total. It is a standard assumption that government activity cannot be measured because it lacks a marketable output. But the time has come to reckon with government productivity, if not to try to measure it. For government jobs in 1968 amounted to 12 million or 15 percent of all employment (including the armed forces, more than 15 million and 18 percent), and may climb above 20 percent by 1980.

Nearly 70 percent of the federal government's three million employees work in the Defense Department or the Post Office, and it would be a fool-hardy calculator indeed who would essay to demonstrate that these employees are improving their output by anything at all. As for the other federal employees, they are probably doing only a little better. But state and local governments now employ 9,400,000, or more than three times as many as the federal government. Nearly five million of these 9,400,000 are educators of one kind or another; their number, up from about 1,500,000 in 1947, has increased ten times as fast as the population and three times as fast as the number of pupils and students. Measured quantitatively, productivity of education has obviously declined. Since there are now on the average a good many fewer students per teacher, the quality of education may be rising. But if so, few experts are yet prepared to argue that it has. And a long time may elapse before any noticeable improvement will be discernible.

THE HANDSOME-PSYCHOANALYST EFFECT

Taking one opinion with another, it appears that the productivity of government as a whole is rising by no more than 1 percent a year, and probably less. If total employment is redefined to include government jobs, and if the productivity of these jobs is rising all of 1 percent a year, national productivity is increasing not by 3 percent or more but by only 2.7 percent a year, and by 1980 it will be increasing at only 2.5 percent. Merely revising the figures, of course, will not change projections for the private economy, but revising the figures to include government is realistic and salutary. It verifies statistically the extent to which low-productivity service employment is eating up more and more of total working time. And it also tells us we are deluding ourselves when we suppose the economy is growing as fast as the figures say it is.

Quite possibly, the government is overestimating the real value of some service production. Statisticians in the Labor and Commerce departments measure the production of an industry in terms of its contribution to gross national product, or the value of its production minus the value of materials and services it buys from others. Then they divide the industry's contribution to G.N.P. by the man-hours consumed by the industry, and so arrive at its output per man-hour. Because the official man-hour figures are accurate and production figures are carefully adjusted for rising prices, changes in output per man-hour probably show up pretty accurately in the statistics.

But estimates of service *production* are often tautological. The contributions of medical and business services to G.N.P., for example, are derived from income figures. This means that a handsome dog of a psychoanalyst, specializing in wealthy matrons whose chief ailment is that they have nothing worthwhile to do, may contribute ten times as much to G.N.P. as a hard-working psychologist in a clinic. Or a brilliant management consultant with the bearing of a Churchill may set his tariffs twice as high as an equally brilliant consultant with a stutter. If both men are increasing their productivity at the same rate, then the former is contributing, on paper, more to the economy's growth than the latter. A man or company in what is in effect a monopoly position, in other words, can produce less and yet contribute more to G.N.P. and national growth than a man or company competing in the market.

Even if the productivity of services is rising at 2 percent a year—an exceedingly generous estimate—the time appropriated by them is increasing, and will continue to increase, at a very rapid rate. Since time is money, services obviously cost more and more. What may not be immediately obvious is that their costs and prices must rise even faster than those of goods. For wages in service industries are going up at least as fast as in goods industries. As a matter of fact, organized teachers and hospital employees, despite their slight or nonexistent gains in productivity, have made up for previously depressed rates by negotiating even bigger percentage increases than employees in goods industries. Low-efficiency service industries thus find themselves burdened with permanently rising costs. Unlike industries wherein productivity is increasing briskly, they cannot offset rising pay per worker with rising output per worker. Because service industries account for more than half the U.S. employment and must pass on all or most cost increases as price increases, their inferior productivity performance is one of the nation's prime inflationary forces.

A KIND OF MONOPOLY POSITION

When the cost of anything rises inordinately and disproportionately, the demand for it tends to soften or decline. But as measured by the Department of Commerce, output of services (and demand for them) is rising at least as fast as output of goods. If services are growing so infernally expensive, why is the country buying more and more of them? The obvious answer is that it needs or wants them badly enough to pay the price. As the economists put it, the demand for them is price-inelastic.

The prices paid for services are also inelastic: when they move, they usually move upward. One reason is that services are not very competitive. To a considerable extent, it is true, services are provided by small owner-managed firms with little market power. But about a third of service employment is accounted for by government and private nonprofit organizations. All told, producers accounting for more than half of total service employment enjoy some kind of monopoly position that encourages them to increase their output but does not pressure them to improve their efficiency. Thus they tend to expand existing services or introduce new ones—as the federal government does when it enlarges a bureau or establishes a new one. Or they try to improve the quality of their output—as departments of education do when they raise the ratio of teachers to pupils. Sometimes the result is better output, sometimes not; often there is no way of telling. When a producer or supplier improves "quality" in this special economic sense, quality means more *input* per unit of output; it does not, alas, necessarily mean better output.

Even competitive services are obliged to improve quality at the cost of higher prices. Motels that used to offer bare lodging, for example, can now meet the competition only by providing wall-to-wall carpeting, color TV, and swimming pools. In one way or another, most services seem driven to expand their output more than twice as fast as their productivity, and thus to keep enlarging their payrolls, their costs, and their prices.

Manufacturing industries provide an edifying contrast. Most manufactured goods are produced by large corporations that are supposed to wield a lot of market power. All would certainly like to get more for their production. Failing that, they would like to justify higher prices by improving the quality of their goods. Auto manufacturers, for example, would love to put so much car into each car that the cheapest models would fetch $3,000. But for all their legendary market power, the auto makers keep getting hauled up by competitors both at home and abroad. So with appliance makers, food processors, and on down the long list of manufacturing industries. Unlike so many suppliers of services, they add relatively few people to their payrolls even while tripling and quadrupling their production.

THE GOVERNMENT AS MONOPOLIST

All the negative characteristics of most services—low productivity growth, rising comparative costs, lack of market discipline, limited consumer sovereignty, and a pervasive compulsion to expand—are combined in government. In a general way, people demand schools, highways, hospitals, adequate armed forces and police, medical care, and so on. But the size and disposition of government programs have only the most tenuous connections with consumer demand properly describable as such. The consumer's sovereignty over government spending, never very strong, seems to be growing weaker as government spending mounts. As a supplier of services, the government finds itself in the role of a monopolist aiming to meet demand and improve quality without worrying much about costs. Even if government chooses the right services for the public, its immunity to anything resembling market discipline ensures that they will be costly. And no sector of the economy is growing so fast as government. In 1948 federal, state, and local governments employed nearly 5,700,000. The figure more than doubled by 1968 and may exceed 20 million by 1980.

About 50 percent of all civilian government employment is accounted for by education, which provides a splendid example of how increased quantity and quality will use up more time. Although education's share of employment may decline a trifle by 1980, the number of people on education payrolls will probably rise from nearly 5 million in 1968 to 7,500,000 in 1980. Enrollment in public elementary and secondary schools, reflecting slower growth in the numbers of school-age children, will increase only 1.2 percent a year between now and 1980. But this low rate will be more than offset by enrollment in higher education, which will increase enormously. The emphasis, moreover, will be on quality. For the ratio of students to teachers will decline, bigger and presumably better schools will be built, and new programs will be inaugurated for disadvantaged youths. The National Planning Association has estimated that 58 cents of every additional dollar spent on education between 1968 and 1980 will represent quality improvement.

In a way not generally understood, the low productivity of government services imposes a heavy burden on the cities. Professor William Baumol of Princeton, writing in *The American Economic Review*, has described the basic problem of the cities as one of supplying services in which productivity is rising very little if at all and whose costs are therefore rising cumulatively and endlessly: police, schools, social services, hospitals, subways, and buses. Most also suffer from what might be called the Quill-Guinan effect. Both the late Mike Quill and Matthew Guinan, past and present presidents of New York City's Transport Workers Union, pursued a policy of demanding work-rule concessions calculated to reduce productivity. At the same time they demanded wage increases that raised transit labor costs at least as fast as manufacturing labor costs. Faced with a similar situation, U.S. railroads and steamship lines got out, or want to get out, of the passenger business. The cities cannot get out of passenger transportation, and hardly anything else. Inexorably and cumulatively, inflation or not, municipal budgets will therefore mount. Aside from standing up to the unions, there is only one way out. Since raising property-tax rates will quickly produce negative returns as taxpayers leave the cities, Baumol argued, the federal government must supply the resources to prevent the crisis.

Probably the most flagrant example of how a nongovernment service can waste time and money is provided by medical and health services. Here employment more than doubled between 1950 and 1967, jumping from 1,400,000 to 3,500,000, and by 1980 will probably increase another two-thirds, or to 5,300,000. Outlays for medical care in current dollars rose from $10 billion in 1947 to $63 billion in 1969 (in constant 1969 dollars, from $24 billion to nearly $63 billion). By 1980 this spending may well rise to $200 billion. Statistical and conceptual difficulties have prevented satisfactory measurement of the output and productivity of the medical-care industry. But Victor Fuchs of the National Bureau of Economic Research has interpreted official industry figures on expenditures, price, and employment to show that real output per man declined between 1947 and 1956, and racked up only a slight gain between 1956 and 1965.

Quality improvements, moreover, have often increased the amount of time it takes medical personnel to do a given job. These days the average doctor is equipped with myriad devices to increase his proficiency and productivity, but precisely because he has so many gadgets and techniques on tap, he takes longer to perform a thorough physical examination than he ever did. "The modern patient usually wants proof from some expensive machine that he's O.K.," says Dr. John Knowles, director of Massachusetts General Hospital. "That takes time and money."

FIREWORKS IN FIRE

Because many of the services that could behave like competitors have neglected to do so, the Antitrust Division of the Department of Justice is beginning to move in on them. There has been much more inflation in personal services than in commodity prices, and a major cause of this inflation, says Richard W. McLaren, head of Antitrust, is price fixing in the services. Some of the cases doubtless will be found in what the Department of Commerce calls "miscellaneous business services," a swiftly growing group that includes business consultants, advertising agencies, janitorial services, and research and testing laboratories. All provide services that business needs and obviously is willing to pay well for. Except perhaps for advertising agencies, they do not have to compete very strenuously; and in any event their fees—and accordingly their measured output and contribution to G.N.P.—keep rising inordinately.

Other targets for Antitrust are "educational services" and "nonprofit organizations." The former category includes commercial and trade schools, libraries, and establishments offering academic and technical courses, nearly all of them nonprofit. They employed fewer than 700,000 in 1958, but will probably employ more than two million by 1980. Nonprofit "membership" organizations, such as trade associations, labor unions, and charitable and religious organizations, now provide about 1,600,000 jobs, and will provide perhaps two million by 1980.

Finally, Antitrust appears ready to set off some fireworks in the service category sometimes labeled F.I.R.E. (finance, insurance, and real estate), whose total employment rose from slightly more than two million in 1948 to 3,700,000 in 1968, and will probably top 4,600,000 in 1980. Early this year Antitrust fired a preliminary salvo against a Maryland association of real-estate brokers, charging it with setting minimum commissions on the sale of real estate and denying listing privileges to noncooperating brokers.

THE ELUSIVE LUXURIES

Some personal services are trying to survive with few forces, natural or artificial, working for them. They are the products, so to speak, of theatres, concert halls, opera houses, bars, restaurants, bespoke tailoring shops, barbershops, ateliers of various kinds, and hotels and lodgings. Their labor costs are rising as fast as other industries' labor costs, they benefit from no appreciable productivity increase, and most get no subsidy, at least not yet. Some do possess monopoly power; after all, a recital hall featuring Artur Rubinstein is selling a unique product for which it can theoretically charge all the traffic will bear. But monopoly power or not, all these personal services face cumulative higher costs and the necessity of charging endlessly higher prices.

Suppose, for example, that wages henceforth go up at only 4 percent a year. Rising productivity would enable manufacturers, utilities, and communication companies to absorb all or most of the increase, and the general price level would probably rise less than 2 percent a year. But those forlorn low-efficiency personal services will just have to charge more and more. In ten years their tariffs will be up 50 to 75 percent. The chateaubriand that is a bargain today at $7 will set the *feinschmecker* back $12 or $13; the $250 tailor-made suit will fetch $450, the $8 symphony orchestra ticket $13 or more, and the $7 theatre ticket $12.

As it has in the past, this kind of escalation will be hard on, and baffling to, young executives and others who look forward to salary increases more than large enough to offset inflation. Suppose inflation settles down at the rate of 2 percent a year, and that a bright young executive gets raises averaging 4 percent a year after taxes. This is a high figure; according to a study by Professor Wilbur G. Lewellen for the National Bureau of Economic Research, recent executive pay gains have averaged only 3 percent after taxes. Such an incentive nevertheless drives the young executive to work hard and long and to use his brain power effectively. It also leads him to hope he can enjoy now and then a few more of the luxuries that other lucky people enjoy. To his dismay, he finds that their prices move up just about as fast as his ability to buy them. As a matter of fact, other demands on his salary, such as the expense of rearing children who consume a lot of low-efficiency services like schooling, may put these luxuries further than ever beyond his everyday reach.

THE HIGH COST OF DISTRIBUTION

Some services are not sheltered from market discipline, and the outstanding example is wholesale and retail trade, which in 1968 provided no fewer than 16,700,000 jobs, or 35 percent of all service employment. Here competition has forced employers to find ways of improving their productivity, and they have come up with advances such as computerized warehousing and inventory controls, new accounting methods, and self-service. Wholesaling accordingly has achieved some impressive productivity increases, and to a lesser extent so has retailing. A lot of the chain stores' success in reducing the cost of retailing, however, is the result not so much of real productivity increases as of making the manufacturer and the consumer perform services formerly performed by the storekeeper. The manufacturer prepackages, prelabels, and presells. The consumer does his own selection, delivery, and financing (i.e., he often pays a charge for credit).

There is little likelihood that large capital investments can pay off in improving the productivity of retail trade. It seems forever burdened with the rising cost of personal contacts. Unless some wholly new impersonal technique of distribution is invented, the cost of distributing goods is bound to keep on mounting faster than the cost of making them. Mail order is no alternative, for it uses enormous amounts of labor and so costs even more than store sales. Appropriately enough, therefore, employment in trade is rising considerably faster than employment in manufacturing. In 1948 trade employed 12 million people, 70 percent as many as manufacturing; by 1980 it will employ nearly 21 million, nearly as many as manufacturing. And by 1990 trade may employ more than manufacturing. Distribution accordingly will become more expensive, and offset to some extent the high productivity growth and lower cost of making goods.

BUT COMES THE REVOLUTION

The only way to counter the tendency of services to gorge themselves on time is to see that productivity in both goods and services grows as fast as the optimistic projections assume it will grow. This is easier said than done. You cannot cheerlead people into improving their efficiency. You can cheerlead them into being saved, or into joining a revolution to end poverty, or to put the "people" in charge of things. But once you've got your revolution, as all Communist regimes have discovered, the only way you can begin to tackle poverty is to shun cheerleading and set up a profit-and-loss system that rewards producers who use resources efficiently and penalizes those who do not.

The problem in the U.S. is to provide the equivalent of market incentives where markets are weak or nonexistent. One of the biggest opportunities for improving output per man-hour lies in raising productivity in government. As every schoolboy should know, government cannot deliver goods and services efficiently. It habitually sets up self-perpetuating bureaucracies that put statistical output ahead of everything else. Since government has no incentive to use resources efficiently, it doesn't do so.

Happily, a growing number of experts are exploring means of raising government efficiency. Professor John W. Kendrick of George Washington University, a leading authority on productivity trends and a long-time advocate of measuring and increasing government productivity, believes that pressures for improving it can be built into public administration; and he estimates that its productivity can be improved significantly. Others would turn government bureaus over to private business, putting them up for competitive bidding. In his recent book, *The Age of Discontinuity*, which was required reading in high Administration circles, Peter Drucker argues for what he calls the reprivatization of government, or farming out its routine functions to outside organizations, such as foundations and corporations. Drucker would establish a government agency something like the Bureau of the Budget, and would charge it with setting objectives, choosing means, and redefining tasks.

BUILT-IN HANDICAPS

Maintaining the high rate of productivity growth in TUC and the goods industries is of prime importance. Only if these industries can maintain or come reasonably close to maintaining their recent average of 4 percent will there be enough manpower to keep real disposable income rising and at the same time power all the programs for improving the quality of U.S. life. It is a common assumption that a sufficient addition of capital, new technology, and better educated employees will automatically raise the productivity of the goods industries. This assumption is valid in mining, TUC, construction, and some manufacturing. Modern and efficient power plants operated by a few highly skilled workers almost automatically raise utility output per man-hour. Bigger volume and enormous drafts of capital do the same for communications. Better equipment, combined with plenty of competition, keeps up efficiency in freight transportation.

But other auguries are not quite so bright. Farming automatically expanded its productivity as marginal farmers left the land, but by 1980 agricultural employment will be down to about three million, close to an irreducible minimum, and any improvement in productivity there will release very few people for other activities. Mining too is close to rock bottom; by 1980 the whole sector will employ only 580,000. Manufacturing, on the whole, still looks promising. The productivity of some manufacturing industries, such as petroleum refining, responds handsomely to capital and technology. And in most of them—machinery, food, apparel, chemicals, metals, motor vehicles, and so on—measured productivity is linked to performance in the market. Even when the market is very imperfect, the goal of profitability abets the efficiency with which they combine resources. But manufacturing statistics turn up one trend that could handicap productivity growth: the number of employees producing what are essentially services has been steadily increasing, and now probably accounts for more than a third of the manufacturing labor force.

The goods industries, on the face of it, will probably have a harder time maintaining their productivity growth than they have had. Thus the job of raising living standards and improving greatly the quality of American life will not be as easy as many think. Even if the performance of the services gets better, the prospects for reducing the hours on life's treadmills very much will keep receding into the future.

READING 46

A PRODUCT LIFE CYCLE FOR INTERNATIONAL TRADE?*

Louis T. Wells, Jr.

The lowering of barriers to international trade has resulted in many opportunities for American companies to profit from exports. Clearly, the businessman needs ways of analyzing the potential exportability of his products and, equally important, tools for predicting which products are likely to be threatened by import competition.

Until recently, the manager was dependent on the explanations of trade offered by the classical and neo-classical economists. Their reasoning generally led to the conclusion that each country will concentrate on exporting those products which make the most use of the country's abundant production factors. The economic theory is elegant—it can be stated mathematically or geometrically and it can be manipulated to yield, under certain assumptions, answers to questions such as what is the value of free trade to a country, or what are the costs and benefits of certain restrictions. So long as the problems posed are of a very broad nature, the theory provides a useful way of analyzing them. However, when the theory is applied to the detailed problems facing the businessman it becomes of limited value.

THE TRADE CYCLE MODEL

A new approach to international trade which appears most promising in aiding the business executive is closely related to the product life cycle

*Reprinted from *The Journal of Marketing,* published by the American Marketing Association, vol. 32, no. 3 (July 1968), pp. 1–6.

concept in marketing. The model claims that many products go through a trade cycle,[1] during which the United States is initially an exporter, then loses its export markets and may finally become an importer of the product. Empirical studies of trade in synthetic materials,[2] electronic products,[3] office machinery,[4] consumer durables,[5] and motion pictures[6] have demonstrated that these products follow a cycle of international trade similar to the one which the model describes.

According to the trade cycle concept, many products follow a pattern which could be divided into four stages:

Phase I: *U.S. export strength*
Phase II: *Foreign production starts*
Phase III: *Foreign production competitive in export markets*
Phase IV: *Import competition begins*

A brief look at the reasoning underlying each of these stages will give some clues which will help the businessman to identify the stage in which particular products may be. The concept can then be an aid in predicting the product trade performance to come and in understanding what actions the manager can take to modify the pattern for certain products and to profit from different stages of the cycle.

Phase I: U.S. export strength

What kinds of new products are likely to be introduced first in the United States? It can be assumed that American entrepreneurs have no particular monopoly on scientific know-how or on very basic technical ability. What they do have, however, is a great deal of knowledge about a very special market—one which is unique in having a large body of very high-income consumers. Products which satisfy the special demands of these customers are especially likely to be introduced in the United States. Moreover, due to a monopoly position of the United States as a supplier of the new products which satisfy these unique demands, they offer the best opportunities for export.

Empirical studies have failed to show a very simple relationship between demand and invention. However, there can be little doubt that certain products are simply more likely to be developed in America. Automatic transmissions for automobiles promised to be pretty expensive additions

---

[1]For a more complete theoretical support of a similar model, see Raymond Vernon, "International Investment and International Trade in the Product Cycle," *Quarterly Journal of Economics,* Vol. LXXX (May, 1966), pp. 190–207.
[2]Gary C. Hufbauer, *Synthetic Materials and the Theory of International Trade* (Cambridge: Harvard University Press, 1966).
[3]Seev Hirsch, *Location of Industry and International Competitiveness* (Oxford: Clarendon Press, 1967).
[4]U.S. Senate, Interstate and Foreign Commerce Committee, *Hearings on Foreign Commerce,* 1960, pp. 130–139.
[5]Louis T. Wells, Jr., *Product Innovation and Directions of International Trade,* unpublished doctoral thesis (Harvard Business School, 1966).
[6]Gorden K. Douglass, *Product Variation and Trade in Motion Pictures,* unpublished doctoral thesis (Department of Economics, Massachusetts Institute of Technology, 1963).

to cars. If an inventor considers the chances of his brain-child's being purchased by consumers, a U.S. inventor would be more likely to pursue an automatic transmission than a European. The European inventor would more probably concern himself with ideas suitable to European demands. He might respond to high fuel taxes and taxes on engine displacement by developing engines which produce more horsepower per cubic inch. He might develop better handling suspensions in response to the road conditions. An inventor usually comes up with products suitable to his own market. It is even more likely that the final product development leading to commercial production will be achieved by an entrepreneur responding to his own national demand.

Even if an American is most likely to be the first to produce a high-income product, why does he not set up his first plant abroad where labor is cheaper? Certainly for many products the cost of materials and of capital is not sufficiently higher in Europe to offset the advantages offered by cheaper labor. Moreover, the burden of tariffs and freight are light enough now for many items. And the uncertainties of manufacture abroad are diminishing as more American companies gain experience. There are, though, very rational reasons why the American entrepreneur might prefer to start manufacture at home.

At the early stages of a product's life, design is often in a constant state of flux. There is a real advantage which accrues to a manufacturer who is close to the market for his products so that he can rapidly translate demands for design changes into more suitable products. Moreover, these changes often require the availability of close communication with specialized suppliers. Hence, the instability of product design for new products argues for a location in the United States—near to the market and close to a wide range of specialized suppliers.[7] The entrepreneur is less likely to be concerned with small cost differences for very new products. The existence of a monopoly or the significant product differentiation at the early stage of the product life cycle reduces the importance of costs to the manufacturer. The multitude of designs and the lack of standard performance specifications make it very difficult for the consumer to compare prices. Also, in the early stage of the product life cycle the consumer is frequently not very concerned with price. Success comes to the manufacturer who can quickly adjust both his product design and marketing strategy to consumers' needs which are just beginning to be well identified.

At this point, the American manufacturers have a virtual monopoly for the new product in the world market. Foreigners who want the good must order it from the United States. In fact, wealthy consumers abroad, foreigners with particular needs for the product, and Americans living abroad seem to hear about it very quickly. Unsolicited orders begin to appear from overseas. U.S. exports start to grow—initially from the trickle created by these early orders—to a steady stream as active export programs are established in the American firms.

[7]Same reference as footnote 3.

Phase II: foreign production starts

Incomes and product familarity abroad increase, causing overseas markets eventually to become large enough that the product which once appealed primarily to the U.S. consumer has a broad appeal in the wealthier foreign countries. Not only does a potential foreign producer now have a market close-at-hand, but some of his costs will be lower than those of the U.S. producer. Imports from America have to bear duty and overseas freight charges—costs which local products will not carry. Moreover, the potential foreign producer may have to invest less in product development—the U.S. manufacturer has done part of this for him. Some measure of the size of his potential market has been demonstrated by the successful sale of imports. Favorable profit projections based on a demonstrated market and an ability to underprice imports will eventually induce an entrepreneur in a wealthy foreign market—usually first in Western Europe—to take the plunge and start serious manufacture. Of course, this manufacturer will, in some cases, be an American subsidiary which starts production abroad, realizing that if it does not, some other company will.

However, the calculations that yield favorable costs projections for competition with imports from the United States in the foreign producer's home market do not necessarily lead to the conclusion that the foreign producer will be a successful competitor in third markets. For many modern manufactured goods he is likely to be at a serious disadvantage due to the small size of his plant in a market where he also must bear the burdens of freight and tariffs. Scale-economies are so important for many products that the U.S. manufacturer, with his large plants supplying the American market, can still produce more cheaply than the early foreign producers who must manufacture on a significantly smaller scale.

During this second stage American exports still supply most of the world's markets. However, as foreign producers begin to manufacture, U.S. exports to certain markets will decline. The pattern will probably be a slowdown in the rate of growth of U.S. exports. The slowdown in the rate of growth of exports of home dishwashers in the last few years as European manufacturers have begun production provides an example of a product in this phase of the cycle.

Phase III: foreign production competitive in export markets

As the early foreign manufacturers become larger and more experienced their costs should fall. They will begin to reap the advantages of scale economies previously available only to U.S. manufacturers. But, in addition, they will often have lower labor bills. Hence, their costs may be such that foreign products become competitive with American goods in third markets where goods from both countries have to carry similar freight and duty charges.

During this stage, U.S. producers will be protected from imports in their domestic market where they are not faced with duty and overseas transportation costs. However, foreign goods will gradually take over the markets abroad which were previously held by American exports. The rate of growth of

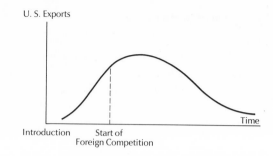

Figure 1
Export Cycle

U.S. exports will continue to decline. The success of European ranges and refrigerators in Latin America points out that these products are in this phase.

Phase IV: import competition begins

As the foreign manufacturer reaches mass production based on his home and export markets, his lower labor rates and perhaps newer plant may enable him to produce at lower costs than an American manufacturer. His cost savings may be sufficient that he can pay ocean freight and American duty and still compete with the American in his own market. This stage will be reached earlier if the foreign producer begins to think in terms of marginal costs for export pricing. If he believes that he can sell above full costs in his home market and "dump" abroad to use up his excess capacity, he may very quickly undercut the U.S. producers pricing on full costs.

During this final stage, U.S. exports will be reduced to a trickle, supplying very special customers abroad, while import competition may become severe. The bicycle is a product which has been in this phase for some time.

The cycle

Thus the cycle is complete—from the United States as a strong exporter to the stage where imports may capture a significant share of the American market. Figure 1 shows schematically the U.S. export performance for an hypothetical product.

The early foreign producers—usually Western Europeans—will face a cycle similar to that of the U.S. manufacturer. As still lower-income markets become large enough, producers in these countries will eventually become competitive—displacing the dominance of the early foreign manufacturers. The manufacture of products moves from country to country in what one author has called a "pecking order."[8]

So far, there are only relatively few examples of the less-developed countries' becoming exporters of manufactured goods. The classic example is standardized textiles. Another interesting example is the export of certain

---

[8]Same reference as footnote 2.

standardized computer components from Argentina. However, the current growth rate of over 12% per year for exports of manufacturers from less-developed countries may indicate that they will soon become an important factor for the American businessman.

HOW DIFFERENT PRODUCTS BEHAVE

Obviously, the export patterns are not identical for all products. Three variables were critical to the argument supporting the trade cycle concept: the uniqueness of the appeal of the product to the U.S. market, the reduction in unit costs as the scale of production increases, and the costs of tariffs and freight. Differences in these variables will be very important in determining how a particular product behaves as an export or import—and thus what the profit opportunities or threats will be.

High-income products

The advantage of the United States in export markets in certain products was said to be dependent on the uniqueness of the appeal of the product to the American consumer. The cycle would be more "stretched out" if this demand is particularly unique. For such products, the U.S. manufacturer will probably remain an exporter for a longer period of time and can postpone his fears of import competition.

It is possible to categorize some products for which the U.S. demand is "unique":

Luxury Function: Certainly products which perform functions people are willing to do without until they are comparatively wealthy have a particularly large demand in the United States. Movie cameras and room air-conditioners come immediately to mind. In fact, a classification of

Table 1

Ratio of value of 1962–1963 exports to value of 1952–1953 exports

Necessity		Discretionary		Luxury	
Refrigerators	0.47	Automobiles	0.99	Movie Cameras	4.14
Ranges	0.87	Electric Clocks	1.04	Freezers	0.74
Radios	1.42	Still Cameras	4.66	Air Conditioners	3.59
Irons	1.56	Washers	1.35	Slide Projectors	4.66
Televisions	1.04	Vacuum Cleaners	1.78	Dishwashers	8.50
		Mixers	1.25	Outboard Motors	4.18
		Record Players	1.81	Recreational Boats	4.40
Average	1.07		1.84		4.32

$F = 7.0$ (Significant at 0.95 level)

Note: Adjustments for freezer exports to Canada and 1963 still camera exports raise significance to 0.99 level. Same reference as footnote 5.
Source: Classification of products from James Gately, Stephen Gudeman, and George Moseley, "Take-Off Phenomenon," unpublished paper submitted to Consumer Behavior Research Seminar (Harvard Business School, May 27, 1965). Export data from U.S. Department of Commerce, Bureau of the Census, FT 410 Reports.

consumer durables into luxury, discretionary, and necessity shows a remarkable correlation with the U.S. export performance of the products. Exports increased 330% over a ten-year period for the luxury products, compared to an almost 84% increase for the discretionary items and only a 7% increase for the necessity products. (See Table 1.)

Expensive to Buy: Products that cost significantly more than other products which perform similar functions appeal primarily to a high-income market. Electric knife sharpeners are an example of this type of product. A study by Time Marketing Service[9] showed that 21.5% of households with incomes of over $10,000 (where the heads were white collar, college educated) owned electric knife sharpeners. In contrast, only 11.6% with incomes under $10,000 owned them.

Expensive to Own: Similarly, products that are expensive to maintain or to operate compared to alternative products which perform similar functions are uniquely suited to a high-income market. The American automobile provides an example. The disadvantage of its high fuel consumption more than offsets the advantages of more space and higher horsepower for most low-income foreign consumers.

Labor Saving: Products which save labor by substituting a relatively large amount of capital are particularly appealing to the American market. The high cost of labor, a function of high American incomes, makes it very attractive to buy items such as heavy road building equipment and computers which substitute capital for labor.

Of course, the businessman can influence the appeal of his products through his product policy. For example, he can build larger or smaller cars, automatic record players or simple ones.

Scale economies

The trade cycle is also influenced by the amount of savings in cost, which can be achieved by increasing the scale of production. If a small plant is equally as efficient as a large one for a given product, a foreign producer will start to manufacture while his market is still relatively small. U.S. exports will not be as successful, and import competition will probably soon begin.

The effect of scale economies is well illustrated by the cases where a product goes through several stages of manufacture. In refrigerator production, for example, low costs can be reached in assembly operations at a much lower volume than in the manufacture of compressors. This difference shows up in the performance of U.S. exports for one period where exports of completed refrigerators fell drastically, but exports of compressors for inclusion in refrigerators assembled abroad held their own.

Tariffs and freight

If tariffs or other trade barriers overseas are high for a particular product, foreign production is encouraged. Hence U.S. exports will receive early

[9]Time Marketing Services, *Selective Mass Markets for Products and Services,* Time Marketing Information, Report No. 1305.

competition from foreign production. Developing countries have frequently raised tariffs to encourage local production while their markets are still small. However, if the American tariff is high, it follows that the United States manufacturers need worry less about import competition.

High freight costs, usually for products which are heavy or bulky compared to their value, tend to discourage trade. Not only will foreign production occur earlier, but foreign competition is unlikely to become a serious threat in the U.S. market. In the extreme cases of very high transportation costs, trade never occurs, or occurs almost entirely along borders where a foreign source is closer than a domestic one. For example, trade in gravel has never been significant because of transportation costs.

Exceptions to the cycle

Not all products can be expected to follow the cyclical pattern described. The model says little about products which do not have a particularly strong demand in the United States. In addition, for some products the location of manufacture is tied to some particular natural resource—agricultural, to certain types of land; mining and initial processing, to areas containing the mineral. The manufacturing processes for some products such as the traditional handicraft goods have only slightly increasing returns to scale. Moreover, some products appear to remain sufficiently differentiated so that price discrepancies play only a slight role. For example, American cigarettes have continued to command a price-premium in Europe.

There are also manufactured goods for which even the U.S. market is not large enough to allow significant scale economies. Such products tend to be produced in various locations close to market clusters, and no one area achieves a large cost advantage. Trade tends to be more on the basis of product differentiation or specialization. However, as demand in the United States grows, a standard version may be produced in quantity, bringing the cost down so that the product moves into the cycle under discussion.

High-performance sports cars and sail boats may be examples of this type product. Until recently, much of the production for such sports cars was located in various areas of Europe and was based on small production quantities. Recently both of these products have seen some large-scale manufacture in the U.S. and significant cost-reductions. General Motors led the way with mass manufacture of the Corvette. More American manufacturers will probably enter the high-performance sports car market and compete with the virtually hand-produced, expensive European sports cars.

THE TRADE CYCLE AND BUSINESS PLANNING

Obviously, no simple model can explain the behavior of all products in international trade. However, the trade cycle model does appear to be useful for understanding trade patterns in a wide range of manufactured goods. Although no such model should be used by the businessman without a careful examination of individual products, it does provide some very useful hints as to which products might be exportable and which might suffer import competition. The concept can give some clues as to the success of various product policies.

Market segmentation

The model provides some insights into the role which market segmentation can play in increasing exports and protecting against imports. Design modifications can be made for certain products which can change the appeal of the product to different kinds of customers and thus modify the trade cycle. In fact, the manufacturer often makes such changes for reasons unrelated to international trade but rather as a response to changes in the nature of his home market. As the American consumer becomes wealthier and more sophisticated, and as domestic competition becomes more severe, the manufacturer often makes his products more automatic, more powerful, more luxurious. The marketer may be trying to differentiate his product from those of his competitor, or he may simply be responding to the demands of a wealthier consumer. These changes may make the product more suited to the growing incomes of the American customer, but they will also affect its exportability. The item may become too expensive for the majority of foreign consumers, hastening competition from foreign-produced goods.

This gradual product sophistication may, however, provide some protection against imports in the United States. No doubt, the size and automatic features of the American automobile have had a special appeal to the high-income American market and have consequently held back the flow of imports. The product design has, however, had another effect: simpler, cheaper foreign cars have been able to capture a part of the U.S. market more concerned with economy of operation and lack of style obsolescence than with luxury, fashion, and automatic features—second cars, student cars, etc.

The American automobile industry did not respond to imports by trying to produce a real economy car in competition with the Volkswagen and Renault, but rather produces a middle-range product (the compacts) which competed with Volvo and Peugeot, for example. The move was probably a wise one. No doubt, the producers of the economy cars abroad had reached cost savings from scale economies equivalent to anything the U.S. producers could hope to obtain. Moreover, they had lower labor costs. By choosing to attack the middle range, the American manufacturers chose a market where they could have a scale advantage for a time, until the higher-income segment of the European market was so large that middle-range cars would be more important. Perhaps the U.S. manufacturers simultaneously created a more exportable product for the future.

For products where design sophistication consists of adding special features to a basic model, export versions can be produced simply by eliminating some of the extras. Thus, some producers can extend the exportability of their products while simultaneously satisfying the more sophisticated needs of their home market.

The existence of segmented markets leads to Americans' exporting and importing the same product: exporting large automobiles to high-income consumers abroad while importing small, economy cars; exporting large refrigerators while importing small ones for campers and summer homes. The relative competitiveness of the United States in 1965–66 in the higher-quality versions of a product stands out well in the case of home freezers. Prices were contrasted for comparable home freezers of different sizes in Germany and in the United States. For each model the lowest-priced unit was chosen for comparison. The larger models were cheaper in the United States and the smaller models in Germany. American manufacturers did not yet need to worry about imports of large freezers, but they were already beginning to experience competition from smaller models.[10]

Product roll-over and foreign investment

Of course, the point is finally reached for many products where design changes can no longer make the American product competitive abroad or safe from imports. The U.S. firms may follow two strategies for survival: a continual product roll-over, shifting resources to new products more suited to the unique demands of the American market; and manufacturing abroad to take advantage of lower production costs and to save tariffs and transportation charges. The strategies are not mutually exclusive, but both require advanced planning and constant surveillance of the future of individual products and assessments of the company's capabilities.

CONCLUSION

Companies can no longer afford failure to analyze opportunities for profit offered by exports and the possible threats to their own market posed by imports. The trend of international events indicates an increased importance of trade to businessmen. In response to this changing environment, the manager must have a continuing program to analyze the future directions of international trade in his products so that he may plan early enough for appropriate policies. The product cycle model provides a useful tool in this analysis.

[10]Sears, Roebuck and Co. catalog (Fall and Winter, 1965) and Neckermann Katalog, No. 169 (September 1, 1965–March 1, 1966).

PART
EIGHT

PLANNING AND EVALUATING THE MARKETING EFFORT

The first selection, "Are You Really Planning Your Marketing?", by Leon Winer reviews planning steps as they are used by many large firms. He argues that they are unsound and then presents a basis for sound market planning. Professor Bright, from Harvard Business School, insists that we can forecast technology; however, not one business in a thousand attempts to forecast technology. Kotler's article, "Corporate Models, Better Marketing Plans," demonstrates how a company can analyze its marketing system, express various relationships explicitly in a model, and then simulate alternative plans on the computer.

An evaluation of the marketing effort must include the consumer. Today, United States business has bred a reaction. There is now a movement called consumerism. Day and Aaker, in their article "A Guide to Consumerism," analyze causal factors which provide a basis for projections of the future of consumerism. Taylor next argues that the marketing practitioner has a commitment to economic development not only to a nation but also to the unemployable. Next, Lavidge takes up the case of the social responsibilities of marketing. He indicates that until recently the expectation that marketing should, or could contribute to society in a significant way was held by few.

E. B. Weiss next illustrates how instantaneous communication will affect all businesses and all marketing. The final selection deals with a complex subject that will be evaluated in great detail during the seventies—the FTC and the regulation of advertising in the consumer interest.

During the sixties we heard a lot about the battle of the brands; during the seventies, we will have need to deal with "the battle of consumerism." The active participants will not be big company brands against other big company brands, but instead big companies against consumers, and federal, state, and local governments.

READING 47

ARE YOU REALLY PLANNING YOUR MARKETING?*

Leon Winer

The biggest problem in marketing planning is the *planning*. Many companies have a marketing "plan," yet few of these plans represent any real planning. To demonstrate this point, five steps will describe practices encountered frequently. These practices were observed through intensive interviews with manufacturing firms and their advertising agencies, and have been reported by executives at meetings and seminars attended by the author.

*Reprinted from *The Journal of Marketing,* published by The American Marketing Association, vol. 29, no. 1 (January 1965), pp. 1–8.

Step 1: Set the market share objective of your brand by adding to its present market share, depending on how ambitious you are.

Step 2: Project total sales volume, for *all* brands of the product, in dollars, for the following year.

Step 3: Multiply the result of Step 1 by the result of Step 2. (Market share objective X projected total dollar market.) This gives the dollar sales objective for the brand.

Step 4: Subtract from the dollar sales objective: (a) total factory cost, (b) an allocated portion of the company's fixed marketing costs, and (c) desired profit. What is left, if anything, is "planned" marketing expenditure.

Step 5: Compose a "marketing mix" of advertising, marketing research, personal selling, price concessions, public relations, package design, point of sales materials, dealer aids, and so on, that will (a) just use up all the marketing funds and (b) yield exactly the forecasted sales volume.

These five steps represent the procedures of many companies, yet they are thoroughly unsound, for three reasons:

First, this procedure assumes that an increase in market share is profitable or, for that matter, possible. By definition, not *all* brands of a product can increase their market shares.

Second, this method of marketing planning reverses the cause-and-effect relationship between marketing effort and sales volume. Clearly, the sales volume forecast should depend on the amount of effort expended on marketing, not the other way around.

Third, this method requires the manager to select the "right" marketing mix from among the hundreds, or thousands, of possible marketing mixes. In other words, the manager is given a sales volume objective and a fixed amount of money for marketing, and he is expected to devise the combination of advertising, price reductions, personal selling, marketing research, public relations, point of sale materials, and so on, that will just use up the available money and will attain the sales objective. No human being has the knowledge or the calculating ability to do this, even if it were *theoretically* possible.

If the argument presented above is correct, and widely-followed practice is inadequate, what alternatives are available?

To answer this question, a study was made of the marketing planning practices of companies recognized as leaders in this area, and of planning books and articles. The conclusion was that while a certain amount of adaptation is required in each case, a general procedure exists that is applicable to marketing planning. This procedure is presented as a flow model in Figure 1. The discussion of the steps in the model will follow the sequence shown, except that "assigning responsibility for planning" will be discussed last instead of first.

SETTING MARKETING OBJECTIVES

In setting marketing objectives, planners should keep in mind three properties of objectives: (1) multiplicity, the fact that organizations have many objectives;

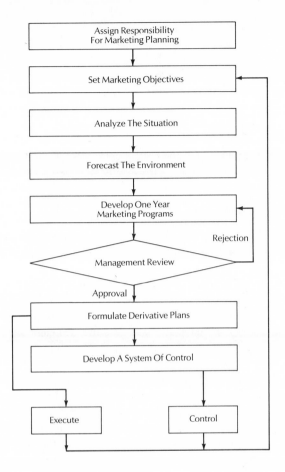

Figure 1
Flow model of a marketing planning procedure

(2) time, objectives need to be set for varying lengths of time; and (3) level, the firm should have many levels of objectives, or a hierarchy of objectives.

Multiplicity

Generally speaking, marketers tend to focus on maximizing next year's profits as being the only proper objective for their efforts. Actually a company may be equally interested in stabilizing profits, or in seeking opportunities for investments for the longer term. Therefore, before doing any marketing planning, it is necessary to explore thoroughly with the company's management what *it* views the company's objectives to be and to derive marketing objectives from those of the company.

Objectives and time

Given the company's objectives, it does not necessarily follow that these can be realized directly. A firm may not be able to capture a larger share of the market, economically, unless it has an improved product. Therefore, in order to attain a more distant objective of increasing its market share, it will set an intermediate objective of developing an improved product.

Since the firm possesses only limited management and financial resources, in setting the objectives described above, it will very probably have to forsake such alternative objectives as entering a foreign market or acquiring a potentially profitable competitor.

Therefore, in setting long-range objectives, and the intermediate objectives that will lead to their attainment, the firm must consider the alternatives it is forsaking, and select those most suitable to its circumstances.

Hierarchy of objectives

Even though a firm sets long-term objectives and determines the appropriate intermediate objectives, that may not be enough. It does not do much good to tell the advertising department that the objective of the company is to increase its rate of return on investment unless this objective is translated into specific strategies. Therefore, it is necessary to develop a hierarchy of objectives.

Development of such a hierarchy of objectives is not a simple task. Careful study is required to make sure that sufficient alternatives are considered at each level and that suitable criteria are discovered for deciding which alternatives are to be selected, or emphasized.

An example, showing how a hierarchy of objectives may be derived through flow-modeling, is shown in Figure 2. This is the case of the business market (offices, factories, stores, hospitals, and so on) of the Interstate Telephone Company (a fictitious name for a real company). At the top of the chart is one of the Company's permanent objectives, that of increasing return on invested capital. A rate of return of $7\frac{1}{2}\%$ is believed to be attainable. Two possible objectives were derived from this one: (1) increase return, or net profit, and (2) reduce the investment base on which return is computed. The second possibility was not believed to be attainable because of (1) population growth, (2) rapidly growing communication needs, and (3) trend toward mechanization and automation. Therefore, attention was focused on the first.

To increase profits, two objectives may be set, following the reasoning of the Interstate Company: (1) increase billings, or (2) reduce costs. Again, the second objective is unlikely to be attained because one of the important sources of the return on investment problem is the rising cost of labor and materials. (One exception should be noted, however. Costs may be reduced by reducing the rate of disconnections due to customer dissatisfaction, since the cost of installing complex equipment often exceeds installation charges.) This leaves the alternative of increasing billings.

To increase billings, the Interstate Company may (1) try to raise rates and risk reduction in usage, (2) persuade customers to increase usage of existing equipment, or (3) sell additional equipment and services in order to increase equipment rentals and, to some extent, usage. However, a public service commission will not grant a rate increase unless return on investment is *below* a certain minimum, say $5\frac{1}{2}\%$. Then a commission is not likely to grant a raise

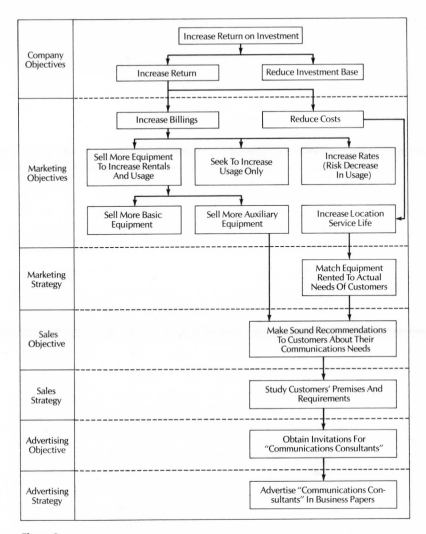

Figure 2

Hierarchy of objectives for the Interstate Telephone Company

that will increase return by as much as two percentage points. The next alternative objective, persuading customers to increase usage, has been used as an objective for promotional efforts of the Company. The third objective, that of selling additional equipment and services, has been selected for particular emphasis. In particular, because of the saturation of the business market with respect to basic equipment, the marketing effort has focused on the sale of auxiliary services and equipment, such as "Call Directors," teletype units, modern switchboards, and interior dialing.

To achieve the objective of selling more auxiliary services and equipment, and reducing disconnections due to customer dissatisfaction, the Company needs to match equipment and services to the *needs* of the customers, by making recommendations based on careful study of these needs. To do this, it seeks to persuade customers, through advertising, to invite "Communications Consultants" to survey their communications problems. In this way, by deriving a hierarchy of objectives, Interstate identifies the specific marketing strategies that will lead to attainment of the Company's highest objectives.

ANALYZING THE SITUATION

Once the planner has a well-developed set of objectives, the next step is to begin discovering ways of attaining them. To do this, he has to form some ideas about what *actions* of the firm, under what *environmental conditions*, have brought about the *present* situation. He will then be able to identify courses of action that may be used in the future.

Logan[1] has suggested a four-step procedure for conducting the situation analysis:

Investigation—A wide range of data that may be relevant should be sought, with care being taken to distinguish between facts and opinions.

Classification—The planner sorts the data collected during the investigation.

Generalization—Classes of data are studied to discover relationships. Statistical techniques such as correlation analysis are used to determine whether dependable associations exist between types of events. For example, a distributor may find that leased outlets are more profitable than owned outlets to a degree that prevents attributing the differences to chance.

Estimate of the Situation—Causes are sought for the associations discovered in the previous step. The planner now has some ideas about what actions under past conditions have resulted in the present situation. In this way he has learned several courses of action that he may follow to achieve his objectives. In the example cited previously, the distributor may find, on searching further, that the higher profitability of leased outlets is caused by the superior location of the leased outlets. In other words, the fact that the outlet was leased was *not* the cause of the higher profitability. Rather *both* the leasing *and* the higher profitability were caused by a third factor—superior location. (Owners of well-located outlets were not willing to sell them and therefore the distributor had been forced to lease.) Consequently, the appropriate strategy for the future would not be to prefer leasing to owning, but to seek good locations and leasing, if necessary. Inadequate search for causes might have led to very poor results.

Ideally, the situation analysis should cover other firms in the industry, so that the company may benefit from their experiences, both successes and failures.

FORECASTING THE FUTURE ENVIRONMENT

The forecasting problem, from the viewpoint of the planner, is to determine *what* conditions he should forecast and *how* to do it. In this article we will

[1]James P. Logan, "Economic Forecasts, Decision Processes, and Types of Plans" (unpublished doctoral dissertation, Columbia University, 1960), pp. 14–19, 76.

limit ourselves to the first part of the problem because the literature of fore-casting techniques is too vast to be reviewed adequately here.

Frey[2] has listed five factors that may affect purchases of a product:

1. Population changes.

2. Improvements in, and new-use discoveries for competing types of products.

3. Improvements in, and new-use discoveries for the company's own type of product.

4. Changed consumer attitudes and habits.

5. Changes in general business conditions.

Howard[3] suggests four criteria for identifying *key* factors:

1. Variability. If a factor is stable over time, there is no need to make a fore-cast of it.

2. Co-variation. There must be a relationship between changes in the factor and changes in demand.

3. Measurability.

4. Independence. The factor must not be closely related to another factor already considered.

Essentially, this means that the planner has to find out *which* uncontrollable factors, such as personal income, occupation of consumers, educational level, attitudes, affect sales of his brand, and then he has to forecast the future of these factors. Here, as in situation analysis, statistical methods must be used with care, to avoid erroneous conclusions.

DEVELOPING ONE-YEAR MARKETING PROGRAMS

Development of marketing programs requires three steps: (a) formulating alternative courses of action, (b) examining these alternatives, (c) comparing alternatives and selecting the ones to be recommended.

Formulating alternatives

The first step in conceiving alternative courses of action was described in an earlier section on situation analysis. We reviewed a four-step process for dis-covering factors that had brought about the present situation, and presumably could be manipulated to achieve future objectives.

However, in addition to the cause-and-effect relationships discovered in situation analysis, there is usually room for innovation, or the development of new courses of action.

[2]Albert W. Frey, *The Effective Marketing Mix: Programming for Optimum Results* (Hanover, New Hampshire: The Amos Tuck School of Business Administration, 1956), p. 11.
[3]John Howard, *Marketing Management* (Homewood, Illinois: R. D. Irwin, Inc., 1957), Chapter VI.

The importance of the creative process cannot be under-estimated, because a plan can only be as good as the best of the alternatives considered. Therefore, it is highly rewarding to spend time evolving alternatives. Unfortunately, there is a strong human tendency to stop the search for alternatives as soon as an apparently acceptable course of action is discovered. This is a tendency that planners must guard against.

Examining alternatives

This step consists of projecting all the outcomes of each alternative course of action evolved above. The outcomes considered should include (1) desirable and undesirable; (2) immediate and long range; (3) tangible and intangible; and (4) certain and only possible.[4]

Clearly, one of the outcomes that must be projected in every case is sales volume and/or profit. In making this projection, errors in both directions are possible. Eldridge[5] discusses the probable consequences of these errors and suggests a solution to the problem.

If (the marketing manager) overestimates his sales volume and gross profit, and bases his marketing expenditures on that overestimate . . . he is likely to find . . . that profits are running well below the forecast. . . .

If he underestimates his volume and gross profit, he runs the risk of spending less than the product needs—and thereby . . . makes certain that the results are less than hoped for.

Nevertheless, it is probably preferable for the marketing manager, when weaving his way perilously between the devil and the deep sea, to err on the side of conservatism in budgeting sales, his marketing expenditures, and his profits. . . .

For himself, his associates, the advertising agency, and the field sales department, it is wholly desirable that objectives should be set on the high side, in order that the attainment of those objectives shall require "reaching. . . ."

In other words, Eldridge suggests "keeping two sets of books." The implications of this suggestion will be discussed subsequently.

Comparing and selecting alternatives

In this step the planner compares the projected outcomes of the various alternative courses of action. The purpose is to rank the alternatives on the basis of the extent to which they achieve objectives and avoid undesirable results. Then the most desirable alternatives are recommended to management.

This point, after programs are prepared, and before they are reviewed by top management, is suitable for writing down the plans.

[4]William H. Newman and Charles E. Summer, Jr., *The Process of Management* (Englewood Cliffs, New Jersey: Prentice Hall, Inc., 1961), p. 302.
[5]Clarence E. Eldridge, "Marketing Plans," in E. R. French (editor), *The Copywriter's Guide* (New York: Harper & Bros., 1958), pp. 3–28, on pp. 24–25.

On the basis of the argument presented here, the written plan should discuss the following topics, if it is to enable management to evaluate it:

1. Specific objective(s) of the plan.

2. Relationship between the specific objective(s) and the objectives of the firm, or an explanation of the extent to which this plan will advance the higher-level and longer-term objectives of the firm. Quantitative measures should be included, if possible.

3. Other specific objectives considered, and the planner's opinion of the relative values of these specific objectives. This evaluation should also include quantitative measures, if possible.

4. Costs of executing the plan.

5. Forecasts of the firm's environment.

6. Course of action recommended: first, briefly, then in detail.

7. Alternative courses of action and reasons why they were considered inferior to the action recommended.

8. Projected results of the plan, if it is executed.

9. Listing of control standards and procedures to be used for controlling execution of the plan.

Before leaving this discussion of preparation of programs, an important point should be emphasized:

Marketing planning should not be done function by function, as has been the tradition for a long time and still is the practice in many firms. (By "functions" we mean the activities normally performed by a marketing department, such as advertising, personal selling, pricing, marketing research,and product and package development. *Within* these functions are many sub-functions. For example, within personal selling is recruitment, selection, and training of salesmen; assignment of territories; design of compensation systems; sales analysis, and so on. At least 50 functions and sub-functions could easily be listed.)

Marketing planning should be oriented to achieving objectives. Of course, if objectives may be fulfilled entirely within one function, the objective-directed plan will also be "functional." But the approach, even then, will still be from objectives to means rather than from means to objectives.

MANAGEMENT REVIEW

Criteria of reviewing executives may be grouped conveniently as follows: (1) economic, or financial; and (2) subjective.

Economic or financial criteria, such as return on investment, present discounted value of future income, alternative uses of funds, and cut-off rates, are sufficiently well known that they do not require comment here.

Subjective criteria, on the other hand, may require some discussion. Smith[6] has commented on the role of management as follows: "Management may simply accept the goals indicated. . . . More frequently . . . management's reaction will be one expressed by such comment as: 'Surely we can do better than that. . . .'"

In the case of the National Paper Company (a fictitious name for a real firm), during one year, management reduced the recommended marketing expenditures by 23%, *without* reducing the sales volume objective. Other, similar, reviewing actions could be cited. Therefore, it appears that management, in reviewing marketing plans, asks itself: "How much 'fat' does this plan contain?" and answers the question somehow, probably subjectively.

Are such reviewing actions justified? In other words, is it fair to the planner to suspect him of "padding" his plan? We have noted earlier the view that: "When it comes to budgeting (setting sales, profit and marketing expenditure goals), the situation is different (from setting objectives for the advertising agency, the sales force, and the like). The forecasts for financial budgeting should be sufficiently conservative that . . . they are certain to be made. . . ."[7] This commentator appears to be suggesting that the planner should overstate consistently the expenditure needed to achieve the goals of the plan. This appears to recognize that a conflict may exist between the objectives of the planner and those of the firm.

The management literature has emphasized repeatedly that differences exist between the objectives of the employee and those of the employing organization. Therefore, it seems fair to conclude that the planner, in trying to achieve his personal goals of continued employment and approval of his superiors, may undermine organizational objectives such as maximum return on marketing expenditures. Following this, the problem of the reviewing manager would then appear to be not to decide *whether* there is "fat" in the plan, but rather to estimate the percentage.

FORMULATING DERIVATIVE PLANS

Ultimately, at the lowest level in the hierarchy, the result of planning has to be a list of actions, or a program, to be carried out.

For drawing up this program, Newman and Summer[8] suggest six steps:

1. Divide into steps the activities necessary to achieve the objective.

2. Note relations between each of the steps, especially necessary sequences.

3. Decide who is to be responsible for each step.

4. Determine the resources needed for each step.

---

[6]Wendell R. Smith, "A Rational Approach to Marketing Management," in Eugene J. Kelley and William Lazer (editors), *Managerial Marketing* (Homewood, Illinois: R. D. Irwin & Co., 1958), p. 154.
[7]Eldridge, same reference as footnote 5, p. 25.
[8]Newman and Summer, same reference as footnote 4, pp. 415–416.

5. Estimate the time required for each step.

6. Assign definite dates for each part.

In formulating its derivative plans, the Finchley (a fictitious name for a real company) Drug Company, uses the individual plans prepared for each of 50 products. The pertinent information is pulled out of each product plan and reassembled in three derivative plans: (a) detailing (personal selling) schedule, (b) advertising program, and (c) financial summary. These derivative plans are described below:

Detailing Schedule—The Detailing Schedule is structured very much like a calendar. For each month, three products are listed in the order in which they are to be presented to physicians. The schedule serves as a working document for the sales force. As the year passes, 500 copies of each page are made and distributed to Finchley's detail men to be carried out.

Advertising Program—The Advertising Program describes several thousand items of direct mail and journal advertising to be prepared during the course of the year. The items are arranged by month and by day of the month when they are to appear, or to be mailed. As the year progresses, this information is used by technicians and artists in the Advertising Department and the Company's agency to prepare advertisements, buy space and materials, and so on.

Financial Summary—The Financial Summary, unlike the other two documents, is not used by any functional department as a basis for action. Instead, it is essentially a communication and control device. Probably the best way to describe the contents of this document is to list the information presented for *each* actively promoted product:

1. Total market ($).

2. Company's share (%).

3. Company's sales ($).

4. Advertising expenditure ($).

5. Allocated detailing cost ($).

6. Total marketing cost ($).

7. Marketing cost as a % of sales.

8. Gross profit ($).

9. Gross profit as a % of sales.

This information is presented both for the current year and the following year.

As plans are executed, the Financial Summary is used for comparing actual results with plans, or controlling the execution of the plan. The point is that advertising, sales, and financial plans are derived from objective-directed product marketing plans and *not* prepared independently by the separate functions: Advertising, Sales, and Finance.

DEVELOPING A SYSTEM OF CONTROL

A system of control should (1) establish standards, (2) measure activities and results, (3) compare these measurements to standards, and (4) report variances between measurements and standards.

Control is relevant to planning because control standards have a greater effect in determining actual results than the objectives of the plan. Therefore, it is necessary that the standards which *are* set, reflect very closely the objectives of the plan.

In addition, a system of control informs the planner of the results obtained from execution of his plans. This is helpful because it becomes possible to change plans if they are found to be ineffective either because (1) the cause and effect premise on which they were based turns out to be faulty, or (2) the actual environment is sufficiently different from the forecast environment.

In the first instance, the objectives are still valid, but the method of attaining them needs to be changed. In the second instance, the objective may no longer be appropriate. Therefore, new objectives and strategies may be required, and with them, new courses of action.

ASSIGNING RESPONSIBILITY FOR MARKETING PLANNING

In practice, the management decision of assigning responsibility for marketing planning is the first step performed. In this paper, we have postponed discussion of this topic until the end, because organization of the planning function may depend on the kind of planning to be done. Therefore, it was necessary to describe first the steps in marketing planning.

Writers on the subject of marketing planning organization have described several alternatives:

1. Delegation of planning to functional executives, such as managers of the advertising, sales, pricing, sales promotion, marketing research divisions of the marketing department.

2. Planning done by a planning staff group.

3. Planning done by everyone who has a part to play in marketing the brand, including outside organizations.

4. Planning done by brand, or product managers.

However, criteria are lacking in the literature for selecting the appropriate planning organization.

Leading firms often rely on product or brand managers for planning, although the practice is not universal, and where such managers are used, their responsibilities are not always the same.

To illustrate this point:

1. At the drug company discussed earlier, product managers plan advertising of two kinds, and personal selling.

2. At the household paper products company, brand managers plan consumer advertising and temporary reductions in price charged to retailers and consumers.

3. The telephone company, on the other hand, does not employ product managers. Instead, planning is assigned to sales and advertising executives, for their individual functions.

Possibly these differences in planning organization can be attributed to differences in the means used for communicating with the market. The telephone company needs to communicate with business market customers (that is, business firms, government agencies, and so on) on an individual basis. The reason is that no two customers (other than the very smallest) are likely to need exactly the same combination of products and services. Therefore, a centrally-conceived, uniform approach, used alone, would not be suitable. The household paper products company and the drug company deal with mass markets where the potential profit made from individual customers is small. This rules out the possibility of tailoring a specialized approach to each customer. In addition, the needs and desires of large numbers of potential and actual customers are relatively similar. Therefore, grouping large numbers of customers into a market for a brand is an economical way of approaching the planning problem.

It follows that the "brand" manager is really a *market* manager, the market being the totality of actual and potential consumers of the brand. We may conclude, therefore, that a brand or product manager has a role to play whenever there is an opportunity to use standardized appeals in communicating with numerous customers.

Nevertheless, not all firms require brand managers, even though they may use mass communication media. For example, the Interstate Telephone Company permits all the advertising planning to be done in its advertising department, and delegates the major part of its sales planning to sales executives. The question arises then: what are the key differences that cause such marked differences in planning organization?

The answer that suggests itself is that there are important differences in the marketing objectives of these firms. Two illustrations can be given.

1. At the paper company, two of the important objectives are increase in market share, and product distribution in certain areas. Programming for these objectives requires crossing of functional lines. Therefore there appears to be a need for a special planning executive.

2. At the telephone company the important marketing objectives are: (1) to increase auxiliary equipment and service billings; and (2) to increase location service life of auxiliary equipment. These objectives are interpreted to require that "communications consultants" survey the operations and premises of business market customers. To achieve this, the company tries to persuade

customers to avail themselves of the free services of these consultants. Thus, we have three levels of objectives: (a) persuade the customer to invite the communications consultant, in order to (b) have the communications consultant advice the customer, in order to (c) increase billings and service life.

Achieving objectives (a) and (b), the objectives that can be achieved by direct action—(c) obviously cannot—does not require any coordination among functions. Objective (b) is achieved by the Sales Department, and objective (a), by the Advertising Department.

The conclusion is that the planning organization should mirror the hierarchy of objectives: a planning manager is needed wherever there is an objective whose achievement requires coordination of, or selection from among, several functions. In practice, the existing organization may satisfy this requirement, in which case, no new responsibilities need be assigned. However, if existing planning responsibilities do not allow for this type of selection, or coordination, new ones need to be created.

IMPLICATIONS FOR MARKETING MANAGERS

When a new idea or concept is presented to the business world, its *form* often receives more attention than its *substance*. While attempts are made to adopt the new concept, old habits of thought, and procedures, are continued even though they may not be consistent with the new idea.

The central idea of marketing planning is to develop marketing objectives that will lead to attainment to the objectives of the firm, and then to devise programs and controls that will help to achieve these marketing objectives. In deciding to plan its marketing activities, a business firm has to stand ready to scrap its traditional budgeting and functional planning procedures and to re-think and reorganize its marketing. Only those methods and procedures should be retained that fit logically with the pattern of starting with the highest objectives of the firm and refining successive steps of instrumental objectives until courses of action are specified. Any other approach, or procedure, will give inferior results.

Admittedly, it is much easier to go through the five steps outlined in the first few paragraphs, and say that marketing is being planned, than to follow the procedure described in the body of this paper. However, in this instance, as in most, there are no easy short-cuts to the development of good, effective, and profitable plans. Also, there really is no escape from the need to plan conscientiously. Leading companies *are* planning in this way, with obvious financial success. Those who wish to attain similar success will have to apply themselves equally. Successful procedures will not be developed overnight, or even in one year. Most likely, it will take from three to five cycles of planning to establish an effective, smoothly-working procedure. However, nothing will be accomplished if a sincere beginning is not made.

READING 48

CAN WE FORECAST TECHNOLOGY?*

James Bright

Despite the widespread conviction that the dominant force in today's environment is technological progress, not one business in a thousand attempts to forecast technology.

Literally thousands of economists demonstrate the value of *economic* forecasting for industry and government; yet one can name barely a dozen *technological* forecasters. And while economic forecasting is a respected and useful industrial function, the notion of technological forecasting generally is ignored or received with skepticism.

The reason is simple. As a discipline, technological forecasting (TF) is in its infancy. Today, it stands where economic forecasting stood perhaps 50 years ago. Yet, the roots of a systematic methodology exist, and many technologists, economists, sociologists, and managers now are eager to see the field developed. They want better tools than the "guesstimate" or "expert" opinion.

Business and government long have been committed to the value of being able to anticipate the character, intensity, and timing of environmental changes. Since technology now plays such a major role, and because its influence is growing, should we not attempt to determine its growth and directions by systematic analysis? Isn't it time firms established formal approaches to technological forecasting?

The response to TF from an average audience encompasses an astonishing range: disbelief, wild enthusiasm, sober appreciation, antagonism, gross misunderstanding, and misrepresentation. And the viewpoints are distributed liberally, without regard to profession or industry.

The trouble with technological forecasting today is *confusion*—confusion as to need, objective, interpretation, and application. In this short article, I hope to dispel some of this confusion, give readers a brief picture of the state of the art, and a personal reaction to it.

The traditional approach to planning—sometimes deliberate, sometimes unconscious—is to ignore future technological change, or to hold technology constant. This attitude is disappearing rapidly in government and high-science industry. Others are also convinced of the need to do much more than has been done about corporate planning and increased technological progress.

The assumption of stasis, which is actually the projection of a negligible rate of change, is quite realistic and useful in some stable activities for periods of one to five years; new technology apparently requires five to 15 years to diffuse throughout society significantly. A company thus may have time to recognize and adjust to technical progress. Economists, concerned with projections of a few years, traditionally have been able to ignore technology for this reason. On the other hand, the assumption is not satisfactory for activities

*Reprinted by permission from *Industrial Research*, March 5, 1968, p. 2.

in advanced technology such as electronics, drugs, plastics, computers, aerospace, or energy conversion. It also is an unrealistic view at those times when relatively stable industries are being inundated by new technology. This is currently the situation in the materials field—steel, paper, glass, and textiles. Food retailing, medicine, and education typify service industries facing explosive technical advancements in the near future.

A variation of this approach is an attitude more common to businessmen and top managers than to technologists: that anything of technological significance can be dealt with after it has materialized and been proven in practice.

In some cases, this may be satisfactory: it has the advantage of certainty, of not leading the firm down false trails. Yet, lead time and vital patent positions may be lost, leaving the firm hopelessly behind.

Another potentially serious result is that the firm meanwhile may commit itself to products, processes, personnel, capital expenditures, and research programs that ultimately reduce its ability to respond to the new technology when it finally does materialize.

Once the waiting is over, numerous hazards remain, with a potential for horrendous economic errors. First is the "crash" program fiasco. When management believes it is behind, there is a tendency to spend any sum, and to go to any extreme, to buy its way into a competitive position. But, by this time others also have seen the merit of the new technology, and a seller's market is likely to exist. The "bandwagon effect" that pervades this atmosphere, coupled with the high cost of haste, distorts judgment and leads to overenthusiastic or overfearful attitudes and painful expense. The policy of insisting on materialization as the only guide to technological progress is dangerous and unsatisfactory.

It commonly is believed that simply looking into the future and expressing a thoughtful opinion about it constitutes a "technological forecast." This is no more TF than is one's opinion about rain next week. Opinion may be right or wrong—but the conclusion is not systematically reproducible.

Some are critical of TF because many opinions on technological progress are not logical and/or contain countless errors. Such critics are correct on the weakness of opinion, but dead wrong in citing this as a fault of TF. Opinion is not forecast; only those ignorant of the subject believe that it is! This is precisely what supporters of TF are concerned about.

"EXPERT OPINION"

What's the matter with expert opinion? The technological forecaster is not against the use of opinion. He merely wants to be sure that the opinion user realizes what he is dealing with.

When one turns to the brilliant technologist for his opinion (some would prefer to call it prophecy), one hopes it will be a happy blend of wisdom, experience, and imagination. Unfortunately, history shows that such opinions often are wrong. The error seems to be traceable to several causes.

● *Bias*: For one thing, technologists are human, and may be biased, perhaps unconsciously, toward their own accomplishments, academic disciplines, and vested intellectual or financial interests. They find it hard to visualize or accept approaches that invalidate their accumulated knowledge and careers of solid accomplishment.

● *Conservatism*: Technologists appreciate physical limitations and technical difficulties. Their experience and training have taught them to be conservative in certain areas of their own knowledge and fields of work. They find it difficult to believe that obstacles that delayed them so long can be readily overcome.

● *Limits of Present Knowledge*: The scientifically inclined naturally judge from known scientific laws and principles, and what is known about science apparently still is much less than what is to be learned. While the technologist often sees possibilities far ahead of others, the record suggests that very often he is too pessimistic regarding the materialization of a technological capability, its effective duplication by others, and too optimistic about its economic benefits. For an extremely disturbing example of this phenomenon consider how the Dept. of Defense, presumably sparing neither brain power nor money in the U.S. technical and military establishments, frequently has underestimated Russian and Chinese progress in the development of nuclear weapons.

● *Poor Understanding of Progress Mechanics*: With rare exceptions, the technologist is not a student of technological progress, any more than the rest of us. Like the economist, he has not had courses on how technological progress evolves; what encourages and impedes it; or how social and political factors, personalities, and the interaction of technologies can speed or delay the progress of a given technology.

Furthermore, the technologist may have his mythologies about technological progress. The brilliant Dr. Norbert Weiner stated that it took radar only two years to get on the battlefield "with a high degree of effectiveness," and a vice president of research at Bell Telephone Laboratories recently claimed that radar was "developed" in five years. Yet, radio detection of obstacles was suggested by Nikola Tesla in 1900, was resuggested by Gugliemo Marconi in 1922, was demonstrated by the Navy Research Laboratory in vessel detection on the Potomac River in 1922, and was the subject of military research and development programs for at least 15 years in the United States alone.

● *Outside Influence*: The technologist and the manager may confuse and compound the forecasting problem by asking such questions as: "How soon will technology X be in use?" or "Is technology X going to replace existing technology Y?" Such questions imply three predictions: that the new technology will be reduced to practice; that it will be adopted by society to a significant degree; and that no economically superior competitor will emerge meanwhile. The technologist often is no wiser than anyone else in foreseeing the many developments outside technology that will influence the diffusion of an advance.

Prophecy or opinion, therefore, may be the most common means of technical anticipation, and it may be very useful, but it does not meet the definition of a forecast. It lacks rigor and logic, even when done by experts.

The "Delphi method," developed by Dr. Olaf Helmer, senior mathematician at the Rand Corp., is an important attempt to improve validity by obtaining the consensus of a number of experts who are successively reacting to questions and refining the reasons for their opinions in a climate that eliminates the influence of personalities. Provided the questions are well chosen (and the experts), the method promises to be a distinct improvement for using opinion to make predictions. Strictly speaking, it is not a forecasting technique, but I believe it has great promise for achieving a much better opinion and in advancing usefulness for corporate communications.

This critique in no way implies that nontechnical opinion is superior to the expert's opinion. Rather, my point is that the very best technologists lack a satisfactory crystal ball, and the allusion to oracular powers in the name of the method can't compensate for this lack.

WHAT IS TF?

The principal misunderstandings about technological forecasting arise out of failure to clarify the forecast objectives relative to the process of technological innovation (*i.e.*, the conversion of technical knowledge into economic reality).

It is not the goal of the *technological* forecast to predict economic or social impact. These may be desirable forecasting goals, but they involve still other —and more difficult—forecasts. Much confusion and criticism of TF arises because predictions about scientific progress, engineering applications, diffusion of technology, economic merit, and social impact are thoughtlessly mingled.

A technological forecast is a probabilistic prediction of future technological attributes, forms, or parameters, reproducible according to a system of analysis resting on quantitative relationships—or other logic—rather than on intuitive opinion. The dozen or so techniques of forecasting largely rest on one of three bases:

Forecasts based on the past: Here one identifies past trends and relates the future to those trends. There are a number of variations worth noting.

● Trend extrapolation: This is done by developing the past time-series data of the parameter and projecting the trend line, possibly with various modifications such as change in the rate of advance, tapering off toward a known limit, e.g., physical or economic. This is an old and familiar tool to engineers and applied scientists. The novelty today lies in aggressive application to product planning, facilities planning, and corporate strategy.

● Precursor events, or leading indicators: The idea is to find an indicator that leads the parameter to be predicted. Then, by developing time-series data for the leading indicator, it is possible to forecast approximate future performance.

As an obvious but useful example of precursor events, consider how the speed of bombers leads the speed of civilian transport planes.

● Envelope curves: Records suggest that most technical parameters for a given device, such as the strength of a type of material, follow an S-curve of growth; or they seem to form the upper part of such a curve, which tapers off against a physical or economic limit. One may infer that a given device reaches a point of diminishing returns; the supposition is that it will be replaced by a superior technological device. This replacement will follow its own S-curve of growth and the pattern will be repeated.

An envelope curve is the master curve roughly tangent to these successive performance curves. The envelope curve extension thus may predict the growth of a technical capability, without specifying the technical device that may be used to achieve it. The efficiency of a succession of prime movers, or sources of light, for instance, seems to follow this pattern.

● Analogy: By developing an analogy to technological patterns in the past, or an analogy to a natural phenomenon, such as biologic growth or the spread of epidemics, a valid forecast might be produced. Scientists at TRW have forecast the growth of electrical power systems in spacecraft by analogy to their growth in aircraft. There undoubtedly is a pattern in these data; and it can assist the designer and his firm to set general targets of size and timing. Obviously, these predictions are only guides.

Forecasts based on the future: This type of technique describes the future, and from this extracts the most probable conditions. Given these probable conditions one can attempt to identify the technological advances that will be needed. The most valuable, timely, or feasible technical targets can be derived. Then a program to achieve the most promising technology is launched. The original analysis of future needs becomes, in effect, a technological forecast.

Forecasts based on dynamic models: Obviously, technological progress is the result of complex interactions of many factors. If it were possible to develop accurate models, and to transfer coefficients of this process, one could mathematically develop a forecast by the industrial dynamics concept of Dr. Jay Forrester of MIT. I know of no such real world application to technological forecasting. However, on a much simplified scale, something approaching dynamic forecasting has been done using games and scenarios, with the computer presenting alternatives and effects of decisions about future conditions and actions.

The thoughtful reader will observe that the forecasts based on the concept of the future and on dynamic models are heavily involved with technological planning, sometimes called "normative forecasting." Furthermore, some of the techniques do not strictly meet the definition of TF proposed earlier.

True enough; but the important point is that they lead to predictions about future technology based on an explicable logic and stated assumptions. This forces the reasoning out into the open, and enables one to challenge assumptions and consider the adequacy of factors that were included.

SCHIZOID

The study of technological forecasting thus leads one to a somewhat schizophrenic frame of mind.

On one hand, it is perfectly apparent that improvement in technical parameters, such as engine horsepower per pound, and in functional capability regardless of devices, such as explosive power, is an evolutionary process, organic-like in growth. While individual additions seem minuscule or revolutionary in the hindsight of years, these improvements blend together and generate technological progress at amazingly definite rates of advance. These rates seem to accelerate gradually, generally under some form of exponential growth. (Unfortunately, one does not know how to choose the right exponents to apply!)

On the other hand, it is equally obvious that future environmental conditions will determine very heavily (but not solely) what technology is needed and what will be supported. To which direction shall we look? The past or the future? My answer is: "Both ways." We cannot deny the insight provided by a record of steady change, but we dare not ignore the demands of society, which will substantially influence what is to be brought into economic reality.

Arguments over the "best" way to forecast are pointless, at least at this time. What is needed is both better understanding and practice of this infant art. Given even this imperfect state of knowledge, however, it is possible to make some systematic anticipation of the directions, character, and timing of some kinds of technical and economic progress. With the quantitative results, technological forecasting becomes useful to industry for purposes such as:

- Assisting in the planning of research programs—amount, direction, scientific skills needed, etc.

- Guiding engineering programs toward the use of new technology, and adjustment to new technical demands.

- Identifying areas where product improvement will be needed, and revealing the need for new products.

- Setting quantitative performance standards for new products, processes, and materials.

- Helping to establish the timing of new technology.

- Assisting in identifying economic potential and impact of technological progress.

- Guiding technological planning in its contribution to long-range corporate planning.

- Helping to identify major opportunities and threats in the technological environment.

No one pretends that technological forecasting is precise, infallible, or capable of accomplishing all these functions singly. But I do claim that it can make a substantial contribution to technological planning, and to the selection of corporate goals. Though still in its infancy, some leading firms and government agencies are proving that TF eventually will become a powerful planning tool.

Any imaginative organization is certain to benefit by considering these forecasting concepts and applying them to its products, its industry conditions, its customer's technologies, and its own tools and processes. If nothing else, technological forecasting forces us to challenge past practice, to look to the future in the hope of controverting the adage that history repeats itself by introducing variations that will be to the benefit of all.

READING 49

CORPORATE MODELS: BETTER MARKETING PLANS*

Philip Kotler

The market planner's task may seem no more onerous or complex than that of the plant manager who must plan the best utilization of the company's labor, equipment, and raw materials, or of the financial officer who must plan the flow of company funds. These other managers, however, generally work with better data, more measurable and dependable input-output relationships, and more direct control.

In marketing, information is poor, expenditures affect demand and costs simultaneously, and human factors play a large role. Thus it is no wonder that marketing management is considered essentially an art by both its practitioner and its critics.

The need to make order out of chaos may be answered by one of management science's newest and most promising developments—the corporate marketing planning model, which is:

- Computerized.

- Industry-specific.

- Data-based.

- Comprehensive.

- Designed for developing and evaluating alternative company marketing plans.

In this article, I shall describe and illustrate a specific, seven-step procedure for mapping and programming such a marketing model for a typical company. . . .

*Reprinted by permission from *Harvard Business Review,* vol. 48, no. 4, July–August 1970. Copyright, 1970 by the President and Fellows of Harvard College: all rights reserved, pp. 135–149.

CHARTING THE SYSTEM

Every company is a pioneer in this area because it must start fresh to create its own concepts, data base, and means of validation. I have found the following seven concepts and tools to be basic to any such system:

1. Core marketing system model.

2. Comprehensive marketing systems model.

3. Input-output models.

4. Functional relationship models.

5. Four-quadrant profit-forecasting and -planning model.

6. Mathematical sales and profit-model.

7. Computer model and output.

Before discussing these concepts in detail, I think it is important to emphasize that the development of a marketing system (or, indeed, of any system) must be undertaken with the full participation of the marketing and other company executives who will be the future users of the corporate marketing model. Education is one of the important by-products of model-building activity, and participation will help to expose the blind spots of various executives about the overall operation of the marketing system.

Executives in the same company tend to see the marketing system in different terms. It is not exceptional to find executives omitting or deemphasizing critical elements in the marketing system. The cooperative attempt to build a corporate marketing model should yield, as one of its major products, a comprehensive and consensual view of the company's marketing system.

CORE SYSTEM MODEL

The most elementary marketing system is made up of a company and a market. The company is related to the market through a set of four basic flows, those shown in Exhibit 1. The company dispatches goods, services, and communications to the market; in return it receives dollars and information. The inner loop is an exchange of money for goods; the larger, outer loop is an exchange of information.

A modern marketing system includes additional institutions that play a crucial role in the operation of the system. For instance, the behavior of suppliers has many direct and indirect effects on the company's marketing program and its ability to serve its customers. Furthermore, the company typically faces competitors who are seeking to satisfy the same market needs. Between the company and its market stands a host of selling, facilitating, and consulting intermediaries who add time, place, form, and possession utility to the marketplace. Finally, all of these institutions interact with the larger social forces of public policy, economics, technology, and culture.

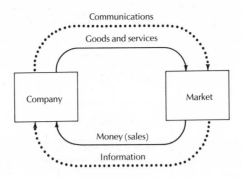

Exhibit I
An elementary marketing system

To illustrate these concepts, let us examine each one in relation to an actual, but disguised, company. We will assume that the company is a leading candy producer, and we want to develop the marketing model for one of its major products—a soft-centered chocolate-covered candy bar.

A diagram of the company's core marketing system can be constructed, showing the company, the market, and the linking channels of distribution (see Exhibit 2).

We assume that the company has already made a major *product-market decision* to produce and sell this candy bar. Such a decision is not made lightly or frequently; it is, rather, a *strategic* decision that is followed by sizable resource commitments to its pursuit. Only at long-run intervals will the company evaluate and decide whether to continue or drop the product.

The right side of the diagram attempts to expand the generic market underpinnings of this particular product. It can provide clues to spotting other opportunities and also to understanding the sources of competition. Thus:

● A candy bar is part of a larger market, the candy market, which contains many other forms of candy that may constitute potential opportunities or threats.

● In turn, the candy market itself is embedded in a much larger market, known as the snack and treat market, which represents all products that provide nourishment or taste satisfaction between major meals. Seen in this light, candy is in competition with such sundries as potato chips, soft drinks, pastry, and chewing gum.

● Finally, the snack and treat market represents only a small part of the food industry. The company must see itself as primarily in the food business. Further analysis will reveal that the product is also deeply involved in the pleasure market as well.

To reach candy bar consumers, the company some time ago decided to use the three major channels of distribution shown in Exhibit 2. The *channels-of-distribution decision* is another *strategic* decision that will have a major effect on current operations. The relative importance of these various channels has

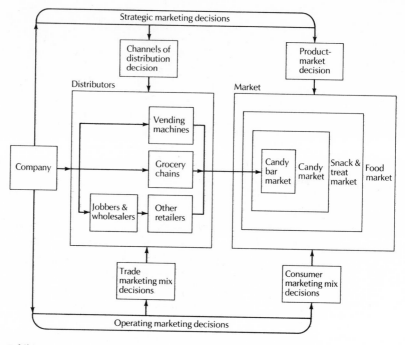

Exhibit 2
Core marketing system model

been changing through time, and management will want to periodically evaluate the channels with respect to at least five measures of performance:

1. Relative sales volume.

2. Relative profit volume.

3. Expected growth in sales.

4. Expected growth in profits.

5. Degree of control and adaptability of each distribution channel.

Within the context of these two major strategic decisions on the product market and the channels lies the whole area of *marketing operations planning.* This company has the dual problem of developing marketing plans for the trade and for the consumers.

Strategic vs. tactical decisions

From a model-building point of view, it is useful to recognize the distinction between strategic marketing decisions and tactical marketing decisions (in the marketing operations planning area). It may be that quite different models have to be built for these two categories of decisions. A General Mills executive recently articulated his view of the difference between the two as follows:

At General Mills, our marketing activities can be classified in two basic ways. The first of these would be the tactical operations which are continually going on with the objective of getting the right balance between elements in the marketing mix. This type of operation can result in spending efficiencies, proper tactical responses to competitive thrust, etc. To a certain extent, you might classify it as the money-saving end of the marketing business as opposed to the money-making end of the business.

We feel that the second basic marketing activity, strategic innovation, is probably more likely to create major increases in profit than optimizing tactical operations. At General Mills the responsibility for strategic innovation is primarily shared by the marketing groups and the R&D groups. We feel most strongly that only by creating major discontinuities in established marketing patterns are we going to be able to grow in profit at our targeted rate.[1]

Clearly, if strategic innovation involves changing the system itself, the model necessary for its evaluation may be quite different from that required for evaluating marketing operations planning that takes place within a stable system.

COMPREHENSIVE SYSTEM MODEL

The next step is to diagram the company's marketing system more comprehensively to show other marketing entities and decisions and the feedback-control relationships. Exhibit 3 illustrates how such a model could be constructed for the candy company. The system is logically divided into six aspects:

1. The environment, or, more precisely, those forces in the environment that affect candy demand, such as population growth, per-capita income, attitudes toward candy, and so on.

2. The company and competitors' marketing decision models.

3. The major categories of decision making in this market—product characteristics, price, sales force, physical distribution and service, and advertising and sales promotion.

4. The three major distribution channels that the company uses for this product.

5. The buyer behavior model which shows customer response to the activities of the manufacturers and the distribution channels, as well as to the environment.

6. Total industry sales and market shares for each company.

---

[1] H. B. Atwater, Jr., "Integrating Marketing and Other Information Systems," a paper presented to the National Industrial Conference Board, New York City, October 18, 1967, p. 7.

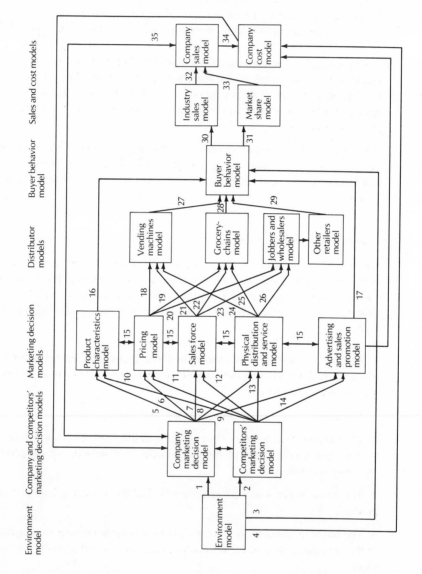

Exhibit 3

Comprehensive marketing system model

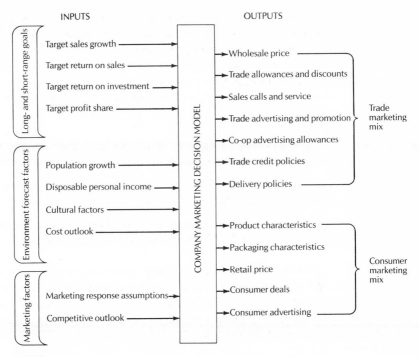

Exhibit 4

Input-output model of company marketing decisions

The various arrows show the flows which connect the major elements in the marketing system. The flows are numbered for ease of reference by the company subsequently. Flow "5," for example, would refer to a detailed diagram and description showing types of product characteristic decisions, the inputs used to influence each of the decisions, the sources of data for each of the inputs, and so forth. Using this device, the company can develop a detailed documentary analysis of its marketing system.

INPUT-OUTPUT MODELS

At this stage the marketing system is further refined by preparing diagrams of the inputs and outputs shown in the boxes of Exhibit 3.

As an illustration of this technique, consider the company marketing-decision box which is singled out and featured in Exhibit 4. To obtain the information shown in such an exhibit, company executives are asked to list the major types of marketing decisions made in the company. A variety of answers can be expected, which again emphasizes the fact that managers in the same company carry in their heads only partial models of the total marketing system.

Note that their answers generally seem to relate to either trade decisions or consumer decisions. The two kinds of decisions are called outputs and are listed on the right side of the exhibit. To influence the trade, the company uses the wholesale price, trade allowances, sales calls and service, trade advertising, co-op advertising allowances, credit policy, and delivery policy. To influence the consumer, the company uses product characteristics, packaging characteristics, retail price, consumer deals, and consumer advertising.

Having identified the major decision outputs, management then lists the various inputs and influences on these decisions, which fall into one of three groups:

1. The company's long- and short-range goals for sales growth, return on sales, and return on investment.

2. Forecastable factors in the environment, such as population growth, disposable personal income, cultural factors, and the cost outlook.

3. Various assumptions about the sales effectiveness of different marketing instruments as well as expectations concerning competition.

The inputs listed at the left represent one possible way to classify the factors affecting the company marketing decisions listed at the right. Each input and output can be elaborated further. For example, in the area of cultural factors, it is possible to isolate three such factors that will have a significant effect on future candy consumption:

Weight consciousness—if there is any relaxation of the pressures in American society toward the idea that "slimness is beautiful," and we return to a Peter Paul Rubens view of feminine beauty, this will lead to a substantial increase in the sales of candy.

Cavity-consciousness—as better dentrifices are developed, people will worry less about the negative effects of sugar on their teeth, and this will reduce their inhibitions against eating candy; nevertheless, worry about sugar may remain a factor, and some companies will see this as an opportunity to develop a tasty, sugarless candy which will offer the double appeal of not contributing either to tooth decay or to overweight.

Cigarette consumption—as people reduce their cigarette consumption in response to the publicity given to the health hazards, we can expect candy, gum, and other "oral" gratifiers to take the place of cigarettes.

All this adds up to the fact that the traditional economic-demographic factors used in marketing forecasting should be supplemented whenever possible with forecasts of cultural factors. Cultural forecasting, like technological and public policy forecasting, is a field that is just beginning to be developed.

Flow of information

Having identified the major inputs and outputs of the company marketing decision model, we now proceed to trace how these data feed into other parts of the system. Consider the output described as the trade marketing mix. This output now becomes input into each of the distribution channels—for example, the grocery chain model (Exhibit 5).

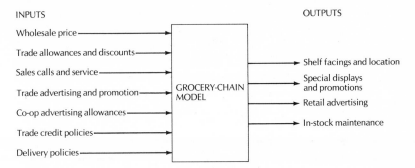

Exhibit 5
Input-output model of grocery-chain decisions

The next step is to consider the major outputs of the grocery chain model —that is, the decisions which grocery chains independently make that affect the purchase rate of this candy bar. These include:

● The amount and location of shelf facings that will be devoted to this candy bar product.

● The extent of store cooperation in special displays and promotions.

● The amount of retail advertising of this candy product that each store decides to undertake.

● The policy of the stores toward maintaining good inventories and keeping the shelves filled with the product.

These are store decisions that vitally affect the sales of this candy bar through the stores, especially considering that candy bar sales have a large impulse component. The manufacturer, however, has no direct control over the stores' decisions in this area.

This is why it is vitally important to identify the factors on the left, since they represent the "handles" the manufacturer can use to influence the store decisions shown on the right. That is, the manufacturer will develop wholesale price, trade allowances, sales calls and service, trade advertising, cooperative advertising, credit policies, and delivery policies in such a way as to exert the maximum amount of influence on the grocery chains to feature its product.

The influence of the dealers' decisions on the final consumers is shown in Exhibit 6, along with influences coming from other parts of the marketing system. The various influences are classified into product and promotion factors (outputs coming from the company marketing decision model), distribution factors (outputs coming from the channels of distribution models), and environmental factors (outputs coming from the environment model). These factors shape consumers' buying behavior to bring about a certain level of industry sales and brand share sales of candy bars.[2]

[2]For a review and comparison of some recent buyer behavior models, see James F. Engel, David T. Kollat, and Roger D. Blackwell, *Consumer Behavior* (New York, Holt, Rinehart & Winston, Inc., 1968), Chapter 3.

INPUTS

OUTPUTS

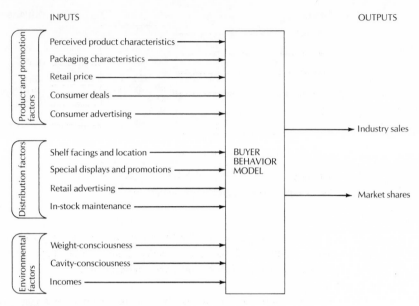

Exhibit 6
Input-output model of buyer behavior

FUNCTIONAL RELATIONSHIPS

I have illustrated how each model component can be analyzed in greater detail to define its inputs and outputs, and how the outputs of one component become the inputs to other components. The next task is to measure the functional relationships between various key elements. For instance, it is obvious that the retail price and advertising affect the rate of consumer purchase; the real task is to measure by how much.

Let us look at two examples of measured functional relationships. Part A of Exhibit 7 shows the estimated effect on candy bar sales of an important characteristic—i.e., the relative amount of chocolate (measured as a percent of the total weight of the candy bar). In our case example, the candy bar is chocolate-covered, and the question is: How thick should this chocolate covering be?

The company would like to keep this percentage down because chocolate is an expensive ingredient compared with the ingredients that make up the soft center. However, consumer tests reveal that, as the chocolate content of the bar is reduced, preference and sales decline. The soft center begins to appear through the chocolate in places and leads the average consumer to feel that the bar is poorly made. Furthermore, his palate desires more chocolate to offset the soft center.

Surprisingly, when the layer of chocolate gets too thick (above 35% of the weight of the bar), consumer preference for the bar also falls, but for a different reason. The consumer begins to think of this, not as a soft-centered candy bar, but as a chocolate bar with "some stuff in it." He relates this bar to pure chocolate bars, and it suffers by comparison.

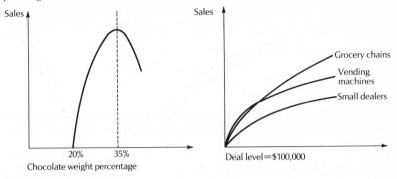

A. Relationship between chocolate weight percentage and sales

B. Relationship between deal level and sales response of different channels

Exhibit 7

Functional relationship models

To the best of management's knowledge, then, sales have the parabolic relationship to percentage chocolate weight that is shown in Part A of Exhibit 7.

Given this functional relationship, what is the optimum level of chocolate? If the company wishes to maximize sales, then chocolate should constitute 35% of the candy bar's weight. However, since the company is primarily interested in maximizing profit, management needs the ingredient cost functions, as well as the sales response function, to determine the profit-maximizing amount of chocolate.

Part B of Exhibit 7 shows another functional relationship—namely, the one between the amount of trade allowance (deal level) and sales. It appears that the channels of distribution differ in their response to deal offers. Small retailers are less responsive to deals than are other channels. They do not handle as high a volume, nor do they calculate as closely the profit implicit in various deals. The grocery chains, on the other hand, are quick to take advantage of deals. These functional relationships can be useful in determining the optimal allocation of deal money to the different distribution channels.

PROFIT-FORECASTING MODEL

At some point, the various functional relationships must be put together into a model for analyzing the sales and profit consequences of a proposed marketing plan. Let us first look at a graphical method of integrating major relationships in the marketing model. Then, in the following section, we will use this to develop a computerized version of the marketing model.

The graphical-analytical device is shown in Exhibit 8. It has been adapted for the candy company example from an idea of Robert S. Weinberg's.[3]

[3]"Multiple Factor Break-Even Analysis: The Applications of Operations-Research Techniques to a Basic Problem of Management Planning and Control," *Operations Research,* April 1956, pp. 152–186. (This idea has an even earlier origin in macroeconomic literature for analyzing equilibrium levels of investment and savings.)

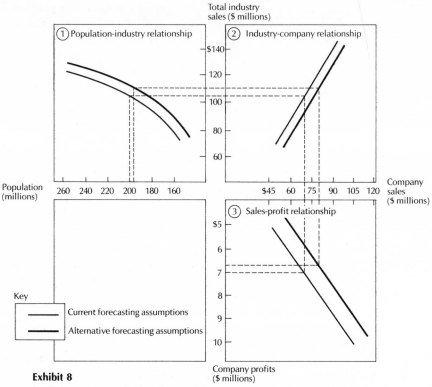

Exhibit 8

Profit-forecasting and -planning model

Quadrant I shows the relationship between population and the total sales of chocolate-covered soft-centered candy bars. (We are assuming for the sake of illustration that the only important environmental variable is population. If two or more environmental variables are involved, a weighted combination of them may be portrayed on this axis, or a mathematical analysis can be substituted for the graphical one.)

The functional relationship shows that sales tend to increase with population, but at a decreasing rate. The part of the curve describing candy consumption for stages where the U.S. population was under 200 million is historically derived through least-squares regression analysis. The part of the curve showing sales for future sizes of the U.S. population is extrapolated and is influenced by anticipated cultural and economic trends. The curve indicates that a population of 200 million consumes approximately $105 million of soft-centered candy bars.

Quadrant 2 shows the relationship between total sales of soft-centered candy bars and company sales. When industry sales are $105 million, this particular company enjoys sales of $70 million, i.e., a market share of 67%. The part of the curve toward the lower level of industry sales is derived from historical information; the part toward the higher levels of sales is extrapolated on the assumption that there will be no dramatic changes in company and competitors' marketing efforts.

Although the function is linear, it does not necessarily indicate that the company expects its market share to remain constant. This would be true only if the line started at the 0,0 origin of this quadrant (not shown). Actually, the line indicates that the company expects its share of market to fall slightly as total sales increase. For example, when industry sales are $140 million, the expectation of company sales is $90 million, or an estimated market share of 64%, as compared with 67% now.

Quadrant 3 shows the relationship between company sales and company profits. Here, again, the company assumes that the relationship is basically linear. At the present time, profits are $7 million on company sales of around $70 million, or 10%. If company sales go up to $105 million, the company expects profits of approximately $10.2 million, i.e., 9.7%.

This kind of graphical device, which assumes that all the underlying relationships have been combined and expressed in terms of three basic relationships, allows us to visualize the effect of a particular level of an environmental factor and continued marketing program on company sales and profits. To this extent, it is a forecasting device.

Its use extends beyond this, however, into marketing planning as well. Suppose, for example, that the company expects the new anti-smoking campaign to have a big impact on candy bar sales, shifting the curve in Quadrant 1 higher (see Exhibit 8). Furthermore, suppose the company is considering intensifying its marketing effort to increase its market share even further. The anticipated effect of this on company market share can be seen by shifting the function in Quadrant 2, to the right. At the same time, the company's marketing costs increase, and that shifts the sales-profit curve to the right, as shown in Quadrant 3.

What is the net effect of this complicated set of shifts? The result is that, although sales have increased, profits have fallen. Apparently, the cost to the company of attaining a still higher market share exceeds the profits on the extra sales. The company would be wise not to intensify its marketing effort, at least according to the specific plan it is considering and its estimated effects.

MATHEMATICAL PROFIT MODEL

The four-quadrant profit-forecasting and -planning model helps one to visualize the impact of a complex set of developments on final company sales and profits. It is also a very useful device for explaining a forecast or a plan to others in the company. At the same time, however, it is quite limited with respect to the number of factors that can be handled directly. For more detailed modeling, we need a mathematical formulation of the candy company's marketing system.

A simplified version of such a model is shown in Exhibit 9. The starting point for any marketing planning model is an equation that expresses profits as a function of the variables under the company's control. Equation #1 shows a profit equation for Company i where profit is gross profit margin $(P - c)$ times quantity (Q), minus the fixed costs (F), advertising and promotion expenditures (A), and distribution expenditures (D). It is possible to spell out the profit equation in greater detail, but this form will suffice for illustration.

#1 Company i's profit equation

$$Z_{i,t} = (P_{i,t} - c_{i,t})Q_{i,t} - F_{i,t} - A_{i,t} - D_{i,t}$$

#2 Company i's sales equation

$$Q_{i,t} = s_{i,t}Q_t$$

#3 Industry sales equation

$$Q_t = m_t k_t N_t \text{ , where . . .}$$
$$m_t = \textbf{parameter}$$
$$k_t = 24(1 - .25^t)$$
$$N_t = 200(1.03)^t$$

#4 Market share equation

$$S_{i,t} = \frac{R_{i,t}{}^{e_{R,i}}P_{i,t}{}^{-e_{P,i}}(a_{i,t}A_{i,t})^{e_{A,i}}(d_{i,t}D_{i,t})^{e_{D,i}}}{\sum_i [R_{i,t}{}^{e_{R,i}}P_{i,t}{}^{-e_{P,i}}(a_{i,t}A_{i,t})^{e_{A,i}}(d_{i,t}D_{i,t})^{D,i}]}$$

$Z_{i,t}$ = Profits in dollars of Company i in year t
$P_{i,t}$ = Average price per lb. of Company i's product in year t
$c_{i,t}$ = Variable cost per lb. of Company i's product in year t
$Q_{i,t}$ = Number of lbs. sold of Company i's product in year t
$F_{i,t}$ = Fixed costs of manufacturing and selling Company i's product in year t
$A_{i,t}$ = Advertising and promotion costs for Company i's product in year t
$D_{i,t}$ = Distribution and sales force costs for Company i's product in year t
$s_{i,t}$ = Company i's average market share in year t
Q_t = Industry sales of soft-centered candy bars in year t
m_t = Soft-centered candy bar poundage as a share of total candy poundage
k_t = Per-capita candy consumption in lbs. in year t
N_t = Millions of persons in U.S.A. in year t
$R_{i,t}$ = Preference rating of Company i's product in year t
$a_{i,t}$ = Advertising effectiveness index
$d_{i,t}$ = Distribution effectiveness index
$e_{R,i}$ = Elasticities of preference, price, advertising, and distribution, respectively, of Company i
$e_{P,i}$
$e_{A,i}$
$e_{D,i}$

Exhibit 9
Mathematical sales and profit model

Typically, the most difficult variable to estimate is company sales (Q_i). The model builder's skill comes into play here as he tries to formulate an explanatory and predictive equation for company sales. Equation #2 is such an equation. It appears that the model builder took the easy way out by defining company sales as the product of company market share (s_i) and total sales of soft-centered candy bars (Q). However, when doing this, it is necessary to account for the two new variables, total sales and market share.

To explain total sales, we formulate the relationship shown in Equation #3. Total soft-centered candy bars sales are the product of the population (N), the per-capita candy consumption rate in pounds (k), and the ratio of soft-centered candy bar sales to total candy sales (m). But now it appears that we have traded the variable Q for three new variables. Fortunately, the three variables are fairly easy to account for exogenously. The ratio of soft-centered candy bar sales to total sales is a fairly stable number. The per-capita candy consumption rate is expected to rise asymptotically in the United States from its present level $(t = 1)$ of 18 pounds per capita to 24 pounds per capita, which happens to be the per-capita candy consumption level of the highest candy-consuming country in the world, Great Britain. The population itself (N) is rising at the rate of 3% a year.

The other variable in the company's sales equation, market share, is typically the hardest of the elements to formulate; yet it is crucial in that it will reflect all of the assumptions about the company marketing decision variables.

There are several ways to formulate the equation for market share.[4] Equation #4 is one example. It shows market share as the ratio of the weighted value of the company's marketing mix to the sum of all candy companies' weighted marketing mixes. The weighted value of a marketing mix is the product of the company's effective preference level, price, advertising, and distribution raised to their respective elasticities. Further refinements can be introduced to reflect the carryover effects of past promotions. The market share model, whatever its form, must synthesize the functional relationships described earlier.

Additional refinements can and should be introduced into this model. For example, cost per pound (c) may not be constant but, rather, may vary with the scale of sales (via production), the preference rating for the company's product (to the extent that this involves better quality ingredients), and time itself, because of inflation. This means some formulation of $c = f(Q,R,t)$ would be desirable. Furthermore, fixed costs may not be independent of the level of sales and production, and therefore some formulation of the form $F = g(Q)$ might be necessary. These and other refinements are introduced as part of the evolution of the model into an increasingly accurate instrument for forecasting and planning.

The model not only must be formulated, but also must be fitted and updated according to the best available information and statistical techniques. Objective data are preferred, but, when they are not available, carefully collected subjective data may be used. The effect of uncertain data inputs on the results can be tested through sensitivity analysis.

COMPUTER MODEL & OUTPUT

At some stage the model should be programmed for the computer and made available to management, preferably on an on-line basis. Marketing planners should be able to sit at a terminal, type in the latest research data, along with specific proposed settings of the marketing decision variables, and get back an estimate of the plan's expected sales and profits. The computer program should also contain, if possible, a subroutine which can search for the best plan possible.

For an illustration of the print-out from one such computer program, see Exhibit 10. The particular model that underlies this output is much simpler than the one discussed earlier. Instead of using a sales model to derive sales estimates from planned levels of marketing decision variables, management supplies subjective estimates of sales.

The print-out shows the inputs and expected payoffs for a seven-year

[4]See, for example, Doyle L. Weiss, "The Determinants of Market Share," *Journal of Marketing,* August 1968, p. 290.

```
        INTERNAL RATE OF RETURN (AFTER TAXES) = 45          PCNT

                          TIME HORIZON = 7                  YEARS
    REMAINING UNDEPR. P&E INVEST. AT BEGIN. YR.1 = 900000   DOLLARS
    REMAINING NO. OF YEARS OF P&E DEPRECIATION   = 3        YEARS
    REMAINING UNDEP. BLDG INVEST. AT BEGIN. YR.1 = 210000   DOLLARS
    REMAINING NO. OF YEARS OF BLDG DEPRECIATION  = 21       YEARS

        DEPRECIATION HORIZON FOR P&E INVESTMENTS  = 10      YEARS
        DEPRECIATION HORIZON FOR BLDG INVESTMENTS = 30      YEARS

    OPPORTUNITY COST (AT BEGINNING OF PERIOD) = 2.E+06      DOLLARS
                        WORKING CAPITAL = 13                PCNT SALES
            SALVAGE VALUE (AT END OF PERIOD) = 10           X EARNINGS
```

	1	2	3	4
YEAR	RET.PRICE($)	RET.MAR.(PCNT)	WHOLE.PRICE($)	WHOLE.MAR.(PCNT)
1969	.577	18	.473	0
1970	.602	18	.494	0
1971	.621	18	.509	0
1972	.639	18	.524	0
1973	.659	18	.54	0
1974	.675	18	.554	0
1975	.698	18	.572	0

	5	6	7	8
	FACTORY PRICE($)	VARIABLE MAN. COST($)	VARIABLE MAN. COST(PCNT)	VARIABLE MKTG COST(PCNT)
1969	.473	.191	40.4	5
1970	.494	.196	39.7	5
1971	.509	.202	39.7	5
1972	.524	.208	39.7	5
1973	.54	.214	39.6	5
1974	.554	.221	39.9	5
1975	.572	.227	39.7	5

	9	10	11	12
YEAR	CONTRIB. TO FIXED COSTS AND PROFIT ($)	(PCNT)	FIXED MAN. COST($)	FIXED MKTG. COST($)
1969	.258	54.6	915000	4.25E+06
1970	.273	55.3	971000	4.9E+06
1971	.282	55.3	1.028E+06	5.5E+06
1972	.29	55.3	1.31E+06	5.75E+06
1973	.299	55.4	1.386E+06	6.25E+06
1974	.305	55.1	1.471E+06	6.85E+06
1975	.317	55.3	1.824E+06	7.6E+06

	13	14	15
YEAR	P&E INVEST.	BLDG.INVEST.	DEPREC.EXPENSE
1968	850000	0	
1969	0	0	395000
1970	0	0	395000
1971	850000	1.E+06	395000
1972	0	0	213333
1973	0	0	213333
1974	850000	1.E+06	213333
1975	0	0	331666

	16	17	18	19
YEAR	INDEX OF COMPANY SALES	COMPANY SLS(UNITS)	INDUSTRY SLS(UNITS)	MARKET SHARE
1969	1	3.E+07	1.166E+09	2.6
1970	1.1	3.3E+07	1.182E+09	2.8
1971	1.2	3.6E+07	1.198E+09	3
1972	1.3	3.9E+07	1.215E+09	3.2
1973	1.4	4.2E+07	1.23E+09	3.4
1974	1.5	4.5E+07	1.247E+09	3.6
1975	1.6	4.8E+07	1.265E+09	3.8

	20	21	22	23
YEAR	MKTG EXP.(PCNT SLS)	P.A.T.(PCNT SLS)	P.A.T.($)	CSH FLOW(A.T.)
1968				-2.85E+06
1969	34.9	7.7	1.097245E+06	-353001
1970	35.1	8.4	1.370807E+06	1.493337E+06
1971	35	8.8	1.610162E+06	-110272
1972	33.1	9.9	2.014062E+06	1.953967E+06
1973	32.5	10.4	2.361914E+06	2.281351E+06
1974	32.5	10.4	2.591395E+06	667228
1975	32.7	9.9	2.723974E+06	2.722089E+06
1976				

Exhibit 10

Sample print-out from computer program

plan being considered for a cereal product. (This plan calls for the continuation of the past marketing strategy; other plans were also considered.)

The first item printed out is the calculated internal rate of return after taxes for the particular plan. (The computer program is set up to give two other payoff measures—i.e., the present value of the after-tax cash flow, and the sales and market share needed to achieve a 10% ROI after taxes.)

The next line shows that this calculation is for a seven-year planning horizon. Some details are then printed out on the initial value of the undepreciated plant and equipment and building investment devoted to this product line and the remaining number of years of depreciation. The depreciation horizons are also printed out, as well as the current opportunity cost of this investment and its expected salvage value at the end of the period.

The rest of the print-out shows the expected or planned year-to-year levels of important variables that ultimately affect the internal rate of return. Column I shows the retail price per unit, which is expected to rise from $.58 to $.70 in the course of seven years. Column 2 shows that the retail margin for this product (18%) is not expected to change. Column 3 shows the resulting wholesale prices. Since this company sells direct to the retailers, there is no wholesale margin (Column 4), and the factory price (Column 5) is the same as the wholesale price.

Column 6 shows estimated variable manufacturing costs, and they too are expected to rise over the period, from a present level of $.19 to $.23 in 1975. The ratio of variable manufacturing costs to factory prices is shown in Column 7, followed by the planned ratio of variable marketing costs to factory prices (Column 8). Subtracting variable manufacturing and marketing costs per unit from the price, the result is the contribution to fixed costs and profits, which is shown in dollar and percentage form in Columns 9 and 10 respectively.

The next step calls for estimating fixed manufacturing costs and fixed marketing costs over the next seven years, which are shown in Columns 11 and 12. The symbol E+06 is computer print-out shorthand and means that the reader should move the decimal place, in the associated number, six places to the right. Thus $1.028E+06 means $1,028,000. Columns 13 and 14 show the anticipated investments in plant, equipment, and building over the next seven years, and Column 15 shows the estimated total depreciation expense.

We now arrive at the estimated sales and profits. Columns 16 and 17 show management's estimates of sales (in percentage and in unit terms, respectively) over the next seven years. The figures indicate that management expects company sales (in units) to rise at the rate of about 10% a year, on the basis of its planned levels of marketing expenditures. Column 18 presents management's estimates of industry sales for the next seven years.

The figures in Column 19, market share, are derived by dividing estimated company sales (Column 17) by estimated industry sales (Column 18). We see that management expects market share to grow from 2.6% to 3.8% over a seven-year period. Column 20 expresses total marketing expenditures (Columns 8 and 12) as a percent of sales, and this percentage is expected to fall. Examining this more closely, we see that management expects sales to rise faster than marketing expenditures; hence it is assuming an increase in marketing productivity.

Columns 21 and 22 are a derivation of the implied yearly profits after taxes in percentage and dollar terms. The computer program uses the following formula to calculate dollar profits after taxes:

$$Z = (I - T)(CQ - F - D)$$

where Z = Profits after taxes;

T = Tax rate;

C = Contribution to fixed costs and profit;

Q = Sales in units;

F = Fixed manufacturing and marketing costs;

D = Depreciation.

For example, the profits after taxes for 1969 are:

$(I - .4944)[(\$.258)(30,000,000) - \$5,165,000 - \$395,000]$, or \$1,097,245[5]

Column 23 shows the results of the conversion of profits after taxes to cash flow after taxes. The formula for cash flow can be expressed as:

$$L = Z + D - W - Y$$

where L = Cash flow after taxes;

Z = Profits after taxes;

D = Depreciation;

W = Working capital in dollars (i.e., working capital as a percent of sales, times wholesale price, times sales in units);

Y = New investment expenditure.

For example, the cash flow after taxes for 1969 is:

$\$1,097,245 + \$395,000 - [.13(\$.473)(30,000,000)] - 0$, or $-\$353,001$.[5]

Having calculated the cash flow after taxes, the computer now calculates the internal rate of return implicit in the cash flow in Column 23. This is found by taking the opportunity cost at the beginning of the period and searching for the interest rate that would discount the future cash flows so that the sum of the discounted cash flows is equal to the initial opportunity cost; this rate turns out to be 45%.

Thus computer programs such as this one enable the marketing planner to determine the financial consequences implied by a particular set of costs, investments, and sales. He can easily calculate the impact on profit of any alterations in his data or assumptions. This particular computer program could be improved further by:

● Including separate estimates of each marketing decision variable, rather than lumping them together as total marketing expense.

● Incorporating a sales model that estimates sales analytically from the marketing plan variables and from environmental and competitive assumptions, instead of requiring direct estimation.

● Introducing a subroutine for planning territorial allocations of the marketing budget.

● Introducing risk explicitly into the program by including pessimistic, optimistic, and normal estimates.

● Introducing a profit-maximizing algorithm which will search for the best marketing plan in the light of the assumptions and data.

CONCLUDING NOTE

In this article I have outlined one rational approach to building a model for determining and evaluating marketing strategies. With such a model for a

---

[5]This figure is the computer output and differs slightly from the arithmetic result of the formula as presented, because of certain simplifications of input data.

given product within its total environment, the marketing executive can experiment with any number of detailed plans to determine the best one. While computerized models will not guarantee success in marketing, they are likely to produce better results than intuition alone.

Marketing plans will always be subject to unknown risks and so must be tempered by the judgment and experience of the decision maker. But a systematic analysis of market forces and their probable effects on a particular product will go a long way toward keeping the risks within tolerable limits.

READING 50

A GUIDE TO CONSUMERISM*

George S. Day and David A. Aaker

Consumerism has played an expanding role in the environment of business decision makers. Despite wishful thinking by some, the following analysis of consumerism is as relevant today as it was in 1964 when it was written:

1. As evidenced by consumer agitation at the local-state-federal levels, business has failed to meet the total needs and desires of today's consumers.

2. Into this business-created vacuum, government forces have quickly moved to answer this consumer need.

3. The areas of consumer interest are so diverse that they offer government agencies and legislators almost limitless reasons for additional regulation of business and commerce.

4. If business managers want to avoid such new government regulations (with the attendant possibilities of excessive and punitive legislation), they will have to take positive action to demonstrate that the business interest is in more general accord with consumer's needs and wants.[1]

The ensuing six years has seen the passage of considerable consumerism legislation and a substantial broadening of the concept's scope. During this period one constant factor has been a lack of agreement on the extent of the influence of consumerism or its long-range implications. Businessmen have suffered from a myopia that comes from perceiving consumerism primarily in terms of markets with which they are very familiar. Their emphasis on the peculiarities of these few markets often leads them to overlook similar problems in other contexts and, thus, to discount the seriousness of the overall

---

*Reprinted from *The Journal of Marketing*, published by the American Marketing Association, vol. 34, no. 3 (July 1970), pp. 12–19.
[1]Tom M. Hopkins, "New Battleground—Consumer Interest," *Harvard Business Review*, Vol. 42 September–October, 1964), pp. 97–104.

problem they face. Legislators and members of the consumer movement are more responsive to the broad problems facing consumers, but their lack of understanding of specific market situations too often leads to inappropriate diagnoses and solutions. Fortunately the two basic perspectives are demonstrating a healthy convergence. The goal of this paper is to encourage this convergence by putting consumerism into a perspective that will facilitate understanding.

THE SCOPE OF CONSUMERISM

The term *consumerism* appears to be uniquely associated with the past decade. Even in this short period it has undergone a number of changes in meaning. Vance Packard, one of the earliest adopters of the term, linked consumerism with strategies for persuading consumers to quickly expand their needs and wants by making them "voracious, compulsive (and wasteful)."[2] His usage clearly reflected the concerns of the fifties with planned obsolescence, declining quality, and poor service in saturated consumer goods markets. The term was not put to wider use until 1963 or 1964, when a variety of commentators identified it with the very visible concerns triggered indirectly by Rachel Carson, and directly by Ralph Nader's auto safety investigations and President Kennedy's efforts to establish the rights of consumers: to safety, to be informed, to choose, and to be heard.[3]

The most common understanding of consumerism is in reference to the *widening* range of activities of government, business, and independent organizations that are designed to protect individuals from practices (of both business and government) that infringe upon their rights as consumers. This view of consumerism emphasizes the direct relationship between the individual consumer and the business firm. Because it is an evolving concept, there is no accepted list of the various facets of this relationship. The following is representative:

1. *Protection against clear-cut abuses.* This encompasses outright fraud and deceit that are a part of the "dark side of the marketplace,"[4] as well as dangers to health and safety from *voluntary use of a product.* There is substantial agreement in principle between business and consumer spokesmen that such abuses must be prevented, but there is often a wide divergence of opinion on the extent of the problem. As a result the government has taken the initiative in this area, usually after the divulgence of a sensational abuse. This has been the case with much of the legislation dealing with drug, tire, auto, and pipeline safety, and meat and fish inspection. Even so, this is the least controversial and oldest aspect of consumerism.

[2]Vance Packard, *The Waste Makers* (New York: David McKay, 1960), p. 23.
[3]Rachel Carson, *Silent Spring* (Boston, Mass: Houghton Mifflin Company, 1962); Ralph Nader, *Unsafe At Any Speed* (New York: Pocket Books, 1966); and "Consumer Advisory Council, First Report," Executive Office of the President (Washington, D.C.: U.S. Government Printing Office, October, 1963).
[4]Senator Warren Magnuson and Jean Carper, *The Dark Side of the Marketplace* (Englewood Cliffs: Prentice-Hall, 1968).

2. *Provision of adequate information.* The concern here is with the economic interests of the consumer. The question is whether the right to information goes beyond the right not to be deceived, to include the provision of performance information that will ensure a wise purchase. Much of the controversy and confusion over consumerism revolves around this basic issue.[5] The two polar positions identified by Bauer and Greyser are the business view that the buyer should be guided by his judgment of the manufacturer's reputation and the quality of the brand, versus the view of the consumer spokesmen that information should be provided by impartial sources and reveal performance characteristics.[6]

3. *The protection of consumers against themselves and other consumers.* Some of the thrust behind consumerism comes from the growing acceptance of the position that paternalism is a legitimate policy. Thus, the National Traffic and Motor Vehicle Safety Act of 1966 is not concerned with the possibility that the buyer has an expressed but unsatisfied need for safety, and emphasizes instead that carelessness may have undesirable consequences for innocent participants.[7] There is a sound basis in economic theory for such intervention whenever the action of a buyer serves only his own best interest and fails to take into account the effects on others. However, this principle is being extended to situations of "implied consumer interest" where the individual is deemed unable to even identify his own best interest (e.g., the mandatory installation of seat belts and the provision for a "cooling off" period after a door-to-door sale). This is a strong justification for the protection of inexperienced, poorly educated, and generally disadvantaged consumers. More controversial by far is the extension of this notion to all consumers on the grounds that manipulated preferences may be disregarded when the consumer is not acting in his best interest.[8]

The above three facets of consumerism suggest the current thrust of the movement. Yet, it would be naive to portray consumerism as a static entity. It has had a dynamic past and continues to evolve and change at an increasingly rapid rate. For example, the emphasis of the consumer movement of the thirties and later was on dangerous and unhealthy products and "dishonest or questionable practices which are believed to hamper the consumer in making wise decisions . . . and obtaining useful information."[9] The emphasis today is clearly much broader.

There is a high probability that the scope of consumerism will eventually subsume, or be subsumed by two other areas of social concern; distortions and inequities in the economic environment and the declining quality of the physical environment. The forecast of a greater identity between these social

[5]*Freedom of Information in the Market Place* (Columbus, Mo.: F.O.I. Center, 1967).
[6]Raymond A. Bauer and Stephen A. Greyser, "The Dialogue That Never Happens," *Harvard Business Review*, Vol. 45 (November–December, 1967), p. 2.
[7]Robert L. Birmingham, "The Consumer As King: The Economics of Precarious Sovereignty," *Case Western Reserve Law Journal*, Vol. 20 (May, 1969).
[8]Same reference as footnote 7, p. 374.
[9]Fred E. Clark and Carrie P. Clark, *Principles of Marketing* (New York: The Macmillan Company 1942), p. 406.

problems and consumerism rests on the fact that they are associated with many of the same basic causes, have common spokesmen, and seem to be moving in the same direction in many respects. Yohalem has indicated that the ultimate challenge of consumerism to industry is "toward ending hunger and malnutrition . . . toward alleviating pollution of the air, water and soil . . . toward educating and training the disadvantaged . . . toward solving these and other problems of a society rather than strictly of an industrial nature."[10]

Concern over the *economic environment* dates back to the end of the last century. The long-run manifestation of this concern has been antitrust law and enforcement, which has swung back and forth between protecting competition and protecting competitors. Despite various ambiguities in antitrust interpretation, this has been a major effort to ensure consumers' "right to choose" by increasing the number of competitors. Some regard it as "the fundamental consumer edifice on which all other measures are bottomed."[11] Judging from the recent intensification of concern over the economic role of advertising and promotion (insofar as they increase price and raise barriers to entry to new markets), reciprocity, restrictive distributive arrangements, conglomerate mergers, and related topics, it appears that antitrust issues will be a continuing impetus to consumerism. In a period of rapid inflation it is not surprising that advertising and promotion costs have come under additional scrutiny for their role in contributing to high prices, particularly food prices. This promises to be a durable issue, considering a task force of the White House conference on food, nutrition, and health has recommended lower food prices, by reducing promotion not related to nutritional or other food values, as a major item in a national nutrition policy.[12]

More recently, consumerism has become identified with the widespread concern with the quality of the *physical environment*. The problems of air, water, and noise pollution have become increasingly salient as the tolerance of the public for these abuses has decreased. In effect a "critical mass" of explosive concern has suddenly been created. The consumer movement has rapidly rearranged its priorities to become a part of this critical mass. This shift is not surprising in view of the desire to broaden consumerism to include problems arising from indirect influences on the consumer interest. It also follows naturally from the long standing concern with built-in obsolescence and poor quality and repairability, for these problems contribute to pollution in a "disposable" society.

As the consumer movement joins with conservationists and interested legislators there is a growing likelihood of government action. The argument for such intervention has been well stated by Andrew Shonfield:

---

[10]Aaron S. Yohalem, "Consumerism's Ultimate Challenge: Is Business Equal to the Task?" address before the American Management Association, New York, November 10, 1969.

[11]Statement of Leslie Dix (on behalf of the Special Committee on Consumer Interests), Federal Trade Commission, *National Consumer Protection Hearings* (Washington: U.S. Government Printing Office, November, 1968), p. 16.

[12]"Food Ads to Get Wide Ranging Scrutiny at White House Session," *Advertising Age,* Vol. 41 (December 1, 1969), p. 1.

Increasingly the realization is forced upon us that the market, which purports to be the reflection of the way in which people spontaneously value their individual wants and efforts, is a poor guide to the best means of satisfying the real wishes of consumers. That is because market prices generally fail to measure either social costs or social benefits. In our civilization these grow constantly more important. Simply because some amenity—let it be a pleasant view or an uncongested road or a reasonably quiet environment—is not paid for directly by those who enjoy it, there is no measure of the cost of the disinvestment which occurs when a profitable economic activity destroys what already exists. Unless the State actively intervenes, and on an increasing scale, to compel private enterprise to adapt its investment decisions to considerations such as these, the process of economic growth may positively impede the attainment of things that people most deeply want.[13]

The result may well be increased controls on producer-controlled emittants and, perhaps, "quality standards . . . or other regulatory devices in the interest of upgrading product quality and repairability."[14]

THE UNDERLYING CAUSES OF CONSUMERISM

Additional insights come from a consideration of the factors underlying the recent upsurge of interest in consumerism. It appears that increasingly discontented and aroused consumers have combined with a growing number of formal and informal institutions capable of focusing discontent, to create enough pressure to overcome the advantage of the traditionally more effective lobbies representing the producer's interests. Since a particular government action means much more to the individual producer (who will be totally affected), than to the individual consumer (who divides his concern among many items), this clearly involved a significant effort.

The discontented consumer

The discontented consumer is not part of a homogeneous group with easily described complaints. The fact is great variation exists among consumers in the extent of their discontent and there is a wide variety of underlying causes. Nonetheless, it is possible to distinguish specific sources of discontent that are traceable to the marketing environment from other more pervasive concerns with the nature of society.

Problems in the marketplace. To some observers the leading problem is imperfections in the state of information in consumer markets.[15] They believe consumers would be adequately cared for by competition *if* they could learn

[13]Andrew Shonfield, *Modern Capitalism: The Changing Balance of Public and Private Power* (New York: Oxford University Press, 1965), p. 227.
[14]Stanley E. Cohen, "Pollution Threat May Do More for Consumers Than Laws, Regulations," *Advertising Age*, Vol. 41 (March 2, 1970), p. 72.
[15]Richard H. Holton, "Government-Consumer Interest: The University Point of View," in *Changing Marketing Systems*, Reed Moyer, ed. (Chicago, Ill.: American Marketing Association, Winter, 1967), pp. 15–17.

quickly about available brands and their prices and characteristics. However, as products and ingredients proliferate, each consumer is less and less able to make useful price and quality comparisons. This inability leads to "increasing shopper confusion, consequent irritation and consequent resentment."[16] The problem is most severe for products which are purchased infrequently, exhibit a rapid rate of technological change, and whose performance characteristics are not readily apparent. Hence, increasing pressure is applied for tire standards, unit prices, truth-in-lending, truth-in-funds, information about the design-life of durable goods, and so on. The truth-in-packaging bill is another manifestation of this problem, for it aims to help the consumer cope with the volume of information available relative to grocery and drug products. Since advertising has not been notable as a source of adequate, or even accurate information that could alleviate the problem, it has been under continuing attack.[17] To the extent that retailing is becoming more and more impersonal, the whole situation may become worse. Thus,

As a result of the character of contemporary retail establishments, the vastly increased number of consumer products, and the misleading, deceptive and generally uninformative aspects of advertising and packaging, the consumer simply lacks the information necessary to enable him to buy wisely.[18]

This is not an unusually intemperate charge; nor is it denied by the finding that 53% of a sample of adults disagreed with the statement that, "In general, advertisements present a true picture of the product advertised." This response measures both a concern over genuine deception and differences in people's tolerance for fantasy.[19] Nonetheless the potential for dissatisfaction is large.

The proliferation and improvement of products, resulting from attempts to better satisfy specific needs and/or reduce direct competition, has also had other consequences. As one appliance executive noted, "The public is staging a revolt of rising expectancy. Customers today expect products to perform satisfactorily, to provide dependable functional performance and to be safe. This threshold of acceptable performance is steadily rising. . . ."[20] Unfortunately the complexity and malfunction potential of many products has also been rising.[21] The result is an uncomfortable level of dissatisfaction with quality, compounded by inadequate service facilities.[22] This situation is not confined to hard goods, for one result of rapidly rising sales is overburdened

[16]E. B. Weiss, "Line Profusion in Consumerism," *Advertising Age*, Vol. 39 (April 1, 1968), p. 72.
[17]Louis L. Stern, "Consumer Information Via Increased Information," *Journal of Marketing*, Vol. 31 (April, 1967), pp. 48–52.
[18]Richard J. Barber, "Government and the Consumer," *Michigan Law Review*, Vol. 64 (May, 1966), p. 1226.
[19]Raymond A. Bauer and Stephen A. Greyser, *Advertising in America: The Consumer View* (Boston: Graduate School of Business Administration, Harvard, 1968), p. 345.
[20]Robert C. Wells, quoted in James Bishop and Henry W. Hubbard, *Let The Seller Beware* (Washington: The National Press, 1969), p. 14.
[21]"Rattles, Pings, Dents, Leaks, Creaks—and Costs," *Newsweek*, Vol. 45 (November 25, 1968), p. 93.
[22]See, Federal Trade Commission, "Staff Report on Automobile Warranties" (Washington: no date), and "Report of the Task Force on Appliance Warranties and Service" (Washington: January, 1969).

retail and manufacturing facilities, which leads to deteriorating quality and service for almost all mass-merchandised goods.[23]

These problems are occurring at a time when consumers are generally less willing to give industry the benefit of the doubt—an understandable reaction to the well-publicized shortcomings of the drug, auto, and appliance manufacturers. Even without these problems, more skepticism is to be expected from consumers who have found that their assumptions about the adequacy of laws covering reasonable aspects of health, safety, and truthfulness are wrong. Recent disclosures involving such vital issues as meat inspection and auto and drug safety have hurt both government and industry by contributing to an atmosphere of distrust. According to Stanley Cohen, the meat inspection battle was particularly important here, "because for the first time the public had a clear cut demonstration of the jurisdictional gap (between state and federal governments) that limits the effectiveness of virtually all consumer protection legislation."[24]

Problems in the social fabric. The present imperfections in the marketplace would probably not have generated nearly the same depth of concern in earlier periods. The difference is several changes deep in society that have served as catalysts to magnify the seriousness of these imperfections.

The first catalyst has been the new visibility of the low-income consumer. These consumers suffer the most from fraud, excessive prices, exorbitant credit charges, or poor quality merchandise and service. Unfortunately, solutions oriented toward improving the amount and quality of product information have little relevance to low-income buyers who lack most of the characteristics of the prototype middle-income consumer.[25]

● Low income consumers are often unaware of the benefits of comparative shopping.

● They lack the education and knowledge necessary to choose the best buy, even if it were available. Because of their low income they have fewer opportunities to learn through experience.

● They often lack the freedom to go outside their local community to engage in comparative shopping.

● They lack even a superficial appreciation of their rights and liabilities in post-sale legal conflicts.

● Nothing in their experience has reinforced the benefits of seeking better value for their money; consequently, the low-income buyer lacks the motivation to make improvements in his situation.

Thus, the low-income consumer environment is a perfect breeding ground

[23]"Consumers Upset Experts," *New York Times* (April 13, 1969), F. 17.
[24]Stanley E. Cohen, "Business Should Prepare for Wider Probe of Consumer Protection Laws," *Advertising Age*, Vol. 39 (January 8, 1968), p. 59.
[25]Lewis Schnapper, "Consumer Legislation and the Poor," *The Yale Law Journal*, Vol. 76 (1967).

for exploitation and fraud. The extent of the distortion in the ghetto market-place has only recently been widely comprehended and related to the overall failure of society to help the disadvantaged.[26]

The second catalyst is best described as a basic dissatisfaction with the impersonalization of society in general, and the market system in particular. Evidence for this point of view is not difficult to find, particularly among young people. A survey of college student opinion found 65% of the sample in strong or partial agreement with the statement that "American society is characterized by injustice, insensitivity, lack of candor, and inhumanity."[27] Similar levels of disenchantment were reported among parents and non-students of the same age. The need seems to be felt for social organizations that are responsive—and perhaps the impression of responsiveness is as important as the specific responses that are made.

There is little doubt that large American corporations are not regarded as responsive by their customers. According to Weiss, both manufacturers and retailers are "turning a deaf ear," while increasingly sophisticated consumers are demanding more personal relationships and security in their purchases.[28] This situation stems from a series of changes in the marketing environment —the rise of self-service and discounting (in part because of the difficulty of obtaining good sales employees), the high cost of trained service personnel, and the intervention of the computer into the relationship with consequent rigidifying of customer policies and practices. The prospects for improvement are dim, because the benefits of good service and prompt personal attention to complaints are difficult to quantify and consequently are given low priority when investment decisions are made. As more consumers are seeing the government as being more sympathetic, if not more helpful, the prospect for arbitration procedures to settle complaints is increased.

The most disturbing feature of the catalyzing effects of the recently visible low-income consumer, the growing dissatisfaction with the impersonaliza-tion of society, and concern over the quality of the physical environment is their intractability. These problems are almost impervious to piecemeal at-tempts at correction. In view of the small likelihood of large-scale changes in social priorities or social structures, these problems will be a part of the environment for the foreseeable future.

The final and most enduring catalyst is the consequence of an increasingly better educated consumer. The Chamber of Commerce recently noted that the consumer of the present and future "expects more information about the products and services he buys. He places greater emphasis on product per-formance, quality and safety. He is more aware of his 'rights' as a consumer and is more responsive than ever before to political initiatives to protect these rights."[29]

[26] David Caplovitz, *The Poor Pay More* (New York: The Free Press, 1963).
[27] Jeremy Main, "A Special Report on Youth," *Fortune*, Vol. 79 (June, 1969), pp. 73–74.
[28] E. B. Weiss, "The Corporate Deaf Ear," *Business Horizons*, Vol. XI (December, 1968), pp. 5–15.
[29] Report of Council on Trends and Perspective on, "Business and the Consumer—A Program for the Seventies" (Washington, D.C.: Chamber of Commerce of the United States, 1969).

The activist consumer

The discontented consumer found many more effective ways to express feelings and press for change during the 1960s than ever before. The development of means of translating discontent into effective pressure distinguishes recent consumer efforts from those of the 1910 and 1935 eras.

The consumer has been more ably represented by advocates such as Ralph Nader, Senator Warren Magnuson, and a number of journalists who pursue similar interests. These men are able to identify and publicize problems, and to follow up with workable programs for improvement. In a real sense, they are self-elected legal counsels to a typically unrepresented constituency. Many consumer problems would have remained smoldering but unfocused discontents without their attention. New product researchers have frequently found consumers do not seem to know what is bothering them or realize that others are similarly troubled until the extent of the problem is publicized or an alternative is provided.

The institutional framework has also been expanded and strengthened in recent years. Traditional bodies, such as Consumers Union and Consumers Research, Inc., have now received support from permanent bodies in the government such as the Consumer Advisory Council and the Office of the Special Assistant to the President for Consumer Affairs. These agencies have been specifically developed to avoid the problems of excessive identification with regulated industries which plague some of the older regulated bodies.

This decade has also seen greater willingness on the part of consumers to take direct action. Consider the protest of housewives in Denver over the costs of trading stamps and games. While this was probably due to general dissatisfaction over the effects of inflation on food prices, it did represent an important precedent. More sobering is the extreme form of protest documented by the National Commission on Civil Disorders:

Much of the violence in recent civil disorders has been directed at stores and other commercial establishments in disadvantaged Negro areas. In some cases, rioters focused on stores operated by white merchants who, they apparently believed, had been charging exorbitant prices or selling inferior goods. Not all the violence against these stores can be attributed to "revenge" for such practices. Yet, it is clear that many residents of disadvantaged Negro neighborhoods believe they suffer constant abuses by local merchants.[30]

The changing legal and political scene

Pressures for change have been directed at a legal and political structure that is much more willing to take action than before:

1. Overall, there is more acceptance of government involvement in issues of

---

[30]"Exploitation of Disadvantaged Consumers by Retail Merchants," *Report of the National Commission on Civil Disorders* (New York: Bantam Books, 1968), pp. 274–277.

consumer protection. Also, the federal government has been more prepared to take action because the state and local governments have generally defaulted their early legal responsibility in this area.[31]

2. A combination of factors has contributed to the expanded role of the federal government. Congress is no longer so dominated by the rural constituencies who appear less interested in these matters; consumer legislation is relatively cheap and appears to generate goodwill among voters; and various tests of the influence of business lobbyists have shown that their power is not as great as originally feared.[32] In fact, many observers feel that industry may have been its own worst enemy by often opposing all consumer legislation without admitting any room for improvement or providing constructive alternatives.[33] Worse, they may have demonstrated that industry self-regulation is not workable.[34]

3. The consequence is a Congress that is responsive to the economic interests of consumers. A significant proportion of the enacted or pending legislation is a result of Congressional initiative and is directed toward ensuring that consumers have adequate and accurate shopping information. This is very different from earlier legislation which was enacted because a tragedy dramatized the need to protect health and safety.[35]

4. A large number of legal reforms have been slowly instituted which attempt to correct the imbalance of power held by the manufacturers; e.g., the expansion of the implied warranty, and the elimination of privity of contract.[36] Of special interest are current efforts to give the individual consumer more leverage by making the practice of consumer law profitable for attorneys. The mechanism being promoted is the consumer class action which permits suits by one or a few consumers on behalf of all consumers similarly abused.[37] This will make fraud cases, where individual claims are smaller than legal costs, much more attractive to investigate and litigate.

THE FUTURE OF CONSUMERISM

One of the main conclusions from past efforts to forecast social phenomena is that naive extrapolations are likely to be wrong. A better approach in this

---

[31]Ralph Nader, "The Great American Gyp," *New York Review of Books*, Vol. 9 (November 21, 1968), p. 28.

[32]Stanley E. Cohen, "Giant Killers' Upset Notions That Business 'Clout' Runs Government," *Advertising Age*, Vol. 40 (July 14, 1969), p. 73.

[33]Jeremy Main, "Industry Still has Something to Learn About Congress," *Fortune*, Vol. 77 (February, 1967), pp. 128–130.

[34]Harper W. Boyd, Jr., and Henry J. Claycamp, "Industrial Self-Regulation and the Consumer Interest," *Michigan Law Review*, Vol. 64 (May, 1966), pp. 1239–1254.

[35]Philip A. Hart, "Can Federal Legislation Affecting Consumers' Economic Interests Be Enacted?" *Michigan Law Review*, Vol. 64 (May, 1966), pp. 1255–1268.

[36]David L. Rados, "Product Liability: Tougher Ground Rules," *Harvard Business Review*, Vol. 47 (July–August, 1969), pp. 144–152.

[37]David Sanford, "Giving the Consumer Class," *The New Republic*, Vol. 40 (July 26, 1969), p. 15. Partial support for this concept was given by President Nixon in his "Buyer's Bill of Rights" proposal of October 30, 1969.

situation is to utilize the interpretation that consumerism is, at least partially, a reflection of many social problems that are certain to persist, and perhaps be magnified in the future. This diagnosis rules out the possibility that consumerism activity will decline significantly in the future; the unanswered questions concern the rate of increase in this activity and the areas of greatest sensitivity.

One index of activity, the amount of federal consumer legislation pending, should slow its rate of increase. Only a limited number of consumer bills can be considered at a time; over 400 such bills were pending in Congressional committees at the end of 1969.[38] Also more attention will have to be given to implementing and improving existing legislation, rather than writing new legislation. For example, there is evidence that the truth-in-lending bill will not achieve its original goals; partly because of lack of understanding of the problem and partly because of inadequacies and confusion in the enacted legislation.[39] Similarly, it is dismaying that after two years of experience with the truth-in-packaging bill it is being referred to as "one of the best non-laws in the book."[40] In this particular situation the problem seems to lie with the interest and ability of the various regulatory agencies to implement the law. This is not an isolated example of enforcement failures. The Food and Drug Administration (FDA) recently estimated that fewer than two-thirds of all food processors have complied with standards to prevent some forms of food contamination. One result has been an increased pressure for a powerful central consumer agency[41] to implement, modify and coordinate the 269 consumer programs that are presently administered by 33 different federal agencies.[42]

The very nature of the contemporary marketplace will probably continue to inhibit basic changes in business operations. Weiss points out some manufacturers and retailers will always equate responsible with legal behavior.[43] These tendencies are reinforced by the competitive structure of many markets where success depends on an ability to appeal directly to the "marginal float." One view of this group is that they constitute a minority who are "fickle . . . particularly susceptible to innovation that may not be relevant, and to attention getters such as sexy TV jokes or giveaway games."[44] While research support is lacking, this widely held view helps explain some of the behavior consumerists complain about.

There are signs that concerned parties are making efforts to rise above emotion to rationally identify and realistically attack the problems. Two major,

[38] See, "Nixon shops for consumer protection," *Business Week* (November 1, 1969), p. 32.

[39] "A Foggy First Week for the Lending Law," *Business Week* (July 5, 1969), p. 13. This result was accurately forecasted by Homer Kripke, "Gesture and Reality in Consumer Credit Reform," *New York University Law Review*, Vol. 44 (March, 1969), pp. 1–52.

[40] Stanley E. Cohen, "Packaging Law Is on Books, But Ills It Aimed to Cure Are Still Troublesome," *Advertising Age*, Vol. 40 (September 1, 1969), p. 10.

[41] Same reference as footnote 18, and Louis M. Kohlmeier, Jr., "The Regulatory Agencies: What Should Be Done?" *Washington Monthly*, Vol. 1 (August, 1969), pp. 42–59.

[42] "Wide Gaps Exist in Consumer Food Safety," *Congressional Quarterly* (November, 1969).

[43] E. B. Weiss, "Marketeers Fiddle While Consumers Burn," *Harvard Business Review*, Vol. 46 (July–August, 1968), pp. 45–53.

[44] See Stanley E. Cohen, "Consumer Interests Drift in Vacuum as Business Pursues Marginal Float," *Advertising Age*, Vol. 40 (March 24, 1969), p. 112.

if embryonic, research efforts are under way which aim at providing decision makers in business and government with empirically based knowledge to supplement the intuition on which they now too often solely rely. The first is the Consumer Research Institute sponsored by the Grocery Manufacturers Association, and the second is an effort by the Marketing Science Institute.[45] Although both research organizations have close ties with business, neither was established to justify or defend vested interests. Their objectives are to promote basic, academic research that will be respected by all parties. The MSI group specifically proposes to obtain participation at the research-design phase of each project of those who would potentially disagree about policy. Although the government now has no comparable effort, it is reasonable to expect movement in this direction. Cohen has suggested that the FTC should establish a Bureau of Behavioral Studies "whose function would be to gather and analyze data on consumer buying behavior relevant to the regulations of advertising in the consumer interest."[46]

An early study, which might be regarded as a prototype to the CRI and MSI efforts, experimentally examined the relationship between deceptive packaging (with respect to content weight) and brand preference.[47] It demonstrated that experimentation can provide useful information to policy makers.

These research approaches and the forces behind them should not only generate influential information, but should also help stimulate some basic changes in orientation. We can expect to see, for example, the simplistic "economic man" model of consumer behavior enriched.[48] The last decade has seen great progress made in the study of consumer behavior. This progress should contribute directly to a deeper analysis of consumerism issues. Hopefully, the dissemination of relevant knowledge will help eliminate present semantic problems.[49] Such a development must accompany rational discourse.

Business managers, whether progressive or defensive, can be expected to develop new, flexible approaches toward insuring that the rights of the consumer will be protected. Even though the motives may be mixed, there is no reason why effective programs cannot be developed.

[45]"Business Responds to Consumerism," *Business Week* (September 6, 1969), p. 98, and Robert Moran, "Consumerism and Marketing," *Marketing Science Institute Preliminary Statement* (May, 1969).

[46]Dorothy Cohen, "The Federal Trade Commission and the Regulation of Advertising in the Consumer Interest," *Journal of Marketing*, Vol. 33 (January, 1969), pp. 40–44.

[47]James C. Naylor, "Deceptive Packaging: Are Deceivers Being Deceived?" *Journal of Applied Psychology*, Vol. 6 (December, 1962), pp. 393–398.

[48]David M. Gardner, "The Package, Legislation, and the Shopper," *Business Horizons*, Vol. 2 (October, 1968), pp. 53–58.

[49]Same reference as footnote 6.

READING 51

ON THE MARKETING PRACTITIONER'S COMMITMENT TO ECONOMIC DEVELOPMENT*

John R. Wish and Jack L. Taylor, Jr.

Marketing is committed to economic development more than marketing practitioners realize. Knowledgeable economists and marketers have analyzed, discussed, and suggested solutions to economic development problems.[1] They have studied countries at various stages of development to gain familiarity with the phenomena.[2]

These studies, until recently, have been oriented toward production rather than marketing.[3] The contributions from the production approach to economic development have been useful. They have pointed out that an infrastructure, a production system, and an exchange system are needed to cause development; and that these structures and systems need skilled personnel. Formal education and training have been stressed.[4] Only recently have researchers suggested that economic development plans must provide the motivation, the zest, and the relevancy for an active participation by members of an underdeveloped economy.[5]

THE MARKETING MISSION

The stimulation, coordination, and control of an economic development program requires a consensus on goals, means, and priorities by government and industry.[6] Marketing has and will continue to provide the zest and relevancy needed to stimulate the market demand. Marketers are charged with the responsibility of analyzing and assessing the market opportunity and selling customer satisfaction. This notion is derived from two tenents of marketing thought—the "mission of marketing" and the "marketing concept."

Marketings mission is threefold—to find the shortest path to the market, to bring new products into the market, and to bring new people into the

*Unpublished paper.

[1]Benjamin Higgins, *Economic Development*, rev. ed., W. W. Norton & Company, Inc., New York, 1968; also see William E. Cox, Jr., "A Commercial Structure Model for Depressed Neighborhoods," *Journal of Marketing*, vol. 33, July, 1969, pp. 1–9.

[2]W. W. Rostow, *The Process of Economic Growth*, 2d ed., W. W. Norton & Company, Inc., New York, 1962, pp. 311–328.

[3]Douglas Felix Lamont, "A Theory of Marketing Development: Mexico," *Proceedings of the American Marketing Association*, p. 44, Fall, 1965.

[4]Cyril S. Belshaw, *Traditional Exchange and Modern Markets*, Prentice-Hall, Inc., Englewood Cliffs, N.J., 1965.

[5]Deborah S. Freedman, "The Impact on Development of the Consumption of Modern Durables," *Proceedings of the American Marketing Association*, p. 488, fall, 1968.

[6]Michael J. Thomas, "The Role of Marketing in Irish Development Planning," *Proceedings of the American Marketing Association*, p. 494, fall, 1968.

market.[7] It is the third marketing mission which commits the marketer to plan an active role in economic development.

It is the marketers search for profitable markets with people, money, and willingness to buy that commits him to economic development.[8] The people and willingness to buy are present in the United States ghettos and depressed neighborhoods. The purchasing power is not. Marketing know-how is being used to suggest to ghetto populations that there is a way out that can preserve the dignity of the man and that can provide the zest and relevancy needed to motivate people to want to learn, to be trained, and to become active participants in the market.[9] Marketing companies need these underdeveloped markets. They will be forced to develop the capacity to serve these markets just to sell the output produced by advancing technologies. This means a commitment to develop capacities to serve by understanding the issues, problems and sociocultural facets of underdeveloped economies. It means a commitment to the United States ghetto problem as well as that of underdeveloped nations—a commitment to find ways to bring these areas and nations more fully into the market. Also, it means a commitment to provide the knowledge to participate.

THE MARKETING CONCEPT IS NOT SUFFICIENT

In advanced economies the marketer has done his job well.[10] He has developed the capacity to understand consumption process, exchange systems, production systems, and sociocultural facets of advanced economies.[11] The essence of this development is captured in the marketing concept—to sell satisfaction at a profit. The concept demands a consumer perspective—to find the needs and wants of the market and develop it with the right products, at the right time, at the right price, and at the right place. But this is not enough, for it assumes that the market is there, in all its dimensions—people, money, and willingness to buy. "Develop it" now means that new capacities must be developed to educate, to train, to motivate, and to show them the "way out." The job is more than industry can handle alone. It is and will continue to be a joint government-industry domain. The domain is defined as the range of products offered, the population serviced, and the services rendered.[12] It is a domain that requires consensus by those involved on goals, means and priorities. We have some evidence.

[7]Wroe Alderson and Michael H. Halbert, *Men, Motives and Markets*, Prentice-Hall, Inc., Englewood Cliffs, N.J., 1968, pp. 45–63.
[8]William J. Stanton, *Fundamentals of Marketing*, 2d ed., McGraw-Hill Book Company, New York, 1967, p. 77.
[9]W. Leonard W. Evans, Jr., "Ghetto Marketing: What Now?" *Proceedings of the American Marketing Association*, p. 488, fall, 1968.
[10]George Katona, *The Mass Consumption Society*, McGraw-Hill Book Company, New York, 1964.
[11]John Kenneth Galbraith, *The New Industrial State*, Houghton Mifflin Company, Boston, 1967.
[12]James P. Thompson, *Organizations in Action*, McGraw-Hill Book Company, New York, p. 26.

SOME FINDINGS

In Chile, the government has effectively promoted efficiency in retail food marketing. Government activities ranged from purely regulation to the provision of infrastructure, to control of participation in the market, and to direct entry as an entrepreneur in the marketing process. The results suggest that government participation as an entrepreneur in the marketing process holds significant promise.[13] Economic development researchers in Tawain report that the consumption of modern durables has influenced their development.[14] This suggests that marketing can be a positive factor in the development process. American ghetto marketers have proposed that marketers teach black people how to become entrepreneurs; they have challenged marketing to teach them how to develop the capacity to serve and to provide the know-how on how to motivate active participation.[15] Others have suggested community development corporations to reduce the risk of ghetto marketing.[16] Legislation has been proposed and will be enacted to bring about the economic development of these peoples and areas. Again, marketing has a "mission" responsibility to complete.

The Irish have written a success story in economic development by planning their marketing in cooperation with the government.[17] They have had significant success in export market development as a result of cooperative planning. Also, some marketers have found in Brazil that, although there are economic and cultural differences between the United States and Brazil, the thought process in developing market strategy should not differ.[18] Perhaps these are the "universals," as Cox suggests.[19] Even the Soviet economy is responding to the needs and wants of the customers.[20] The factory quota systems are out, and the market system seems to have replaced them. Since the essence of marketing is to be found in the exchange system and since this system does and will continue to play a vital role in economic development, marketing practitioners will find that they are committed to an *active* role in this process that they never realized they had in the past.

[13]Peter D. Bennett, "The Role of Government in the Promotion of Efficiency in Retail Marketing of Food Products in Greater Santiago Chile," *Proceedings of the American Marketing Association,* p. 105, fall, 1965.

[14]Deborah S. Freedman, "The Impact on Development of the Consumption of Modern Durables," *Proceedings of the American Marketing Association,* p. 488, fall, 1968.

[15]W. Leonard Evans, Jr., "Ghetto Marketing: What Now?" *Proceedings of the American Marketing Association,* p. 528, fall, 1968.

[16]Frederick D. Sturdivant, "Retailing in the Ghetto: Problems and Proposals," *Proceedings of the American Marketing Association,* p. 523, fall, 1968.

[17]Michael J. Thomas, "The Role of Marketing in Irish Development Planning," *American Marketing Association,* p. 494, fall, 1968.

[18]Donald A. Taylor, "Marketing in Brazil," *Proceedings of the American Marketing Association,* p. 110, fall, 1965.

[19]Revies Cox, "The Search for Universals in Comparative Studies of Domestic Marketing Systems," *Proceedings of the American Marketing Association,* p. 143, fall, 1965.

[20]Marshall I. Goldman, "The Soviet Economy at the Crossroads," *Proceedings of the American Marketing Association,* p. 83, fall, 1965.

CONCLUSION

Their search for new market opportunities will force marketers to develop the capacity to serve these underdeveloped markets. Whether the marketer knows it or not, he is committed to this, not so much by current legislation as by his own search for a market in all its dimensions: money, people, and willingness to buy.

The evidence discussed suggests that stimulation, coordination, and control of an economic development program requires a consensus on goals, means, and priorities between government and industry. This is possible, workable, and will lead to goal accomplishment. Market practitioners who understand this commitment will be able to take advantage of market opportunities and develop the capacity to serve these markets by (1) finding the shortest path to the market and (2) bringing new products into the market.

READING 52

THE GROWING RESPONSIBILITIES OF MARKETING*

Robert J. Lavidge

Marketing is being widely criticized for its failure to contribute more to the solution of social as well as economic problems. This is a new phenomenon. Until recently, the expectation that marketing should, or could, contribute to society in a significant way was held by few.

AREAS OF GROWING RESPONSIBILITY

As a result of changes in both marketing and its environment, it is likely that marketing people will have an expanding opportunity, *and responsibility,* to serve society during the 1970s. Examples relate to:

1. Consumerism.

2. The struggle of the poor for subsistence.

3. The marketing of social and cultural services.

4. The day-to-day functioning of the economy.

5. The use and pollution of society's resources.

Efficiency and social justice

Marketing has a key role to play in the drive for increased efficiency within our economy. It also has an opportunity to play a significant role in the drive

*Reprinted from *The Journal of Marketing,* published by the American Marketing Association, vol. 34, no. 1 (January 1970), pp. 25–28.

for social justice which is replacing the drive for security or affluence among many members of our society. There is a need for more vigorous action in both of these areas, efficiency and social justice. There also is a need, which is likely to grow during the 1970s, for truly responsible marketing practitioners and educators to vigorously resist action proposed in the cause of either efficiency or social justice which is likely to damage the economy and to do more harm than good in the long run.

Consumerism

The "social concerns" of marketing men and women have been focused primarily on sins of commission—especially on fraudulent or deceptive advertising, packaging, pricing, and credit practices. Although some progress is being made, marketing leaders must do a more effective job during the next decade, of identifying and reducing these practices. Moreover, history suggests that standards will be raised. Some practices which today are generally considered acceptable will gradually be viewed as unethical, then immoral, and will enventually be made illegal. Rather than resisting such changes, marketing leaders have a responsibility to provide intelligent guidance in bringing them about. But that is not enough.

"Consumerism" related to sins of omission, as well as those of commission, will continue to grow during the 1970s. There will be further expansion in the demand for more useful information to help consumers decide what to buy. Both consumers and marketers will increasingly be concerned with warranties and guaranties, with the handling of consumer complaints, and with product performance testing. Marketing men and women also have a responsibility to provide intelligent *leadership* in this movement rather than to stand aside, to cast themselves in the role of obstructionists, or to go to the other extreme and lend support to actions in the name of social justice which are well-intentioned but reflect a lack of understanding of marketing.

The struggle for subsistence

For much of the United States' population the struggle for material subsistence no longer provides direction. But the subsistence struggle will continue during the 1970s throughout most of the world. Socially concerned marketing men and women will not be content with their role in satisfying other needs while a large share of the world's population struggles with hunger and starvation. With vastly improved communications and increased education, we will become increasingly conscious of the unsatisfied needs of people in the economically underdeveloped nations of the world and in the poverty areas of the United States. Growing recognition of these unsatisfied needs will continue to provide ammunition to those who think of marketing activities primarily in terms of stimulating selfish desires rather than satisfying both physical and psychological needs. Marketing people must work simultaneously in cultures of affluence and of poverty during the 1970s. The dual culture problem will pose difficulties because actions appropriate for one culture could be very inappropriate for the other.

More than a decade ago, Peter Drucker noted marketing's opportunity in connection with the

> . . . race between the promise of economic development and the threat of international world-wide class war. The economic development is the opportunity of this age. The class war is the danger. . . . And whether we shall realize the opportunity or succumb to danger will largely decide not only the economic future of this world—it may largely decide its spiritual, its intellectual, its political and its social future. Marketing is central in this new situation. For marketing is one of our most potent levers to convert the danger into the opportunity.[1]

Walt Rostow, while serving as chairman of the Policy Planning Council of the Department of State, told the members of the American Marketing Association: "I can tell you—without flattery—that I believe the skills this organization commands and represents are going to prove critical in the generation ahead to the development of countries and regions which contain a clear majority of the world's population.[2] The opportunity and the challenge about which Drucker and Rostow spoke remain to be met in the 1970s.

Social and cultural services

The coming decade also will witness an expansion of the role of marketing in connection with "markets based on social concern, markets of the mind, and markets concerned with the development of people to the fullest extent of their capabilities."[3] Kotler and Levy have pointed out that the work of marketing people is contributing to the enrichment of human life through improved marketing of educational, health and religious services, better utilization of natural resources, and enjoyment of the fine arts.[4] Marketing people are helping the institutions which provide such social and cultural services to improve the tailoring of their services to their "customers" and to improve the "distribution," "pricing," and "promotion" of them.

The day-to-day functioning of the economy

During the coming decade, marketing people will be responsible for helping bring material rewards to more members of society. Ethical, creative, efficient day-to-day marketing activities help the economy function more effectively

[1]Peter F. Drucker, "Marketing and Economic Development," *Journal of Marketing,* Vol. XXII (January, 1958), pp. 252–259, at p. 254 and 255.

[2]Walt W. Rostow, "The Concept of a National Market and its Economics Growth Implications," in *Marketing and Economic Development,* Peter D. Bennett, ed. (Chicago, Ill.: American Marketing Association, September, 1965), pp. 11–20, at p. 11.

[3]William Lazer, "Marketing's Changing Social Relationships," *Journal of Marketing,* Vol. 33 (January, 1969), pp. 3–9, at p. 4.

[4]Philip Kotler and Sidney J. Levy, "Broadening the Concept of Marketing," *Journal of Marketing,* Vol. 33 (January, 1969), pp. 10–15, at p. 10.

to serve mankind. And, as William Lazer noted in a recent *Journal of Marketing* article, ". . . it is clear that when abundance prevails individuals and nations can afford to, and do, exercise increasing social concern."[5] It is when basic needs are met that men can turn attention to other needs and values, to the higher aspirations of mankind.[6] Nevertheless, it is likely that marketing people will find themselves increasingly under fire and working in what seems to be a hostile environment during the coming decade. There are likely to be continued increases in the importance of noneconomic values with growing resistance to competitive activity and resultant attacks on marketing. This may be intensified during the latter part of the decade by movement toward the checkless, cashless society. This could result in changes affecting marketing institutions which make the distribution revolution of the 1950s and '60s seem like a period of relative stability. The resultant dislocations may lead to attacks on marketing from within, as well as outside, the marketing community.

Marketing leaders will have to respond to broader attacks on marketing, as well as to issues related to consumerism. The marketing leaders who truly serve society will be those who search for, seize, and act on opportunities for improvement rather than merely defend themselves or take popular actions in the name of social justice regardless of their impact on society.

The use and pollution of society's resources

During the 1970s, marketing men and women will become increasingly concerned with the pollution of our air, water, and land (by others as well as by business firms). With greater emphasis on business ecology, there will be expanding opportunities for marketing people to assist in the adoption and use of new techniques for preserving and improving the environment.

Marketing teachers and practitioners have a responsibility to play a role in discouraging activities which are generally agreed to be harmful to society. During the next decade, marketing leaders also will be much more concerned with the impact of their actions and inactions on society in connection with a host of goods and services which cannot be clearly labeled either good or bad. The automobile, for example, has contributed enormously to economic development and to the enrichment of human life during the past half-century. But this contribution has not been without cost. The automobile is a major factor in the pollution of our air. It contributes to a staggering number of accidental deaths and injuries, and its land utilization cost has reached significant levels in many urban areas. Marketing people will become increasingly involved in questions of the type to which this inevitably leads. In evaluating the opportunities for new products and services, for example, the role of marketing people heretofore has focused largely on the question: Can it be sold? During the 1970s there will be increasing attention to: *Should it be sold? Is it worth its cost to society?*

[5]Same reference as footnote 3, at p. 6.
[6]A. H. Maslow, *Motivation and Personality* (New York: Harper and Row, 1954).

THE CHANGING NATURE OF MARKETING

The areas in which marketing people can, and must, be of service to society have broadened. In addition, marketing's functions have been broadened. Marketing no longer can be defined adequately in terms of the activities involved in buying, selling, and transporting goods and services. The role of marketing in determining what goods and services will be offered now is also widely, although not universally, accepted. In addition, the coordinating and integrating roles of marketing are being given more attention. Increasingly, we are recognizing that the organization—business, educational, governmental, religious, or other—functions to serve people, its "customers." This, of course, is the essence of the "customer concept" (a term I prefer to "marketing concept").

Planning and the systems approach

The next decade is likely to witness a significant increase in the use of marketing planning, with emphasis on integrating coordinated marketing activities into the total fabric of the organization. There will be greater use of the systems approach, with planning based on the "customer concept" to solve both business and nonbusiness problems and to take advantage of opportunities for improvement. This offers much that is good. Marketing people must be prepared to play a central role in this important advance. But in doing so, they must be alert to the danger of introducing rigidities which strangle our economy in the interest of efficiency. The type of problem which can be created was illustrated by J. B. McKitterick in "Planning the Existential Society,"[7] He cited the person who chose the right course in school in order to gain admission to the right college where he could study the right subjects and move on to the right graduate school in order to work in the right career—only to discover that it really wasn't the right career for him. This, of course, is an argument for liberal education. It also illustrates the danger of commitment to a plan or a system which does not provide for revision of goals and the roads to them in the light of changing objectives and changing environmental factors. This is a danger to which marketing leaders must be alert in the '70s as planning based on the customer concept is adopted more widely by both business and nonbusiness organizations.

Moreover, marketers must avoid letting their desire for more and better information on which to base their plans blind them to the dangers to society which lie in the *improper* use of data banks and new surveillance techniques. Marketing men and women have a clear responsibility to provide leadership in avoiding the threats that George Orwell invisioned in *1984*,[8] as well as in making proper use of such tools.

[7]J. B. McKitterick, "Planning the Existential Society," in *Marketing and the New Science of Planning*, Robert L. King, ed. (Chicago, Ill.: American Marketing Association, August, 1968), pp. 3–9, at p. 3.
[8]George Orwell, *1984* (New York: Harcourt, Brace & World, Inc., 1949).

CONCLUSIONS

Marketing practitioners and marketing educators who are sincerely concerned about the impact of their actions and inactions on society will have no shortage of challenges during the 1970s. Facing the kinds of changes which can be anticipated plus those we do not now foresee, marketing people will have an opportunity to make a significant contribution to society in their day-to-day activities—influencing decisions about what goods and services are offered, as well as helping bring them efficiently to their end users in a climate which is increasingly hostile to competitive activity and to many of the functions of marketing. At the same time, socially concerned marketing men and women will strive during the '70s: (1) to reduce marketing abuses and upgrade standards; (2) to help mitigate and ultimately eliminate the effects of poverty; (3) to aid in improving the marketing of social and cultural services; (4) to reduce the pollution of our environment; and (5) to develop international marketing institutions which will contribute to improved utilization and distribution of the world's resources and, hopefully, as a result, to world peace. In all these efforts, the truly responsible marketing leader will vigorously resist actions which would damage the economy that serves society imperfectly but increasingly well—whether those actions are proposed in the interests of profits, efficiency, or social justice.

It has been said that the "social responsibilities of businessmen arise from the amount of social power they have. The idea that responsiblity and power go hand-in-hand appears to be as old as civilization itself."[9] As it matures, as it broadens in function and scope, marketing will become increasingly relevant during the 1970s to the fulfillment of man. And as the impact of marketing on society increases, so does the social responsibility of marketing people.

READING 53

THE COMMUNICATIONS REVOLUTION AND HOW IT WILL AFFECT ALL BUSINESS AND ALL MARKETING*

E. B. Weiss

Fourteen years ago, in my four-installment *Advertising Age* series on cybernetics and its future impact on marketing, I prophesied:

Technologically, our social and business society is deep in a total revolu-

[9]Keith Davis, "Understanding the Social Responsibility Puzzle," *Business Horizons*, Vol. 10 (Winter, 1967), pp. 45–50, at p. 48.
*Reprinted from *The Communications Revolution and How It Will Affect All Business and All Marketing*, published by Advertising Publications, Inc., Copyright 1966, pp. 5–10.

tion—the cybernetics revolution. This is a three-pronged revolution: (1) automation; (2) computerization; and (3) instantaneous communication. Marketing cannot remain immune from the impact of these three electronic horsemen.

That was in 1953. The very term, "automation," had just been coined. Only three computers were in use. And instantaneous global communication was still a mote in the scientific eye.

Fourteen years later, there is no need to spell out automation's progress —particularly in production.

But today the communications-information revolution, sparked by the computer, is poised for a leap ahead that will make automation's 14-year progress seem like slow-motion—and that will radically alter our total civilization.

An old proverb (overlooked by Khrushchev) states: "One pound of learning requires ten pounds of common sense to apply it." The world's accumulation of knowledge has presumably doubled in the past decade. It will double again in the next decade. Clearly, the application of this new knowledge could become a staggering task.

The fundamental contribution of the new communications revolution is to put knowledge to work more promptly than ever before, more effectively than ever before, over more of the world than ever before. That includes marketing information.

Technology carried us from local, to regional, to national instantaneous communication. Now we are advancing toward true universality, embracing global audiences, global enterprises, global markets—and global marketing and advertising programs.

Through communication satellites and other remarkable communications breakthroughs, it will be possible to communicate with anyone, anywhere, at any time, by voice, sight or written message—instantaneously. Moreover, all communications will be instantly recorded—instantaneously retrievable —and instantly reproducible.

Hundreds of millions of individuals will be in full sight and sound of one another. Ultimately, individuals equipped with miniature TV transmitter-receivers will communicate directly with one another worldwide, using personal channels similar to today's personal telephone—and just as simply.

Overseas mail will be transmitted through facsimile reproduction via satellites. Satellite television could mean that several hundred million viewers may be watching the same program aided by instantaneous language translation. Magazines and newspapers will be electronically typeset over vast distances and will achieve worldwide simultaneous editions.

When?

NO FAR-OFF DREAM

By the end of 1966, satellites will be communicating with two-thirds of the world. By 1968, television will be technologically (if not economically) able to reach most of the world—live!

Clearly, we have already moved far past the threshold of a new era in both mass and personal communications. A worldwide system of instant sight and sound linking governments, business and billions of people is now becoming a reality.

This awesome revolution will ultimately enable the marketing process to reach the entire population of the earth simultaneously!

For the nearer term, global mass communication will radically change our international marketing programs in the more advanced nations—as well as at home.

Lack of communication brought about the babel of tongues. Instantaneous global communications will, in time, bring about a universal language. This new language will stem largely from English. (Even today, English is the most widely used of the 4,000 or more languages. Some 300,000,000 people use it as their primary tongue, and another 600,000,000 speak or understand it in some degree.)

With a single language accessible to practically all people, new opportunities will open to marketing.

Our new communications technology offers us, at least in theory, the possibility that all the world can share the same experience simultaneously. And that may help weld together our fractured world.

Yet, what science knows today about communications is merely "threshold" knowledge. Even more awesome developments are being explored.

For example, the laser is a device that produces an intense, highly-directional light beam. A Bell System report states:

"Coherent" laser light has the potential of carrying a tremendous volume of communications. Bell System scientists are, right now, contemplating laser "pipes" with a capacity millions of times greater than today's most advanced communications systems, connecting major population centers and enabling any individual to have his private "line" for sound-and-sight communication across any distance, just as he now has his private telephone line.

Then there is the new communication science called holography, a process hailed by some scientists as the most important photographic event since the invention of photography itself more than 100 years ago.

Holography photographs objects by laser light. When a viewer looks through the film into the light of a laser, a three-dimensional image of the original object suddenly springs into view, floating in mid-air behind the film. (I saw a demonstration at the Bell Laboratories; it is a startling experience.)

Holography promises three-dimensional television and other visual uses. It can be used on high-speed readers or scanners for computers. Other potential uses range from information storage to materials testing.

IMAGE OR REALITY?

And now hear this: It is entirely possible that electronic communication will, in time, achieve a degree of realism that will make it somewhat difficult for one's sensory apparatus to distinguish between an *electronically-created* visual experience and an *in-person* one!

How? Like so:

Scene: A luxury apartment in the city. A woman sits in her living room. On the curved walls she sees ocean-surf—a sea gull wheeling in the sky. She is talking with a friend. The surf's boom and the cry of the gull impinge on their conversation.

But the friend is not physically present. She was brought into that living room by laser beam from a satellite. She is recreated, in color and full dimension (you could walk around her image and see the back of her head by holography).

Where does "reality" begin and end in that scene? Obviously, we are entering a new world of experience—sired by new communications technology.

"*Custom* communication" is a term that may become as common as "*mass* communication." Under the custom communication concept, communications in the home—and in business, school, laboratory, library, etc.—will be under the complete control and discretion of the user.

A broad spectrum of information and entertainment services will be available—sight, sound, graphic. These custom services may be fed into home, office, or school through a coaxial cable or "microwave pipe" similar to other utility pipes. This "pipe" could deliver, among other services:

1. Color TV and radio—worldwide.

2. Facsimile newspapers and other graphic media from all over the world.

3. Direct access to libraries.

4. Telephone services with remarkable new degrees of sophistication.

5. Medical diagnostic services.

6. Computer services.

7. Business, weather and market information.

The individual user will be able to exercise complete discretion in determining the information of his choice. The "on-off" knob will no longer be the full range of his options.

A computer authority has stated:

Already, we have the technology to lessen the need to commute to work by providing the business man at home with closed-circuit television, remote-access computers, facsimile machines, etc. Some business meetings could certainly be conducted via a home-to-office system of electronic communication.

Indeed some conservative scientists have concluded that the office may tend to go into a decline—and that the core of the metropolitan city may, as a consequence, go into a decline. Remote? I think so.

But when William Haber, Dean of the College of Literature, Science and

Arts, University of Michigan, flatly predicts that in 20 years "50% of the work force will be employed on types of jobs which are not even in existence—and the overwhelming majority of these jobs are not yet *even in our imagination*" —it would be wise to take an "it *can* happen" stance.

And when Dean Myron Tribus of Dartmouth's Thayer School of Engineering predicts: "If there's one conclusion which I should offer as most firm, it is this—these things will happen *sooner*, and on a *larger scale*, than most of us now think likely"—don't conclude "not in my lifetime."

VAST CHANGES FOR MARKETING MANAGEMENT IN BUSINESS

Marketing unquestionably is to become an electronic-communications based enterprise. This will lead, in time, to the creation of a new department—the Information Management Department. That department will control the Electronic Information Management Center.

Marketing executives will meet in this center and scan information displayed visually on demand. They will be able to call for wanted data through a control console and to feed results of decisions and other information back into the system. They will be able to evaluate a series of alternative marketing plans by simulation. Consequently, relationships between marketing executive, scientist and technician will be of prime importance. All three must be able to understand each other. Each must look to the others to supplement the strengths he does not have.

Electronic communication will transform the traditional world of publishing—a potentiality I explore in depth in the next installment, as well as later in this installment. Indeed, electronic communication makes inevitable a foreseeable slowdown in the rate of growth in the use of the mails—and an eventual downturn. The future of the mail is no longer to be a strong, persistent growth situation!

Concurrently, check writing will be cut by 90%—this is the prediction of our major banks!

SATELLITES PROMISE WORLD DATA

It is the satellite that promises marketing its greatest degree of change—and in the foreseeable future.

The list of potential applications for communication satellites goes on and on, with each prophet trying to outdo the previous one. But certainly such an idea as world information centers, which would catalog and make instantly available vast quantities of information, are made feasible by communication satellites. This is particularly true in light of the tremendous capabilities of our present-day computers.

In 1961, IBM used 28,900 miles of domestic telephone circuitry; by 1966 it was using 380,000 miles, and two voice channels across the Atlantic. On the basis of that volume, IBM petitioned the FCC for the right to bypass the common carriers, AT&T and ITT, and have direct access to the Comsat satellite. The petition was turned down in July, 1966.

But the experience opened a new window to the future for the company. IBM now has the vision of the communications of tomorrow, with machines talking to machines across the oceans. IBM feels sure it is a market that does not have to be controlled completely by the entrenched carriers.

IBM makes a careful distinction between data transmission—the simple function of carrying electrical impulses—and *data transformation*, which it defines as the analyzing, correlating and sorting of those impulses. IBM does not want to be considered merely the manufacturer of a device that would be only a part of the common carriers' communication system. It sees itself playing a critical role in a brand new kind of *international data processing*, composed of computers that communicate with each other.

In a decade or sooner, large satellites will be put in orbit with enough power to broadcast TV and radio programs *direct to individual homes*. What happens to present TV-radio stations and networks?

Federal Communications Commission Chairman E. William Henry warned the broadcast industry last March that the day may come when direct-broadcast satellites would eliminate "overnight" the need for local radio and television stations.

A step toward a direct-to-home TV satellite system that could cover an area of up to half a million square miles was proposed by Radio Corp. of America engineers early in 1966. RCA engineers said achievement of such a system is entirely within the capability of today's space technology. If detailed studies were started in 1966, they said, launch could occur in 1969 or 1970. Unmodified, standard TV receivers would be used with minimal additions to the home antenna.

Remember the live Gemini 6 and 7 telecasts? They were achieved as the result of the development of a transportable satellite-communication earth station, mounted on the deck of the recovery vessel. These unprecedented broadcasts sent over great distances from a remote location, without access to a permanent earth station or cables, marked the beginning of a new era of broadcasting. In that era it will be possible to transmit live television pictures instantaneously from any point on the globe to any other point—and ultimately *directly* into the home.

(The transportable station transmitted pictures from the cameras aboard the "Wasp" by microwave signal to the Comsat Early Bird satellite which, in turn, relayed them to the ground station at Andover, Me. The signals were then distributed by land line facilities by the television networks in the U.S., which broadcast them to American homes coast-to-coast. Early Bird re-transmitted signals from Andover to ground stations in Europe.)

An American and a European computer will talk with each other for a month via the Early Bird satellite some time in 1967 in a communications test with broad social and economic implications. (One can foresee a time when a European or Asian office might be able to receive and store records as complete as those of the home office.)

The use of the home (and office) television set *as an instrument of reproduction which would be independent of a broadcasting station* is clearly in view. This involves a recording-playback apparatus attached to the TV receiver which would enable the viewer to select visual material of his own choice, record it and play it back at his own convenience. It is nothing less than a visual version of the long-playing phonograph record. This could prove a revolutionary supplement to existing TV. (TV records could be sold, exchanged or circulated with the same ease as books or music recordings.)

This prospect was discussed by a group of educators and industrialists at Stanford University recently. The group concluded that television stations, some day, will use "video records" to provide low-cost programs, the way radio stations now use phonograph records. The group also predicted that "video records" will be used by many home owners for entertainment, culture and education, to be played on the home set at the viewer's convenience.

Already, equipment that records television programs on tape and plays back on command is being marketed. Efforts are being made to reduce the cost of this equipment.

THE HOME BECOMES AN OFFICE AND COMMUNICATIONS CENTER

The recently introduced television tape recorder, which will be in general use by 1975, will provide an electronic solution to the No. 1 shopping irritant —the lack of competent, courteous salespeople. One fine day, a taped demonstration of a product, flashed on a TV tape recorder, will be doing what the present crop of I'll-do-you-a-favor-when-I-take-your-order clerks just don't do.

As the car telephone becomes more common, and as television sets in autos become more numerous, these communication marvels will be developed in ways that will permit shopping from a *moving* car. This will be even more practical when Detroit gives us automated cars that drive themselves (lab models are being tested now) and which will be computer controlled.

Everything that goes into the home by telephone, television, radio, magazines, newspapers, etc., consists of information. The volume of this information is increasing enormously. The pace of increase will accelerate. Adult education—and education is now to become a life-long process—will complicate the problem.

In brief, the knowledge explosion presents to the *public* the same problems of absorption and understanding facing science, industry, etc. Therefore, it will become just as necessary for the home to have an information system as for the business office.

The home is to be tied into the communication revolution in fascinating ways. For example, the newest computer systems may appear as input-output units in the home. They would use small televisionlike screens with keyboards and copying devices.

When you ask a question, you see the answer almost simultaneously on the screen. If you want a copy of the answer, a photocopying device will make the copy immediately.

As the cost of the computer is brought down, as its use is simplified, as its miniaturization continues, as the ease and speed with which the home computer and the "big brother" computer can "talk" to each other improves, and as the giant "shared-time" computer becomes still more common and versatile, the user of the computer in the home will become more common.

STAY AT HOME; OPERATE BUSINESS, STUDY, AND SHOP

Millions at home—and, of course, at business, too—may use such systems at the same time. They will not need to know any more about the operation of the system than the average person knows about the telephone (which, incidentally, may be an integral part of this communication system).

Home copiers will become widespread. It will be as common to have a personal copying machine as a portable typewriter. People will duplicate things that they like, building personal libraries of copied material just as they now collect tape recordings. The home copier will also be used for business purposes.

There is a trend among business men toward performing more work at home. The still shorter work week accelerates this trend. And the home computer, hooked into a central computer at the office, plus other electronic communication facilities, will still further accelerate the trend by making it possible to carry on at home functions that previously could be performed only in business offices.

Concurrently, other social, economic and political changes will make the office in the home as common as the library was in better homes some decades ago. It will become a new type of "study" in the home. And this will come about as well from the new freedoms and responsibilities of the distaff side of the family, as from the presumed head of the family.

There is a parallel development at home involving what is just now being called "the learning room." According to the editor of *Practical Builder*, the "learning room" presumably will be equipped for one basic purpose—the pursuit of knowledge. It will serve students of all ages—adults as well as children—as education becomes a life-long process.

No stretching of the demonstrated technology is required to envision computer consoles installed in every home and connected to public-utility computers through the telephone system. The console might consist of a typewriter keyboard and a television screen that can display text and pictures. Each subscriber will have his private file space in the computer that he can consult and alter at any time. The system will serve as each person's memory. Full reports on current events will be available for the asking—and for home recording and reproduction if wanted.

Income tax returns will be automatically prepared on the basis of continuous, cumulative annual records of income, deductions, contributions and expenses.

Cookbooks will be computerized so the housewife can select a recipe and follow audio-visual directions through a sight-and-sound system in the home.

COMPUTER'S MODEL T ERA IS PAST

I have stated that the computer is one of the key factors in the communication-information revolution. Dr. Jerome B. Weisner, dean of science at the Massachusetts Institute of Technology and former science adviser to President Kennedy, writing in the *New York Times* on the computer, said:

The computer, with its promise of a million-fold increase in man's capacity to handle information, will undoubtedly have the most far-reaching social consequence of any contemporary technical development. The potential for good in the computer, and the danger inherent in its mis-use, exceed our ability to imagine . . . We have actually entered a new era of evolutionary history, one in which rapid change is a dominant consequence.

Fifteen years ago, there existed only a few trouble-plagued Model T models of the computer. Today, some 40,000 are in operation—some operating with unbelievable speed and capable of remarkably sophisticated uses. At least 75,000 computers will be in use by 1970.

More significant than a mere count of hardware is the fact that many of the computer systems now coming along are enormously more sophisticated, enormously faster, and are time-sharing systems. Hundreds of users can have access to them simultaneously.

But as remarkable as the third-generation computers are, still more remarkable advances are being planned. Information that currently costs 20¢ to store in core memory will cost .005¢ in less than a decade. The average cost of 10,000 computer instructions, now at around a half-mill to two mills, will drop to one-fiftieth of those amounts by 1975.

Another set of related figures works out this way: In 1945 (at a labor cost of $1 per hour and at a rate of 16 operations per minute, with no overhead or capital cost) it cost about $1,000 to do a million operations on a computer keyboard. Today, one can do such operations for about 8¢. In about five years the cost will drop by at least a factor of 100!

Between 1963 and 1972—a single decade—there will be a decrease of 85% in the cost of completing a typical data-processing job. During this period, the cost of storage by magnetic tape will go down by 97%; the cost of image storage by 96%; and communication line costs, because of increased speeds of transmission, will decrease by 50%. These changes in economics will mean that the computer will be able to do more with information at a lower cost than we now can possibly imagine.

COMPUTERS WORKING ORALLY SEEN COMING 'ROUND THE BEND

Voice recognition by the computer—in other words, a computer that will respond to oral command—while rife with problems, is making significant engineering progress. No serious forecast about computer systems in the 1970s can omit voice recognition systems.

Thus, General Electric reports that its scientists:

are trying to arrange for the user to communicate with the computer in ordinary English. The computer will understand a question that you ask in English and give you an answer in English.

The goal is to make the computer readily available to people who do not wish to learn the specialized language which the computer can now understand. By analogy, what we are thinking about is this: If it were necessary for you to have a two-year course in auto mechanics before you could get a driver's license, the use of the automobile would be severely restricted.

Likewise, to make the computer truly useful to a wide variety of people, we must essentially remove it from the status of the oracle, surrounded by monks and lamas, and make it available to the user in his own language. The boss is not going to learn FORTRAN or COBOL or any one of those formalized or specialized languages.

If we can develop satisfactory schemes for putting people in touch with computers and give them an easy-to-use language, ten years from now we will be handling thousands of times as much information by electronic means as we do now.

The oral command concept is making rapid technical strides—several years ago, in national advertising, the Bell System predicted the orally-actuated telephone. It is now possible to predict not only a machine that would permit voice control of computers and of telephone dialing, but also of typewriters.

RCA said its voice command machine responds to 28 of the basic sounds in the English language. The machine causes a typewriter to print a phonetic symbol for each sound it recognizes. (Thomas B. Martin, an RCA engineer, said the next step is recognition of words in conversational speech, an achievement believed to be "just a few years away.")

Until the oral command concept is farther advanced, "programed languages" (and eventually basic English) will widen the use of computers. These languages, which are being simplified, enable men to "converse" with, and develop programs for, the machines without being skilled computer technicians.

Already, a computer can transpose a *rough* design into *exact* specifications. If an engineer makes a free-hand drawing of a bridge on such a system's television-like screen, the computer will convert the drawing into exact engineering specifications, will calculate and display materials and stress, and show the design in whole, or in part, or in any perspective, in immediate response to the engineer's needs.

The time-sharing computer system is still in its early stage of technological development. For example, a portable keyboard terminal that can provide full access to *any* time-sharing computer system in the country has been developed at Carnegie Institute of Technology. The device, called Dataport, plugs into regular AC electrical outlets, and can be quickly set up over an ordinary telephone.

A marketing man in his home, a salesman in a motel, or an engineer at a remote test site could simply dial into the big central computer system with no need for a permanent teletypewriter hookup. This means it will be economically feasible for all employes to have direct access to the computer at any place, at any time.

We are clearly coming into an age in which computers will "talk" with each other—negotiate with each other—come to mutual decisions. (AT&T has declared there will be more communications between machines than between humans.)

Computers that can read handwritten numbers are well advanced. The next step is toward machines that can read handwriting. Researchers are at work on this.

Moving information hundreds of thousands of miles in split seconds is the exciting new potential of data communications—so-called "real time." This is literally the art of putting computers "on the phone" so that you can use information while it's still "live" and make decisions on what "is," not on what "was."

Engineers at Bell Telephone Laboratories have completed production by computer of seven animated black-and-white movies. The movies range from simple line drawings to complex patterns—all produced by computer. Five of the experimental movies were shown by Bell at a computer symposium to demonstrate the *growing potential of machines to express themselves graphically* as well as in torrents of equations and formulas. (The animated films, used for education and research, can be produced faster and more economically by computers than by human draftsmen!)

OTHER DEVELOPMENTS ARE EQUALLY EXCITING

I am seriously tempted to continue, here and now, to explore the fantastic new world of the computer. However, in a later installment, which is concerned exclusively with the computer, as well as in other installments, including the installment on marketing, the role of the computer in the communications-information revolution will be covered in greater detail.

Let us move on, then, to other marvels in the communications-information revolution.

The Bell System has poured millions into the development of its Picturephone—and continues to pour more millions into this remarkable leap ahead in telephonic communications. AT&T is convinced that the potential uses of Picturephone service, which combines sight and sound for the telephone, are almost limitless.

The Picturephone, a Bell Laboratories scientist told me, is currently aimed at a very simple function—*face-to-face dialog*:

In its second stage of growth, and we can do it today technically but we can't do it economically as yet—we will give the Picturephone graphic capability. What do I mean by graphic capabilities? Simply enough, resolution to hold up a page in front of one Picturephone that could instantaneously be seen and read *on the screen of another Picturephone! We aim to have a Picturephone that can transmit and receive over ordinary telephone wires, at reasonable cost,* anything *that involves sight.*

We want color in the Picturephone. We aim to add the new dimension of visible emotion to mass communications!

AT&T hopes the cost for Picturephone can be brought down to $15 or $20 a month. Said this same Bell scientist:

When the first long-distance call was made, it cost about $25 to call cross country for a minute—to say nothing about the quality. Today, if you call at any time, it costs $2; if you call at certain hours, it's $1—to say nothing about the quality.

On the Picturephone the cost will come down; we think we have to reach the $50 monthly figure to open the market. This will open the business market and will have a limited appeal to the home market.

When you have it in businesses, business men will require one at home in order to communicate. And this is the way it will start in the home. Really, to take hold in the consumer market, it will have to come down to about $20 and we expect to achieve that figure.

The Bell System believes its Touch-Tone telephone, plus the Picturephone, will enable shoppers to make purchases from home by phoning a computer at a store. The Bell System describes that form of robot retailing this way:

Housewives will be conveniently shopping from their homes by phoning a computer or related facility at a store and dialing numbered codes corresponding to items desired. These codes would be furnished by merchants in catalogs or advertisements. At the store, the receiving machine would automatically produce a sales order as well as shipping, billing, inventory and related records.

In the future, people also may be paying their bills from their homes by using the phone to transmit information to machines at their bank. The receiving machine would automatically produce a record authorizing payment for funds and, at the same time, produce a record of the transaction for the caller.

ORDER BY PUSH-BUTTON TELEPHONE

Standard Oil Co. (Ohio) used Touch-Tone phones to reduce inventory costs and shorten delivery intervals. Sohio furnishes each service station owner with a new kind of catalog with which he can order tires, batteries and accessories. The catalog is made up entirely of cards, one of each different item he sells. When he has an order to transmit, he inserts a telephone punched card into the Touch-Tone phone which automatically calls a teletypewriter station at the regional office.

Next, with another punched card, he identifies his station. Then, for each item he wants to order, he selects the appropriate card and inserts it into the Touch-Tone phone, adding the only variable, quantity, *by using the buttons of the Touch-Tone telephone.*

By making this use of the existing telephone system with Touch-Tone phones, Sohio has been able to reduce the number of order errors, improve delivery schedules, eliminate an estimated 60% of the paper work formerly required, and cut inventory.

It is expected that the Touch-Tone service, tied into the Picturephone service, will combine to furnish a complete mass communication service of immense potentials ranging from a "checkless" society to innumerable new dimensions for traditional business and home communications.

UNITY IN COMMUNICATIONS SCORING BREAKTHROUGHS

Now suppose we restate the broad terms of the communications revolution before we move on; it will help clarify the additional innovations to be covered in this initial broad coverage.

Until recently, our progress in communication was measured in terms of *separate and distinct* new services. In the use of the airwaves, wireless telegraphy was first on the scene. Then came radio broadcasting and radio telephony.

Next, television was developed and advanced from black-and-white to color. Today, the computer operates as a highly sophisticated communications tool for data processing. These momentous communications advances occurred *separately* in time and context.

But now the new communications technology is imposing *unity* upon this assortment of *random* developments. With the introduction of microwave channels and the appearance of communications satellites, etc., *there is no longer any technical need for distinction among the various forms of communications.* All of them can pass through the same relays in the form of identical electronic pulses.

This means that not only television and telephone, but books, magazines and newspapers will be converted into identical bits of energy for transmission over any distance. At the receiving end, these electronic signals will be converted back into their original form or into any desired form: visual display, recorded sounds, processed pages, etc.

This suggests that we will have one major channel of news, information and entertainment that will be a single integrated system combining *all*, or *most* of the separate electronic instruments and printed means of communications today. I do not mean to suggest that this single unified system will *eliminate* all other forms of communication—but it will certainly profoundly reshape existing communication media.

The future effects of the electronic communications revolution on the publishing industry are intriguingly forecast in the recent wave of mergers and affiliations of publishing houses with electronics corporations (Random House with RCA, General Electric and *Time*, Sylvania and *Reader's Digest*, Xerox and the several publishing organizations it has absorbed, and Science Research Associates with IBM).

CARRY ENCYCLOPEDIA IN WALLET

This trend will continue—perhaps resulting in only a few large "publication networks," as is the case right now in radio and television. (These mergers suggest that the publishing networks of the future may partly coincide with the present radio-television systems. There may even have to be new federal regulations to insure freedom of expression in the public interest.)

The *Wall Street Journal* recently predicted:

The reader of the not-too-distant future may carry in his pocket the complete works of Shakespeare, the whole Encyclopaedia Britannica, and a filing cabinet full of office paperwork—all on a few wallet-size plastic cards.

This is the dream of the companies now producing microforms—tiny pieces of plastic that can hold a staggering amount of printed information reduced to microscopic size. . . .

The microform is fast becoming a major tool of business in its struggle to cope with the paperwork explosion. Across the country, corporations and other users are compressing scores of cubic feet of conventional documents into microforms that would barely fill a shoe box. They are finding it a lot easier to store, update and retrieve information from microforms than from roll microfilm, a principal medium for record storage since the 1920s. In some cases, they have launched a double-barreled attack on paperwork bulk by having computers print their output on the tiny pieces of film.

Microforms—or microfiche, as such super-reduced film transparencies are often called—got a mighty boost from Uncle Sam in July, 1964, when the government decided to use them in distributing technical reports from defense agencies to businesses.

Fiche producers' dreams of a wallet-size library for the general reader may become reality before too long. At least two major popular publishers are considering putting out reference and education volumes on fiche, at sharply reduced prices. "This could mean a revolution in the book and magazine field," says one fiche manufacturer.

Such a development would hinge on the perfection of a low-priced device to "blow up" the microform images so they could be read.

VAST IMPACT ON LIBRARIES AND PUBLISHERS IS FORESEEN

The development of inexpensive copiers, and deep cuts in the cost per copy, plus color and still greater speed, suggest that the copier will also bring about vast changes in publishing. Xerox is producing books by photocopy. As one printing expert put it: "Some of the copying machines are miniature printing plants."

Libraries have only begun to realize the potential of copying machines. Since photocopies will soon be produced at less cost than acquiring books, there may be little need for any well-equipped and well-organized library to have more than one copy of any book! (This has begun in college libraries.)

Nor will there be much need to maintain the costly apparatus of general library circulation; it will be cheaper to provide a library-borrower with his own copy of whatever he wants. Books will not leave the librarian's direct control—a librarian's dream! (Some libraries now follow this practice with scientific journals.) The library, itself, may largely take the form of microcards or microfiche arranged for easy projection and copying.

Moreover, the copier will not be limited to the reproduction of printed documents. Its possible future linkage to television for copying pictures off the screen already is being discussed.

Publishers are now realizing that the traditional division between editing and composition is disappearing under the impact of computer technology. Use of computers to compose type has led to the realization that maximum benefit can be obtained if the machines are used also to reshape editorial material into new forms. This, in essence, is editing.

Microfilm publishing already has attained amazing growth and acceptance in the U.S. as part of the total business publishing industry. In just six years, a microfilm technical data system developed by one company has matured into a marketing communications bridge between some 16,000 industrial suppliers and the key buying influences in their customer companies.

Publishers are also anxious about the development of scientific, library and business information networks centered on electronic memory systems with accompanying printout of material as required—the so-called "information utility" which I cover in a later installment. A logical development is that information from books will be fed into these data networks, thus reducing the number of books needed for reference.

The data utility is analogous in some ways to the electrical utility. It is cheaper for many people to use a central electric power utility than for each individual to have his own generator. The same economic reasoning applies to the data utility industry. The technology of real-time processing, time-sharing, and communication will allow this to happen. We will just plug in for data as we now do for electricity.

The data utility concept would include the inquiry concept—in some ways, the "publishing" of the future. This will allow the sale of data over a communications system in answer to a query placed by the customer. The possibilities are unlimited; practically any information can be provided. This is another reason for the purchase of publishing companies by electronic companies.

Then there are the computer-based educational systems. Technology now allows a dynamic or "live" relationship between a student and a machine system. The system answers questions as they are posed and discerns gaps in a student's basic grasp of a subject. Such systems are already at work in some industrial situations—IBM's Maintenance Training is a good example.

Academic libraries are laying plans to tie themselves together electronically so that each can benefit from the resources of the others. The medical libraries of Harvard, Yale and Columbia have been preparing for such a network for three years.

Clearly the marketing function will now be shaped by electronics. Even salesmen will be hooked into a feedback system—and marketing departments and advertising agencies will be tapping scores and even hundreds of data banks.

The future of the computer, of the data bank, of electronic education, of electronically-controlled marketing, the marriage between publishing and electronics—each will be analyzed in depth.

READING 54

THE FEDERAL TRADE COMMISSION AND THE REGULATION OF ADVERTISING IN THE CONSUMER INTEREST*

Dorothy Cohen

It is the purpose of this article to review the present means by which the Federal Trade Commission regulates advertising for the protection of the consumer, as well as the adequacy of the criteria which underlie the regulatory process. Further, it is suggested that additional measures be taken that would increase the effectiveness of the advertising regulatory process.

In implementing its responsibility to regulate advertising for the protection of consumers, the Federal Trade Commission has developed informal decision criteria. In broad terms, the Commission's judgments have been consistent with an "economic man" concept of consumer purchase behavior. It views the consumer as an informed, reasoning decision maker using objective values to maximize utilities. This is essentially a normative concept.

The basic assumptions of the Commission's regulatory design or criteria are maximization of the consumer's utilities and rational choice. A necessary ingredient to fulfill these assumptions is full, accurate information. The Commission, therefore, protects the consumer by identifying and attacking information which is insufficient, false, or misleading. These deficiencies are uncovered by relating the objective characteristics of a product, as determined by the Commission, to its advertising representations.

The Commission, therefore, operates under the legally and economically acceptable premise that the consumer is to be assured full and accurate information which will permit him to make a reasoned choice in the marketplace. Nonetheless, examination of the results of the Commission's activities utilizing this concept reveals the existence of several gaps in its protection. For example, the poor are not always protected from excessive payments because of lack of information about true cost or true price. The health and safety of the consumer are not always assured, since information concerning the hazards of using particular products is not always available. The belief that added protection is needed was reinforced by a report of the Consumer Advisory Council to President Johnson which states "that although this is an era of abundance . . . there is also much confusion and ignorance, some deception and even fraud. . . ."[1]

The need for added protection does not necessarily suggest discarding the Commission's regulatory framework, because a more effective structure currently does not exist. The elimination of the present regulatory design would in fact create a void in the consumer protection network. It does suggest, however, that steps should be taken as a basis for stronger protection in the

---

*Reprinted from *The Journal of Marketing,* published by the American Marketing Association, vol. 33, no. 1 (January 1969), pp. 40–44.
[1]*Consumer Issues '66,* A Report Prepared by the Consumer Advisory Council (Washington, D.C.: U.S. Government Printing Office, 1966), p. 1.

future. The current movement to improve regulation through stressing full disclosure, while serving to eliminate some deficiencies, is not sufficient.[2] The Consumer Advisory Council's report, for example, in summarizing the outlook for the future, observes:

Technological change is so rapid that the consumer who bothers to learn about a commodity or a service soon finds his knowledge obsolete. In addition, many improvements in quality and performance are below the threshold of perception, and imaginative marketing often makes rational choice even more of a problem.[3]

Full disclosure of pertinent facts is one step in improving the protection network. Additional steps are needed to assure that the consumer understands the significance of the facts. It has been noted, for example, that the consumer is selective in his acceptance of information offered. This selectivity is due, in part, to a difference between the objective environment in which the consumer "really" lives and the subjective environment he perceives and responds to.[4] The consumer reacts to information not only with his intelligence, but also with habits, traits, attitudes, and feelings. In addition, his decisions are influenced significantly by opinion leaders, reference groups, and so on. There are predispositions at work within the individual that determine what he is exposed to, what he perceives, what he remembers, and the effect of the communication upon him.[5]

It has been noted that appeal to fear (emphasizing the hazards of smoking or of borrowing money) may not deter the chronically anxious consumer, nor will it necessarily protect his health or pocketbook. Valid communications from a non-authoritative source may not be believed, whereas questionable communications from an authoritative source may be readily accepted. Thus, the extensive use of "sufficient" truth may take on an aura of non-believability and be rejected. Attempts to avoid conflicting evidence may result in ignoring the information completely.

The Commission's efforts to provide the consumer with economic information concerning value are not completely effective, since the consumer does not measure value in economic terms alone. Brand loyalties create values in the eyes of the consumer as does the influence of social groups and opinion leaders within these groups. His desire to attain certain levels of aspiration may lead the consumer to be a "satisficing animal . . . rather than a maximizing animal,"[6] that is, one who chooses among values that may be currently suitable, rather than those which maximize utilities. In order for the Commission to improve the consumer protection network, it must reflect an understanding of the behavioral traits of consumers.

[2]See The J. B. Williams Co., Inc. and Parkson Advertising Agency, Inc. v. F.T.C., 5 *Trade Regulation Reporter #72, 182* (Chicago, Ill.: Commerce Clearing House, Inc., August, 1967); and several aspects of truth-in-packaging and truth-in-lending legislation.
[3]Same reference as footnote 1, at p. 6.
[4]Herbert A. Simon, "Economics and Psychology," in *Psychology: A Study of a Science,* Simon Koch, editor, Vol. 6 (New York: McGraw-Hill Book Co., Inc., 1963), p. 710.
[5]Joseph T. Klapper, "The Social Effects of Mass Communication," in *The Source of Human Communication,* Wilbur Schramm, editor (New York: Basic Books, Inc., 1963), p. 67.
[6]Same reference as footnote 4, at p. 716.

Adapting the regulatory design to handle behavioral traits is no easy task. An examination of a behavioral model of consumer performance reveals the existence of many intervening variables, so that the creation of standards for this non-standardized consumer becomes exceedingly difficult. Moreover, current knowledge of the consumer as a behavioralist is far from complete. Indeed, the feasibility and success associated with the practical uses of this model are dependent upon future research.

It is, therefore, recommended that attention be directed toward current and future research in the behavioral sciences to devise means for amending the advertising regulatory framework. This would lead to improvements in the communication process and the elimination of protection gaps. The application of behavioral characteristics to the regulatory model is not intended as a panacea, but is a suggestion for improving some regulatory ailments. In broad policy terms the Commission can initially do little more than establish closer contact with the consumer and analyze behavioral data which may be relevant to the regulation of advertising. Suggestions for improved administrative procedures are limited to applications of current behavioral knowledge of the consumer. Future research may suggest more precise administrative action, for increased knowledge of the consumer's buying behavior should lead to the development of more effective mechanisms for his protection.

RECOMMENDATIONS

The following specific recommendations are suggested as guidelines for future governmental activities relative to consumer advertising.

Bureau of behavioral studies

A Bureau of Behavioral Studies should be established within the Federal Trade Commission (similar to the Commission's Bureau of Economics) whose function would be to gather and analyze data on consumer buying behavior relevant to the regulation of advertising in the consumer interest.

Consumer complaint offices

The Federal Trade Commission should establish "consumer complaint" offices throughout the United States. One method of gathering more information about the consumer is to provide closer contact between the Federal Trade Commission and the public. Complaints about advertising abuses may originate with consumers, but these have been at a minimum; and lately the Commission has accentuated its industry-wide approach to deceptive practices. Although the industry-wide approach is geared toward prevention and permits the FTC to deal with broad areas of deception, it minimizes the possibility of consumer contact with the Commission. In 1967, awareness of this fact resulted in an action in which the Commission's Bureau of Field Operations and its 11 field offices located in cities across the United States intensified its program of public education designed to give businessmen and consumers a better understanding of the work of the agency.[7]

If the Commission is to operate satisfactorily in the consumer interest, it must develop a closer relationship with consumers. Most consumers are still uncertain about the protection they are receiving, and the Federal Trade Commission appears to be an unapproachable body with little apparent contact with the "man-on-the-street."

Consumer complaint offices would identify the Federal Trade Commission's interest in the consumer and act as a clearing house for information. Consumers could be informed about steps to take if they believe they have been deceived, what recourse is open, and how to secure redress for grievances. The Commission could secure evidence about deception direct from consumers. Moreover, the complaints of these private individuals might be based on noneconomic factors, permitting clearer delineation of the behavioral man and the ways in which he might be protected.

Priority of protection

The Federal Trade Commission should establish a definitive policy of priority of protection based on the severity of the consequences of the advertising. While appropriations and manpower for the Federal Trade Commission have increased in recent years, they are still far from adequate to police all advertising. Therefore, the ability to protect is limited and selective. In its recent annual report the Commission did indicate, however, that it had established priorities:

A high priority is accorded those matters which relate to the basic necessities of life, and to situations in which the impact of false and misleading advertising, or other unfair and deceptive practices, falls with cruelest impact upon those least able to survive the consequences—the elderly and the poor.[8]

Nevertheless, in the same year the Commission reported that approximately 20% of the funds devoted to curtailing deceptive practices were expended on textile and fur enforcement (noting that the Bureau of Textiles and Furs made 12,679 inspections on the manufacturing, wholesaling, and retailing level).[9]

Priority may be established in two ways. First, it may be considered relative to the harmful consequences of deceptive advertising. This approach could suggest, for example, that the Federal Trade Commission devote more of its energies to examining conflicting claims in cigarette advertising than to examining conflicting claims in analgesic advertising (which seems to focus on the question of whether one pain reliever acts faster than the other). Exercising such priorities might accelerate the movement toward needed reforms (such

---

[7]Federal Trade Commission, *Annual Report*, 1967, p. 67.
[8]Same reference as footnote 7, at p. 17.
[9]Same reference as footnote 7, at pp. 30 and 81.

as the current safety reforms in the automobile industry) by pinpointing the existence of inadequately protected consumer areas.

A second method of establishing priority could be to delineate the groups that are most susceptible to questionable advertising. This is where the behavioral model may play an important role. Sociologists are trying to discover common aspects of group behavior, and research has disclosed that each social class has its own language pattern.[10] Special meanings and symbols accentuate the differences between groups and increase social distance from outsiders.[11]

Disclosure of special facets of group behavior should be helpful to the Commission in designing a program of protection. As noted earlier, the poor cannot be adequately protected by the disclosure of true interest rates because their aspirations may provide a stronger motivating influence than the fear of excessive debt. Knowledge of the actual cost of borrowing would offer no protection to the low-income family which knows no sources of goods and credit available to it other than costly ones. Nor would higher cost of borrowing deter the consumer who, concerned mostly with the amount of the monthly payment, may look at credit as a means of achieving his goals. In fact, the Federal Trade Commission concluded, in a recent economic report on installment sales and credit-practices in the District of Columbia, that truth-in-lending, although needed, is not sufficient to solve the problem of excessive use of installment credit for those consumers who are considered poor credit risks and are unsophisticated buyers.[12]

The problems of the poor extend beyond the possible costs of credit. They include the hazards of repossession, the prices paid for items in addition to credit costs, and the possibility of assuming long-term debt under a contractual obligation not clear at the outset. It is possible that behavioral studies may disclose a communication system that would be a more effective deterrent to the misuse of credit than the disclosure of exorbitant interest rates. Until then, the Commission should give priority to investigations where the possibility of fraudulent claims, representations, and pricing accompany the offering of credit facilities to low-income groups. For example, advertisements of "three complete rooms of furniture for $199.00, easy payments" continue to appear despite the Commission's ruling that "bait and switch" tactics are unfair. Thus, the possibility exists that the low-income consumer may be "switched" to a much more expensive purchase whose costs become abnormally high due to the exorbitant interest rates included in the "easy payments." In its monitoring and review of advertising the Commission's staff should give precedence to investigations of such "bargain, easy payments" advertising, since much of it is especially designed to attract the low-income groups.

[10]Léonard Schatzman and Anselm Strauss, "Social Class and Modes of Communication," *American Journal of Sociology*, Vol. 60 (January, 1955), pp. 329–338.

[11]Tamotsu Shibutani, "Reference Groups as Perspectives," *American Journal of Sociology*, Vol. 60 (May, 1955), p. 567.

[12]5 *Trade Regulation Reporter* #50,205 (Chicago, Ill.: Commerce Clearing House, Inc., July, 1968).

Improvement of the communication process

The consumer's cognitive capacity (the attitudes, perceptions, or beliefs about one's environment) and its effect on the communication process should be reflected in designing advertising controls so that the inefficient mechanisms can be improved or eliminated.

Currently the concept of full disclosure is being expanded as the major means of offering the consumer additional protection. This is particularly evident where the objective is to dissuade the consumer from the use of or excessive use of a product or service. Little attention is paid, however, to determining whether the selective consumer is taking note of these disclosures.

An examination of behavioral man reveals that he is less "perfect" than economic man. His values are not based on objective realities alone, nor are his choices always what may be objectively considered as best among alternatives. In legislative design the regulatory authorities should come to grips with the question of whether protection of the consumer includes "protection from himself." There are indications that the latter concept is considered a legitimate area for regulatory activities—as evidenced in legislation affecting cigarette advertising and in some elements of the truth-in-lending and truth-in-packaging bills.

While questions may be raised about the legitimacy of interfering with the consumer's "freedom of choice," there is evidence that the methodology devised for this interference is deficient. In the current regulatory design, the proposed method of securing these different kinds of protection is the same, although the kinds of protection offered to the consumer may differ. For example, the consumer is currently protected against deceptive advertising by laws requiring that he be provided with truthful disclosure as to the product and its features. Where authorities believe that the advertising claims of certain products or services should be minimally used or completely avoided, the consumer is again protected by non-deceptive "full disclosure" as to the product and its features. Yet a quick review of consumer behavior and persuasibility reveals that a strategy designed to change or dissuade must, of necessity, differ from a strategy designed to reinforce. The consumer may be quite willing to accept information which supports his beliefs or preconceptions and yet be unwilling to accept evidence which refutes these same beliefs. Moreover, research has disclosed that adherence to recommended behavior is inversely related to the intensity of fear arousal. Intense fear appeal may be ineffective since it arouses anxiety within the subject which can be reduced by his hostility toward the communication and rejection of the message. It has also been noted that the tendency toward dissonance reduction can lead to failure to understand the information disclosed. Thus "full disclosure" cannot be a completely effective control mechanism when its main purpose is to protect the consumer from using a particular product or service, for the consumer may simply ignore these disclosures.

Based on current research, one approach the Commission might take toward an improved program of dissuasion would be to reinforce the negative information through an authoritative source, such as the Commission itself. Although the agency has a number of publications—*Annual Report, News Summary, Advertising Alert*—none of these is specifically geared to provide the consumer with information. A monthly report to consumers, initially available at "consumer complaint" offices, might serve as an effective mechanism for denoting the existence of hazardous products, excessive claims, questionable representations, and so forth. Specifically, this report could detail information of particular interest to consumers concerning advertising abuses that had been curtailed, cease and desist orders, questionable advertising practices currently under investigation, and so on. It is also suggested that this printed publication occasionally be supplemented by reports through a more pervasive medium—television.

It is not recommended that the Commission become a product-testing service, since the latter implies governmental control over competitive offerings and could place excessive restrictions on freedom of choice. Instead the report is to be considered a communication device, designed to insure that consumers take more note of available information on the premise that the information emanates from an authoritative governmental source.

Behavioral criteria

The Federal Trade Commission should use behavioral as well as economic criteria in evaluating consumer interest. Subjective as well as objective claims should be examined in determining whether a "tendency to deceive" exists. Due to insufficient knowledge of consumer behavior, an accurate blueprint for defining products in terms of consumer choice is not available. Future research may present more precise propositions about consumer behavior which would facilitate the development and implementation of behavioral criteria. However, currently there are areas wherein the adaptation of behavioral factors in establishing criteria for advertising regulation may provide for more adequate protection in the consumer interest.

Assuming it were possible to provide the consumer with complete information based on economic criteria, the individual may still be unable to exercise informed choice. A recent report by the National Commission on Food Marketing stated: "Given complete price information, the help of computers and all the clerical help needed, it is impossible to say which retailer in a particular community has lower prices."[13] Moreover, as noted earlier, individuals do not choose on the basis of price appeal alone.

Advertising today, to a great extent, stresses non-economic or promotional differences. Products are denoted as being preferred by groups, individuals, society, motion picture stars, sports leaders, and the average man. Since consumers may make their selections on the basis of these promotional representations, adequate protection requires that advertisements be subject to as

[13]*Organization and Competition in Food Retailing, Technical Study No. 7*, a report prepared by the National Commission on Food Marketing (Washington, D.C.: U.S. Government Printing Office, 1966), p. 169.

close an examination for deceptive representation as they are for deceptive price claims.

Insufficient emphasis has been placed in the advertising regulatory design on the importance of testimonials in influencing consumer choice. In the examination of the selective consumer it has been noted that his choice is influenced by a desire for group membership and by the opinion of leaders within these groups. It has also been noted that the consumer engages in selective exposure and selective perception, suggesting that when the consumer finally does accept an "opinion leader," the latter exerts significant pressure on the consumer's choice.

The use of testimonials in advertising takes account of this fact of consumer behavior, but the regulatory design does not. Those who are deemed to be opinion leaders and dominant members of groups are selected and paid for their "testimonials." Moreover, where the selected figure does not perform well, for example, on television, an actor is used to replace him. The consumer may be deceived into believing an "opinion leader" is evaluating a product or service. These opinions may be used by the consumer to substantiate the suitability of this particular item in his own value structure.

Currently, the basic legal requirement is that testimonials be truthful. However, if someone declares that he prefers "Brand X," validation of this statement is necessarily subjective. Adequate consumer protection requires more stringent regulations which should extend into evidence of truthfulness of this testimonial and disclosure as to the way in which it was secured. It is suggested that in using a testimonial no substitute attestors be allowed; and if payment has been made for the endorsement, the advertisement should so state. If evidence is available that the individual does not use the product (such as a cigar recommendation by a non-cigar smoker), his testimonial should not be permitted.

SUMMARY

In its efforts to protect the consumer against advertising abuse, the Federal Trade Commission has developed a protective network in the consumer interest primarily based on economic standards. There are gaps in this protection network, which result from the fact that the consumer does not appraise his interest solely in economic terms. Rather, the consumer develops patterns of buying behavior that reflect the influence of non-economic values and the individual's cognitive capacity. The Federal Trade Commission should take cognizance of this "behavioral" man in its consumer interest activities.

It is recommended that the Commission become more familiar with and establish closer contact with the consumer through a Bureau of Behavioral Research, consumer complaint offices, and through the distribution of consumer publications to disclose advertising irregularities. In addition, it is recommended that the Commission adapt regulatory criteria to current knowledge of the behavioral man in order to assure that federal regulation of advertising is accurately functioning in the consumer interest.